Lecture Notes in Computer Science 7963

Commenced Publication in 1973
Founding and Former Series Editors:
Gerhard Goos, Juris Hartmanis, and Jan van Leeuwen

Editorial Board

David Hutchison
Lancaster University, UK

Takeo Kanade
Carnegie Mellon University, Pittsburgh, PA, USA

Josef Kittler
University of Surrey, Guildford, UK

Jon M. Kleinberg
Cornell University, Ithaca, NY, USA

Alfred Kobsa
University of California, Irvine, CA, USA

Friedemann Mattern
ETH Zurich, Switzerland

John C. Mitchell
Stanford University, CA, USA

Moni Naor
Weizmann Institute of Science, Rehovot, Israel

Oscar Nierstrasz
University of Bern, Switzerland

C. Pandu Rangan
Indian Institute of Technology, Madras, India

Bernhard Steffen
TU Dortmund University, Germany

Madhu Sudan
Microsoft Research, Cambridge, MA, USA

Demetri Terzopoulos
University of California, Los Angeles, CA, USA

Doug Tygar
University of California, Berkeley, CA, USA

Gerhard Weikum
Max Planck Institute for Informatics, Saarbruecken, Germany

T0224050

Mei Chen   Bastian Leibe
Bernd Neumann (Eds.)

Computer
Vision Systems

9th International Conference, ICVS 2013
St. Petersburg, Russia, July 16-18, 2013
Proceedings

 Springer

Volume Editors

Mei Chen
Carnegie Mellon University, Pittsburgh, PA, USA
E-mail: mei.chen@intel.com

Bastian Leibe
RWTH Aachen University, Germany
E-mail: leibe@vision.rwth-aachen.de

Bernd Neumann
University of Hamburg, Germany
E-mail: neumann@informatik.uni-hamburg.de

ISSN 0302-9743   e-ISSN 1611-3349
ISBN 978-3-642-39401-0   e-ISBN 978-3-642-39402-7
DOI 10.1007/978-3-642-39402-7
Springer Heidelberg Dordrecht London New York

Library of Congress Control Number: 2013942398

CR Subject Classification (1998): I.5, I.4, I.3, I.2.10, I.5.4, C.3

LNCS Sublibrary: SL 1 – Theoretical Computer Science and General Issues

© Springer-Verlag Berlin Heidelberg 2013
This work is subject to copyright. All rights are reserved by the Publisher, whether the whole or part of
the material is concerned, specifically the rights of translation, reprinting, reuse of illustrations, recitation,
broadcasting, reproduction on microfilms or in any other physical way, and transmission or information
storage and retrieval, electronic adaptation, computer software, or by similar or dissimilar methodology
now known or hereafter developed. Exempted from this legal reservation are brief excerpts in connection
with reviews or scholarly analysis or material supplied specifically for the purpose of being entered and
executed on a computer system, for exclusive use by the purchaser of the work. Duplication of this publication
or parts thereof is permitted only under the provisions of the Copyright Law of the Publisher's location,
in ist current version, and permission for use must always be obtained from Springer. Permissions for use
may be obtained through RightsLink at the Copyright Clearance Center. Violations are liable to prosecution
under the respective Copyright Law.
The use of general descriptive names, registered names, trademarks, service marks, etc. in this publication
does not imply, even in the absence of a specific statement, that such names are exempt from the relevant
protective laws and regulations and therefore free for general use.
While the advice and information in this book are believed to be true and accurate at the date of publication,
neither the authors nor the editors nor the publisher can accept any legal responsibility for any errors or
omissions that may be made. The publisher makes no warranty, express or implied, with respect to the
material contained herein.

Typesetting: Camera-ready by author, data conversion by Scientific Publishing Services, Chennai, India

Printed on acid-free paper

Springer is part of Springer Science+Business Media (www.springer.com)

Preface

Understanding the computational processes of visual perception and constructing vision systems has been a prominent goal of computer scientists since the advent of computers. In 1955, Oliver Selfridge proclaimed to build "eyes and ears for the computer," marking the beginning of a long development, guided by changing paradigms and leading to exciting insights. While the enormous complexity of human vision is still being explored, technological developments have reached a state where computational vision processes can be integrated into operational systems, realizing a spectrum from ambitious applications to advanced experimental cognitive systems.

Whereas research on methods and theories has been well supported by scientific journals and major international conferences such as CVPR, ICCV, and ECCV from early on, the challenges of building complex operational vision systems received less attention. Therefore, a new conference series, titled "International Conference on Computer Vision Systems" (ICVS), was created, with the first conference taking place at Las Palmas on the Canary Islands in 1999. The idea of this conference series is to primarily address issues arising in the design and deployment of comprehensive computer vision systems for a broad spectrum of applications, such as robotics, monitoring, video analysis, and scene interpretation.

This volume contains the contributions to the 9th ICVS hosted in St. Petersburg, Russia. The focus is on diverse aspects of computer vision systems, ranging from video capture to high-level image interpretation, typically treated in the context of a realistic application or system building task. It is worth noting that a major fraction of the contributions deal with robot vision, mirroring the increasing support and interest for artificial cognitive systems and robotic applications. For example, several papers address the challenging task of analyzing a mobile world by moving sensors. While there is impressive progress, it is also apparent that much more work will be needed in this field and hopefully be presented at future ICVS conferences.

There were 94 submissions to ICVS 2013, out of which the Program Chairs selected 16 papers for oral presentation at the conference and 20 papers for presentation as posters, based on the careful reviews of the Program Committee and additional reviewers. All accepted papers have been revised by their authors to address reviewers' comments and are presented in this volume. We would like to thank all the authors for their submissions and all the reviewers for their valuable comments.

May 2013

Mei Chen
Bastian Leibe
Bernd Neumann

Organization

General Chair

Markus Vincze   Vienna Institute of Technology, Austria

Local Organization

Alexandr Redkin   Intel, St. Petersburg, Russia

Program Co-chairs

Mei Chen	Intel, Carnegie Mellon University, Pittsburgh, USA
Bastian Leibe	RWTH Aachen University, Germany
Bernd Neumann	University of Hamburg, Germany

Program Committee

Michael Arens	Fraunhofer IOSB, Germany
Antonios Argyros	University of Crete, Greece
Christian Bauckhage	Fraunhofer IAIS, Germany
Eduardo Bayro-Corrochano	CINVESTAV, Guadalajara, Mexico
Alexandre Bernardino	Instituto Superior Técnico, Portugal
Alain Boucher	IFI, Vietnam
Richard Bowden	University of Surrey, UK
François Bremond	INRIA, France
Jorge Cabrera	University of Las Palmas de Gran Canaria, Spain
Régis Clouard	GREYC Laboratory, France
Daniel Cremers	TU Munich, Germany
James Crowley	I.N.P. Grenoble, France
Kostas Daniilidis	University of Pennsylvania, USA
Larry Davis	University of Maryland, USA
Bruce Draper	USA
Gian Luca Foresti	Colorado State University, Italy
Jannik Fritsch	Honda Research Institutes, Germany
Antonios Gasteratos	Democritus University of Thrace, Greece
Rolf-Rainer Grigat	Technical University Hamburg-Harburg, Germany
Guodong Guo	West Virginia University, USA

Riad Hammoud   DynaVox Technologies, USA
Vasek Hlavac   Czech Technical University in Prague,
                                    Czech Republic
Jesse Hoey   University of Dundee, UK
David Hogg   University of Leeds, UK
Costas Kotropoulos   Aristotle University of Thessaloniki, Greece
Ivan Laptev   INRIA Paris-Rocquencourt, France
Dan Lee   University of Pennsylvania, USA
Ales Leonardis   University of Ljubljana, Slovenia
Bärbel Mertsching   University of Paderborn, Germany
Giorgio Metta   University of Genova/Instituto Italiano di
                                    Tecnologia, Italy
Lazaros Nalpantidis   Aalborg University, Denmark
Ramakant Nevatia   University of Southern California, USA
Lucas Paletta   Joanneum Research, Austria
Theodore Papadopoulo   INRIA, France
Nikolaos Papamarkos   Democritus University of Thrace, Greece
Claudio Pinhanez   IBM T.J. Watson Research Center, USA
Axel Pinz   Graz University of Technology, Austria
Fiora Pirri   University of Rome "La Sapienza", Italy
Ioannis Pratikakis   Democritus University of Thrace, Greece
Carlo Regazzoni   University of Genova, Italy
Paolo Remagnino   Kingston University, UK
Yoichi Sato   University of Tokyo, Japan
Silvio Savarese   University of Michigan, USA
Gerald Schaefer   Loughborough University, UK
Bernt Schiele   Max-Planck-Institut für Informatik, Germany
Konrad Schindler   ETH Zürich, Switzerland
Yaser Sheikh   Carnegie Mellon University, USA
Alexander Stoytchev   Iowa State University, USA
Agnes Swadzba   University of Bielefeld, Germany
Anastasios Tefas   Aristotle University of Thessaloniki, Greece
Monique Thonnat   INRIA Sophia Antipolis, France
Qi Tian   University of Texas, San Antonio, USA
Panos Trahanias   University of Crete, Greece
John Tsotsos   York University, Canada
Emre Ugur   ATR, Kyoto, Japan
Marc Van Droogenbroeck   University of Liege, Belgium
Sergio Velastin   Kingston University, UK
Sven Wachsmuth   University of Bielefeld, Germany
Christian Woehler   Technical University Dortmund, Germany
Sebastian Wrede   University of Bielefeld, Germany
Zhaozheng Yin   Missouri University, USA
Hongbin Zha   Peking University, China
Li Zhang   University of Wisconsin Madison, USA

Additional Reviewers

Wongun Choi	University of Michigan, USA
Srikanth Kallakuri	ATR, Japan
Dennis Mitzel	RWTH Aachen University, Germany
Zhen Zeng	University of Michigan, USA

Visual Processing and Understanding of Human Faces and Bodies

Takeo Kanade

Robotics Institute
Carnegie Mellon University
Pittsburgh, PA 15213, USA

Abstract. A human face and body convey important information to understand a person: her identity, emotion, action, and intention. Technologies to process video of human faces and bodies have many applications, ranging from biometrics to medical diagnosis and from surveillance to cognitive human-robot interaction. This talk will give highlights of the recent work at the CMU Vision Group, in particular, to robust face (and object) alignment, real-time face tracking, facial Action Unit (AU) recognition for emotion analysis, 2D and 3D body tracking, and facial video cloning for understanding human dyadic communication.

Active Pedestrian Safety: From Research to Reality

Dariu M. Gavrila

Dept. of Environment Perception, Daimler R&D, Ulm, Germany
dariu.gavrila@daimler.com

Abstract. One of the most significant large-scale deployments of intelligent systems in our daily life nowadays involves driver assistance in smart cars. The past decade has witnessed a steady increase of interest in the plight of the vulnerable road users, i.e. pedestrians and bicyclists. Accident statistics show that roughly one quarter of all traffic fatalities world-wide involve vulnerable road users; most accidents occur in an urban setting. Devising an effective driver assistance system for vulnerable road users has long been impeded, however, by the "perception bottleneck", i.e. not being able to detect and localize vulnerable road users sufficiently accurate. The problem is challenging due to the large variation in object appearance, the dynamic and cluttered urban backgrounds, and the potentially irregular object motion. Topping these off are stringent performance criteria and real-time constraints. I give an overview of the remarkable research progress that has been achieved in this area and discuss its main enablers: the algorithms, the data, the hardware and the tests. Our long-standing research on vulnerable road users has recently paid off. Our company, Daimler, deploys an advanced set of driver assistance functions for its Mercedes-Benz 2013 E- and S-Class models, termed "Intelligent Drive", using stereo vision sensing. It includes a pedestrian safety component which facilitates fully automatic emergency braking - the system works day and night. I conclude by discussing future research directions, on the road towards accident-free driving.

Addressing Some of the Challenges in Building Vision Systems

Martial Hebert

Robotics Institute
Carnegie Mellon University
Pittsburgh, PA 15213, USA
hebert@ri.cmu.edu

Abstract. Despite considerable progress in the past two decades in all aspects of computer vision, building vision systems for practical applications remains a considerable challenge. This is especially true in applications such as robotics and autonomous systems, in which even a small error rate in the perception system can have catastrophic effects on the overall system. This talk will review a few ideas that can be used to start formalizing the issues revolving around the integration of vision systems. They include a systematic approach to the problem of self-assessment of vision algorithm performance and of predictive quality metrics on the inputs to vision algorithms, ideas on how to manage multiple hypotheses generated from a vision algorithm rather than relying on a single "hard" decision, and methods for using external (non-visual) domain- and task-dependent information and constraints to boost the performance of the vision system. These ideas will be illustrated with examples of recent vision systems for scene understanding, depth cueing, and object recognition for robotics and HRI applications.

•

Deep Hierarchies in Human and Computer Vision

Norbert Krüger

University of Southern Denmark
norbert@mmmi.sdu.dk

Abstract. In the last decade, computer vision - although being still a rather young scientific discipline - was able to provide some impressive examples of artificial vision systems that outperform humans (for example in terms of speed in well defined industrial inspection tasks or in terms of precision as for example in the latest vision based technology for goal decisions in football). However, the human visual system is still superior to any artificial vision system in visual tasks requiring generalization and reasoning (often also called 'cognitive vision') such as extraction of visual based affordances or visual tasks in the context of tool use and dexterous manipulation. Two decades ago, there has been a strong connection between the two communities dealing with human vision research and computer vision. This link however has been somehow lost recently and computer vision has been more and more developed into a sub-field of machine learning. In this talk, I argue that the reason for the superiority of human vision for 'cognitive vision tasks' is connected to the deep hierarchical architecture of the primate's visual system which contradicts the 'flat design' of many of the most successful artificial vision systems available today. I will ponder on this somehow disturbing fact and will give arguments in favor of establishing deep structures as the only way to be able to solve cognitive vision tasks. The talk is divided into three parts: First, I will give an overview about today's knowledge about the primate's (and by that the human's) visual system primarily based on neurophysiological research. In the second part of the talk, an 'Early cognitive Vision' (ECV) system is described. The ECV system is a deep hierarchical visual representation designed as a visual front-end facilitating the realization of higher level processes, in particular on intelligent robot systems. Basic design choices of the system have been motivated by analogies to the human visual system. The current status of the ECV system is presented as well as a number of applications, in particular in the context of certain learning tasks connected to robotics. In the last part, I will summarize current research attempts on deep hierarchies in computer vision made by other groups and will formulate a number of open research questions related to the design of artificial cognitive vision systems. By that I also hope to help to facilitate a renewal of a fruitful interaction between biological and computer vision.

Table of Contents

Image and Video Capture

Automatic Unconstrained Online Configuration of a Master-Slave
Camera System 1
David Münch, Ann-Kristin Grosselfinger, Wolfgang Hübner, and Michael Arens

A Five-Camera Vision System for UAV Visual Attitude
Calculation and Collision Warning 11
Akos Zarandy, Zoltan Nagy, Balint Vanek, Tamas Zsedrovits, Andras Kiss, and Mate Nemeth

An Integrated 4D Vision and Visualisation System 21
Csaba Benedek, Zsolt Jankó, Csaba Horváth, Dömötör Molnár, Dmitry Chetverikov, and Tamás Szirányi

Compensation for Multipath in ToF Camera Measurements Supported
by Photometric Calibration and Environment Integration 31
Stefan Fuchs, Michael Suppa, and Olaf Hellwich

Coloured Video Code for In-Flight Data Transmission 42
Falk Schubert, Thilo Fath, and Harald Haas

Vision-Based Magnification of Corneal Endothelium Frames 52
Dario Comanducci and Carlo Colombo

Visual Attention and Object Detection

FACTS - A Computer Vision System for 3D Recovery and Semantic
Mapping of Human Factors 62
Lucas Paletta, Katrin Santner, Gerald Fritz, Albert Hofmann, Gerald Lodron, Georg Thallinger, and Heinz Mayer

Anytime Perceptual Grouping of 2D Features into 3D Basic Shapes 73
Andreas Richtsfeld, Michael Zillich, and Markus Vincze

Model-Based Pose Estimation for Rigid Objects 83
Manolis Lourakis and Xenophon Zabulis

A Web-Service for Object Detection Using Hierarchical Models 93
Domen Tabernik, Luka Čehovin, Matej Kristan, Marko Boben, and Aleš Leonardis

Fast Detection of Multiple Textureless 3-D Objects.................... 103
   Hongping Cai, Tomáš Werner, and Jiří Matas

Biological Models for Active Vision: Towards a Unified Architecture 113
   Kasim Terzić, David Lobato, Mário Saleiro, Jaime Martins,
   Miguel Farrajota, J.M.F. Rodrigues, and J.M.H. du Buf

Real-Time Image Recognition with the Parallel Directed Enumeration
Method... 123
   Andrey V. Savchenko

Self-Localization and Pose Estimation

Simultaneous Localization and Mapping for Event-Based Vision
Systems 133
   David Weikersdorfer, Raoul Hoffmann, and Jörg Conradt

Dimensionality Reduction for Efficient Single Frame Hand Pose
Estimation 143
   Petros Douvantzis, Iason Oikonomidis, Nikolaos Kyriazis, and
   Antonis Argyros

A Head Pose Tracking System Using RGB-D Camera................. 153
   Songnan Li, King Ngi Ngan, and Lu Sheng

A New Hierarchical Method for Markerless Human Pose Estimation 163
   Yuan Lei, Huawei Pan, Weixia Chen, and Chunming Gao

Autonomous Robot Navigation: Path Planning on a Detail-Preserving
Reduced-Complexity Representation of 3D Point Clouds 173
   Rohit Sant, Ninad Kulkarni, Ainesh Bakshi, Salil Kapur, and
   Kratarth Goel

Motion and Tracking

High Frame Rate Egomotion Estimation 183
   Natesh Srinivasan, Richard Roberts, and Frank Dellaert

Is Crowdsourcing for Optical Flow Ground Truth Generation
Feasible?... 193
   Axel Donath and Daniel Kondermann

A Comparative Study on Multi-person Tracking Using Overlapping
Cameras.. 203
   Martijn C. Liem and Dariu M. Gavrila

Visual Tracking Using Superpixel-Based Appearance Model 213
   Shahed Nejhum, Muhammad Rushdi, and Jeffrey Ho

Carried Object Detection and Tracking Using Geometric Shape
Models and Spatio-temporal Consistency............................ 223
   Aryana Tavanai, Muralikrishna Sridhar, Feng Gu,
   Anthony G. Cohn, and David C. Hogg

Robust Multi-hypothesis 3D Object Pose Tracking 234
   Georgios Chliveros, Maria Pateraki, and Panos Trahanias

Automatic Parameter Adaptation for Multi-object Tracking 244
   Duc Phu Chau, Monique Thonnat, and François Brémond

Probabilistic Cue Integration for Real-Time Object Pose Tracking...... 254
   Johann Prankl, Thomas Mörwald, Michael Zillich, and
   Markus Vincze

3D Reconstruction

Depth Estimation during Fixational Head Movements in a Humanoid
Robot 264
   Marco Antonelli, Angel P. del Pobil, and Michele Rucci

LaserGun: A Tool for Hybrid 3D Reconstruction 274
   Marco Fanfani and Carlo Colombo

Accurate Dense Stereo Matching of Slanted Surfaces Using 2D Integral
Images 284
   Gwnag Yul Song, Seong Ik Cho, Dong Yong Kwak, and
   Joon Woong Lee

Integrating Multiple Viewpoints for Articulated Scene Model
Aquisition 294
   Leon Ziegler, Agnes Swadzba, and Sven Wachsmuth

Features, Learning and Validation

Explicit Context-Aware Kernel Map Learning for Image Annotation.... 304
   Hichem Sahbi

Integrating Cue Descriptors in Bubble Space for Place Recognition 314
   Özgür Erkent and Işıl Bozma

A Hierarchical Scheme of Multiple Feature Fusion for High-Resolution
Satellite Scene Categorization 324
   Wen Shao, Wen Yang, Gui-Song Xia, and Gang Liu

A Validation Benchmark for Assessment of Medial Surface Quality
for Medical Applications 334
   Agnés Borràs, Debora Gil, Sergio Vera, and Miguel Angel González

When Is a Confidence Measure Good Enough?........................ 344
 *Patricia Márquez-Valle, Debora Gil, Aura Hernàndez-Sabaté, and
 Daniel Kondermann*

Parallel Deep Learning with Suggestive Activation for Object Category
Recognition 354
 Karthik Mahesh Varadarajan and Markus Vincze

Author Index... 365

Automatic Unconstrained Online Configuration of a Master-Slave Camera System

David Münch, Ann-Kristin Grosselfinger, Wolfgang Hübner, and Michael Arens

Fraunhofer IOSB, Gutleuthausstraße 1, 76275 Ettlingen, Germany
david.muench@iosb.fraunhofer.de

Abstract. Master-slave camera systems – consisting of a wide-angle master camera and an actively controllable pan-tilt-zoom camera – provide a large field of view, allowing monitoring the full situational context, as well as a narrow field of view, to capture sufficient details. Unconstrained calibration of such a system is a non-trivial task. In this paper a fully automatic and adaptive configuration method is proposed. It learns a motor map relating image coordinates from the master view to motor commands of the slave camera. First, a rough initial configuration is estimated by registering images from the slave camera onto the master view. In order to be operational in poorly textured environments, like hallways, the motor map is online refined by utilizing correspondences originating from moving objects. The accuracy is evaluated in different environments, as well as in the visual and the infrared spectrum. The overall accuracy is significantly improved by the online refinement.

Keywords: Master-slave camera system. Self calibration. Semi-stationary camera system. Video surveillance. Weak calibration.

1 Introduction

In content-based video analysis the goal is a holistic understanding of an observed scene. We assume a surveillance scenario which means that any situation of an observed agent of interest – an object, a person, a vehicle, etc. – is automatically recognized and logged. If a situation is considered dangerous or unusual an automated warning should be raised in order to assist the human operator. Being visually supported by the surveillance system, the human operator is able to pay attention on specific predefined situations of interest.

Master-slave camera systems are a practical trade-off in order to overcome limitations of cameras with a single focus. They provide a large field of view (FOV), allowing to monitor the full situational context, as well as a narrow FOV, used to capture sufficient details of individual objects, at the same time. A typical setup consists of a wide-angle master camera with a fixed focus and an actively controllable pan-tilt-zoom (PTZ) camera.

Figure 1 depicts the camera setup and the envisioned application scenario in which detailed information about people, interactions, etc. are automatically captured by a detailed close-up view. Close-up views are required for more detailed detection and identification of objects. As mentioned in [9] there is a lower

M. Chen, B. Leibe, and B. Neumann (Eds.): ICVS 2013, LNCS 7963, pp. 1–10, 2013.
© Springer-Verlag Berlin Heidelberg 2013

(a)   (b)

Fig. 1. Application scenario and camera setup. The master camera captures a scene with automatically increasing the information in potentially interesting areas. (a) In this image a master camera detects several unspecified objects, while close-up views from the PTZ-camera allow, e.g. the identification of a car (red) or person (orange) or what the persons are doing (blue). (b) The master-slave camera system used in this work consists of an Axis P5534, Q1755, and Q1922.

bound of the size of detecting a person in an image. Other demands for close-ups might stem from pose reconstruction [6] for action recognition of persons. Face detection for person identification can also be applied [4]. The system is intended to support a rule-based inference machine [20], which fuses all the mentioned methods above and performs semantic feedback to the active controllable cameras to even further specialize the situations of interest in a scene.

This article is structured as follows: Section 2 provides an overview of related work on multi-camera systems and their configuration. Our proposed system and the whole processing pipeline are presented in Section 3. Section 4 gives a comprehensive evaluation and explains the online refinement. Section 5 provides a conclusion. The contribution of this article is (a) a comprehensive vision system working under low constraints (b) in different spectral ranges and (c) the automatic online refinement followed by a comprehensive evaluation.

2 Related Work

In the literature active multi-camera systems which were mainly well-defined and calibrated are addressed in [12]. Here, we mainly address the problem of setting up multi-camera systems in unconstrained environments, without extrinsic calibration and without precise knowledge about the geometry of the cameras.

Multi-camera Systems. There can be differentiated between different kinds of multi-camera systems with active components. In [4] several PTZ-cameras cooperate in a scene observed by one master camera. Several master cameras and several PTZ-cameras are investigated in [23]. In an indoor environment, such as a smart control room, there are dozens of cameras among them one with a fisheye objective and two PTZ-cameras [13]. Another possibility instead of a fix master camera is the use of only PTZ-cameras with one of them operating as master camera [8].

Motivation and Organization of Camera Control. In addition to different hardware configurations, there is a clear distinction in terms of the motivation and organization of the purpose and control of a multi-camera system. One application of a multi-camera system is to track objects over several cooperative cameras [10]. Another application is to increase the information of certain objects, such as number plate recognition [24] or person identification [27]. In [4] both methods, multi-camera object tracking and the generation of close-up views are combined in one system.

According to Bellotto et. al. [4] the organization of multi-camera control can be divided in three parts: First, there is the *Picture Domain Camera Control*, which means that the control of the cameras is only based on low-level information from 2D images. Second, there is the *Scene Domain Camera Control* making use of 3D scene models etc. And finally, there is the *Conceptual Level Camera Control* using extracted higher-level information to control the cameras intelligently.

Configuration and Calibration. In a multi-camera system the mapping from a point in one camera to the corresponding point in the other camera is essential. For that the calibration of the camera system is needed. Calibration methods can be divided into weak and strong calibration methods.

Strong calibration means that both internal and external parameters of all cameras have to be determined. This allows determining the correspondences of a point in a 2D image to another point in a 2D image via 3D world coordinates. The calibration can be done for every camera [25], or as a pair-wise stereo setup [11]. In outdoor scenarios often georeferences are added [23]. Compensating the deficiencies of low-budget cameras, Jain et. al. [14] use an extended set of calibration equations, in contrast to [22] where a simplified camera model is used. Other methods need manual assistance, such as hand-drawn gridlines, or light-points [7].

Weak calibration avoids the mapping from one image to the other via 3D world-coordinates. Instead a lookup-table (LUT) with the corresponding 2D image coordinates and the PTZ motor coordinates is generated. Early approaches (e.g. [28]) make use of manually selected correspondences, such as annotated persons [18]. The interpolation of sparse LUTs can be performed e.g. geometrically [16] or with splines [1]. Other methods use specific properties of certain scenes as e.g. lane markings or vanishing points.

Methods based on local image features, e.g. [16], avoid scene dependent specialties and are independent from what is seen in an image. As the FOV of the PTZ-camera is normally only a small fraction of the master camera's FOV, several approaches generate a mosaic image of images from the PTZ-camera while storing the PTZ coordinates. Wu and Radke [26] do not save the mosaic image, instead only the features are stored.

Here we propose a method for automatically calibrating the master-slave camera system, see Figure 1. The proposed method combines several advantages of the above mentioned approaches into one configuration method. The method performs a weak calibration under the constraint that both cameras have a similar view point. In general no further assumptions about the camera geometry are made. Instead of mosaicking, a sparse initial LUT is interpolated using linear regression in order to calculate the mapping from master image coordinates to the motor space of the PTZ camera. As it is not possible to find correspondences in poorly textured regions, therefore, an online refinement using temporarily available objects during operation in these areas to incrementally improve the LUT is proposed. Online refinement turns out to be an essential processing step in most real world scenarios.

3   Methods

In the following section the whole processing pipeline of our proposed master-slave camera system is described in detail.

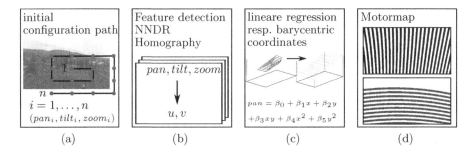

Fig. 2. The overall processing pipeline, used to automatically determine the motor map. (a) A rough initial set of correspondences is determined. (b) The process samples a mapping between the image coordinates (u, v) of the master camera and the motor space of the PTZ camera. (c) A linear regression resp. Barycentric coordinates are used to generate a dense LUT. (d) Visualization of the learned dense motormap (rounded to integers and alternately colored).

3.1   Determining Correspondences between Uncalibrated Cameras

Local image features sampled around view invariant interest points have been proven to be an efficient tool in determining corresspondences without additional constraints. For a comprehensive review on local features see [15,17]; particularly due to their efficient runtime complexity, we decided to use SURF features [2], although the proposed method is not limited to a specific feature type. In order to compensate stronger deviations in view point, our method can also be used with affine invariant features [17,19], or features adapted to the source image [21]. Despite estimating the internal camera parameters no further preprocessing, image correction, photometric correction, or spectral adaption is required.

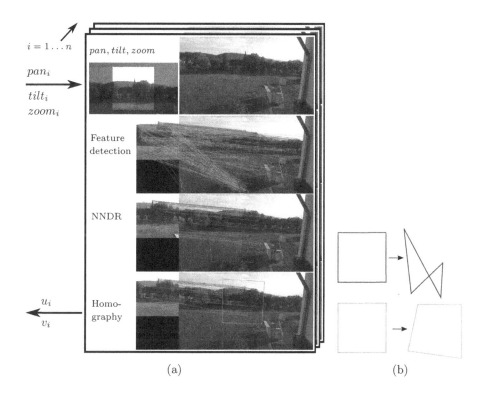

Fig. 3. (a) Visualization of detecting features in master and slave image, matching corresponding features, and estimating the homography. (b) Verifying probably unuseful homographies (upper) and only allowing probably good homographies (lower).

The initialization and matching of the processing pipeline are shown in Figure 2. To start the configuration a rough initial set of correspondences is determined. Thus, the PTZ-camera starts moving in a spiral-like pattern (a) in order to cover its full viewing range. Subsequently, in each correspondences step the features are extracted, matched, and a homography is estimated (b). For feature matching we avoid using fixed thresholds or simple Nearest Neighbor Search. Instead Nearest Neighbor Distance Ratio is used, as it performs best in our setups [17]. Finally, the homography between the two views is computed from the correspondences, see Figure 3 (a).

To reject 'wrong' homographies, see Figure 3 (b), we normalize the transformation matrix H_{sm} according to $detH'_{sm} = 1$: $H'_{sm} = H_{sm} * \frac{sgn(detH_{sm})}{\sqrt[3]{|detH_{sm}|}}$, see also [3]. $H'_{sm} \in SL_3(\mathbb{R})$ thus, we can apply thresholds to avoid outliers, in our case: $-5{,}0 < h'_{11} < 5{,}0$, $\quad -5{,}0 < h'_{22} < 5{,}0$, $\quad 0{,}55 < h'_{33} < 2{,}5$.

3.2 Mapping Image Coordinates to Motor Space

The adaptation process described so far generates a sparse mapping between coordinates in the master image and the motor space of the PTZ camera, see Figure 4. In order to be applicable a dense mapping has to be estimated from the sparse LUT. In general a bijective function is desired, but due to inaccuracies in the motor control of the PTZ-camera, the mapping is only injective.

Minimizing the error over different types of polynoms we get

$$\text{pan} = a_{p0} + a_{p1} * x + a_{p2} * y + a_{p3} * x * y + a_{p4} * x^2 + a_{p5} * y^2.$$

With $(p_1 \cdots p_n)^T = \boldsymbol{X}\boldsymbol{a_p} + \boldsymbol{\epsilon_p}$ and $\boldsymbol{X}$ according to the chosen polynom, the least square estimate is $\hat{\boldsymbol{a}}_{\boldsymbol{p}} = (\boldsymbol{X}^T\boldsymbol{X})^{-1}\boldsymbol{X}^T (p_1 \cdots p_n)^T = \boldsymbol{X}^+ (p_1 \cdots p_n)^T$. The same procedure for tilt. To assure reliable results RANSAC is applied in this step. A prototypical visualization of the initial and dense LUT is shown in Figure 2 (c).

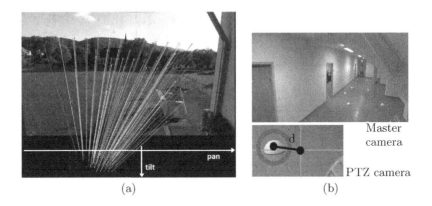

(a)   (b)

Fig. 4. (a) Registering the PTZ view onto the master image. This includes the sparse mapping. (zoom fixed). (b) Evaluating the error d (the distance of the ground truth PTZ motor coordinates and the actual PTZ coordinates) of the learned master-slave configuration.

3.3 Person Detection and Close-Up Image Acquisition

After having learned a dense LUT in the previous section the master-slave camera system is able to communicate between the different cameras. We can differentiate the image processing into the master-camera's part and the slave part.

An elaborated image processing loop starts with background subtraction and blob detection to identify potentially interesting situations.

Having gathered a close-up image with the slave camera, further fine-grained image processing methods are applied, such as person identification, face detection, and object detection. In addition to it human action recognition and high-level situation recognition are applied, too. We will not further detail those methods, as we see them as generic building blocks for the work presented here.

4   Evaluation

As the proposed system operates in a closed control loop, no offline data can be used for evaluation. Therefore, we quantitatively evaluated the performance of the system in different application domains. To evaluate the accuracy more than hundreds of markers were placed all over the FOV of the master camera, see Figure 4 (b). For every marker location the PTZ is moved to a position where the marker is centered in the PTZ's view. This procedure is done manually, in order to achieve ground truth data. Next, the procedure is repeated, using the automated PTZ control. The accuracy is measured in terms of the angular deviation in the position of the PTZ camera.

Robustness with Respect to the Application Domain. We evaluated the proposed system in different domains, see Figure 5. The comprehensive evaluation reveals the specific challenges in each domain.

Fig. 5. The proposed system was evaluated in different domains. In a human-like surveillance scenario (a,d), in an wide-scene surveillance scenario (b,c), in a perimeter protection scenario at night (e), and indoors (f).

Figure 6 summarizes results, measured in exemplary task domains, depicted in Figure 5. Over hundred markers are placed in the FOV of the master camera. For each marker the accuracy of the dense mapping is evaluated, see Figure 4 (b). In Figure 6 (a) resp. (b) the angular errors of pan resp. tilt of the PTZ camera are visualized (star). The x-axis are the pixels in horizontal (a) resp. vertical (b) direction. Thus, in the lower left of the FOV the error is larger than elsewhere. Comparing to Figure 4 (a), no correspondences could be found in that area of the scene.

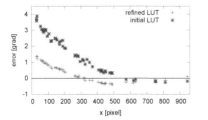
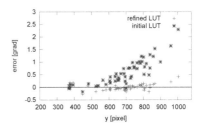

Fig. 6. Evaluation of the accuracy of pan (left) and tilt (right) in scenario Figure 5 (b) with the initial learned LUT (star) and the automatically online refined LUT (plus).

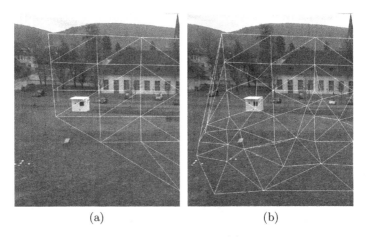

Fig. 7. Triangulation of the initial learned LUT (a); refined by additonally online found correspondences (b). The triangulation is used alternatively for interpolation with Barycentric coordinates instead of linear regresssion.

Incremental Online Refinement. Having evaluated the proposed system in the above domains reveals a weak point: In poorly texture regions it is not possible to establish sufficient corresspondeces. Therefore, the dense mapping has to be interpolated over large regions, resulting in an increasingly inaccurate PTZ control. That is a main drawback in the proposed system, as in that case, e.g., it is not applicable in the domains in Figure 5.

In order to overcome this limitation, we use the sparsely sampled FOV as an initial estimate and refine it using correspondences originating from moving objects. In typical scenes these are persons walking around, bikes and cars moving around. The idea is to use the temporal occurrence of persons or objects in low-textured areas to gather further correspondences for the sparse LUT and to refine the dense LUT incrementally and online.

In Figure 7 (a) a triangulation of the initial LUT is shown. In (b) it is extended by additional values gathered during a short time of operation. In Figure 6 the automatically refined LUT is evaluated again (plus). As a result, the error could be decreased by a factor of 5.

5   Conclusion

In this paper we have shown a semi-stationary master-slave camera system which is capable of self-configuration under non-cooperative low textured conditions. The effectiveness of the proposed system has been shown in different scenarios over time. Increasing the amount of cameras should include a georeferencing resulting in a global cover map. Further work include the extension of modalities e.g. [5] and the integration into a situation understanding framework [20], including high-level information inference as semantic feedback for lower level processes, c.f. first work on high-level semantic feedback is presented in [4].

References

1. Badri, J., Tilmant, C., Lavest, J.-M., Pham, Q.-C., Sayd, P.: Camera-to-Camera Mapping for Hybrid Pan-Tilt-Zoom Sensors Calibration. In: Ersbøll, B.K., Pedersen, K.S. (eds.) SCIA 2007. LNCS, vol. 4522, pp. 132–141. Springer, Heidelberg (2007)
2. Bay, H., Ess, A., Tuytelaars, T., Van Gool, L.: Speeded-Up Robust Features (SURF). Computer Vision and Image Understanding 110(3), 346–359 (2008)
3. Begelfor, E., Werman, M.: How to Put Probabilities on Homographies. Transactions on Pattern Analysis and Machine Intelligence 27(10), 1666–1670 (2005)
4. Bellotto, N., Benfold, B., Harland, H., Nagel, H.H., Pirlo, N., Reid, I., Sommerlade, E., Zhao, C.: Cognitive Visual Tracking and Camera Control. Computer Vision Image Understanding 116(3), 457–471 (2012)
5. Bodensteiner, C., Hebel, M., Arens, M.: Accurate Single Image Multi-Modal Camera Pose Estimation. In: Kutulakos, K.N. (ed.) ECCV 2010 Workshops, Part II. LNCS, vol. 6554, pp. 296–309. Springer, Heidelberg (2012)
6. Brauer, J., Hübner, W., Arens, M.: Generative 2D and 3D Human Pose Estimation with Vote Distributions. In: Proc. of 8th International Symposium on Visual Computing, Rethymnon, Crete, Greece (2012)
7. Davis, J., Chen, X.: Calibrating Pan-Tilt Cameras in Wide-Area Surveillance Networks. In: Proc. 9th IEEE Int. Conf. on Computer Vision, pp. 144–149 (2003)
8. Del Bimbo, A., Dini, F., Lisanti, G., Pernici, F.: Exploiting Distinctive Visual Landmark Maps in Pan-Tilt-Zoom Camera Networks. Computer Vision Image Understanding 114(6), 611–623 (2010)
9. Dollar, P., Wojek, C., Schiele, B., Perona, P.: Pedestrian Detection: An Evaluation of the State of the Art. IEEE Transactions on Pattern Analysis and Machine Intelligence 34(4), 743–761 (2012)
10. Everts, I., Sebe, N., Jones, G.: Cooperative Object Tracking with Multiple PTZ Cameras. In: 14th Int. Conf. on Image Analysis and Processing, pp. 323–330 (2007)
11. Horaud, R., Knossow, D., Michaelis, M.: Camera Cooperation for Achieving Visual Attention. Machine Vision and Applications 16(6), 1–2 (2006)

12. Hu, W., Tan, T., Wang, L., Maybank, S.: A Survey on Visual Surveillance of Object Motion and Behaviors. IEEE Transactions on Systems, Man, and Cybernetics, Part C: Applications and Reviews 34(3), 334–352 (2004)
13. IJsselmuiden, J., Stiefelhagen, R.: Towards High-Level Human Activity Recognition through Computer Vision and Temporal Logic. In: Dillmann, R., Beyerer, J., Hanebeck, U.D., Schultz, T. (eds.) KI 2010. LNCS, vol. 6359, pp. 426–435. Springer, Heidelberg (2010)
14. Jain, A., Kopell, D., Kakligian, K., Wang, Y.F.: Using Stationary-Dynamic Camera Assemblies for Wide-area Video Surveillance and Selective Attention. In: 2006 IEEE Computer Society Conference on Computer Vision and Pattern Recognition, vol. 1, pp. 537–544 (2006)
15. Li, J., Allinson, N.M.: A Comprehensive Review of Current Local Features for Computer Vision. Neurocomputing 71, 1771–1787 (2008)
16. Liao, H.C., Pan, M.H., Hwang, H.W., Chang, M.C., Po-Cheng, C.: An Automatic Calibration Method Based on Feature Point Matching for the Cooperation of Wide-Angle and Pan-Tilt-Zoom Cameras. Information Technology and Control 40(1), 41–47 (2011)
17. Mikolajczyk, K., Schmid, C.: A Performance Evaluation of Local Descriptors. Transactions on Pattern Analysis and Machine Intelligence 27(10), 1615–1630 (2005)
18. Mohanty, K., Gellaboina, M.: A Semi-Automatic Relative Calibration of a Fixed and PTZ Camera Pair for Master-Slave Control. In: 3rd European Workshop on Visual Information Processing, pp. 229–234 (2011)
19. Morel, J.M., Yu, G.: ASIFT: A New Framework For Fully Affine Invariant Image Comparison. SIAM Journal on Imaging Sciences 2(2), 438–469 (2009)
20. Münch, D., Michaelsen, E., Arens, M.: Supporting Fuzzy Metric Temporal Logic Based Situation Recognition by Mean Shift Clustering. In: Glimm, B., Krüger, A. (eds.) KI 2012. LNCS, vol. 7526, pp. 233–236. Springer, Heidelberg (2012)
21. Ozuysal, M., Calonder, M., Lepetit, V., Fua, P.: Fast Keypoint Recognition Using Random Ferns. Transactions on Pattern Analysis and Machine Intelligence 32(3), 448–461 (2010)
22. Sinha, S.N., Pollefeys, M.: Pan-Tilt-Zoom Camera Calibration and High-Resolution Mosaic Generation. Computer Vision and Image Understanding 103(3), 170–183 (2006); special issue on Omnidirectional Vision and Camera Networks
23. Szwoch, G., Dalka, P., Ciarkowski, A., Szczuko, P., Czyzewski, A.: Visual Object Tracking System Employing Fixed and PTZ Cameras. Intelligent Decision Technologies 5(2), 177–188 (2011)
24. Tian, Y.L., Brown, L., Hampapur, A., Lu, M., Senior, A., Shu, C.F.: IBM Smart Surveillance System (S3): Event Based Video Surveillance System With an Open and Extensible Framework. Machine Vision and App. 19(5-6), 315–327 (2008)
25. Tsai, R.: A Versatile Camera Calibration Technique for High-Accuracy 3D Machine Vision Metrology Using Off-The-Shelf TV Cameras and Lenses. IEEE Journal of Robotics and Automation 3(4), 323–344 (1987)
26. Wu, Z., Radke, R.: Keeping a Pan-Tilt-Zoom Camera Calibrated. Transactions on Pattern Analysis and Machine Intelligence 99, 1 (2012)
27. Yi, R.D.X., Gao, J., Antolovich, M.: Novel Methods for High-Resolution Facial Image Capture Using Calibrated PTZ and Static Cameras. In: 2008 IEEE International Conference on Multimedia and Expo, pp. 45–48 (2008)
28. Zhou, X., Collins, R.T., Kanade, T., Metes, P.: A Master-Slave System to Acquire Biometric Imagery of Humans at Distance. In: First ACM SIGMM International Workshop on Video Surveillance, IWVS 2003, pp. 113–120 (2003)

A Five-Camera Vision System for UAV Visual Attitude Calculation and Collision Warning

Akos Zarandy[1,2], Zoltan Nagy[1,2], Balint Vanek[1], Tamas Zsedrovits[1],
Andras Kiss[2,1], and Mate Nemeth[1]

[1] Institute for Computer Science and Control, 13-17 Kende Street, Budapest, H-1111, Hungary
zarandy.akos@sztaki.mta.hu
[2] Pazmany Peter Catholic University, 50 Prater Street

Abstract. A five-camera vision system was developed for UAV visual attitude calculation and collision warning. The vision system acquires images by using five miniature cameras, stores, and evaluates the visual data real-time with a multi-core processor system implemented in FPGA. The system was designed to be able to operate on a medium sized UAV platform, which raised numerous strict physical constraints.

Keywords: vision system, UAV, low power, multi-camera, FPGA, multi-core processing, image processing, visual navigation, collision warning.

1   Introduction

Unmanned Aerial Vehicle (UAV) technology reached an advanced level, which enables them technically to fly autonomously a predefined paths and complete different missions. However, legally they are not allowed to fly fully autonomously, since flight authorities identified various safety shortcomings [1]. One of the problems is that they are not robust enough due to the lack of on-board sensor and actuator redundancies. Another missing capability is the collision avoidance [2,3,4,5], because the GPS based control and navigation system makes the UAV flying practically blindly, hence it can collide with any other aircraft, or with any stationary object, which is not correctly on the map (new building, antenna tower, pillar of a bridge, crane, ski lift, etc.). The introduced vision system was designed to help in these problems, by making the Inertial Navigation System (INS) more robust by adding an extra angular velocity sensor source, and by identifying collision threats in time.

Naturally the vision system should fulfill numerous tough specification criteria. Its resolution and field of view (FOV) should be high enough to identify intruder aircraft from large distance; it should be able to perform real-time processing; its size, weight, and power consumption parameters should satisfy on-board UAV operation requirements; and finally, it should be affordable. From functionality point of view, it is expected to calculate the attitude of the aircraft by calculating the differential orientation changes between consequent frames (yaw, pitch, roll angles) and detect intruder aircrafts, which are on a collision course; store all the acquired images in full resolution for archiving and for off-line testing purposes.

M. Chen, B. Leibe, and B. Neumann (Eds.): ICVS 2013, LNCS 7963, pp. 11–20, 2013.
© Springer-Verlag Berlin Heidelberg 2013

The paper is organized on a way that first we describe the state-of-the-art and the related work in this field (Section 2). Then, system specification is given in Section 3 After that the system is described in Section 4. In Section 5 the multi-core processor array implementation is briefly shown. Finally, measurement results are given in Section 6.

2   Related Work

Naturally, avoiding mid-air collisions is not a new problem. Traditionally, there are two different approaches to address the airborne collision avoidance. The first assumes cooperation among the aircrafts. In this case each aircraft transmits its position, velocity, and planned route, and based on a predefined protocol the aircrafts avoids approaching each-other. The nowadays used version of the system is called TCAS (traffic collision avoidance system) [6]. A new version of it, called ADS-B (automatic dependent surveillance-broadcast) is currently introduced, and will be mandatory in most larger aircrafts from 2020 [7]. Though cooperative approaches are relatively simple, and does not require sensing of remote aircrafts, however US and European agencies require having non-cooperating solution on board as well.

Modern big airliners utilize sophisticated radar and computer systems, which identify the position and the velocity of intruder aircrafts, warns the pilot if they are on a collision course, and even make an avoidance maneuver automatically if pilot does not react. However, this solution cannot be applied to small aircrafts due economic and weight considerations.

For large UAVs sensor fusion is a commonly used approach, to make the collision avoidance system operational in all flight conditions. The system, described in [8], is based on a pulsed Ka-band radar, two kinds of visible cameras, two IR cameras, and two PCs. For small UAVs vision only systems are currently developed in different places. One is described in [9], in which one piece of 1024x768 resolution camera and a PC with GPU is used to identify the intruder. Compared to this system, our system has significantly higher resolution, smaller weight, size and power consumption, thanks to its compact design and FPG image processor engine.

3   System Specification

The vision system has two important roles, namely the attitude data calculation and the collision warning. From these, the more challenging task from image acquisition point of view is the collision warning, because detection of potentially dangerous intruder aircrafts in time requires the permanent monitoring of the field of view of $220°×70°$ in front of our UAV [10] with high resolution as we will see below. Fig. 1 illustrates the requirements of the safe avoidance. According to the flight safety requirements [10], there should be a certain separation volume around each aircraft, in which nothing else can be. The size of the separation volume (separation minima) differs from airplane to airplane and situation to situation.

To be able to avoid the separation minima, the intruder should be detected from a distance, which is not smaller than the traffic avoidance threshold. If the intruder is not detected before crossing the traffic avoidance threshold, but detected before the collision avoidance threshold, the collision can be still avoided. For human pilots 12.5 second before collision is the last time instant, when collision can be avoided with high probability [**Hiba! A hivatkozási forrás nem található.**]. Naturally, to avoid scaring the pilots and the passengers of the other aircraft, and to increase the safety level, earlier initialization of the avoidance maneuver is required, which certainly assumes earlier detection. Since the tracks of the small and medium size UAVs do not interfere with streamliners, or high speed jets, we have to be prepared for other UAVs and Cessna 172 type manned crafts. This means that the maximal joint approaching speed is 100 m/s, therefore we need to detect them from 2000 meters (20 seconds before collision), to be able to safely avoid them. In these cases the separation minima is 2000ft (~660m) collision volume is 500ft (~160m).

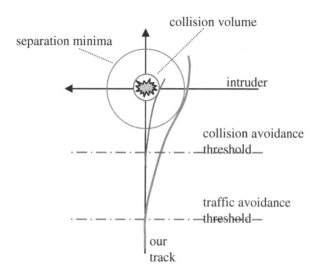

Fig. 1. Traffic (green) and collision (magenta) avoidance courses

To be able to perform robust visual detection of an aircraft, it should be at least 3 pixels large in the captured image. For a Cessna 172 class aircraft, with 10 meters wingspan, 0.1 degree/pixel resolution is minimum required. This means an overall minimum 2200x700 pixel resolution.

Other important system requirement is the speed. The control system is expecting 20 navigation parameter update in a second, therefore, the frame rate should be minimum 20FPS. Naturally, the image processing part of the vision system should be able to perform the complete processing on this speed also.

For real-time attitude calculation the same resolution and speed, but smaller FOV is satisfactory. Therefore the system with the above specification can calculate the angular changes of the aircraft orientation.

The system should be able to fit and operate on a UAV platform, which introduces strong limitations to its size, weight and power parameters. Our target was to fit the device to medium sized UAVs with 3m wingspan, which limits the weight to maximum 0,5kg including batteries. Another important requirement is that the vision and storage system should be resonance tolerant.

4   System Description

In this section first, the selection of the main components is described, then the system architecture, the interconnections of the components, the power distribution, and the system integration are shown.

4.1   Camera Selection

The key component of a special purpose vision system is the camera. During the design phase, one has to consider different types of camera. One would think that the most straightforward solution would be to use one piece of high resolution (like 2500x1000) camera with a low distortion ultra-wide angle optics. However, the problem with this setup is that the size and the weight of the camera and especially the ultra-wide view angle optics is way beyond the acceptable limits.

Therefore we have decided to apply multiple small cameras. We have studied three different classes of cameras:

1. Micro cameras with integrated lenses (mobile phone class);
2. Miniature cameras with S-mount (M12) lenses;
3. Small industrial cameras with C-mount or CS-mount lenses.

Micro Cameras. The advantage of the micro cameras is that they are cheap, have sufficient pixel resolution up to 8 megapixels (e.g. Framos modules: http://www.framos-imaging.com/sensormodules.html?&L=1), and they are ultra-compact and low power. However, the price of the miniaturization is poor optical quality, and rolling shutter sensors, which makes them unusable for UAV navigation application, where it is critical to capture the entire image at the same time.

Miniature Cameras with S-mount (M12) Lenses. Miniature cameras are good candidates for low volume, low weight applications. In this camera class, the optics is already replaceable, and one can find high resolution (megapixel) lightweight optics (http://www.sedeco.nl/sedeco/index.php/lenses/smount) for them with different view angles. The resolution of the rolling shutter ones are going up or beyond 5 megapixels (http://www.mobisensesystems.com/pages_en/aptina_modules.html), while the global shutter ones have lower resolutions, like WVGA or the soon available 1.2 megapixels one (http://www.mobisensesystems.com/pages_en/camera_modules.html). Here the typical power consumption is less than 200mW, and the weight is around 10g including optics.

The output of these cameras is either parallel raw data or USB.

Small Industrial Cameras with C-mount or CS-mount Lenses. There are a very large number of cameras in this class. One can find them in different resolution (from VGA up to 8 megapixels), size (from 3x3x3cm), weight (from 40g), and both rolling and global shutter types (e.g. http://www.ptgrey.com/products/index.asp). However, here the weight of a precision lens is significant as well (60-200g) (http://www.edmundoptics.com/imaging/imaging-lenses/), hence the overall weight is above 100g. This weight is much larger than the cameras in the second category, but as an exchange, the precision of the lens and the optical alignment is much better. The power consumption of these cameras is watts rather than hundred milliwats, mostly because they use power hungry high-speed serial output data channels.

The outputs of these cameras are typically Gige, USB 2, USB 3, Camera Link, or Fire-wire.

Selection. Since we need global shutter sensor, we can select cameras from the second or the third category only. The second category makes possible to build vision system for small and medium sized UAVs, where weight of the vision system should not exceed 500g.

Our other selection criterion was the data interface. For us the parallel digital raw data IO was the optimal, since for short distance it consumes much less power than high speed serial interfaces (Gige, USB, Fire-wire, Camera Link) which were designed for long distance communications.

We have selected 5 pieces WVGA (752x480) cameras (MBSV034M-FFC from Mobisens) to cover the required resolution with necessary overlap. For this ⅓ inch camera module, we have selected 3.66 mm focal length High Resolution Infinite Conjugate μ-Video™ Imaging Lenses from Edmund.

4.2   Data Storage Unit

In an airborne application the data storage can be implemented in some kinds of flash memory device. The options are memory card, USB stick, or solid state disk. The data-rate to save in this device is 5x752x480x20=36Mbyte/sec (2.1 Gbyte/min) raw data assuming 5 cameras, WVGA image size, and 20fps. Though data compression is a widely used option for image storage, in our application, where very small remote objects are needed to be identified, the artifacts introduced by the compression is intolerable.

Therefore we needed a device which can cope with 36Mbyte/sec data flow. This is way beyond the write speed of an SD card (2-10Mbyte/sec) or a USB stick (4-25Mbyte/sec). Moreover, we need to store up to 20 minutes flight data during a test data acquisition flight, hence 45Gbyte data storage space is needed. This fits already to a small sized SSD (64 Gbyte). The system enables easy up scaling, since SSDs go up to 600Gbyte.

4.3   Processor Selection

Nowadays the high-performance image processing platforms are based either on GPUs, or on DSPs, or on FPGAs. In case of strict power, weight, and size budget, the power hungry GPU platforms with their heavy cooling radiators cannot be an option, even though there have been some platforms already developed for military UAVs (http://defense.ge-ip.com/products/gpgpu/c497).

By comparing DSPs and FPGAs, the DSPs are more flexible, and their programming time is much shorter, however, the processing performance of the FPGAs is much higher. Since a five-camera data acquisition, processing and storing system requires high computational speed and flexible data communication channels, the FPGA solution was the better choice. We have selected a small form factor FPGA board with a Spartan 6 XC6SLX45T FPGA (EXPARTAN-6T, http://www. tokudenkairo.co.jp/exp6t/), which had enough user IO ports to collect the data from the five cameras, and had SATA interface to save the acquired image flows.

4.4   System Architecture and Interconnections

The block diagram of the system is shown in **Fig. 2**. It contains off-the-shelf components (the cameras, the FPGA board, and the SSD), and a custom designed interface card. The cameras and the interface card are connected with 30 wire Flexible Flat Cable (FFC). The interface card is connected to the FPGA card with a board to board 80 pin connector. The SSD is connected to the FPGA board with SATA cable.

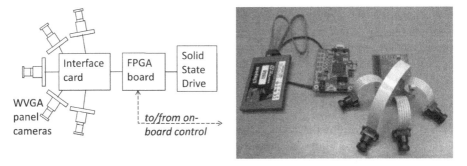

Fig. 2. The block diagram of the vision system and the photo of the connected components

4.5   Operation

The cameras are initialized through separate I^2C bus. They are running synchronized. Their integration times are the same, and they receive the same system clock, and exposure trigger signal. Therefore the individual frames are captured at the same time.

The vision system is connected to the on-bard control computer of the UAV through two I^2C buses. Through these connections, the vision system receives the attitude estimation calculated by the navigation computer, and based on it, the vision system also calculates its yaw, pitch, and roll figures, what is sent back to the navigation system. In case of intruder aircraft detection, its position and size is sent to the navigation and control computer to initialize an avoidance maneuver.

4.6   Power Supply

The total power consumption of vision system is about 7.5 W. Most of it is consumed by the SSD, which is 4.8 W alone (http://www.legitreviews.com/article/1980/1/). The energy source of the entire system is a 1200mAh 7.4V Lithium Polymer battery (2S1P). It can provide continuously 30 amps (25C), which ensures that the battery will not be overloaded. It enables close to 1 hour continuous operation.

4.7   System Integration

Physical system integration is always a key point of a complex embedded system. It is especially true for an airborne vision system with multiple cameras, where the relative camera orientations are critical. Therefore a horseshoe like solid aluminum frame was constructed for holding the cameras and cancelling any cross vibrations (**Fig. 3**). The interface and the FPGA cards were put in and behind the horseshoe between two aluminum planes. The vision system is mounted to the nose of a two engine aircraft on a way that the axis of the front camera is aligned with the horizontal axis of the aircraft (**Fig. 4**).

Fig. 3. Camera holder aluminum frame with the cameras (left), and the entire vision system without the power units (right)

5   Multi-core Processor Architecture in the FPGA

The image processing system should execute the following parallel tasks:

- calculating the attitude changes of the aircraft;
- identifying intrude aircrafts;
- communicating with the control and navigation processor of the UAV;
- and transferring the raw image data towards the SSD.

All of these functionalities are handled by a custom designed multi-core processor architecture implemented in a Spartan 6 LX45T FPGA. The basic concept of the processor design was to mimic the human foveal vision on a way that a pre-processor examines the entire frame and identifies those locations, which needs more attention. Then, the focus of the processing is shifted to these locations one after the other, similarly as our fovea focuses to different important details of a scene.

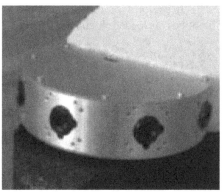

Fig. 4. The vision system mounted on the nose of the aircraft (left) and the enlarged aircraft nose (right)

The architecture of the multi-core foveal processor is shown in **Fig. 5**. As it is shown on the figure, the five parallel 8 bit data flows arriving synchronously from the cameras are combined to one, time multiplexed 8 bit data flow. The combined data flow goes to the SATA core and to the full-frame streaming pre-processor as well.

The pre-processor has a streaming architecture, means that it cannot randomly access the entire frame, but it receives it row-wise sequentially as the image is read out from the sensor. To be able to calculate neighborhood operators, it collects a few lines of the frame and processes those lines together. As the data stream flows through the processor, it finds those high contrast corner-like locations where displacement vector will be calculated when the next frame arrives. It also identifies those objects which might turn out during the post processing phase to be an intruder aircraft. The pre-processor sends the coordinates of the identified locations to the internal microprocessor (MicroBlaze), and saves the raw frame and the some processed data to the external memory.

The MicroBlaze is a general purpose 32 bit soft-core processor implemented in the Xilinx FPGAs. It has relatively low computational power (~200MHz clock speed), which means that it cannot perform image processing tasks. It can be used to be the control processor of the system, and also to perform some decision making and communication.

The MicroBlaze then goes through the identified suspicious locations and performs foveal (region of interest, ROI) processing one after the other, by instructing the binary and the grayscale ROI processors to cut out the required windows, copy them into the internal block memories of the FPGA, and execute the program sequences. The detailed description of the pre-processor and the foveal processor can be found in [11], while the algorithm description in [12].

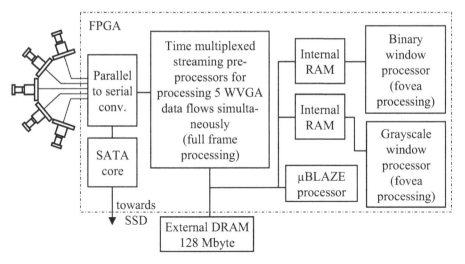

Fig. 5. The block diagram of the image processing architecture

6   Measurement Results

We have executed multiple successful flights for areal image acquisition. The captured image sequences are synchronized with the data recordings of the inertial measurement unit (IMU), hence the aircraft position and attitude at each frame capturing time intend is known.

On these image sequences, the displacement vectors were calculated in 8 different characteristic locations, and based on them, the attitude was calculated using the five-point method [13]. As it can be seen in **Fig. 6** the calculated yaw data of the UAV and the measured results are closely correlated. (Other two angles and the detailed description of the algorithm are shown in [13]. **Fig. 6** also shows an identified intruder aircraft. The algorithm performs well. It can identify all the intruder aircrafts against clear-sky or cloudy background in our image sequences captured from UAV platform or from the ground. On the other hand, we are at the beginning of the algorithm evaluation both in the attitude calculation and the intruder aircraft identification.

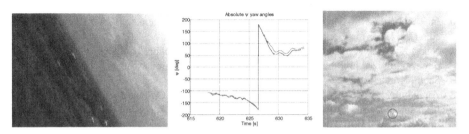

Fig. 6. The local displacement vectors (left), the yaw angle calculation with different methods (middle) (blue: five-point method [13], red: IMU data), and a detected intruder (right)

7 Conclusion

A five-camera vision system was introduced. The system was designed to be able to operate on UAV platforms. Its role is real-time attitude (orientation angle) calculation, vision based collision warning, and visual flight data acquisition. The system has been built and partially verified on a UAV platform.

Acknowledgement. The ONR Grants (N62909-11-1-7039, N62909-10-1-7081) is greatly acknowledged., The authors express their thanks to grants TÁMOP- 4.2.1.B-11/2/KRM-2011-0002 and TÁMOP-4.2.2/B-10/1-2010-0014.

References

1. Felder, W.: Unmanned System Integration into the National Airspace System. Keynote Presented at ICUAS 2012, Philadelphia, PA, USA (June 2012)
2. Dey, D., Geyer, C., Singh, S., Digioia, M.: Passive, Long-Range Detection of Aircraft: Towards a Field Deployable Sense and Avoid System. In: Howard, A., Iagnemma, K., Kelly, A. (eds.) Field and Service Robotics. STAR, vol. 62, pp. 113–123. Springer, Heidelberg (2010)
3. Federal Aviation Administration, Fact Sheet - Unmanned Aircraft Systems, UAS (2010)
4. Department of Defense, Unmanned Aircraft System Airspace Integration Plan. Tech. Rep. Department of Defense (March 2011)
5. Federal Aviation Administration, Integration of Unmanned Aircraft Systems into the National Airspace System Concept of Operations (2012)
6. Livadas, C., Lygeros, J., Lynch Nancy, A.: High-level modeling and analysis of the traffic alert and collision avoidance system (TCAS). Proceedings of the IEEE 88(7), 926–948 (2000)
7. Federal Aviation Administration, Fact Sheet - Automatic Dependent Surveillance-Broadcast (ADB-S) (2010)
8. Fasano, G., Accardo, D., Moccia, A., Carbone, C., Ciniglio, U., Corraro, F., Luongo, S.: Multi-Sensor-Based Fully Autonomous Non-Cooperative Collision Avoidance System for Unmanned Air Vehicles. Journal of Aerospace Computing, Information, and Communication 5(10), 338–360 (2008)
9. Mejias, L., McNamara, S., Lai, J., Ford, J.: Vision-based detection and tracking of aerial targets for UAV collision avoidance. In: International Conference on Intelligent Robots and Systems (IROS), pp. 87–92 (2010)
10. International Civil Aviation Organization, Air Traffic Management, ICAO Doc 4444, 15th edn. (2007)
11. Nagy, Z., Kiss, A., Zarándy, Á., Vanek, B., Péni, T., Bokor, J., Roska, T.: Volume and power optimized high-performance system for UAV collision avoidance. In: ISCAS 2012, Seoul, Korea (2012)
12. Zarándy, Á., Zsedrovits, T., Nagy, Z., Kiss, A., Roska, T.: On-board see-and-avoid system. In: Conference of the Hungarian Association for Image Processing and Pattern Recognition (Kepaf 2013), Bakonybel, pp. 604–617 (2013)
13. Zsedrovits, T., Zarandy, A., Vanek, B., Peni, T., Bokor, J., Roska, T.: Estimation of Relative Direction Angle of Distant, Approaching Airplane in Sense-and-avoid. Journal of Intelligent and Robotic Systems 69(1-4), 407–415 (2013)

An Integrated 4D Vision and Visualisation System

Csaba Benedek, Zsolt Jankó, Csaba Horváth, Dömötör Molnár, Dmitry Chetverikov,
and Tamás Szirányi*

Institute for Computer Science and Control, Hungarian Academy of Sciences
H-1111 Budapest, Kende utca 13-17, Hungary
firstname.lastname@sztaki.mta.hu

Abstract. This paper reports on a pilot system for reconstruction and visualisation of complex spatio-temporal scenes by integrating two different types of data: outdoor 4D data measured by a rotating multi-beam LIDAR sensor, and 4D models of moving actors obtained in a 4D studio. A typical scenario is an outdoor scene with multiple walking pedestrians. The LIDAR monitors the scene from a fixed position and provides a dynamic point cloud. This information is processed to build a 3D model of the environment and detect and track the pedestrians. Each of them is represented by a point cluster and a trajectory. A moving cluster is then substituted by a detailed 4D model created in the studio. The output is a geometrically reconstructed and textured scene with avatars that follow in real time the trajectories of the pedestrians.

Keywords: rotating multi-beam LIDAR, MRF, motion segmentation, 4D reconstruction.

1 Introduction

Efforts on real time reconstruction of 3D dynamic scenes receive great interest in intelligent surveillance [13], video communication and augmented reality systems. Obtaining realistic 4D video flows of real world scenarios may result in a significantly improved visual experience for the observer compared to watching conventional video streams, since a reconstructed 4D scene can be viewed and analysed from an arbitrary viewpoint, and virtually modified by the user. However, building an interactive 4D video system is highly challenging, as it needs in parallel automatic perception, interpretation, and real time visualisation of the environment.

A 4D reconstruction studio is an advanced, intelligent sensory environment, which uses multiple synchronized and calibrated high-resolution video cameras and a GPU to build dynamic 3D models providing free-viewpoint video in real-time. An example for this environment is introduced in [7]. While this system can efficiently record and visualise the model of a single moving person, in itself it is not appropriate to capture a large scenario with several moving people and various background objects.

---

* This work is connected to the i4D project funded by the internal R&D grant of MTA SZTAKI. Csaba Benedek also acknowledges the support of the János Bolyai Research Scholarship of the Hungarian Academy of Sciences and the Grant #101598 of the Hungarian Research Fund (OTKA). Dmitry Chetverikov is also affiliated with Eötvös Loránd Univeristy (ELTE).

M. Chen, B. Leibe, and B. Neumann (Eds.): ICVS 2013, LNCS 7963, pp. 21–30, 2013.
© Springer-Verlag Berlin Heidelberg 2013

Recently a portable stereo system has been introduced [8] for capturing and 3D reconstruction of dynamic outdoor scenes. Here the observed scenario should be surrounded by several (8-9) carefully calibrated cameras beforehand, and the reconstruction process is extremely computation-intensive, as dealing with a short 10 sec sketch takes several hours. In addition, full automation is difficult due to usual stereo artefacts such as featureless regions and occlusions, which can cause significant problems in an uncontrolled outdoor environment.

Time-of-Flight (ToF) technologies, such us LIDAR, offer notable advantages versus conventional video flows for automated scene analysis, since in the provided 2.5D range data sequences geometrical information is directly available, and the measurements are significantly less sensitive on the weather and illumination conditions of the acquisition. High speed Rotating Multi-Beam (RMB) LIDAR systems, such as the Velodyne HDL-64E sensor, are able to provide accurate 3D point cloud sequences with a 15 Hz refreshing frequency, making the configuration highly appropriate for analysing moving objects in large outdoor environments with a diameter up to 100 meters. However, a single RMB LIDAR scan is a notably sparse point cloud, moreover we can also observe a significant drop in the sampling density at larger distances from the sensor and we also can see a ring pattern with points in the same ring much closer to each other than points in different rings [1]. These properties yield poor visual experiences for the observes, when a raw (Fig. 8(a)) or a semantically coloured (Fig. 8(c)) point cloud sequence is displayed in a screen.

The above observations motivated us to develop an unconventional system, called the *integrated 4D* (i4D) system, which combines two very different sources of spatiotemporal information, namely, a RMB-LIDAR and a 4D reconstruction studio. The main purpose of the integration of the two types of data is our desire to measure and represent the visual world at different levels of detail. In our approach, the LIDAR sensor provides a global description of a dynamic outdoor scene in the form of a time-varying 3D point cloud. The latter is used to separate moving objects from static environment and obtain a 3D model of the environment. The 4D studio builds a detailed dynamic model of an actor (typically, a person) moving in the studio. By integrating the two sources of data, which is to our best knowledge a unique attempt up to now, one can modify the model of the scene and populate it with the avatars created in the studio.

2   System Description

This paper introduces the proposed i4D system, describing all major processing steps from the acquisition of the raw data (point clouds and videos) to the creation and visualisation of an augmented spatio-temporal model of the scene. The system configuration consists of the following processing blocks:

- *Data acquisition:* LIDAR based environment scanning for point cloud sequence generation,
- *Data preprocessing:* foreground and background segmentation of the LIDAR sequence by a robust probabilistic approach (Sec. 3.1),
- *Motion analysis:* detection and tracking of moving pedestrians, generating motion trajectories (Sec. 3.2),

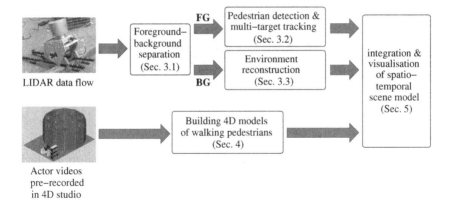

Fig. 1. Flowchart of the integrated 4D reconstruction system. **BG** is background, **FG** foreground.

- *Environment reconstruction:* geometric reconstruction of ground, walls and other field objects. Texturing the obtained 3D models with images of the scene (Sec. 3.3),
- *Pedestrian visualization:* creating textured moving pedestrian models in the 4D reconstruction studio (Sec. 4),
- *Integration:* transforming the system elements into a joint dynamic scene model and visualisation of the 4D scenario, where each avatar moves in the scene according to the assigned trajectory (Sec. 5).

Fig. 1 shows a flowchart of the complete i4D system. Each of the main building blocks is described in the corresponding section of the paper, as indicated in the flowchart.

3   LIDAR Data Processing

In this section, we present a hybrid method for dense foreground-background point labelling in a point cloud obtained by a Velodyne HDL-64E RMB-LIDAR device that monitors the scene from a fixed position. The method solves the computationally critical spatial filtering tasks applying an MRF model in the 2D range image domain. The ambiguities of the point-to-pixel mapping are handled by joint consideration of the true 3D positions and the 2D labels. Then, we execute detection and tracking of moving pedestrians for the foreground points. Next, we transform the background point cloud into a polygon mesh while maintaining the information about individual objects such as ground, walls, and trees. Finally, the models of the environment objects are manually textured using photos taken in the scene. Below, we describe these steps in more detail.

3.1   Foreground-Background Separation

The rotating multi-beam LIDAR device records 360°-view-angle range data sequences of irregular point clouds. Examples of measured point clouds will be shown later in this paper. To separate dynamic foreground from static background in a range data sequence, we apply a probabilistic approach [2].

range image   foreground mask

Fig. 2. Example of foreground-background segmentation

To ensure real-time operation, we project the irregular point cloud to a cylinder surface yielding a depth image on a regular lattice, and perform the segmentation in the 2D range image domain. A part of a range image showing several pedestrians is demonstrated in Fig. 2. Spurious effects are caused by the quantisation error of the discretised view angle, the non-linear position corrections of sensor calibration, and the background flickering, e.g., due to vegetation motion.

One can model the dynamic range image as a Mixture of Gaussians and update the parameters similarly to the standard approach [14]. This provides a segmentation of the point cloud which is quite noisy because of the spurious effects. These effects are significantly decreased by the dynamic MRF model [2] that describes the background and foreground classes by both spatial and temporal features. The model is defined in the range image space. The 2D image segmentation is followed by a 3D point classification step to resolve the ambiguities of the 3D-2D mapping. Using a spatial foreground model, we remove a large part of the irrelevant background motion which is mainly caused by moving tree crowns. Fig. 2 shows an example of foreground segmentation.

3.2   Pedestrian Detection and Multi-target Tracking

In this section, we present the pedestrian tracking module of the system. The input of the module step is a point cloud sequence, where each point is marked with a segmentation label of foreground or background. The output consists of clusters of foreground regions so that the points corresponding to the same person receive the same label over the sequence. We also generate a 2D foot point trajectory of each pedestrian to be used by the 4D scene reconstruction module.

First, the point cloud regions classified as foreground are clustered to obtain separate blobs for each moving person. We fit a regular lattice to the ground plane and project foreground regions onto this lattice. Morphological filters are applied in the image plane to obtain spatially connected blobs for different persons. Then we extract appropriately sized connected components that satisfy area constraints determined by lower and higher thresholds.

This procedure is illustrated in Fig. 3. The centre of each extracted blob is considered as a candidate for foot position in the ground plane. Connected pedestrian shapes may be merged into one blob, while blobs of partially occluded persons may be missed or broken into several parts. Instead of proposing various heuristic rules to eliminate these artefacts at the level of the individual time frames, we developed a robust multi-tracking module which efficiently handles the problems at the sequence level.

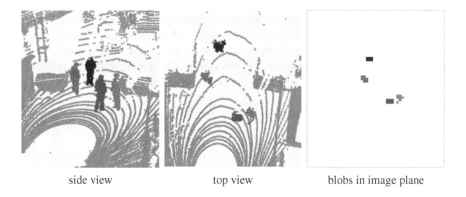

| side view | top view | blobs in image plane |

Fig. 3. Illustration of pedestrian separation

Our multi-tracking algorithm receives the measured ground plane positions and for each frame iterates three basic operations, namely, data assignment, Kalman filter correction and Kalman filter prediction. The assignment operation assigns the candidate positions to objects, then the object positions are corrected and, finally, predictions for the subsequent positions are made and fed back to the assignment procedure. The algorithm can handle false positives as well as tracks starting and terminating within a sequence. Temporary track discontinuities are bridged in a post-processing step, while short false tracks are removed based on their length.

Fig. 4. Example of pedestrian tracking in a LIDAR sequence. Top row: point clusters whose colours identify the tracked persons. Bottom row: corresponding video frames displayed for verification.

The tracker module provides a set of pedestrian trajectories, which are 2D foot centre point sequences in the ground plane. To determine the points corresponding to each pedestrian in a selected frame, the connected foot blobs around a given trajectory point should be vertically back-projected to the 3D point cloud. A result of tracking is demonstrated in Fig. 4 that shows two segmented point cloud frames from a measurement sequence in a courtyard. It also shows the video frames taken in parallel as reference. One can observe that during the tracking the point cluster of a pedestrian preserves its colour.

3.3   Environment Reconstruction

In this section, we describe our method for static environment reconstruction. First we accumulate the background points of the LIDAR sequence collected over several frames, which results in a dense point cloud that represents the ground, walls, trees, and other background objects. Assuming that the ground is reasonably flat and horizontal, we fit an optimal plane to this point cloud using the robust RANSAC [6] algorithm that treats all other objects as outliers. Points close to this plane are considered as ground points in the following. For vegetation detection and removal, we have developed an algorithm, which calculates a statistical feature for each point in the merged point cloud based on the distance and irregularity of its neighbors, and also exploits the intensity channel which is an additional indicator of vegetation, which reflects the laser beam with a lower intensity. The remaining points are then projected vertically to the obtained ground plane, where projections of wall points form straight lines that are extracted by the Hough transform [5]. Applying the Ball-Pivoting algorithm [3] to the 3D points that project to a straight line, we create a polygon mesh of a wall.

In the reconstruction phase, static background objects of the scene, such us trees, containers or parking cars are replaced with 3D models obtained from Google's 3D Warehouse. The recognition of these objects from the point cloud is currently done manually, and we are now working on the automation of this step. For example, one can adopt here the machine learning based approach of [10], which extracts various object level descriptors for point cloud blobs representing the detected objects, while to obtain similar representations of the training models from the 3D Warehouse, they perform ray casting on the models to generate point clouds, finally the classification is performed in the descriptor space.

Sample results of our environment reconstruction are shown in Fig. 8. Model texturing is based on a set of photographs taken in the scene.

4   Creating 4D Models of Walking Pedestrians

Relatively small objects such as pedestrians cannot be reconstructed from the LIDAR range data in sufficient detail since the data is too sparse and, in addition, it only gives 2.5D information. Therefore we create properly detailed, textured dynamic models indoors, in a 4D reconstruction studio. The hardware and software components of such a studio can be found in [4,7]. For completeness, we give below a brief description of the reconstruction process.

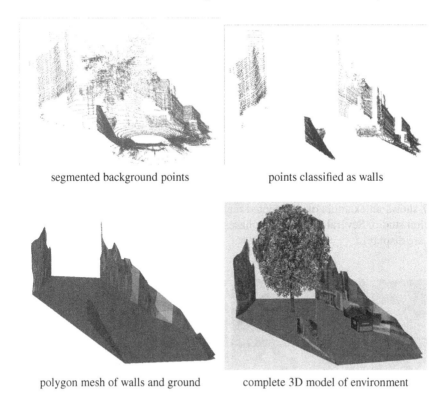

segmented background points   points classified as walls

polygon mesh of walls and ground   complete 3D model of environment

Fig. 5. Point cloud segmentation and environment reconstruction

Fig. 6 shows a sketch and a panorama of the studio where green curtains and carpet form homogeneous background to facilitate segmentation of the actor. The frame carries 12 calibrated and synchronised video cameras placed uniformly around the scene, and one additional camera on the top in the middle. The cameras are surrounded by programmable LEDs that provide direct illumination. The studio has ambient illumination, as well. Seven PC-s provide the computing power and control the cameras and the lighting.

Currently, each set of 13 simultaneous video frames captured by the cameras is processed independently from the previous one. For a set of 13 images, the system creates a textured 3D model showing a phase of actor's motion. The main steps of the completely automatic 3D reconstruction process are as follows:

1. Colour images are extracted from the captured raw data.
2. Each colour image is segmented to foreground and background. The foreground is post-processed to remove shadows [4].
3. A volumetric model is created using the Visual Hull algorithm [11].
4. A triangulated mesh is obtained from the volumetric model using the Marching Cubes algorithm [12].
5. Texture is added to the triangulated mesh based on triangle visibility [7].

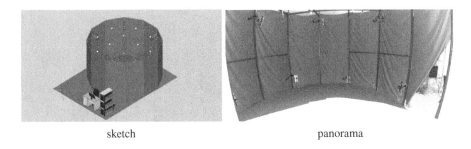

sketch   panorama

Fig. 6. Sketch and panorama of a 4D reconstruction studio

Fig. 7 shows an example of augmented reality created with the help of the 4D reconstruction studio. Several consecutive phases of an avatar walking in a virtual environment are displayed.

Fig. 7. A 4D studio actor walking in virtual environment

5   Integrating and Visualising the Spatio-temporal Scene Model

The last step of the workflow is the integration of the system components and visualisation of the integrated model. The walking pedestrian models are placed into the reconstructed environment so that the center point of the feet follows the trajectory extracted from the LIDAR point cloud sequence. Currently, we use the assumptions that the pedestrians walk forward along their trajectories. The top view orientation of a person is calculated from the variation of the 2D track.

To combine the 3D-4D data of different types arriving in different formats and visualise them in a unified format, we have developed a customised software system. All models are converted to the general-purpose OBJ format [15] which is supported by most 3D modelling programs and enables user to specify both geometry and texture.

Our visualisation program is based on the VTK Visualisation Kit [9]. Its primary goal is to efficiently support combining static and dynamic models allowing their multiplication and optimising the usage of computational resources. One can easily create mass scenes that can by viewed from arbitrary viewpoint, rotated and edited. Any user interaction with the models, such as shifting and scaling, is allowed and easy to perform.

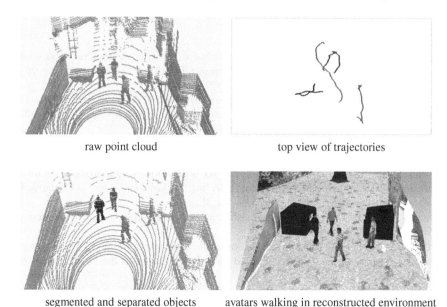

raw point cloud   top view of trajectories

segmented and separated objects   avatars walking in reconstructed environment

Fig. 8. Sample results of object tracking and integrated dynamic scene reconstruction

The dynamic shapes can be multiplied not only in space, but in time, as well. Our 4D studio is relatively small. Typically, only two steps of a walking sequence can be recorded and reconstructed. This short sequence can be multiplied and seamlessly extended in time to create an impression of a walking person. To achieve this, the system helps the user by shifting the phases of motion in space and time while appropriately matching the sequence of the models.

An important requirement was to visualise the 3D motions of the avatars according to the trajectories provided by the LIDAR pedestrian tracking unit. An avatar follows the assigned 3D path, while rotation of the model to the left or right in the proper direction is automatically determined from the trajectory. Sample final results of the complete 4D reconstruction and visualisation process are demonstrated in Fig. 8.

6   Conclusion and Outlook

In this paper, we have introduced a complex system on the interpretation and 4D visualisation of dynamic outdoor scenarios containing multiple walking pedestrians. As a key novelty, we have connected two different modalities of perception: a LIDAR point cloud stream from a large outdoor environment, and an indoor 4D reconstruction studio, which is able to provide detailed models of moving people. The proposed approach points towards real-time free-viewpoint and scalable visualisation of large scenes, which will be a crucial point in future augmented reality and multi modal communication applications. As future plans, we aim to extend the investigations to point cloud sequences collected from a moving platform, and also implement automatic field object recognition and surface texturing modules.

References

1. Behley, J., Steinhage, V., Cremers, A.: Performance of histogram descriptors for the classification of 3D laser range data in urban environments. In: IEEE International Conference on Robotics and Automation (ICRA), pp. 4391–4398 (May 2012)
2. Benedek, C., Molnár, D., Szirányi, T.: A dynamic MRF model for foreground detection on range data sequences of rotating multi-beam lidar. In: International Workshop on Depth Image Analysis, Tsukuba City, Japan. LNCS (2012)
3. Bernardini, F., Mittleman, J., et al.: The Ball-Pivoting algorithm for surface reconstruction. IEEE Transactions on Visualization and Computer Graphics 5(4), 349–359 (1999)
4. Blajovici, C., Chetverikov, D., Jankó, Z.: 4D studio for future internet: Improving foreground-background segmentation. In: IEEE International Conference on Cognitive Infocommunications (CogInfoCom), pp. 559–564. IEEE (2012)
5. Duda, R., Hart, P.: Use of the hough transformation to detect lines and curves in pictures. Comm. of the ACM 15, 11–15 (1972)
6. Fischler, M., Bolles, R.: Random sample consensus: A paradigm for model fitting with applications to image analysis and automated cartography. Comm. of the ACM 24, 381–395 (1981)
7. Hapák, J., Jankó, Z., Chetverikov, D.: Real-time 4D reconstruction of human motion. In: Perales, F.J., Fisher, R.B., Moeslund, T.B. (eds.) AMDO 2012. LNCS, vol. 7378, pp. 250–259. Springer, Heidelberg (2012)
8. Kim, H., Guillemaut, J.Y., Takai, T., Sarim, M., Hilton, A.: Outdoor dynamic 3-d scene reconstruction. IEEE Trans. on Circuits and Systems for Video Technology 22(11), 1611–1622 (2012)
9. Kitware: VTK Visualization Toolkit (2013), http://www.vtk.org
10. Lai, K., Fox, D.: Object recognition in 3D point clouds using web data and domain adaptation. International Journal of Robotic Research 29(8), 1019–1037 (2010)
11. Laurentini, A.: The visual hull concept for silhouette-based image understanding. IEEE Transactions on Pattern Analysis and Machine Intelligence 16, 150–162 (1994)
12. Lorensen, W., Cline, H.: Marching cubes: A high resolution 3D surface construction algorithm. In: Proc. ACM SIGGRAPH, vol. 21, pp. 163–169 (1987)
13. Roth, P., Settgast, V., Widhalm, P., Lancelle, M., Birchbauer, J., Brandle, N., Havemann, S., Bischof, H.: Next-generation 3D visualization for visual surveillance. In: IEEE International Conference on Advanced Video and Signal-Based Surveillance (AVSS), August 30-September 2, pp. 343–348 (2011)
14. Stauffer, C., Grimson, W.E.L.: Learning patterns of activity using real-time tracking. IEEE Transactions on Pattern Analysis and Machine Intelligence 22, 747–757 (2000)
15. Wavefront Technologies: OBJ file format. Wikipedia, Wavefront.obj file (2013)

Compensation for Multipath in ToF Camera Measurements Supported by Photometric Calibration and Environment Integration

Stefan Fuchs[1], Michael Suppa[1], and Olaf Hellwich[2]

[1] DLR, Robotics and Mechatronics Center, Weßling, Germany
[2] Technische Universität Berlin, Computer Vision & Remote Sensing, Germany

Abstract. Multipath is a prominent phenomenon in Time-of-Flight camera images and distorts the measurements by several centimetres. It troubles applications that demand for high accuracy, such as robotic manipulation or mapping. This paper addresses the photometric processes that cause multipath interference. It formulates an improved multipath model and designs a compensation process in order to correct the multipath-related errors. A calibration of the ToF illumination supports the process. The proposed approach, moreover, allows to include an environment model. The positive impact of this process is demonstrated.

Keywords: ToF camera, calibration, multipath, 3d modelling.

1 Introduction

As an active 3d sensor a **T**ime-**o**f-**f**light camera emits sinusoidally modulated **N**ear-**I**nfra-**R**ed (NIR) light. The NIR light is reflected by the observed scene and projected onto a pixel matrix. The distances and amplitudes are computed within every pixel. Thus, the ToF camera provides range and intensity images at high frame rates independent of textures or illumination. Thanks to their small-sized design, ToF sensors are an option to laser-scanners and stereo cameras.

Early ToF cameras came along with numerous error sources, such as the distance- and the amplitude-related error. These effects are widely discussed by now, and there are proper error models with effective calibration procedures [1]. Thereby, the ToF sensors became more reliable and more accurate. There is, however, still a prominent effect that depends on the vicinity: *Interference*. Each pixel spans and samples a 3d surface. Ideally, the surface receives the NIR light from the camera and directly reflects it to the pixel. Contrary to this assumption, the pixel further receives light, that took a circuit due to reflection and scattering in the scene or in the optics. As a result, the ToF pixel demodulates an interference of several incoming NIR signals.

Interference caused inside the camera optics is called *Scattering*. It stems from lens material inhomogeneities and internal reflections. In particular, it is generated by very bright surfaces close to the camera, which cause a haze across the image. This haze infects all pixels in relation to the distance information that

M. Chen, B. Leibe, and B. Neumann (Eds.): ICVS 2013, LNCS 7963, pp. 31–41, 2013.
© Springer-Verlag Berlin Heidelberg 2013

comes from the bright surface. Normally, pale areas, such as the background, are affected with a negative distance offset and drift towards the camera.

Interference caused outside the camera by inter-reflections in the scene is called *Multipath*. A ToF camera illuminates its field of view, wherein the light propagates and scatters without hindrance. As a result, the modulated NIR signal reaches the camera via multiple paths. Hence, the ToF pixel recognises a super-positioned signal and produces an erroneous measurement. Commonly, the offset is positive and the measurement drifts off the camera. For instance, corners are baggy or boxes are ballooned [2]. Multipath deteriorates 3d mapping results or it causes collisions or grasping failures in robotic tasks [3]. Effectively approaching the multipath phenomenon is integral for establishing the ToF camera in applications that demand for accuracy, e.g. manipulation and modelling.

2   Related Work

Compared to the other systematic ToF camera errors, the interference issue has not been intensively investigated so far. The nature of multipath and scattering is similar, but the latter gained more attention. Mure-Dubois et al. [4] analysed scattering effects in ToF cameras. They interpret scattering as a linear additive contribution to a complex signal. The scattering is modelled as a space invariant point-spread-function (PSF) in order to reduce the scattering effect on average from 330 mm to 120 mm. Kavli et al. [5] introduce a more generally shaped PSF by paying attention to the scattering's dependency on the pixel location. As a result, they report an average reduction of scattering by 60 %. In [6] Falie experiments with differently shaded planes. By tagging scene objects with a calibration pattern, made of a dark and bright area at known contrast, the accurate distances are computed and the error is reduced to 20 mm.

Against this, multipath cannot be treated by knowledge gained a-priori. Fuchs et al. [7] proposed an approach to automatically compensate for the multipath-related errors. They estimate the error distribution on the basis of the amplitude and distance measurements. By means of ray tracing the interfering signal components of each visible pixel are determined. Fuchs et al. experimentally showed an improvement of about 60 %. Their multipath model, however, has a drawback: It does not consider reflectance and area. Hence, the approach only applies for scenes with homogeneous and constant reflectance. Jimenez et al. [8] further developed this multipath model. They consider the surface areas, and the multipath-related error is computed iteratively by means of an optimisation step. Core of this method is a cost function that evaluates, if the multipath simulation outcome corresponds to the measurement. In two exemplary scenes, the effectivity in reducing the error to about 10 mm is demonstrated. This approach has high computational costs, because the number of parameters to optimise agrees with the number of pixels. Furthermore, the authors do not consider the multipath-related error in the amplitudes, which are used to compute the reflectance. Therefore, an reflectivity coefficient is introduced.

Against the background of these ideas, we contribute four innovations: First, the multipath model is revised and formulated by means of the relevant quantities radiance and radiant flux. Therewith, the actual physical and radiometric processes are considered. Second, the strength of the ToF camera illumination is determined in a calibration step. The camera radiance is the only constant quantity in the system and allows to reliably identify the reflectance of textures in the scene without manually adjusted reflectivity coefficients. Third, the impact of multipath-related error to the amplitudes is estimated iteratively. Fourth, we include an environment model and an efficient visibility check. Surfaces outside the camera view port cause multipath as well. Expanding the multipath simulation to this "unseen" environment yields more accurate results.

The remainder of this paper is structured as follows: Sec. 3 introduces the relevant quantities and the photometric law. Sec. 4 adapts these basics to the measurement process. At that, the ToF illumination, the reflections within the scene, and the ToF measurement process is related to the photometric and spatial configuration of the environment. Sec. 5 formulates an improved multipath model followed by the outline of the compensation algorithm, which comprises an environment model and an efficient visibility check.

3 Photometric Law with Radiance and Radiant Flux

The majority of computer vision problems is solved without considering the radiometric mechanisms of the image generation process. In the context of compensation for multipath in ToF images, tracing the propagation of the NIR light is an essential key. This paper applies radiance L and radiant flux Φ to describe the propagation. The radiance describes the amount of light that is emitted from a particular area and falls within a given solid angle in a specified direction. Assuming ideal Lambertian emitters, the radiance is equal in each direction. The radiant flux is a measure of the total power of radiation that is emitted from a surface, e.g. the NIR light. The integral transfer of radiant flux $d\Phi_{i \to j}$ between two integral surfaces is described by the *Photometric Law*:

$$d\Phi_{i \to j} = L_i \frac{dA_i \cos \beta_{ij} dA_j \cos \beta_{ji}}{d_{ij}^2} \quad . \tag{1}$$

The amount of flux depends on the incident and exit angles $\{\beta_{ij}, \beta_{ji}\}$, the surface areas $\{A_i, A_j\}$, and the distance d_{ij} between the two surfaces. Both the emitted and received flux are on par, provided there is no medium in between.

4 Adaption to Time-of-Flight Camera Measurements

In order to set up a model that describes the origin of the multipath-related error, the photometric law is adapted to the ToF camera measurement process. For this purpose the environment, observed by the ToF camera, is discretised into Lambertian surface elements (surflets). Fig. 1 sketches the ToF camera with two exemplary surflets κ_i and κ_j. The ToF device illuminates the surflets with a constant radiance $L_\otimes$. Depending on a surflets's reflectance, the incident NIR

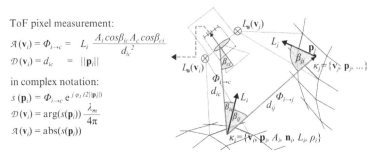

ToF pixel measurement:

$$\mathcal{A}(\mathbf{v}_i) = \Phi_{i \to c} = L_i \frac{A_i \cos\beta_{ic} A_c \cos\beta_{ci}}{d_{ic}^2}$$

$$\mathcal{D}(\mathbf{v}_i) = d_{ic} = ||\mathbf{p}_i||$$

in complex notation:

$$s(\mathbf{p}_i) = \Phi_{i \to c} e^{j \varphi_s (2||\mathbf{p}_i||)}$$

$$\mathcal{D}(\mathbf{v}_i) = \arg(s(\mathbf{p}_i)) \frac{\lambda_m}{4\pi}$$

$$\mathcal{A}(\mathbf{v}_i) = \mathrm{abs}(s(\mathbf{p}_i))$$

Fig. 1. The scene is illuminated with radiance $L_\otimes$. The radiances L_i and L_j depend on the reflectance of the surflets κ_i and κ_j. Flux $\Phi_{i \to j}$ between κ_i and $kappa_j$ depends on the areas A_i and A_j, the exit and incident angles β_{ij} and β_{ji}, and the distance d_{ij}. Flux $\Phi_{i \to c}$ is going from κ_i to the camera pixel $\mathbf{v}_i$ and it is measured as $\mathcal{A}(\mathbf{v}_i)$.

light is scattered with the radiance L_i or L_j. The radiant flux $\Phi_{i \to c}$ that goes from surflet κ_i to the camera pixel $\mathbf{v}_i$ is measured as amplitude value $\mathcal{A}(\mathbf{v}_i)$

$$\mathcal{A}(\mathbf{v}_i) = \Phi_{i \to c} = L_i \frac{A_i \cos\beta_{ic} A_c \cos\beta_{ci}}{d_{ic}^2} \quad , \tag{2}$$

wherein d_{ic} denotes the distance of κ_i to the origin of the camera coordinate system. This distance is equivalent to the pixel's ToF range measurement $\mathcal{D}(\mathbf{v}_i)$. The surflets κ_i and κ_j, moreover, interact, which causes multipath. The portion of radiant flux $\Phi_{i \to j}$ that goes from κ_i to κ_j is an important parameter for the strength of the multipath-related error. It depends on the distance d_{ij} between the two surflets, their orientation w.r.t. each other and their areas. These three attributes are obtained from the range image $\mathcal{D}$.

By means of the intrinsic ToF camera parameters $\mathbf{\Pi}_L$ the depth image $\mathcal{D}$ is transformed into a point cloud. Therewith the central points of all surflets are available. In Fig. 1 the distance d_{ij} between emitter κ_i and receiver κ_j is the Euclidean norm of $||\mathbf{p}_i - \mathbf{p}_j||$. A principal component analysis is performed on the basis of the neighbouring 3d points and gives the normal $\mathbf{n}$. The normal is useful to obtain the surflet orientation and the surflet area. Given the normals and the line-of-sight between κ_i and κ_j the incident and exit angles are computable. The normal is further a decision criteria, whether a surflet is visible from a particular surflet of the 3d scene. The surflet area A_i corresponds to the area that is spanned by the camera pixel $\mathbf{v}_i$. The area A_i is computed from the quadrilateral, which is generated by four rays that start in the principal point, pass the vertices of $\mathbf{v}_i$ and intersect with the surflet plane. The area A_c refers to the aperture of the camera and is negligible, because it is a constant factor for all computations.

As stated in Eq. 2 the amplitude $\mathcal{A}(\mathbf{v}_i)$ is a measure for the radiant flux $\Phi_{i \to c}$ coming from surflet κ_i. Provided a suppression of background illumination, the complete radiant flux $\Phi_i = \pi A_i L_i$, that leaves the surflet κ_i, only originates from the NIR spotlight $\otimes$. Basically, Φ_i corresponds to $\Phi_{\otimes \to i}$, but it is attenuated by the surflet's rate of absorption ρ_i. Given this albedo ρ_i, the radiance L_i, and the 3d features of κ_i, one can obtain the the the spotlight's radiance $L_\otimes$:

$$L_\otimes = \frac{\pi L_i \, d_{ic}{}^2}{\rho_i \, \cos\beta_{i\otimes} \, \cos\beta_{\otimes i}} \quad . \tag{3}$$

Since the area of the NIR illumination is constant, it is negligible and not present in this equation. According to the ToF principle, this formulation presupposes a Lambertian spotlight, which is located at the origin of the camera coordinate system. In reality, there is a LED array, whose superposition causes uneven lighting. For this reason, the camera radiance $L_\otimes(\mathbf{v})$ is computed for each single pixel $\mathbf{v}$. Each $L_\otimes(\mathbf{v})$ illuminates a fraction of the camera's field of view (FOV), which is congruent with the solid angle spanned above the camera pixel $\mathbf{v}$. Fig. 1 shows $L_\otimes(\mathbf{v}_i)$ and $L_\otimes(\mathbf{v}_j)$ shining on κ_i and κ_j respectively. These radiances are identified in a photometric calibration, wherein the camera captures a plane with known albedo. Once performed, this camera radiance calibration allows to translate $\mathcal{A}(\mathbf{v}_i)$ into a constant attribute ρ_i, which is the reflectance of κ_i and obtained by reorganising Eq. 3.

5   Multipath Model

The discrete surflets tagged with spatial and photometric attributes allow for understanding the generation of multipath. Fig. 2(a) sketches the proposed multipath model with the aid of three surflets and an ideal and an distorted signal path. The emitters $L_\otimes$ illuminate the scene with NIR light, sinusoidally modulated at frequency λ_m. The beam B_i goes from $L_\otimes$ to surflet κ_i. Ideally, the light is reflected by κ_i and goes back only to the camera. As proposed by [4] the received signal $s(\mathbf{p}_i)$ is formulated in complex notation:

$$s(\mathbf{p}_i) = \Phi_{ic} \exp\left(j \; \phi_\Delta(2\|\mathbf{p}_i\|)\right) \quad \text{with} \quad \phi_\Delta(x) = x\frac{2\pi}{\lambda_m} \quad .$$

The absolute value denotes the radiant flux Φ_{ic}, which is transmitted from the surflet κ_i to pixel $\mathbf{v}_i$. The phase $\phi_\Delta(x)$ denotes the overall covered distance, which is twice $\|\mathbf{p}_i\|$. A second beam B_j radiates κ_j. The surflet κ_j scatters partially towards κ_i, illustrated by beam C. Hence, B_j generates via κ_j an additional distance component $s^+(\mathbf{p}_i, \mathbf{p}_j)$

$$s^+(\mathbf{p}_i, \mathbf{p}_j) = \Phi_{i,jc}^+ \exp(\phi_\Delta(\|\mathbf{p}_i\| + \|\mathbf{p}_i - \mathbf{p}_j\| + \|\mathbf{p}_j\|)) \quad ,$$

which is added to the true signal $s(\mathbf{p}_i)$ and yields the measured signal $\hat{s}(\mathbf{p}_i)$. The strength of $s^+(\mathbf{p}_i, \mathbf{p}_j)$ is defined by the additional radiant flux $\Phi_{i,jc}^+$, which depedends on L_j and is transmitted to κ_i within beam C. Only a fraction is forwarded by κ_i and finds the way to the camera pixel $\mathbf{v}_i$. On the one hand, κ_i absorbs a part of the light depending on the albedo ρ_i. On the other hand, the solid angle in the direction of the camera is limited. Hence, $\Phi_{i,jc}^+$ is

$$\Phi_{i,jc}^+ = \rho_i \frac{\Phi_{ic}}{L_i \pi A_i} \, L_j \frac{A_j \cos\beta A_i \cos\alpha}{\|\mathbf{p}_i - \mathbf{p}_j\|^2} \quad .$$

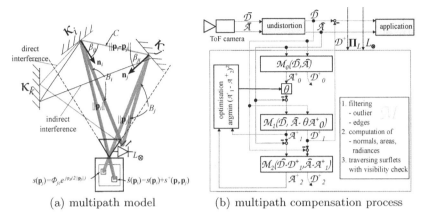

(a) multipath model   (b) multipath compensation process

Fig. 2. (a) depicts the multipath model concentrating on two beams of the luster cone. The unseen surface κ_k can interfere by scattering light that comes directly from the camera's spotlight or indirectly from κ_j. (b) visualises the multipath compensation process. Initially, $\mathcal{A}_0^+$ is incorrect and thus attenuated by θ, which is iteratively estimated by repeatedly applying $\mathcal{M}_1$ and verifying its result with $\mathcal{M}_2$. The optimisation is finished with an optimal θ, when $(\mathcal{A}_2^+ - \mathcal{A}_1^+)^2$ is minimised.

The surflet κ_i is not only radiated by κ_j, but by all surflets $\mathcal{P}$ that are spanned by the camera. To estimate the true signal $s(\mathbf{p}_i)$, the additional components are summed and subtracted from the measured signal $\hat{s}(\mathbf{p}_i)$:

$$s(\mathbf{p}_i) = \hat{s}(\mathbf{p}_i) - \sum_{q \in \mathcal{P}} s^+(\mathbf{p}_i, \mathbf{q}) \quad . \tag{4}$$

Fig. 2(a), moreover, depicts an exteriorly located surflet κ_k, which scatters light coming from the scene. Surflet κ_k is not in the camera's FOV. An environment model $\mathcal{E}$ can provide the pose, area and albedo of κ_k in order to estimate its contribution to multipath. First, κ_k is seen as a receiver and the incoming flux from the surflets in $\mathcal{P}$ is accumulated. Second, κ_k is seen as a transmitter, whose accumulated flux is scattered to the surflets in $\mathcal{P}$. Doing this for all surflets in $\mathcal{E}$ completes the multipath compensation.

6   Multipath Compensation Process

The compensation method $\mathcal{M}(\mathcal{D}, \mathcal{A})$ merges the insights of Sec. 4 and Sec. 5 and computes the multipath-related errors $\mathcal{D}^+$ and $\mathcal{A}^+$ for a given depth and amplitude image pair. Eq. 4 assumes knowledge of the true images $\mathcal{D}$ and $\mathcal{A}$, which are the object of the procedure. Therefore, a two-step algorithm is implemented.

The *first step* performs a computation on the basis of the measurements $\hat{\mathcal{D}}$ and $\hat{\mathcal{A}}$. It yields the initial guesses $\mathcal{D}_0^+$ and $\mathcal{A}_0^+$. We suppose a small multipath-related error in comparison with the true value. This holds an issue, because the surflet reflectance is obtained from $\hat{\mathcal{A}}$. The albedo is a crucial component for a

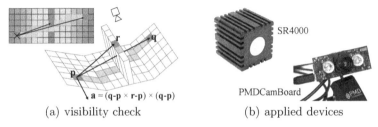

(a) visibility check   (b) applied devices

Fig. 3. (a) Visibility check at an exemplary scene (bottom) with its surflets and the depth image (top). An obstacle intersects the valley and **p** is not visible from **q**. The line of sight is projected into the depth image. The highlighted pixels are traversed. At sample **r** the vector **a** does not point at the camera. Thereby, it indicates an obstacle for the line-of-sight. (b) SR4000 and the PMDCamBoard used for the experiments.

reasonable estimation of $\mathcal{D}^+$, because it decides the amount of scattered light. Applying the erroneous $\hat{A}$ yields incorrect and scaled results (see Fig. 6(b)).

The *second step* approaches this issue. $\mathcal{A}_0^+$ is multiplied with the scale factor θ. Subsequently, $\mathcal{M}(\hat{\mathcal{D}}, \hat{A} - \theta \, \mathcal{A}_0^+)$ computes the solution $\mathcal{D}_1^+$ and $\mathcal{A}_1^+$. Ideally, Eq. 4 can predict the erroneous measurement on the basis of the true figures and the result of $\mathcal{M}(\hat{\mathcal{D}} - \mathcal{D}_1^+, \hat{A} - \mathcal{A}_1^+)$ should comply with the actual measurement. Hence, the optimal θ is acquired by minimising the difference $(\mathcal{A}_1^+ - \mathcal{A}_2^+)^2$.

Fig. 2(b) depicts the flow chart of the complete approach. Method $\mathcal{M}$ encapsulates the pre-processing and the ray-tracing. First, the pre-processing eliminates the spurious measurements and outliers by means of an edge filter and a median filter. Such artifacts strongly deteriorate the normal estimation and thus the angles, areas and albedo. These quantities define the signal attenuation and decide on the visibility of two surflets. Following the normal computation, the radiance and albedo of the surflets are derived from $\hat{\mathcal{D}}$ and $\hat{A}$. Afterwards, the surflets are traversed. For each surflet (**p**) the interacting surflets (points $\mathbf{q} \in \mathcal{P} \cup \mathcal{E}$) are determined and the sum $s^+(\mathbf{p})$ is computed according to Eq. 4.

More complex scenes require an *visibility check*. We propose an efficient approach that suits for range cameras. Fig. 3(a) shows a surflet κ_i whose visibility to surflet κ_j is tested. If κ_i is seen from κ_j and vice versa, none of the surflets highlighted in Fig. 3(a) has to be in the line-of-sight. The line-of-sight is projected into the depth image by means of the Bresenham-Algorithm and sampled. An auxiliary vector **a** is computed for each sample and its direction is compared with the viewing direction of the camera. If it is pointed towards the camera, the line-of-sight is not interrupted.

7   Experiments and Results

The experiments are performed with two camera devices that differ in illumination power and modulation frequency (see Fig. 3(b)): The SR4000 comes with 30 MHz and the PMDCamBoard 20 MHz. The multipath compensation is performed on a desktop computer with 2.79 GHz clock rate. The complexity is

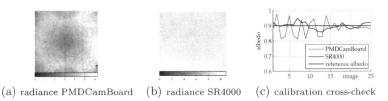

(a) radiance PMDCamBoard   (b) radiance SR4000   (c) calibration cross-check

Fig. 4. Photometric calibration result. (a) and (b) display the radiance matrices of the ToF cameras used for the experiments. (c) plots the cross-check. Based on the radiance matrices the albedo of a white plane is estimated for various poses. The radiance calibration is valid with a slight deviation up to 10 %.

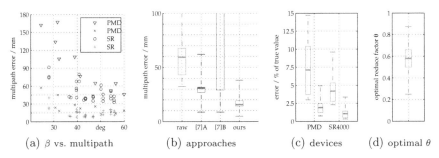

(a) β vs. multipath   (b) approaches   (c) devices   (d) optimal θ

Fig. 5. 44 experiments at a corner with evenly and unevenly shaded planes. (b) Comparison of our approach with the method of [7]. [7]A refers to evenly shaded planes and performs reasonably, but, for unevenly shaded planes [7]B fails. (c) Our approach on average reduces the RMS error to 16 mm or 2 % w.r.t. to the true distance.

quadratic, but down-sampling the ToF image can reduce the computational cost. The sampling-rate for the optimisation and the estimation of $\mathcal{D}_1^+$ is set to 10 and 2, respectively. Thereby, the SR4000 and PMDCamBoard images are processed in 60 s and 150 s, respectively. The starting value for θ is 0.8.

Photometric Calibration. Initially, a photometric calibration is performed. The camera is pointed at a plane with known pose and known albedo. The first is a by-product of the intrinsic camera calibration, the latter is white paper with $\rho = 0.9$. Fig. 4 displays the outcomes. The SR4000 features 24 LEDs and the PMDCamBoard features 2 LEDs. Consequently, the radiance of the SR4000 is stronger and more homogeneous (see Fig. 4(a) and 4(b)). Five captures are used to determine the radiances. Fig. 4(c) plots the cross-check at various other camera poses to demonstrate the validity of the photometric calibration.

Basic Experiments. The effectivity of the approach is evaluated in a basic setup and compared with [7] and [8]. For this purpose a corner is captured at distances of 0.7 m to 1.3 m and the cutting angles α and the viewing angles β are varied. The 44 experiments reveal an average multipath-related error of 7 % w.r.t. the true distance or 60 mm.. Fig. 5(a) plots error vs. viewing angle. It shows: the smaller β the less is the direct illumination and the larger is the multipath-related error. Fig. 5(c) demonstrates that the modulation frequency has a bearing on the error. The PMDCamBoard comes with a larger multipath-

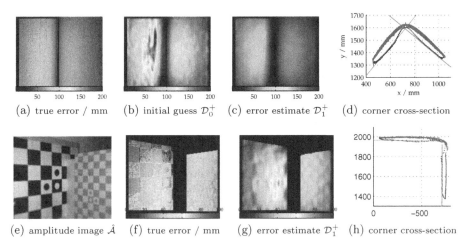

(a) true error / mm   (b) initial guess $\mathcal{D}_0^+$ (c) error estimate $\mathcal{D}_1^+$ (d) corner cross-section

(e) amplitude image $\hat{\mathcal{A}}$ (f) true error / mm   (g) error estimate $\mathcal{D}_1^+$ (h) corner cross-section

Fig. 6. The two rows present a corner experiment with homogeneous (top) and heterogeneous (bottom) texture. The images in the rightmost column depict a cross section through the Ground Truth (green), the fixed (black) and the erroneous (red and bulgy) measurement. Due to the different viewing angles, the multipath-related error differs with 65 mm (left) / 55 mm (right). 6(b) plots the initial guess $\mathcal{D}_0^+$, which strongly deviates from the actual error. With optimal $\theta = 0.66$ the improved error estimation $\mathcal{D}_1^+$ is plotted in 6(c). Our approach decreases the error to 14 mm (left) / 16 mm (right). The second row demonstrates that our approach handles surfaces with uneven albedo. The planes intersect at $\alpha = 90\,°$ and the viewing angles are on par with $\beta = 45\,°$. 6(g) illustrates estimated error $\mathcal{D}_1^+$ at optimal $\theta = 0.57$, which very good matches the actual error depicted in 6(f). Our approach reduces the RMS error from 40 mm to 8 mm.

related error under the same conditions. For the two devices the remaining error is below 2.5 %. The variance is larger for the PMDCamBoard, because measurement noise is stronger and compromises the normal estimation. On average, the error is reduced by 75 %. The optimal θ varies between 0.5 and 0.7 . Fig. 5(b) also plots the results of our approach against the outcomes of [7]. For evenly shaded planes [7] performs reasonably, but for unevenly shaded planes it fails, because [7] does not consider different reflectance. Fig. 6 details two measurements and allows to compare our results with [8], who reduced the multipath-related error to about 10 mm in similar setups. This corresponds to our results, although we reduced the computational cost drastically by optimising one parameter only.

Including the Environment. The SR4000 camera observes a rack, which stands close to a wall. The board is only partially visible (see Fig. 7(a)). The camera lights on it and the light is scattered between the board and the walls. In Fig. 7(b) the multipath-related error up to 80 mm is plotted. Resolving the multipath on the basis of the measurement is not effective and only decreases the RMS error to 50 mm. Including the walls and the neighbouring shelf boards improves the result to an RMS error of 10 mm. Fig. 7(c) plots the multipath estimate $\mathcal{D}_1^+$, which corresponds to the actual multipath-related error. Fig. 7(d) displays the environment made of 2544 surflets. The shelf board acts as a light source and scatters the NIR light. The walls feature a realistic radiance.

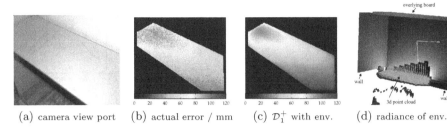

(a) camera view port   (b) actual error / mm   (c) $\mathcal{D}_1^+$ with env.   (d) radiance of env.

Fig. 7. 7(a) illustrates a part of the shelves in limited field-of-view of the camera. The actual multipath-related error is at average 65 mm and depicted in 7(b). Including the environment model drastically decreases the RMS error 10 mm and $\mathcal{D}_1^+$ in 7(c) matches the actual error. 7(d) shows the surflets of the environment model. The measurement (red) acts as a light source and illuminates the surflets. The brighter the surflets the more light they receive and reflect. The processing time increases to 164 s.

8   Conclusion

Multipath distorts the measurements by several centimetres and is critical for tasks that demand for high accuracy, such as robotic manipulation or mapping. This paper discusses an enhanced approach to compensate for multipath-related errors in ToF camera images. First, the approach considers the physics of ToF illumination in terms of radiance and radiant flux. Second, a calibration of the ToF illumination is introduced. Third, the compensation process features an optimisation to accurately estimate the multipath-related error. Fourth, the indirectly interfering environment is included into the multipath model. The effectivity of this approach is demonstrated. The multipath-related error is reduced by 75 % in scenes with both evenly and unevenly textured surfaces. Furthermore, including the environment drastically improves the results. The radiosity simulation proves the multipath model and its radiometric assumptions. Our method improves on [7] by 50 % and matches the outcomes of [8] at less computational cost.

Acknowledgment. This work is funded partially by the European Community's Seventh Framework Programme (FP7/2007-2013) within the TAPAS project (www.tapas-project.eu).

References

1. Lindner, M., Schiller, I., Kolb, A., Koch, R.: Time-of-flight sensor calibration for accurate range sensing. Journal of Computer Vision and Image Understanding (CVIU) (2010)
2. Gudmundsson, S.A.: Environmental effects on measurement uncertainties of time-of-flight cameras. In: Proceedings of the International Symposium on Signals Circuits and Systems (ISSCS), Iasi, Romania (July 2007)
3. May, S., Fuchs, S., Droeschel, D., Holz, D., Nüchter, A., Hertzberg, J., Malis, E.: 3d mapping with time-of-flight cameras. Journal of Field Robotics, Special Issue on Three-dimensional Mapping 26, 934–965 (2009)

4. Mure-Dubois, J., Huegli, H.: Optimized scattering compensation for time-of-flight camera. In: Proceedings of the SPIE Three-Dimensional Methodes for Inspection and Metrology, Boston, Massachusetts, USA (September 2007)
5. Kavli, T., Kirkhus, T., Thielemann, J.T., Jagielski, B.: Modelling and compensating measurement errors caused by scattering in time-of-flight cameras. In: Proceedings of SPIE 7066 Two- and Three-Dimensional Methods for Inspection and Metrology VI, San Diego, California, USA (August 2008)
6. Falie, D.: 3d image correction for time of flight (tof) cameras. In: Proceedings of the International Conference of Optical Instrument and Technology (OIT), Beijing, China (2008)
7. Fuchs, S.: Multipath interference compensation in tof-camera images. In: Proceedings of the International Conference on Pattern Recognition (ICPR), Istanbul, Turkey (August 2010)
8. Jimenez, D., Pizarro, D., Mazo, M., Palazuelos, S.: Modelling and correction of multipath interference in time of flight cameras. In: Proceedings of IEEE Conference on Computer Vision and Pattern Recognition (CVPR), Providence, USA (2012)

Coloured Video Code for In-Flight Data Transmission

Falk Schubert[1], Thilo Fath[2], and Harald Haas[2]

[1] EADS Innovation Works, Munich, Germany
[2] The University of Edinburgh, UK

Abstract. We present a new approach for optical data transmission between the in-flight entertainment (IFE) system of aeroplanes and mobile devices. As wireless in-flight applications are subject to strict frequency and electromagnetic compatibility regulations, we propose to transfer the data optically. We display video streams of 2-dimensional black-and-white or coloured visual codes on the IFE screen. To allow robust reconstruction of the transmitted data, we present a new visual code which is captured and processed by mobile devices of passengers. In order to efficiently compensate for frame losses, the visual codes are coupled with a temporal forward error correction (FEC) scheme. The system is evaluated in an Airbus A330 cabin mock-up under realistic conditions employing representative mobile devices like low-cost and high-end smartphones. Performance evaluations show that the developed transmission system achieves data rates of up to 120 kbit/s per individual passenger seat.

Keywords: coloured visual codes, temporal FEC encoding, visual transmission, mobile vision.

1 Introduction

We notice an increasing demand for wireless services during flights in order to transfer general information (*e.g.* in-flight magazines, airport maps, *etc.*) and passenger specific data (*e.g.* information for connecting gates, departure time of connecting flights, *etc.*) to mobile devices of passengers. However, the application of wireless services within aircraft cabins imposes several constraints. As passenger specific data is to be transmitted, security and privacy aspects have to be considered. More importantly, the transmission system has to comply with high safety regulations as potential access to sensitive on-board systems needs to be prevented. Conventional radio frequency (RF) communications cannot be easily employed in sensitive environments like aircraft cabins due to stringent frequency regulations. A few airlines already provide wireless local area network (WLAN) services to their passengers on some selective flights. However, these services require costly installation of dedicated hardware equipment like access points and wireless transceivers. Furthermore, the bandwidth has to be shared between all passengers (up to several hundreds of users) which simultaneously use the data transmission service.

M. Chen, B. Leibe, and B. Neumann (Eds.): ICVS 2013, LNCS 7963, pp. 42–51, 2013.
© Springer-Verlag Berlin Heidelberg 2013

Due to these constraints, we promote to use optical wireless transmission instead of RF-based transmission. Optical signals are not subject to frequency regulations and provide large transmission bandwidth by allowing multiple parallel data transmissions within the same area. Moreover, by applying optical transmission it is possible to reuse the existing hardware within the aircraft cabin, *i.e.* the displays of the in-flight entertainment (IFE) system and the built-in cameras of mobile devices. In detail, we propose an optical wireless data transmission method using a new visual code. The data to be transmitted (*e.g.* text-files or images) is encoded into several visual codes which are displayed on the screen of IFE system like a common video. This sequence is captured and decoded by a mobile device. The proposed visual code is coupled with a new temporal sequence-wise forward error correction (FEC) scheme which allows to recover capturing errors caused by frame transition effects and enables the compensation of entirely lost video frames.

The remainder of this paper is organised as follows: In Section 2, we discuss and review related work. In Section 3, the developed transmission system is presented. A description of the new visual code is given in Section 4. Transmission experiments are presented in Section 5 and evaluation results are discussed. Finally, Section 6 concludes the paper.

2   Related Work – Visual Codes for Data Transmission

Visual codes have become very popular in print media. The most common visual codes are 1-dimensional barcodes [3]. In recent years, more sophisticated 2-dimensional codes such as Data-Matrix-Codes [2] or Quick Response (QR)-codes [1] have received attention. All these codes can be decoded independently of the viewpoint, work under realistic illumination conditions and allow to recover from decoding errors. However, the data rate of conventional visual codes is limited to only a few bytes, thus not allowing a practical application for in-flight communication.

In order to overcome this limitation, some research activity has focussed on spreading data across several visual codes and displaying them in form of a video rather than a single image. In [6], unsynchronised 4-dimensional codes are proposed for optical data transfer between public displays and mobile devices. The authors combine three different 2-dimensional Data-Matrix-codes in the complementary colour channels red, green and blue to one common frame. Several of these frames are displayed in a temporal sequence resulting in a coloured visual code video. The authors propose a simple redundancy concept to enable reliable data transmission. However, the induced redundancy limits the data throughput to only 23 characters per second. In [8], the author also uses coloured visual code videos to transmit data. This system also provides a low data rate of only 430 byte/s. In [9], a system called *PixNet* is proposed. The visual encoding of the image is based on the orthogonal frequency division multiplexing (OFDM) scheme, whereas the actual image detection uses the Data-Matrix detection algorithm. The authors report that applying OFDM encoding makes the system less sensitive to illumination variations. However to our experience, most mobile devices employ robust auto-balancing techniques which provide constant contrast. Moreover, the authors report a data rate of up to 12 Mbit/s at a distance of 10 m. However, this data rate is only achieved for a static setup using high-quality cameras and a large display. Low-cost built-in cameras as well as potential frame loss are not taken into account in their work.

3 System Overview

None of the existing systems employing visual code videos provides the simplicity and the robustness of single frame visual codes, while enabling practical data throughput. Therefore, in this paper, we present an easy to use low-cost optical transmission system which provides a data rate of several kbit/s. Fig. 1 shows the system setup. The user holds a mobile device in front of the IFE screen which is built into the front seat.

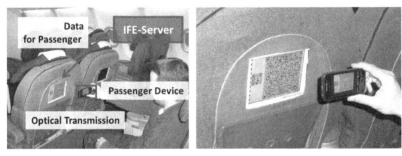

Fig. 1. Left: Setup for the transmission of passenger specific data from the central IFE server to the mobile device. Right: Typical distance between mobile device and display.

The detailed transmission process is illustrated in Fig. 2. First, the data, *e.g.* text documents or images, is compressed and encrypted to provide security and privacy of the passenger specific information. Second, the encrypted and compressed file is FEC encoded to compensate for potential transmission errors. In a third step, the FEC encoded data is segmented into several packets. Each of these packets is visually encoded by our new visual code resulting in a sequence of several visual codes. Fourth, this visual code sequence is displayed in a continuous loop on the IFE screen. The user can start to capture the visual codes at any time without the need for an initial synchronisation. In a fifth step, the captured visual codes are detected and processed. The visually decoded data packets are reassembled in the correct order by means of additionally encoded meta information providing the packet number. The reassembling reconstructs the originally FEC encoded data stream. In a sixth step, the FEC encoded data is decoded. Due to the induced FEC, errors which arise during the transmission and capturing process can be corrected. Finally, the FEC decoded data is

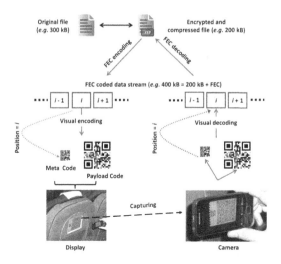

Fig. 2. Data transmission via visual code videos

decrypted and uncompressed and the reconstructed file is stored on the user device.

As the IFE system can display the desired content on-demand [7], the wireless data transfer can be used by each passenger simultaneously. Therefore, bandwidth need not to be shared between the passengers. Moreover, the unidirectional data transfer between display and mobile device provides a fundamental safety feature as there is no uplink connection from the user device to the sensitive on-board systems. The major benefit of the proposed transmission system is that it reuses the existing IFE equipment without the need for any additional hardware installations. The system requires only a software update of the existing IFE system and an application to be installed on the mobile device.

4   Visual Encoding and Decoding

The lack of synchronisation between display and camera of the mobile device comes at the price of several effects. Since cameras often have a rolling-shutter and displays usually build up images line-wise, transition artefacts between two consecutive frames can be observed (*e.g.* two frames can partially overlap or they can overlay each other completely as shown in the centre of Fig. 3). These effects are even emphasised when low-cost cameras are used which can be typically found in smartphones - the target device for our application. These cheap cameras have a small aperture, and hence require long exposure times. However, these long exposure times increase the chance that the camera captures a frame transition. Additionally, long exposure times also cause motion blur (shown on the left side of Fig. 3) as hand-held cameras are never perfectly static. In order to achieve higher data rates, coloured visual codes can be applied. However, colour-channels suffer from cross-talk (*i.e.* a blue photon does not only affect the blue channel but also the green and red channels) and show high sensitivity to bad illumination, which leads to noisy images, especially in the case of low-cost sensors. On the right side of Fig. 3, a coloured visual code is decomposed into its three colour channels of which the blue channel is shown. One can clearly notice the higher noise level compared to pure black-and-white visual codes.

Fig. 3. Left: motion blur, Centre: transition overlay of two frames, Right: Blue colour channel

These artefacts (*i.e.* motion blur, frame transition, pixel noise) can prevent a correct decoding of the visual code. Conventional visual codes (*e.g.* QR-codes [1]), which are primarily designed for print media, have to be robust to decoding errors (*e.g.* due to abrasion or dirt on the printed material). Therefore, conventional visual codes have inherent FEC capabilities to recover from such decoding errors. This FEC coding is performed on a per frame basis, *i.e.* the data and the error correction codewords are contained in the same visual code only allowing to recover from a few decoding errors. However, in our application some artefacts degrade the visual code so much (*e.g.* by motion blur or frame transitions) that these image frames cannot be reconstructed at all. As a result, the transmitted data stream cannot be reconstructed correctly as some packets are completely lost. Consequently, the conventional frame-wise FEC redundancy encoding has to be extended to allow a recovery of completely lost frames. Therefore, a temporal sequence-wise FEC encoding of the complete data stream is proposed. This encoding enables the recovery of lost frames. As a result, the data stream can be reconstructed correctly even if some frames are lost. Our FEC encoding scheme uses a $(127, 67, 30)$ Reed-Solomon code having a data capacity of about 52.8% and a recovery capacity about 23.6%. Thus, the data can be correctly reconstructed if up to about a quarter of the visual code sequence is completely missing. Higher, respectively lower error correction levels can also be employed if higher robustness or higher throughput is required. In order to increae the robustness, the FEC encoded data is interleaved. This means that the FEC part is randomly distributed across all frames within the visual code sequence.

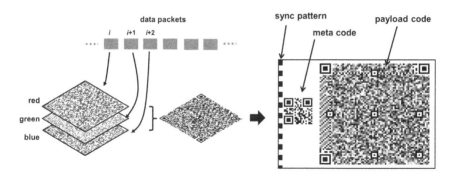

Fig. 4. Left: Three black-and-white payload codes are merged into a single coloured payload code. Right: A single visual code consists of three parts: sync pattern, meta code and payload code.

In the following, we describe the setup of our visual code and how the FEC encoded data stream is stored in it. As illustrated in Fig. 2, each packet of the FEC coded data stream is visually encoded into a single visual code. Fig. 4 shows the actual setup of our visual code. It consists of three parts: a synchronisation pattern, a meta code and the payload code. Each of these parts will be discussed separately:

Meta Code. In order to reassemble the captured frames in the correct order, the receiver has to know the index of the visual code frame within the sequence because the display and camera are not synchronised. As this meta information is required before performing the FEC decoding at the receiver side, we separate this information from the actual payload. We employ a conventional QR-code which we call meta code and which is located on the left side of our visual code (see Fig. 4). As there is only a small amount of meta information (*e.g.* the frame number) to be transmitted, a small QR-code having a low version number (*e.g.* version 1 – 2) is sufficient. We set the FEC level of the meta code to the highest redundancy.

Payload Code. The actual data to be transmitted is stored in the so-called payload code, which is located on the right side of the visual code as shown in Fig. 4. In order to allow viewpoint invariant capturing and decoding of the payload code, we need to detect the outline of the code. We therefore add finder patterns like the ones found in conventional QR-codes. These consist of concentric squares that are located in the corners and in the centre of the payload code. During decoding on the mobile device, the locations of these patterns are identified. We use the detector from the open source implementation *ZXing* [11]. With the detected pixel coordinates, a homography can be calculated that rectifies the visual code using the direct linear transform algorithm [5]. The rectification aligns the patterns from the captured camera image with the known quadratic structure of the payload code. As a result, the pixels corresponding to individual bits of the data packet can be extracted. We group multiple pixels (*e.g.* 8 × 8) into modules which represent a single bit. The extraction is done by binarization using a threshold. This threshold is found by building a histogram from intensity values along a line-scan of the rectified payload code. The two maximal peaks of the histogram are considered as black-and-white points (*i.e.* reference points). The intensity value that optimally separates both reference points in the histogram is used as threshold for the binarization. The resulting binarized values of all modules correspond to binary numbers, *i.e.* the actual data bits. In order to increase the data rate, we combine three black-and-white payload codes (corresponding to three consecutive data packets) to one coloured payload code. Each of the three individual payload codes is interpreted as one of the three colour channels as illustrated on the left side of Fig. 4. At the decoder side, the detection of the finder patterns and the rectification is performed on the coloured visual code. However, the selection of the optimal threshold and the binarization is carried out for each colour channel (*i.e.* red, green and blue) separately.

Synchronisation Pattern. As discussed above, the display and the camera are not synchronised. To ensure that the camera captures all displayed frames, we set the display rate of the visual codes to 10 – 15 frames per second (fps). This rate is half the capturing rate of the camera which is about 30 fps. Given the relative short image build-up time of the display of about 17 ms (60 Hz response-rate), this oversampling ensures that multiple images will be recorded for each displayed visual code. As a result, at least one visual code frame is captured without transition effects. The relation between capturing and displaying is shown in Fig. 5. For correct decoding, we need to filter out the captured frames which contain transition effects (illustrated by "X" in Fig. 5). Furthermore, due to the oversampling usually more than one copy of the same visual code frame is captured without transition effects. However these frames may still vary in terms of quality (*e.g.* contrast). Hence, only the best copy should be selected to ensure optimal processing. This filtering and selection process keeps the number of decoding operations at a minimum. The process is described in the following: A black-and-white pattern (called synchronization pattern) is added to the left side of each visual code (see Fig. 4) which alternates between two versions (called even-pattern s_e and odd-pattern s_o) from displayed frame to frame. For each captured frame, the recorded pattern q is extracted from the rectified image. In order to determine its version, synthetically constructed patterns of both versions (*i.e.* s_e and s_o) are correlated with the captured one. The version of the pattern which provides the highest correlation score is assigned to q. The score for the even-pattern is calculated as follows:

$$r_e = \frac{\sum_i (s_e(i) - \hat{s}_e)(q(i) - \hat{q})}{\sqrt{\sum_i (s_e(i) - \hat{s}_e)^2 \sum_j (q(j) - \hat{q})^2}}$$

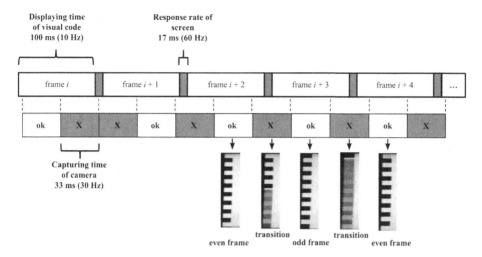

Fig. 5. The upper time-line shows how the screen displays the visual code sequence. The lower time-line shows the capturing times of the camera. At the bottom the enlarged synchronization pattern are depicted for frames free of artefacts ("ok") and for frames containing transition artefacts ("X").

where the intensity values of the black-and-white patterns are linearized into the vectors s_e and q. $\hat{s}_e$ and $\hat{q}$ are the mean intensity values of the patterns. The score r_o for the odd-pattern is calculated in analogous manner.

While processing consecutively captured frames, the scores and frames are added to a buffer as long as no new version is assigned to the current frame compared to the previous one. As soon as a new frame version is detected, the frame with the highest correlation score is taken from the buffer and passed on to the decoder.

5   Transmission Experiments

In the following, the results of our transmission experiments are presented. The aim of the experiments is to find the achievable data throughput for different variations of our visual code (*i.e.* black-and-white *vs.* coloured) and for different mobile devices (*i.e.* low-end *vs.* high-end smartphone). The data to be transferred consists of typical passenger specific information. All experiments have been carried out in an Airbus A330 aircraft cabin mock-up under realistic illumination and geometric conditions (see Fig. 1). The cabin mock-up is equipped with an IFE system. The display has a size of about 17 cm × 13 cm with a resolution of 1024 × 768 pixels. Fig. 1 shows the setup of the transmission experiments within the considered application scenario. The distance between the screen and the mobile device is about 20 – 30 cm. The passenger holds the mobile device in the hand during the transmission, roughly aligning it with the display.

Table 1. Performance bounds derived from transmission experiments

User Device	Colour of Visual Code	Frame-Rate (fps)	Bit-Rate (kbit/s)
Samsung Galaxy Ace	black-and-white	10	22.40
Apple iPhone 4	black-and-white	13	54.29
Apple iPhone 4	coloured	13	120.43

First, the transmission performance of the developed application is evaluated using a low-cost smartphone [10]. The built-in camera of this smartphone has a resolution of 640 × 480 pixels in the video mode. In order to reduce transition artefacts, the frame rate of the IFE display has been limited to 10 fps. Transmission experiments have shown that this is the largest frame rate which ensures that each frame is captured once without transition effects. Moreover, only black-and-white visual codes are used due to the poor quality of the camera. In this setup each frame can contain a maximum amount of 280 bytes of actual payload data (*i.e.* without FEC overhead). Hence, at 10 fps we achieve a maximum bit rate (throughput) of about $10 \cdot 280 \cdot 8 = 22.40$ kbit/s (see Table 1).

Second, the transmission performance is analysed if a high-end user device (an Apple iPhone 4 smartphone [4]) is used instead of a low-cost device. The built-in camera of this smartphone has a higher resolution of 1280 × 720 pixels in video mode. Moreover, for this user device, the frame rate of the display can be increased to 13 fps. This transmission rate ensures that each frame is captured at least once without transition effects. Due to the higher quality of the built-in camera, 522 bytes of real data can be encoded in each frame ensuring that the whole data can be reconstructed correctly. This results in a bit rate of $13 \cdot 522 \cdot 8 = 54.29$ kbit/s (see Table 1). This data rate exceeds the achievable data rate of the low-cost smartphone by a factor of about 2.42.

Finally, the data rate can be additionally increased by using coloured visual codes. By using the three independent colour channels red, green and blue for parallel data transmission, the data rate can be theoretically increased by a factor of three. However, as shown in Section 4, the coloured visual codes suffer from optical cross-talk and colour mixing. Therefore, coloured visual codes are subject to increased error rates. In this case, 1158 bytes of real data can be encoded in each frame, resulting in a bit rate of about $13 \cdot 1158 \cdot 8 = 120.43$ kbit/s (see Table 1). Compared to the black-and-white visual code, this is an increase by a factor of about 2.22.

6   Summary and Conclusions

A novel approach for optical wireless data transmission within an aircraft cabin has been presented. The developed system reuses the display of the IFE system to transfer passenger specific data to mobile devices. A new visual code has been introduced that is displayed as a video stream which contains the data to be transferred. The new visual code is coupled with a temporal FEC encoding scheme allowing robust transmission. The transmitted frames consist of a meta code, which contains supplementary information like the frame number, and the payload code, which contains the actual information to be transmitted. In a future implementation, these two codes might be combined to one common visual code. Furthermore, a selection algorithm has been presented which uses a synchronisation pattern to detect frame transitions and to select the best captured frame for the decoding process. Transmission experiments within an actual aircraft cabin mock-up have demonstrated the functionality of the developed application under realistic conditions. The performance evaluation shows that a throughput of up to 120 kbit/s can be achieved with current smartphones. Further tests have shown that 30 seconds are a tolerable time which is accepted by a passenger to capture the IFE screen with a mobile device. During this time, up to 450 kB can be transmitted by a single visual code sequence. This file size is sufficient to transfer the required amount of data for the proposed application. In order to increase the data rate, the black-and-white visual codes have been extended to coloured visual codes. In future work, we will evaluate the performance of visual codes with more than 8 different colours which currently result from combining only the three colour channels.

References

1. Information technology – Automatic identification and data capture techniques – Bar code symbology – QR Code. ISO/IEC 18004:2000(E) (2000)
2. Information technology – Automatic identification and data capture techniques – Data Matrix bar code symbology specification. ISO/IEC 16022:2006 (2006)
3. Information technology – Automatic identification and data capture techniques – EAN/UPC bar code symbology specification. ISO/IEC 15420:2009 (2009)
4. Apple Inc. Technical specification: iPhone 4 (2012),
   http://www.apple.com/uk/iphone/iphone-4/specs.html (retrieved October 25, 2012)
5. Hartley, R., Zisserman, A.: Multiple View Geometry in Computer Vision, 2nd edn. Cambridge University Press (2004)
6. Langlotz, T., Bimber, O.: Unsynchronized 4d barcodes: coding and decoding time-multiplexed 2d colorcodes. In: International Conference on Advances in Visual Computing, Lake Tahoe, NV, USA (2007)
7. Liu, H.: Deliverable D4.1: State of Art of In-flight Entertainment Systems and Office Work Infrastructure. Sixth Framework Programme Project: Smart Technologies for Stress Free Air Travel (2006)
8. Memeti, J.: Data Transfer Using a Camera and a Three-Dimensional Code. Bachelor's thesis, University of Zurich (2012)
9. Perli, S.D., Ahmed, N., Katabi, D.: Pixnet: interference-free wireless links using lcd-camera pairs. In: International Conference on Mobile Computing and Networking, Chicago, Illinois, USA (2010)
10. Samsung. Technical specification: Galaxy Ace GT-S5830 (May 2012),
    http://www.samsung.com/uk/support/model/GT-S5830OKAXEU   (retrieved October 25, 2012)
11. ZXing. Multi-format 1D/2D barcode image processing library, release 1.7,
    http://code.google.com/p/zxing/ (retrieved September 27, 2011)

Vision-Based Magnification
of Corneal Endothelium Frames

Dario Comanducci and Carlo Colombo

Computational Vision Group
Dipartimento di Ingegneria dell'Informazione
Università di Firenze – Via S. Marta 3, 50139 Firenze, Italy
{comandu,colombo}@dsi.unifi.it

Abstract. We present a fast and effective method to compute a high-resolution image of the corneal endothelium starting from a low-resolution video sequence obtained with a general purpose biomicroscope. Our goal is to exploit information redundancy in the sequence so as to achieve via software a magnification power and an image quality typical of dedicated hardware, such as the confocal microscope. The method couples SVM training with graph-based registration, and explicitly takes into account the characteristics of the application domain. Results on long, real sequences and comparative tests against general-purpose super-resolution approaches are presented and discussed.

Keywords: Biomedical imaging, Machine learning, Super-resolution, Video mosaicing.

1 Introduction

The density and shape of endothelium cells change with age and are related with the health of the cornea; checking them is nowadays a routine diagnostic test, performed either in manual or automatic way. For this purpose, dedicated *confocal microscopes* capable to obtain a high quality image of the endothelium cells, are often used. Nevertheless, the endothelium is also visible, at lower resolution, with less powerful and expensive instruments such as the slit lamp biomicroscope. A typical low-resolution frame obtained with a slit lamp biomicroscope is shown in Fig. 1(a): Only a little portion of the frame contains a visible part of the endothelium area, enclosed by the rectangle in the picture. The white area on the left is due to the corneal reflection of the slit lamp light used to illuminate the cells. For the sake of comparison, Fig. 1(b) shows an image of the endothelium obtained with a confocal microscope. Here the endothelium is visible in better detail, thanks to the higher resolution of the instrument.

The goal of this work is to generate a high-resolution (HR) image (with confocal microscope quality, i.e., a zooming factor of at least $3\times$) of the endothelium cells, given a low-resolution (640×480 pixels) video sequence of the endothelium area obtained with a slit lamp biomicroscope. Coping with low resolution images is practically unavoidable for general *in vivo* analysis with a biomicroscope,

M. Chen, B. Leibe, and B. Neumann (Eds.): ICVS 2013, LNCS 7963, pp. 52–61, 2013.
© Springer-Verlag Berlin Heidelberg 2013

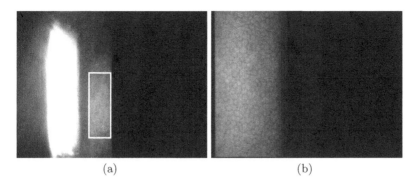

(a)   (b)

Fig. 1. (a): A typical endothelium image obtained with the slit lamp biomicroscope. (b): A confocal image of the endothelium.

where a real-time frame rate (30 fps) is required to ensure that the frames are acquired without significant motion blur. As of course the required image quality cannot be achieved by mere bicubic interpolation of a single frame, in this work *all* frames are exploited within a super-resolution (SR) framework based on photo-mosaicing. As shown in the experimental tests section, our solution drastically reduces computations with respect to classical multi-frame SR approaches (see [1] for a general overview, and [2] for a survey on the use of SR methods in medical imaging). More details on theoretical and implementation aspects can be found, together with additional experimental results, in an extensive technical report devoted to this work [3].

2   The Magnification Method

The proposed method can be split into the following steps: (1) Automatic segmentation of the visible endothelium within each frame; (2) Selection of the best endothelium subsequence via a trained SVM; (3) Image alignment and mosaicing of the selected visible endothelium segments; (4) HR image generation by exploiting all the pixels from the aligned images.

Raw Endothelium Segmentation. Fig. 2 shows the result of endothelium region segmentation for Fig. 1. The endothelium is contained in the image rectangle $[x_l, x_r] \times [y_-, y_+]$, whose extremes are computed by analyzing the shape and slope of cumulative horizontal and vertical histograms of pixel intensity.

SVM-based Selection of Effective Endothelial Images. The quality of the HR image depends on the quality of the images contributing to it. Hence, a quality measurement is required in order to select the best images to be used. In order to identify endothelial images with good visual quality, color and texture descriptors compliant with the MPEG-7 standard are used to train an SVM with a radial basis function as kernel. Furthermore, SVM classification is combined

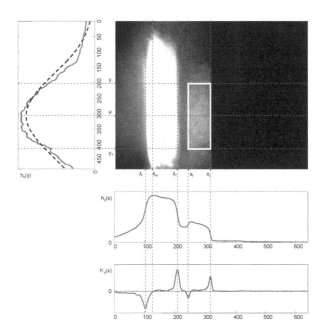

Fig. 2. The cumulative histograms $h_y(x)$ and $h_x(y)$, together with the derivative $h'_y(x)$, computed for Fig. 1(a). **Best viewed in color.**

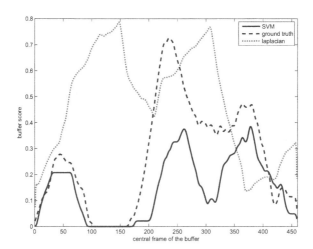

Fig. 3. Score of being a good visual quality subsequence. Bold line: Buffer score based on SVM average probability. Dotted line: Buffer score based only on average Laplacian energy. Dashed line: Buffer score based on ground truth.

with the average energy of *image Laplacian* of the segmented frames. Such an operator, usually employed in digital photography as a pixel-based autofocusing heuristic [4], is used here to identify the most focused images. Indeed, the main factor that can affect the quality of the endothelium image is blur, either due to fast eye/lamp motion or out of focus. The synergy between SVM-based classification and Laplacian-based ranking is exploited since they have complementary strengths and weaknesses. On the one hand, SVMs can discriminate between segments with endothelial content and images where the endothelium is absent, but cannot provide any quality ranking among the images within the same class. On the other hand, the Laplacian operator is a powerful sharpness indicator, but is unreliable when applied to images without endothelium.

SVM classification is employed here to select a buffer of good consecutive frames (i.e. a subsequence) as input to our SR method. In all the experiments presented in this paper the buffer is composed of 60 frames, corresponding (at 30 fps) to 2 seconds of acquisition time. This is a reasonable number of frames since, due to fast eye saccades/lamp jumps, the superposition of the endothelium segments is likely to be lost with larger buffers. Extensive tests show that the best SVM performance (92.58% correct classification in the validation set) is obtained by using just two labels, "useful" and "not useful", and concatenating the CLD (Color Layout), CSD (Color Structure) and HTD (Homogeneous Texture) MPEG-7 descriptors. Frame buffer selection is obtained by averaging the SVM probability of the "useful" frames inside a sliding window running along the segmented sequence. The closer such a buffer score to 1, the higher the chance that the buffer is composed of good images. Fig. 3 shows an example of the buffer score obtained with the SVM classification applied to a video sequence of 470 frames, compared with the same score using manual ground truth. The sequence contains several frames without visible endothelium regions. Although the SVM score is often lower than the ground truth score, local maxima (good buffers) and minima (bad buffers) are located at approximately the same frames of the sequence, thus allowing us to select the best subsequence. When local maxima are comparable, as in the case of Fig. 3, the final decision is taken by looking at the highest average energy of image Laplacian (red dotted curve) of the segmented frames in each subsequence.

Photo-mosaicing. Since the cornea can be regarded as locally planar, photo-mosaicing can be exploited as a way to obtain the HR image of the endothelium region. The resulting mosaic covers the endothelium area visible during the whole scanning session. The quality of the HR image depends on the quality of the images contributing to the mosaic. Again, a quality measurement is required in order to select the best images to use for the purpose of mosaic creation. Since the SVM classification has already found a good subsequence made by (almost) all useful images, the average modulus of the image Laplacian can be directly applied as quality measure. A robust, graph-based implementation of the mosaicing algorithm, akin to the one proposed in [5], is employed, so as to cope with possible outlier frames of class "not useful" that can occur in the subsequence.

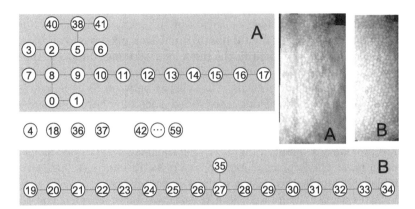

Fig. 4. A case of multiple trees for a sequence of 60 frames. The tiles composing subgraph A have an average quality lower than the quality of the tiles in subgraph B. Hence the latter is selected, even if the former has more nodes.

The algorithms is summarized as follows. First, each segmented image I_k is roughly aligned w.r.t. the next frame I_{k+1} by means of an affine transformation. Since in some frames the endothelium area can be very blurred or not visible at all, the registration of subsequent frames can fail, thus producing several distinct chains of linked images. Each chain is a tree composed by a set of subsequent image nodes. Chains are then merged together to build wider trees. Two chains are merged if an alignment transformation is found between any two nodes belonging to them. Multiple trees arise when it is not possible to merge all the chains in an unique connected graph. When this happens, each tree corresponds to a different mosaic, one of which is chosen to produce the HR image. The criterion for the tree selection is based on the size (i.e. the number of nodes) of the tree and average quality of its images. By default the selected tree is the largest, unless a second one has a better average quality (Fig. 4 shows an example of this situation). The reason for this strategy is that the value of every pixel of the HR image will be estimated on as many samples as possible, and it is convenient that the samples come from low resolution images of good quality. In Fig. 5, the mosaic obtained at the end of the raw alignment step is shown, together with the frame-by-frame apparent motion of the slit lamp with respect to the mosaic.

After the raw, affine registration, a finer image alignment takes place. For this purpose, a node I_r is selected, among the frames of the chosen tree, as root. This root acts as the reference frame of the finer mosaic and all the other images are registered w.r.t. it, according to a full projective warping transformation (2D homography).

Once all the low-resolution (LR) images have been registered w.r.t. the reference frame, the creation of the HR image can start. The HR image is a magnified version of the reference frame. Hence, the transformation W_k mapping the HR image onto each LR image I_k is obtained as $W_k = \mathrm{diag}(\rho^{-1}, \rho^{-1}, 1) H_k^{-1}$, where

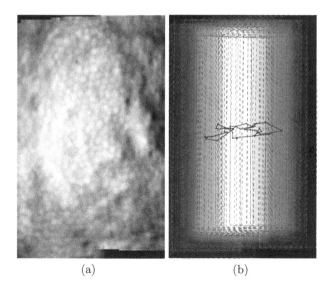

(a)   (b)

Fig. 5. (a): The mosaic after raw image alignment. (b): The overlap of all the tiles, and the path made by the slit lamp over the mosaic. The whiter the pixel, the higher the number of overlapping images. Note the sudden jumps that can arise during the scanning session. **Best viewed in color.**

$\rho > 1$ is the magnification factor and $\mathtt{H}_k$ is the homography mapping I_k onto the reference frame. Our method recovers the HR image J in closed form as a linear combination of several pixels coming from the LR images. The solution can be written as

$$\mathbf{j} = \mathtt{U} \sum_k \lambda_k \mathtt{N}_k \mathbf{i}_k \ , \tag{1}$$

where vectors $\mathbf{j}$ and $\mathbf{i}_k$ contain (in lexicographic order) the pixel values of the HR and I_k image, respectively. In Eq. 1 the λ_k's are Laplacian weights; each matrix $\mathtt{N}_k$ has size $n_j \times n_k$, while $\mathtt{U}$ is a square matrix of dimensions $n_j \times n_j$, being n_j and n_k the number of elements of $\mathbf{j}$ and $\mathbf{i}_k$ respectively. The matrices $\mathtt{N}_k$ and $\mathtt{U}$ take into account respectively the number of pixels that influence each HR pixel value, and the local amount of unsharp filtering. They can easily be computed as shown in [3]. The effects of matrix $\mathtt{U}$ applied to Fig. 6(a) are visible in Fig. 6(b). For the sake of comparison, Fig. 6(d) shows the effect of unsharp filtering on the image in Fig. 6(c), that was obtained by standard bicubic interpolation of the reference frame. Note that the results of bicubic magnification are much inferior than those obtained with our method. In fact, on the one hand, unlike Fig. 6(b), Fig. 6(d) contains artifacts due to high frequency noise. On the other hand, the bicubic-magnified image contains the same information than the LR frame it comes from, and therefore its fine details are not realistic. Conversely, the high-frequency details obtained with our method are realistic, as they summarize the information coming from the whole LR image sequence.

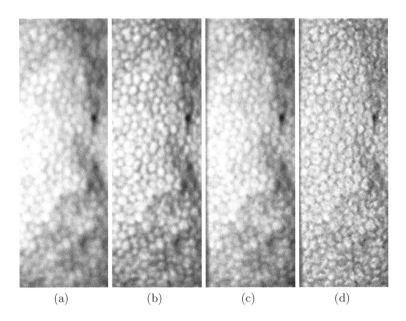

(a)   (b)   (c)   (d)

Fig. 6. (a): The first guess for the HR image. (b): The final HR image after sharpening.
(c): The bicubic interpolation of the corresponding LR frame after image equalization.
(d): image (c) after sharpening; note how the noise is enhanced too.

3   Experimental Results

In this section, results of comparative experiments are presented and discussed.

The first experiment compares our ad hoc mosaicing approach against a commercial state-of-the-art software (Photoshop^{TM} CS3). As shown in Fig. 7, both algorithms are able to successfully register almost all the frames containing the endothelium region (in the case of Photoshop, frames already cropped by our segmentation algorithm were provided to the software). The key difference is in the merging step: in fact, the result provided by Photoshop (Fig. 7(a)) has a wide region (enclosed by the black curve) that appears blurred, while in our solution the same region is of good quality. This is due to the fact that our solution merges the images by Laplacian averaging, while Photoshop is less selective. As a result, the quality of the Photoshop mosaic is highly affected even by very few blurred frames. Hence, for the special class of corneal endothelium images, using an information selection criterion based on the relative frame quality (as done in our approach) is undoubtedly beneficial.

A second comparison is made with a standard classical super-resolution method, according to which the HR image is generated by using a standard MAP super-resolution framework and exploiting the Huber function as prior [6]. The best MAP result, shown in Fig. 8(b), is clearly of less quality with respect

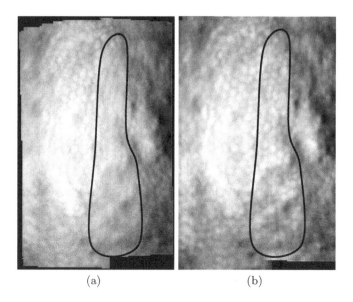

(a)   (b)

Fig. 7. Comparison of mosaic images. (a): Photoshop CS3. (b): Our result. The encircled area shows the mosaic portion where Photoshop fails to attain good image quality (see text).

to ours, as it suffers of a posterization effect, that flattens the appearance of the endothelium cells, and makes cell boundaries much less definite. It is likely that the Huber prior, although providing excellent results in other contexts (see again [6]), is less suitable for endothelial images. For the sake of completeness, Fig. 8(c) shows the best MLE solution to the super-resolution problem. As expected from the theory, being the MLE a simple least squares approach, a lot of high-frequency artifacts are generated in this case, thus making this solution totally unuseful for diagnostic purposes.

3.1 Gallery

Fig. 9 shows fifteen examples of 3× magnification of 60-frame LR sequences with different subjects and acquisition conditions. For each example are shown: one original LR endothelium image (left), the result of image magnification by bicubic interpolation (middle), and the result obtained with our super-resolution approach (right). For our approach, the average execution time for a single magnification process with an off-the-shelf notebook (processor Intel® core i3 CPU M330 at 2.13GHz) is about 7 seconds. In all cases, the HR image obtained with our method looks very detailed w.r.t. the original image, and of much better quality w.r.t. interpolated image.

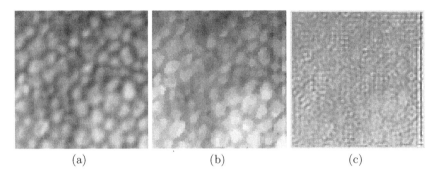

Fig. 8. (a): Our result for the HR image. (b): The best MAP result employing the Huber function as prior. (c): The best MLE result.

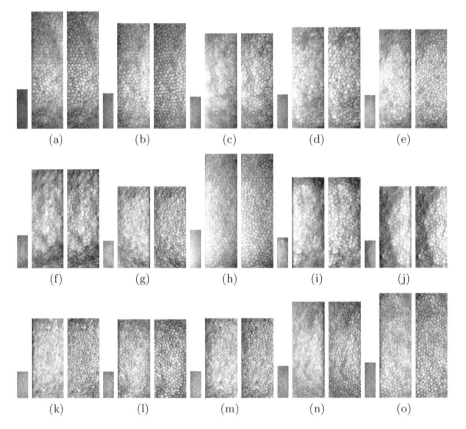

Fig. 9. Several examples with magnification factor 3×. Images are of variable size, due to different illumination conditions. For each group of images, from left to right: original endothelium image; enhanced bicubic-interpolated image; HR image obtained with our method.

4 Conclusions and Future Work

In this work, a fast and efficient method for obtaining good quality magnified images from a low resolution slit lamp biomicroscope was proposed. Compared against classical super-resolution techniques based on multiple images of the same scene, our method produces images of higher quality, as it is specifically tailored to the endothelial image domain.

Future work will address the development of a more general framework suitable for different applications. Indeed most of the computational steps of the pipeline could be adapted to new (medical and not) image domains, after a proper training of SVMs. For the sake of generalization, the ad hoc endothelium segmentation procedure described in section 2 could be replaced by a cascade of classifiers line in [7] to perform endothelium detection. Such classifiers could be trained again to detect the region of interest in each frame if the super-resolution pipeline is applied to a different domain.

Improvements to speed up the registration process will be addressed as well.

References

1. van Ouwerkerk, J.: Image super-resolution survey. Image and Vision Computing 24(10), 1039–1052 (2006)
2. Greenspan, H.: Super-resolution in medical imaging. The Computer Journal 52(1), 43–63 (2009)
3. Comanducci, D., Colombo, C.: A Super-Resolution Based Pipeline for the Magnification of Corneal Endothelium Images. Technical Report #CVG-10/2011, Università di Firenze, Dipartimento Sistemi e Informatica (October 2011) (submitted for publication)
4. Ng, K.-C., Poo, A.N., Ang, M.H.: Practical issues in pixel-based autofocusing for machine vision. In: Proc. IEEE International Conference on Robotics and Automation (2001)
5. Marzotto, R., Fusiello, A., Murino, V.: High resolution video mosaicing with global alignment. In: Proc. Conf. Computer Vision and Pattern Recognition (2004)
6. Capel, D.: Image Mosaicing and Super-Resolution (Cphc/Bcs Distinguished Dissertations). Springer (2004)
7. Viola, P., Jones, M.: Robust real-time face detection. International Journal of Computer Vision 57(2), 137–154 (2004)

FACTS - A Computer Vision System for 3D Recovery and Semantic Mapping of Human Factors

Lucas Paletta, Katrin Santner, Gerald Fritz, Albert Hofmann,
Gerald Lodron, Georg Thallinger, and Heinz Mayer

JOANNEUM RESEARCH Forschungsgesellschaft mbH,
DIGITAL - Institute for Information and Communication Technologies
Steyrergasse 17, 8010 Graz, Austria
{lucas.paletta,katrin.santner,gerald.fritz,albert.hofmann,
gerald.lodron,georg.thallinger,heinz.mayer}@joanneum.at

Abstract. The study of human attention in the frame of interaction studies has been relevant for usability engineering and ergonomics for decades. Today, with the advent of wearable eye-tracking and Google glasses, monitoring of human attention will soon become ubiquitous. This work describes a multi-component vision system that enables pervasive mapping of human attention. The key contribution is that our methodology enables full 3D recovery of the gaze pointer, human view frustum and associated human centered measurements directly into an automatically computed 3D model. We apply RGB-D SLAM and descriptor matching methodologies for the 3D modeling, localization and fully automated annotation of ROIs (regions of interest) within the acquired 3D model. This methodology brings new potential into automated processing of human factors, opening new avenues for attention studies.

Keywords: Visual attention, 3D information, SLAM, human factors.

1 Introduction

The study of human attention in the frame of interaction studies has been relevant in usability engineering and ergonomics for decades [1]. Today, with the advent of wearable eye-tracking and Google glasses, monitoring of human visual attention and the measuring of human factors will soon become ubiquitous. This work describes a multi-component vision system that enables pervasive mapping and monitoring of human attention. The key contribution is that our methodology enables full 3D recovery of the gaze pointer, human view frustum and correlated human centered measurements directly into an automatically computed 3D model. It applies RGB-D SLAM and descriptor matching methodologies for 3D modeling, localization and automated annotation of ROIs (regions of interest) within the acquired 3D model. This innovative methodology will open new opportunities for attention studies in real world environments, bringing new potential into automated processing for human factors technologies.

This work presents a computer vision system methodology that, *firstly*, enables to precisely estimate the 3D position and orientation of human view frustum and gaze

M. Chen, B. Leibe, and B. Neumann (Eds.): ICVS 2013, LNCS 7963, pp. 62–72, 2013.
© Springer-Verlag Berlin Heidelberg 2013

and from this enables to precisely analyze human attention in the context of the semantics of the local environment (objects [18], signs, scenes, etc.). Figure 1 visualizes how accurately human gaze is mapped into the 3D model for further analysis. *Secondly*, the work describes how ROIs (regions of interest) are automatically mapped from a reference video into the model and from this prevents from state-of-the-art laborious manual labeling of tens / hundreds of hours of eye tracking video data. This will provide a scaling up of nowadays still small sketched attention studies – such as, in shop floors, the analysis of navigation, and human-robot interaction – with ca. 10-15 users and thus enable for the first time large scale, statistically significant usability studies.

(a)

(b)

(c)

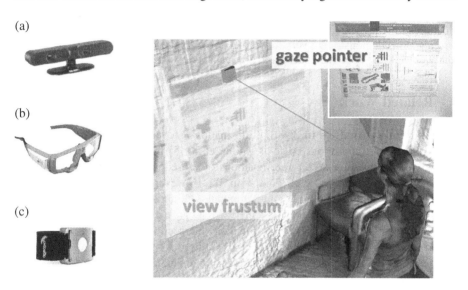

Fig. 1. Sketch of sensors used in the study (left) and typical gaze recovery (right). A full 6D recovery of the view frustum and gaze (right) is continuously mapped into the 3D model. (a) RGB-D scanning device, (b) eye tracking glasses (ETG) and (c) bio-electrical signal device.

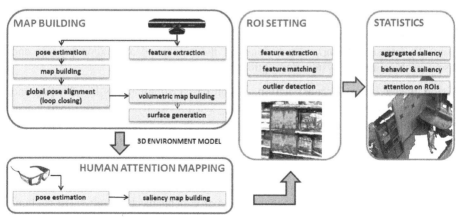

Fig. 2. Sketch of workflow for 3D gaze recovery and semantic ROI analytics

The methodology for the recovery of human attention in 3D environments is based on the workflow as sketched in Figure 2: For a spatio-temporal analysis of human attention in the 3D environment, we firstly build a spatial reference in terms of a three-dimensional model of the environment using RGB-D SLAM methodology [2]. Secondly, the user's view is gathered with eye tracking glasses (ETG) within the environment and localized from extracted local descriptors [3]. Then ROIs are marked on imagery and automatically detected in video and then mapped into the 3D model. Finally, the distribution of saliency onto the 3D environment is computed for further human attention analysis, such as, evaluation of the attention mapping with respect to object and scene awareness. Saliency information can be aggregated and, for example, being further evaluated in the frame of user behaviors of interest. The performance evaluation of the presented methodology firstly refers to results from a dedicated test environment [4] demonstrating very low projection errors, enabling to capture attention on daily objects and activities (package logos, cups, books, pencils).

2   Related Work

Human Attention Analysis in 3D. 3D information recovery of human gaze has recently been targeted in various contexts. Munn et al. [5] introduced monocular eye-tracking and triangulation of 2D gaze positions of subsequent key video frames, obtaining observer position and gaze pointer in 3D. However, they reconstructed only single 3D points without reference to a 3D model with angular errors of $\approx 3.8°$ (compared to our $\approx 0.6°$). Voßkühler et al. [6] analyzed 3D gaze movements with the use of a special head tracking unit, necessary for their intersection of the gaze ray with a digitized model of the surrounding. Pirri et al. [7] used for this purpose a mass marketed stereo rig that is required in addition to a commercial eye-tracking device, and attention cannot be mapped and tracked. The achieved accuracy indoor is ≈ 3.6 cm at 2 m distance to the target compared to our ≈ 0.9 cm (Paletta et al. [4]). Waizenegger et al. [19] tracked 3D models of conferees for the provision of virtual eye contact; Park et al. [20] presented 3D 'social saliency fields' to be established in human communication from head mounted camera views – however, they refer to dynamic in contrast to static parts of the 3D environment as in this work. In general, we present a straight forward solution of mapping fixation distributions onto a 3D model of the environment. The presented work extends through the automated annotation process and discusses the complete system description with shop floor scenario.

Vision Based Dense Reconstruction. Vision based Simultaneous Localization and Mapping (SLAM) aims at building a map of a previously unknown environment while simultaneously estimating the sensors pose within this map. In the last years SLAM has been performed using a huge variety of visual sensor such as single cameras, stereo or trinocular systems [8]. With the launch of range image devices, large scale dense reconstruction of indoor environments has been proposed [9], with real-time dense tracking and mapping system of small desktop scenes (KinectFusion). Dense reconstruction of large cyclic indoor environments has been presented via bundle adjustment techniques and fusion of probabilistic occupancy grid maps with loop closing (Pirker et al. [2]).

Vision Based Localization. Recently, several authors proposed a least-squares optimization routine minimizing the re-projection errors, others perform a perspective n-Point pose estimation algorithm. Both groups rely on correspondences established between 3D model points and 2D image points. In case of a large scale map consisting of thousands of model points, correspondence estimation becomes computationally too expensive. Therefore, image retrieval techniques [3] have been proposed to reduce the number of possible matching candidates.

Logo Detection. Logo detection is done on more general reference material in our work. The base for reference logos is packaging similar to those contained in the Surrey Object Image Library. An evaluation of state-of-the-art algorithms in machine vision object recognition on image databases shows that SIFT performs best on comparative image databases (SOIL-47 dataset [15]).

3 Gaze Localization in 3D Models

Visual Map Building and Camera Pose Estimation. For realistic environment modeling we make use of an RGB-D sensor (e.g. ASUS Xtion ProLive[1]) providing per pixel color and depth information at high frame rates. After intrinsic and extrinsic camera calibration, each RGB pixel can be assigned a depth value. Since we are interested in constructing a 3D environment in reasonable time, we perform feature based visual SLAM relying on the approach of [2]. Our environment consists of a sparse pointcloud, where each landmark is attached with a SIFT descriptor for data association during pose tracking and for vision based localization of any visual device within this reconstructed environment. Estimated camera poses (keyframes) are stored in a 6DOF manner. Incremental camera pose tracking assuming an already existing map is done by keypoint matching followed by a least-square optimization routine minimizing the reprojection error of 2D-3D correspondences. We decided to use the current frame for map expansion if the camera has moved for a certain amount or if the number of positive matches falls below a certain threshold. New landmarks are established using the previously estimated camera pose and the depth information stemming from the RGB-D device. Finally, sliding-window bundle adjustment is performed to refine both camera and landmark estimates. To detect loop closures we use a bag-of-words approach [3]. To close the loop we minimize the discrepancy between relative pose constraints through a pose graph optimization routine [10] followed by natural landmark transformation using corrected camera poses.

Densely Textured Surface Generation. For realistic environment visualization, user interaction and subsequent human attention analysis, a dense, textured model of the environment is constructed. Therefore, depth images are integrated into a 3D occupancy grid [2] using the previously corrected camera pose estimates. Hereby, we follow the pyramidal mapping approach implemented on the GPU. In contrast to existing approaches, we are able to reconstruct environments of arbitrary size. Space is not

---

[1] http://www.asus.com/Multimedia/Xtion_PRO_LIVE/

limited by GPU memory but only by the computer's memory resources. The whole volume is divided into subvolumina, whose sizes depend on the memory architecture of the GPU (typically 512^3 voxels). Unused subvolumina (e.g. already mapped or not visible) are cached in CPU memory (or any arbitrary storage devices) and reloaded on demand. Realistic surface construction is done by a marching cubes algorithm [12], where overlapping subvolumina guarantee a watertight surface. To apply realistic texture, we use a simple per vertex coloring approach. Hereby, the visible subset of points for each pose is determined using the z-Buffer together with a color buffer based selection technique. Each vertex' RGB color value is computed by projecting it onto the color image plane and taking the running average over all possible values resulting in a smooth, colored mesh (see Figure 3).

3D Gaze Recovery from Monocular Localization. To estimate the proband's pose, SIFT keypoints are extracted from ETG video frames and then matched landmarks from the prebuilt environment and a *full 6DOF pose* is estimated using the perspective n-Point algorithm [13]. Given the proband's pose together with the image gaze position, we are interested in its fixation point within the 3D map. Therefore, we compute the intersection of the viewing ray through the gaze position with the triangle mesh of the model. For rapid interference detection we make use of an object oriented bounding box tree [14] reporting the surface triangle and penetration point hit by the ray. Fixation hits are integrated over time resulting in a *saliency map* used to study and visualize each user's attention in the 3D environment (see Figure 4). For a smoother visualization of saliency and to account for uncertainties in localization and gaze, we use a Gaussian weighted kernel with nearby surface triangulation.

Automated 3D Annotation of Regions of Interest. Annotation of ROIs in 2D or even 3D information usually causes a process of massive manual interaction. In order to map objects of interests, such as, logos, package covers, etc. into the 3D model, we first use logo detection in the high resolution scanning video to search for occurrences of predefined reference appearances. We apply the SIFT descriptor to find the appropriate logo in each input frame. Visual tracking has been omitted so far in order not to introduce tracking errors into the 3D mapping step (see Figure 5). For robustness, ROI polygons are filtered if the geometric transformation of nearby frames significantly differs from the identity transform. For ROI identification in 3D model space, we use the keyframe poses estimated as described above together with the ROIs automatically detected in the associated image. Each surface point inside the camera's view frustum is projected onto the image plane and checked for being inside the ROI polygon (resulting ROIs in image and 3D domain are depicted in Figure 5).

4   Experimental Results

Eye Tracking Device. The mass marketed SMI™ eye-tracking glasses (Figure 1b) - a non-invasive video based binocular eye tracker with automatic parallax compensation - measures the gaze pointer for both eyes with 30 Hz. The gaze pointer accuracy of $0.5°$–$1.0°$ and a tracking range of $80°/60°$ horizontal/vertical assure a precise localization of the human's gaze in the HD 1280x960 scene video with 24 fps. An accurate three point calibration (less than 0.5° validation error) was performed and the gaze positions within the HD scene video frames were used for further processing. To evaluate our system in a realistic environment we recorded data on a shop floor covering an area of about 8x20m². We captured 2366 RGB-D images and reconstructed the environment consisting of 41700 natural visual landmarks and 608 keyframes. The resulting textured surface is shown in Figure 3c.

Recovery of 3D Gaze. In the study on human attention, 3 proband's were wearing eye-tracking glasses and the Affectiva Q sensor for measuring electrodermal activity (EDA) and accelerometer data. Probands had the task to search for three specific products which define the ROI in 2D and 3D. The ratio of successfully localized versus acquired frames is described in in Table 1: user 1 and 2 are efficiently localized. In general, blurred imagery, images depicting less modeled area in the test environment and too close views of the scenery cause localization outages that will be improved with appropriate tracking methodology as future work. However, the system allows a fully automatic computation of each proband's path within the environment, the full recovery of gaze and aggregation of saliency over time within the 3D model (Figure 3). The accuracy estimation of the proposed 3D gaze recovery has been reported in [4] with an angular projection error of ≈0.6° within the chosen 3D model which is therefore smaller than the calibration error of the eye-tracking glasses (≈1°). The Euclidean projection error was only ≈1.1 cm on average and thus enables to capture attention on daily objects and activities (packages, cups, books, pencils).

Fig. 3. Hardware (a) for the 3D model building process (Kinect and HD camera), (b) study with packages, (c) 3D model of the study environment, a shop floor for experimental studies

Table 1. Performance of localization in two typical user tracks

proband	# frames in total	# frames successfully localized
1	1903	1512 (79.45%)
2	1306	1088 (83.31%)

Fig. 4. Mapping of saliency on the acquired 3D model and automated recovery of the trajectory of ETG camera positions (spheres). Recovery of frustum (view) and gaze (line with blob).

Table 2. Accuracy evaluation of the ROI detection algorithm

performance \ ROI	# 1	# 2	# 3	total
# ground truth annot.	21	87	95	203
# logo detections	19	184	82	285
# true positives	19	86	70	175
precision	1.00	0.47	0.85	0.61
recall	0.90	0.99	0.74	0.86
avrg. spatial overlap (σ)	0.87 (0.02)	0.90 (0.06)	0.86 (0.05)	0.88 (0.06)

Table 3. Evaluation results of the three-dimensional ROI computation

R	O(R) 2D automatic ROI detection	O(R) 2D manual ROI annotation
# 1	0.728369	0.731168
# 2	0.327668	0.848437
# 3	0.611904	0.671895

ROI Detection in 2D and 3D. To evaluate the performance of automated 3D ROI association from HD video, we generated ground truth data (Figure 5). For accuracy evaluation of ROI detection, we are only interested in the detection performance, since tracking is not relevant for 3D mapping and robust detections are preferred instead of continuous tracks containing imprecise regions. ROI may be composed of multiple parts, hence the *temporal coverage* by detections of each gives an indication whether the complete ROI is covered. We have 3 ROIs consisting of 8 parts with temporal coverage between 37% and 98%. The precision and recall values act as a common quality measure of detection performance. Here, we employ an overlap criterion $O(R)$ [18] of a ROI R and its ground truth (R) $O(R) = \frac{A(R \cap G(R))}{A(R \cup G(R))}$, where $A(\cdot)$ denotes of the area of the polygonal region detected in the RGB images. The results are presented in Table 2. While having high precision rates at ROI #1 and #3, very similar products cause the algorithm to produce false positives resulting in a low precision rate for ROI #2 (see Figure 5). Given the high recall and spatial overlap values, the logo detection algorithm provides suitable input for the 3D mapping procedure. To evaluate the reliability, correctness and accuracy of the automatic ROI computation in 3D domain, we manually segmented ROIs in 3D space as ground truth. As an accuracy measure we again employ the overlap criterion defined above, where $A(\cdot)$ denotes the area of the region formed by surface triangles. To show the influence of the accuracy of the ROI detection in the image domain, we compare the 3D ROIs computed out of the *fully automatic* 2D ROI detection algorithm against the *manually annotated* ones (results in Table 3). Clearly, false, missing or imprecise detections in the image domain produce a high error in the 3D space, since the overlap criterion for manually annotated ROIs is higher in each case. This is also visualized in Figure 5, where a single 2D detection outlier results in erroneous 3D ROIs.

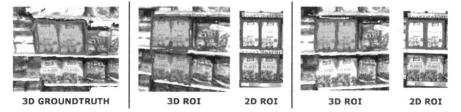

| 3D GROUNDTRUTH | 3D ROI | 2D ROI | 3D ROI | 2D ROI |

Fig. 5. Automated ROI detection in the 2D and 3D domain. (left) 3D ground truth annotation. (mid) ROIs computed in 3D out of automatic 2D detections. (right) 3D ROIs computed out of the 2D ground truth data.

Semantic Mapping of Attention. The proposed system allows a fully automated workflow to evaluate human attention performance entirely within a 3D model. The automatic detection of ROIs in three-dimensional space enables the system to provide the user with statistical evaluation without any manual annotation, which is known to be time consuming and error prone. One of the basic indicators when dealing with ROIs is called AOI hit, which states for a raw sample or a fixation that its coordinate value is inside the ROI [16]. ROI #1 received the maximum hits (287) by all users, with the maximum hits counted for user #1 (112 hits). Another example is the dwell –

often known as 'glance' in human factor analysis – and defined as one visit in an ROI, from entry to exit. The maximum mean dwell time was measured for ROI #1 but by user #3 (133.3 ms). Figure 6 plots the distribution of the dwell times for ROI #1 over all participants. Notice that dwells shorter than 35ms are excluded from the plot to enhance the readability. There are in total 287 hits for ROI #1, 45 visits of the region took at least 35 ms and the longest visit lasted 733.3 ms. From these data we conclude that only a minority of the captured fixations is related to human object recognition since this is known to trigger from 100 ms of observation / fixation [17]. However, the investigation of human attention behavior is dedicated to future work and we believe that we developed a most promising technology, in particular, for the purpose of studying mobile eye tracking in the field, in the real world, and for computational modeling of attention modeling.

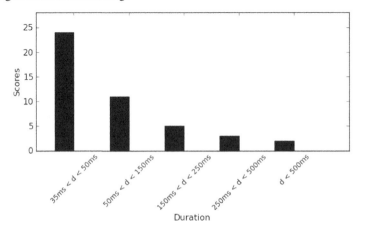

Fig. 6. Distribution of dwell times according to their duration for ROI #1. Human object recognition is known to trigger from 100 ms of observation / fixation [17].

5   Conclusion and Future Work

We presented a complete system for (i) wearable data capturing, (ii) automated 3D modeling, (iii) automated recovery of human pose and gaze, and (iv) automated ROI based semantic interpretation of human attention. The examples from a first relevant user study demonstrate the potential of our computer vision system to perform automated analysis and/or evaluation of the human factors, such as attention, using the acquired 3D model as a reference frame for gaze and semantic mapping, and with satisfying accuracy in the mapping from eye tracking glasses based video onto the automatically acquired 3D model. The presented system represents a significant first step towards an ever improving mapping framework for quantitative analysis of human factors in environments that are natural in the frame of investigated tasks. Future work will focus on improved tracking of the human pose across image blur and uncharted areas as well as on studying human factors in the frame of stress and emotion in the context of the 3D space.

Acknowledgments. This work has been partly funded by the European Community's Seventh Framework Programme (FP7/2007-2013), grant agreement n°288587 MASELTOV, and by the Austrian FFG, contract n°832045, Research Studio Austria FACTS.

References

1. Salvendy, G. (ed.): Handbook of Human Factors and Ergonomics. John Wiley (2012)
2. Pirker, K., Schweighofer, G., Rüther, M., Bischof, H.: GPSlam: Marrying Sparse Geometric and Dense Probabilistic Visual Mapping. In: Proc. 22nd BMVC (2011)
3. Nistér, D., Stewénius, H.: Scalable Recognition with a Vocabulary Tree. In: Proc. Conference on Computer Vision and Pattern Recognition (CVPR) (2006)
4. Paletta, L., Santner, K., Fritz, G., Mayer, H., Schrammel, J.: 3D Attention: Measurement of Visual Saliency Using Eye Tracking Glasses. In: Proc. ACM SIGCHI Conference on Human Factors in Computing Systems (CHI 2013), pp. 199–204 (2013) (extended abstracts)
5. Munn, S.M., Pelz, J.B.: 3D point-of-regard, position and head orientation from a portable monocular video-based eye tracker. In: Proc. ETRA 2008, pp. 181–188 (2008)
6. Voßkühler, A., Nordmeier, V., Herholz, S.: Gaze3D - Measuring gaze movements during experimentation of real physical experiments. In: Proc. Eur. Conf. Eye Mov. (ECEM) (2009)
7. Pirri, F., Pizzoli, M., Rudi, A.: A general method for the point of regard estimation in 3D space. In: Proc. Conf. Computer Vision and Pattern Recognition (CVPR), pp. 921–928 (2011)
8. Marks, T.K., Howard, A., Bajracharya, M., Cottrell, G.W., Matthies, L.: Gamma-SLAM: Using stereo vision and variance grid maps for SLAM in unstructured environments. In: Proc. IEEE International Conf. Robotics and Automation (ICRA) (2008)
9. Izadi, S., Kim, D., Hilliges, O., Molyneaux, D., Newcombe, R., Kohli, P., Shotton, J., Hodges, S., Freeman, D., Davison, A., Fitzgibbon, A.: KinectFusion: real-time 3D reconstruction and interaction using a moving depth camera. In: Proc. 24th Annual ACM Symposium on user Interface Software and Technology (2011)
10. Strasdat, H., Montiel, J.M.M., Davison, A.: Scale Drift-Aware Large Scale Monocular SLAM. In: Proceedings of Robotics: Science and Systems (2010)
11. Pirker, K., Schweighofer, G., Rüther, M., Bischof, H.: Fast and Accurate Environment Modeling using Three-Dimensional Occupancy Grids. In: Proc. 1st IEEE/ICCV Workshop on Consumer Depth Cameras for Computer Vision (2011)
12. Lorensen, W.E., Cline, H.E.: Marching Cubes: A high resolution 3D Surface Construction Algorithm. Computer Graphics 21, 163–169 (1987)
13. Lepetit, V., Moreno-Noguer, F., Fua, P.: EPnP: An Accurate O(n) Solution to the PnP Problem. International Journal of Computer Vision, 155–166 (2009)
14. Gottschalk, S., Lin, M.C., Manocha, D.: OBB-Tree: A Hierarchical Structure for Rapid Interference Detection. In: Proc. Annual Conf. Comp. Graphics & Interact. Techniques (1996)

15. Everingham, M., Van Gool, L., Williams, C.K.I., Winn, J., Zisserman, A.: The PASCAL Visual Object Classes (VOC) Challenge. Intl. Journal of Computer Vision (2010)
16. Holmqvist, K., Nyström, M., Andersson, R., Dewhusrt, R., Jarodzka, H., van de Weijler, J.: Eye Tracking – A Comprehensive Guide to Methods and Measures, p. 187. Oxford University Press (2011)
17. Grill-Spector, K., Sayres, R.: Object Recognition: Insights From Advances in fMRI Methods. Current Directions in Psychological Science 17(2), 73–79 (2008)
18. Fritz, G., Seifert, C., Paletta, L., Bischof, H.: Attentive object detection using an information theoretic saliency measure. In: Paletta, L., Tsotsos, J.K., Rome, E., Humphreys, G.W. (eds.) WAPCV 2004. LNCS, vol. 3368, pp. 29–41. Springer, Heidelberg (2005)
19. Waizenegger, W., Atzpadin, N., Schreer, O., Feldmann, I., Eisert, P.: Model based 3D gaze estimation for provision of virtual eye contact. In: Proc. ICIP 2012 (2012)
20. Park, H.S., Jain, E., Sheikh, Y.: 3D gaze concurrences from head-mounted cameras. In: Proc. NIPS 2012 (2012)

Anytime Perceptual Grouping of 2D Features into 3D Basic Shapes

Andreas Richtsfeld, Michael Zillich, and Markus Vincze

Automation and Control Institute (ACIN),
Vienna University of Technology
Gusshausstrae 25-29, 1040 Vienna, Austria
{ari,mz,mv}@acin.tuwien.ac.at

Abstract. 2D perceptual grouping is a well studied area which still has its merits even in the age of powerful object recognizer, namely when no prior object knowledge is available. Often perceptual grouping mechanisms struggle with the runtime complexity stemming from the combinatorial explosion when creating larger assemblies of features, and simple thresholding for pruning hypotheses leads to cumbersome tuning of parameters. In this work we propose an incremental approach instead, which leads to an anytime method, where the system produces more results with longer runtime. Moreover the proposed approach lends itself easily to incorporation of attentional mechanisms. We show how basic 3D object shapes can thus be detected using a table plane assumption.

Keywords: Computer vision, perceptual organization, object detection, basic shapes, proto-objects.

1 Introduction and Related Work

Recognition methods based on powerful feature descriptors have lead to impressive results in object instance recognition and object categorization. In some scenarios, however, no prior object knowledge can be assumed and more generic object segmentation methods are required. This is the realm of perceptual grouping, the application of generic principles for grouping certain image features into assemblies that are likely to correspond to objects in the scene.

These principles are of course well studied, starting with the pioneering work in Gestalt psychology by Wertheimer, Köhler, Koffka and Metzger. *Gestalt principles* (or *Gestalt laws*) aim to formulate the regularities according to which the perceptual input is organized into unitary forms, also referred to as wholes, groups or Gestalts. Typical Gestalt principles are *proximity, continuity, similarity* and *closure*, as well as *common fate, past experience* and *good Gestalt (form)* ([22,23,7,6,9]). *Common region* and *element connectedness* were later introduced and discussed by Rock and Palmer [12,10,11].

The perceptual grouping literature has largely focused on grouping of edges, especially detecting the enclosing contours of objects. While learning algorithms have been mainly used for object recognition, Sarkar and Soundararajan [16,18]

M. Chen, B. Leibe, and B. Neumann (Eds.): ICVS 2013, LNCS 7963, pp. 73–82, 2013.
© Springer-Verlag Berlin Heidelberg 2013

employ a methodology to learn the importance of Gestalt principles to build large salient edge groupings of visual low-level primitives. Grouping principles, such as proximity, parallelity, continuity, junctions and common region are trained to form large groups of edge primitives that are likely to come from a single object. The approach by Estrada and Jepson [4] uses a measure of affinity between pairs of lines to group line segments into perceptually salient contours in complex images. Compact closed region structure is also identified by bidirectional best-first search with backtracking by Saund [19], but similar to the approach by Estrada et al. many parameters and thresholds have to be set. Graph-based methods to extract closed contours were introduced by Wang et al. [21] and Zhu et al. [24]. Unfortunately both methods suffer from the problem of combinatorial explosion leading to polynomial runtime complexity in the number of edge segments.

Sala and Dickinson [15,14] introduce a method for contour grouping by construction of a region boundary graph and use consistent path search to identify a pre-defined vocabulary of simple part models. These models correspond to projections of 3D objects, but the approach stays at the 2D image level. Song et al. [20] propose a novel definition of the Gestalt principle *Prägnanz* based on Koffkas definition that image descriptions should be both stable and simple. They show a grouping mechanism based on the Gestalt principles *proximity* and *common region*, using straight lines as grouping primitives and color image regions to estimate the common region principle. Benchmark results are shown on the Berkeley Segmentation Dataset (BSD) to demonstrate their method.

Focusing on the runtime behavior of perceptual grouping Mahamud et al. [8] presented an any-time method for finding smooth closed contours bounding objects of unknown shape using the most salient edge segments for incremental processing. Their approach is able to stop processing at any time and delivers the best results (most salient closures) detected up to that time. However, a drawback of the approach is the high computational cost and that the approach does not scale well to bigger problems. Zillich et al. [25] introduced incremental indexing in the image space (as opposed to the more common indexing into a model data base using geometric features) for parameter-free perceptual grouping. Incrementally extending search lines are used to find intersections of straight lines and shortest path search is then used to identify closed convex contours, leading again to an anytime approach that yields the most salient closed convex contours at any processing time. Their approach however only uses straight edges.

In this work we also want to focus on anytime processing, as we believe that having control of the runtime behavior of a method is of high importance if that method is to be used within a larger system context. This is especially true for methods prone to suffering from high runtime complexity (e.g. combinatorial explosions), which is often the case with perceptual grouping approaches. The contributions of this work then are a) the extension of the anytime framework of Zillich et al. [25] to support a wider range of feature primitives; b) the construction of 3D objects from grouped 2D features (for a limited class of shapes);

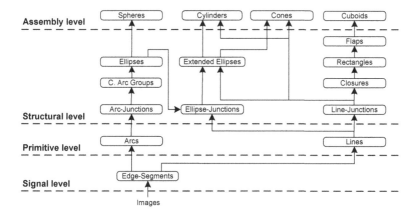

Fig. 1. Our proposed perceptual grouping structure in the classificatory structure introduced by Sarkar and Boyer [17,2]

and c) showing how attention quite naturally fits into this framework and leads to attended objects popping out earlier.

2   Perceptual Grouping Structure

Sarkar and Boyer [17,2] introduced a classificatory structure for perceptual grouping processes with four different levels of data abstraction, namely *signal, primitive, structural* and *assembly level*. Edgels, edge chains or uniform regions are extracted first from image pixels (grey level or RGB image) in the signal level. Parametric image features, such as straight lines and arcs are subsequently estimated in the primitive level, before corners, closed regions, polygons and ribbons are constructed in the structural level. Large arrangements of visual primitives finally form object hypotheses at the assembly level.

Our approach follows the above 4 level structure. Edges are extracted at the signal level followed by the construction of line- and arc-primitives. In the structural level incremental processing is initiated by employing incrementally extending search lines in the image space. Whenever search lines intersect new junctions are created and subsequent modules will be triggered to form new higher level primitives. Bottom-up grouping continues until basic object shapes appear in the assembly level.

3   Implementation

In this section we first present the overall process flow within the structure in Fig. 1. We then outline how incremental indexing drives the process flow, explain the various processing modules in detail, and explain how we arrive at 3D object hypotheses. Finally we show how attentional mechanisms can be tied to the proposed process flow.

3.1   Process Flow

Processing does not happen in a traditional bottom-up pipeline, where each level of primitives is constructed one after another. Instead, following the principle of anytimeness, processing is *incremental*. A processing module for a primitive (e.g. finding closures) is always triggered when the module gets informed about a new lower level primitive (e.g. a junction). This in turn leads to processing at the next higher level (e.g. rectangles), and stops at a level where no more grouping principles can be satisfied, or at the assembly level with the creation of an object hypothesis.

Processing starts with edge extraction, which is the only non-incremental part, as we use an off-the shelf edge detection method to detect all edges (lines and arcs) at once. All subsequent processing is controlled by extending search lines of shape primitives (see Sec. 3.2) to find junctions between primitives.

All created primitives are *ranked* according to significance values derived from geometric constraints (e.g. line length). Ranking serves two purposes. First, primitives at the lower levels, i.e. those triggering higher level processing, are selected for processing according to rank. For example a line is chosen to extend its search line by one pixel. To this end we randomly select ranked primitives using an exponential distribution. This leads to the most salient structures popping out first. Second, ranking allows *masking* to prune unlikely primitives. A higher ranked primitive masks a lower ranked primitive if the two disagree about the interpretation of a common lower-level element (e.g. two overlapping closures sharing an edge). Masking prunes results with poor significance and limits combinatorial explosions in processing modules higher up the hierarchy.

3.2   Incremental Indexing and Anytimeness

Incremental indexing is used in the structural level to form junctions. Search lines emanating from primitives are used to find junctions between primitives. Search lines are defined in the image space for line, arc and ellipse primitives, as shown in Fig. 2. We define tangential and normal search lines for straight lines, tangential search lines at the start and end point for arcs, and normal search lines at the vertex points for ellipses. These search lines are drawn into the so-called vote image one pixel at a time, whenever the respective primitive was selected for processing. Each search line is drawn with the originating primitive's label. Whenever a growing search line intersects another or hits a primitive, a new junction emerges. The different types of junctions for different types of intersecting search lines are shown in Figure 2. Emanating search lines for different processing times can be seen in the result section in Fig. 4.

3.3   Gestalt Principles and Primitives

Primitives are grouped using implicitly and explicitly implemented Gestalt principles. E.g. proximity is implicitly implemented by the search lines for finding junctions, while closure, parallelity or connectedness are explicitly implemented

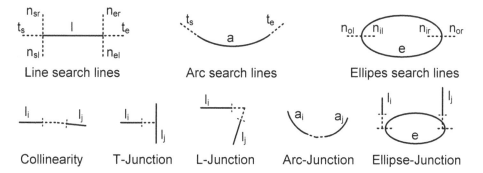

Fig. 2. Definition of search lines (first row) and types of junctions between search lines (second row). Collinearities, T-junctions and L-junctions between lines, arc-junctions between arcs and ellipse-junctions between ellipses and lines.

as geometric constraints within the respective processing modules. In the following we briefly describe the generation of each primitive:

Edge Segments – Edge segments are constructed from the raw color image data with a Canny edge extractor.

Lines and Arcs – Edge segments are split for fitting straight lines and arcs into the segments using the method by Rosin and West [13].

Line Junctions – Junctions between lines are T-Junctions, L-Junctions and Collinearities, as shown in Fig. 2. T-junctions are substituted by two L-junctions and a collinearity for further processing in the grouping framework. Lines form the vertices V_l, and junctions the edges E_l of a graph $G_l = (V_l, E_l)$, which is constantly updated as new junctions are created.

Closures (closed convex contours) – Whenever new junctions appear Dijkstra's algorithm for shortest path search is run on the updated graph $G_l = (V_l, E_l)$. A constraint on similar turning directions during search ensures creation of convex contours.

Rectangles – With rectangles we refer to geometric structures including trapezoids and parallelograms (i.e. perspective projections of 3D rectangles under one-point projection [3]). Four dominant changes of the direction (L-Junctions) and at least one parallel opposing line pair is mandatory to create a rectangle.

Flaps – A flap is a geometric structure built from two non-overlapping rectangles where the two rectangles share one edge. All cuboidal structures under generic views consist of flap primitives.

Arc junctions – Arc junctions are created when two arc search lines with same convexity intersect, as shown in Fig. 2. Again a graph $G_a(V_a, E_a)$ is constructed from arcs and their junctions, and updated whenever a new junction comes in.

Convex arc groups – Shortest path search on $G_a(V_a, E_a)$ leads to convex arc groups, i.e. groups of pairwise convex arcs.

Ellipses – Ellipses are fitted to convex arc groups using least squares fitting [5] as implemented in OpenCV.

Ellipse junctions – Ellipses trigger initialization of ellipse search lines, as shown in Fig. 2), with the goal of finding lines connected to the ellipse's major vertices.

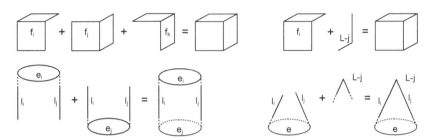

Fig. 3. Construction of basic object shapes: First row: Cuboid from three flaps or from flap and L-junction. Second row: Cylinder from two extended ellipses and Cone from extended ellipse and L-junction.

Extended ellipses – Ellipses with two attached lines (possibly themselves extended via collinearities) form so called extended ellipses.

Cuboids – Figure 3 shows the two options to construct a cuboid. First, from three flaps sharing three different rectangles and second, from a L-junction and two line primitives connecting to a flap.

Cones – Cones are built from extended ellipses by finding an L-junction between the connected lines from the ellipse junctions, see Fig. 3.

Cylinders – Cylinders are also build from extended ellipses with ellipse junctions at each vertex by finding a connection of lines between the ellipse junctions, see again Fig. 3.

Spheres – Spheres are inferred from circles, which are a special type of ellipse.

3.4   From 2D Shapes to 3D Objects

All primitives so far are groups of 2D image features. But the primitives at the assembly levels are highly non-accidental configurations corresponding to projections of views of 3D objects. So with a few additional assumptions we should be able to create 3D object hypotheses.

To this end we assume that the pose of the calibrated camera with respect to the dominant plane on which objects are resting is known. For the indoor robotics scenario we are targeting, this knowledge comes from the known tilt angle and elevation of the camera, together with the assumed (typically standardized) table height. We are then able to calculate the 3D properties of a rectangular cuboid, of upright standing cones and cylinders. We simply intersect view rays through the lowermost junctions with the ground plane and thus obtain 3D position on the plane as well as unambiguous size of the basic object shapes. This restriction to simple symmetric shapes also allows to complete the unseen backside of the object.

3.5   Adding Attention

In Section 3.1 ranking of primitives was based solely on their significance. Sometimes however we might have external clues. The user of our system might provide us with regions of interest (ROIs), perhaps deduced from saliency maps,

Fig. 4. Incremental grouping: Line search lines (first row), arc search lines (second row) and resulting basic shapes (third row) after 150, 200, 300 and 500ms processing time. The last row shows search lines and detected basic shapes when attention (region of interest) is set to the salt box and the tape respectively.

or change detection. Also higher level knowledge might be available such as the gaze direction of a human or the position of a grasping hand.

Including such attentional cues is quite straight-forward. To this end we weight the significance of a primitive with its distance to the provided region(s) of interest, using a Gaussian located at the center of the ROI with sigma equal to 0.25 times image width. Processing is thus concentrated around the region of interest. The ROIs allows us to specify where to look first and more "carefully". Note that we do not exclude other regions of the image, as would be the case if we simply cut out the ROI and then work on the sub-image. Strongly prominent structures outside the ROI will still be detected, albeit a bit later.

4   Experiments

We demonstrate results on a table top scene containing six objects of different shapes. Figure 4 shows the growing search lines of lines (first row) and arcs (second row) and the resulting 3D shapes of the assembly level, after 150ms, 200ms, 300ms and 500ms processing time. As can be seen, with the proposed incremental approach object detection depends on processing time: The longer

Table 1. Average true positive detection rate for objects shown in Fig. 4 with different processing times and results when using an attention point for the sought-after object

	Mug	Salt-Box	Cube	Peanuts	Ball	Tape	Average
150ms	0.0%	0.0%	0.0%	3.3%	33.3%	0.0%	7.8%
150ms with ROI	0.0%	0.0%	36.7%	10.0%	40.0%	13.3%	16.7%
200ms	0.0%	10.0%	83.3%	13.3%	16.7%	0.0%	20.6%
200ms with ROI	3.3%	10.0%	100.0%	20.0%	56.6%	50.0%	39.9%
300ms	0.0%	60.0%	100.0%	40.0%	80.0%	10.0%	48.3%
300ms with ROI	0.0%	30.0%	100.0%	33.3%	90.0%	56.7%	51.7%
500ms	6.7%	100.0%	100.0%	33.3%	90.0%	60.0%	65.0%
500ms with ROI	16.7%	66.7%	100.0%	46.6%	96.6%	80.0%	67.8%

the search lines grow the more primitives are connected and hence the more shapes are found.

The last row of Fig. 4 shows two examples when using attention by specifying a region of interest (ROI) with 300ms processing time. Search lines in the ROI are preferred for extension, leading on average to earlier detection. Table 1 shows the average detection rate (over 30 images) for the different objects shown in Fig. 4. The detection rate is estimated with four different processing times with and without a region of interest (ROI) centered on the object. Note that we are here not concerned with how attention is provided. It could be based on color ("the yellow ball"), generic saliency operators or any other means providing salient locations in the image.

Surprisingly it can be observed that the detection rate actually decreases for some objects when using attention. This can be explained considering the texture on the objects which, being nearest to the attention point, grabs too much attention and lets the system hallucinate objects into the texture. Note that the actual object is typically still found, but masked by the hallucinated texture object, and thus not reported. The main impact of using ROIs can be observed when using short processing times.

5   Conclusion

We presented an anytime system for detecting 3D basic object shapes from 2D images. Anytimeness is provided by incremental indexing, which drives the bottom-up perceptual grouping process. We also showed how attention can quite naturally be integrated into anytime processing. Experimental evaluation shows encouraging results on example images of moderate complexity with objects of different shapes, though a more extensive evaluation on a broader range of scenes and objects is needed. Further images with prototypical real world scenes are shown in Fig. 5.

One limitation of the system is the fact that we rely solely on edge primitives from a standard Canny edge detector. Recent approaches have shown that edge extraction and region segmentation delivers best results when done simultaneously [1]. Also results from more sophisticated edge detectors would certainly

Fig. 5. More detected shape primitives: Office and living room scenes with detected boxes and cylinders (red) as well as the lower-level primitives rectangles (yellow) and closures (blue)

lead to improved results and should be considered for further investigations. Another limitation is the restricted number of detectable shapes at the assembly level (much like [15,14]), but this restriction on the other hand provides the heuristics to generate 3D shapes from the 2D assemblies. To overcome the problem of defining basic shapes, learning algorithms could be employed at the assembly level to group primitives of the structural level according to the principles of perceptual organization as shown in [16,18].

Acknowledgement. The research leading to these results has received funding from the Austrian Science Fund (FWF): project TRP 139-N23, InSitu.

References

1. Arbeláez, P., Maire, M., Fowlkes, C., Malik, J.: Contour Detection and Hierarchical Image Segmentation. IEEE Transaction on Pattern Analysis and Machine Intelligence (PAMI) 33(5), 898–916 (2011)
2. Boyer, K.L., Sarkar, S.: Perceptual organization in computer vision: status, challenges, and potential. Computer Vision and Image Understanding 76(1), 1–5 (1999)
3. Carlbom, I., Paciorek, J.: Planar Geometric Projections and Viewing Transformations. ACM Computing Surveys 10(4), 465–502 (1978)
4. Estrada, F.J., Jepson, A.D.: Perceptual grouping for contour extraction. In: International Conference on Pattern Recognition (ICPR), vol. 2, pp. 32–35. IEEE (2004)
5. Fitzgibbon, A.W., Fisher, R.B.: A Buyer's Guide to Conic Fitting. In: Procedings of the British Machine Vision Conference (BMVC), pp. 513–522. British Machine Vision Association (1995)
6. Koffka, K.: Principles of Gestalt Psychology. International library of psychology, philosophy, and scientific method, vol. 20. Harcourt, Brace and World (1935)
7. Köhler, W.: Gestalt Psychology Today. American Psychologist 14(12), 727–734 (1959)
8. Mahamud, S., Williams, L.R., Thornber, K.K.: Segmentation of multiple salient closed contours from real images. IEEE Transactions on Pattern Analysis and Machine Intelligence (PAMI) 25(4), 433–444 (2003)

9. Metzger, W.: Laws of Seeing, 1st edn. The MIT Press (1936)
10. Palmer, S.E.: Common region: a new principle of perceptual grouping. Cognitive Psychology 24(3), 436–447 (1992)
11. Palmer, S., Rock, I.: Rethinking perceptual organization: The role of uniform connectedness. Psychonomic Bulletin & Review 1(1), 29–55 (1994)
12. Rock, I., Palmer, S.: The legacy of Gestalt psychology. Scientific American 263(6), 84–90 (1990)
13. Rosin, P.L., West, G.A.W.: Segmenting Curves into Elliptic Arcs and Straight Lines. In: Proceedings Third International Conference on Computer Vision (ICCV), pp. 75–78. IEEE Comput. Soc. Press (1990)
14. Sala, P., Dickinson, S.: Contour Grouping and Abstraction Using Simple Part Models. In: Daniilidis, K., Maragos, P., Paragios, N. (eds.) ECCV 2010, Part V. LNCS, vol. 6315, pp. 603–616. Springer, Heidelberg (2010)
15. Sala, P., Dickinson, S.J.: Model-based perceptual grouping and shape abstraction. In: IEEE Computer Society Conference on Computer Vision and Pattern Recognition Workshops, pp. 1–8 (2008)
16. Sarkar, S.: Learning to Form Large Groups of Salient Image Features. In: IEEE Computer Society Conference on Computer Vision and Pattern Recognition (CVPR), pp. 780–786 (1998)
17. Sarkar, S., Boyer, K.L.: Perceptual organization in computer vision - A review and a proposal for a classificatory structure. IEEE Transactions on Systems Man and Cybernetics 23(2), 382–399 (1993)
18. Sarkar, S., Soundararajan, P.: Supervised learning of large perceptual organization: graph spectral partitioning and learning automata. IEEE Transactions on Pattern Analysis and Machine Intelligence (PAMI) 22(5), 504–525 (2000)
19. Saund, E.: Finding perceptually closed paths in sketches and drawings. IEEE Transactions on Pattern Analysis and Machine Intelligence (PAMI) 25(4), 475–491 (2003)
20. Song, Y.-Z., Xiao, B., Hall, P., Wang, L.: In Search of Perceptually Salient Groupings. IEEE Transactions on Image Processing 20(4), 935–947 (2011)
21. Wang, S., Stahl, J.S., Bailey, A., Dropps, M.: Global Detection of Salient Convex Boundaries. International Journal of Computer Vision (IJCV) 71(3), 337–359 (2007)
22. Wertheimer, M.: Untersuchungen zur Lehre von der Gestalt. II. Psychological Research 4(1), 301–350 (1923)
23. Wertheimer, M.: Principles of perceptual organization. In: Beardslee, D.C., Wertheimer, M. (eds.) A Source Book of Gestalt Psychology, pp. 115–135. Van Nostrand, Inc. (1958)
24. Zhu, Q., Song, G., Shi, J.: Untangling Cycles for Contour Grouping. In: International Conference on Computer Vision (ICCV), vol. (c), pp. 1–8. IEEE (2007)
25. Zillich, M., Vincze, M.: Anytimeness avoids parameters in detecting closed convex polygons. In: IEEE Computer Society Conference on Computer Vision and Pattern Recognition Workshops (CVPRW), pp. 1–8. IEEE (June 2008)

Model-Based Pose Estimation for Rigid Objects*

Manolis Lourakis and Xenophon Zabulis

Institute of Computer Science, Foundation for Research and Technology - Hellas
Vassilika Vouton, P.O. Box 1385, GR 711 10, Heraklion, Crete, Greece

Abstract. Determining the pose of objects appearing in images is a problem encountered often in several practical applications. The most effective strategy for dealing with this challenge is to proceed according to the model-based paradigm, which involves building 3D models of objects and then determining object poses by fitting their models to new images with the aid of detected features. This paper proposes a model-based approach for estimating the full pose of known objects from natural point features. The method employs a projective imaging model and incorporates reliable automatic mechanisms for pose initialization and convergence. Furthermore, it is extendable to multiple cameras without the need to perform multi-view matching and relies on sparse structure from motion techniques for the construction of object models offline. Experimental results demonstrate its accuracy and robustness.

Keywords: Pose estimation, feature matching, object detection & recognition.

1 Introduction

Accurate localization of objects in images is a primary requirement for vision systems applied to areas such as robotic manipulation, tracking, augmented reality, tangible interfaces, etc. Such systems are expected to operate reliably in dynamic and unknown environments, delivering accurate object position and orientation estimates despite any variations in the appearance of objects due to changes in viewing position, illumination or occlusion. Object pose estimation is often addressed in the context of model-based matching and recognition [11], for which a vast body of literature is available. According to this paradigm, a collection of geometric object models and their associated features is assembled first. During recognition, features extracted from an image are matched to those stored in a model and the mapping among them is used to determine the pose of the corresponding object.

This paper presents a system for estimating the full, i.e. six degrees of freedom, pose of rigid objects. The system employs an offline stage to build a library of models encoding the 3D geometry and local appearance of objects, followed by an online stage for matching and pose estimation. Stored models consist of

---

* This work has received funding from the EC FP7 programme under grant no. 270138 DARWIN.

M. Chen, B. Leibe, and B. Neumann (Eds.): ICVS 2013, LNCS 7963, pp. 83–92, 2013.
© Springer-Verlag Berlin Heidelberg 2013

sparse sets of 3D points from an object's surface along with the SIFT descriptors [13] of their image projections. During online operation, image features and their SIFT descriptors are extracted from images and matched against those of the models to establish putative correspondences. Owing to the specificity of SIFT, the number of these correspondences usually provides strong evidence regarding the presence of particular modelled objects in an image. Such hypotheses are tested by using the 3D coordinates of matched model points to estimate object poses and thus verify that correspondences occur in a configuration consistent with geometry. The proposed approach is applicable regardless of the relative pose of the object with respect to the camera, is robust to occlusions and mismatches and can easily recover from failures as it maintains very little state information. It makes mild assumptions regarding objects, postulating that they are rigid and textured but arbitrarily complex. Furthermore, it employs a fully projective imaging formulation, mechanisms for reliable pose initialization and convergence, is extendable to multiple cameras without the need to perform multi-view matching and relies on automatic structure from motion (SfM) techniques for the construction of offline models. Related existing work is reviewed in Sect. 2, the components of the proposed method are detailed in Sections 3-5 and experimental results from real and synthetic datasets are presented in Sect. 6.

2   Related Work

Early approaches to model-based matching employed intensity edges as features. Lowe [11], for example, relied on perceptual organization to group features and reduce the size of the search space involved in matching, followed by top-down spatial correspondence aimed at aligning a model with an image and estimating its pose. This work was confined to using straight line segments and employed approximate parallelism as their grouping cue. Since this property is not preserved under perspective, the method is limited to images with affine geometry for which the perspective distortion is small. The approach was subsequently extended to handle objects with arbitrary curved surfaces and internal parameters representing articulations or surface deformations [12].

Later on, developments in covariant detectors and descriptors for image patches [14] were adopted to build local representations. Thus, Vacchetti et al. [18] combine geometric models with feature-based matching against a set of reference keyframes to track rigid objects in 3D. Rothganger et al. [15] capture the appearance of object surface patches using affine invariant local descriptors and their spatial relationships using multi-view geometric constraints. Matching enforcing photometric and geometric consistency achieves object recognition and pose estimation. The approach assumes an affine projection model and incurs high computational cost. Gordon and Lowe [3] describe a system based on SIFT features for recognizing learnt models in new images and solving for their pose. Intended for use in an augmented reality application, this system estimates the pose of the camera with respect to a set of mostly stationary objects in its environment rather than the other way round. As a result, it puts emphasis on the reduction of jitter and drift and can handle only a single model at a time that corresponds to the scene being tracked. The work of Collet et al. [1], who present a system based on natural features capable of estimating the pose of objects in a robot's workspace, is the most relevant to the current paper. Our work differs from [1] in that it does not require alignment of models with the real word prior to estimating pose, it employs more accurate pose initialization, is more resilient to mislocalized feature points, it can tolerate local minima in pose estimation and can be readily extended to multiple cameras.

3 Models and Features

Object models are a key ingredient of the proposed method. To obtain a complete, view independent model of an object, the latter has to be modelled using images from multiple viewpoints. Hence, each object is photographed individually in several images as a hand-held camera circumnavigates around it and then the acquired images are used to estimate the inter-frame camera motion and recover a corresponding 3D point cloud via SfM techniques [17]. An object model comprises of a set of 3D points from this point cloud, each accompanied by a SIFT image descriptor which captures the local surface appearance in the point's vicinity. A SIFT descriptor is available from each image where a particular 3D point is seen. Thus, we select as its most representative descriptor the one originating from the image in which the imaged surface is most frontal and close enough to the camera. This requires knowledge of the surface normal, which is obtained by gathering the point's 3D neighbors and robustly fitting to them a plane. This procedure also identifies isolated 3D points that are filtered out from the final model.

During pose estimation, SIFT keypoints are detected in an image and then matched against those contained in an object model. The robustness of SIFT permits the reliable identification of features that have undergone large affine distortions between the image and the model. The established correspondences are used to associate the 2D image locations of feature locations with the 3D coordinates of their corresponding points on the objects surface. The procedure we initially evaluated for point matching used the standard ratio test for SIFT descriptor distances, as follows. Matches were identified by finding the two nearest neighbors to each descriptor from the image among those in the model, and only accepting a match if the distance to the closest neighbor was less than a fixed threshold of that to the second closest neighbor. This threshold can be adjusted to leniently establish more matches, or conservatively select the most reliable ones. It was observed experimentally that the ratio test yielded substantial proportions of erroneous matches. The F2P strategy from [10], also based on a ratio test, was also tested and found to be a viable choice in terms of the quality of produced matches, hence it was adopted as our matching technique.

Distances among SIFT descriptors are traditionally quantified with the Euclidean (L_2) norm. The SIFT descriptor is a weighted histogram of gradient orientations. Thus, irrespectively of the matching criterion, improvements in matching are attained by substituting L_2 with histogram norms such as the Chi-squared (χ^2) distance [16]. Despite that other, more computationally demanding, distances such as the quadratic-Chi family or the circular Earth Movers were found to yield even better matching results, the χ^2 distance was eventually adopted as it offers the best performance / computational cost trade-off.

4   Pose Estimation

Pose estimation concerns determining the position and orientation of a camera given its intrinsics and a set of n correspondences between known 3D points and their image projections. This problem, also known as the Perspective-n-Point (PnP) problem, has received much attention due to is wide applicability in various domains. PnP is typically solved using non-iterative approaches that involve small, fixed-size sets of 3D-2D correspondences. For example, the basic case for triplets (P3P), was first studied in [4] whereas other solutions were later proposed in [2,8]. P3P is known to admit up to four different solutions, whereas in practice it usually has just two. As a result, a fourth point is used in practice for disambiguation. Minimal solutions to PnP are particularly important for estimating pose in a robust estimation framework, as the cardinality of each random sample is directly related to the total number of samples that need to be drawn in order to find a solution with acceptable confidence. On the other hand, being unable to combine more than the minimal number of correspondences, minimal solutions ignore much of the redundancy present in the data and hence suffer from inaccuracies. This is remedied by non-linear refinement, as follows.

4.1   Monocular Robust Pose Estimation with Non-linear Refinement

This section describes in more detail our approach for pose estimation in a single image. Starting with a set of 2D-3D point correspondences, a preliminary pose estimate is computed first and then refined iteratively. This is achieved by embedding a P3P solver into a RANSAC [2] framework that uses the MSAC redescending cost function for hypothesis scoring. Applied to the problem of pose estimation, RANSAC repetitively draws random quadruples of points and uses one triple with the P3P solver of [4] and the fourth point for verification to obtain a pose estimate. The best scoring pose hypothesis is retained as RANSAC's outcome and used to classify correspondences into inliers and outliers. By minimizing the reprojection error pertaining to all inliers, the pose computed by RANSAC is next refined to take into account more than three correspondences. Since it involves a non-linear objective function, this minimization is carried out iteratively with the Levenberg-Marquardt (L-M) algorithm, as explained next.

Denoting by $\mathbf{K}$ the 3×3 intrinsic calibration matrix and n corresponding 3D-2D points by $\mathbf{M}_i$ and $\mathbf{m}_i$, the pose computed with RANSAC is refined by using it as a starting point to minimize the cumulative image reprojection error

$$\min_{\mathbf{r}, \mathbf{t}} \sum_{i=1}^{n} d(\mathbf{K} \cdot [\mathbf{R}(\mathbf{r}) \,|\, \mathbf{t}] \cdot \mathbf{M}_i - \mathbf{m}_i)^2, \tag{1}$$

where $\mathbf{t}$ and $\mathbf{R}(\mathbf{r})$ are respectively the sought translation and rotation matrix parameterized using the Rodrigues rotation vector $\mathbf{r}$, $\mathbf{K} \cdot [\mathbf{R}(\mathbf{r}) | \mathbf{t}] \cdot \mathbf{M}_i$ is the predicted projection on the image of the homogeneous point $\mathbf{M}_i$ and $d(\mathbf{x}, \mathbf{y})$ denotes the reprojection error, i.e. the Euclidean distance between the image points represented by vectors $\mathbf{x}$ and $\mathbf{y}$. The Jacobians required by L-M were provided analytically using symbolic differentiation.

The minimization in (1) can be made more immune to noise caused by mislocalized image points by employing M-estimators [6]. The former substitute the squared-error of the residuals with a symmetric robust cost function $\rho()$ which increases less steeply than quadratically and/or down-weights points whose residual errors are too large. To ensure that $\rho()$ has a unique minimum at zero, it is common to choose it to be convex. However, non-convex cost functions are more effective in suppressing the influence of large errors at the cost of not guaranteeing uniqueness of minimum. An effective strategy is to start the process with a convex cost function, iterate until convergence, and then apply a few iterations with a non-convex one to eliminate the effect of large errors. Regardless of the exact form of the chosen cost function, it is stressed that M-estimation is robust to outliers due to mislocalization errors but not to false matches (i.e., gross errors which should be filtered out by other techniques like RANSAC prior to M-estimation). In our work, the application of M-estimators to pose refinement proceeds in two stages. The first stage employs the Fair convex cost function and the second Tukey's bi-weight for suppressing outliers.

4.2   Global Optimization for Pose Refinement

An issue with the objective function of (1) is that it is multimodal. Thus, nonlinear refinement with L-M initiated relatively far from the true minimum, runs the risk of getting trapped to a local minimum rather than converging to the true pose. To counter multiple minima, we have investigated the application of global optimization methods to pose estimation. A popular strategy for dealing with global optimization problems is to resort to multi-start procedures, which explore the feasible region by employing multiple runs of a local optimization algorithm started at several different points. More specifically, a multi-start algorithm selects a finite set of sample starting points from the feasible region. Local searches initiated at each of these points produce a set of local optima, the best of which is declared as the global optimum over the feasible region. Multi-start algorithms can make various choices of local search algorithms. Local search being a relatively expensive operation, multi-start methods seek to minimize the number of local searches performed. This is achieved by clustering together sampled points that lie in the region of attraction of the same local optimum. As a result, a single local search suffices for all points within the same cluster and yields considerable computational savings for the multi-start scheme. Among the various clustering methods available, the Multi Level Single Linkage (MLSL) algorithm [7] is one of the best, incorporating effective mechanisms for determining when to link sample points and when to terminate. SobolOpt [9] is an efficient MLSL variant that selects starting points with the aid of Sobol sequences, which are pseudo-random low-discrepancy sequences that guarantee a good spatial distribution of samples. In this work, we have applied our implementation of SobolOpt to pose refinement, employing the L-M algorithm as its local search method. As a result, the pose estimation is rendered capable of escaping local minima and converging to the correct pose which would otherwise remain unreachable by plain L-M.

4.3   Binocular Pose Refinement

Estimating the pose as described in Sect. 4.1 employs a single camera. To improve accuracy with little additional overhead, a second viewpoint can be employed and the estimation can be extended to the binocular case by combining the reprojection error in two images. More specifically, assuming that two calibrated cameras are available, monocular pose estimation for each image is carried out as in Sect. 4.1. The pose of an object in one of the cameras (e.g. right) can be related to that in the other (i.e., left) with the aid of the extrinsic stereo calibration parameters. Indeed, if the pose of the object in the left camera is defined by $\mathbf{R}$ and $\mathbf{t}$, its pose in the right camera equals $\mathbf{R_s R}$ and $\mathbf{R_s t} + \mathbf{t_s}$, where $\mathbf{R_s}$ and $\mathbf{t_s}$ correspond to the pose of the right camera with respect to the left. Assuming a rigid stereo rig, $\mathbf{R_s}$ and $\mathbf{t_s}$ remain constant and can be estimated offline via extrinsic calibration. The binocular reprojection error consists of two additive terms, one for each image. Denoting the intrinsics for the left and right images by $\mathbf{K}^L$ and $\mathbf{K}^R$, the binocular reprojection error for n corresponding 2D-3D points in the left image and m in the right is defined as

$$\min_{\mathbf{r,t}} \left(\sum_{i=1}^{n} d(\mathbf{K}^L \cdot [\mathbf{R(r)} \,|\, \mathbf{t}] \cdot \mathbf{M}_i - \mathbf{m}_i^L)^2 + \sum_{j=1}^{m} d(\mathbf{K}^R \cdot [\mathbf{R}_s\mathbf{R(r)} \,|\, \mathbf{R}_s\mathbf{t} + \mathbf{t}_s] \cdot \mathbf{M}_j - \mathbf{m}_j^R)^2 \right),$$
(2)

where $\mathbf{t}$ and $\mathbf{R(r)}$ are the sought translation and rotation, $\mathbf{K}^L \cdot [\mathbf{R(r)} \,|\, \mathbf{t}] \cdot \mathbf{M}_i$ is the projection of homogeneous point $\mathbf{M}_i$ in the left image, $\mathbf{K}^R \cdot [\mathbf{R}_s\mathbf{R(r)} \,|\, \mathbf{R}_s\mathbf{t} + \mathbf{t}_s] \cdot \mathbf{M}_j$ is the projection of homogeneous point $\mathbf{M}_j$ in the right image and $\mathbf{m}_i^L$, $\mathbf{m}_j^R$ are the 2D points corresponding to $\mathbf{M}_i$ and $\mathbf{M}_j$ in the left and right images, respectively. It is noted that (2) circumvents the error-prone reconstruction of points via triangulation and does not limit the baseline of the two views nor calls for sparse feature or 3D point matching. It can also be extended to an arbitrary number of cameras. Similarly to the monocular case, a M-estimate of the reprojection error is minimized rather than its squared Euclidean norm. The minimization of (2) employs only the inliers of the two monocular estimations and can be started from the monocular pose computed for the left camera. Since this is assumed to be already close to the true minimum, application of the global optimization scheme of Sect. 4.2 is not essential. Nevertheless, this initialization does not treat images symmetrically as it gives more importance to the left image. Therefore, if the pose with respect to the left camera is erroneous, there is a risk of the binocular refinement also converging to a suboptimal solution. To remedy this, the refinement scheme is extended by also using the right image as reference and refining pose in it using both cameras, assuming a constant transformation from the left to the right camera. Then, the pose yielding the smaller overall binocular reprojection error is selected as the most accurate one.

5   Object Detection and Recognition

Assume that a set of models corresponding to known objects and a strongly calibrated binocular camera system are available. SIFT features and their corresponding descriptors are extracted independently from each image. Optionally, and in order to increase efficiency, feature detection can be restricted only within certain regions of interest (ROIs) in images. Such regions are intended as a means for directing the system's attention to where objects might approximately be and need not be very accurate or in 1-1 correspondence with the objects actually contained in an image. In this work, ROIs are determined by a color-based foreground extraction process [20]. SIFT descriptors are matched against those of the models to establish putative correspondences. For each model giving rise to sufficiently many such correspondences, a hypothesis concerning the presence of the corresponding object in the image is formed. Such hypotheses are tested by using the 3D coordinates of matched model points to estimate object pose as detailed in Sections 4.1 & 4.2 and verify that the model accounts for the observed arrangement of features with adequate confidence. Confidence is quantified by considering the proportion c_p and number c_n of pose estimation inliers supporting a hypothesis and considering an object to be present if $c_p > 90\%$ and $c_n > 40$. A by-product of this process is an estimate of the pose of each detected object. Evaluation of all hypotheses for an image identifies all objects in it. Being independent of each other, the evaluation of each hypothesis in our implementation runs in parallel with the rest, using different CPU cores. Applied to each image, the aforementioned process yields two sets S_L and S_R comprised of the objects found in each. To increase accuracy, the system strives to perform pose estimation using both cameras for objects in the intersection of S_L and S_R, using the approach of Sect. 4.3. For the remaining objects found only in one image, their monocular poses are employed.

6   Experiments

Two groups of experiments were performed. The first employed synthetic images generated with poses known beforehand. The second group utilized real images for which the true poses were inferred via careful object placement on a calibration grid. To generate synthetic images, a textured mesh model of an object was obtained in addition to its sparse keypoint model recovered as in Sect. 3. Utilization of a mesh enables dense rendering of the object while taking into account its self-occlusions. The mesh was obtained using the ARC3D service [19] and was aligned with the sparse keypoint model. Finally, a conventional OpenGL renderer was employed to render the mesh at selected poses against a black background. The object rendered for the experiment was the green parallelepiped of Fig. 1 with size $45 \times 45 \times 90 \, mm^3$. The virtual camera orbited it in 60 frames with its optical axis oriented towards the object's centroid. The experiment was conducted in four conditions, in which the radius of the circular trajectory was modulated at $500, 750, 1000$ and $1500 \, mm$ from the object's centroid. The camera moved

Table 1. Mean and standard deviation for the translational ($\mathbf{t}$, mm) and rotational ($\mathbf{R}$, °) pose errors for methods (a), (b), and (c)

Radius	$\mathbf{t}_a$	$\mathbf{R}_a$	$\mathbf{t}_b$	$\mathbf{R}_b$	$\mathbf{t}_c$	$\mathbf{R}_c$
500 mm	9.40 (7.33)	0.38 (0.25)	9.01 (5.85)	0.34 (0.20)	6.56 (4.21)	0.26 (0.17)
750 mm	15.02 (12.82)	0.58 (0.41)	10.42 (7.31)	0.43 (0.27)	8.20 (5.23)	0.34 (0.18)
1000 mm	17.07 (13.71)	0.70 (0.45)	11.63 (9.68)	0.48 (0.43)	9.05 (6.36)	0.40 (0.23)
1500 mm	16.96 (12.24)	0.73 (0.49)	13.09 (11.57)	0.50 (0.39)	10.65 (7.22)	0.48 (0.26)

on a plane that was 185 mm above that upon which the object was placed. The ground truth pose was compared against the estimates obtained from three methods: (a) monocular pose estimation (Sect. 4.1 and 4.2), (b) binocular pose estimation using 3D points reconstructed with stereo triangulation followed by absolute orientation [5], and (c) binocular pose estimation using the joint reprojection error of points in two views (Sect. 4.3). Only one image was employed for each application of method (a). Methods (b) and (c) employed a binocular pair comprised of the same image as in (a) and a second image which was four frames ahead of the first. Thereby, the two cameras are verging at the object at a relative angle of 24°. Table 1 summarizes the mean and standard deviation of the error pertaining to the translational and rotational components of the pose estimates for the four conditions of the experiment. The translational error between an estimate $\widehat{\mathbf{t}}$ and the true translation $\mathbf{t}$ is computed as $||\mathbf{t} - \widehat{\mathbf{t}}||$, whereas the rotational error between $\widehat{\mathbf{R}}$ and $\mathbf{R}$ is $\arccos((\mathrm{trace}(\mathbf{R}^{-1}\widehat{\mathbf{R}}) - 1)/2)$ and corresponds to the amount of rotation about a unit vector that transfers $\mathbf{R}$ to $\widehat{\mathbf{R}}$. Clearly, method (c) outperforms the other two in all conditions and, expectedly, error grows with the camera distance from the target. Both binocular methods (b and c) outperform the monocular one (a), as expected.

The binocular method of Sect. 4.3 is evaluated next with the aid of real images. To obtain ground truth for object poses, a checkerboard was used to guide the placement of a target object that was systematically moved at locations aligned with the checkers. The camera pose with respect to the checkerboard was estimated through conventional extrinsic calibration, from which the locations of the object on the checkerboard were transformed to the camera reference frame. Note that these presumed locations include minute calibration inaccuracies as well as human errors in object placement. The green object of Fig. 1 was placed and aligned upon every checker of the 8 × 12 checkerboard visible in the image. The checkerboard was at a distance of approximately 1.5 m from the camera, with each checker being 32 × 32 mm^2. Camera resolution was 960 × 1280 pixels, and its FOV was 16° × 21°. The mean translational error in these 96 trials was 2.4 mm with a deviation of 1.5 mm. Total running time per frame was around 600 ms on an Intel Core i7 CPU 950 @ 3.07GHz.

The accuracy of pose estimation was also evaluated in the presence of modulated occlusions. In this experiment, objects have been occluded in both images of a binocular pair by applying an increasingly larger mask to each bounding box of an object. This mask was expanded from the bottom of the bounding box

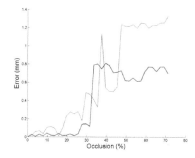

Fig. 1. Estimation error in the presence of increasing occlusions. Left: an image from a binocular pair (courtesy of Profactor GmbH). Right: translational components of pose estimation errors, plotted as functions of the occlusion percentage for the two objects.

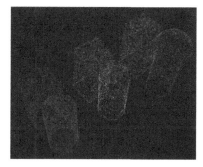

Fig. 2. Pose estimation under occlusions. Left: an image from a binocular pair. Right: point clouds transformed with their estimated poses to the checkerboard coord. frame.

towards its top, masking out object pixels. The experiment was performed for both objects of Fig. 1. We observe that the method is quite robust to occlusions, as it provides less than 5 mm of translational error wrt the unoccluded pose for occlusions up to 70% in the images. In another qualitative experiment, we employed six objects severely occluding each other. In addition, a cardboard box was also placed in front of the objects (see Fig. 2). Despite the severity of occlusions, top faces of objects provided sufficiently many features to the binocular method which, as shown in the right figure, yields fairly accurate pose estimates.

7   Conclusion

The paper has presented an approach for rigid object detection and pose estimation that was shown experimentally to be very accurate and robust to occlusions. Future work will address the incorporation of geometric constraints in the feature matching process and the extension of the method to track moving objects.

References

1. Collet Romea, A., Berenson, D., Srinivasa, S., Ferguson, D.: Object Recognition and Full Pose Registration from a Single Image for Robotic Manipulation. In: Proc. of ICRA 2009 (May 2009)
2. Fischler, M., Bolles, R.: Random Sample Consensus: A Paradigm for Model Fitting with Applications to Image Analysis and Automated Cartography. CACM 24, 381–395 (1981)
3. Gordon, I., Lowe, D.G.: What and Where: 3D Object Recognition with Accurate Pose. In: Ponce, J., Hebert, M., Schmid, C., Zisserman, A. (eds.) Toward Category-Level Object Recognition. LNCS, vol. 4170, pp. 67–82. Springer, Heidelberg (2006)
4. Grunert, J.: Das pothenotische Problem in erweiterter Gestalt nebst über seine Anwendungen in Geodäsie. Grunerts Archiv für Mathematik und Physik (1841)
5. Horn, B.: Closed-Form Solution of Absolute Orientation Using Unit Quaternions. J. Optical Soc. Am. A 4(4), 629–642 (1987)
6. Huber, P.: Robust Statistics. Wiley (1981)
7. Kan, A.R., Timmer, G.: Stochastic Global Optimization Methods, Part I & II (Clustering Methods & Multi-Level Methods). Math. Program. 39(1), 27–78 (1987)
8. Kneip, L., Scaramuzza, D., Siegwart, R.: A Novel Parametrization of the Perspective-three-Point Problem for a Direct Computation of Absolute Camera Position and Orientation. In: Proc. of CVPR 2011, pp. 2969–2976 (2011)
9. Kucherenko, S., Sytsko, Y.: Application of Deterministic Low-Discrepancy Sequences to Nonlinear Global Optimization Problems. Comput. Optim. Appl. 30(3), 297–318 (2005)
10. Li, Y., Snavely, N., Huttenlocher, D.P.: Location Recognition Using Prioritized Feature Matching. In: Daniilidis, K., Maragos, P., Paragios, N. (eds.) ECCV 2010, Part II. LNCS, vol. 6312, pp. 791–804. Springer, Heidelberg (2010)
11. Lowe, D.: Three-Dimensional Object Recognition from Single Two-Dimensional Images. Artificial Intelligence 31(3), 355–395 (1987)
12. Lowe, D.: Fitting Parameterized Three-Dimensional Models to Images. IEEE Trans. Pattern Anal. Mach. Intell. 13(5), 441–450 (1991)
13. Lowe, D.: Distinctive Image Features from Scale-Invariant Keypoints. Int. J. Comput. Vis. 60(2), 91–110 (2004)
14. Mikolajczyk, K., Tuytelaars, T., Schmid, C., Zisserman, A., Matas, J., Schaffalitzky, F., Kadir, T., Gool, L.V.: A Comparison of Affine Region Detectors. Int. J. Comput. Vis. 65(1-2), 43–72 (2005)
15. Rothganger, F., Lazebnik, S., Schmid, C., Ponce, J.: 3D Object Modeling and Recognition Using Local Affine-Invariant Image Descriptors and Multi-View Spatial Constraints. Int. J. Comput. Vis. 66(3), 231–259 (2006)
16. Rubner, Y., Puzicha, J., Tomasi, C., Buhmann, J.: Empirical Evaluation of Dissimilarity Measures for Color and Texture. Comput. Vis. Image Und. 84(1), 25–43 (2001)
17. Snavely, N., Seitz, S., Szeliski, R.: Photo Tourism: Exploring Photo Collections in 3D. ACM Trans. Graph. 25(3), 835–846 (2006)
18. Vacchetti, L., Lepetit, V., Fua, P.: Stable Real-Time 3D Tracking Using Online and Offline Information. IEEE Trans. Pattern Anal. Mach. Intell. 26(10), 1385–1391 (2004)
19. Vergauwen, M., Gool, L.V.: Web-based 3D Reconstruction Service. Mach. Vision Appl. 17(6), 411–426 (2006)
20. Zivkovic, Z.: Improved Adaptive Gaussian Mixture Model for Background Subtraction. In: Proc. of ICPR, vol. (2), pp. 28–31 (2004)

A Web-Service for Object Detection
Using Hierarchical Models

Domen Tabernik[1], Luka Čehovin[1], Matej Kristan[1], Marko Boben[1],
and Aleš Leonardis[1,2]

[1] Faculty of Computer and Information Science, University of Ljubljana, Slovenia
[2] CN-CR Centre, School of Computer Science, University of Birmingham
domen.tabernik@fri.uni-lj.si

Abstract. This paper proposes an architecture for an object detection system
suitable for a web-service running distributed on a cluster of machines. We build
on top of a recently proposed architecture for distributed visual recognition system and extend it with the object detection algorithm. As sliding-window techniques are computationally unsuitable for web-services we rely on models based
on state-of-the-art hierarchical compositions for the object detection algorithm.
We provide implementation details for running hierarchical models on top of
a distributed platform and propose an additional hypothesis verification step to
reduce many false-positives that are common in hierarchical models. For a verification we rely on a state-of-the-art descriptor extracted from the hierarchical
structure and use a support vector machine for object classification. We evaluate
the system on a cluster of 80 workers and show a response time of around 10
seconds at throughput of around 60 requests per minute.

1   Introduction

Improvements in the field of computer vision and the available processing power from
hardware improvements are enabling many new web-services to rely on computer vision algorithms. While many services work very well in most cases, they still have
certain limitations. In particular, in the context of the content-based image search, addressed by services such as Google Image Search[1], many services work great for images
found on the internet but fail completely for images not available on the internet. For
instance, querying a Google Image Search with an image of a coffee mug captured by
a cell-phone camera will not return any related images even though there are millions
of images of coffee mugs found on the internet.

To improve content-based image retrieval the authors of [9] proposed to include more
advanced computer vision algorithms. By finding semantic meaning of object(s) a system could utilize this information to improve content-based image retrieval. They provide an architecture for building a web-service that could achieve this but focus only on
object categorization which requires object annotations. This service may be adequate
for applications where user can easily input location of object, but when user cannot
provide location or there might be more different objects in the image then simple categorization cannot return proper image description. This problem can be addressed by

---

[1] http://images.google.com/

M. Chen, B. Leibe, and B. Neumann (Eds.): ICVS 2013, LNCS 7963, pp. 93–102, 2013.
© Springer-Verlag Berlin Heidelberg 2013

adding localization capabilities to obtain additional regions of interest which can provide more accurate image description.

A first candidate for object detection would be the current popular state-of-the-art algorithm which utilizes HOG descriptor with a discriminatively trained deformable part models [2]. But running an algorithm as a web-service imposes fairly strict constraints on the processing speed. A web-service must quickly respond to each request since the user is not willing to wait for the results for too long. In [9], the authors achieve response time of two seconds for their service of object categorization, but response time for object detection can be higher due to localization and multiscale processing. With sliding-window being the main technique for the current state-of-the-art method a testing with hundreds of thousands of windows over different scales becomes computationally prohibitive. Certain optimization techniques [7,10] have been presented to mitigate this problem but they require dedicated hardware (FPGA,GPU) and do not address the problem of scaling to higher number of categories. Given those constraints a much more viable approach is using a hierarchical models such as [5,6,11], which enable sharing of parts among different categories [4]. This allows for more efficient object encoding and faster inference of multiple categories while avoiding the sliding windows. A significant drawback of hierarchical models are false-positive detections that occur in highly textured or cluttered images.

In this work we build on top of an architecture proposed by [9] and use their system to implement object detection web-service. As our first contribution, we demonstrate a detection using hierarchical models for a fast processing in a web-service. To achieve fast and distributed real-time processing we utilize the same Storm[2] platform as was used in [9]. As a second contribution, we propose a hypothesis verification step to address the problem of false-positives in hierarchical methods. The presented system can function not only as support for category-oriented content-based image retrieval, but as a standalone web-service it can also serve as a backend to multitude of different applications, such as providing a backend support for a robotic vision system.

The remainder of the paper is structured as follows. In Section 2 we present detection with hierarchical model and a hypothesis verification step. We provide a detailed implementation of the algorithm as a Storm topology in Section 3 and present performance analysis in Section 4. We conclude the paper in Section 5.

2   Object Detection with Hierarchical Models

Hierarchical models follow the principle of modeling shapes with hierarchical compositions. They are arranged in layers where each layer represents shapes composed of simpler shapes from the previous layer. The lower layer usually represent small and simple shapes while higher layer capture shapes complex enough for object description. While many different hierarchical models exist, we demonstrate object detection on learnt-hierarchy-of-parts [5] (LHOP) model.

In the following we will denote the library of hierarchical parts trained for up to L layers as a set of N compositions $\mathcal{L} = \{P_i^l\}_{i=1:N}$, where P_i^l is an identifier of i-th composition and belongs to the l-th layer of the library. At the last layer L, in our case

---

[2] http://storm-project.net

LHOP library was learnt with up to 6 layers, each composition directly identifies one trained category, i.e. for each category we have only one corresponding composition on the L-th layer. Applying the library $\mathcal{L}$ on a given image $\mathcal{I}$, the algorithm of hierarchical model infers a set of K detected parts, $\mathcal{C}(\mathcal{I}, \mathcal{L})$,

$$\mathcal{C}(\mathcal{I}, \mathcal{L}) = \{\pi_k^l\}_{k=1:K}, \tag{1}$$

where the k-th detected part on the l-th layer $\pi_k^l = [P_k, \mathbf{c}_{\pi_k}, \lambda_k]$ is defined by its library identifier P_k^l, its location $\mathbf{c}_{\pi_k}$ in the image and its detection score λ_k. All the inferred parts from the last layer L directly correspond to detected objects in the image:

$$\mathcal{D}(\mathcal{I}, \mathcal{L}) = \{\pi_j^L\}_{j=1:J} \tag{2}$$

where $\mathcal{D}(\mathcal{I}, \mathcal{L})$ is a set of J detected objects in the image $\mathcal{I}$ processed with the library $\mathcal{L}$. While each detected object is defined the same as detected part at L-th layer $\pi_j^L = [P_j^L, \mathbf{c}_{\pi_j}, \lambda_j]$, we can also add a category information since a library identifier P_j^L from the L-th layer always directly matches to one learning category. We can also obtain a bounding box location of detected object simply by tracing down sub-parts of detected part π_j^L to the first layer. Minimal and maximal locations of all traced sub-parts define a bounding box of detected image. We can therefore define a set of detected objects from a given image $\mathcal{I}$ as:

$$\mathcal{D}(\mathcal{I}, \mathcal{L}) = \{(\pi_j^L, c_j, r_j)\}_{j=1:J}, \tag{3}$$

where c_j is detected category and $r_j = (x, y, w, h)$ is a detection bounding box.

2.1 Hypothesis Verification

A common problem of many hierarchical models is occurrence of false-positive detections. In the LHOP false-positives occur due to allowed flexibility between detected sub-parts in the image and corresponding composition in the library and as such the constellation of sub-parts can slightly vary. This causes false objects to appear mostly in textured or cluttered images. To reduce the problem we introduce hypothesis verification by computing a descriptor from each detected hypothesis and use Support Vector Machine to verify the detected category. As descriptor we use Histogram of Compositions [8] (HoC), which relies on the same hierarchical structure as the LHOP model.

For each detected object from $\mathcal{D}(\mathcal{I}, \mathcal{L})$ we discard category information c_j and retain only detected bounding box r_j. Within a bounding box r_j we calculate a HoC descriptor $\mathcal{H}_j$ from detected parts of second and third layer. In [8] the authors use library pre-trained on a general set of images but since the HoC descriptor incorporates the same LHOP model as we use for the detection we can easily compute descriptor on the same library of compositions. This also eliminates the time required to reprocess the image with different library. All computed descriptors $\mathcal{H}_j$ are in the end sent to the Support Vector Machine for classification. We use LIBSVM [1] with an RBF-kernel and χ^2 distance function. As the final step we perform a non-maximum suppression using simple greedy approach.

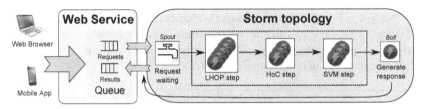

Fig. 1. Storm topology overview. Incoming requests from a web browser or a mobile application are received by the Web Service. Requests are pushed into a ***requests queue***, where main spout from storm topology listens for new requests. The final response is generated by the last bolt, which pushes the response into a ***results queue*** for web service to forward it back to the user.

3   A Distributed Implementation in Storm

In this section we detail the detection as a Storm application. Storm is a distribute platform for real-time stream processing of BigData. Its computational model consists of a directed graph, a topology, with vertices representing parallel processing elements and edges represening direction of data stream. We build our topology for this computational model from three main steps: (i) an LHOP step where we process the image and produce hierarchical compositions π_k^l, (ii) a HoC step where we extract detected regions r_j and produce HoC descriptor $\mathcal{H}_j$ for each detected object π_j^L and (iii) an SVM step where we classify each descriptor into pre-trained categories (see, Fig. 1 for overview).

3.1   The LHOP Step

We first define one main *Spout* termed *Request waiting spout* which communicates with a web-service through a queuing system. In our case we are using Beanstalk[3] queues. When a request is initiated by the user it is first received by the web-service which forwards it to the requests queue. The request comes in a form of a meta-data and a query image $(Metadata, Image)$. Meta-data defines additional information about request and among other contains a request identification and type of service requested by the user. Type of service is used to select the proper library for LHOP processing and for selecting proper group of SVM models for classification. The process of this spout is summarized in Algorithm 1. We assign only one worker for this spout as its workload is small and one worker can quickly handle multiple requests.

Algorithm 1. Request waiting spout running as a single worker

Input tuple: /
Output tuple: $(Metadata, Image)$
1: **loop**
2:     $request = $ pop_queue($requests\_queue$)
3:     $\mathcal{I} \leftarrow$ extract_image($request$)
4:     $Metadata \leftarrow$ extract_metadata($request$)
5:     **emit** $(Metadata, \mathcal{I})$
6: **end loop**

---

[3] http://kr.github.com/beanstalkd/

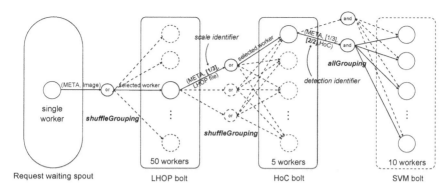

Fig. 2. Request from web-service is received by the *Request waiting spout* that emits it to the *LHOP bolt*. Due to **shuffle grouping** a single LHOP worker is selected for processing of the tuple. Selected LHOP worker emits scale compositions as separate tuples. Three scales are emitted in this example. Each is sent to the *HoC bolt* using **shuffle grouping**. Following the first scale, this tuple is assigned to one of HoC workers. The HoC worker processes compositions and emits a tuple with the descriptor for each detection. Two detections are emitted in this example. Following the second detection, this tuple is sent to all workers of the *SVM bolt* by using **allGrouping**.

As a second part of this step we implement the *LHOP bolt* (see, Algorithm 2). We connect it to the Request waiting spout therefore this bolt receives $(Metadata, Image)$ tuple as input from the spout. The connection between this spout and bolt is a shuffle grouping which ensures optimal load balancing between processes assigned for the LHOP. This is achieved since with shuffle grouping for each request emitted by the spout the LHOP worker chosen to process it is selected using even distribution of workload (see, Fig. 2). The work for LHOP bolt consists of computing LHOP compositions $\{\pi_k^l\}_i$ from input image $\mathcal{I}$ for each scale i and emitting each scale to next bolt. We emit result as multiple new tuples, for each scale separately, to ensure detections of each scale can be processed in parallel. As an output tuple we pass along result together with original meta-data and scale identifier. We use meta-data as request identifier since there will always be multiple requests in the system and each bolt has to know associated request for every input tuple it receives. We also use a scale identifier, which is composed out of a scale index i and a max scale number, to help succeeding bolts associate input tuple with correct scale. The LHOP processing is the most consuming part of the system, therefore we assign 50 workers for this bolt.

Algorithm 2. LHOP-processing bolt running as 50 workers

Input tuple: $(Metadata, Image)$
Output tuple: $(Metadata, scale\_indexing, LHOP\_file)$
1: $\mathcal{L} \leftarrow$ select_library($Metadata$)
2: $\mathcal{I} \leftarrow Image$
3: **for** $i = 1$ to max_scale **do**
4:     $\{\pi_k^l\}_i =$ construct_LHOP_hierarchy($\mathcal{I}, \mathcal{L}, i$)
5:         **emit** $(Metadata, [i/max\_scale], \{\pi_k^l\}_i)$
6: **end for**

Algorithm 3. HoC-processing bolt running as 5 workers

Input tuple: $(Metadata, scale\_indexing, LHOP\_file)$
Output tuple: $(Metadata, scale\_indexing, detection\_indexing, HoC\_descriptor)$
1: $\mathcal{L} \leftarrow$ select_library$(Metadata)$
2: $[i/max\_scale] \leftarrow scale\_indexing$
3: $\{\pi_k^l\}_i \leftarrow LHOP\_file$
4: $\{\pi_j^L\}_i =$ find_detections$(\{\pi_k^l\}_i)$
5: $num\_detections =$ size$(\{\pi_j^L\}_i)$
6: **for** $j = 1$ to $num\_detections$ **do**
7:      $r_{i,j} =$ get_bounding_box(π_j^L)
8:      $\mathcal{H}_{i,j} =$ compute_HoC$(\{\pi_k^l\}_i, r_{i,j})$
9:      **emit** $(Metadata, [i/max\_scale], [j/num\_detections], (\mathcal{H}_{i,j}, r_{i,j}))$
10: **end for**

3.2   The HoC Step

In the second main step we extract locations of all detected object of each scale, generate a HoC descriptor for each detection and pass it along to next step. The process of *HoC bolt* is described in Algorithm 3. We connect this bolt to the LHOP with shuffle grouping to allow for even distribution of workload (see, Fig. 2). Each HoC bolt worker will receive tuple with meta-data (i.e. request identifier), scale identifier and LHOP compositions for that scale. This bolt will output multiple new tuples, one for each detection, containing meta-data, scale identifier, detection identifier and a HoC descriptor with bounding box information. We assign only 5 workers for this bolt as this process is not computationally expensive.

3.3   The SVM Step

The last main step in our topology consists of classifying each detection with a Support Vector Machine. We implement this in the *SVM bolt* as described in Algorithm 4 and connect it to the HoC bolt using *allGrouping* (see, Fig. 3). This type of grouping is used for sending tuple not only to one worker but to all workers at once, meaning that all workers of the SVM bolt will receive the same tuple with the descriptor from

---

Algorithm 4. SVM-processing bolt running as 10 workers

Input tuple: $(Metadata, scale\_indexing, detection\_indexing, HoC\_descriptor)$
Output tuple: $(Metadata, scale\_indexing, detection\_indexing, svm\_score\_array)$
1: $task\_id \leftarrow$ running_process_id()
2: $\{svm\_model_m\} \leftarrow$ select_svm_category_subset$(Metadata, task\_id)$
3: $[i/max\_scale] \leftarrow scale\_indexing$
4: $[j/num\_detections] \leftarrow detection\_indexing$
5: $(\mathcal{H}_{i,j}, r_{i,j}) \leftarrow HoC\_descriptor$
6: **for** $m = 1$ to size$(\{svm\_model_m\})$ **do**
7:      $score_m =$ svm_classify$(\mathcal{H}_{i,j}, svm\_model_m)$
8: **end for**
9: **emit** $(Metadata, [i/max\_scale], [j/num\_detections], (\{score_m\}_{i,j}, r_{i,j}))$

Algorithm 5. SVM-grouping bolt running as 5 workers

Input tuple: $(Metadata, scale\_indexing, detection\_indexing, svm\_score\_array)$
Output tuple: $(Metadata, scale\_indexing, detection\_indexing, best\_svm\_score)$
1: $[i/max\_scale] \leftarrow scale\_indexing$
2: $[j/num\_detections] \leftarrow detection\_indexing$
3: $(\{score_m\}_{i,j}, r_{i,j}) \leftarrow svm\_score\_array$
4: save_scores_to_memory$((Metadata, i, j), \{score_m\})$
5: **if** saved all scores for $(Metadata, i, j)$ **then**
6: $\quad saved_scores_{i,j} = $ get_saved_scores_from_memory$(Metadata, i, j)$
7: $\quad (c_{i,j}, score_{i,j}) = $ select_best_category$(saved\_scores_{i,j})$
8: $\quad$ **emit** $(Metadata, [i/max\_scale], [j/num\_detections], (c_{i,j}, score_{i,j}, r_{i,j}))$
9: **end if**

---

one detection. We can exploit this feature and instruct each worker to test descriptor not on all categories but only on a subset of categories. This allows us to achieve distributed processing of a single detection and lower the response time for one request. We assign 10 workers for this bolt meaning each worker should handle every 10th category. When testing for more then 10 categories the processing time should reduce to 1/10th of the processing time with all the categories, while for less then 10 categories the improvement would not be noticeable.

To merge the classifications of a single detection from multiple workers we introduce additional bolt termed *SVM-grouping bolt*. We connect it to the output of the SVM bolt using field grouping. This type of grouping always sends tuple with the same field values to the same worker. We use this grouping to send tuples with the classifications belonging to the same detection to only one worker (see, Fig. 3). Worker can then save partial classifications to memory until all classifications for a single detection have been collected and after that worker outputs the collected classifications as a new single tuple. This bolt is described in Algorithm 5. We use only 5 workers for this bolt.

Algorithm 6. Detection grouping bolt running as 5 workers

Input tuple: $(Metadata, scale\_indexing, detection\_indexing, best\_svm\_score)$
Output tuple: $(Metadata, detections)$
1: $[i/max\_scale] \leftarrow scale\_indexing$
2: $[j/num\_detections] \leftarrow detection\_indexing$
3: $(c_{i,j}, score_{i,j}, r_{i,j}) \leftarrow best\_svm\_score$
4: save_detections_to_memory$(Metadata, (i, j, c_{i,j}, score_{i,j}, r_{i,j}))$
5: **if** saved all detections for $(Metadata)$ **then**
6: $\quad saved_detections = $ get_saved_detections_from_memory$(Metadata)$
7: $\quad merged_detections = $ non_maximus_suppression$(saved\_detections)$
8: $\quad$ **emit** $(Metadata, merged\_detections)$
9: **end if**

3.4 The Detection Merging Step

In the LHOP and HoC bolts a single detection has been split into multiple tuples for optimal computation and they need to be merged back into a single tuple before user

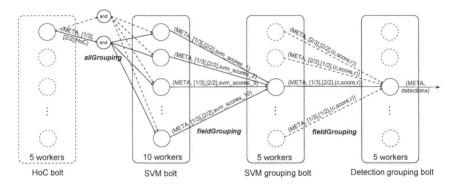

Fig. 3. The *SVM bolt* receives tuple with a HoC descriptor. Due to **allGrouping** connection between bolts a descriptor is sent to all workers where at each worker it is tested with the SVM models of a specific subset of categories. Next, using **field grouping** all classifications of a single detections are always sent to a single worker of the *SVM-grouping bolt*. There, classifications are merged together and sent to the *Detection grouping bolt*. Due to **field grouping** all detections from a single image are sent to a single worker where they are merged together into final result that will be returned to user.

response can be generated. We implement merging in the *Detection grouping bolt*, which is connected to the SVM-grouping bolt using a field grouping. We use field grouping to ensure all tuples belonging to the same request are always sent to the same worker (see, Fig. 3). Within this worker we save each detection $(c_{i,j}, score_{i,j}, r_{i,j})$ belonging to scale i and detected object j. To detect when all the tuples have been collected we rely on the numbers defining how many scales (max_scale) and how many detection $(num\_detections)$ were initially created. When all detections are collected we additionally run a non-maximum suppression to eliminate any multiple detections and send a tuple with meta-data and a list of detections to our final bolt. This process is described in Algorithm 6. The worker of the final bolt encapsulates the results and pushes it to the result queue where web-service is waiting. For the final two bolts we use 5 workers for each of them.

4   Performance

We evaluated our topology on a cluster of three high performance machines: one machine with 16 CPU cores and two machines with 32 CPU cores. Combined together we allocated 80 workers for the Storm topology. We generated one LHOP library with two visual categories selected from the *ETHZ Shape Classes* [3] dataset: apple logos and mugs.

The response time of our topology is composed of computation time of each individual bolt. Testing on a sample image of 750x560 pixels with 10 scales and 500 repeated requests we achieved average response time of around 45 seconds. To improve response time we also enabled parallelization of LHOP code using OpenMP [4] and utilized a multicore support of our processing units. This reduced processing time for LHOP by a factor of 4 and lowered the response time to around 10 seconds.

---

[4] http://openmp.org

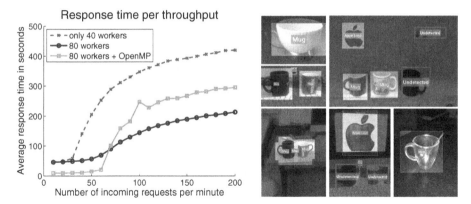

Fig. 4. Left: performance figures for three different configurations (i) 40 workers with disabled OpenMP, (ii) 80 workers with disabled OpenMP, (iii) 80 workers with enabled OpenMP. Right: examples of query images with correct (cropped gray) and missing (uncropped red) detection.

We computed average response time in relation to throughput of the topology using three different configurations: (i) using only 40 workers, (ii) using all 80 workers and (iii) using all 80 workers and with OpenMP enabled. The results of our test are shown in Fig. 4. The average response time of topology without OpenMP is slightly less than 50 seconds, while with OpenMP the response time lowers to around 10 seconds. This response time is maintained until requests cannot be processed at the faster rate than the rate at witch they arrive. With 40 workers this rate is around 30 requests per minute while with 80 workers the rate doubles to around 60 requests per minute until additional requests start to queue. Increasing the throughput by adding the hardware is an indication of efficient scalability of this system. We can also notice that OpenMP implementation is able to maintain response time of around 10 seconds for up to 60 requests per minute. After that, the additional requests require more running workers which compete with OpenMP parallel implementation for CPU time, therefore the response time increases even more than without OpenMP.

The max throughput of the system can be expressed with equation $\lambda_{max} = c \cdot m / t_{res}$, where t_{res} is response time for a single detection and m is a parallel factor defining number of parallel computation units. In our case we are using 80 workers for topology but workers are assigned for different tasks and are distributed unevenly. We added an adjustment factor c to the equation and can calculate $c = 0.5625$ based on values from graph: $m = 80$, $t_{res} = 45\,sec$ and $\lambda_{max} = {}^{60}/_{min}$. The relation between max throughput λ_{max} and number of workers m for this system can then be expressed as:

$$\lambda_{max} = \frac{0.5625 \cdot m}{45}, \tag{4}$$

from which we can estimate the parallelization to satisfy specific traffic requirements, e.g. 800 workers would be needed for throughput of 10 requests per second.

5   Conclusion

In this paper we presented an implementation of visual object detection on a distributed processing platform. We implemented an hierarchical model, specifically learnt-hierarchy-of-parts [5], for localization and used Support Vector Machine with HoC descriptor [8] as verification of each detection. We presented our implementation as a Storm application and provided an evaluation on a cluster of 80 workers. We have achieved response time of around 45 seconds using single core in the LHOP code and around 10 seconds with multicore processing enabled in the LHOP code. We have also shown ability to handle 60 requests per minute without considerable increase of response time and demonstrated a scalability of our system with the increase of processing power.

The achieved response time of 10 seconds can still be a limiting factor for many web-service applications and will therefore be the focus of further optimization in our future work. As the main bottleneck is LHOP processing we will focus on optimizing this bolt even further. As our future work we also plan to implement a content-based image search which will be connected with this service to provide category information and improve retrieval of relevant images.

Acknowledgments. This work was supported in part by ARRS research program P2-0214 and ARRS research projects J2-4284, J2-3607 and J2-2221.

References

1. Chang, C.C., Lin, C.J.: Libsvm: A library for support vector machines. ACM Transactions on Intelligent Systems and Technology 2, 27:1–27:27 (2011), Software available at http://www.csie.ntu.edu.tw/~cjlin/libsvm
2. Felzenszwalb, P.F., Girshick, R.B., McAllester, D., Ramanan, D.: Object detection with discriminatively trained part-based models. IEEE Transactions on PAMI 32, 1627–1645 (2010)
3. Ferrari, V., Tuytelaars, T., Van Gool, L.: Object detection by contour segment networks. In: Leonardis, A., Bischof, H., Pinz, A. (eds.) ECCV 2006. LNCS, vol. 3953, pp. 14–28. Springer, Heidelberg (2006)
4. Fidler, S., Boben, M., Leonardis, A.: Evaluating multi-class learning strategies in a generative hierarchical framework for object detection. In: NIPS (2009)
5. Fidler, S., Leonardis, A.: Towards scalable representations of object categories: Learning a hierarchy of parts. In: CVPR. IEEE Computer Society (2007)
6. Kokkinos, I., Yuille, A.: Inference and learning with hierarchical shape models. Int. J. Comput. Vision 93(2), 201–225 (2011)
7. Lampert, C.H., Blaschko, M.B., Hofmann, T.: Beyond sliding windows: Object localization by efficient subwindow search. In: CVPR, pp. 1–8 (2008)
8. Tabernik, D., Kristan, M., Boben, M., Leonardis, A.: Learning statistically relevant edge structure improves low-level visual descriptors. In: ICPR (2012)
9. Tabernik, D., Čehovin, L., Kristan, M., Boben, M., Leonardis, A.: Vicos eye - a webservice for visual object categorization. In: Proc. of the 18th Computer Vision Winter Workshop (2013)
10. Wojek, C., Dorkó, G., Schulz, A., Schiele, B.: Sliding-windows for rapid object class localization: A parallel technique. In: Rigoll, G. (ed.) DAGM 2008. LNCS, vol. 5096, pp. 71–81. Springer, Heidelberg (2008)
11. Zhu, L., Chen, Y., Torralba, A., Freeman, W., Yuille, A.: Part and appearance sharing: Recursive compositional models for multi-view. In: CVPR, pp. 1919–1926 (June 2010)

Fast Detection of Multiple Textureless 3-D Objects

Hongping Cai, Tomáš Werner, and Jiří Matas

Center for Machine Perception, Czech Technical University, Prague

Abstract. We propose a fast edge-based approach for detection and approximate pose estimation of multiple textureless objects in a single image. The objects are trained from a set of edge maps, each showing one object in one pose. To each scanning window in the input image, the nearest neighbor is found among these training templates by a two-level cascade. The first cascade level, based on a novel edge-based sparse image descriptor and fast search by index table, prunes the majority of background windows. The second level verifies the surviving detection hypotheses by oriented chamfer matching, improved by selecting discriminative edges and by compensating a bias towards simple objects. The method outperforms the state-of-the-art approach by Damen et al. (2012). The processing is near real-time, ranging from 2 to 4 frames per second for the training set size $\sim 10^4$.

1 Introduction

We address scalable near real-time localization and detection of multiple rigid textureless 3-D objects with complex shapes. The objects may be presented in an arbitrary pose and the algorithm should provide an approximate estimate of the pose. Problems of this type arise, for instance, in robotics, where one needs to recognize and localize objects to facilitate manipulation.

The problem is challenging. Impressive results have been achieved in recognition of textured objects using affine-covariant detectors [15] and descriptors attached to them [13,3], but these methods do not apply to textureless objects.

Scanning window methods have shown significant progress in two-class object detection [19,3,12,5]. These methods are robust but not easily extendable to a large number of objects and poses. Moreover, the two-class detectors often need many training samples per object-pose which is unrealistic to assume.

The most informative local features on textureless objects are edges, caused mainly by discontinuities in depth or curvature and thus carrying information about shape. Our representation is thus edge-based, requiring a single training image per object-pose, acquired by an uncalibrated camera. No other information than edges (such as color or intensity) is used.

We propose a new two-stage cascaded detection method, combining a scanning window approach with an efficient voting procedure and a verification stage. At each position of the scanning window, novel edge-based features, computed in constant time, vote for each object-pose. This first stage prunes a vast majority

M. Chen, B. Leibe, and B. Neumann (Eds.): ICVS 2013, LNCS 7963, pp. 103–112, 2013.
© Springer-Verlag Berlin Heidelberg 2013

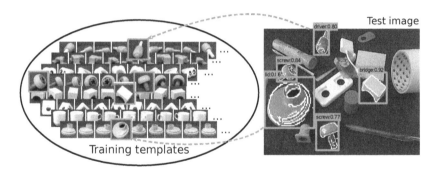

Fig. 1. A part of the training set and a detection result. Of the training images, only edges are used for detection. Color is shown only for illustration.

of windows as plausible hypotheses for location of any object. The second stage of the cascade, verification, is more time-consuming but limited only to a small fraction of windows. It is implemented by oriented chamfer score [18], improved by selection of discriminative edges based on their stability and orientation frequency, and by a compensation of the bias of the chamfer matching towards simpler objects. Fig. 1 shows an example training set and detection result.

Related Work. The approaches to textureless object detection and/or pose estimation divide into two broad categories, model-based and image-based. Model-based approaches have used CAD 3-D models [9,10] which is common in industrial applications, or depth information [8,11].

Image-based viewpoint classification has been addressed in [17,7]. In these works, the number of viewpoints is limited and the task is solved by viewpoint classifier. Unfortunately, this approach does not scale to a larger number of viewpoints or objects.

There are not many works on image-based textureless 3-D detection that would be scalable to many objects and poses. Due to only one training image for one specific viewpoint, this problem is usually tackled by nearest neighbor search on a large training set [2,4,8]. In [2], an early research on 3-D object textureless object detection was done, both model-based and image-based. A shape is represented here by a set of grouped straight lines and efficiently searched for the nearest neighbor using the k-D tree. The recent work [4] uses a similar idea, achieving real-time detection. A shape is represented by a rotation- and scale-invariant descriptor, which records the relations among each edgelet constellations. Unlike [2], which considers only a limited set of relations among lines such as parallelism and co-termination, the relations in [4] are much richer. The work [8] focused on achieving real-time performance in detection of multiple objects and thousands of templates from gradient orientations and 3-D surface normal orientations, using highly optimized implementation.

Speed is a key challenge in such works due to a large set of templates. They utilize fast techniques such as k-D tree [2], hash table [4], hierarchical search [20], look-up table and parallel techniques [8]. In contrast, we achieve high speed using a cascaded approach with fast index table search.

2   Fast Pruning of Object-Pose Hypotheses

The first stage of the cascade efficiently prunes object-pose hypotheses with low similarity to the scanning window. This is done by attaching to each window a sparse descriptor and then finding nearest neighbors in the feature space.

Sparse Edge-Based Image Descriptor. In the scanning window and each training template, we define m *reference points* $p_1, \ldots, p_m$ placed on a regular grid, excluding the margin near the image border (Fig. 2). A window I is assigned the feature vector $(d_I(p_1), \ldots, d_I(p_m), \phi_I(p_1), \ldots, \phi_I(p_m))$, where $d_I(p)$ denotes the distance of point p to the nearest edge in I and $\phi_I(p)$ is the orientation of this edge. This is computed efficiently using the distance transform.

The similarity of a scanning window I and a training template T is defined as the number of matched reference points, where a reference point is matched if both its features are similar up to some tolerances:

$$c(T, I) = \left| \left\{ i \in \{1, \ldots, m\} \mid |d_T(p_i) - d_I(p_i)| \leq \theta_d, \ |\phi_T(p_i) - \phi_I(p_i)|_\pi \leq \theta_\phi \right\} \right|. \tag{1}$$

The distance of two angles is measured modulo π, which is denoted $| \cdot |_\pi$.

Fast Voting with Quantized Features. To obtain detection hypotheses, we need to find training templates that are similar, in the sense of (1), to the scanning window. Doing this exhaustively is infeasible. As the function $-c(T, I)$ is not a metric, algorithms like k-D tree cannot be used. Instead, we solve this task approximately using an index table with quantized features. The distance features $d_T(p_i)$ and the orientation features $\phi_T(p_i)$ are quantized into n_d and n_ϕ bins, respectively. For the scanning window I and a template T, a reference point p_i is matched if the distances $d_T(p_i)$, $d_I(p_i)$ and the orientations $\phi_T(p_i)$, $\phi_I(p_i)$ have the same quantized values.

In the training phase, an index table of size $n_d \times n_\phi \times m$ is built. A cell (q_d, q_ϕ, i) of this table contains the list of indices j of all training templates T_j in which the quantized value $d_{T_j}(p_i)$ is q_d and the quantized value of $\phi_{T_j}(p_i)$ is q_ϕ. Thus, the index of each training template occurs in the table m times. To find nearest training templates to a scanning window, each template collects the votes from the cells corresponding to the quantized features of I. The templates with at least θ_v votes are accepted as hypotheses. In order to decrease the risk of discarding true positives, we find the nearest neighbor for each object instead of the single nearest neighbor for the whole training set.

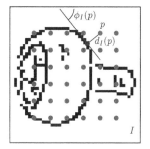

Fig. 2. The novel sparse image descriptor designed for textureless objects, used at the first cascade level. The m reference points are shown in red. Each reference point p in image I is assigned two features, the distance $d_I(p)$ to the nearest edge and the orientation $\phi_I(p)$ of this edge.

The average number of index visits per query is $mn/(n_d n_\phi)$. This number can be large. It can be decreased by grouping several reference points, at the expense of a larger table. In particular, we group triplets of points. A triplet is matched if all its three points match. The feature vector is obtained by randomly picking a triplet of reference points L times, yielding the table size $(n_d n_\phi)^3 L$ and the average number of index visits $Ln/(n_d n_\phi)^3$. In experiments, we refer to this modification as *Table-3pt*, while the single-point search is *Table-1pt*.

3   Verification by Improved Oriented Chamfer Matching

Detection hypotheses generated at the first stage of the cascade are verified at the second stage by a more precise but more expensive method, based on *oriented chamfer matching (OCM)* [18].

3.1   Compensating the Bias Towards Simples Shapes

In [18], the oriented chamfer distance between images I and T is defined as the weighted average $\sum_{e \in T}[\alpha d_I(e) + (1-\alpha)|\phi_I(e) - \phi_T(e)|_\pi]/|T|$ of the distance and orientation components. Here, $\phi_T(e)$ is the orientation of edge e in T and $|T|$ is the number of edges in T. We observed that when $|T|$ has large variance over the training set, this distance is biased towards simpler objects. To compensate this bias, we use the oriented chamfer score in a different form as

$$s_\lambda(T, I) = \frac{\left|\left\{ e \in T \mid d_I(e) \leq \theta_d, \; |\phi_T(e) - \phi_I(e)|_\pi \leq \theta_\phi \right\}\right|}{\lambda|T| + (1 - \lambda)\overline{|T|}}, \qquad (2)$$

where $\overline{|T|} = \frac{1}{n}\sum_{i=1}^{n}|T_i|$ is the average number of edges over all training templates and $\lambda \in [0, 1]$ is a parameter. The numerator of (2) is the number of edges from T that have a match in I (this yielded slightly better results than the weighted average of distances). For $\lambda = 1$, the score corresponds to the distance used in [18]. Setting $0 < \lambda < 1$ decreases the score for templates with fewer edges than average (Fig. 3 shows an example). As shown in the experiments, this has a significant positive impact on detection performance.

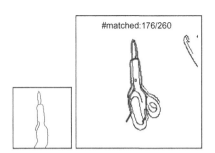
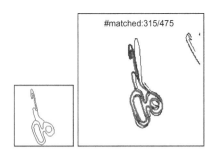

Fig. 3. Compensation of the bias towards simpler shapes. The matched template points are shown in red, the unmatched points in blue. (a) the score s_λ for the driver template: $s_1 = 0.68$, $s_{\frac{1}{2}} = 0.47$. (b) the score for the scissors template: $s_1 = 0.64$, $s_{\frac{1}{2}} = 0.64$. Before resp. after the compensation, the test image is classified as driver resp. scissors.

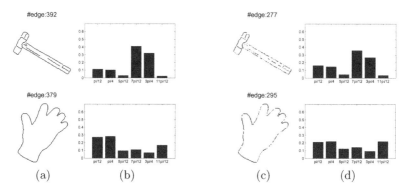

Fig. 4. Selection by edge orientation: $\alpha = 40\%$ of edges corresponding to the two highest bins are randomly removed. (a) original edges, (b) their orientation histogram, (c) selected edges, (d) their orientation histogram.

3.2   Selecting Discriminative Edges

For efficiency, [18] computed OCM on only a subset of randomly selected edge points in the template without drop of performance. In contrast, we want to use only edges that are discriminative for object detection. It has been an important topic in shape matching and detection to learn discriminative edges and discard unstable ones [14,16]. We use two criteria to select edges: stability to viewpoint and frequency of edge orientations.

Selection by Stability to Viewpoint. We define an edge in a training template to be *stable* if it matches, via oriented chamfer matching, the corresponding edge in any image obtained by a slight change of viewpoint (possibly, also of illumination, edge detector parameters, etc.). Stable edges are approximately selected as follows. As our training set does not contain explicit information which training templates are 'similar', we substitute this information. For each template T, we define $\mathcal{N}(T)$ to be the set of k templates that are most similar to T in the sense of the oriented chamfer score (2). We assume that $\mathcal{N}(T)$ will mostly contain templates differing by a small change of viewpoint. For every edge point $e \in T$ we define the score

$$n_T(e) = \left|\left\{ T' \in \mathcal{N}(T) \,\middle|\, |d_T(e) - d_{T'}(e)| \leq \theta_d, \; |\phi_T(e) - \phi_{T'}(e)|_\pi \leq \theta_\phi \right\}\right|. \quad (3)$$

We keep only the edges from T that have the score greater than a threshold, $n_T(e) \geq \tau k$ where $0 < \tau < 1$.

Selection by Edge Orientations. The similarity score (2) tacitly assumes that the positions and orientations of all edges in the template are independent. Sometimes this is far from true. In particular, if the template contains long straight lines, the edges forming these lines are highly dependent and therefore carry less information than edges originating from small and irregular parts of the object. Take a hammer as an example, as shown in Fig. 4. The handle makes up for about 70% of all the edge points. However, these long lines do not discriminate a hammer from a screw driver or from just a few parallel lines.

We propose the following simple heuristic to account for this effect. First, the histogram of edge orientations in the template is computed. Then, a part, α, of edges in the two highest bins is removed. This is justified by the fact that the edge orientation histogram with long straight lines is likely to have a dominant peak. This method can be understood as a partial equalization of the orientation histogram. Note in Fig. 4 that 70% edges of the hammer fall into the highest two bins. After the selection, most edges of the hammer head are kept, while the handle edges have become notably sparser.

Non-maxima Suppression. After the verification, we obtain a set of detection candidates for scanning windows at various locations and scales. This set of hypotheses is finally filtered by a version of non-maxima suppression, which repeats the following step till no hypotheses are left: find the hypothesis with the highest score (2) and remove all windows that have a large overlap with it.

4   Experiments

4.1   The CMP-8objs Dataset

Due to the lack of suitable public datasets, we created a new *CMP-8objs* dataset of 8 objects with no or little texture. Each object was placed on a turntable with a black background and 180 views were captured by an uncalibrated hand-held video camera, covering approximately a hemisphere of views. The training templates were obtained from these images by cropping and scaling to the common size 48×48 pixels. To achieve partial invariance to image-plane rotation, the templates were synthetically rotated in range $[-40, 40]$ degrees in 9 steps. This resulted in 12,960 training templates. Some of them are shown in Fig. 5(a).

For testing, we captured 60 images of the size 640×480. Some examples are shown in Fig. 8 (top). Each image contains multiple objects in arbitrary poses with partial occlusion. Some of the objects are not in the training set and serve as distractors. The first 30 images have black background while the last 30 images were captured on a desktop with a light wood texture. We manually labeled the ground truth (354 objects in total) with bounding boxes.

We used the following parameters: $\theta_\phi = \pi/9$, $\theta_d = 3.1$, $N_d = 4$, $N_\phi = 6$, $m = 36$, $\theta_v = 12$ in Table-1pt and $\theta_v = 3$, $L = 50$ in Table-3pt. We ran the

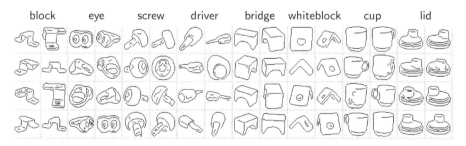

Fig. 5. Examples of training templates for the *CMP-8objs* dataset

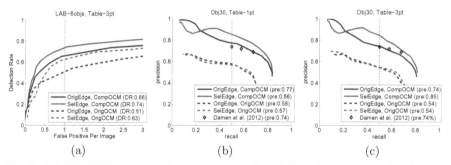

Fig. 6. (a) DR/FPPI curves of Table-3pt on the CMP-8objs dataset. (b)(c) Precision/recall curves on the Obj30 dataset with Table-1pt and Table-3pt. In both methods, applying edge selection (§3.2) and OCM compensation (§3.1) lead to significant increase of performance. The results of Damen et al. were copied from [4, Figure 7].

detector at every position of the scanning window with 3 pixel steps, and at 10 scales with scale factor 1.2. On average, the first cascade stage decreased $\sim 10^9$ training-test pairs per image to $\sim 10^4$.

The performance is quantified by DR/FPPI (detection rate *vs.* the number of false-positives per image) curves, obtained by varying the similarity threshold. This score has been commonly used in shape-based detection [6,12]. The detection is considered correct if the detected object label is the same as the ground-truth label and the detected rectangle and the ground-truth rectangle overlap by more than 50% of the area.

We ran the detectors with four settings obtained by applying or not applying OCM compensation (§3.1) and edge selection (§3.2). We only show the performance for Table-3pt, as Table-1pt yields very similar results. As shown in Fig. 6(a), both techniques improve the performance significantly. With both techniques applied, the detection rate is 74% at FPPI=1, which outperforms the standard OCM without edge selection by 24%.

On average, Table-3pt needed 0.63 s per image, compared to 1.77 s for Table-1pt (on Intel Core i7-3770 at 3.40 GHz). Fig. 8 (top) shows example detections.

4.2 The Obj30 Dataset

We further evaluated our method on the *Obj30* dataset from [4], which contains 1433 training images of 30 textureless 3-D objects. As our detector is not natively invariant to rotation, we expanded the training set to 7056 templates by synthesizing rotated images. The test set has 1300 frames. Unlike CMP-8objs, each test image contains at most two objects on a clear background, as shown in Fig. 8 (bottom). The main challenge of this dataset is in more complex objects and in larger variance of shape complexity.

Because objects on average occupy relatively larger image area in Obj30 than in CMP-8objs, we used larger training templates (120×120) and fewer scales (8). Since the first cascade stage is independent on the template size, this had little effect on the detection time. All the other parameters were the same.

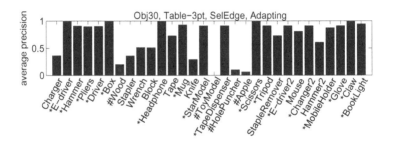

Fig. 7. The average precision (AP) for each object in the Obj30 dataset with the Table-3pt indexing method. Note that 17 objects (*) achieve AP above 85%, and 4 objects (#) are difficult to detect with AP below 20%.

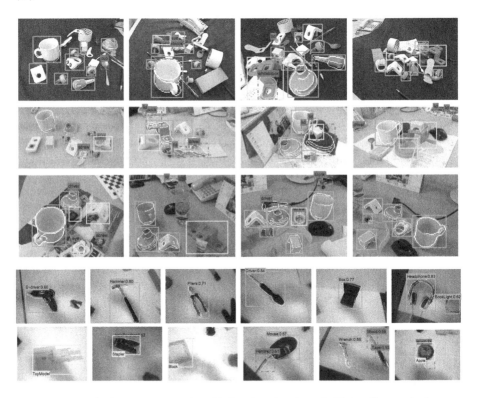

Fig. 8. Example detections for the CMP-8objs (top) and Obj30 (bottom) dataset. True positives, false positives and false negatives are shown in green, red and yellow, respectively. The edges of the found training templates are superimposed.

For evaluation, we used precision/recall curves obtained by varying the matching score threshold. The results are in Fig. 6(b)(c). The figures also show the performance of the algorithm [4].

We again evaluated the effect of OCM compensation (§3.1) and edge selection (§3.2). The edge selection was done only by edge orientation, since this dataset does not contain enough training images for each objects to select by stability. The OCM compensation improves the performance significantly; not using it results in many false positives with small number of edges. Edge selection without OCM compensation has only a small positive effect. However, the effect of simultaneous OCM compensation and edge selection is very significant.

For the recall fixed to 50%, the precision is 86%/85% with Table-1pt/Table-3pt. This is significantly more than 74% achieved in [4]. This improvement is mainly due to OCM compensation and edge selection. The average running time per frame is 0.37 s for Table-1pt and 0.26 s for Table-3pt, which is less than for CMP-8obj due to fewer training-test pairs, clearer scenes, and fewer scales. This is to be compared to 0.14 s reported in [4].

In Fig. 7, we further report the average precision (APs) for each object, which is commonly used to evaluate visual detection and retrieval. For 17 objects, AP is greater than 85%. Similarly as in [4], objects with more distinctive shapes are more easily detected and less confused, such as E-driver, box, headphone, scissors, and claw. In contrast, false positives tend to be caused by elongated objects, such as knife, wood, hammer and tape (on the side view), though this effect is largely reduced by OCM compensation and edge selection. Example detections are shown in Fig. 8 (bottom).

5   Conclusion

We have proposed a new method for near real-time detection of textureless objects. Each object is represented by a set of training templates with different object poses. Of the training images, only edge information is used. Since the method finds the object-pose template nearest to the scanning window, it provides for free also a rough estimation of object pose.

The detector, applied to all scanning windows at various locations and scales, is a two-level cascade. The first level efficiently prunes the vast majority of background windows. It is based on a novel sparse image descriptor inspired by oriented chamfer matching. The second level verifies the surviving scanning windows by improved oriented chamfer matching. The improvements consist in compensating a bias towards simpler objects and in selecting discriminative edges.

The method outperforms the state-of-the-art approach [4] by 11% on the Obj30 dataset, publicly available with [4]. Good results have been achieved also on the CMP-8obj dataset, which we created newly for this paper. The CMP-8obj dataset with the ground truth is publicly available [1]. The processing is near real-time, on average 4 fps on the Obj30 dataset (with 7,000 training templates) and 1.5 fps on the CMP-8objs dataset (with 13,000 training templates).

We have deliberately used no other information than edges. However, the found detections could be easily filtered based on other cues, such as color, to further improve the performance. This verification could afford to be time-consuming thanks to only a small number of hypotheses.

Acknowledgement. The authors have been supported by EC project FP7-ICT-270138, the Technology Agency of the Czech Republic project TE01020415, and EPSRC project EP/K015966/1.

References

1. http://cmp.felk.cvut.cz/data/textureless
2. Beis, J.S., Lowe, D.G.: Indexing without invariants in 3D object recognition. PAMI 21(10), 1000–1015 (1999)
3. Dalal, N., Triggs, B.: Histograms of oriented gradients for human detection. In: CVPR, vol. 2, pp. 886–893 (2005)
4. Damen, D., Bunnun, P., Calway, A., Mayol-Cuevas, W.: Real-time learning and detection of 3D texture-less objects: a scalable approach. In: BMVC (2012)
5. Felzenszwalb, P.F., Girshick, R.B., McAllester, D., Ramanan, D.: Multiscale categorical object recognition using contour fragments. PAMI 30(9), 1627–1645 (2008)
6. Ferrari, V., Fevrier, L., Jurie, F., Schmid, C.: Groups of adjacent contour segments for object detection. PAMI 30(1), 36–51 (2008)
7. Gu, C., Ren, X.: Discriminative mixture-of-templates for viewpoint classification. In: Daniilidis, K., Maragos, P., Paragios, N. (eds.) ECCV 2010, Part V. LNCS, vol. 6315, pp. 408–421. Springer, Heidelberg (2010)
8. Hinterstoisser, S., Cagniart, C., Ilic, S., Sturm, P., Navab, N., Fua, P., Lepetit, V.: Gradient response maps for real-time detection of texture-less objects. PAMI 34(5), 876–888 (2012)
9. Hinterstoisser, S., Lepetit, V., Ilic, S., Holzer, S., Bradski, G., Konolige, K., Navab, N.: Model based training, detection and pose estimation of texture-less 3D objects in heavily cluttered scenes. In: Lee, K.M., Matsushita, Y., Rehg, J.M., Hu, Z. (eds.) ACCV 2012, Part I. LNCS, vol. 7724, pp. 548–562. Springer, Heidelberg (2013)
10. Liebelt, J., Schmid, C., Schertler, K.: Viewpoint-independent object class detection using 3D feature maps. In: CVPR (2008)
11. Liu, M., Tuzel, O., Veeraraghavan, A., Taguchi, Y., Marks, T.K., Chellappa, R.: Fast object localization and pose estimation in heavy clutter for robotic bin-picking. International Journal on Robotic Research 31(8) (2012)
12. Liu, M.Y., Tuzel, O., Veeraraghavan, A., Chellappa, R.: Fast directional chamfer matching. In: CVPR (2010)
13. Lowe, D.G.: Distinctive image features from scale-invariant keypoints. Intl. Journal of Computer Vision 60(2), 91–110 (2004)
14. Maji, S., Malik, J.: Object detection using a max-margin hough transform. In: CVPR, pp. 1038–1045 (2009)
15. Mikolajczyk, K., Tuytelaars, T., Schmid, C., Zisserman, A., Matas, J., Schaffalitzky, F., Kadir, T., Van Gool, L.: A comparison of affine region detectors. Intl. Journal of Computer Vision 65(1), 43–72 (2005)
16. Opelt, A., Pinz, A., Zisserman, A.: A boundary-fragment-model for object detection. In: Leonardis, A., Bischof, H., Pinz, A. (eds.) ECCV 2006. LNCS, vol. 3952, pp. 575–588. Springer, Heidelberg (2006)
17. Savarese, S., Fei-Fei, L.: 3D generic object categorization, localization and pose estimation. In: ICCV (2007)
18. Shotton, J., Blake, A., Cipolla, R.: Contour-based learning for object detection. In: ICCV (2005)
19. Viola, P., Jones, M.: Rapid object detection using a boosted cascade of simple features. In: CVPR (2001)
20. Wiedemann, C., Ulrich, M., Steger, C.: Recognition and tracking of 3D objects. In: Rigoll, G. (ed.) DAGM 2008. LNCS, vol. 5096, pp. 132–141. Springer, Heidelberg (2008)

Biological Models for Active Vision: Towards a Unified Architecture

Kasim Terzić, David Lobato, Mário Saleiro, Jaime Martins, Miguel Farrajota, J.M.F. Rodrigues, and J.M.H. du Buf

Vision Laboratory (LARSyS), University of the Algarve, Faro, Portugal
{kterzic,dlobato,masaleiro,jamartins,mafarrajota,jrodrig,dubuf}@ualg.pt

Abstract. Building a general-purpose, real-time active vision system completely based on biological models is a great challenge. We apply a number of biologically plausible algorithms which address different aspects of vision, such as edge and keypoint detection, feature extraction, optical flow and disparity, shape detection, object recognition and scene modelling into a complete system. We present some of the experiments from our ongoing work, where our system leverages a combination of algorithms to solve complex tasks.

1 Introduction

The problem of understanding complex visual scenes has been tackled from two main directions: computational approaches from computer vision, and the study and imitation of biological vision systems. Scene understanding systems attempt to provide the best explanation of the observed scene in terms of a semantic, meaningful description of low-level image data, typically by describing scene objects and relations between them. They combine different vision algorithms and use top-down and bottom-up processing in order to solve what is known to be an NP-complete problem [1].

It is known that primate brains solve this problem with apparent ease, so the study of biological vision has played an important role since the beginnings of computer vision and the insights from neurological observations have resulted in many biologically inspired algorithms addressing sub-problems of scene understanding, primarily in the fields of object recognition and robotics. However, to our knowledge there is no vision system combining many different aspects of vision into an integrated and comprehensive biologically plausible system for active real-time vision. In this paper, we present our work towards such a system and provide examples of our system solving a number of different vision problems. We concentrate on the system architecture and algorithms working in combination. More detailed descriptions of individual methods can be found in our previous publications.

2 Related Work

There is a wealth of scene understanding systems roughly divided into four major streams: grammars [2–4], blackboard architectures [5, 6], probabilistic models

M. Chen, B. Leibe, and B. Neumann (Eds.): ICVS 2013, LNCS 7963, pp. 113–122, 2013.
© Springer-Verlag Berlin Heidelberg 2013

[7–9], and artificial intelligence methods based on ontologies and description logics [10–12]. Some systems perform active vision tasks by controlling cameras [13].

Many biologically-inspired algorithms for solving sub-tasks of the complete vision problem have been proposed, particularly for feature extraction and early vision [14, 15], attention [16], and object recognition, with hierarchies based on Gabor responses [17], convolutional nets [18], and a number of connectionist architectures [19–21]. Recently, complete plausible models of the ventral (object recognition) pathway have appeared, based on the HMAX model [22]. Modern robotics has also embraced biological algorithms, with biologically-inspired SLAM algorithms [23, 24], obstacle avoidance, and complete robotic architectures [25]. Attempts to build a comprehensive biologically plausible system have focussed on dynamic field-based models of different aspects of vision [26] and cognitive robots [25]. A good comparative summary of computer vision and biological vision is given in [27].

3   System Overview

Figure 1 gives an overview of our system, which is a simplified model of the mammalian brain (for an excellent overview of different visual processing pathways we refer to [28]). All modules share information in the form of maps of neural activations (population codes) which excite or inhibit neuron populations within each module. In the rest of this section, we briefly describe individual modules of our system. For more detailed information on individual algorithms, we refer to our previous publications.

3.1   Early Vision

Early vision refers to cortical areas V1 and V2, which perform low-level processing and provide input for both the ventral and dorsal pathways. We do not yet

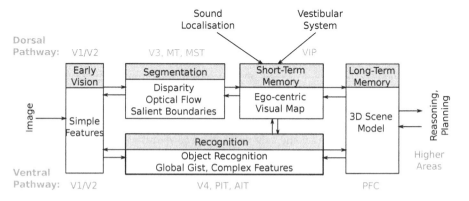

Fig. 1. Overview of our biologically-inspired active vision system. The top path models the dorsal pathway (localisation, motion and attention), bottom path the ventral pathway (recognition). Grey text indicates corresponding cortical areas.

Fig. 2. Filter kernels in V1. From left to right: even simple cell, odd simple cell, single-stopped cell, double-stopped cell, tangential inhibition cell, radial inhibition cell.

model earlier processing in the retina and the lateral geniculate nucleus, notably the non-standard retinal ganglion cells.

For our V1 model, we use a multi-scale adaptation of Heitger's work [29]. Simple cells are modelled as complex Gabor filters, with a cosine-based real part, and a sine-based imaginary part. Complex cells are modelled by the magnitude of the simple cell responses, while the phase contains important information for disparity processing. We apply simple and complex cells at multiple scales (different Gabor wavelengths) and eight orientations. Complex cells are the basis for line/edge and keypoint detection. Line and edge detection is performed at locations where the complex cell response is maximum along the filter orientation. If at such a location one of the two components of the simple cell filter contains a zero crossing and the other one is maximum or minimum, an event is detected. There are four possible combinations of zero crossing and extrema, corresponding to four types of events: positive line, negative line, positive edge and negative edge. For each detected event, we keep the event type and the orientation of the strongest complex cell response.

For keypoint extraction, we use models of end-stopped cells. Single-stopped and double-stopped cells are modelled as a mixture of Gaussians, which respond to line/edge terminations and corner/blob-like features. We apply two types of inhibition to suppress responses along lines and edges. An overview of the cell models is given in Fig. 2, and example results in Fig. 3. For a detailed mathematical model, we refer to [29]. At V2 level, we extract curve segments based on Gestalt principles of good continuity, extract symmetries and group low-level events into simple descriptors.

We have three implementations of our V1 model. The CPU version is competitive with computational interest point detectors like SIFT and SURF, while the two GPU versions (based on CUDA and OpenCL) easily run in real time.

3.2 Segmentation and Attention

The dorsal "where" pathway deals with attention, localisation, and tracking of scene objects. We have three modules implementing various functions of the dorsal pathway: shape-based image pre-segmentation, stereo disparity and optical flow. These three modules interact in order to produce a rough layout of the scene and guide the attention of the slower ventral pathway for object recognition.

Fig. 3. Results of our V1 model. From left to right: input image, complex cell response (one orientation), detected edges, and detected keypoints, all at one scale.

Fig. 4. Disparity Energy Model. Left: an image from the Middlebury dataset. Middle: depth image (ground truth). Right: Depth map produced by our algorithm.

Symmetry and Shape Modelling. We use two methods for detecting salient shapes in images. We model a set of symmetry cells which are active where line and edge segments with compatible orientations are detected at equal distances from the cells. It is known from biology that there are strong cell activations around symmetry axes. We also model a set of salient line and edge segment cells at V2 and V3. Shape grouping cells tuned selective to a set of common geometric shapes are activated when specific segments and symmetry axes are detected at equal distances. Strong activations of populations of these cells correspond to detected shapes. Gestalt-like grouping of salient boundaries is used as an aid for segmentation, attention, and local gist.

Disparity. We use a combination of two main biological disparity estimation algorithms. Some disparity information is available as left-right phase difference of simple cell responses in V1. Early phase-based disparity models gave poor results around discontinuities because the phase of Gabor responses is different for different types of lines and edges [30], but phase can provide exact disparities at line and edge locations as long as the line/edge type is considered during phase calculation. We combine this early phase-based wireframe model with a Disparity Energy Model which works well with large regions. Our DEM consists of about 8000 binocular cells trained using random dot stereograms (see Fig. 4).

Optical Flow. Tracking corner-like features has a long history in computer vision [31]. Our method builds on end-stopped cell responses from V1 [32]. A circular descriptor is calculated for each keypoint by examining simple cell responses around the keypoint and classifying the keypoint as a K, L, T or +

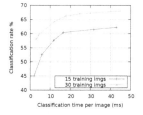

Fig. 5. Recognition performance on Caltech 101 as a function of classification time. Good performance is obtained even at 50 frames per second.

junction. Each keypoint activates the cells of the same class in its neighbourhood so they fire if the same type of keypoint is detected in the following frame. A scale-space tree of keypoints is constructed to group keypoints into objects moving in the same direction, providing rough object segmentation and tracking.

3.3   Recognition

The ventral "what" pathway is in charge of recognition and categorisation. It acts both for extracting the global gist of a scene (scene categorisation) and for accurate recognition of individual objects once a potential object position has been focused on. Complex hierarchical features are extracted but much of the localisation is lost in higher areas like the inferotemporal cortex.

The most influential computational model of the ventral pathway is HMAX [22] in which simple and complex cells are alternated several times, leading to the extraction of stable features. We follow a slightly different approach. We extract keypoints at many scales and extract descriptors around these regions. We then use a Naive Bayes Nearest Neighbour classification algorithm [33] for approximating a MAP classifier. The NBNN classifier only uses a similarity measure, summation and thresholding, which can all be performed by neurons. Our previous work has shown that by using our cortical keypoints instead of a dense descriptor grid, we can significantly cut down on the amount of needed data while maintaining state-of-the-art categorisation performance (see Fig. 5). At the moment, our algorithm uses the SIFT descriptor, which is not completely biologically plausible, but we are currently working on using HMAX-based features constructed from our V1 outputs.

3.4   Short-Term Visual Memory

Our visual system is capable of maintaining a vivid visual description of the scene across saccades and head movements (or pan and tilt action of a stereo camera). This ego-centric representation is somewhere between low-level features and a full semantic scene model (which is maintained in world coordinates). While image representation in V1 is completely retinotopic, there is evidence for a representation which is stable across saccades in higher cortical regions [34].

Fig. 6. Panoramic image stitched from 30 camera views. Our V1 keypoints were used together with SIFT descriptors.

Since saccades and movements are inherent in an active vision system, we build a stable representation of V1/V2 responses by stitching together images from different camera views into a panoramic whole (Fig. 6). Since our V1 features are based on wavelets, we can reconstruct the original image with reasonable accuracy from keypoints, lines and edges, so the stitched representation acts as short-term visual memory. Currently, we use standard computational stitching methods with our biological keypoints, but we are working on a fully biological algorithm. We use this intermediate ego-centric memory for robot localisation. Since we are using a pan and tilt unit and not an omni-directional camera (in order to more closely approximate primate vision), locating landmarks requires camera movement and a stable representation is needed to self-localise and estimate a mapping between the current view and the 3D scene model.

3.5 Long-Term Memory and High-Level Reasoning

Our 3D world model is object-based and represented in a 3D coordinate system. For each detected object, we store the position (determined by disparity and triangulation from the short-term visual memory), size, class, shape, primary colours and possibly other features. Each object is updated as the scene changes. In the near future, we will extend this simple model with a biologically motivated dynamical-field represenation [26]. For autonomous robots, we also use a dynamical 2D spatial map of obstacles which is actively updated (using reinforcement learning) and fades with time (see Fig. 9).

High-level reasoning is currently limited to a simple path-finding algorithm in the 3D scene used for our visual SLAM experiments, but we are actively working on sequence learning and task planning. Our 3D model could theoretically be combined with any computational reasoning system such as [11] to infer new information, but reasoning and inference in primates is a field of active research with many unknowns.

3.6 Additional Modules

Non-visual cues can play an important role in active vision, so our system currently also includes two additional modules. The first one is a biological model for binaural sound source localisation, which can detect the direction from which a sound is coming and make a rough guess at the object class. The second module is a dynamical model of the mammalian vestibular system which models head direction cells in the hippocampus in order to estimate the heading direction based on gyroscope readings and can estimate travelled distance based on accelerometer readings.

4   Experiments

Benchmarking generic vision systems is known to be difficult due to a large number of possible scenarios and the work-in-progress nature of most systems. Thus, instead of detailed benchmarks of individual modules, we show our system being used in a number of different scenarios, illustrating the versatility of the system and the ability to leverage different visual processes. The focus is on complex tasks which must be solved by a combination of different modules.

4.1   Real-Time Pose and Gesture Recognition

Figure 7 shows our system detecting and recognising hand gestures in real time. The process begins with the extraction of keypoints, lines and edges (early vision), followed by biologically-inspired optical flow for grouping moving objects together (dorsal stream). Grouped objects are then processed in turn by our object recognition module (ventral stream). The system can successfully distinguish between 5 hand gestures and 5 head gestures at several frames per second.

4.2   Disparity-Based Scene Segmentation

Segmentation of objects in cluttered and textured environments is very difficult, and object detection using sliding windows is expensive. We can apply our system for real-time object recognition in a common robotic table-top scenario (Fig. 8). We start by extracting V1 responses from a complete image (early vision), followed by depth estimation using the Disparity Energy Model (dorsal stream). Disparity produces a rough segmentation corresponding to objects. We then zoom onto each object in turn (foveation), extract keypoints again using our V1 model (early vision), and then perform object recognition using our model (ventral stream). Objects were learned from several views beforehand, but online learning is easy with our approach. The 3D scene model is updated with the size, location, and classes of the detected objects after each frame. Apart from the Disparity Energy Model which is currently being optimised, the system runs in real time.

Fig. 7. Optical flow for object detection

Fig. 8. Real-time object recognition with disparity-based segmentation

Fig. 9. Robot navigation and SLAM. Left: robot's environment. Right: dynamic world map. Grey areas are detected obstacles which fade with time. Coloured rectangles are detected landmarks overlaid on top of the obstacle map. The yellow line shows the robot's path.

4.3   Vision-Based SLAM

We have updated our robot SLAM algorithm to make full use of the proposed system. The robot can navigate in a simplified environment and look for known objects and use them as landmarks. The process uses coarse-scale V1 keypoints (early vision) to construct a complexity map and guide attention to promising regions (dorsal stream). These regions are then processed sequentially by the object recognition system (ventral stream). The floor is not strongly textured, so areas with many keypoints are assumed to be objects or obstacles. Relative sizes and positions of the recognised landmarks are used to self-localise in world coordinates. A dynamical 2D obstacle map is updated in real time, while landmarks and their coordinates are kept in a separate, object-oriented represenation. Figure 9 illustrates the process.

5   Discussion

We have presented a biologically motivated and plausible system for active vision which combines state-of-the-art biological models into a coherent whole. We have tried to maintain a biological representation as much as possible, with interfaces between modules modelled as maps of neural activations.

Despite years of research on complex computer vision systems, combining different algorithms remains a difficult and unresolved challenge. In the field of biological vision research, this problem is even more pronounced, with a lot of work going into understanding specific areas of the visual cortex, but with little research into combining existing algorithms into a complete vision system. We believe that such work is important, both for understanding the complex interplay between vision subsystems, and for creating practical vision systems.

The system presented in this paper is work in progress. We have evaluated our system in several scenarios and shown that it is capable of solving complex problems which require a combination of visual processes, but there are still many challenges on the road to a complete biological active vision system. Our current work focuses on making all parts of the system biologically plausible and the migration to a larger robot platform which will allow for more challenging experiments in less constrained environments.

Acknowledgement. This work was supported by the EU under the grant ICT-2009.2.1-270247 *NeuralDynamics* and the Portuguese FCT under the grant PEst-OE/EEI/LA0009/2011.

References

1. Tsotsos, J.K.: Analyzing vision at the complexity level. Behav. Brain Sci. 13, 423–445 (1990)
2. Fu, K.S.: Syntactic Pattern Recognition and Applications. Prentice Hall (1982)
3. Leyton, M.: A process-grammar for shape. Artif. Intell. 34, 213–247 (1988)
4. Zhu, S., Mumford, D.: A Stochastic Grammar of Images. Foundations and Trends in Computer Graphics and Vision. Foundations and Trends in Computer Graphics and Vision. Prentice-Hall (2006)
5. Hanson, A., Riseman, E.: Visions: A computer system for interpreting scenes. In: Computer Vision Systems, pp. 303–333 (1978)
6. Guhl, T.P., Shanahan, M.P.: Machine perception using a blackboard architecture. In: International Conference on Computer Vision Systems (2007)
7. Ommer, B., Buhmann, J.: Learning the compositional nature of visual object categories for recognition. IEEE T-PAMI 32, 501–516 (2010)
8. Li, L.J., Socher, R., Fei-Fei, L.: Towards total scene understanding: Classification, annotation and segmentation in an automatic framework. In: CVPR (2009)
9. Fei-Fei, L., Fergus, R., Perona, P.: One-shot learning of object categories. IEEE T-PAMI 28, 594–611 (2006)
10. Nagel, H.H.: From image sequences towards conceptual descriptions. Image and Vision Computing 6, 59–74 (1988)
11. Neumann, B., Möller, R.: On scene interpretation with description logics. Image and Vision Computing 26, 82–101 (2008)
12. Maillot, N., Thonnat, M.: Ontology based complex object recognition. Image Vision Comput. 26, 102–113 (2008)
13. Fusier, F., Valentin, V., Bremond, F., Thonnat, M., Borg, M., Thirde, D., Ferryman, J.: Video understanding for complex activity recognition. Machine Vision and Applications (MVA) 18, 167–188 (2007)
14. Heitger, F., Rosenthaler, L., von der Heydt, R., Peterhans, E., Kuebler, O.: Simulation of neural contour mechanisms: from simple to end-stopped cells. Vision Res. 32, 963–981 (1992)

15. Hansen, T., Neumann, H.: Neural mechanisms for the robust representation of junctions. Neural Computation 16, 1013–1037 (2004)
16. Tsotsos, J.: Neurobiological Models of Visual Attention, pp. 229–238 (2003)
17. Fidler, S., Leonardis, A.: Towards scalable representations of object categories: Learning a hierarchy of parts. In: CVPR, Minneapolis (2007)
18. LeCun, Y., Bottou, L., Bengio, Y., Haffner, P.: Gradient-based learning applied to document recognition. Proceedings of the IEEE, 2278–2324 (1998)
19. Fahlman, S.E., Hinton, G.E.: Connectionist architectures for artificial intelligence. IEEE Computer 20, 100–109 (1987)
20. Fukushima, K.: Neocognitron for handwritten digit recognition. Neurocomputing 51, 161–180 (2003)
21. Do Huu, N., Paquier, W., Chatila, R.: Combining structural descriptions and image-based representations for image, object, and scene recognition. In: IJCAI, pp. 1452–1457 (2005)
22. Serre, T., Wolf, L., Bileschi, S., Riesenhuber, M., Poggio, T.: Object recognition with cortex-like mechanisms. IEEE T-PAMI 29, 411–426 (2007)
23. Milford, M., Wyeth, G.: Mapping a suburb with a single camera using a biologically inspired slam system. IEEE Transactions on Robotics 24, 1038–1053 (October)
24. Siagian, C., Itti, L.: Biologically inspired mobile robot vision localization. IEEE Transactions on Robotics 25, 861–873 (2009)
25. Erlhagen, W., Bicho, E.: The dynamic neural field approach to cognitive robotics. Journal of Neural Engineering 3, 36–54 (2006)
26. Zibner, S.K.U., Faubel, C., Iossifidis, I., Schöner, G.: Dynamic neural fields as building blocks for a cortex-inspired architecture of robotic scene representation. IEEE Transactions on Autonomous Mental Development (in print 2013)
27. Kruger, N., Janssen, P., Kalkan, S., Lappe, M., Leonardis, A., Piater, J., Rodriguez-Sanchez, A.J., Wiskott, L.: Deep hierarchies in the primate visual cortex: What can we learn for computer vision? IEEE T-PAMI 99, 1 (2012) (in print)
28. Felleman, D.J., Essen, D.C.V.: Distributed hierarchical processing in the primate cerebral cortex. Cereb Cortex, 1–47 (1991)
29. Rodrigues, J., du Buf, J.: Multi-scale keypoints in V1 and beyond: Object segregation, scale selection, saliency maps and face detection. BioSystems 86, 75–90 (2006)
30. Frohlinghaus, T., Buhmann, J.M.: Regularizing phase-based stereo. In: ICPR, vol. 1 (1996)
31. Shi, J., Tomasi, C.: Good features to track. In: CVPR, pp. 593–600 (1994)
32. Farrajota, M., Saleiro, M., Terzic, K., Rodrigues, J., du Buf, J.: Multi-scale cortical keypoints for realtime hand tracking and gesture recognition. In: Proc. 1st Int. Workshop on Cognitive Assistive Systems, Vilamoura, pp. 9–15 (2012)
33. Boiman, O., Shechtman, E., Irani, M.: In Defense of Nearest-Neighbor Based Image Classification. In: CVPR, Anchorage (2008)
34. Turi, M., Burr, D.: Spatiotopic perceptual maps in humans: evidence from motion adaptation. Proc. Biol. Sci. 1740, 3091–3097 (2012)

Real-Time Image Recognition with the Parallel Directed Enumeration Method

Andrey V. Savchenko

National Research University Higher School of Economics, Nizhniy Novgorod,
Russian Federation
avsavchenko@hse.ru

Abstract. The parallel computing algorithms are explored to improve
the efficiency of image recognition with large database. The novel parallel version of the directed enumeration method (DEM) is proposed. The
experimental study results in face recognition problem with FERET and
Essex datasets are presented. We compare the performance of our parallel DEM with the original DEM and parallel implementations of the
nearest neighbor rule and conventional Best Bin First (BBF) k-d tree. It
is shown that the proposed method is characterized by increased computing efficiency (2-10 times in comparison with exhaustive search and
the BBF) and lower error rate than the original DEM.

Keywords: Real-time image recognition, face recognition, directed enumeration method, probabilistic neural network with homogeneity testing.

1 Introduction

One of the well-known issues of vision systems building [1], [2] is a processing of
large databases [3], [4]. Unfortunately, nearest neighbor (NN) rule and exhaustive search usually cannot be implemented in real-time applications. Conventional approach to speed up recognition is based on either parallel computing or
an approximate NN algorithms [5] which return the NN for a large fraction of
queries and a very close neighbor otherwise [3], [6]. K-d tree (and its modifica-
tions such as the Best Bin First (BBF) [3]), spill tree, triangle tree are widely
used in object recognition. Approximate NN search has been recently combined
with parallel/distributed implementation to process very large databases in high
dimensions [7], [8]. Most of such algorithms are usually implemented only with
the Minkowski metric [3]. Also, they cannot be used to solve the difficult cases
in which models are at very similar distances [3]. However, this problem is quite
acute in several tasks such as face recognition [2].

To overcome these problems the directed enumeration method (DEM) has
been proposed [4]. It was proved [9] to reach essentially higher recognition performance than brute force and the BBF. Meanwhile, almost no studies have
addressed the possibility to combine the parallel computing with the DEM.
This paper seeks to fill this gap by presenting the novel parallel DEM (PDEM).

M. Chen, B. Leibe, and B. Neumann (Eds.): ICVS 2013, LNCS 7963, pp. 123–132, 2013.
© Springer-Verlag Berlin Heidelberg 2013

We experimentally demonstrate that our method increases recognition speed if multi-core CPU is available.

The rest of the paper is organized as follows: in Section 2 we recall the HOG (Histogram of Oriented Gradients) [10] and the DEM [4]. In Section 3, the PDEM is introduced. In Section 4, the experimental results of face recognition with FERET[1] and Essex[2] datasets are presented. Concluding comments are given in Section 5.

2   Image Recognition with Large Database

Let a set of $R > 1$ greyscale images $\{X_r\}$, $r \in \{1, ..., R\}$ be specified. Each r-th image corresponds to a class $c(r) \in \{1, ..., C\}$, $C \leq R$ is the count of classes in the database. It is required to assign a query image X to one of C classes. We assume that objects of interests (say, faces in face recognition) are preliminary detected, hence, each image contains only one object. The first part of this problem is feature extraction. There are several popular feature sets - color intensities, HSV representation of color, texture representation, shape, etc. We use gradient orientation - illumination invariant texture feature showed good results in image recognition [1], [10]. Then local features are calculated by dividing images into a regular grid ($K \times K$ equal cells, K rows and K columns) to provide illumination and outlier robust appearance-based correspondence [9]. The HOG is evaluated $H^{(r)}(k_1, k_2) = \{h_1^{(r)}(k_1, k_2), ..., h_N^{(r)}(k_1, k_2)\}$ for each cell $k_1, k_2 \in \{1., ,, .K\}$. Here N is the number of bins in the histogram. The same procedure to extract histograms $H(k_1, k_2)$ is applied to query X.

The second part is classifier design. If $C \approx R$ and the number of classes and feature vector size are large, the NN rule is usually applied as other state-of-the-art classifiers (MLP, SVM, etc) do not outperform the NN in this particular case. Namely, X is assigned to the closest class (in terms of some similarity measure $\rho(X, X_r)$). In view of the small spatial deviations due to misalignment after object detection, high accuracy is shown [9] by the following similarity measure which performs mutual alignment of the HOG features and compares histograms in Δ-neighborhood of each cell

$$\rho(X, X_r) = \sum_{k_1=1}^{K} \sum_{k_1=1}^{K} \min_{|\Delta_1| \leq \Delta, |\Delta_2| \leq \Delta} \rho_H(H(k_1 + \Delta_1, k_2 + \Delta_2), H^{(r)}(k_1, k_2)). \quad (1)$$

Here $\rho_H()$ is any distance between HOGs. In this paper, we explore the square of Euclidean distance and implementation of the probabilistic neural network with homogeneity testing (PNNH) proposed in [11]

$$\rho_{PNNH}(H, H^{(r)}) = \sum_{i=1}^{N} \left(h_i ln \frac{2h_{K;i}}{h_{K;i} + h_{K;i}^{(r)}} + h_i^{(r)} ln \frac{2h_{K;i}^{(r)}}{h_{K;i} + h_{K;i}^{(r)}} \right) \quad (2)$$

---

[1] http://face.nist.gov/colorferet/request.html
[2] http://cswww.essex.ac.uk/mv/allfaces/index.html

where $h_{K;i}^{(r)} = \sum_{i=1}^{N} K_{ij} h_i^{(r)}, h_{K;i} = \sum_{i=1}^{N} K_{ij} h_i$ is the convolution of the HOGs with any kernel K_{ij}. Here the conventional Gaussian Parzen window is used [11].

It is assumed that the database is large (hundreds of classes C, thousands of images R) so that exhaustive search with the NN rule cannot be implemented in real-time applications, such as face recognition from video which sometimes requires to process 20-30 frames in a second. Even if detected face is tracked, high accuracy cannot be achieved if the face is recognized only once. Really, most successful techniques combine decisions obtained from several frames to improve the recognition reliability. To speed-up the image recognition procedure (1), approximate NN algorithms [6] as the BBF kd-tree [3] are successfully implemented in general object recognition. Unfortunately, they demonstrate poor performance in complex recognition tasks and impossibility to be combined with similarity measures (1) if $\Delta > 0$ [9]. In this case, other methods (e.g., the DEM [4]) could be applied. The DEM (Algorithm 1) seeks for a model, distance to which does not exceed a fixed threshold ρ_0.

Algorithm 1. The directed enumeration method

Data: query image X, database X_r
Result: model X^* which is either the NN to X or $\rho(X, X^*) < \rho_0$
1 **begin**
2   Define X_μ as undefined, priority queue Q is empty, $c = 0$, $s = 0$
3   **while** X_μ is undefined or $\rho(X, X_\mu) \geq \rho_0$) and ($c < E_{\max}$ or $s < E_s$)
    do
4        $s = s + 1$
5   **if** queue Q is empty **then**
6   Insert random database image X_{rand} into the queue Q
7   Pull the highest priority item from the queue Q into X_i
8   Fill the set of potential candidates $X_i^{(M)} = \{X_{i_1}, ..., X_{i_M}\}$
9   **for** $X_j \in X_i^{(M)}$ **do**
10   **if** distance $\rho(X, X_j)$ has not been calculated **then**
11   Insert X_j into queue Q, $c = c + 1$
12   **if** X_μ is undefined or $\rho(X, X_j) < \rho(X, X_\mu)$ **then**
13   Define X_μ as X_j, $s = 0$

14   Put X_μ into result X^*

Here Q is the priority queue of images sorted by the distance to X, $E_{\max}$ is the maximum count of model images to check (see similar parameter of the BBF [3]) and the set of $M = const \ll R$ images $X_i^{(M)}$ is determined from

$$\left(\forall X_j \notin X_i^{(M)} \right) \left(\forall X_k \in X_i^{(M)} \right) \Delta\rho(X_j) \geq \Delta\rho(X_k) \qquad (3)$$

where $\Delta\rho(X_j) = |\rho_{ij} - \rho(X, X_j)|$ is the deviation of $\rho_{ij} = \rho(X_i, X_j)$ relative to the distance between X and X_j. The most significant limitation of this method is its need to store the distance matrix $P = \|\rho_{ij}\|$. However it was shown in [4] that it is possible to modify the DEM and store only the most valuable part of this matrix. Such a modification is characterized by similar to the original DEM computing efficiency, but with 90% economy of the RAM.

Algorithm 1 is an implementation of widely used in artificial intelligence greedy best first search algorithm with heuristic (3). This algorithm differs from the DEM [9] as the termination condition is made more complex. Namely, we introduce parameter E_s which stands for the count of iterations to achieve stable decision X^*. Really, the original DEM could terminate after checking for E_{max} model images even if the candidate X_μ has been recently changed. Our modification helps to prevent the brute force if there is no image in the database distance to which is less than ρ_0, but do not stop exact after E_{max} iterations.

3   Parallel Directed Enumeration Method

In this section it is assumed that parallel environment is available to improve the image recognition performance [7], [8]. Thus, we have $T = const$ tasks (cores of CPU, nodes in a cluster, machines in distributed environment) which can be executed in parallel. The obvious way to increase the recognition speed is to use the parallel NN rule. Each model image is assigned to one of T tasks (randomly or sequentially) so that each task t is associated with a set of model images $X^{(t)} \subset \{X_r | r = \overline{1, R}\}$. The sizes of sets should be approximately equal to achieve the best parallelism effect.

However, if we try to apply such approach to the DEM described in the previous section, we face with two issues. At first, it is necessary to evaluate threshold ρ_0. If it is computed by each task separately, then each task will have its own threshold. It leads to a lower accuracy of either threshold estimation or further recognition. Thus, we suggest to calculate the matrix of distances between all model images P (or its part which contains several models for each class, if the database size R is really large). The threshold is evaluated in one major node and then ρ_0 and P are transmitted to each task (node). If false-accept rate (FAR) is fixed $\beta = const$, then ρ_0 is evaluated as a β-quantile of the distances between images from distinct classes $\{\rho_{ij} | i = \overline{1, R}, j = \overline{1, R}, c(i) \neq c(j)\}$. Such training needs to be executed only once for each database.

Second problem is the division of the database into T clusters to achieve the best performance. It is known [4] that the DEM's efficiency is increased if the model images are distant to each other in terms of applied similarity measure. Hence, there are two possible types of algorithms. One of them is based on the hierarchical agglomerative clustering [12]. Unfortunately, even complete link algorithm does not lead to approximately equal clusters. Thus, we propose another algorithm, namely, an adaptive choice of distant clusters (Algorithm 2) so that an average sum of distances between each model and all other images in each cluster. It is quite similar to the GAAC (group-average agglomerative clustering) [12] but we look for a *maximum* sum of distances (not *minimum*, as in the GAAC). Also, the sizes of each cluster are chosen identical.

Algorithm 2. The choice of distant clusters

Data: tasks count T, database X_r

Result: set of distinct model images sets $\{X^{(i)}|t = \overline{1,T}\}$

1 **begin**
2   **for** $r \in 1, ..., R$ **do**
3      $\lfloor\ I[r] = 0$
4    $Size = R/T$
5   **for** $t \in 1, ..., T - 1$ **do**
6   Put r_1 with first r for which $I[r] = 0$
7   Put $I[r_1] = t$, $X^{(t)} = \{X_{r_1}\}$
8   **for** $i \in 2, ..., Size$ **do**
9        $r_i = \underset{r=\overline{1,R},I[r]=0}{argmin} \sum_{X \in X^{(t)}} \rho(X, X_r)$
10        $I[r_i] = t$, $X^{(t)} = X^{(t)} \cup \{X_{r_i}\}$
11    $X^{(T)} = \{X_r | r = \overline{1,R}, I[r] = 0\}$

The complete PDEM is described in Algorithm 3. Here we assume that it is possible to send a termination event to all tasks so that they stop the search and return the best found image. If all tasks are executed as threads in a single process, this action is implemented with a global variable and obvious modification of termination condition in Algorithm 1. For multi-core CPU and the tasks count T comparable with the count of cores the proposed PDEM could increase the accuracy and computing performance in comparison with either parallel NN, or the original (nonparallel) DEM. The next section provides experimental evidence to support this claim.

Algorithm 3. The parallel directed enumeration method

Data: query image X, tasks count T, database X_r

Result: model image X^*

1 **begin**
2   Define X^* as undefined, $Found = false$
3   Estimate threshold ρ_0
4   Obtain $\{X^{(i)}|t = \overline{1,T}\}$ by Algorithm 2 and transmit $X^{(t)}$ to t-th task
5   Perform the DEM (Algorithm 1) by each task in parallel
6   **for** $i \in 1, ..., T$ **do**
7   Wait for completion of any task t which result is X_t^*
8   **if** X^* *is undefined or* $\rho(X, X_t^*) < \rho(X, X^*)$ **then**
9   Define X^* as X_t^*
10   **if** $\rho(X, X^*) < \rho_0$ *and* $Found = false$ **then**
11          $\lfloor\ Found = true$, Send termination event to remaining tasks

---

4   Experimental Results

In this experiment Essex and FERET datasets were used. From Essex dataset $R = 881$ images of $C = 395$ different people were selected. Other 5519 photos of the same people were put to a test set to evaluate recognition accuracy. From FERET dataset $R = 1432$ face-to-face images of $C = 994$ persons populated the database (i.e. a training set), other 1288 frontal photos of the same persons formed a test set. The faces were detected with the OpenCV library. The median filter with window size (3x3) was applied to remove noise in detected faces. The faces were divided into 100 fragments ($K = 10$). The number of bins in the HOG $N = 8$. To obtain threshold ρ_0, the FAR is fixed to be $\beta = 1\%$. The count of iterations to achieve stable decision $E_s = 10$. These parameters provide the best accuracy for both datasets [9]. The error rate obtained by cross-validation with the NN rule and similarity measure (1) with Euclidean and the PNNH (2) distances is shown in Table 1 in the format average error rate $\pm$ its standard deviation. From this table one could notice that, first, the error rate for conventional Euclidean distance exceeds the error for the PNNH (2). And, second, mutual alignment of features (1) with $\Delta > 0$ usually improves the recognition accuracy, especially, for FERET dataset.

Table 1. Brute force error rate

Dataset	Euclidean, $\Delta = 0$	PNNH, $\Delta = 0$	Euclidean, $\Delta = 1$	PNNH, $\Delta = 1$
Essex	$0.74\% \pm 0.04\%$	$0.7\% \pm 0.1\%$	$0.41\% \pm 0.01\%$	$0.32\% \pm 0.01\%$
FERET	$13.7\% \pm 0.4\%$	$10.5\% \pm 0.3\%$	$11.7\% \pm 0.34\%$	$8.1\% \pm 0.27\%$

In the next experiment we compare the performance of OpenCV's implementation (cvCreateKDTree) of the BBF (only available for Euclidean distance in (1), $\Delta = 0$), brute force, the DEM and the proposed PDEM. We evaluate the error rate (in %) and the average time (in ms) to recognize one test image with a modern laptop (4 core i7, 6 Gb RAM) and Visual C++ 2010 compiler with optimization by speed. The count of parallel tasks T varies from 1 (nonparallel case) to 2, 4 and 8 (parallel case). Each task is implemented as a separate thread by using the Windows ThreadPool API

After several experiments [3], [9] the best (in terms of speed) value of parameter M was chosen $M = 64$ for nonparallel case and $M = 16$ for parallel one. The following strategies to divide the database into T clusters were used: sequential (images $1, ..., T$ were assigned to the task 1, images $T, ..., 2T$ - to the task 2, etc.), random choice (each image is assigned to one of T nodes at random), complete link clustering and proposed Algorithm 2. Parameter E_{max} was chosen to achieve the recognition accuracy which is not 0.5% less than the accuracy of brute force. If such accuracy could not be achieved, E_{max} was set to be equal to the count of models assigned to each task.

Table 2. Average recognition time (in ms) per image (Essex dataset)

Tasks count T	Method	Euclidean, $\Delta = 0$	PNNH, $\Delta = 0$	Euclidean, $\Delta = 1$	PNNH, $\Delta = 1$
1	Brute force	0.97 ± 0.0004	10.5 ± 0.018	8.9 ± 0.02	84.4 ± 0.218
	BBF	0.73 ± 0.002	-	-	-
	DEM	$\mathbf{0.17 \pm 0.0009}$	$\mathbf{1.09 \pm 0.013}$	$\mathbf{1.19 \pm 0.007}$	$\mathbf{10.7 \pm 0.08}$
2	Brute force	0.55 ± 0.0015	5.6 ± 0.061	4.8 ± 0.011	43.3 ± 0.023
	BBF	0.47 ± 0.0039	-	-	-
	PDEM, sequence	0.13 ± 0.0005	0.94 ± 0.0008	0.92 ± 0.003	10.4 ± 0.008
	PDEM, random	0.12 ± 0.0016	0.91 ± 0.0036	0.96 ± 0.0015	9.2 ± 0.064
	PDEM, complete link	0.2 ± 0.0007	1.2 ± 0.0034	1.26 ± 0.004	13.7 ± 0.067
	PDEM, distant clusters	$\mathbf{0.11 \pm 0.0002}$	$\mathbf{0.89 \pm 0.0088}$	$\mathbf{0.9 \pm 0.001}$	$\mathbf{9.0 \pm 0.025}$
4	Brute force	0.35 ± 0.003	3.5 ± 0.141	2.98 ± 0.007	27.1 ± 0.33
	BBF	0.23 ± 0.0041	-	-	-
	PDEM, sequence	0.096 ± 0.0007	0.87 ± 0.01	0.68 ± 0.0036	8.7 ± 0.036
	PDEM, random	0.095 ± 0.002	0.88 ± 0.048	0.7 ± 0.0053	7.9 ± 0.041
	PDEM, complete link	0.17 ± 0.001	1.7 ± 0.021	0.91 ± 0.011	8.9 ± 0.038
	PDEM, distant clusters	$\mathbf{0.091 \pm 0.0003}$	$\mathbf{0.86 \pm 0.0136}$	$\mathbf{0.66 \pm 0.004}$	$\mathbf{7.3 \pm 0.03}$
8	Brute force	0.3 ± 0.0047	2.88 ± 0.0075	2.02 ± 0.061	21.9 ± 0.054
	BBF	0.24 ± 0.0016	-	-	-
	PDEM, sequence	$\mathbf{0.085 \pm 0.001}$	0.77 ± 0.007	$\mathbf{0.57 \pm 0.0001}$	8.5 ± 0.011
	PDEM, random	0.086 ± 0.0017	0.77 ± 0.021	0.62 ± 0.0056	8.5 ± 0.117
	PDEM, complete link	0.11 ± 0.0005	0.9 ± 0.01	0.66 ± 0.0037	9.8 ± 0.079
	PDEM, distant clusters	$\mathbf{0.085 \pm 0.0017}$	$\mathbf{0.75 \pm 0.006}$	0.59 ± 0.0098	$\mathbf{6.6 \pm 0.013}$

Table 3. Error rate of approximate NN methods (Essex dataset)

Tasks count T	Method	Euclidean, $\Delta = 0$	PNNH, $\Delta = 0$	Euclidean, $\Delta = 1$	PNNH, $\Delta = 1$
1	BBF	$0.9\% \pm 0.1\%$	-	-	-
	DEM	$0.98\% \pm 0.3\%$	$0.82\% \pm 0.15\%$	$0.57\% \pm 0.15\%$	$0.49\% \pm 0.1\%$
2	BBF	$0.74\% \pm 0.05\%$	-	-	-
	PDEM	$0.98\% \pm 0.1\%$	$1.06\% \pm 0.2\%$	$0.74\% \pm 0.2\%$	$0.41\% \pm 0.08\%$
4	BBF	$0.9\% \pm 0.05\%$	-	-	-
	PDEM	$1.14\% \pm 0.2\%$	$0.98\% \pm 0.1\%$	$0.74\% \pm 0.16\%$	$0.49\% \pm 0.1\%$
8	BBF	$0.74\% \pm 0.05\%$	-	-	-
	PDEM	$0.94\% \pm 0.15\%$	$1.06\% \pm 0.15\%$	$0.57\% \pm 0.15\%$	$0.4\% \pm 0.11\%$

Table 4. Average recognition time (in ms) per image (FERET dataset)

Tasks count T	Method	Euclidean, $\Delta = 0$	PNNH, $\Delta = 0$	Euclidean, $\Delta = 1$	PNNH, $\Delta = 1$
1	Brute force	1.6 ± 0.012	18.6 ± 0.202	14.2 ± 0.021	147.5 ± 0.36
	BBF	1.3 ± 0.007	-	-	-
	DEM	$\mathbf{0.\ 74 \pm 0.003}$	$\mathbf{4.2 \pm 0.01}$	$\mathbf{3.5 \pm 0.014}$	$\mathbf{30.9 \pm 0.025}$
2	Brute force	0.91 ± 0.009	9.6 ± 0.049	7.3 ± 0.047	79.9 ± 0.121
	BBF	0.94 ± 0.006	-	-	-
	PDEM, sequence	0.61 ± 0.0029	4.2 ± 0.037	$\mathbf{4.1 \pm 0.006}$	$\mathbf{30.6 \pm 0.035}$
	PDEM, random	0.73 ± 0.066	4.3 ± 0.045	4.2 ± 0.036	31.1 ± 0.438
	PDEM, complete link	0.78 ± 0.005	4.6 ± 0.081	5.9 ± 0.02	36.7 ± 0.04
	PDEM, distant clusters	$\mathbf{0.6 \pm 0.041}$	$\mathbf{3.7 \pm 0.024}$	$\mathbf{4.1 \pm 0.005}$	31.0 ± 0.045
4	Brute force	0.75 ± 0.005	7.1 ± 0.334	4.56 ± 0.022	59.1 ± 0.578
	BBF	0.73 ± 0.0011	-	-	-
	PDEM, sequence	$\mathbf{0.37 \pm 0.01}$	3.1 ± 0.021	2.7 ± 0.081	30.2 ± 0.401
	PDEM, random	0.39 ± 0.016	3.3 ± 0.054	2.74 ± 0.132	30.9 ± 0.543
	PDEM, complete link	0.42 ± 0.009	3.7 ± 0.03	3.01 ± 0.054	34.3 ± 0.301
	PDEM, distant clusters	$\mathbf{0.37 \pm 0.007}$	$\mathbf{2.7 \pm 0.029}$	$\mathbf{2.69 \pm 0.098}$	$\mathbf{30.1 \pm 0.355}$
8	Brute force	0.71 ± 0.006	5.04 ± 0.035	3.1 ± 0.004	47.9 ± 1.69
	BBF	0.54 ± 0.006	-	-	-
	PDEM, sequence	0.343 ± 0.005	2.47 ± 0.026	2.0 ± 0.0004	24.2 ± 0.063
	PDEM, random	0.358 ± 0.031	3.3 ± 0.071	2.05 ± 0.045	25.7 ± 0.321
	PDEM, complete link	0.41 ± 0.0025	2.9 ± 0.098	2.8 ± 0.031	28.9 ± 0.074
	PDEM, distant clusters	$\mathbf{0.27 \pm 0.0026}$	$\mathbf{1.96 \pm 0.003}$	$\mathbf{1.46 \pm 0.0027}$	$\mathbf{23.9 \pm 0.059}$

Table 5. Error rate of approximate NN methods (FERET dataset)

Tasks count T	Method	Euclidean, $\Delta = 0$	PNNH, $\Delta = 0$	Euclidean, $\Delta = 1$	PNNH, $\Delta = 1$
1	BBF	$17.0\% \pm 1.6\%$	-	-	-
	DEM	$15.9\% \pm 2.4\%$	$12.7\% \pm 1.8\%$	$15.8\% \pm 2.7\%$	$12.1\% \pm 0.8\%$
2	BBF	$13.7\% \pm 0.9\%$	-	-	-
	PDEM	$13.9\% \pm 1.1\%$	$10.9\% \pm 0.6\%$	$11.9\% \pm 0.6\%$	$8.8\% \pm 0.5\%$
4	BBF	$13.7\% \pm 0.9\%$	-	-	-
	PDEM	$13.7\% \pm 0.5\%$	$10.7\% \pm 0.7\%$	$11.8\% \pm 0.5\%$	$8.4\% \pm 0.4\%$
8	BBF	$13.7\% \pm 0.9\%$	-	-	-
	PDEM	$13.8\% \pm 0.5\%$	$10.6\% \pm 0.5\%$	$12.2\% \pm 0.7\%$	$8.2\% \pm 0.4\%$

Average recognition time per one image (in ms) for Essex dataset is shown in Table 2. Here we use Algorithm 2 to form the clusters for both brute force and the BBF as these methods do not have any requirements to the model database. The best results for particular distance and tasks count are marked by bold. The corresponding error rates are presented in Table 3. Here we do not distinct the methods of clusters' choice as they are characterized by similar accuracy. In this experiment with Essex dataset we can see that though the performance of the conventional DEM ($T = 1$) is quite high (5-10 times more than brute force and 4 times better than the BBF), the proposed PDEM is 1.5-2 times more effective (for $T = 8$). Second, proposed Algorithm 2 looks to be the most effective in comparison with other algorithms used here (with one exception for Euclidean distance with $\Delta = 1$ and $T = 8$). Third, the accuracy of the DEM and the PDEM is similar to the accuracies of brute force (Table 1) and the BBF (Table 3) though we assumed that the 1%-FAR is appropriate. However, from our point of view, in this case (for particular hardware) the NN rule (brute force) with Euclidean distance ($\Delta = 0$) is satisfactory for its practical usage as it requires only 1 ms (Table 2) to recognize one person in one task with 99.26% accuracy (Table 1).

The situation is different for FERET dataset as the error rate of Euclidean distance is essentially high (Table 1). The results for this dataset are summarized in Table 4 (error rate) and Table 5 (recognition time). Here, first, the accuracy (Table 5) of the nonparallel approximate NN methods (the BBF and the DEM) is much lower than the accuracy of the brute force (Table 1). At the same time, parallel implementation provides better exploration of the whole decision space, thus, the accuracy of the PDEM is approximately equal to the exhaustive search. Second, face recognition with FERET seems to be more complex than the recognition with Essex (see Table 1). Thus, the recognition with the BBF takes even more time than the NN rule. It is not surprising as the BBF requires the NN to be quite closer to input image than the second-nearest neighbor [3]. However, our PDEM with $T = 8$ exceeds nonparallel brute force in 6-10 times and the NN parallel implementation (with $T = 8$ tasks) in 2-2.5 times with practically the same accuracy. Here the recognition time of the NN with the complex PNNH (2), $\Delta = 1$ (47.9 ms per image for $T = 8$ tasks, see Table 4) may be unsatisfactory in real-time face recognition if face detection takes much time or frame contains several faces. At the same time, this similarity measure is efficiently implemented with the PDEM (23.9 ms) if the error rate of other distances (10-14%, see Table 1) was assumed to be unsatisfactory.

5   Conclusion

To this end, we proposed the novel modification of the DEM and argued that it increases recognition performance with large database if multicore processor and parallel environment is available. We suggested Algorithm 2 to form the model databases for each node (thread). It was shown that our approach allows to achieve adequate accuracy and high computing efficiency (Tables 2, 4) in comparison with either exhaustive search or the widely used in computer vision BBF kd-tree [3]. Our modification saves all advantage of the original DEM. Moreover, the PDEM's accuracy may be much better (see Table 5) as it examines several model images simultaneously. The PDEM seems to be more computing efficient than the approximate NN methods currently used for real-time face recognition in parallel environment.

In this article we focus on databases which contain only thousand of models. We do not explore face recognition with much larger sizes of the database as modern image feature sets seem to be not satisfactory for such a complex task. Hence, it is really difficult to estimate an adequate threshold ρ_0 for the PDEM's termination condition. However, from the performance point of view, the main direction for further research of the PDEM is its application in recognition with the database (probably, synthetic) which contains hundreds of thousands of images.

Acknowledgement. This study was carried out within "The National Research University Higher School of Economics Academic Fund Program in 2013-2014, research grant No. 12-01-0003".

References

1. Forsyth, D.A., Ponce, J.: Computer Vision: A Modern Approach. Prentice Hall (2011)
2. Li, S.Z., Jain, A.K. (eds.): Handbook of Face Recognition, 2nd edn. Springer (2011)
3. Beis, J., Lowe, D.G.: Shape indexing using approximate nearest-neighbour search in high dimensional spaces. In: Conference on Computer Vision and Pattern Recognition, pp. 1000–1006 (1997)
4. Savchenko, A.V.: Directed enumeration method in image recognition. Pattern Recognition 45(8), 2952–2961 (2012)
5. Liu, T., Moore, A.W., Gray, A., Yang, K.: An Investigation of Practical Approximate Nearest Neighbor Algorithms. In: NIPS-2004, pp. 825–832 (2004)
6. Kleinberg, J.: Two algorithms for nearest-neighbor search in high dimensions. In: Twenty-Ninth Annual ACM Symposium on Theory of Computing, pp. 599–608 (1997)
7. Novak, D., Zezula, P.: M-Chord: A Scalable Distributed Similarity Search Structure. In: Infoscale, pp. 149–160 (2006)
8. Haghani, P., Michel, S., Aberer, K.: Distributed similarity search in high dimensions using locality sensitive hashing. In: EDBT 2009, pp. 744–755 (2009)
9. Savchenko, A.V.: Face Recognition in Real-Time Applications: Comparison of Directed Enumeration Method and K-d Trees. In: Aseeva, N., Babkin, E., Kozyrev, O. (eds.) BIR 2012. LNBIP, vol. 128, pp. 187–199. Springer, Heidelberg (2012)
10. Dalal, N., Triggs, B.: Histograms of Oriented Gradients for Human Detection. In: Conference on Computer Vision and Pattern Recognition, pp. 886–893 (2005)
11. Savchenko, A.V.: Statistical Recognition of a Set of Patterns Using Novel Probability Neural Network. In: Mana, N., Schwenker, F., Trentin, E. (eds.) ANNPR 2012. LNCS, vol. 7477, pp. 93–103. Springer, Heidelberg (2012)
12. Sneath, P., Sokal, R.: Numerical Taxonomy: The Principles and Practice of Numerical Classification. Freeman (1973)

Simultaneous Localization and Mapping for Event-Based Vision Systems

David Weikersdorfer, Raoul Hoffmann, and Jörg Conradt

Neuroscientific System Theory
Technische Universität München
weikersd@in.tum.de, raoul.hoffmann@mytum.de, conrad@tum.de

Abstract. We propose a novel method for vision based simultaneous localization and mapping (vSLAM) using a biologically inspired vision sensor that mimics the human retina. The sensor consists of a 128x128 array of asynchronously operating pixels, which independently emit events upon a temporal illumination change. Such a representation generates small amounts of data with high temporal precision; however, most classic computer vision algorithms need to be reworked as they require full RGB(-D) images at fixed frame rates. Our presented vSLAM algorithm operates on individual pixel events and generates high-quality 2D environmental maps with precise robot localizations. We evaluate our method with a state-of-the-art marker-based external tracking system and demonstrate real-time performance on standard computing hardware.

1 Introduction

Estimating your position within an environment is a crucial task for any autonomous artificial mobile system. In mobile robotics, intense research and development efforts have been devoted to systems that localize themselves on a map while creating and maintaining such an a-priori unknown map (simultaneously localization and mapping, SLAM, [1]). Typical engineered systems rely on a combination of sensors, such as ego-motion estimation (e.g. odometry or inertial measurements), distance sensors (e.g. laser range finders or RGB-D cameras), or on vision based feature tracking to create precise environmental representations for self-localization. An example of a visual SLAM method is KinectFusion [2], a dense surface mapping and tracking algorithm which requires highly optimized code and GPU hardware to run in real-time for a quite small spatial volume. This is typical for many state-of-the-art vision SLAM systems which perform extremely well with the drawback of high computational requirements: typical algorithms by far exceed the computing power provided by small autonomous robots and often perform offline, time-delayed data interpretation.

In this paper we present a novel approach to visual SLAM in unknown environments for a biologically inspired event-based vision sensor that operates in real time. The integrated Dynamic Vision Sensor (DVS) [3] is a neurobiologically inspired pixel-wise asynchronous vision sensor that generates elementary events

M. Chen, B. Leibe, and B. Neumann (Eds.): ICVS 2013, LNCS 7963, pp. 133–142, 2013.
© Springer-Verlag Berlin Heidelberg 2013

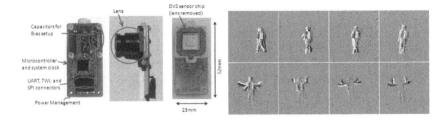

Fig. 1. Left: The event-based embedded Dynamic Vision Sensor (eDVS). Right: An example data reading. Each image shows the 128x128 sensor with pixel events integrated over 0.1 seconds. Light pixels indicate change of illumination from dark to light - dark pixels a change from light to dark.

("pieces of information") only for every temporal illumination change perceived by any pixel (see fig. 1). Such a visual representation generates small amounts of data with high temporal precision, typically faster than 30 micro-seconds. Each individual event contains very little reliable information, as the underlying cause for this event might be any one of a large collection of possible state changes, or even pure noise. Frame based visual SLAM methods which operate on sequences of traditional camera images have nearly full localization information in each new image. With event-based sensors we only marginally update the systems belief about the true underlying state with every new event. This allows a more efficient system design, but most classic computer vision algorithms need to be redesigned as they require full images at fixed frame rates.

In [4] an event-based particle filter algorithm for visual, event-based self-localization using the eDVS sensor has been proposed. In that work a fixed and pre-build map stitched from photos has been used for navigation. This is a severe restriction for real world applications as the map should be generated directly by the acting robotic system without need for manual intervention or additional sensors. In this paper we extend this event-based tracking algorithm to a complete event-based simultaneous localization and mapping method which generates a map automatically during self-localization (see fig. 2).

The rest of the paper is outlined as follows: In §2 we describe the concept behind our event-based simultaneous localization and mapping method. Details about our main contribution - the mapping - will be presented in §3 in general and specialized to the case of 2D SLAM. We evaluate our method on a large dataset in §4 and show that we can achieve excellent tracking and mapping results.

2   Event-Based SLAM

In [4] a novel event-based tracking algorithm which adapts the particle filter Condensation algorithm [5] to the characteristics of an event-based sensor like the eDVS is proposed. An event-based sensor provides a continuous stream of events $e^{(k)}, e^{(k+1)}, \ldots \in \mathcal{R}$. $\mathcal{R}$ denotes the range of possible pixel positions on the

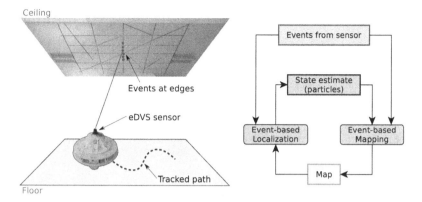

Fig. 2. Schematic overview of our tracking scenario for event-based tracking (left) and corresponding program flow (right)

sensor, i.e. $\mathcal{R} = [0, 127]^2$, and upper subscription is used to indicate event index. Due to the fact that the number of events created by the event-based sensor depends on movement and rotation speed, the event index does not correspond to system time.

For each event $e^{(k)} \in \mathcal{R}$, the event-based tracking algorithm in [4] uses a particle set $P^{(k)} \subset \Omega \times \mathbb{R}^+$ for a multivariate probabilistic estimate of the current system state. Each particle $p = (x, s) \in P^{(k)}$ consists of the corresponding state estimate $x \in \Omega$ (position and orientation of the sensor) and a score value $s \in [0, 1]$ representing the likelihood of the state estimate. State likelihoods sum up to 1 for a given particle set.

Towards the goal of simultaneous localization and mapping, we introduce a dynamic map over the map domain Γ ($\Gamma = \mathbb{R}^2$ for a two-dimensional map), which our event-based SLAM method will continuously update during localization. This is a major extension of the event-based tracking method in [4] as it is no longer required to manually provide an a priori map. For each location $u \in \Gamma$ on the map we represent the likelihood that the event-based sensor will generate an event when one of it pixels observes this location while the sensor is moving. Formally we model this likelihood as

$$\mathcal{M}(u) = \frac{\text{\# of occurred events for } u}{\text{\# of possible obervations for } u} =: \frac{\mathcal{O}(u)}{\mathcal{Z}(u)} \tag{1}$$

It is important to note the difference between the event-based sensor and a classic image sensor: While a classic image sensor reports observations at fixed time intervals which can also be easily repeated by measuring multiple times, the event-based sensor generates events only if one of its pixels detects a change in illumination. This happens either when objects move in the scene or, as in our case, when the sensor moves within a static environment and one of its pixels traverses an edge in the perceived brightness of the scenery. Therefore

Fig. 3. Example for occurrence map $\mathcal{O}$ (left), normalization map $\mathcal{Z}$ (middle) and final likelihood map $\mathcal{M}$ (right)

map likelihood $\mathcal{M}$ measures the number of events generated at a map location with respect to the number of sensor pixel crossings. As locations on the map can be observed several times with varying frequency, the occurrence map $\mathcal{O}$ needs to be normalized using a normalization map $\mathcal{Z}$ in order to get stable and comparable map likelihoods.

Our event-based localization and mapping method is outlined as follows: For every event, we alternately update the state estimates using the latest map and update the map using the new state estimate (see fig. 2). First, for event-based localization, we update the particle set $P^{(k)}$ using the current event $e^{(k)}$ and the likelihood map $\mathcal{M}^{(k-1)}$ from the previous step provided by event-based mapping. State estimates x_i are propagated using a diffusion model specific to the event-based sensor and state probabilities s_i are computed using the likelihood map:

$$s_i^{(k)} = s_i^{(k-1)} + \alpha\,\mathcal{M}^{(k-1)}(\mu^{-1}(e^{(k)}|x_i^{(k)})) \tag{2}$$

(see [4] for details). The projection function $\mu : \Gamma \times \Omega \to \mathcal{R}$ and its inverse are discussed in more detail in §3. Second, the map $\mathcal{M}^{(k)}$ is updated using the current event $e^{(k)}$ and the current state estimate $P^{(k)}$. The second step, event-based visual mapping, is the major contributions of this paper and explained in more detail in section §3.

3   Event-Based Visual Mapping

For the computation of the likelihood map $\mathcal{M}$, we iteratively compute three maps over the map domain Γ during the mapping phase of our event-based SLAM method (see fig. 3): First, the occurrence map $\mathcal{O} : \Gamma \to \mathbb{R}^+$ where observation probabilities for events are summed up as events occur. Second, the normalization map $\mathcal{Z} : \Gamma \to \mathbb{R}^+$ which records the possibility of observations depending on the magnitude of movement of the sensor. Finally occurrence and normalization map are combined to the likelihood map $\mathcal{M} : \Gamma \to \mathbb{R}^+$ with eq. 1.

3.1   Computation of the Occurrence Map $\mathcal{O}$

For the computation of the occurrence map, we project events from the sensor position back onto the map domain and integrate them using a Gaussian sensor model. The current event $e^{(k)}$ and the current state estimate $P^{(k)} = \{p_1^{(k)}, \ldots, p_n^{(k)}\}$, $p_i^{(k)} = (x_i^{(k)}, s_i^{(k)})$, are used to compute corresponding observed map locations $\mu^{-1}(e^{(k)}|x_i^{(k)})$. Here we use the inverse of a projection function $\mu : \Gamma \times \Omega \to \mathcal{R}$ which projects a map location onto the sensor given a fixed state. We assume that μ^{-1} has a unique solution - for a discussion see §3.3. Thus the occurrence map is computed iteratively as

$$\mathcal{O}^{(k)}(u) = \mathcal{O}^{(k-1)}(u) + \sum_{i=1}^{n} s_i^{(k)} \mathcal{N}\left(u \,\middle|\, \mu^{-1}(e^{(k)}|x_i^{(k)}), \sigma\right), \ \mathcal{O}^{(0)} = 0. \quad (3)$$

The Gaussian normal distribution $\mathcal{N}$ is used to represent measurement and discretization uncertainties. The standard deviation σ depends on camera parameters and the distance of the sensor to event location. As generally done in SLAM algorithms, it can be beneficial to not use all particles for updating the occurrence map, but only a fraction with highest probabilities.

3.2   Computation of the Normalization Map $\mathcal{Z}$

The number of possible observations for the normalization map $\mathcal{Z}$ can be computed by considering the special properties of the event-based sensor: Assuming a strong edge in the perceived light intensity, the sensor will generate one event for every pixel which passes over the edge. Thus the fractional number of possible generated events for a map location $u \in \Gamma$ is proportional to the length of its path on the sensor in pixel coordinates. Given a state estimate $x \in \Omega$, we compute the corresponding fractional pixel position on the sensor using the projection function μ. Note that this position does not necessarily lie inside the sensor boundaries as not all areas of the map are visible by the sensor at all times. If a map point is not visible by the sensor under the current or previous state estimate the normalization map is not updated at this map location. Otherwise the normalization map is computed as

$$\mathcal{Z}^{(k)}(u) = \mathcal{Z}^{(k-1)}(u) + \|\mu(u|x_*^{(k)}) - \mu(u|x_*^{(k-1)})\|, \ \mathcal{Z}^{(0)} = 0. \quad (4)$$

$x_*^{(k)}$ denotes the expected state which is computed as the weighted mean of the whole particle set $P^{(k)}$. Due to noise in the expected state and the high rate at which events are generated by the sensor, it is sensible to update the normalization map only periodically and not for every event.

3.3   Implementation Example: Event-Based SLAM for 2D Scenarios

In this section we briefly explain how the general formulation of our event-based SLAM algorithm can be specialized for a 2D localization and mapping scenario as presented in the introduction (see fig. 2). In this case, the state domain is the position of the robot on the floor and its rotation, i.e. $\Omega = \mathbb{R}^2 \times SO(2)$. The map is constructed for a flat ceiling parallel to the floor on which the robot is moving, i. e. $\Gamma = \mathbb{R}^2$.

For this setting the projection function μ is realized using the pinhole camera model:

$$\mu : \mathbb{R}^2 \times \mathbb{R}^2 \times SO(2) \to \mathcal{R}, \ (u, x, \theta) \mapsto \mathrm{proj}\left(R_z(\theta)^{-1}\left((u, D)^T - (x, 0)^T\right)\right) \quad (5)$$

with

$$\mathrm{proj} : \mathbb{R}^3 \to \mathcal{R}, \ v \mapsto \left(f\frac{v_x}{v_z} - c_x, f\frac{v_y}{v_z} - c_y\right) \quad (6)$$

where f and c are the usual camera model parameters and $R_z(\theta)$ is rotation about the z-axis by an angle θ. D is the constant height of the ceiling over the floor.

The standard deviation σ in eq. 3 is chosen equal to half the size of a sensor pixel projected onto the ceiling. This represents the fact that the size of the Gaussian on the occurrence map for an individual pixel event should correspond to the size of a sensor pixel projected onto the map space.

The inverse of the projection function μ^{-1}, which indicates where the occurrence map is updated in eq. 4, has a unique solution when the distance D is constant. For the more general case where the distance of the source of an event to the sensor is not known this is no longer the case. There are several possible strategies to solve this problem which are not further investigated in this paper: The depth information could be provided by additional sensors like Primesens depth-sensing sensors [6], or the depth information could be estimated by using multiple event-based sensors [7,8]. Another approach would be to use the full trace of the back projection μ^{-1} throughout a volumetric map using a cone-like probability distribution instead of a punctual Gaussian distribution in eq. 3.

4   Evaluation

In order to test our method we equipped a mobile robot with an upwards facing event-based dynamic vision sensor (eDVS) as depicted in fig. 2. The robot was remotely driven on varying paths through an indoor environment. For ground truth comparison, the robot was tracked externally by the marker-based motion capture system OptiTrack V100:R2. The event streams from the sensor were recorded and afterwards processed offline by our SLAM algorithm, resulting in estimated trajectories and constructed maps of the ceiling. Our tracking system did not use any additional information such as user driving commands or wheel rotation measurements. Our implementation uses pixel gridmaps for occurrence map $\mathcal{O}$, normalization map $\mathcal{Z}$ and likelihood map $\mathcal{M}$ with a pixel size of 1 cm.

To evaluate the quality of trajectories resulting from our method, we compare them against the ground truth paths from the external tracking system by calculating the Root-mean-square error (RMSE) of the position error and the error in orientation angle. As the world coordinate system of the external tracking system differs from the coordinate system chosen by our SLAM method we can only compare relative coordinates and thus have to first align our path to the ground truth path using a simple optimization over global position, global orientation, time offset and sensor rotation offset.

Fig. 4. Left: Photo of the ceiling. Middle: Resulting map from our method. Darker spots indicating a higher likelihood of events. The green scale bar indicates the size of the field of view of the sensor on the ceiling (ca. 2 meters). Right: Overlay of our map (magenta) and the edge map of the ceiling photo (blue).

We evaluated our method on a dataset with 40 different randomly selected paths. Figure 6 shows three typical examples and depicts the paths and maps created by our system, a comparison against ground truth as tracked by the overhead system and the corresponding error in position and orientation over time. An overview over the mean RMSE in position and rotation, the number of successfully tracked scenarios [1] and the processed events per second is evaluated on the whole dataset against a varying number of particles (table 1). Reported mean errors of 6.0 cm and 5.5 degrees are expected regarding the low sensor resolution of 128x128 pixels and the height of the ceiling of about three meters. The reported number of processed events per second demonstrate the efficiency of our method as in normal operating mode the sensor typical generates only around 25000 events per second.

Table 1. Positional and rotational root-mean-square error (RMSE), failure rate and processing speed for a varying number of particles

Particles	RMSE pos.	RMSE rot.	Failure rate	Events/s
5	35.4 cm	51.2°	18/40	87800
10	5.9 cm	5.5°	5/40	80700
25	6.0 cm	5.5°	4/40	65600
75	6.0 cm	5.4°	3/40	38800

Fig. 4 shows that maps created by our method are clearly resembling reality by comparing against a photo of the ceiling. As our map captures illumination changes we show an overlay of our map and an edge map of the photo created with the Sobel edge detector. As shown on with the scale bar in the figure, the mapped region is multiple times larger than the field of view of the sensor. It is observable that the likelihood $\mathcal{M}$ is higher at points of high local contrast in the photo.

---

[1] Scenarios are marked as not successful if a manual inspection shows a severe deviation of path and map from the the ground truth.

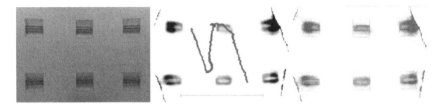

Fig. 5. Left: Photo of an indoor ceiling in a common office. Middle: Map and path created by our method. The green bar indicates the size of the field of view of the sensor on the ceiling (ca. 3 meters). Right: Overlay of our map (magenta) and the edge map of the ceiling photo (blue).

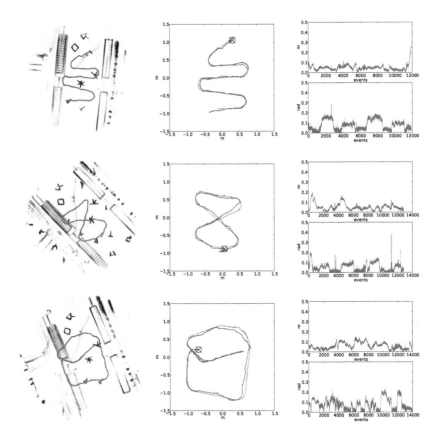

Fig. 6. Top to bottom: Three typical examples out of a total of 40 from the dataset. Left: Map and path as created by our method. Middle: Trajectories resulting from our method (red) and the external tracking system (blue). The trajectory starting point is marked with a X. Right: Positional and rotational error over number of resamples.

The ceiling of the room where the external tracking system is installed has various natural and artificially added distinctive features and edges. To show that our method is also suitable with ceilings with fewer features, e.g. only overhead lamps, we tested it in a common office room. A photo of the ceiling, the estimated robot path and the map created by our method and a map comparison is shown in fig. 5. This demonstrates that even though our method relies on variations of brightness in the scenery, i.e. the ceiling, and works best with high feature density, it also produces correct results for common office ceilings with a low feature density.

5 Conclusion

We presented a novel method for simultaneous localization and mapping for systems equipped with an event-based vision sensor (DVS). This sensor asynchronously reports individual events for perceived changes of pixel illumination. Due to the sparse nature of data reported by such a sensor, we achieved a significant reduction in required computing resources compared to current state-of-the-art visual SLAM algorithms [1], allowing faster than real-time localization and map generation (table 1) on a single core desktop computer. We are currently investigating a time-optimized implementation that runs in real time on standalone microcontroller boards for possible commercial applications.

For this paper we applied our method to a 2D visual SLAM scenario where a mobile robot moves on the ground and continuously localizes itself using features on the ceiling. Evaluation on a large recorded dataset demonstrates that our method works reliable with high accuracy already for a small number of particles.

Acknowledgements. The authors would like to thank Nicolai Waniek (NST, TUM) and Jan Funke, Florian Jug, Michael Pfeiffer and Matthew Cook from the Institute of Neuroinformatics (ETH and University Zurich) for valuable discussions.

References

1. Neira, J.P., Davison, A.J., Leonard, J.J.: Special issue on visual slam 24 (2008)
2. Newcombe, R.A., Molyneaux, D., Kim, D., Davison, A.J., Shotton, J., Hodges, S., Fitzgibbon, A.: Kinectfusion: Real-time dense surface mapping and tracking. In: IEEE International Symposium on Mixed and Augmented Reality (2011)
3. Lichtsteiner, P., Posch, C., Delbruck, T.: A 128x128 120db 15us latency asynchronous temporal contrast vision sensor. IEEE Journal of Solid State Circuits (2007)
4. Weikersdorfer, D., Conradt, J.: Event-based particle filtering for robot self-localization. In: IEEE International Conference on Robotics and Biomimetics (2012)
5. Isard, M., Blake, A.: Condensation conditional density propagation for visual tracking. International Journal of Computer Vision (1998)

6. Shotton, J., Fitzgibbon, A., Cook, M., Sharp, T., Finocchio, M., Moore, R., Kipman, A., Blake, A.: Real-time human pose recognition in parts from single depth images. In: IEEE Conference on Computer Vision and Pattern Recognition (2011)
7. Schraml, S., Belbachir, A.N., Milosevic, N., Schön, P.: Dynamic stereo vision system for real-time tracking. In: IEEE International Symposium on Circuits and Systems (2010)
8. Rogister, P., Benosman, R., Ieng, S.H., Lichtsteiner, P., Delbruck, T.: Asynchronous event-based binocular stereo matching. IEEE Transactions on Neural Networks and Learning Systems (2012)

Dimensionality Reduction for Efficient Single Frame Hand Pose Estimation

Petros Douvantzis, Iason Oikonomidis, Nikolaos Kyriazis, and Antonis Argyros

Institute of Computer Scince - FORTH,
Computer Science Department - University of Crete
Heraklion, Crete, Greece

Abstract. Model based approaches for the recovery of the 3D position, orientation and full articulation of the human hand have a number of attractive properties. One bottleneck towards their practical exploitation is their computational cost. To a large extent, this is determined by the large dimensionality of the problem to be solved. In this work we exploit the fact that the parametric joints space representing hand configurations is highly redundant. Thus, we employ Principal Component Analysis (PCA) to learn a lower dimensional space that describes compactly and effectively the human hand articulation. The reduced dimensionality of the resulting space leads to a simpler optimization problem, so model-based approaches require less computational effort to solve it. Experiments demonstrate that the proposed approach achieves better accuracy in hand pose recovery compared to a state of the art baseline method using only 1/4 of the latter's computational budget.

Keywords: Model based hand pose estimation, dimensionality reduction, PCA.

1 Introduction

The problem of estimating the configuration of the human body or its parts has high practical and theoretical interest. Body pose can be calculated at several scales and granularities including full body [13, 17], head [12] and hand pose [3, 9, 11, 18]. Recovering the articulation of a human hand can be proven very useful in a number of application domains including but not limited to advanced HCI/HRI, games, AR applications, sign language understanding, etc. Depending on the application requirements, different variants of the basic hand pose[1] estimation problem can be formulated. If a sequence of poses needs to be estimated, the resulting problem can be described as *hand pose tracking*. If a single hand pose needs to be estimated from a single frame, without prior knowledge resulting from temporal continuity, the problem is referred to as *single frame hand pose estimation*. Clearly, a solution to the single frame hand pose

---

[1] In this work, we use the term *hand pose* to refer to the 3D position, orientation and full articulation of a human hand.

M. Chen, B. Leibe, and B. Neumann (Eds.): ICVS 2013, LNCS 7963, pp. 143–152, 2013.
© Springer-Verlag Berlin Heidelberg 2013

estimation problem can be used to bootstrap hand pose tracking. Additionally, hand pose tracking can be implemented as sequential hand pose estimation.

Several methods have been proposed to solve the hand pose estimation problem using markerless visual data. According to [3] the existing approaches can be categorized as partial or full pose estimation methods, depending on the completeness of the output. The last class is further divided to *appearance-based* and *model-based* methods. Appearance-based methods [14,15,17,19] estimate hand configurations directly from images, using a precomputed mapping from the image feature space to the hand configuration. Model-based methods [2,4,9–11] search the solution space of the problem for the hand configuration that is most compatible to the observed hand. Every hypothesized hand pose is transferred to feature space using a hand shape model that is compared to the observed features.

Appearance-based methods are computationally efficient at estimation phase and usually do not require initialization. However, their accuracy is proportional to the wealth of the training set. Model-based approaches have better resolution since they search the parameter space without discretizing it. Their primary limitation is their computational requirements which are due to the high dimensionality of the problem to be solved: A large number of hypothesized poses must be compared to the observed data during the search of the problem space. For the case of hand pose tracking, due to temporal continuity, the current solution may be searched in the vicinity of the solution of the previous frame. This has resulted in methods that achieve near real time performance [9]. However, in single frame hand pose estimation, the position, orientation and articulation of the human hand needs to be estimated without a prior knowledge of the observed hand's configuration and, thus, the full parametric space needs to be searched.

In this work, we come up with a compact representation of hand articulation that permits model based methods to operate on lower dimensional spaces and become more efficient. Adopting the representation used in [9], the articulation of the human hand can be described by 20 parameters encoding the angles of the human hand joints and thus forming a 20-dimensional space. However, only a fraction of this space contains valid hand configurations [5,16]. For example, if no external forces are applied, the range of motions that can be performed by each finger joint is limited [8]. It may also be the case that a combination of disjointly plausible joint values may result in implausible hand configurations. As an example, a combination of joint values may result in a finger intersecting itself, another finger or the palm. Furthermore, the biomechanics and the physiology of the hand impose inter-finger and intra-finger constraints. For example, bending the pinky causes the ring finger to be bent as well. Last but not least, when a human hand is known to be engaged in specific activities (e.g., grasping, sign language, etc), its configurations are expected to lie in a much lower dimensional manifold.

Most of the mentioned constraints are hard to model analytically. However, they can be learnt by employing dimensionality reduction techniques on sets of training samples. The reduced spaces model implicitly the existing constraints.

In this work we perform dimensionality reduction by employing Principal Components Analysis (PCA). By providing mechanisms to move between representations, model-based methods can operate on the transformed space of reduced dimensionality. Although dimensionality reduction and PCA has been employed in the past for hand pose estimation [1, 6], in this work we evaluate the performance gain obtained for the problem of single frame hand pose estimation and demonstrate its integration with an existing, state of the art baseline method. The model-based method employed as the baseline is that of Oikonomidis et al. [9]. For hand pose tracking, this method achieves an accuracy of $5mm$ and a computational performance of 20 fps. However, due to the dimensionality of the problem, for single frame hand pose estimation the method is more time consuming and less reliable. For this reason, tracking is performed only after the hand is manually initialized for the first frame. In our work we show that by employing dimensionality reduction, the problem's search space is reduced to such a degree that single frame hand pose estimation becomes practical. More specifically, experimental results demonstrate that the proposed approach estimates the hand pose accurately and only at a fraction of the computational budget required by the baseline method. Thus, the need for manual initialization of the pose of the hand is lifted and the potential of model based methods to support hand pose estimation to real-world applications in considerably increased.

2 Proposed Approach

According to the employed baseline method [9], hand pose estimation is formulated as an optimization problem, seeking for the hand model parameters that minimize the discrepancy between the appearance of hypothesized hand configurations and the actual hand observation. Observations come from images acquired by an RGB-D camera and consist of estimated depth and skin color maps. Hypotheses are rendered through graphics techniques that also give rise to features comparable to those of the observations. Hypotheses are evaluated with an objective function that measures their compatibility to the observations. The optimization problem is handled by a variant of Particle Swarm Optimization (PSO) [7] (optimization module), which searches the parametric space of hand configurations.

A hand pose is represented by a 27-dimensional vector. 3 parameters encode the 3D position of the hand, 4 parameters its 3D orientation in quaternion representation and 20 parameters encode its articulation. Thus, the baseline method searches the 27-dimensional space S_{27}.

The proposed method incorporates PCA in the baseline method and creates a reduced dimensionality search space S_{7+M} consisting of $7 + M$ dimensions. 7 parameters encode 3D position and 3D orientation, while M parameters encode the articulation in a M-dimensional PCA space ($M \leq 20$). Two variations are proposed for the problem of single frame hand pose estimation, namely single-PCA and multi-PCA.

2.1   Single-PCA

Single-PCA consists of a training and an estimation phase. At the training phase of the algorithm, a single PCA space of M dimensions is created as follows. A dataset $\boldsymbol{A}$ consisting of N hand configurations $\boldsymbol{h}$ of 20 dimensions each is used as a training set. After the data are standardised, the orthogonal basis $\boldsymbol{W}$ of the PCA space is calculated. The orthogonal basis $\boldsymbol{W}$, along with the mean and standard deviation per dimension contain all the information needed for projection and back-projection to/from the PCA space. From now on, these elements are considered to form a trained PCA model P.

The number of dimensions M of P that are sufficient to describe the articulation information of the training set can be decided by calculating the cumulative variance explained by the first M PCA dimensions. Otherwise, the number of dimensions M can be chosen experimentally. A small number M introduces a representation error in the PCA space, but results in a smaller space to be searched.

Having encoded the articulation in a M dimensional space, we do not know the range of values of the newly defined PCA dimensions. This information is important because PSO requires the knowledge of the ranges of parameter values during optimization. Hence, we calculate the lower and upper bounds per PCA dimension as follows. Using the trained PCA model P, the $N \times 20$ matrix $\boldsymbol{A_{20}}$ is projected to a $N \times M$ matrix A_M. The standard deviation σ per PCA dimension of A_M is calculated and the lower/upper bounds are estimated as

$$[\boldsymbol{b}_L, \boldsymbol{b}_H] = [-2\boldsymbol{\sigma}, +2\boldsymbol{\sigma}] . \tag{1}$$

During the estimation phase, the baseline method is modified as shown in Fig. 1. The optimizer searches the bounded space S_{7+M} using the hypothesis evaluation module to calculate the objective function for the given observation. It should be noted that since the hypothesis evaluation module (see Fig.1) evaluates 27-dimensional parameter hypotheses, a hypothesis in space S_{7+M} must first be back-projected to the original space S_{27}. Finally, the best scoring hypothesis across all PSO generations is back-projected to S_{27} and returned as the solution.

2.2   Multi-PCA

PCA is not sufficient to represent non linearly correlated data such as multiple hand configurations. However, since most hand motions reside in some linear subspace [3], a different PCA model can be trained for each of them. This idea is used in multi-PCA.

More specifically, during the training phase, we use multiple articulation training sets $\boldsymbol{A^i}$, $i = 1, 2, .., F$. Each set consists of data that are linearly correlated. A different PCA model P^i is trained for each set $\boldsymbol{A^i}$, producing F bounded spaces S^i to be searched by the optimizer. Thus, during the estimation phase, F single-PCA optimization problems are solved independently. The hypothesis with the lowest error across all F solutions is chosen as the final solution.

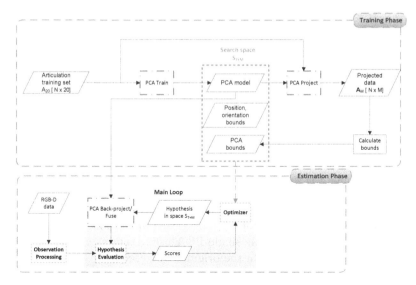

Fig. 1. Graphical illustration of the proposed methodology. At training phase, the reduced dimensionality search space S_{7+M} is created. At estimation phase, an RGB-D frame is used as input and the best hypothesis is searched for. The enclosed modules at the bottom, form the algorithm's main loop which runs for each generation of the optimizer (PSO).

3 Experimental Evaluation

The quantitative evaluation of single-PCA and multi-PCA is based on synthetic data, which enable the assessment of the proposed method against known ground truth. In this direction, a test set consisting of 27-dimensional configurations was rendered as RGB-D images, simulating a real sensor acquiring hand observations.

To quantify the accuracy in hand pose estimation, we employ the metric adopted in [9]. More specifically, the hand pose estimation error Δ is the averaged Euclidean distance between the respective phalanx endpoints of the ground truth and the estimated hand pose.

All the experiments ran offline on a computer equipped with a quad-core intel i7 930 CPU, 6 GBs RAM and an Nvidia GTX 580 GPU with 1581 GFlops processing power and 1.5 GBs memory.

3.1 Dataset Creation

The single-PCA algorithm requires a single training set, while the multi-PCA algorithm requires multiple. In our experiments, single-PCA was trained on the union of the training sets of multi-PCA. More specifically, we created three sequences of 100 hand poses each corresponding to one of the following three different hand motions: pinching, open hand closing towards a cylindrical grasp, open hand closing towards a closed fist. For each of the datasets, a training set was

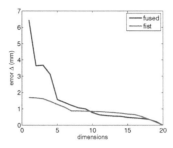

Fig. 2. The representation error of PCA with respect to the number of dimensions for the fused dataset and the fist dataset

created by adding uniform noise of 0.1 rad in each dimension. Multi-PCA used each training set separately, while single-PCA used them as a unified training set. The test set was created from the original three sequences by adding noise as before and by providing a position and orientation for each pose. The final test set contained 75 poses, uniformly sampled from each of the three sequences.

Since a representation error is introduced due to dimensionality reduction, it is useful to examine the PCA's behaviour when applied to the employed dataset. This enables us to roughly estimate the proposed method's accuracy in single frame hand pose estimation, since the representation error can be considered as a lower limit to the error achieved by single-PCA and multi-PCA. We are interested in the behaviour of PCA on the three separate datasets (multi-PCA case) and on the fused dataset (single-PCA case). We expect the latter to perform worse due to its more complicated contents, because more complex data need more PCA dimensions to account for their variance.

Towards this direction, PCA models are learned for each training set with varying numbers of PCA dimensions $M = 1, 2, .., 20$. In order to measure the error introduced by the reduced dimensionality, each data sample h of the test set is projected to the PCA space S_{7+M} and then back-projected to a point h^{bp} onto the original space S_{27}. The error $\Delta(h, h^{bp})$ is calculated for all samples. The averaged error is shown in Fig. 2. More dimensions are required by the fused dataset to achieve as low representation error as the fist dataset. Thus, we can expect multi-PCA to require a smaller number of dimensions than single-PCA for the same estimation accuracy.

3.2   Results

We evaluated the single-PCA and the multi-PCA method comparatively to the baseline method. The algorithms ran three times for each frame of the test set. The algorithms' behaviour is examined with respect to the parameters that affect the computational budget and the number of dimensions of the search space. The parameters that affect the computational budget of the method are the number of particles and generations of the PSO. More particles per generation search more densely the search space, while more generations improve the possibility that the

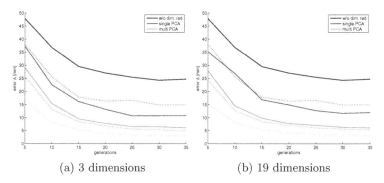

(a) 3 dimensions   (b) 19 dimensions

Fig. 3. Error Δ with respect to the number of PSO generations and particles: solid line for 16 particles, dotted line for 64 particles. PCA algorithms ran in (a) 3 PCA dimensions and (b) 19 PCA dimensions.

particles converge and the global optimum is found. PCA dimensions can vary from 1 to 20. When no dimensionality reduction is used (baseline method), the articulation dimensions are 20. In both cases, the dimensions encoding position and orientation are 7 and will not be displayed in the following figures, even though they are subject to optimization.

In Fig. 3 the effect of the computational budget on the algorithms is shown. A first observation is that Δ decreases monotonically with the number of generations. Additionally, as the particles per generation increase, the resulting error decreases. However, multi-PCA seems to reach its performance peak at $20 - 25$ generations, which is sooner than the others. The results demonstrate that multi-PCA performs better than single-PCA, which in turn outperforms the baseline method. Furthermore, single-PCA with 16 PSO particles performs better that the baseline method with 64 PSO particles. Similarly, multi-PCA employing 16 particles has almost the same accuracy with single-PCA using 64 particles. Moreover, for an accuracy around $15mm$, the baseline method requires at least 30 PSO generations, while single-PCA requires only 16.

In Fig. 4 the horizontal axis refers to the number of PCA dimensions. The results show that the number of dimensions has a low impact on the single-PCA algorithm for the current dataset. It performs better in three dimensions than one, which was expected from the representation error analysis in Fig. 2. However, the best choice on the number of dimensions for a given accuracy cannot be safely estimated. The multi-PCA algorithm is less affected by the number of dimensions and approximates a straight horizontal line in the plots.

In order to examine the distribution of the error, the histogram of the estimation error Δ for all 3×75 estimations, using 35 PSO generations and 3 PCA dimensions, has been computed and is shown in Fig. 5. When using 16 particles, the baseline method has a small number of successful estimations on

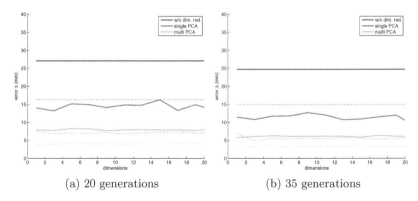

(a) 20 generations   (b) 35 generations

Fig. 4. The error Δ for the the 3 algorithms with respect to the number of PCA dimensions and the number of particles: 16 particles drawn as solid line, 64 particles drawn as dotted line. PSO generations are (a) 20 and (b) 35.

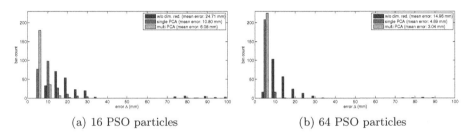

(a) 16 PSO particles   (b) 64 PSO particles

Fig. 5. Histogram of the error Δ for all the 3×75 estimations per algorithm running for 35 PSO generations with (a) 16 PSO particles and (b) 64 PSO particles. Single-PCA and multi-PCA algorithms used 3 PCA dimensions.

the $10mm$ error bin. Some estimations with error around $80mm$ correspond to wrong orientation estimation and usually a mirrored pose was returned. Single-PCA performs significantly better but with most of its estimations lying in the $10mm$ bin, it cannot be considered quite accurate. Multi-PCA performs exceptionally well, having 80% of its estimations in the $5mm$ bin, and has increased accuracy in more difficult poses.

When 64 particles are employed for each PSO generation, the baseline method's performance is improved but still 47% of the estimations exhibit an error greater than $12.5mm$. Single-PCA manages to almost reach the performance levels of the multi-PCA algorithm, while the latter could not make use of the extra computational budget since its performance was already very good. Figure 6 provides sample results obtained from the baseline and the two proposed methods for various PSO budgets.

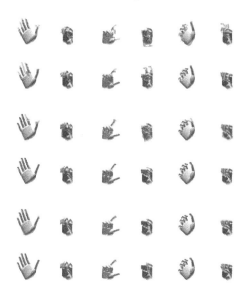

Fig. 6. Sample hand pose estimations for no dimensionality reduction (rows 1, 2), single PCA (rows 3, 4) and multi PCA (rows 5, 6) rendered in blue. True poses are rendered in red color. For each method, the algorithms ran for 35 generations and for 16 (top) and 64 (bottom) particles. PCA algorithms used 3 dimensions.

4 Conclusions

In this work the usage of PCA in single frame hand pose estimation was assessed. The proposed single-PCA algorithm, given a dataset consisting of hand poses, calculates a space S_{7+M} of reduced dimensionality and implicitly learns some of the underlying hand configuration constraints. As indicated by the experimental evaluation, the results outperform the baseline algorithm. The estimated pose has an accuracy up to $5mm$ depending on the employed computational budget, and can be used to bootstrap automatically hand pose tracking. PCA, being a linear technique, cannot effectively describe complicated datasets with non linear data. To face this fact, we also proposed a multi-PCA algorithm which uses more than one training sets to learn multiple PCA subspaces. Multi-PCA performed better than single-PCA and required a quarter of the PSO particles to achieve slightly better accuracy. The obtained results demonstrate that model based methods can efficiently solve the single frame hand pose estimation problem in spaces of reduced dimensionality. This lifts one of their drawbacks, that is the need of manual initialization. Thus, their practical exploitation in the context of vision systems and applications is improved considerably.

Acknowledgments. This work was supported by the EU FP7-ICT-2011-9-601165 project WEARHAP.

References

1. Bowden, R., Heap, T., Hart, C.: Virtual data gloves: Interacting with virtual environments through computer vision. In: Proc. 3rd UK VR-Sig Conference, DeMontfort University, Leicester, UK (1996)
2. de La Gorce, M., Paragios, N., Fleet, D.J.: Model-based hand tracking with texture, shading and self-occlusions. In: IEEE CVPR, pp. 1–8. IEEE (2008)
3. Erol, A., Bebis, G., Nicolescu, M., Boyle, R.D., Twombly, X.: Vision-based hand pose estimation: A review. CVIU 108(1-2), 52–73 (2007)
4. Hamer, H., Schindler, K., Koller-Meier, E., Van Gool, L.: Tracking a hand manipulating an object. In: IEEE ICCV, pp. 1475–1482. IEEE (2009)
5. Ingram, J., Kording, K., Howard, I., Wolpert, D.: The statistics of natural hand movements. Experimental Brain Research 288, 223–236 (2008)
6. Kato, M., Wei Chen, Y., Xu, G.: Articulated hand tracking by PCA-ICA approach. In: 7th International Conference on Automatic Face and Gesture Recognition, FGR 2006, pp. 329–334 (April 2006)
7. Kennedy, J., Eberhart, R.: Particle swarm optimization. In: IEEE ICNN, vol. 4, pp. 1942–1948. IEEE (1995)
8. Lin, J., Wu, Y., Huang, T.S.: Modeling the constraints of human hand motion. In: Workshop on Human Motion, pp. 121–126. IEEE (2000)
9. Oikonomidis, I., Kyriazis, N., Argyros, A.A.: Efficient model-based 3D tracking of hand articulations using Kinect. In: BMVC (2011)
10. Oikonomidis, I., Kyriazis, N., Argyros, A.A.: Full DOF tracking of a hand interacting with an object by modeling occlusions and physical constraints. In: IEEE ICCV, pp. 2088–2095. IEEE (2011)
11. Oikonomidis, I., Kyriazis, N., Argyros, A.A.: Markerless and efficient 26-DOF hand pose recovery. In: Kimmel, R., Klette, R., Sugimoto, A. (eds.) ACCV 2010, Part III. LNCS, vol. 6494, pp. 744–757. Springer, Heidelberg (2011)
12. Padeleris, P., Zabulis, X., Argyros, A.A.: Head pose estimation on depth data based on Particle Swarm Optimization. In: IEEE CVPRW, pp. 42–49 (June 2012)
13. Poppe, R.: Vision-based human motion analysis: An overview. CVIU 108(1), 4–18 (2007)
14. Romero, J., Kjellstrom, H., Kragic, D.: Monocular real-time 3D articulated hand pose estimation. In: 9th IEEE-RAS International Conference on Humanoid Robots, Humanoids 2009, pp. 87–92. IEEE (2009)
15. Rosales, R., Athitsos, V., Sigal, L., Sclaroff, S.: 3D hand pose reconstruction using specialized mappings. In: IEEE ICCV, vol. 1, pp. 378–385. IEEE (2001)
16. Santello, M., Flanders, M., Soechting, J.: Patterns of hand motion during grasping and the influence of sensory guidance. Journal of Neuroscience 22, 1426–1435 (2002)
17. Shotton, J., Fitzgibbon, A., Cook, M., Sharp, T., Finocchio, M., Moore, R., Kipman, A., Blake, A.: Real-time human pose recognition in parts from single depth images. In: IEEE CVPR, pp. 1297–1304 (June 2011)
18. Stenger, B., Mendonça, P.R., Cipolla, R.: Model-based 3D tracking of an articulated hand. In: IEEE CVPR, vol. 2, p. II–310. IEEE (2001)
19. Wu, Y., Huang, T.S.: View-independent Recognition of Hand Postures. In: IEEE CVPR, pp. 88–94 (2000)

A Head Pose Tracking System Using RGB-D Camera

Songnan Li, King Ngi Ngan, and Lu Sheng

The Chinese University of Hong Kong, Hong Kong SAR

Abstract. In this paper, a fast head pose tracking system is introduced. It uses iterative closest point algorithm to register a dense face template to depth data captured by Kinect. It can achieve 33fps processing speed without specific optimization. To improve tracking robustness, head movement prediction is applied. We propose a novel scheme that can train several simple predictors together, enhancing the overall prediction accuracy. Experimental results confirm its effectiveness for head movement prediction.

Keywords: head movement prediction, K-means like retraining, head pose tracking, iterative closest point algorithm.

1 Introduction

RGB-D cameras like Kinect capture both color and depth information in real time. They turn many complex computer vision algorithms into practical systems. In this paper, we introduce a fast Kinect-based head pose tracking system which uses user-specific 3D face template to track head pose. As using 3D face template, eye positions are also provided by the system. Therefore, the system can be used as a natural human computer interface in many attractive applications. For example, it can be applied in gaming or free-viewpoint video to provide user viewpoints; it can be used to control cursor with head motion, which will facilitate people with disabled arms; it can serve as a preprocessing step for free-head-movements gaze estimation, and so on.

In the literature, head pose estimation, face tracking, and eye localization have been investigated intensively. Most of previous studies are based on color information only. Related surveys can be found in [9]. As RGB-D camera becomes affordable, more and more researchers start to base their studies on depth data. For example, depth could be used to locate nose [8] or several nose position candidates [3] to infer head pose. In [5], the head pose estimation algorithm learned a regression model from a large amount of depth patches. In [4], a sparse face model was used for 3D deformable face tracking. Both color and depth information were exploited.

The prior study that is most closely related to our work is perhaps [13]. Although the system introduced in [13] aims at tracking facial expression, rigid head pose tracking is one of its essential processing steps. Like in [13], we generate

M. Chen, B. Leibe, and B. Neumann (Eds.): ICVS 2013, LNCS 7963, pp. 153–162, 2013.
© Springer-Verlag Berlin Heidelberg 2013

user-specific dense face template, and try to register this 3D template to depth data using ICP algorithm [2]. The contribution of the paper mainly comes from the registration process. We propose a novel method to train head movement predictors. These head movement predictors can provide a good initialization result for ICP and help it converge more easily. They make our head pose tracking system more robust in case of fast head movements.

This paper is structured as follows. Section 2 describes the system. Functionality and implementation details of each processing component are discussed. Section 3 focuses on the design of head movement predictors. A "K-means" like re-training scheme is proposed, which can be used when several predictors cooperate with each other for prediction. Experimental results verify its effectiveness for head movement prediction. Section 4 concludes the paper.

2 System Description

We use a commercial product to obtain the user-specific face template, which is then segmented manually to exclude regions that typically exhibit strong deformations. This is the offline part of the system which will be investigated further in a future work. Our current research work is only related to the rest of the system, and will be elaborated below.

The workflow of the online part is illustrated in Fig. 1. Either face and nose detection or head movement prediction is used to provide initialization result for ICP tracking, depending on whether or not the previous tracking results are available.

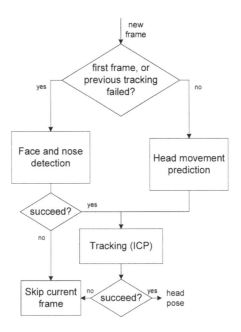

Fig. 1. Workflow of the head pose tracking system

2.1   Face and Nose Detection

As shown in Fig. 1, when it is the first frame or tracking of the previous frame fails, detection using color information is performed. It serves as an initialization/ re-initialization step for tracking. Using Haar-like features and cascade classifiers [12], the system detects the first face region across its search path. Then a nose region is detected using a similar method. To accelerate this detection process, the video resolution is down-sampled from 640×480 to 160×120. The search of nose uses original video resolution, but the search region is constrained to the detected face region.

The 3D position of nose tip $\mathbf{d}_{nose}$ is found by assuming that it is the closest point to the camera in the nose region. Pose of the face template is initialized by registering its nose tip position $\mathbf{f}_{nose}$ to the detected one $\mathbf{d}_{nose}$, and forcing that the template faces towards the camera center. This pose initialization result will be refined in the following step (Section 2.3) using the ICP algorithm.

Besides using detection, previous tracking results if available may be used to predict head pose more accurately. It will help the ICP algorithm to converge quickly. This paper will focus on this part in Section 3.

2.2   Tracking Using the ICP Algorithm

In this system, the face template is considered as a 3D point cloud, $\mathbf{f}_i$, $i \in [1, 2, ..., N_f]$. Given the camera calibration results, the depth image captured by Kinect can be easily transformed into another 3D point cloud, $\mathbf{d}_i$, $i \in [1, 2, ..., N_d]$. ICP algorithm is applied to register the two point clouds, and accordingly generates the head pose information.

The ICP algorithm [2] typically consists of several iteratively processing steps. In our system, it can be summarized as follows:

(1) For each point of the face template $\mathbf{f}_i$, find its matching point $\mathbf{d}_i$ in the point cloud captured by Kinect.
(2) Reject matching pairs $\{\mathbf{f}_i, \mathbf{d}_i\}$ according to predefined conditions.
(3) For the remaining matching pairs $\{\mathbf{f}_i, \mathbf{d}_i\}$, $i \in [1, 2, ..., N_r]$, find an optimal transform matrix $\mathbf{T}$ by minimizing a matching error metric, which quantifies the matching quality of $\{\mathbf{T} \times \mathbf{f}_i, \mathbf{d}_i\}$, $i \in [1, 2, ..., N_r]$.
(4) If the algorithm does not converge, repeat step 1 to 3.

Different approaches can be taken for each processing step, so there are many ICP variants [11]. In our system, projective data association [7] is used to find point correspondences in step one. The choice is mainly because of its superior efficiency compared with, for example, the typically used nearest neighbor method. In step two, a matching pair will be rejected if (a) the distance between $\mathbf{f}_i$ and $\mathbf{d}_i$ is too large (>50mm in our implementation) or (b) $\mathbf{f}_i$ does not have correspondence because of occlusion. Since our face is highly curved, part of it will be self-occluded. The occluded part will not be captured by Kinect, so some of $\mathbf{f}_i$s cannot find their correspondences. The self-occlusion can be detected by analyzing the normal vector of $\mathbf{f}_i$, which is also included in the face template file.

The homogeneous 4×4 transform matrix $\mathbf{T}$ is determined by minimizing this matching error metric:

$$\mathbf{T} = argmin_{\mathbf{T}} \sum_{i=1}^{N_r} \|\mathbf{q}_i \cdot (\mathbf{T} \times \mathbf{f}_i - \mathbf{d}_i)\|^2 \tag{1}$$

where $\mathbf{q}_i$ is the unit normal vector of $\mathbf{f}_i$. A numerical method BFGS [10] is used to optimize this metric. ICP using Eq. (1) as the matching error metric is called point-to-plane ICP. We found experimentally that it performs much better than point-to-point ICP [2] which does not employ normal information. Steps 1 to 3 are repeated until Eq.(1) reaches a local optimum.

With a dual-core 2.33GHz CPU, the face & nose detection algorithm runs at around 15 frames per second (fps). It is only used occasionally for tracking re-initialization. Without specific optimization, tracking using ICP runs at around 33fps. It can be optimized easily using multi-core CPU or GPU due to the parallel nature of the ICP algorithm. The tracking results are very accurate and robust to fast head motion. Fig. 2 illustrates some tracking and re-initialization results. A demo video can be found on the project website[1].

3   Head Movement Prediction

To predict movements, Kalman filter is typically used. Kalman filter is good at modeling linear systems. But head movement is typically nonlinear. For non-linear movements, usually particle filter is applied. But particle filter needs a large number of samples to estimate a probability distribution, which makes it time consuming. In this section, a new method is proposed for head movement prediction. It uses only three samples and can provide quite accurate prediction results.

3.1   Prediction Model

Perhaps the most intuitive method for 1-dimensional variable prediction should be this simple linear model:

$$x_k = a_0 + a_{-1}x_{k-1} + a_{-2}x_{k-2} + ... + a_{-L+1}x_{k-L+1} \tag{2}$$

where a_is, $i \in \{0, -1, ..., -L+1\}$ are model parameters, x_k is the variable value (e.g., position in millimeter or orientation in degree) at time k, and L is the predictor length. Clearly it cannot model nonlinear head movement. But in our system, the prediction result is not directly used as the head pose of the next frame (as in applications such as head mounted display [1] which directly uses the prediction result as the next head pose to reduce display latency), but as an initialization result for ICP tracking. Therefore, we can use several simple linear models which work together to compensate for their disadvantages.

---

[1] http://www.ee.cuhk.edu.hk/~snli/HeadTracking.htm

Fig. 2. Illustration of tracking and re-initialization results

In practice, we use the following prediction model instead of (2):

$$\nabla x_k = a_0 + a_{-1}\nabla x_{k-1} + a_{-2}\nabla x_{k-2} + ... + a_{-L+1}\nabla x_{k-L+1} \qquad (3)$$

where ∇x_k is equal to $x_k - x_{k-1}$ which indicates change of position or orientation between adjacent frames. Using the same number of parameters, Eq. (3) can better model natural movement. For example, using two parameters, Eq. (3) can model constant velocity ($a_0 = 0$ and $a_{-1} = 1$ assuming the frame sampling rate is constant), while Eq. (2) cannot. As introduced below, parameters are derived by training. It is better to use less parameters, since there will be less possibility for the model to over-fit the training data.

Head motion prediction aims to provide a good initial transform matrix $\mathbf{T}$ in Eq. (1), so that the ICP algorithm can converge robustly. The 4×4 homogenous transform matrix $\mathbf{T}$ has only 6-degrees of freedom: $\mathbf{T}_k = [\nabla x_k, \nabla y_k, \nabla z_k, \nabla \phi_k, \nabla \theta_k, \nabla \omega_k]^t$ which corresponds respectively to transitions and rotations along the XYZ axes. For computational efficiency, we assume independence between these six variables and use the same model parameters for prediction:

$$\mathbf{T}_k = a_0\mathbf{1} + a_{-1}\mathbf{T}_{k-1} + a_{-2}\mathbf{T}_k - 2 + ... + a_{-L+1}\mathbf{T}_{k-L+1} \qquad (4)$$

3.2   Training

Head movement should have its unique characteristics, which can be captured by tuning the predictor parameters (a_0, a_{-1}, etc.) according to real-world head

Table 1. Three linear predictors with different lengths (L=1, 2, 3), and their prediction errors measured by MSE

	a_0	a_{-1}	a_{-2}	MSE
Predictor A (L=1)	0.009	-	-	240.3
Predictor B (L=2)	0.004	0.585	-	138.7
Predictor C (L=3)	0.005	0.469	0.198	127.7

movement data. As a preliminary experiment, we captured a head movement sequence with $N = 1829$ frames, trying to include many typical head movements. Exhaustive search is used to find a good initialization result for ICP, which converged successfully for all frames in this video sequence. Such a scheme cannot be applied in practice considering its complexity, but can be used to derive ground truth when more accurate tracking devices are unavailable.

It should be noted that transitions $(\nabla x_k, \nabla y_k, \nabla z_k)$ are measured in millimeter, while rotations $(\nabla \phi_k, \nabla \theta_k, \nabla \omega_k)$ are measured in degree. The six variables have different variances in the training data. To prevent the training result to be biased towards variables that exhibit larger variances, they are normalized by their respective standard deviation values[2]. Then the predictor parameters are obtained by optimizing this least square equation:

$$\min_{[a_0,a_{-1},\dots,a_{-L+1}]^t} \left\| \begin{bmatrix} \mathbf{T}_N \\ \mathbf{T}_{N-1} \\ \vdots \\ \mathbf{T}_L \end{bmatrix} - \begin{bmatrix} 1 & \mathbf{T}_{N-1} & \mathbf{T}_{N-2} & \dots & \mathbf{T}_{N-L+1} \\ 1 & \mathbf{T}_{N-2} & \mathbf{T}_{N-3} & \dots & \mathbf{T}_{N-L} \\ \vdots & & & \ddots & \vdots \\ 1 & \mathbf{T}_{L-1} & \mathbf{T}_{L-2} & \dots & \mathbf{T}_1 \end{bmatrix} \times \begin{bmatrix} a_0 \\ a_{-1} \\ \vdots \\ a_{-L+1} \end{bmatrix} \right\|^2 \quad (5)$$

or

$$\min_{\mathbf{V}} \|\mathbf{P} - \mathbf{Q} \times \mathbf{V}\|^2 \quad (6)$$

which has a closed form solution: $\mathbf{V} = (\mathbf{Q}^t \times \mathbf{Q})^{-1} \times \mathbf{Q}^t \times \mathbf{P}$.

We trained three linear predictors with different lengths L. Their parameters are shown in Table 1. The prediction error is measured by MSE:

$$MSE = \frac{\sum_{k=L}^{N} \|\mathbf{T}_k - \hat{\mathbf{T}}_k\|^2}{6(N - L + 1)} \quad (7)$$

where $\mathbf{T}_k$ is the ground truth, $\hat{\mathbf{T}}_k$ is the predicted one with each of its elements rescaled (by multiplying the corresponding standard deviation value). As expected, the prediction error gradually decreases as the predictor length increases. However, to prevent over-fitting training data, predictor should not be too long. In practice, we chose the maximum predictor length to be 3, as shown in Table 1.

As explained above, in our application we can evaluate several predictions and select the best one as initialization for ICP. Therefore, all three predictions A, B and C can be used together. The notation $\min(A, B, C)$ indicates a new

---

[2] $\sigma_{\nabla x} = 12.86$, $\sigma_{\nabla y} = 8.33$, $\sigma_{\nabla z} = 1.80$, $\sigma_{\nabla \phi} = 0.67$, $\sigma_{\nabla \theta} = 0.97$, $\sigma_{\nabla \omega} = 0.77$.

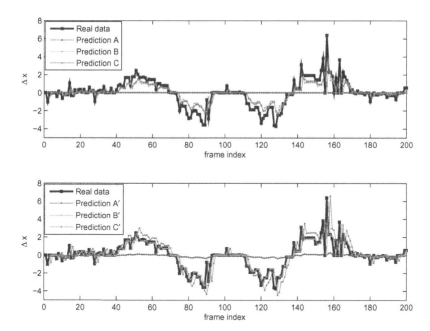

Fig. 3. 200 frames of predictions on ∇x. Upper subfigure illustrates prediction results using predictors A, B, and C as given in Table 1. Bottom subfigure illustrates prediction results using predictors A', B', and C' as given in Table 2.

predictor that combines all three predictors together, and only uses the best predictor among A, B and C for each frame. Compared with the smallest MSE value in Table 1, i.e., 127.7, $\min(A, B, C)$ further reduces it to 102.8.

3.3 A "K-means" Like Re-training

The upper subfigure of Fig. 3 shows an example of prediction results, i.e., 200 frames of predictions on ∇x, using three predictors A, B and C given in Table 1. It can be observed that although predictors B and C have different lengths, they have similar prediction results. None of predictors A, B and C can predict large transitions accurately. The reason is that they intend to cope with all types of data, balancing performances of predicting both large and small transitions. This should be difficult for any simple linear predictor.

Therefore, we propose a model re-training scheme. It aims to construct a better prediction algorithm by considering the fact that in practice, several simple predictors may cooperate with each other rather than working alone. It takes a "K-means" like approach. Limited by the paper length, readers interested in K-means cluster algorithm please refer to [6]. A conceptual description of this re-training scheme is given in Fig. 4. In practice, the re-training of predictors A, B and C is conducted in the following way: (1) Set the initial parameters of new predictors A', B', and C' according to Table 1. Parameters of A' are a_0=0.009, a_{-1}=0 and a_{-2}=0. Parameters of B' are a_0=0.004, a_{-1}=0.585 and a_{-2}=0. C'

| 1. Choose K predictors, and tune their parameters using all the training data. |
| 2. Compare prediction results, and accordingly divide the training data into K sets, in a way that all training data in set j are best predicted by predictor j. |
| 3. Re-train each predictor j with its specific training set j. |
| 4. If parameters do not converge, go to step 2. |

Fig. 4. A "K-means" like re-training scheme

Table 2. Predictors after re-training. The last column shows the ratio of best prediction number to all training data for each predictor.

	a_0	a_{-1}	a_{-2}	best/all
Predictor A'	-0.054	0.041	0.039	30%
Predictor B'	-0.008	0.927	0.003	52%
Predictor C'	0.088	0.352	0.888	18%

is the same as C. Notice that the lengths of A', B' and C' are all 3 now. (2) Compare the prediction results, and divide the training data into 3 sets accordingly. Training data in 1st, 2nd and 3rd sets are best predicted by predictors A', B' and C', respectively. (3) Re-train A', B' and C' using training set 1, 2, and 3, respectively. (4) Repeat steps 2 and 3 until the parameter values converge.

The final parameters are shown in Table 2. Table 2 also lists the ratio of best prediction count to all training frames for each predictor. The bottom subfigure of Fig. 3 shows an example of their prediction results. It can be seen that compared with B and C, B' and C' exhibit larger diversity. This will be helpful when using them together to construct a better prediction algorithm, e.g., $\min(A', B', C')$. On the training data, $\min(A', B', C')$ further reduces the smallest MSE from $\min(A, B, C)$'s 102.8 to 80.3.

3.4   Performance Test

To test the performance, another head movement sequence is used. It has 717 frames. The ground truth tracking result is derived using exhaustive search as introduced before. The prediction error is measured by MSE as given in Eq. (7) [3]. The model parameters of A, B, C, A', B', C' are shown in Table 1 and 2. From Table 3, it can be seen that the re-training reduces prediction error on this test sequence significantly.

The prediction result is used as an initialization for ICP. The matching error metric of ICP as given by Eq. (1) can be used to evaluate prediction performance. Fig. 5 compares three predictors on this test video. "Identity" corresponds to a naive predictor given by $\mathbf{T}_k = 0$, i.e., all a_i of Eq. (4) are set to zero. Using "Identity", the previous head state is used as an initialization for the next frame. $\min(\text{Identity}, B, C)$ is similar with $\min(A, B, C)$ but A is replaced with

---

[3] Input data are normalized by the standard deviation values obtained from the training data before prediction. After prediction, the predicted values are rescaled before calculating MSE.

Table 3. Prediction errors of five predictors on a test sequence

	A	B	C	Min(A, B, C)	Min(A', B', C')
MSE	391.0	168.9	153.3	135.7	93.06

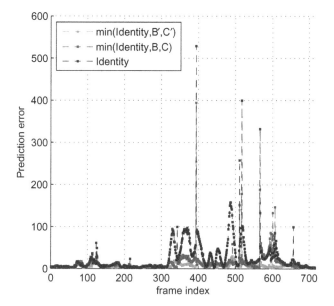

Fig. 5. Prediction errors measured by Eq. (6) on the test sequence

"Identity". It is believed that if the training data is large enough, A should be close to "Identity". And in practice, we find that "Identity" indeed performs better than A. Similarly, min(Identity, B', C') is min(A', B', C') with A' replace by "Identity". It should be noted that for the same frame, inputs of these predictors ($\mathbf{T}_{k-1}$ and $\mathbf{T}_{k-2}$) are different. So it is possible that occasionally "Identity" even performs better than min(Identity, B, C).

As shown in Fig. 5, min(Identity, B', C') outperforms the other two for most frames. Specially, for those extremely difficult frames (head movement with burst acceleration) which are associated with very large prediction errors, min(Identity, B', C') always produce the smallest prediction error, which verifies that the retraining indeed enhances the prediction capability.

4   Conclusion

In this paper, we introduced a Kinect-based head pose tracking system. Point-to-plane ICP is used to register a user-specific face template to the point cloud captured by Kinect. To make sure that ICP can converge robustly even with fast head motion, a reliable head movement prediction algorithm is required to provide ICP with a good initialization result. Our head movement prediction algorithm uses three simple linear predictors. To enhance overall prediction accuracy, a novel method is proposed to train these simple predictors. We name this method as "K-means" like re-training to emphasize its similarity with the K-means clustering algorithm. It automatically clusters the training data into K groups and trains K predictors, respectively. Although any one of these predictors trained using this method cannot provide a good estimate for every frame, there will be one of them that can predict quite accurately. Therefore, when they are used together, good performance can be expected. It should be noted that the proposed training method can also be applied to other predictors, such as Kalman filters. This is one aspect of our future work. Other aspects include using professional tracking device to obtain accurate training data, and code optimization.

References

1. Azuma, R., Bishop, G.: Improving static and dynamic registration in an optical see-through hmd. In: Proceedings of the 21st Conference on Computer Graphics and Interactive Techniques, pp. 197–204. ACM, USA (1994)
2. Besl, P., McKay, H.: A method for registration of 3-D shapes. IEEE Transactions on Pattern Analysis and Machine Intelligence 14(2), 239–256 (1992)
3. Breitenstein, M., Kuettel, D., Weise, T., Van Gool, L., Pfister, H.: Real-time face pose estimation from single range images. In: Proceedings of IEEE Conference on Computer Vision and Pattern Recognition, pp. 1–8 (2008)
4. Cai, Q., Gallup, D., Zhang, C., Zhang, Z.: 3D deformable face tracking with a commodity depth camera. In: Daniilidis, K., Maragos, P., Paragios, N. (eds.) ECCV 2010, Part III. LNCS, vol. 6313, pp. 229–242. Springer, Heidelberg (2010)
5. Fanelli, G., Weise, T., Gall, J., Van Gool, L.: Real time head pose estimation from consumer depth cameras. In: Mester, R., Felsberg, M. (eds.) DAGM 2011. LNCS, vol. 6835, pp. 101–110. Springer, Heidelberg (2011)
6. Hartigan, J.: Clustering algorithms. John Wiley Sons (1975)
7. Izadi, S., Kim, D., Hilliges, O., Molyneaux, D., Newcombe, R., Kohli, P., Shotton, J., Hodges, S., Freeman, D., Davison, A., Fitzgibbon, A.: Kinectfusion: real-time 3D reconstruction and interaction using a moving depth camera. In: Proc. UIST, pp. 559–568 (2011)
8. Malassiotis, S., Strintzis, M.G.: Robust real-time 3D head pose estimation from range data. Pattern Recognition 38, 1153–1165 (2005)
9. Murphy-Chutorian, E., Trivedi, M.: Head pose estimation in computer vision: A survey. IEEE Transactions on Pattern Analysis and Machine Intelligence 31(4), 607–626 (2009)
10. Nocedal, J., Wright, S.: Numerical optimization. Springer series in operations research. Springer (2006)
11. Rusinkiewicz, S., Levoy, M.: Efficient variants of the ICP algorithm. In: Proceedings of International Conference on 3-D Digital Imaging and Modeling, pp. 145–152 (2001)
12. Viola, P., Jones, M.J.: Robust real-time face detection. Int. J. Comput. Vision 57(2), 137–154 (2004)
13. Weise, T., Bouaziz, S., Li, H., Pauly, M.: Realtime performance-based facial animation. In: ACM SIGGRAPH 2011, pp. 1–10. ACM, USA (2011)

A New Hierarchical Method for Markerless Human Pose Estimation

Yuan Lei, Huawei Pan*, Weixia Chen, and Chunming Gao

School of Information Science and Engineering, Hunan University, Changsha,410082,
Hunan, China
38697014@qq.com

Abstract. We present a system for markerless human motion capture through a hierarchical method from multiple camera views. In the absence of markers, the task of recovering the human pose is challenging and requires strong image features and robust algorithm. We propose a solution which integrates the 2D posture information and the volumetric reconstruction. Firstly, the model's initia posture is obtained through the method of segmenting silhouette. After that, we track the human pose by using a hierarchical method, which is divided into three steps: head detection, torso prediction and limb matching. In order to gain the robust results, we discard the interior voxel data, use the middle voxel data for motion tracking, and use the surface voxel data for global optimization. The experiment results show that the method is valid and robust.

Keywords: hierarchical, markerless, tracking, Iterative Closest Point.

1 Introduction

Markerless human motion capture is an active topic in the areas of computer vision with many applications in animation, interactive games, motion analysis (sport, medical) and surveillance. One of the key technologies of motion capture is the pose estimation, which recovers 3D human body pose parameters from 2D videos. There has been significant work in recovering the full body pose from images and videos in the last ten-fifteen years. Most human pose estimation methods are divided into two categories: monocular [1, 2]and multi-view [3, 4]. Although the technology of 2D skeleton extraction is well enough to use for pose estimation, self-occlusion problem is still unresolved. Therefore, most researchers adopt based on multi-view method to estimate 3D human pose from voxels. The human pose estimation methods are divided into two: model-free[5]and model-based[6]. According to the experience, most of human pose estimation systems usually adopt the model-based method. Analysis method using synthesis technique is usually applied in the model-based method. Its basic principle is predicting the posture of the human model, fitting it to the feature extracted from images and updating the parameters of the human model.

---

* Corresponding author.

M. Chen, B. Leibe, and B. Neumann (Eds.): ICVS 2013, LNCS 7963, pp. 163–172, 2013.
© Springer-Verlag Berlin Heidelberg 2013

In general, due to the inability of recovering the optimal parameters by global searching, we recover the human posture by searching around the initial values. And then, we can obtain the posture from each frame by the "predict-fit-update" processing. Thus, the initialization of the human body model (HBM) is an essential step in the human motion tracking process. So, the automatic initialization in the markerless motion capture system has become a problem that should be solved urgently. To solve this issue, this paper puts forward a method that can automatically acquire human posture based on the silhouette segmentation.

The problem of tracking the pose of human body is to estimate the position and configuration of the HBM from the video data and take them as the parameters of the tracked human body. Due to high dimensionality of the pose space, it is challenging to search the true body configurations for any search strategy. The existing literature for model-based tracking either approach the problem using a Bayesian filtering formulation[7–9], or as an pure optimization problem [10–12]. L. Sigal et al.[9] formulated the human pose and motion estimation by solving using a non-parametric belief propagation, which uses a variation of particle filtering that can be applied over a general graphical model with loops. Zheng Zhang et al.[10] estimated human posture by matching the voxels to the barrel model updated by Particle Swarm Optimization (PSO) algorithm.

2   System Flow

The flow chart of this motion capture system is shown in Fig.1. It mainly consists of initialization and tracking parts. The initialization part includes the system initialization, such as camera calibration using Zhang's method[13], and the model initialization, which is expounded in 3. The initial parameters of the human model are retrieved from labelled voxels, which is obtained by integrating the features extracted from a segment silhouette into reconstructed 3D volume data. The motion tracking can be complete through three steps. Firstly, the head information is searched by iteration of encircling, which is detailed in Sec.4.1. Then, the main vector of torso is predicted in Sec.4.2. At last, we introduce a method of tracking the limbs by matching them to the labelled voxels using ICP(Iterative Closest Point) algorithm described in Sec.4.3.

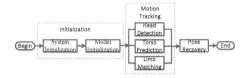

Fig. 1. The system flow chart

3   Model Initialization

For a model-based markerless motion capture method, an articulated body model is needed. The Cylinder model are flesh out by 10 cylinder, as shown in Fig.2, and contains 15 joints: head, neck, root, shoulders, elbows, wrists, hips, knees, and ankles. P_{joint} denotes the joint coordinate in the world coordinate system.

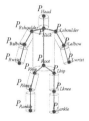

Fig. 2. 3D cylinder Model

According to the issue of pose initialization, we propose a method for model initialization, which consists of three steps: segmenting silhouette into different parts, labelling 3D voxels, and then extracting 3D human parameters, as shown in Fig.3. The core principle of our algorithm is recovering human 3D posture by combining the 3D information with the 2D features, which is extracted from one appropriate silhouette.

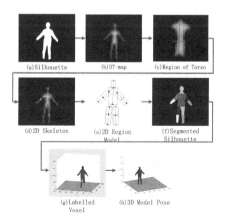

Fig. 3. Flow chart of pose initialization

3.1 Silhouette Segment

In order to obtain human pose features from image, we segment the silhouette to different parts by matching the pixels of the silhouette to a region model. The region model is built with a 2D skeleton which is extracted from 2D silhouette based on Distance Transformation and PCA(Principal Component Analysis) algorithm.

Step1.2D Skeleton Extraction. We present a robust method to extract 2D skeleton parameters from a silhouette, as shown in Fig.3(a). Firstly, we process the silhouette with the Fast Distance Transformation(Fast DT). The definition of the Fast DT can be described as a map whose value in each pixel p of the predicted contour, called Region of Interesting, satisfies the following condition:

$$D(p) = min\{d(p, q)|I(q) = 0\}. \tag{1}$$

Where I means a binary image, p is the foreground pixel, q is the background pixel. After then, we can obtain the DT map of the silhouette, as shown in Fig.3(b). Because of the torso is much broader than other parts of human bodies such as limbs and head, the DT value is higher. In our experiments, we also find that the DT value of the torso is very static, which attributes to the similar of the size between human beings mainly. Thus, the simple constant threshold can be used to separate the torso from the silhouette, as shown in Fig.3(c).

After that, PCA will be introduced to compute the principal normal vector of the torso and its orthogonal vector, represented by v_1 and v_2. We denote the point which has the maximum value in the DT map as P_{dt_max}. Therefore, with the length of the human vertebra, we can gain the general location of P_{root2d} by $P_{root2d} = P_{dt_max} + L_{torso} * v_1$, where the L_{torso} is the estimated length, P_{root2d} is estimated point. In order to gain the optimal location of P_{root2d}, we introduce a method based on the constraints:$\arg\max \sum_{i=1}^{n} \{i|i \in Rect(P_1, P_2, \delta)\}$,where $Rect(P_1, P_2, \delta)$ is the rectangle region built with the P_1 and P_2, its width is 2δ, as shown in Fig.4(a). Fig.4(b) shows the situation of satisfying constraints, and Fig.4(c) is the situation of non-satisfying constraints.

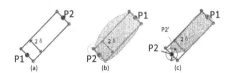

Fig. 4. Estimate articulation using energy constraint

Finally, we can extract the 2D joints from the silhouette, as shown in Fig.3(d), by combining the remaining pixels projection to the orientation of vector v_1 and v_2, with the human prior information.

Step2.Pixel Classification. We establish an adaptive human region model according to the 2D joint points. The human region model consists of 10 regions $I_n, (n = 1, \cdots, 10)$, as shown in Fig.3(e). Then, we match each pixel of the silhouette to the region model by calculating the minimum distance from the pixel to every part of the region model. The pixels can be labeled to the different values by the following function:

$$SL(p) = n, if D(p, I_n) = min\{D(p, I_1), \cdots, D(p, I_{10})\}. \tag{2}$$

where $n = 1, 2, \cdots, 10$,each region I_n is formed by four vertex t_1, t_2, t_3, t_4 , $D(p, I_n)$ is the minimum distance from the pixel p to the region, and can be computed by the algorithm of distance from point to polygon, as shown in the following equation.

$$D(p, I_n) = min\{d(p, L_k)\}. \tag{3}$$

Finally, each pixel is classified to 10 groups by the above method, and is labelled by different values, as shown in Fig.3(f), where different color regions represent different body parts.

3.2   Labelled Voxel Reconstruction

We gain 3D voxel by SFS(Shape-From-Silhouette) algorithm [14]based on a look-up table. In our paper, we establish a look-up table between voxels and their correspond projection pixels in each camera view. In general, the labelled silhouette is recorded as SL(Silhouette Labelled). According to the previous results, our look-up table of the SL is different from the traditional table. The pixel has different value when it is on different body part regions. If the voxel's projection in the SLwhich is belong to the head region, the voxel is marked as head. After that we can obtain human body part segmented and labelled voxels, as shown in Fig.3(g).

3.3   Initial Pose Extraction

According to the above results, 3D voxel data can be segmented into different parts, such as head, torso and limbs. Based on the topology of human, we figure out all junction voxels between two body part data that has the different $f(x, y, z)$. After that, we can get the rest point, such as the end of limbs and head, according to the information of the rest voxel data and the human skeleton prior length.

We can obtain the human 3D skeleton information by the previous method. Then, the skeleton parameter is modified by the body rigid constraint as the recovered human model parameters. Then, we can get the initial posture of the model, as shown in Fig.3(h).

4   Tracking

Motion tracking can be defined as pose estimation from image sequences with the temporal and volumic information . We introduce a hierarchical method for tracking human poses based on the human body model. Due to its unique shape and size, the head is easiest to find and is located firstly. After then, the torso vector can be predicted through the iteration of searching. Finally, we label the voxels of the frame t based on the Mahalanobis distance between the voxels and the predicted positions of the model parts. For each part of the model, we gain the rotate matrix and translation vector by using ICP algorithm. Finally the model parameters is recovered using the global optimization of the objective function.

According to the connectivity, we divided the voxels to three : surface, middle, interior. In order to reduce the computation, we subtract the interior voxels, and use the middle voxels for motion tracking, the surface voxels for global optimization.

4.1   Head Detection

We create a spherical crust template whose center is P_{head}^{t-1} and radius is r_{head}. P_{head}^{t-1} is the head position of frame t-1. The template initial center location of frame t that maximizes the number of the voxels, which are inside the crust, is represented by C_0^t. The sphere fitting algorithm is then applied by updating the center of the template (as shown in Fig.5). The updated center N_i^t is given as:

$$N_i^t = P_{head}^{t-1} + i(C_0^t - P_{head}^{t-1})/|C_0^t - P_{head}^{t-1}|. \tag{4}$$

where i is the step length. Then we recount the center C_i^t of the voxels which fall into this new sphere.

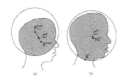

Fig. 5. Shpere fitting procedure Left: iteration begins; Right: iteration stops

The algorithm iterates until $\|C_n^t - N_n^t\| < Thresh$. The head position of the frame t is obtained by $P_{head}^t = N_n^t$. We obtained the junction voxels between body and head, defined by V_{neck}. Therefore, the $B^t = \frac{1}{N}\sum_{i=1}^{N} V_{neck}(i)$ is chosen as the neck point of frame t.

4.2   Torso Vector Prediction

Between the plane which is perpendicular to torso and passes neck point P_{neck}^{t-1} and the plane passes pelvis point P_{root}^{t-1} at t-1 time, we can build a spatial direction set as shown in Fig.6. For each point which distributes uniform in the neighborhood area with radiusδ in the neck and pelvis planes can train $(N+1)$ strips vectors. N is the number of sampling points in the neighborhood area of neck or root.

Each trained vector is used as a predictive torso direction at t time. For each vector, count up the t time voxel data number which falls into the section $[P_{neck}^t, P_{root}^{'t}(n)], n = 1, \cdots, (N+1)$ and vertical distance is less than torso radius. The vector corresponds to the maximum number is as the optimal solution,which is direction of torso at the t time. And that, we can obtain P_{root}^t by the optimal torso direction.

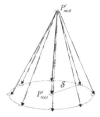

Fig. 6. Prediction vector set

4.3   Limb Matching

We first divided the voxels into two types: the surface and interior. The interior voxels are used for motion tracking, and surface voxels are used for global optimization. Acorrding to the previous sections, we got three points of skeleton, such as head, neck, and root. $X^t = \{x_1^t, x_2^t, \cdots, x_{12}^t\}$ notates the rest joint points. $V^t = \{v_1^t, v_2^t, \cdots, v_{12}^t\}$ and $M^t = \{m_1^t, m_2^t, \cdots, m_{12}^t\}$ denotes the voxel data and model sampled points of each body part respectively.

Step1.Update X^t and M^t. According to the previous section, the body parameter is assumed by $x_i^t = x_i^{t-1}, i = 1, \cdots, 12$. M^t is the points sampled from the HBM, which is established via the skeleton parameters X^t .

Step2.Label voxels. The voxels of frame t are labelled to different body parts, by matching it to the model M^t , according to the Mahalanobis distance, is as follows.

$$d(v, m_i^t) = (v - u_i)k_i(v - u_i)^T. \tag{5}$$

where v is the voxel, u_i is the mean value, k_i is the covariance matrix. The voxel is belonged to the part which has minimum distance value.

Step3.Bottom-up fitting. We employ a hierarchical method for fitting the voxel to the model points, using the ICP algorithm for the local optimization. As the HBM is a topological structure, we can figure out the skeleton point by the bottom-up method. The constraints is applied to the local optimization using ICP algorithm. As the right forearm for example(as shown in Fig.7), it includes two endpoints, right elbow and right wrist, which are represented as x_4^t, x_5^t at frame t. In our method, the x_4^t is computed first. So, the R and T is chosen as the local optima when it is satisfied the condition: $\arg\min \|(Rx_4^{t-1} + T) - x_4^t\|$. Then, the endpoint of wrist can be acquired by $x_5^t = Rx_5^{t-1} + T$. Finally, we can obtain the optical parameters of X^t gradually.

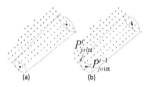

Fig. 7. Body Tracking

Step4.Global optimization. The fittness function is

$$f(R,T) = \sum_{i=1}^{N_i} \sum_{j=1}^{N_s} \left\| (RP_i + T) - P_j' \right\|^2. \tag{6}$$

where P is the point of the updated model, P' is the point of surface voxels. We use the Singular value decomposition (SVD) algorithm to calculate the optimal value of R, T. Finally, the human pose of each endpoint can be recovered by $P^t = RP^{t-1} + T$.

5   Experimental Results

We evaluate the performance of our hierarchical human pose estimation approach using the HumanEva-II dataset [15]. The dataset consists of synchronized video streams from 4 color cameras at 60 Hz along with ground truth 3D body poses obtained using a commercial motion capture system. We assess the accuracy of recovered poses using the evaluation metric proposed in Sigal et al. which measures the sum of the Euclidean distances to $K = 15$ virtual markers corresponding to the locations of the major joints. The error in the voerall estimated pose $X'_{mrk}$to the ground truth poseX_{mrk} (in mm) is expressed as the average absolute distance between individual markers, $X_{mrk} = \{p_1, p_2, \cdots, p_K\}$.

$$Error(X_{mrk}, X'_{mrk}) = \frac{1}{K} \sum_{k=1}^{K} \| p_k - p_k' \| \tag{7}$$

When computing the result, we ignored 40 frames(298-337) for Subject 4 where the ground truth is not available. Fig.8 and Fig.9 gives the sample frames of the experimental results. Fig.10 shows the plots of the mean errors over the sequences. We conducted a quantitative comparison of our method against the method 1: L.Sigal et al.[15]provided a baseline algorithm that used a relatively standard Bayesian framework with optimization in the form of annealed particle filtering. Method 2: Poppe et al.[16]took an example-based approach to pose recovery. This approach is somewhat person specific and does not generalize well to unseen actions. The errors of the three algorithms performed on the HumanEva-II dataset. Compared with the results from Methods 1 and 2, our method provides more accurate results. This illustrates that our method can improve the performance of other human pose estimation methods. The Table.1 shows the time cost of the our method and the Method 1. The disadvantage of our method is large amount of calculation, due to the ICP algorithm we used.

Fig. 8. The experimental results of human pose estimation on HumanEvaII with S2 subject

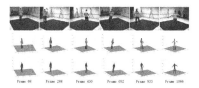

Fig. 9. The experimental results of human pose estimation on HumanEvaII with S4 subject

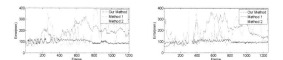

Fig. 10. Error analysis chart on S2 and S4 subject

Table 1. Running Time Comparison

Method	My method	Method 1
Time(second)	45.23	18.74

6   Conclusion

This paper proposes human motion initialization and motion tracking approach based on labelled voxels. Fisrtly we get the initial skeleton information by segmented silhouette, and then label the next frame body voxel data by tracking algorithm which includes head template fitting algorithm and body part tracking. Experimental results verify that the subsequent motion voxel data can be tracked easily and robustly precisely. Because the ICP algorithm is time costly, the deficiency of the method is that we cannot accelerate the running time, on the premise of the accuracy. And lacking of hardware equipment, we can not tackle the tracking procedure really in real time. We will focus the future work on parallel computing with our method, and make markless motion capture effectively in real time.

Acknowledgement. Project is supported by National Natural Science Foundations of China (No. 11201136). Project is supported by Guangdong Province's

Ministry of Education projects for Industry-Academy-Research cooperation (No 2011B090400002).

References

1. Mykhaylo, A., Stefan, R., Bernt, S.: Monocular 3D pose estimation and tracking by detection. In: IEEE Computer Society Conference on Computer Vision and Pattern Recognition, pp. 623–630 (2010)
2. Ankur, A., Bill, T.: Recovering 3D human pose from monocular images. IEEE Transactions on Pattern Analysis and Machine Intelligence 28, 44–58 (2006)
3. Atul, K., Niels, H., Graham, T., et al.: 3D human pose and shape estimation from multi-view imagery. In: IEEE Computer Society Conference on Computer Vision and Pattern Recognition Workshops, pp. 49–56 (2011)
4. Hofmann, M., Gavrila, D.M.: Multi-view 3D human pose estim-ation in complex environment. International Journal of Computer Vision 96, 103–124 (2012)
5. Smith, B.A.: Model Free Human Pose Estimation with Application to the Classification of Abnormal Human Movement and the Detection of Hidden Load. Virginia Polytechnic Institute and State University, Virginia (2010)
6. Caillette, F., Howard, T.: Real-Time Marklerless Human Body Tracking with Multi-View 3-D Voxel Reconstruction. In: Proc. BMVC, vol. 2, pp. 597–606 (2004)
7. Gall, J., Potthoff, J., Schnörr, C., Rosenhahn, B., Seidel, H.-P.: Interacting and annealing particle filters: Mathematics and a recipe for applications. Journal of Mathematical Imaging and Vision, 1–18 (2007)
8. Kaliamoorthi, P., Kakarala, R.: Human pose tracking by parametric annealing. In: IEEE Conference on Computer Vision and Pattern Recognition Workshop (2012)
9. Sigal, L., Isard, M., Haussecker, H., Black, M.J.: Loose-limbed People: Estimating 3D Human Pose and Motion Using Non-Parametric Belief Propagation. Internal Journal of Computer Vision 98, 15–48 (2012)
10. Zhang, Z., Seah, H.S., Quah, C.K.: Particle swarm optimization for markerless full body motion capture. In: Panigrahi, B.K., Shi, Y., Lim, M.-H. (eds.) Handbook of Swarm Intelligence. ALO, vol. 8, pp. 201–220. Springer, Heidelberg (2011)
11. Kehl, R., Van Gool, L.: Markerless tracking of complex human motions from multiple views. Computer Vision and Image Understanding 104, 190–209 (2006)
12. Shen, J.-F., Yang, W.-M., Liao, Q.-M.: Multiview human pose estimation with unconstrained motions. Pattern Recognition Letters 32, 2025–2035 (2011)
13. Zhang, Z.Y.: A flexible new technique for camera calibration. IEEE Transactions on Pattern Analysis and Machine Intelligence 22, 1330–1334 (1998)
14. Cheung, K.M., Kanade, T., Bouguet, J.-Y., Holler, M.: A Real-Time System for robust 3D voxel reconstruction of human motions. In: CVPR, vol. 2, pp. 714–720 (2000)
15. Sigal, L., Balan, A.O., Black, M.J.: HumanEva: Synchronized video and motion capture dataset and baseline algorithm for evaluation of articulated human motion. International Journal of Computer Vision 87, 4–27 (2010)
16. Poppe, R.: Evaluating example-based pose estimation: Experiments on the HumanEva sets. In: CVPR EhuM2: 2nd Workshop on Evaluation of Articulated Human Moition and Pose Estimation (2007)

Autonomous Robot Navigation: Path Planning on a Detail-Preserving Reduced-Complexity Representation of 3D Point Clouds

Rohit Sant, Ninad Kulkarni, Ainesh Bakshi, Salil Kapur, and Kratarth Goel

BITS-Pilani, K.K. Birla Goa Campus, Goa, India
{rhsant,ninadk1092,aineshbakshi,salilkapur93,
kratarthgoel}@gmail.com

Abstract. Determination of a collision free, optimal path achieved by performing complex computations on an accurate representation of the terrain, is essential to the success of autonomous navigation systems. This paper defines and builds upon a technique – Spatially Important Point (SIP) Identification – for reducing the inherent complexity of range data without discarding any essential information. The SIP representation makes onboard autonomous navigation a viable option, since space and time complexity is greatly reduced. A cost based, dynamic navigation analysis is then performed using only the SIPs which culminates into a new time and space efficient Path Planning technique. The terrain is also retained in the form of a graph, with each branch of every node encountered, indexed in a priority sequence given by its cumulative cost. Experiments show the entire dataflow, from input data to path planning, being done in less than 700ms on a modern computer on datasets typically having 10^6 points.

Keywords: Autonomous navigation, path planning, range data, dynamic programming, spatially important points.

1 Introduction

Autonomous navigation on partially unknown terrains is a very popular problem statement in the field of robotics. Representation of a terrain in the robots configuration space is intricately related to deliberative path planning algorithms. Terrain can be represented in great detail with modern sensors, but the computational cost associated with real-time navigation on such terrain is often too much for onboard processing. It is with this background and the subsequent motivation that we propose an integrated approach towards terrain representation and path planning. In our technique for terrain data representation we work towards reducing its complexity while preserving the powerful nature of geometric 3D Models of the scene. We detect points essential to the representation of the terrain and refer to them as Spatially Important Points (SIPs). This is done by comparing 'importance' values of each point to those in its neighborhood and also to a template. This algorithm ensures retention of essential features which results in detail preserving, vastly compressed datasets which are easily reconstructable by simple linear interpolation. Our customized Navigation

M. Chen, B. Leibe, and B. Neumann (Eds.): ICVS 2013, LNCS 7963, pp. 173–182, 2013.
© Springer-Verlag Berlin Heidelberg 2013

Analysis works with the minimal terrain representation, forming clusters which are ascertained to be both absolutely and relatively navigable subject to mechanical and topological constraints as well as to the current state of the robot. Finally, it performs a modular cost based path planning implementation to obtain an optimal path on the same.

The organization of the paper is as follows: Section (2) describes related work in the field of autonomous navigation, Section (3) describes, in detail, the working of our Spatially Important Point algorithm, Reconstruction and Path Planning and their implementation is discussed. Results are tabulated in Section (4) and Section (5) concludes the paper.

2   Review of Existing Techniques

Reduced-complexity representation of 3D data is an implicit requirement for almost all research concerning 3D range data. Early work, for example that by Martin et al. [5] uses a median value to represent each 3D grid in an octree. Though this reduces complexity, it results in indiscriminate loss of detail. A variation on the same theme by Lee et al. [6] incorporates non-uniform grids, but the results still suffer due to the downsampling technique. A technique described in [3] uses multiple scans to identify redundancy, but this adds an unwanted restriction on the input and severely limits its usefulness in situations where multiple scans cannot be obtained. Moenning and Dodgson [4] have a different motivation; in context of our target, our results overshadow theirs. A notable implementation can be seen in [7], in which the authors approach this problem using curvature.

Since this is usually an interim step in a larger problem statement, most researchers do not bother with operating on raw data, preferring to use clustering [2], [13] usually with a k-nearest neighbors approach.

Path Planning has been studied continuously from the 1970's leading to extensive research in the field. Configuration Space approach originates in the work of Lorenzo-Perez [8] and underlies most Path Planning research. Brooks's planner [9] decomposes the configuration space into a graph of free, blocked, and mixed cuboids. Takahashi and Schilling [16] plan for a rectangular robot with polygonal obstacles via heuristic search of the generalized Voronoi diagram. Heuristic searches will try to find any path, but will do so faster than blind search [10]. This has led to a range of heuristic algorithms being adopted by or developed for autonomous navigation, such as A*, Dijkstra's, D* and D* Lite [9], [10]. Best first search algorithms such as these work with numerous types of configuration spaces to find the optimal path yet does not localize the effect of obstacles in the representation. Probabilistic algorithms such as artificial potential field algorithm and road map algorithms, modified A* search algorithm, and genetic algorithms are also used yet they are plagued by local minima problems a work around to which has been given by Hussein [9].

Like existing techniques Nashashibi [11], we approach 3D terrain representation and subsequent path planning as a composite problem statement.

2.1   Our Contribution

We develop a completely new technique for autonomous navigation starting from basic geometry, which enables our algorithm to achieve better efficiency, due to its specialized nature. With our reconstruction technique we demonstrate that our algorithm's low-complexity range data representation is accurate. We introduce the concepts of the dichotomy of navigability (relative and absolute), as also the technique of base detection. All these techniques are then used in an integrated manner to carry out a fast, structured navigation which uses dynamic programming and a graph storage format for path planning. The computations saved by our terrain representation [1] and the on-demand nature of our path planning technique provides a unique and useful solution to the problem statement. The technique is completely portable, and may be implemented on any robot equipped with a laser rangefinder.

3   Algorithm Description

The flowchart shown here gives a basic block diagram of our technique in full. Each component is subsequently explained in detail.

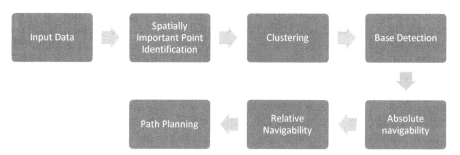

Fig. 1. Workflow of the technique described in the paper

3.1   Overview of Spatially Important Point Technique

An in-depth discussion on the Spatially Important Point Technique can be found in our supplementary material [1]. We summarize it here.

A Spatially Important Point, as defined by us, is a point where the terrain changes appreciably. The Spatially Important Point Technique finds points of significance in a terrain by carrying out a sort based on importance, where the importance function f is defined as in equation (1) in [1].

The defining characteristic of this function is that it identically equals zero for any consecutive point-pair on a flat terrain. Hence deviations of f from zero provide a good measure of the absolute change in the terrain. Comparisons with neighboring values of f is a good way of judging the relative change in the terrain. Using these concepts, equations (2-5) in [1] describe the procedure of identifying SIPs.

We discard everything but the Spatially Important Points got from the above procedure. All points which lie between two such consecutive constant-elevation Spatially Important Points can be regenerated by a linear interpolation between the said Spatially Important Points, thus eliminating the need to store them explicitly. We therefore hypothesize that a representation of the terrain by its Spatially Important Points is a complete representation. We hereon refer to this technique as Spatially Important Point Representation (SIPR). Our hypothesis is tested using the reconstruction technique which is built around linear interpolation; results can be seen in [1].

Unlike [12], [4], [5] and [6] which build upon more expensive constructs like meshes, grids, triangulations and /or expensive post-processing using ICP [3], we develop a completely new technique starting from basic geometry and build up on it. Our algorithm achieves better efficiency, due to its specialized nature. To the best of our knowledge, our algorithm for low-complexity range data representation does indeed provide a unique and useful solution for detail preserving reduction of point data – thus removing the final drawback of range data.

3.2   Building on SIPR – The Navigation Algorithm

The output of SIPR is still a point cloud consisting of raw points belonging to the original dataset, with no aberrations. On this point cloud we perform mild clustering using the DBSCAN clustering algorithm. A cluster is a collection of Spatially Important Points belonging to the same geometric or topological feature. It is important because it imparts strong connectivity to the SIPs. We then perform a two-step navigability analysis on these clusters and retain those which are traversable given inherent mechanical constraints on the robot. The Navigation analysis initially marks out regions of the dataset which are absolutely non-navigable regardless of the position, orientation and state of the robot. The output of this stage is a portion of the dataset which is evaluated for navigability based on the current state of the robot. Novel procedures such as Base Detection and Cross Cluster Planing are used to determine vital distance and slope parameters. Our algorithm integrates path planning with this navigability analysis thereby greatly reducing the number of computations. We finally take a cost based approach to choose the best available path and retain a graph of all nodes previously visited. We define separate costs for separate outcomes, and the final composite cost can be chosen in accordance with the purpose of the navigation, which is a highlight of the modularity of this algorithm.

Clustering. Clusters are obtained by using the DBSCAN [14] algorithm while preserving a bias for obtaining smaller cluster size. The basis for this is averting misclassification of points into clusters to which they do not inherently belong.

Base Detection. Since the SIPR algorithm removes all regularity, the clusters obtained must be interpreted carefully- a cluster implies irregularity in the terrain and the robot must travel in the intervening region between clusters for maximum stability. The base detection algorithm finds 'ground level' points for each cluster to facilitate navigation given that all intervening spatial information between clusters has been done away with. The algorithm description is as follows:

- The centroid for each cluster is calculated using the standard centroid formula.
- The cluster is then divided into sectors of 10 degrees each, centered on the centroid, and the point with the least z coordinate is chosen in each of these sectors if one happens to exist.
- This computation is carried out for each cluster that is present thereby obtaining the base points for each cluster.

Absolute Navigability. This analysis removes all clusters that are absolutely non navigable subject to mechanical constraints of the robot. These clusters are obstacles that cannot be navigated under any actual circumstance by the robot, independent of direction of approach. The algorithm description is as follows:

- Check whether the height of a cluster, calculated by the absolute value of the maximum difference in the Z co-ordinates of the points, is less than a given height threshold. If it is, then the cluster is absolutely navigable.
- If a point is greater than the height threshold, we calculate the average of the maximum slope between all base point and this point and repeat it for all such points. If the average of all maximum slopes is greater than given slope threshold then the cluster is not navigable otherwise it is.
- All absolutely non navigable clusters are discarded while the others are retained.

Mathematical Expression:
Cluster C_j is retained

If

$$(z_{max} - z_{min}) < \tau_h \tag{1}$$

Else

$$avg(max(Sl(z', B(C_j)))) < \tau_s \tag{2}$$

Where
  z' is the z-co-ordinate for a general point belonging to cluster C_j s.t. $z' > \tau_h$
  $Sl(a, b))$ denotes the slope between points a and b measured w.r.t. the XY plane
  $B(C_j)$ denotes the set of base points of cluster C_j
  τ_h denotes the height threshold
  τ_s denotes the slope threshold

Relative Navigability. Relative Navigability analysis is done on clusters retained after absolute navigability analysis. It proposes a technique to perform the reachability analysis for each cluster in the dataset. Reachability analysis ranks all clusters, found in a fixed radius search around a given cluster, in accordance with their reachability index.

- The reachability index of a neighbor of a given cluster is calculated whereby two parameters are taken into consideration: distance and slope.

- The minimum distance parameter $\mathcal{D}$ is obtained by selecting each base point of the given cluster and calculating the minimum Euclidian distance to all base points of the neighboring cluster.
- In a similar manner, the slope parameter $\mathcal{S}$ is obtained by calculating the average of the maximum slope between a set of all base points of the given cluster to those of the neighboring cluster. Mathematical expression:

$$\forall\, P_i \in \mathcal{B}(\mathbb{C}_r) \text{ and } \forall\, Q_k \in \mathcal{B}(\mathbb{C}_s), \tag{3}$$

$$\mathcal{D}(\mathbb{C}_r, \mathbb{C}_s) = min\,(d(P_i, Q_k)) \tag{4}$$

$$\mathcal{S}(\mathbb{C}_r, \mathbb{C}_s) = avg\big(ma\,x\big(Sl(P_i, Q_k)\big)\big) \tag{5}$$

Where
$B(\mathcal{C}_j)$ denotes the set of base points of cluster $\mathcal{C}_j$
$Sl(a, b))$ denotes the slope between points a and b measured w.r.t. the XY plane
$d(a, b)$ denotes the Euclidean distance between points a and b

Path Planning. This section amalgamates two concepts namely region growing and path planning into one. These regions are representative of the traversable path on a macro level. The exact traversable path can determined by performing a simple Voronoi path detection algorithm on the regions that are grown. Since we use a cost based approach, we begin by defining the various costs.

The costs, as defined by us are navigability cost, direction cost and destination cost.

Navigability Cost. $(\mathcal{C}_N)$ This cost is determined by multiplying the distance and slope parameters. This is because both contribute equally to reach a subsequent cluster and large increase in either one would increase mechanical effort by the same factor.

Direction Cost. $(\mathcal{C}_D)$ Direction Cost is defined as the dot product of the vector joining current cluster centroid to the subsequent cluster centroid and the vector joining current cluster centroid and destination cluster centroid. A weighted average of these two costs is then taken and to it we add the destination cost.

Destination Cost. $(\mathcal{C}_F)$ It is defined as the Euclidian distance between the current cluster centroid and destination cluster centroid, thus forming a cumulative cost.

Cumulative Cost. $(\mathcal{C}_T)$ The weighted sum of the above costs is the cumulative cost given as

$$\mathcal{C}_T = a_1.\mathcal{C}_N + a_2.\mathcal{C}_D + a_3.\mathcal{C}_F \tag{6}$$

The constants a_1 and a_2 are chosen according to the purpose of the navigation. a_3 is chosen for scaling purposes.

Each cluster can now be considered as a node in a graph and paths connecting it to its neighboring clusters as its branches.

Starting from the current position of the robot, which we consider as the starting node, regions are grown on the basis of evaluating all branches, each of which have a cumulative cost (heuristically defined) assigned to them. From here on the words cluster and node will be used interchangeably. The algorithm description is as follows:

- Starting with the initial position, all clusters in the reachability index of the current cluster are considered by sorting the distance array. If the distance parameter of the neighboring cluster is greater than bot size it checks the slope parameter and finally ranks according to the product of the distance parameter $\mathcal{D}$ and the slope parameter $\mathcal{S}$ each cluster. This is to provide equal importance to both the parameters.
- The most favorable branch to the subsequent node from the current node is chosen based on the least cumulative cost and added to the optimum path. All other branches of the current node are sorted based on the same cost and are retained.
- Repeated recursively in order to get to the lowest cost node while continuously checking whether the subsequent node already exists in the optimum path. If it does, then this node is called a blacklist node, to which the robot doesn't traverse again as it would get stuck in a continuous loop.
- In the case where all subsequent nodes to a current node have already been black listed, it has to retrace its path to the previous node in the optimal path.
- Terminating condition is to reach the target node as set initially.

4   Results

The algorithm was applied on a number of datasets, and the entire flow for a single dataset has been tabulated below. We deal with an input terrain represented as a point cloud in 3D. For the purposes of this research, we used the Canadian Planetary Emulation Terrain 3D Mapping Dataset [5]. This data is represented as co-ordinates on a spherical (Range, Elevation, Azimuth) system. All images are screenshots of point clouds viewed in the PCD viewer, part of Point Cloud Library [15].

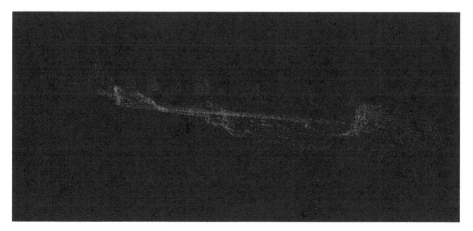

Fig. 2. A side view of a terrain intended to showcase the heights of the clusters rejected (in blue) by the absolute navigability algorithm

4.1   Absolute Navigability

Figures 2 and 3 show the results of absolute navigability on a terrain, with segments
in blue indicating absolutely non-navigable sections of the terrain. The algorithm does
a good job of picking out parts of the terrain which cannot be scaled by a typical hex-
apod (the dimensions of the robot determine the limits of absolute navigability). Trees
and large contours are well left out.

Since our clustering is very light, it is possible that a single feature gets broken into
multiple small clusters which may individually be absolutely navigable. However our
treatment of relative navigability ensures these clusters are never chosen for traversal.

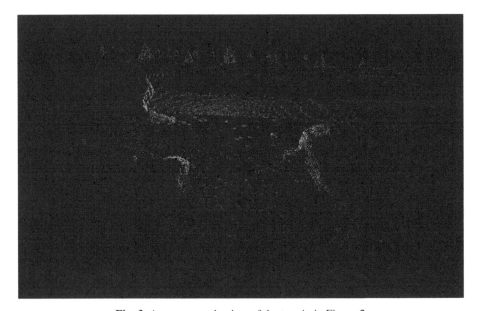

Fig. 3. A reverse angle view of the terrain in Figure 2

4.2   Path Planning

This image (Figure 4) is the final path generated by our algorithm with $a_1 = 100$ and
$a_2 = 800$. The destination cost coefficient a_3 was set to -10, and appropriate
scaling was done on the costs to bring them to the same order of magnitude. The blue
pixels indicate the original terrain, the red pixels denote the Spatially Important Points
and the white line corresponds to the path that will be traversed. (The white line
actually merely indicates the clusters around which the path is to be planned. The
actual step-by-step path can be found by further analysis using these clsuters as
obstacles between which Voronoi regions may be found.)

The costs chosen above correspond to a real-world scenario for a robot that need
not map and need not carry payloads – the objective being reaching the destination in
a short path. . The high contribution of the navigability ensures that the path taken by

the robot does not correspond to a difficult to traverse path; we can argue that this sort of value will be permissible, given that the robot will already have removed the non-navigable regions through its absolute and relative navigability analyses.

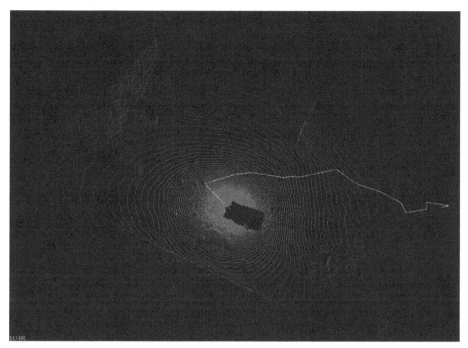

Fig. 4. Output image showing the final path (in white) overlaid on the dataset (blue) and its SIPs (red)

5   Conclusions and Future Work

The navigation algorithm described in this paper, incorporating Spatially Important Point Identification (SIPI) is a tailored and fundamentally strong approach towards a grassroots path planning algorithm. The algorithm has been broken down into stages and explained through this paper, and results at the outputs of various blocks in the workflow have been shown for one terrain.

The applications of this algorithm are immediate in the fields of robotic rescue, reconnaissance, mapping and exploration. It is a complete, self-sufficient system that has been built from the ground up, with integrated systems from the sensor inputs stage to the final navigation stage. It hence achieves the kind of efficiency that non-native systems cannot achieve.

As future work, the authors have laid the foundations for a machine learning module that seamlessly integrates with the path planning module, creating an efficient robot that can truly autonomously navigate a terrain, and continue to learn while on the job.

References

1. Sant, R., Goel, K., Kulkarni, N., Bakshi, A., Kapur, S.: Spatially Important Point Identification: A New Technique for Detail-Preserving Reduced-Complexity Representation of 3D Point Clouds (March 22, 2013), Retrieved from Google Drive, http://goo.gl/gUGgJ

2. Zhao, Y., He, M., Zhao, H., Davoine, F., Zha, H.: Computing Object-based Saliency in Urban Scenes Using Laser Sensing. In: International Conference on Robotics and Automation, pp. 4436–4443. IEEE, Saint Paul (2012)

3. Swadzba, A., Vollmer, A., Hanheide, M., Wachsmuth, S.: Reducing noise and redundancy in registered range data for planar surface extraction. In: 19th International Conference on Pattern Recognition, pp. 1–4. IEEE, Tampa (2008)

4. Moenning, C., Dodgson, N.A.: A New Point Cloud Simplification Algorithm. In: Proceedings of 3rd IASTED Conference on Visualization, Imaging and Image Processing, pp. 1027–1033. IASTED, Benalmádena (2003)

5. Tong, C., Gingras, D., Larose, K., Barfoot, T.D., Dupuis, E.: The Canadian Planetary Emulation Terrain 3D Mapping Dataset. International Journal of Robotics Research (IJRR) (2012)

6. Lee, K.H., Woo, H., Suk, T.: Data Reduction Methods for Reverse Engineering. Int. J. Adv. Manuf. Technol., 735–743 (2001)

7. Song, W., Cai, S., Yang, B., Cui, W., Wang, Y.: A Reduction Method of Three-Dimensional Point Cloud. In: 2nd International Conference on Biomedical Engineering and Informatics, pp. 1–4. IEEE, Tianjin (2009)

8. Brooks, R.A., Lorenzo-Perez, T.: A subdivision algorithm in configuration space for find-path with rotation. IEEE Transactions on Systems, Man and Cybernetics SMC-15(2), 225–233 (1985)

9. Jensen, R.M., Bryant, R.E., Veloso, M.M.: SetA*: An efficient BDD-based heuristic search algorithm. Tech. rep., Computer Science Department, Carnegie Mellon University, 5000 Forbes Ave, Pittsburgh, PA (August 2002)

10. Beginners guide to pathfinding algorithms, http://aidepot.com/Tutorial/PathFinding.html (visited on September 3, 2006)

11. Nashashibi, F., Fillatreau, P., Dacre-Wright, B., Simeon, T.: 3-D autonomous navigation in a natural environment. In: Proceedings of the 1994 IEEE International Conference on Robotics and Automation, May 8-13, vol. 1, pp. 433–439 (1994)

12. Moorthy, I., Millert, J.R., Hut, B., Berni, J.A., Zareo-Tejada, P.J., Lit, Q.: Extracting tree crown properties from ground-based scanning laser data. In: IEEE International Geoscience and Remote Sensing Symposium, pp. 2830–2832. IEEE, Barcelona (2007)

13. Zhao, H., Liu, Y., Zhu, X., Zhao, Y., Zha, H.: Scene Understanding in a Large Dynamic Environment through Laser-Based Sensing. In: International Conference on Robotics and Automation, pp. 127–133. IEEE, Anchorage (2010)

14. Ester, M., Kriegel, H.-P., Sander, J., Xu, X.: A Density-Based Algorithm for Discovering Clusters in Large Spatial Databases with Noise. In: 2nd ACM International Conference on Knowledge Discovery and Data Mining (KDD), pp. 226–231. ACM, Portland (1996)

15. Rusu, R.B., Cousins, S.: 3D is here: Point Cloud Library (PCL). In: 2011 IEEE International Conference on Robotics and Automation (ICRA), pp. 1–4. IEEE, Shanghai (2011)

16. Takahashi, O., Schilling, J.: Motion planning in a plane using generalized Voronoi diagrams. IEEE Transactions on Robotics and Automation 5(2), 143–150 (1989)

High Frame Rate Egomotion Estimation

Natesh Srinivasan, Richard Roberts, and Frank Dellaert

Georgia Institute of Technology

Abstract. In this paper, we present an algorithm for doing high frame rate egomotion estimation. We achieve this by using a *basis flow model,* along with a novel inference algorithm, that uses spatio-temporal gradients, foregoing the computation of the slow and noisy optical flow. The inherent linearity in our model allows us to achieve fine grained parallelism. We demonstrate this by running our algorithm on GPUs to achieve egomotion estimation at $120Hz$.

Image motion is tightly coupled with the camera egomotion and depth of the scene. Hence, we validate our approach by using the egomotion estimate to compute the depth of a static scene. Our applications are aimed towards autonomous navigation scenarios where, it is required to have a quick estimate of the state of the vehicle, while freeing up computation time for higher level vision tasks.

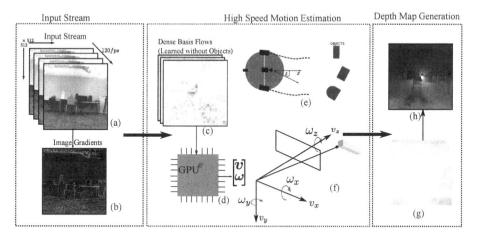

Fig. 1. (a) Input Stream from a high frame rate camera (b) Spatio-temporal gradients as an RGB image, r- $\mathcal{D}^x$, g-$\mathcal{D}^y$, b-$\mathcal{D}^t$. (c) Learned Dense basis flows corresponding to pitch, yaw and forward motion (e) Platform showing typical motion during autonomous navigation (f) Estimated translational and rotational velocity (g) Recovered translational flow (h) Depth map of the scene.

M. Chen, B. Leibe, and B. Neumann (Eds.): ICVS 2013, LNCS 7963, pp. 183–192, 2013.
© Springer-Verlag Berlin Heidelberg 2013

1   Introduction

As high frame rate cameras are becoming commodity hardware, they may play a very important role in the future of vision algorithms. This is because of the several obvious benefits [6] that it offers over its lower frame rate counterparts such as reduced motion blur, smaller inter-frame baseline, etc. However, these cameras also pose different challenges that necessitate developing new models while taking a close look at the underlying imaging process. This paper develops one such model and demonstrates its application to robot egomotion estimation.

In a high frame rate setting, a vision-only solution to egomotion estimation is advantageous as compared to the traditional way of doing egomotion estimation by fusing IMUs (Inertial Measurement Units) and cameras. This is because, from a system standpoint, it is simpler to deal with a single sensor due to fewer integration and synchronization issues. Approaches that fuse multiple sensors [3] works well in a low frame rate setting, however this might be superfluous when using high frame rate cameras. State estimates from high speed cameras are more accurate because they have more measurements for the same trajectory, reducing the dependency on IMUs for high frequency state estimates.

The primary objective of this paper is to develop and evaluate a fast egomotion estimation method which run upwards of $120Hz$. This is possible because of the small inter-frame displacements and brightness variations across images. As a result, *continuous time models*, such as the well known constant brightness model [8] are a near exact representation of the underlying imaging process. These models enable us to develop closed form analytic expression for the unknown egomotion that can be computed in a single step. In contrast, models that rely on image warping or feature tracking require multiple iterations of non-linear estimation to converge to the correct solution.

The first contribution of this paper is to exploit the idea of *Basis Flows* in a continuous time model to compute egomotion directly from image gradients. We take a two-tiered approach, where a slower learning algorithm learns a mapping from egomotion to optic flow by using a dense version of the Basis Flow model developed by Roberts et al. [14]. However, rather than using sparse flow as in that paper, we develop a fully dense approach using spatio-temporal gradients.

A significant advantage of using learned basis flows is that they are independent of camera calibration. In fact, such an approach is not restricted to using a projective camera model at all. The trade-off is that, while rotational basis flows are scene independent, translational basis flows depend on the typical scene structure [14].

The second contribution of this paper is to rapidly estimate the motion and the depth map of a rigid scene, at better-than-framerate operation, using a consumer-grade graphics processing unit (GPU). This is possible because the bulk of the arithmetic to solve our linear model amounts to per-pixel operations. In the depth estimation stage, we reuse the basis flow model to first obtain the optical flow corresponding to translational motion. We then exploit the linearity that exists between the translational flow and inverse-depth to estimate the depth map in a single step. We further use a Kalman filter model to incrementally refine our estimate of depth map over time.

This work was developed to serve as a harness to explore the idea of mental rotations in robot navigation. The depth maps obtained from this paper serve as a quasi-instantaneous snapshot of the environment that enable the robot to reach a goal location (an x, y, z co-ordinate location) by iteratively aligning itself with an abstract representation of the goal state. A similar approach to navigation is believed to exist among primates [2]. However, the details of this work is beyond the scope of this paper and we will address this in a subsequent paper.

2   Related Work

A brief survey on egomotion estimation methods starts with the works of Gibson. This was followed by a series of methods developed during the 80s and 90s. They are mostly classified based on the constraints and the underlying optimization techniques used to solve them. The constrains can either be *differential* epipolar [11], which map the 3D velocity of a point in the real world onto a 2D velocity vector in the image plane, or they can be *discrete* epipolar [10], which map a 3D rigid egomotion between views onto the corresponding 2D image points in each view. A variety of optimization techniques have been developed using these two fundamental constraints. These techniques attempt to solve for the egomotion quickly and robustly, a challenging task due to the non-linear relationship between depth, camera motion, and optical flow. Heeger et al. [7] solve this by sampling possible translations from a unit sphere and then deriving an equation that is linear in the inverse depth and the rotational velocity. Bruss and Horn [4] directly use the bi-linear constraint that exists between the depth and the translational velocity. Other approaches include the use of motion parallax [13] and the epipolar geometry constraints [10,11].

However, in most of these methods, estimation of either optical flow or feature correspondences is an intermediate step. This can be noisy and slow because of wrong feature matches and high-dimensional search spaces. This led to the advent of a class of methods called the direct methods, [9]. In these methods, the optical flow is treated as a hidden variable and camera motion is directly estimated using only image intensity gradients. The estimation is thus reduced to at most 6 parameters with each pixel providing a single constraint, resulting in a highly-overdetermined system. A more detailed analysis on the current state of the art on egomotion estimation can be found in the works of Florian et al. [5].

3   Approach

In this section, we will briefly revisit the basis flow model described in [14] (Sec 3.1), then derive a closed form expression for estimating egomotion (Sec 3.2). We will then show how we can use this egomotion to compute scene depth (Sec 3.3).

3.1   Basis Flows

Basis flows are a powerful model that represent a linear relationship between optical flow and camera motion. They are a learned mapping that is derived by exploiting the following bi-linear relationship that exists between camera motion, $(\mathbf{v}, \omega)$, inverse depth, ρ_i and the optic flow, $u_i = \begin{pmatrix} u_{xi} & u_{yi} \end{pmatrix}^T$ at the ith pixel

$$u_i = \rho_i A_i \boldsymbol{v} + B_i \boldsymbol{\omega} \tag{1}$$

where $\mathbf{v} = \begin{pmatrix} v_x & v_y & v_z \end{pmatrix}^T$ is the translational component of egomotion and $\omega = \begin{pmatrix} \omega_x & \omega_y & \omega_z \end{pmatrix}^T$ is the rotational component. $A_i \in \mathcal{R}^{2\times3}$ and, $B_i \in \mathcal{R}^{2\times3}$ are matrices that depend on the camera parameters and pixel co-ordinates. This idea was first observed by Longuet et al. [11,10] who called it a differential epipolar constraint to distinguish from the discrete epipolar case.

Roberts et al. [14] developed a calibration-free, probabilistic version of this idea by making certain simplifying assumptions about depth, namely approximate constancy per-pixel over time. This simplifies Eq 1 to

$$u_i = W_i \begin{pmatrix} \mathbf{v} \\ \omega \end{pmatrix} \tag{2}$$

where the columns of W_i are the learned basis flows. This method also works for non-projective camera models as discussed in [14].

Basis flows have several interesting and intuitive properties and afford a fine-grained parallelism in the computation of egomotion. During the inference phase, Roberts et al. use a sparse optical flow as measurements from which to compute egomotion. In this paper we take an alternate approach, which leverages high frame-rate, using image gradients.

3.2   Gradient-Based Inference

In this section we develop a probabilistic model for estimating egomotion directly from image gradients. This is the key contribution of this paper which enables us to leverage the computational power of GPUs to estimate egomotion.

In a probabilistic sense, the computation of egomotion is the maximization of the posterior probability of egomotion, $y_t = (\mathbf{v_t}, \omega_t)$ given the image gradients, $Z_t = \{\mathcal{D}_t^{\mathbf{x}}, \mathcal{D}_t^{\mathbf{t}}\}^1$ and the basis flow, W at time, t

$$\hat{y}_t = \arg\max_{y_t} p\left(y_t | Z_t, W\right). \tag{3}$$

Rewriting this as a product of the measurement likelihood and prior and using the independence between the basis flows, W, and the egomotion, y_t, we get

$$\hat{y}_t = \arg\max_{y_t} \mathcal{L}\left(\mathcal{D}_t^{\mathbf{t}} | \mathcal{D}_t^{\mathbf{x}}, y_t, W\right) p\left(y_t\right). \tag{4}$$

---

[1] $\mathcal{D}^{\mathbf{x}} \in \mathcal{R}^{1\times2}$ and $\mathcal{D}^{\mathbf{t}} \in \mathcal{R}$ represent the spatial and temporal gradients.

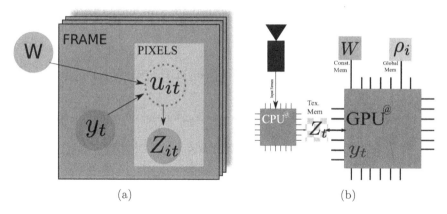

Fig. 2. (a) Bayes-Net Representation of our generative model for pixel i , showing the relation between the basis flow, W, image gradients, Z_i, the camera egomotion, y_t and the optical flow, u_i (b) Memory distribution of the GPU implementation of our model

We use $\mathcal{L}(\cdot)$ to represent the likelihood (unnormalized probability) to distinguish it from a probability, $p(\cdot)$. Eq. 4 states that the temporal gradient, $\mathcal{D}_t^t$ can be independently computed given the spatial gradient, $\mathcal{D}_t^x$, camera egomotion, y_t and the basis flows, W.

The basis flow model given in Eq. 2 provides us with a way to compute the flow, u_t, given the egomotion, y_t However, the model does not provide an explicit relationship between the image gradients, Z_t and egomotion, y_t. In order to evaluate Eq. 4, we exploit the brightness constancy assumption [8] stated as

$$\mathcal{D}_{ti}^t + \mathcal{D}_{ti}^x u_{ti} = 0 \tag{5}$$

where the subscript i corresponds to the ith pixel. This provides us with a additional constraint between the flow, u_{ti} and the image gradients $Z_{ti} = \{\mathcal{D}_{ti}^t, \mathcal{D}_{ti}^x\}$.

An important observation at this point is that the temporal gradient at each pixel, $\mathcal{D}_{ti}^t$ is independent of every other pixel, **iff** we are given the spatial gradient, $\mathcal{D}_{ti}^x$ at that pixel[2]. This allows us to re-write Eq. 4 as a per-pixel product given by

$$\hat{y}_t = \arg\max_{y_t} p(y_t) \prod_i \mathcal{L}\left(\mathcal{D}_{ti}^t | \mathcal{D}_{ti}^x, y_t, W_i\right) \tag{6}$$

where the subscript i refers to the ith pixel.

The Bayes' net representation of our model is shown in Fig. 2a. It tells us that the hidden flow term u_{ti}, provides a link between the egomotion, y_t and the image gradients, Z_{it}. This suggests that we can factorize the measurement likelihood (Eq. 4) as

$$\mathcal{L}\left(\mathcal{D}_{ti}^t | \mathcal{D}_{ti}^x, y_t, W_i\right) = \mathcal{L}\left(\mathcal{D}_{ti}^t | \mathcal{D}_{ti}^x, u_{ti}\right) \mathcal{L}\left(u_{ti} | y_{ti}, W_i\right) \tag{7}$$

---

[2] This is however not completely true, since the spatio-temporal Sobel kernel used in the computation of gradients induces some correlation between adjacent pixels

Since our goal is to get rid of the intermediate flow term, we compute the marginal corresponding to the joint distribution given in Eq. 7 by integrating out the hidden flow term u_{ti}

$$\arg\max_{y_t} p\left(y_t\right) \prod_i \int_{u_{ti}} \left(\mathcal{L}\left(\mathcal{D}_{ti}^{\mathbf{t}} | \mathcal{D}_{ti}^{\mathbf{x}}, u_{ti}\right) \mathcal{L}\left(u_{ti} | y_{ti}, W_i\right)\right) du_{ti}$$

which provides us with the following expression for the marginal distribution:

$$\int_{u_{ti}} \left(\mathcal{L}\left(\mathcal{D}_{ti}^{\mathbf{t}} | \mathcal{D}_{ti}^{\mathbf{x}}, u_{ti}\right) \mathcal{L}\left(u_{ti} | y_{ti}, W_i\right)\right) du_{ti} = \mathcal{L}\left(\mathcal{D}_{ti}^{\mathbf{t}} | \mathcal{D}_{ti}^{\mathbf{x}}, y_t, W_{ti}\right) \qquad (8)$$

Taking the negative log-likelihood of Eq. 8 and maximizing with respect to $y_t = (\mathbf{v}, \omega)$ gives us the following maximum likelihood estimate:

$$y_t = \left(\sum_i (1/J_{ti}^2) \left(W_i^T \left(\mathcal{D}_{ti}^{\mathbf{x}}\right)^T \mathcal{D}_{ti}^{\mathbf{x}} W_i\right)\right)^{-1} \sum_i \left((1/J_{it}^2) \mathcal{D}_{ti}^{\mathbf{x}} \mathcal{D}_{ti}^{\mathbf{t}} W_i\right)^T \qquad (9)$$

where $J_i = \left(\left(\mathcal{D}_{ti}^{\mathbf{x}}\right)^T \Sigma_{ui} \mathcal{D}_{ti}^{\mathbf{x}} + \sigma_I\right)$ where Σ_{ui} is the covariance matrix of the flow at pixel i.

Evaluation of J_{ti} is a per-pixel independent operation. $\mathcal{D}_{ti}^{\mathbf{x}}, \mathcal{D}_{ti}^{\mathbf{t}}$ can be pre-computed in parallel. Each pixel provides an completely independent constraint as detailed in the MAP estimate given in Eq. 9 .

3.3   Depth Maps

In this section we develop a Kalman filter model for computing the scene depth. The depth map is used as a qualitative measure of the accuracy of the estimated egomotion. Eq. 1 provides a bi-linear constraint between the egomotion, depth and flow at each pixel. However the problem is greatly simplified if the optical flow corresponding to **any** of the translational component of egomotion is known. This is because the following linear model exists between the forward flow, u_{ti}^f and the inverse depth ρ_i, given the forward velocity, v_t of the camera

$$u_{ti}^f = \begin{bmatrix} u_{xti}^f \\ u_{yti}^f \end{bmatrix} = \begin{bmatrix} x \\ y \end{bmatrix} \rho_i v_t + \eta \qquad (10)$$

where $\eta = \mathcal{N}\left(0, P_m\right)$ is the noise on flow. The subscript t refers to time, and the superscript f indicates that it is the forward component of flow. (x, y) are co-ordinates of pixel i.

In order to get the forward flow, u^f, we subtract the rotational component of flow, u^ω, from the total flow, u. The rotational component of flow is obtained by scaling the basis flows corresponding to rotation, W^{ω},[3] by our estimate of rotational velocity, ω.

---

[3] Note that $W = \begin{bmatrix} W^{\mathbf{v}} & W^{\omega} \end{bmatrix}$, implying that there is a basis for each component of egomotion. Ex: For 6 DOF motion, we have 6 basis flows.

Matthies et al. [12] talk about the various techniques to refine the depth map estimate using a Kalman filter. Assuming that the camera calibration is known, we get the set of equations shown in Fig. 3, borrowed from [12].

MEASUREMENT

$$d = \left(H^T P_m^{-1} H\right)^{-1} H^T P_m^{-1} u_t^f$$

$$\sigma_d^2 = \left(H^T P_m^{-1} H\right)^{-1}$$

$$H = \begin{bmatrix} x v_t \\ y v_t \end{bmatrix}$$

σ_d = MEASURED VARIANCE IN DISPARITY
p = VARIANCE OF INVERSE DEPTH
d = MEASURED DISPARITY
K = KALMAN GAIN
ρ = INVERSE DEPTH
P_m = MEASURED FLOW VARIANCE

PREDICT

$$\rho_{t+1}^- = \frac{\rho_t^+}{\alpha - T_z u_t^+}$$

$$p_{t+1}^- = (1 + \epsilon)\, p_t^+, \epsilon = 0.1$$

$$\alpha = (1 - \omega_x y + \omega_y x)$$

UPDATE

$$p_t^+ = \left(\left(p_t^-\right)^{-1} + \left(\sigma_d^2\right)^{-1}\right)^{-1}$$

$$K = \frac{p_t^+}{\sigma_d^2}$$

$$\rho_t^+ = p_t^+ \left(\frac{\rho_t^-}{p_t^-} + \frac{d}{\sigma_d^2}\right)$$

Fig. 3. Kalman Filter Equations for estimating inverse depth from the measured disparity d. The set of equations are borrowed from [12] .

4   Experimental Evaluation

Fig. 5a shows the experimental setup. The test platform is a Pioneer3 P3-DX. We use a Flea 3 - USB 3.0 high speed camera running at 512×512 resolution. The on-board computer has a Quad-Core CPU and a Nvidia Quadro K2000M GPU. The platform has 3 degrees of freedom at any time t, namely forward velocity, v_t, yaw, ω_y and pitch, ω_x (due to rough terrain). We first do a quantitative evaluation of the accuracy of the estimated egomotion and the we do a qualitative evaluation by generating depth maps.

4.1   Accuracy of Egomotion Estimation

Fig. 4 shows the accuracy of the estimated egomotion on two test datasets - (1) indoor scene and (2) outdoor scene. The learning stage is done offline and we obtain the basis flows, W at a resolution of 32×32. They are then upscaled to match the resolution of the image (512×512). The covariance term of the flow, Σ_u was assumed to be 1 and the pixel intensity variance, σ_I was assumed to be 0.1. The spatial gradients, $\mathcal{D}_x$ were computed with a 3×3 Sobel operator. The temporal gradients, $\mathcal{D}_t$ was computed by taking difference of adjacent frames after blurring by a 3×3 Gaussian kernel. The accuracy of the estimated egomotion was compared with the wheel odometry as shown in Fig. 4 (d) & (e).

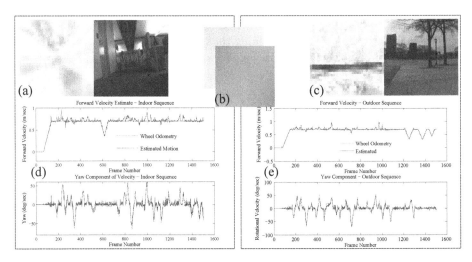

Fig. 4. (a) Learned translational basis flow [left] (color coding of flow can be found in Fig. 5b) for indoor scene [right]. (c) Learned translational basis flow [left] for outdoor scene [right]. (b) computed rotational basis flow, which is same for both sequence because it is independent of scene structure. (d) & (e) comparison of egomotion estimation with wheel odometry.

The estimated motion is quite robust for rotational components but the translational estimates incur errors when robot is undergoing rotations. This is because, rotations drastically change the heading of the camera and as a result, the scene structure. The learned translational basis do not deal well with this kind of transformation. It is also to be noted that the method described here is sensitive to passing objects, especially if they form a significant portion of the camera's field of view. However, we are currently working on a robust, outlier rejection model using the method described in [14]. The core computation time of the motion estimation for each frame was measured at $3.24\,ms$ which is much better than the required $8.33\,ms$ for an input stream of $120\,Hz$.

4.2   Application: Dense Depth Maps

We demonstrate the application of our egomotion estimation by obtaining the depth map of the scene. The pipeline for evaluating the depth map is shown in Fig. 5b. The goal is to first compute the magnitudes of the egomotion components and then estimate the depth from the translational component of flow. We use the TV-L1 dense flow [1] (Fig. 5b (i)) to compute the total flow and then use the method described in section 3.3 to subtract the rotational flow (Fig. 5b (e)). The translational flow(Fig. 5b (h)), that is obtained, is used to get a rudimentary depth map (Fig. 5b (f)) which is then refined using the Kalman filter equations to get the final depth(Fig. 5b (j)).

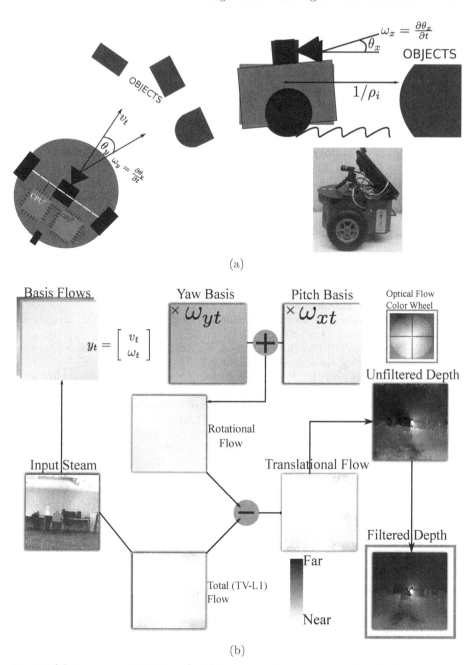

Fig. 5. (a) Experimental Setup. [Left]Diagrammatic representation of the top view, platform is directly moving toward the object with a velocity v_t and yaw, ω_{yt}. It has 3 degrees of freedom at any instant of time. [Top Right] The side view showing the pitching motion due to rough terrain. [Bottom Right] Picture of the setup.(b) Depth Map Generation Pipeline [See section 4.2]. We first computes the egomotion , y_t. Using this estimate, we then get the flow corresponding to translation. We then use this to get a rudimentary depth maps which is refined using the Kalman filter equation to get the refined depth map.

5   Conclusions and Acknowledgments

We have presented a novel, fully probabilistic model for doing egomotion estimation directly from image gradients. We have further demonstrated its applicability in the estimation of depth of a static, rigid scene. From a system level perspective we have shown that we can exploit the GPUs to achieve better-than frame rate performance. While the primary objective of the paper is to estimate motion, the end result was to obtain quick estimates of the depth of the scene.

This research is supported by the Office of Naval Research under grant #00014 − 11 − 1 − 0593. The authors would like to thank Prof. Ronald Arkin for his significant contributions to this project. We would also like to acknowledge the other student team members for their roles: Ivan Walker and Ryan Kerwin.

References

1. Wedel, A., Pock, T., Zach, C., Bischof, H., Cremers, D.: An Improved Algorithm for TV-L1 Optical Flow. In: Cremers, D., Rosenhahn, B., Yuille, A.L., Schmidt, F.R. (eds.) Statistical and Geometrical Approaches to Visual Motion Analysis. LNCS, vol. 5604, pp. 23–45. Springer, Heidelberg (2009)
2. Arkin, R.C.: The role of mental rotations in primate-inspired robot navigation. Cognitive Processing 13, 83–87 (2012)
3. Beall, C., Nguyen, T.H.D., Ok, C., Dellaert, F.: Attitude heading reference system with rotation-aiding visual landmarks (2012)
4. Bruss, A.R., Horn, B.K.P.: Passive navigation. Computer Vision, Graphics, and Image Processing 21, 3–20 (1983)
5. Florian, R., Heiko, N.: A review and evaluation of methods estimating ego-motion. Comput. Vis. Image Underst. 116(5), 606–633 (2012)
6. Handa, A., Newcombe, R.A., Angeli, A., Davison, A.J.: Real-time camera tracking: when is high frame-rate best? In: Fitzgibbon, A., Lazebnik, S., Perona, P., Sato, Y., Schmid, C. (eds.) ECCV 2012, Part VII. LNCS, vol. 7578, pp. 222–235. Springer, Heidelberg (2012)
7. Heeger, D., Jepson, A.: Subspace methods for recovering rigid motion I: Algorithm and implementation. International Journal of Computer Vision 7(2), 95–117 (1992)
8. Horn, B.K.P., Schunck, B.G.: Determining Optical Flow. Artificial Intelligence 17(1-3), 185–203 (1981)
9. Irani, M., Anandan, P.: All about direct methods (1999)
10. Longuet-Higgins, H.C.: A computer algorithm for reconstructing a scene from two projections. Nature 293, 133–135 (1981)
11. Longuet-Higgins, H.C., Prazdny, K.: The Interpretation of a Moving Retinal Image. Proceedings of the Royal Society of London. Series B, Biological Sciences (1934-1990) 208(1173), 385–397 (1980)
12. Matthies, L., Szeliski, R., Kanade, T.: Kalman filter-based algorithms for estimating depth from image sequences. International Journal of Computer Vision 3, 209–236 (1989)
13. Rieger, J.H., Lawton, D.T.: Sensor motion and relative depth from difference fields of optic flows. In: IJCAI, pp. 1027–1031 (1983)
14. Roberts, R., Potthast, C., Dellaert, F.: Learning general optical flow subspaces for egomotion estimation and detection of motion anomalies. In: IEEE Conf. on Computer Vision and Pattern Recognition (CVPR) (2009)

Is Crowdsourcing for Optical Flow Ground Truth Generation Feasible?

Axel Donath and Daniel Kondermann*

Heidelberg Collaboratory for Image Processing, IWR, University of Heidelberg,
Speyerer Strasse 6, 69115 Heidelberg, Germany
{axel.donath,daniel.kondermann}@iwr.uni-heidelberg.de
http://hci.iwr.uni-heidelberg.de

Abstract. In 2012, three new optical flow reference datasets have been published, two of them containing ground truth [1,2,3]. None of them contains ground truth for real-world, large-scale outdoor scenes with dynamically and independently moving objects. The reason is that no measurement devices exists to record such data with sufficiently high accuracy. Yet, ground truth is needed to assess the safety of e.g. driver assistance systems. To close this gap, based on existing, accurate ground truth, we analyse the performance of uninformed human motion annotators. Feature annotation bias and non-rigid motions are a major concern, limiting our results to pixel-accuracy. Our approach is the only way to create ground truth for dynamic outdoor sequences and feasible whenever pixel-accuracy is sufficient for performance analysis and piecewise rigid motions dominate the scene. Finally, we show that our approach is highly effective with respect to annotation cost per frame compared to our baseline method [4].

1 Introduction and Related Work

Ground truth generation for optical flow is a challenging task but mandatory for any advances in the field. It is also necessary for the evaluation of security-relevant applications such as driver assistance systems, medical imaging, robotics, surveillance and more.

Our aim is to find a method for generating optical flow ground truth for large-scale, dynamic outdoor scenes which was first addressed in [4]. Often, ground truth is understood as reference data with perfect accuracy. But the definition of *perfect* is solely defined by the application domain. For example, the flow vectors in the real scenes of the Middlebury flow dataset [6] are up to 1/60 px accurate with unreported error distributions. The KITTI dataset [1] can be assumed to be around 3 px accurate due to LIDAR quality which is sufficient for automotive scenarios.

Yet, the goals of ground truth generation are not only to carefully validate its **accuracy**, but also to reduce **cost** and **creation time**.

---

* We thank Daniel Scharstein for highly valuable discussions about the topic and the high-resolution Middlebury images.

M. Chen, B. Leibe, and B. Neumann (Eds.): ICVS 2013, LNCS 7963, pp. 193–202, 2013.
© Springer-Verlag Berlin Heidelberg 2013

Fig. 1. Color-coded flow (HSV) overlaid on example scene without known ground truth. *Left:* Best-performing publicly available optical flow algorithm (Classic+NL [5]) *Right:* Ground truth generated by crowdsourcing.

Three principal approaches to ground truth generation with different tradeoffs can be identified:

First, ground truth can be created by measurement setups which are known to be at least one magnitude more accurate than the method to be evaluated. A first approach was to use a high resolution camera and a hidden texture only visible in ultraviolet light [6]. Here, the dynamic motions of the scene can be measured, but the method is limited to a stop-motion approach in a lab.

Alternatively, we can resort to well-known devices known from measurement sciences. For static scenes, e.g. 3D scanners can be used to capture point clouds. These devices usually are very expensive (in the order of $50k). Yet, this approach is time-consuming and dynamic scenes still cannot be measured with sufficient accuracy. To reduce cost and increase capture speed, devices such as Microsoft Kinect can be used [3] which in turn decreases accuracy.

Second, computer graphics can generate complex, dynamic scenes. These sequences can also be systematically modified, e.g. by changing textures, exposure, light or weather. The disadvantages are that (a) the content creation (geometry, textures, materials, animations etc.) can be very time consuming and costly [2] and (b) it is unclear, whether the rendered images simulate real data well enough [7].

Third, real data can be annotated by humans. No measurement devices are used at all. This enables practitioners to record many sequences of any application domain. Semantic annotations via crowdsourcing, e.g. for object detection, are common by now. Yet, to date it is unclear how expensive, time consuming and accurate the manual labelling of optical flow fields is.

We contribute with this paper as follows. We show the first approach to create optical flow ground truth for large-scale, dynamic outdoor scenes. We analyse accuracy, bias and repeatability (precision) of optical flow data annotated by uninformed users. We study time and cost of optical flow ground truth generation per frame. We developed open source MTurk interfaces for optical flow annotation[1].

---

[1] Code and Instructions can be found at
http://hci.iwr.uni-heidelberg.de/Staff/dkonderm/MTurkAnnotation

The creation of an actual ground truth dataset consists of many more design choices which is beyond the scope of this paper. Here, we focus on the analysis of a method anyone can use to create her own ground truth in arbitrary quantities in any application domain.

Related Work. The first ground truth sequences for optical flow were the Marbled Block as well as the Yosemite sequence. These single sequences were short and of limited geometrical complexity. A more systematic approach based on synthetic data was implemented by [8], who not only created a whole set of new sequences but also published the source code of the computer graphics system used to generate the data. However, using computer graphics for ground truth was often criticised due to the limited realism of the images at this time. A seminal work in the field was the Middlebury database [6]. Here, not only ground truth was acquired for real sequences. The authors also created a benchmarking website which is still popular to date. A method for more realistic synthetic scenes was published by [9]. Most recently, a large naturalistic synthetic dataset based on open data was generated [2]. For automotive applications several datasets exist for stereo as well as for optical flow, partly synthetic and partly containing ground truth [10,1,3].

Human-assisted motion annotation was first proposed in [4]. In this tool, the first frame of an image sequence is decomposed by the user into layers or objects with a smooth flow field. The layers can then be tracked automatically to the following frames. The user can also annotate feature correspondences and choose a motion model which matches the motion of the layer best. For many sequences the tracking of the objects outlines does not work properly, especially when objects are partly occluded or the tracking is hampered by shadows or blur. In this case an extensive correction by hand is necessary by adjusting badly tracked outlines and finding suitable feature correspondences.

We build on this work by extending the freely available interface by a back end to Amazon Mechanical Turk (MTurk).

Using MTurk has become a common method to annotate image data with labels, bounding boxes, object contours and feature points; a review of these methods is not within the scope of this paper.

To the best of our knowledge, crowdsourcing has not yet been used for optical flow annotation. The closest work is [11] where the authors let users annotate feature tracks in sequences.

2   Ground Truth via Mechanical Turk

The bottlenecks of the motion annotation tools described in [4] are (a) the repeated adjustment of motion contours when tracking the annotation of the first frame fails and (b) the manual annotation of feature points to fit a motion model to each contour. For our data, we estimate about 1-2 hours for the annotation of the first frame, 2-3 hours for a careful correction of the tracking and selection of feature correspondences for *each* following frame and about 1-2 hours of selection and fine-tuning of motion models to create the flow fields from the user annotations (flow fields are created based on annotations and not on the image data). As in the authors' country of residence a student assistant costs around $20 per hour (including overhead), the amount of time spent for motion annotation directly translates into large costs per frame. Since the initial annotation and final tuning of the motion field should be carried out by trained user, we focused on a replacement for the repetitive work on each frame of the sequence.

Motion Contours. After the initial frame is annotated by a trained user, by click on a button this data is exported to MTurk. For every object and frame in the scene a Human Intelligence Task (HIT) is created with the challenge to correct the contour shapes. The associated web interface consists of two large screens: A working screen that allows adjusting, adding and removing single points of the outline and provides also a zoom function for precise working. The second screen shows the initial segmentation of the object, which serves as a guideline for the worker[2]. To enforce the modification of the outlines by the workers, we added Gaussian noise with 4 px variance to our initial segmentation. Experiments showed that this actually increases the accuracy of the worker annotations as they are no more biased towards accepting our inaccurate initial segmentation. Every outline was uploaded for correction five times.

In the first step the results are manually reviewed. This is mainly necessary to sort out outliers and assure a fair judgement of the Turker's work. Based on this review the workers where paid. In the second step the pairwise agreement between the five different contours of a single object were computed. Therefore, we introduced the ratio of the areas of the difference and union of two contour polygons as a measurement for the agreement. Finally, the two outlines with the best agreement were merged by computing the intersection. This way we obtained a final segmentation which was imported again in the motion annotation tool of [4].

Feature Correspondences. To obtain the feature correspondences we set up the following work flow: The image was chopped into small patches of size 50×50 px where we asked the worker to find corresponding points. On the first screen of the web interface the user sees such a patch of the frame and a second screen shows the same area in the following frame. The main screens of the web interface have a size of 300×300 px, so principally one could obtain feature points with a sub-pixel accuracy of $1/6$ px. Below are three magnifying screens that help the user to find the points as accurate as possible. As the shown region is large, the user can utilize high-level semantic context to find the correct correspondences. Additionally, we applied an high-pass filter to enhance structure in the test image and thus ease the locating of good feature points. A guided screencast [3] shows the web interface in action.

Afterwards, every patch with feature points was shortly reviewed by a trained user to sort out outliers. Then the feature points were assigned to the corresponding object and imported in the motion annotation tool. Single feature points

---

[2] An example video can be found at `http://www.youtube.com/watch?v=KOrn7gLjW3Q`
[3] `http://www.youtube.com/watch?v=gqqVK3RhDzM`

were sorted out again by hand to tweak the result. The optical flow was then determined following motion estimation methods in [4]. Please note, that these methods fit a flow field to the user annotations and not to the images.

3   Experiments and Results

We tested the approach on real as well as on synthetic data with known ground truth. As the accuracy of the KITTI dataset is well below the accuracy we expected to achieve with our approach, we opted for more accurate ground truth known from real and synthetic scenes from the Middlebury dataset [6] and synthetic images from the newly proposed Sintel dataset [2]. For a first detailed test we chose frame 10 and 11 of the Rubber Whale sequence [6], which has distinct objects and rather small motion. It also contains rigid as well as non-rigid motions which helps assessing the accuracy in both situations.

For the feature point annotation we asked the worker only to find eight points in each given patch. This value proved to be sufficient in early experiments, reducing the total cost of feature annotation to a minimum.

Accuracy. We carried out six complete runs on sequences with medium resolution, each time determining the resulting flow field. Table 1 shows the Average Endpoint Error (AEE) and Average Angular Error (AAE) compared with the Middlebury ground truth [6] on every run. The AEE ranges from 0.37 px to 0.79 px. The spatial error distribution is shown in Fig. 3. One can notice that the outline correction delivered in all cases good results. The objects are very accurate in the boundary regions even for more complicated outlines. The precision (repeatability) of the outlines are discussed in the paragraph *Precision*. As

Fig. 2. Outlines before (*left image*) and after (*right image*) correction by the MTurk workers. Accuracy as well as precision are in the order of less than one pixel.

can be seen in Fig. 3, the main contribution to the endpoint errors stems from bias due to bad feature correspondences. Here, in some cases entire objects are slightly shifted. For different runs this bias is very different for each object and independent of the amount of texture. This clearly shows that workers do not care too much about subpixel accuracy in their feature matches. The bias still amounts to an AEE below one pixel in all cases. Hence, this error can only be ignored if pixel-accuracy is sufficient for performance analysis.

To improve the results we chose to obtain a denser field of feature points and performed two runs where we let the patches overlap by 25 px. Again, we asked

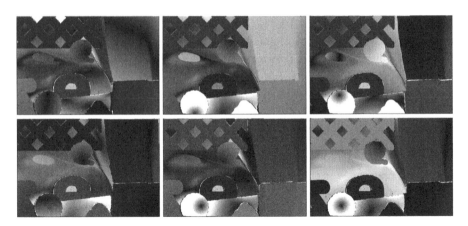

Fig. 3. Endpoint error of six different runs on the Rubber Whale sequence with non-overlapping patches. Biases significantly vary from run to run, visualizing inaccurate annotations by workers. The images are normalised to a maximal endpoint error of 2 px.

the worker to find eight points per patch. In the best run, we obtained an AEE of 0.19 px and AAE of 4.2°. This is worse by a factor of around 2 than the result obtained by [4] on the same sequence with informed users. To test the effect of uninformed users, we very carefully annotated the whole sequence ourselves with the same segmentation and reached an AEE of 0.18 px. It is most likely that we choose another, maybe unfavourable, segmentation and therefore obtained a slightly worse result.

The second run with overlapping patches resulted in an AEE of 0.38 px which is comparable to the best results with non-overlapping patches. However it is considerably better than the mean AEE (0.51 px) of the six runs with non-overlapping patches. We conclude that a higher feature density improves the results significantly. Both endpoint error images can be seen in Fig. 4. The largest deviations are in the region of the background fabric due to non-rigid motion.

To further improve the accuracy we asked the workers to annotate the high resolution images of the Rubber Whale sequence which we obtained from the authors of [6]. To obtain the feature points we had to change our approach slightly: Instead of 50×50 patches we doubled the size and used 100×100 patches. The reasons were to have a manageable number of HITs and to keep the cost in a reasonable range, as the latter increases quadratically with the size of the image. For the same reason we only asked for 4 points, and therefore paid less for each HIT. Surprisingly, the result was not as good as we expected. Again, after downsampling the flow, we achieved an AEE of 0.20 px, similar to the best result on the low resolution images. Based on the chosen feature parameters and the six times higher resolution of the test images, we expected an improvement by a factor of three. Taking a look at the endpoint error on this run (Fig. 4) one notices that the largest deviations are again in the region

Table 1. Average Endpoint Errors (AEE), Angular Errors (AAE), standard Deviation (SD), 25% and 75% quantiles of the endpoint error on the six different runs of the Rubber Whale sequence. Average errors are well below one pixel accuracy, but vary from 0.37 px to 0.79 px. The best fully automatic algorithms in the Middlebury dataset clearly outperform humans by about an order of magnitude. Yet, systematic errors such as bad motion boundaries are handled much better by humans (see discussion). Larger errors are discussed in the text.

Run	#1	#2	#3	#4	#5	#6	Run	OL #1	OL #2	HR	Dim.	Urb.	Sint.
AEE	0.37	0.79	0.51	0.37	0.47	0.63	AEE	0.19	0.38	0.20	0.86	1.13	0.46
AAE	4.7°	9.8°	10.2°	8.5°	11.4°	10.3°	AAE	4.7°	5.8°	4.6°	8.5°	8.7°	7.8°
SD	0.36	0.67	0.63	0.46	0.51	0.58	SD	0.30	0.36	0.31	0.52	1.57	0.65
A25	0.48	1.22	0.67	0.50	0.52	0.91	A25	0.23	0.50	0.24	1.12	1.47	0.49
A75	0.16	0.24	0.14	0.11	0.26	0.14	A75	0.08	0.17	0.04	0.53	0.38	0.11

of the background fabric, while the endpoint error for simple moving objects such as the yellow box, or the letter "Z" is well below 0.10 px. It seems that the non-rigidly moving fabric sets a lower limit to the overall accuracy even with non-rigid motion models. As we annotated the background as a single object, it may be more reasonable to divide it into several regions that move in a similar way. This was done in the next experiment with high resolution images (see below) with no significant improvements.

Precision. Precision is defined as the variance of the results in multiple runs of the same experiment. After sorting out outliers we computed an average outline by computing the intersection of all annotated polygons. We then determined the minimal distance from the average outline for every single polygon point of an annotated outline and computed its mean. More than 70% of all annotations differed less than 0.5 px from the average outline. For the high resolution images we also determined the variation of the corrected outlines. The result was similar to the first runs. The largest part of the outlines was corrected with a precision better than 0.5 px, yielding a precision of 0.08 px in the downsampled image respectively.

Other Sequences. We tested our approach on three more image sequences containing different challenges. The first sequence is called Dimetrodon and contains more non-rigid motion. During the initial motion boundary annotation, we divided the background fabric into regions of similar motion confined by the creases, hoping to achieve better results on regions with non-rigid motions. In contrast, the Urban 2 sequence more resembles driver assistance scenarios: It contains distinct and rather simply shaped objects but large motion, which increases the challenge of finding the right correspondences. Figure 4 summarizes the resulting endpoint errors.

For the Dimetrodon sequence we obtained an AEE of 0.86 px and AAE of 8.4°. One can notice that the error inside the dimetrodon is rather small (around 0.20 px) whereas the non-rigidly moving background shows larger deviations.

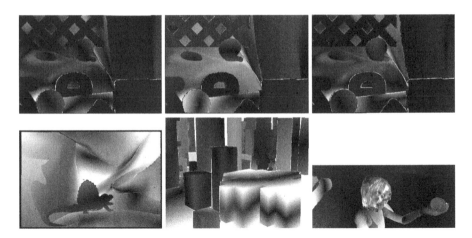

Fig. 4. *Upper row*: Endpoint errors of the Rubber Whale sequence with overlapping patches with an AEE of 0.19 px (left) and 0.38 px (middle) respectively. The difference in AEE is mainly due to the biased annotation of the non-rigidly moving cloth in the background. No significant improvement can be seen on the high res. image (right). *Lower row*: Endpoint errors on frame 10 of the Middlebury Dimetrodon (left) and Urban 2 (middle) sequence. The large endpoint error in the lower right of the Urban 2 image stems from a wrong outline (excluded from average). The AEE of the Sintel Alley 1 (right) sequence is about 1 px. All images are normalised to a maximal endpoint error of 2 px.

Hence, the fragmentation of the background fabric into several regions did not yield a significant improvement.

For the Urban 2 sequence we obtained an AEE of 1.13 px and AAE of 8.7°. The large error on this sequence is mainly due to a wrong outline in the foreground, where the right part of the large building is missing. This can be most likely explained by a user that accidentally got the same image again for correction and missed the right part of the building. In the statistics we excluded this region. Also this building shows the largest endpoint errors, because we annotated it as single object. To further increase the accuracy on could set up the different surfaces of the building as individual layers, with different depths.

As another test we asked the workers to annotate more recent test data. Therefore we chose a "clean" sequence (i.e. without motion blur) of the Sintel [2] dataset. We considered frame 18 and 19 of the Alley 1 sequence as suitable, as it includes easy distinguishable objects, like the wooden boards on the left, as well as more complex objects like the hair. We tried to set up a very detailed initial segmentation, with even the hair divided into several streaks. To reduce cost we excluded the large background region, which moves homogeneously, from the feature point annotation and focused on the foreground. Apart from that we applied the same setting with overlapping patches of size 50×50 px. The resulting AEE was around 0.5 px.

Finally, we asked for an annotation of our application scenario in driver assistance systems. We chose a scene from [3] were all publicly available optical flow methods fail completely due to motion blur, flow vectors larger than 70 px, intricate occlusion patterns and small structures. No ground truth is available for such data, but visual inspection clearly shows high quality human annotations as can be seen in Fig. 1. Large motions and flow boundaries have high quality even in difficult situations. Considering our reference results with known ground truth and thereof especially the Urban 2 sequence, we estimate the endpoint error to be in the order of one pixel.

Cost And Time Effort. A trained user first creates an initial segmentation and afterwards reviews results and creates the flow field. All other tasks are carried out by workers. The annotation of the first frame of an image sequence takes us about $1 - 2$ hours for rather simple sequences such as Rubber Whale, until several hours for more complicated image sequences such as Sintel. The main challenge is to choose a trade-off between what is a region of similar motion and what is a region that can easily be recognised. This choice strongly depends on the number, complexity and rigidity of the objects.

The main part of the correction by the MTurk workers is usually done within $1-2$ days, depending on how well the HITs are paid. The workers spent between $2-4$ minutes per HIT. A run on a low resolution image requires about 500 HITs for outline correction and feature points together. High resolution images require up to 1000 HITs. For the review process we developed a simple review tool which allows rejecting or approving the result within seconds. This takes about 10 minutes per 200 HITs. Computing the flow using the motion annotation tool of [4] also takes us $1 - 2$ hours, depending on the number of objects and amount of tweaking.

For the low resolution (584×388 px) Rubber Whale experiment we spend $\approx \$3.50$/frame for the outline correction and $\approx \$10$/frame for the feature points. For the high resolution (3504×2336 px) Rubber Whale experiment we spent $\approx \$9$ /frame for the outline correction and $\approx \$20$/frame for the feature points. The outline correction of the Sintel dataset (1024×436 px) cost $\approx \$17$/frame, as it included many more objects. For the feature points we paid $\approx \$25$/frame. As that the outline correction and finding of feature points is exclusively done by MTurk workers, we save around 40% compared to paying a student. The time saving effect increases with the number of frames that are being corrected, as many Turkers work in parallel.

4   Conclusion and Future Research

We studied accuracy, precision and cost of optical flow ground truth generation via Amazon Mechanical Turk. In automotive systems accuracies of one to three pixel are acceptable[1]. Our results are around twice as accurate than the ground truth in the KITTI database. Hence, our approach can be used to generate ground truth for this application. An additional advantage of our approach is that we can also create ground truth for dynamically moving objects in unconstrained scenes, which cannot be achieved by any other method. Still, the results are not good enough for comparisons of methods in the subpixel-range. Experiments show that uninformed users can be as good as trained users, but the variance in the quality of the results is more pronounced. We also showed that for single-frame tasks we can cut in half the cost from around $120 to $65 per frame. For more than one frame this ratio becomes even better: for around 10 frames, we would only pay a third of the cost compared to employing a trained user.

We conclude that, although accuracy and bias are downsides of our approach, MTurk-based motion annotation is a feasible, cost-effective and currently the only method for ground truth generation for large-scale outdoor scenes with dynamically moving objects.

References

1. Geiger, A., Lenz, P., Urtasun, R.: Are we ready for autonomous driving? The kitti vision benchmark suite. In: Computer Vision and Pattern Recognition (CVPR), Providence, USA (June 2012)
2. Butler, D.J., Wulff, J., Stanley, G.B., Black, M.J.: A naturalistic open source movie for optical flow evaluation. In: Fitzgibbon, A., Lazebnik, S., Perona, P., Sato, Y., Schmid, C. (eds.) ECCV 2012, Part VI. LNCS, vol. 7577, pp. 611–625. Springer, Heidelberg (2012)
3. Meister, S., Jähne, B., Kondermann, D.: Outdoor stereo camera system for the generation of real-world benchmark data sets. Optical Engineering 51 (2012)
4. Liu, C., Freeman, W.T., Adelson, E.H., Weiss, Y.: Human-assisted motion annotation. In: IEEE Computer Society Conference on Computer Vision and Pattern Recognition (CVPR 2008), pp. 1–8 (2008)
5. Sun, D., Roth, S., Black, M.J.: Secrets of optical flow estimation and their principles. In: Proc. IEEE Computer Society Conference on Computer Vision and Pattern Recognition (CVPR 2010), pp. 2432–2439. IEEE (2010)
6. Baker, S., Scharstein, D., Lewis, J.P., Roth, S., Black, M.J., Szeliski, R.: A database and evaluation methodology for optical flow. International Journal of Computer Vision 92(1), 1–31 (2011)
7. Meister, S., Kondermann, D.: Real versus realistically rendered scenes for optical flow evaluation. In: Proceedings of 14th ITG Conference on Electronic Media Technology, Informatik Centrum Dortmund e.V. (2011)
8. McCane, B., Novins, K., Crannitch, D., Galvin, B.: On benchmarking optical flow (2001), http://of-eval.sourceforge.net/
9. Mac Aodha, O., Brostow, G.J., Pollefeys, M.: Segmenting video into classes of algorithm-suitability. In: Proceedings of the IEEE Conference on Computer Vision and Pattern Recognition (CVPR 2010), pp. 1054–1061 (2010)
10. Vaudrey, T., Rabe, C., Klette, R., Milburn, J.: Differences between stereo and motion behaviour on synthetic and real-world stereo sequences. In: Proc. of 23rd International on Conference Image and Vision Computing New Zealand (IVCNZ 2008), pp. 1–6 (2008)
11. Spiro, I., Taylor, G., Williams, G., Bregler, C.: Hands by hand: Crowd-sourced motion tracking for gesture annotation. In: 2010 IEEE Computer Society Conference on Computer Vision and Pattern Recognition Workshops (CVPRW), pp. 17–24. IEEE (2010)

A Comparative Study on Multi-person Tracking Using Overlapping Cameras

Martijn C. Liem and Dariu M. Gavrila

Intelligent Systems Laboratory, University of Amsterdam, The Netherlands
{m.c.liem,d.m.gavrila}@uva.nl

Abstract. We present a comparative study for tracking multiple persons using cameras with overlapping views. The evaluated methods consist of two batch mode trackers (Berclaz et al, 2011, Ben-Shitrit et al, 2011) and one recursive tracker (Liem and Gavrila, 2011), which integrate appearance cues and temporal information differently. We also added our own improved version of the recursive tracker. Furthermore, we investigate the effect of the type of background estimation (static vs. adaptive) on tracking performance. Experiments are performed on two novel and challenging multi-person surveillance data sets (indoor, outdoor), made public to facilitate benchmarking. We show that our adaptation of the recursive method outperforms the other stand-alone trackers.

1 Introduction

Tracking multiple persons in dynamic, uncontrolled environments using cameras with overlapping views has important applications in areas such as surveillance, sports and behavioral sciences. We are interested in scenes covered by as few as 3-4 surrounding cameras with diagonal viewing directions, maximizing overlap area. This set-up makes establishing individual feature correspondences across camera views difficult, while inter-person occlusion can be considerable.

Various methods have been proposed recently for such a multi-person tracking setting using overlapping cameras, but few quantitative comparisons have been made. In order to improve visibility regarding performance characteristics, we present an experimental comparison among representative state-of-the-art methods.[1] We selected one recursive method [15] and two batch methods [2,1] for this comparison. Furthermore, we made some performance improving adaptations to [15]. The trackers were combined with the static background estimation method from [18] and the adaptive background estimation method from [24].

2 Related Work

In recent years, various methods performing multi-person detection and tracking using overlapping cameras have been presented. In [16], person positions

---

[1] This research has received funding from the EC's Seventh Framework Programme under grant agreement number 218197, the ADABTS project.

M. Chen, B. Leibe, and B. Neumann (Eds.): ICVS 2013, LNCS 7963, pp. 203–212, 2013.
© Springer-Verlag Berlin Heidelberg 2013

are found by matching colors along epipolar lines in all cameras. Foreground images are projected onto horizontal planes in the 3D space in [13], detecting objects at ground plane locations where multiple foreground regions intersect in multiple planes. Similarly, [20] uses images containing the number of foreground pixels above each pixel to create 3D detections at positions with the highest accumulated score. In [5], people's principal axis are matched across cameras. In [8], a Probabilistic Occupancy Map (POM) is presented for person detection. A generative model using a discretized ground plane and fixed size regions of interest approximates the marginal probability of occupancy by accumulating all evidence received from foreground images from every camera. Detections in [15] are generated using a volume carving [22] based 3D scene reconstruction, projected onto the ground plane. Similar to [15], [11] proposes a model in which multiple volume carving based scene configuration hypothesis are evaluated. Instead of solving hypothesis selection in 3D, the graph cut algorithm is used to label the pixels of each camera image as background or one of the people in the scene. In [10], an iterative model is presented labeling individual voxels of a volume reconstruction as either part of an object, background or static occluder.

Combining detections into long-term tracks can be approached in several ways. *Recursive* trackers perform on-line tracking on a frame-to-frame basis, often using well known algorithms like Mean-Shift [6], Kalman filtering [11] or particle filtering [4]. When tracking multiple objects simultaneously, the issue of consistently assigning tracks to detections should be solved. Well known solutions are the Joint Probabilistic Data Association Filter [9,12] and Multiple Hypothesis Tracking [19]. In [15], matching tracks to detections is approached as an assignment problem in a bipartite graph, but evaluation is focused on track assignment instead of tracking performance like this paper. Particle filters have also been extended for multi-target tracking [14,7].

Batch mode trackers optimize assignment of detections to tracks over a set of multiple frames at once. Tracking is often modeled as a linear or integer programming problem or as an equivalent graph traversal problem. Flow optimization is used for tracking in [23], finding disjoint paths in a cost flow network defined using observation likelihoods and transition probabilities. In [2], flow optimization is combined with POM. This is extended with an appearance model in [1].

3   Methods

This section gives an overview of the tracking methods and background models to be compared. We will refer to the method from [15] as Recursive Combinatorial Track Assignment (RCTA), while the batch methods from [2] and [1] will be referred to as K-shortest paths (KSP) and K-shortest paths with appearance (KSP-App), respectively. Our adaptation of RCTA will be referred to as RCTA$^+$.

3.1   Recursive Combinatorial Track Assignment

RCTA [15] uses volume carving to create a 3D reconstruction of the scene. This reconstruction is projected vertically onto the ground plane and segmented using

EM clustering such that N person location hypotheses $\mathcal{P}^n$ (i.e. detections) with sufficient size and vertical mass for a hypothetical person remain. Using the M tracks $\mathcal{T}^m$ from the previous frame, an assignment hypothesis $\mathcal{A}^i$ consists of the assignment of ν person hypotheses to a track, with $0 \leq \nu \leq min(N, M)$. $\mathcal{A}^i$'s likelihood uses the positions of $\{\mathcal{P}^n, \mathcal{T}^m\} \in \mathcal{A}^i$, appearances (separately computed for head, torso, legs) of $\mathcal{P}^n \in \mathcal{A}^i$ and foreground segmentation. Selection and tracking of actual persons is solved jointly by finding the most likely assignment hypothesis $\mathcal{A}^*$. Occlusions between different $\mathcal{P}^n$ make features like the appearance of $\mathcal{P}^n$ depend on all other $\mathcal{P}^n \in \mathcal{A}^i$, making finding $\mathcal{A}^*$ intractable. A two-step approach solves this problem.

In the *preselection* step, Munkres' algorithm [17] computes the top K candidates for $\mathcal{A}^*$ using an approximation of the likelihood based on a subset of features independent of occlusion. In the *verification* step, $\mathcal{A}^*$ is selected by evaluating all K candidates using all features. More details can be found in [15].

We propose a number of improvements to the algorithm. The most important changes are related to way the foreground observation likelihood (the likelihood of the segmented foreground given a person hypothesis) is computed. This likelihood is based on the overlap between the binary foreground segmentation B for each camera and synthetic binary foreground images S created by drawing 1.8×0.5 m rectangles in each camera at the locations of all $\mathcal{P}^n \in \mathcal{A}^i$. The overlap score is quantified as $\sum S \oplus B$, with $\oplus$ the per-pixel XOR operator. In [15], this score is normalized by $\sum S$. We choose not to normalize, allowing computation of the score for empty S. This lets creation of new tracks in an empty scene be guided by the foreground segmentation instead of a default value for the score. We also change the way S is constructed in the *preselection* step, where all $\mathcal{P}^n$ are evaluated independently. In [15], the observation likelihood for $\mathcal{A}^i$ is based on S containing only the $\mathcal{P}^n$ being evaluated. When the scene has multiple people, such S do not match B well, resulting in low observation likelihoods. Instead, we use the Kalman filtered person predictions of all tracks other than the one $\mathcal{P}^n$ is currently being assigned to as the basis of S. For track to detection assignment and person creation we add a rectangle at the corresponding $\mathcal{P}^n$ location, while for track deletion the rectangle corresponding to that track is removed. This makes the observation likelihood of $\mathcal{A}^i$ computed in the *preselection* step more similar to the one computed in the *verification* step. Incorrect $\mathcal{A}^i$ will also be pruned more frequently since they increase $\sum S \oplus B$. In [15], any track assigned to the same detection has the same observation likelihood.

Furthermore, an extra term was added to the object creation likelihood, requiring a hypothesis to explain a minimum number of extra foreground pixels when adding a person. This reduces the chance of accepting detections generated by foreground noise as new persons. The value depends on the expected size of a person entering the scene per camera. The 'train station data' (see sec. 4) with cameras relatively close to the scene, uses 10% of the number of pixels in the image. The 'hall data', with cameras further away from the scene, uses 8%.

When computing appearances of $\mathcal{P}^n$ in the *preselection* step, we not only use appearance cues for $\mathcal{P}^n$ guaranteed to be fully visible under any $\mathcal{A}^i$ as in

[15], but relax this constraint and compute the appearance of the visible part of $\mathcal{P}^n$ visible for at least 25%. Furthermore, instead of using a fixed distribution for the likelihood term based on the distance between a track and a detection [15], we use each track's Kalman filter's predictive distribution to evaluate the likelihood of assigning a detection to that track. This increases tracker flexibility and improves the chance of re-establishing a lost track at a later point in time.

Finally, to reason about $\mathcal{P}^n$ occluded by static objects, we opted to use manually created foreground masks to reconstruct a volume space containing static objects (see [10] for an automatic method). The foreground segmented images at each timestep are augmented with the static object foregrounds before volume reconstruction. After reconstruction, the static object volume is subtracted.

3.2   K-Shortest Paths

KSP [2] does tracking by minimizing the flow trough a graph constructed by stacking POMs [8] from a batch of sequential frames. Each POM location is a graph node, connected to its 9 neighbors in the next frame. Tracks are modeled as flows trough this graph with costs defined by the POM probabilities at locations connected by the tracks. Finding the optimal set of disjoint tracks with minimum cost is formulated as a linear programming problem. Like [2], we use consecutive batches of 100 frames. Track consistency between batches is created by adding the last frame of the previous batch in front of the current batch, forcing flows to start at the track locations from the last frame of the previous batch.

KSP-App [1] extends KSP, incorporating appearance information into KSP's linear programing formulation. For this purpose, the KSP graph is stacked L times, creating L 'groups'. Each of these groups is assigned a predefined appearance template and the number of objects that can have a path in each group is limited. Each appearance consists of one color histogram per camera. Using a KSP iteration, the graph is pruned and appearances are extracted at locations along the tracks and at locations where tracks are separated by at most 3 nodes. The extracted appearance information is compared to the templates using KL divergence and the graph's edges are reweighed using these values. KSP is run a second time using the new graph to determine the final paths. More detailed descriptions of KSP and KSP-App are found in [2] and [1].

3.3   Background Estimation

The datasets used in our experiments contain significant amounts of lighting changes and background clutter. An *adaptive* background estimation method, compensating for changes in the scene over time by learning and adapting the background model on-line, would be preferred in this case. The method presented in [24] uses a Mixture of Gaussians per pixel to model the color distribution of the background and is to some extent robust with respect to illumination. In our scenarios however, where people tend to stand still for some time (up to a minute), preliminary experiments have shown that the adaptive nature of the method causes them to dissipate into the background, creating false negatives.

RCTA solves this by adding tracker feedback into the learning process, updating the background model only at locations without tracks. For the KSP methods, this type of feedback is not straightforward since tracking results are only available after processing the full batch, preventing frame-to-frame reinforcement of the learned background model. Therefore, we use the foreground segmentation method from [18], implemented by [21], as a second, *static* background estimation method. It models the empty scene using eigenbackgrounds constructed from images of the empty scene under different lighting conditions. Nevertheless, foreground segmentations created by this method show more noise than foregrounds generated by RCTA+'s adaptive method. For comparison we used the static background model for both KSP and RCTA methods. Furthermore, we used the foreground segmentations from RCTA+'s adaptive background model as input for the KSP methods, effectively cascading KSP and RCTA+.

4   Experiments

Datasets. Experiments were done on two datasets (fig. 1)². The outdoor 'train station data' has 14 sequences of in total 8529 frames, recorded on a train platform. Between two and five actors enact various situations ranging from persons waiting for a train to fighting hooligans. The scenes have dynamic backgrounds with trains passing by and people walking on the train platform. Lighting conditions vary significantly over time. The area of interest (a.o.i.) is 7.6×12 m and is viewed by 3 overlapping, frame synchronized cameras recording 752×560 pixel images at 20 fps. Ground truth (GT) person locations are obtained at each frame by labeling torso positions, annotating the shoulder and pelvis locations of all persons in all cameras and projecting these onto the ground plane.

The indoor 'hall data' is one 9080 frame sequence recorded in a large central hall. During the first half, actors move in and out of the scene in small groups. After this, two groups of about 8 people each enter one by one and start arguing and fighting. Fig. 2(a) shows the number of people in the scene over time. The 12×12 m a.o.i. is viewed by 4 overlapping, frame synchronized cameras recording 1024×768 pixel images at 20 fps. GT positions are generated every 20th frame by annotating every person's head location in every camera, triangulating these points in 3D and projecting them onto the ground plane. This data is considerably more difficult than the previous dataset, since it contains more, similarly clothed people forming denser groups, and the cameras are placed further away from the scene. Furthermore, many people wear dark clothing, which combined with the dark floor of the hall and multiple badly lit regions complicates foreground segmentation.

Evaluation Measures. Tracking performance is evaluated using the same metrics as in [1]. A missed detection (*miss*) is generated when no track is found within 0.5 m of a GT location, while a false positive (*fp*) is a track without a GT

---

² The data set is made available for non-commercial research purposes. Please follow the links from http://isla.science.uva.nl/ or contact the second author.

Fig. 1. All viewpoints of the train station data (top) and the hall data (bottom)

location within 0.5 m. The mismatch error (mme) counts the number of identity switches within a track and is increased when a track switches between persons. The global mismatch error ($gmme$) is increased for every frame a track follows a different person than the one it was created on. The number of GT persons (gt) is the total number of annotated person positions within the area covered by all cameras. Annotations outside this area and cases where a track is on one side of the area boundary and the ground truth on the other are not counted. This results in small differences between gt for different experiments.

Multi Object Tracking Precision (MOTP) and Multi Object Tracking Accuracy (MOTA) [3] summarize performance. MOTP describes the average distance between tracks and GT locations, while MOTA is defined as $1 - \frac{fp+miss+mme}{gt}$.

Implementation Details. For the train station data, POM settings are taken from [8], using 20 cm grid cells and person ROI of 175×50 cm. For the hall data, 40 cm grid cells are used. Smaller cells cause POM to detect too few people in the dense second half of the scenario. POM's person prior was set to 0.002 in all experiments. RCTA parameters were taken from [15], using voxels of $7 \times 7 \times 7$ cm. Appearance templates for KSP-App are sampled at manually selected POM locations for the train station dataset. For the hall dataset, running KSP-App turned out to be problematic. The density of people, combined with the 40 cm grid cells enlarging the spatial neighborhood of each cell, limit graph pruning, increasing the problem complexity. Even when using a reduced set of 5 instead of 23 templates, we were only able to process a small part of the scenario after a day. Therefore, we were unable to get KSP-App results on the hall dataset.

Most scenarios in the train station dataset start with persons in the scene. Because RCTA has a low probability of creating new tracks in the middle of the scene, tracking is bootstrapped using GT detections. For a fair comparison, the batch mode methods use ground truth initialization for the first frame as well.

All methods are implemented in C^{++}.[3] Experiments were performed on a 2.1 GHz CPU and 4 GB RAM. Computation time was measured on a 960 frame sequence with 4 persons. KSP took ± 8.9 seconds per frame (s/f) while KSP-App

---

[3] KSP and RCTA implementations were kindly provided by the authors. For KSP-app we used our own implementation as it could not be made available.

Table 1. Performance of all methods and background models, on both datasets. MOTA: accuracy, higher is better. MOTP: precision (cm), lower is better. *miss*: misses. *fp*: false positives. *mme*: mismatch error. *gmme*: global *mme*. *gt*: ground truth persons.

(a) Results on the train station data

method	background	MOTA	MOTP	miss	fp	mme	gmme	gt
RCTA$^+$	adaptive	0.89	15	655	2296	53	2749	28348
KSP-App	static	0.84	17	2478	1907	43	5173	28410
KSP	static	0.84	17	2515	1945	57	9940	28409
RCTA$^+$	static	0.74	14	5779	1467	44	3851	28348
RCTA	adaptive	0.72	16	3203	4559	76	9689	28348
RCTA	static	0.67	15	3872	5321	120	9176	28348
KSP-App	RCTA$^+$ adaptive	0.92	16	1070	1248	29	4983	28429
KSP	RCTA$^+$ adaptive	0.91	16	1182	1358	46	8997	28429

(b) Results on the hall data

method	background	MOTA	MOTP	miss	fp	mme	gmme	gt
RCTA$^+$	adaptive	0.54	18	1203	747	97	1371	4419
RCTA$^+$	static, low thr.	0.38	20	1537	1030	186	1839	4419
KSP	static, low thr.	-0.16	29	2702	2286	126	1364	4414
RCTA$^+$	static, high thr.	0.12	18	3839	55	15	371	4419
KSP	static, high thr.	0.28	28	1996	917	252	1966	4411
RCTA	adaptive	0.30	17	2654	361	62	1536	4419
RCTA	static, low thr.	0.24	16	3085	250	27	1085	4419
RCTA	static, high thr.	0.24	17	3084	199	58	1248	4419
KSP	RCTA$^+$ adaptive	0.22	28	1902	1188	344	2148	4415

needed ± 9.7 s/f. Of these times, ± 8.8 s/f is used by POM (this is longer than stated in [8] because we use more ground plane locations and higher resolution images). RCTA and RCTA$^+$ perform detection and tracking at ± 6.5 s/f.

Tracking Results. Table 1 shows the results per dataset. For the train station data, scores are accumulated over all scenarios. Table 1(a)'s top 6 rows show results of the stand-alone trackers combined with each background estimation method. RCTA$^+$ shows overall improvement over RCTA. Combining RCTA$^+$ and the adaptive background model gives the highest MOTA and lowest *gmme*. Static background experiments suffer from foreground segmentation errors. For the train station data, the static background model was configured to minimize false positives from strong illumination changes and shadows, classifying as few people as possible as background. This trade off results in higher *miss* rates for methods using static backgrounds. Because both RCTA methods assume a person to be well segmented in all cameras for reliable volume carving, foreground segmentation errors have most effect here. The POM detector has no such assumption, making it more robust to these artifacts.

MOTP is worse for the KSP methods since volume carving, allowing higher spatial resolutions than POM, offers more positional flexibility. KSP-App's main improvement over plain KSP is in the *mme* and *gmme*. This is to be expected, since KSP-App performs extra processing of the KSP tracks to correct id switches.

RCTA$^+$'s slightly higher *mme* reduces the number of *gmme*. Part of the extra id changes switch the tracker back to its original target. This also accounts for some of RCTA$^+$'s *fp*. When a detection disappears, RCTA$^+$ often switches to an untracked hypothesis with similar appearance instead of removing the track,

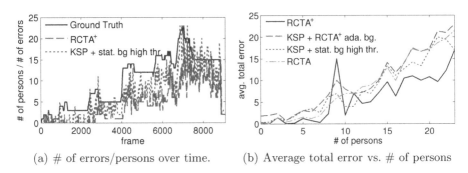

(a) # of errors/persons over time.   (b) Average total error vs. # of persons

Fig. 2. People and error statistics over time for the hall dataset

especially when the track is at some distance from the scene's boundaries. When the original target re-emerges some time later, RCTA$^+$ switches back.

The last two rows of table 1(a) show that using adaptive backgrounds generated by RCTA$^+$ as input to the KSP marginally improves performance over RCTA$^+$. KSP benefits from the cleaner foregrounds, while KSP-App improves on this result by providing more stable tracking results. The *gmme* for this last method is still higher than for pure RCTA$^+$, as a side-effect of the reduced *mme*.

Table 1(b) shows the results on the hall dataset. The large number of people and their close proximity in the second half of the scenario results in lower performance compared to the train station data. Standard RCTA's failure creating tracks is seen in the high *miss* rate but lower number of *fp*. This can to a large extent be blamed on the overlap computation as discussed in sec. 3.1. RCTA$^+$ using its adaptive background model again outperforms the other methods, this time including the RCTA$^+$-KSP cascade. This shows a more fundamental issue of KSP and the POM detector with crowded scenarios. When persons' foreground segmentations are not separated in any view, POM will detect too few persons, assuming the rest of the foreground regions are noise. Enlarging the POM grid to 40 cm cells partially compensates this, but causes missed detections when people are very close together and lowers detection precision. RCTA$^+$'s volume carving and clustering approach has less problems splitting dense groups, but also creates incorrect detections when the volume space is incorrectly clustered. KSP's lack of appearance model makes it is more prone to track switches as well.

Because of the challenging conditions of the hall dataset described earlier, using the same configuration for the static background model as for the train station data results in many missing foreground segments. Therefore, we did additional experiments using a lower segmentation threshold, detecting more people but increasing the foreground noise from illumination and shadows. Results using the 'high' and 'low' threshold settings are marked as resp. 'high thr.' and 'low thr.' in table 1(b). Again, RCTA$^+$ shows sensitivity to missing detections, resulting in a lower MOTA for the high threshold static backgrounds. KSP shows bad performance when using the low threshold however, producing more errors than the *gt*, resulting in a negative MOTA. When using the high threshold, KSP shows better results, but also suffers from the missing detections.

Fig. 3. Examples of tracking results. (top) Train station data: RCTA$^+$, KSP-App, KSP and KSP-App/RCTA$^+$ cascade. (bottom) Hall data: RCTA$^+$, KSP with low background threshold, KSP with high background threshold and KSP-RCTA$^+$ cascade.

Fig. 3 shows some examples of tracking results from one of each dataset's viewpoints. In fig. 2(b) the average total error ($fp + miss + mme$) per frame containing a certain number of people is shown for the hall data for the best performing versions of each method. The figure shows a relatively constant error up to 7 people, after which it starts to increase linear with the number of people in the scene. The RCTA$^+$ error shows an outlier at 9 people because the dataset has only 1 annotated frame containing 9 people, at the end of the scenario. At that point, multiple fp of people who just exited the scene still linger. Fig. 2(a) shows the evolution of both the number of people during the scene, and the error per frame for RCTA$^+$ and KSP with static background and high threshold.

5   Conclusion

In this paper, three state-of-the-art tracking methods and our adaptation of one have been compared in combination with two types of background estimation. RCTA$^+$ with adaptive backgrounds consistently outperforms the other stand-alone methods, including RCTA. For lower person-density scenarios, KSP-based methods give competitive results. For higher person-density scenarios, KSP-based methods suffer from the limitations of the POM detector when persons overlap in many cameras. RCTA$^+$ with adaptive backgrounds outperforms the latter by a MOTA score of 0.26.

References

1. Ben Shitrit, H., et al.: Tracking multiple people under global appearance constraints. In: Proc. of the ICCV, pp. 137–144 (2011)
2. Berclaz, J., et al.: Multiple object tracking using k-shortest paths optimization. IEEE Trans. on PAMI 33(9), 1806–1819 (2011)
3. Bernardin, K., Stiefelhagen, R.: Evaluating multiple object tracking performance: the clear mot metrics. JIVP 2008, 1–10 (2008)

4. Breitenstein, M.D., et al.: Online Multi-Person Tracking-by-Detection from a Single, Uncalibrated Camera. IEEE Trans. on PAMI 33(9), 1820–1833 (2011)
5. Calderara, S., Cucchiara, R., Prati, A.: Bayesian-Competitive consistent labeling for people surveillance. IEEE Trans. on PAMI 30(2), 354–360 (2008)
6. Collins, R.: Mean-shift blob tracking through scale space. In: Proc. of the IEEE CVPR, vol. 2, p. II–234 (2003)
7. Du, W., Piater, J.: Multi-camera people tracking by collaborative particle filters and principal axis-based integration. In: Yagi, Y., Kang, S.B., Kweon, I.S., Zha, H. (eds.) ACCV 2007, Part I. LNCS, vol. 4843, pp. 365–374. Springer, Heidelberg (2007)
8. Fleuret, F., et al.: Multicamera people tracking with a probabilistic occupancy map. IEEE Trans. on PAMI 30(2), 267–282 (2008)
9. Fortmann, T., Bar-Shalom, Y., Scheffe, M.: Sonar tracking of multiple targets using joint probabilistic data association. IEEE JOE 8(3), 173–184 (1983)
10. Guan, L., Franco, J.S., Pollefeys, M.: Multi-view occlusion reasoning for probabilistic silhouette-based dynamic scene reconstruction. IJCV 90(3), 283–303 (2010)
11. Huang, C.C., Wang, S.J.: A bayesian hierarchical framework for multitarget labeling and correspondence with ghost suppression over multicamera surveillance system. IEEE Trans. on ASE 9(1), 16–30 (2012)
12. Kang, J., Cohen, I., Medioni, G.: Tracking people in crowded scenes across multiple cameras. In: ACCV, vol. 7, p. 15 (2004)
13. Khan, S., Shah, M.: Tracking multiple occluding people by localizing on multiple scene planes. IEEE Trans. on PAMI 31(3), 505–519 (2009)
14. Kim, K., Davis, L.S.: Multi-camera tracking and segmentation of occluded people on ground plane using search-guided particle filtering. In: Leonardis, A., Bischof, H., Pinz, A. (eds.) ECCV 2006. LNCS, vol. 3953, pp. 98–109. Springer, Heidelberg (2006)
15. Liem, M., Gavrila, D.M.: Multi-person localization and track assignment in overlapping camera views. In: Mester, R., Felsberg, M. (eds.) DAGM 2011. LNCS, vol. 6835, pp. 173–183. Springer, Heidelberg (2011)
16. Mittal, A., Davis, L.S.: M 2 Tracker: a multi-view approach to segmenting and tracking people in a cluttered scene. IJCV 51(3), 189–203 (2003)
17. Munkres, J.: Algorithms for the assignment and transportation problems. Journal of the Society for Industrial and Applied Mathematics, 32–38 (1957)
18. Oliver, N.M., Rosario, B., Pentland, A.P.: A bayesian computer vision system for modeling human interactions. IEEE Trans. on PAMI 22(8), 831–843 (2000)
19. Reid, D.: An algorithm for tracking multiple targets. IEEE Trans. on Automatic Control 24(6), 843–854 (1979)
20. Santos, T.T., Morimoto, C.H.: Multiple camera people detection and tracking using support integration. PRL 32(1), 47–55 (2011)
21. Sobral, A.C.: BGSLibrary: A opencv c++ background subtraction library (2012), software available at http://code.google.com/p/bgslibrary/
22. Szeliski, R.: Rapid octree construction from image sequences. CVGIP 58(1), 23–32 (1993)
23. Zhang, L., Li, Y., Nevatia, R.: Global data association for multi-object tracking using network flows. In: Proc. of the IEEE CVPR, pp. 1–8 (2008)
24. Zivkovic, Z., van der Heijden, F.: Efficient adaptive density estimation per image pixel for the task of background subtraction. PRL 27(7), 773–780 (2006)

Visual Tracking Using Superpixel-Based Appearance Model

Shahed Nejhum[*1], Muhammad Rushdi[2], and Jeffrey Ho[2]

[1] The MathWorks, 3 Apple Hill Dr, Natick MA 01760, USA
shahed.nejhum@mathworks.com
[2] Department of Computer and Information Science and Engineering
University of Florida, Gainesville FL 32611, USA
{mrushdi,jho}@cise.ufl.edu

Abstract. In this work, we propose a tracking algorithm that robustly handles complex variations in target appearance, scale, occlusion, and background. In particular, the algorithm exploits a novel superpixel-based appearance model for visual tracking. From the initial tracking window, we extract superpixels and compute their histogram features. In subsequent frames, we search for the region that maximizes the similarity of the superpixel features. Our algorithm detects target occlusion and updates the appearance model accordingly. As well, the model is updated to handle large-scale variations. We present experimental results on several publicly available challenging sequences. Qualitative and quantitative evaluation of our tracking algorithm show improved performance over state-of-the-art trackers.

Keywords: superpixel, tracking, image representation, image matching.

1 Introduction

Visual tracking in uncontrolled environments is an important problem in computer vision research because of its applications in many fields including surveillance, human-computer interaction and medical image analysis. Despite significant advances in recent years, visual tracking is still a challenging problem. The main difficulties in tracking a target over a long period of time lie in handling the appearance changes, illumination, pose and scale variations and recovering from target occlusions. Therefore, the target appearance model needs to be updated adaptively to handle these challenges. Adaptive models of the target appearance have been proposed in many visual tracking models [1–4]. In these models, the appearance is continuously updated with new tracking results. Some tracking algorithms also model the background surrounding the target. Depending on the foreground and the background modeling approach, trackers are divided into two classes, namely, generative and discriminative trackers.

Discriminative tracking methods [5, 6] are posed as binary classification problems where the task is to distinguish the target region from the background.

---

[*] This work was completed when the first author was at the University of Florida.

M. Chen, B. Leibe, and B. Neumann (Eds.): ICVS 2013, LNCS 7963, pp. 213–222, 2013.
© Springer-Verlag Berlin Heidelberg 2013

This classification task requires modeling the foreground and the background separately which also helps to handle partial occlusions of the target. However, the update of these appearance models is often very costly. On the other hand, generative tracking methods [2, 7] track a target object by searching for the region that is most similar to the reference model. For these methods, the update of the appearance model is more efficient but the update can cause the tracker to drift away from the target when the target is partially occluded. Without an occlusion detection mechanism in generative tracking algorithms, adaptive target modeling can cause the tracker to drift away. In this paper, we propose a generative tracking algorithm that addresses this problem and provides a solution for robust visual tracking. In particular, our tracking algorithm presents a novel superpixel-based appearance model with a simple but effective model update mechanism. Our algorithm also robustly handles occlusions and scale variations of the target.

2   Related Work

For robust and adaptive appearance modeling, tracking algorithms available in the literature use various high-level, mid-level or low-level image features. In high-level appearance modeling paradigms, the target is considered as a single region and features such as color or intensity histograms are used to describe the region. However, this type of modeling completely disregards the spatial configuration of the target and hence the tracker is often confused by different targets of similar backgrounds. Moreover, this holistic modeling produces jittered tracking results for targets with large shape variations. Low-level image cues (for example SIFT, SURF, and LBP) are mainly used in feature-based tracking. Since these low-level image cues do not persist consistently in long image sequences, their tracking results are not satisfactory in long sequences.

Recently, mid-level cues were effectively used for tracking objects in long and challenging sequences[1, 8]. Specifically, the target region is divided into smaller regions and the appearance model is constructed from the feature vectors describing those regions. In [1], the authors propose a tracker that models the target by dividing the target region into fragments. Local histograms computed from the fragments are used to model the target. This makes the tracker robust against partial occlusion. However, this fragment-based appearance model is not adaptive and hence the tracker fails to track targets having large appearance variations over time. In [8], small image patches are selected from the target to model its appearance. These patches are called Attentional Regions (AR) of the target. The tracker combines vote maps obtained from these attentional regions to decide the target location in the new image frame.

Apart from reliable modeling of the visual target, another important factor of a tracking algorithm is to update the model to adapt to the variations of the target appearance and scale. The PROST tracking algorithm [4] uses three different tracking modules: non-adaptive, fully adaptive and semi-adaptive modules. The PROST algorithm proposes some criteria to update the semi-adaptive module based on the outputs from the two other modules. Although the algorithm can track occluded targets, it does not explicitly detect occlusion. The MILTrack algorithm [6] is considered to be a state-of-the-art discriminative tracking algorithm that uses multiple-instance learning. The foreground and background appearance (positive and negative samples) are updated regularly to deal with the appearance variations of the target.

Our proposed algorithm uses mid-level image features to model the target appearance. In particular, the algorithm models the target using superpixels [9–11]. Our algorithm computes a superpixel map and then superimposes a rectangular grid on top of the map. Each grid point is assigned the feature vector of the covering superpixel. Hence, a superpixel-based similarity measure is evaluated between the model and the candidate windows to find the target in the new frame. In order to account for appearance variations, the model is updated with new tracking results. To keep the model robust, the model uses superpixels from the initial frame and the most recent frame. Using these superpixels, we construct the adaptive appearance model. The proposed algorithm also uses an occlusion detection module that guides the model update process. While using superpixels in tracking has been done before [12], our work is distinguished by three aspects. First, we incorporate spatial information by placing a fine grid on top of the superpixel map. Second, our model update process is much simpler than that of [12]. Third, our model is generative while the previous approaches are discriminative ones. Our experimental results show that the proposed algorithm produces better results. The results will be presented in Section 5.

3   Appearance Model

In this section, we describe the construction of the target appearance model. The initial appearance model is constructed from the first frame of the sequence. The target is manually specified as a rectangular region R in this frame. Inside R, we establish a rectangular grid G as shown in Figure 1. Assuming that the grid G contains N grid points, the collection of these grid points is specified by $G = \{g_i\}_{i=1}^{N}$. The relative location of a grid point g_i is denoted by $p_i = \mathrm{pos}(g_i) - \mathrm{pos}(\mathrm{upperLeft}(R))$, where $\mathrm{pos}(g_i)$ is the pixel location of the grid point g_i and $\mathrm{pos}(\mathrm{upperLeft}(R))$ is the pixel location of the upper left corner of the initial rectangle R. Each grid point g_i is annotated with a feature vector f_i. The collection of these feature vectors over the grid, $F = \{f_i\}_{i=1}^{N}$, constitutes the initial appearance model of the target. The spatial information of the target is thus encoded in the proposed appearance model through the grid G and the feature set F. This spatial model makes the tracker robust against partial occlusions and also helps the tracker to deal with targets of complex appearance.

In this work, we use mid-level image cues to compute the feature vector set F. More specifically, the superpixels computed inside the rectangle R are used for this purpose as shown in Figure 1. To extract the superpixels, we use the energy minimization algorithm proposed in Veksler *et al.* [9]. This algorithm efficiently computes superpixels whose boundaries are aligned with the image edges. We apply this superpixel generation algorithm to produce a superpixel map M for the bounding rectangle R of the target. For each grid point g_i, we determine the associated superpixel from the superpixel map M. In particular, let $m_i = M(p_i)$ specify the covering superpixel of the grid point g_i located at the position p_i. The intensity or color histogram h_{m_i} of the superpixel m_i is used as the feature vector f_i for the grid point g_i.

Fig. 1. Construction of the superpixel-based appearance model. Given an image window, we first generate the superpixels defined by the red boundaries. Secondly, the histogram features are computed for each superpixel. Thirdly, we superimpose a grid on top of the superpixel map. Finally, each grid point (in green) is associated with the covering superpixel and its histogram feature vector.

Instead of computing the superpixels, one possible alternative would have been to use the histogram computed from a rectangular image patch centered at $\text{pos}(g_i)$. Although this way is computationally more efficient, it completely ignores the edges of the frame. Our approach of using the superpixels implicitly encodes the edges in the target appearance model as well. In fact, this edge-aware approach makes our appearance model more informative about the target than the patch-based alternative. Moreover, the superpixel computation algorithm we use runs reasonably fast on the rectangle R whose area is only a small fraction of the entire frame area. Update of our proposed appearance model is also very simple and intuitive. The feature vector set F is updated to handle the target appearance change due to pose or illumination variations. To handle the target scale variations, the grid G is updated as well. In the next section, we present our tracking algorithm using this novel appearance model.

4   Tracking Algorithm

At the beginning of the proposed algorithm, the initial appearance model is constructed using the first frame as described in Section 3. Then, for each subsequent frame I_t of the sequence, the proposed tracking algorithm produces a rectangle R_t enclosing the target. Localizing the target in the new frame is formulated as a search problem in our algorithm (Section 4.1). Briefly, this search is performed as follows. At first, a set of candidate rectangles $\mathcal{R} = \{R^j\}_{j=1}^J$ are generated. Then, the algorithm evaluates the similarity between the current target appearance model and the appearance of the candidate rectangles. Finally, the candidate rectangle having the highest similarity score is selected as the rectangle R_t containing the target. The next step after the localization of the target is to determine whether the target is being occluded or not (Section 4.2). Update of the appearance model is performed next (Section 4.3). This update depends on the outcome of the occlusion step. The final step is to adjust the scale of the appearance model (Section 4.4). These four steps (target localization, occlusion detection, model update and scale update) are repeated in each frame to track the target.

4.1   Target Localization

For target localization, we search for the rectangle R_t in the frame I_t that is the most similar to the current target appearance model. The best rectangle R_t is selected from a set of candidate rectangles $\mathcal{R}$ as follows. Let R_{t-1} be the best window in the frame I_{t-1}. Also let c_{t-1}, w_{t-1} and h_{t-1} be the center, width and height of R_{t-1}, respectively. Any rectangle R^j in the frame I_t whose dimensions are $w_{t-1} \times h_{t-1}$ and whose center lies within d distance from the pixel location c_{t-1} is included in the candidate set $\mathcal{R}$. The union of the rectangles in the set $\mathcal{R}$ forms a rectangular region $\mathbf{R}$ in the frame I_t whose center is at the position c_{t-1} and whose dimensions are $(w_{t-1} + 2d) \times (h_{t-1} + 2d)$. The region $\mathbf{R}$ is superpixelized in order to compute the superpixel-based appearance of each candidate rectangle R^j in the set $\mathcal{R}$. The superpixel generation algorithm [9] divides the region $\mathbf{R}$ into S superpixels $\{s_k\}_{k=1}^S$. The mapping from the image pixels to the generated super-pixels is the superpixel map $\mathbf{M}$ for the region $\mathbf{R}$. The intensity histograms $\{h_k\}_{k=1}^S$ of these superpixels $\{s_k\}_{k=1}^S$ are then estimated. For each pixel p in $\mathbf{R}$, the covering superpixel can be determined from $\mathbf{M}(l)$ where $l = \mathrm{pos}(p) - \mathrm{pos}(\mathrm{upperLeft}(\mathbf{R}))$[1]. The computation of the appearance of the rectangle R^j is done as follows.

First, we superimpose the N-point grid G on the rectangle R^j. This gives us the grid-point locations $\{p_i\}_{i=1}^N$ of R^j. Then, using these locations, we determine the superpixels and histograms associated with each of the grid-points. The resultant histogram set $F^j = \{f_i^j\}_{i=1}^N$ represents the appearance of the candidate rectangle. Then we compute the similarity between the histogram set F^j of the

---

[1] $\mathrm{pos}(x)$ is the position of pixel x.

candidate rectangle R^j and the corresponding set F of the target model. We define the similarity score between two histogram sets $sim(F^1, F^2)$ as

$$sim(F^1, F^2) = \sum_{i=1}^{N} hist\_sim(f_i^1, f_i^2) \tag{1}$$

where $hist\_sim(f_i^1, f_i^2)$ represents the similarity between the histograms f_i^1 and f_i^2. We use histogram intersection [13] to calculate the similarity between the histograms

$$hist\_sim(f_i^1, f_i^2) = \sum_{b=1}^{B} min(f_i^1(b), f_i^2(b)) \tag{2}$$

where B is the number of bins in the histogram. We use Equation 1 to calculate the appearance similarity of each candidate rectangle in the set $\mathcal{R}$. Then, the rectangle with the highest similarity is chosen to be the target rectangle R_t.

4.2   Occlusion Detection

Our tracking algorithm uses an adaptive appearance model of the target. The appearance model is updated when a new tracking result is available. However, the update may cause the tracker to drift away from the target if it is currently under partial occlusion and the appearance model is updated with this partially occluded tracking result. For this reason, our proposed tracking algorithm first detects whether the target is being occluded or not. Then, the algorithm updates the appearance model. Next, we describe the occlusion detection step.

In the target localization step, the rectangle R_t containing the target in the frame I_t is determined. The appearance of R_t is further analyzed in the occlusion detection step. In particular, we estimate the appearance similarity between the target rectangle R_t and recent backgrounds. If this appearance similarity score is large (i.e. the appearance of R_t is highly similar to recent backgrounds), we infer that the target is having occlusion. The recent backgrounds are modeled as a set of rectangles $\mathcal{B}$ taken from the L most recently processed frames $(I_{t-1}, I_{t-2}, ..., I_{t-L})$. At each frame I_{t-j}, we include the rectangle B_{t-j} centered at c_t and whose dimensions are $w_t \times h_t$ in the set $\mathcal{B}$ only if $|c_t - c_{t-j}| > d_{occ}$. (i.e. if the center of the rectangle B_{t-j} is at least d_{occ} away from the center of the rectangle R_{t-j}). We estimate the similarities between R_t and each rectangle in the set $\mathcal{B}$ and calculate the average value θ. If $\theta > \theta_{occ}$, we conclude that, the target is partially occluded. Here, θ_{occ} is the occlusion detection threshold.

4.3   Model Update

As described in Section 3, the proposed target appearance model consists of a grid G and a collection of feature vectors F (Each grid point $g_i \in G$ has a feature vector $f_i \in F$). Let F_1 and F_t denote the feature vector sets obtained by superimposing the grid G on the initial and target rectangles R_1 and R_t, respectively. In order to handle the appearance variations of the target, the model is continuously updated using the initial and target feature sets F_1 and F_t. Using only the initial and most recent frames keeps the model update simple but more importantly robust against any drift [3]. Now, the model feature set F is constructed from F_1 and F_t as follows.

Each feature vector $f_i \in F$ is constructed as a convex combination of the vectors $f_{1i} \in F_1$ and $f_{ti} \in F_t$. The weight of this convex combination depends on the outcome of the occlusion detection step. If the target is not occluded ($\theta \leq \theta_{occ}$), we put more weight on the current features f_{ti}, otherwise, more weight is given to the initial features f_{1i}

$$f_i = \begin{cases} w_1 \times f_{1i} + (1 - w_1) \times f_{ti} & \text{if } \theta > \theta_{occ} \\ w_2 \times f_{1i} + (1 - w_2) \times f_{ti} & \text{if } \theta \leq \theta_{occ} \end{cases} \qquad (3)$$

where $w_1 > w_2$. Also, when the algorithm detects occlusion ($\theta > \theta_{occ}$), the target is more likely to be occluded for sometime. Therefore, for the next few frames, the algorithm skips the occlusion detection step and favors the initial features.

4.4   Scaling

The final step of our algorithm is to determine the scale of the target. The target appearance model is updated accordingly to handle the scale variations. To determine the scale of the target on the current frame, a set of rectangles are generated by varying the size of the rectangle R_t while keeping the new rectangle centers fixed at c_t (center of R_t). The appearances of these rectangles are compared with the target appearance model and the scale of the rectangle having the highest similarity is selected as the updated scale of the target. The update of the model is performed as follows. Firstly, The appearance model is resized with the selected scale. Then, a new grid G_t is created to replace G. And finally, the feature vector set F is recomputed using the new grid G_t.

5   Experimental Results

We evaluated our algorithm using twelve challenging sequences: Sylvester [2], Woman and Faceocc1 [1], Basketball and Singer1 [3], Tiger1, Tiger2 and Faceocc2 [6] and Lemming, Liquor, Box and Board sequences [4]. The tracking performance of our proposed structured superpixel-based tracker (SSP) has been compared with several state-of-the-art tracking algorithms: the Multiple-Instance-Learning tracker (MIL) [6], the Visual Tracking Decomposition tracker (VTD) [3], the SemiBoost tracker (SB) [5], the Super-Pixel Tracker (SPT) [12], the Online AdaBoost tracker (OAB) [14], the Online Random Forest (ORF) tracker [15],the Parallel Robust Online Simple Tracker (PROST) [4], and the Fragment-based tracker (FRAG) [1].

5.1   Experimental Setup

For each video sequence, we computed the superpixel map of the initial frame using the energy minimization framework of Veksler *et al.* [9] where the patch size was set to $8 - 14$ pixels, the smoothness weight term to 100 and the number of iterations to 10. Then a grid with a spacing of $4 - 7$ pixels was placed on top of the superpixel map. This grid spacing was selected based on the size of the target so that number of grid points is roughly 200 in all experiments. The similarity between tracking windows was computed according to Equation 1 and then normalized between 0 and 1. For occlusion detection, the 5 most recent frames were used to model the background. A distance threshold of $10 - 15$ pixels was used to decide whether a window belongs to the background. The occlusion detection threshold was set to $0.6 - 0.7$ depending on the foreground-background similarity of a specific sequence. The model update weights w_1 and w_2 in Equation 3 were set within the ranges $0.8 - 0.9$ and $0.5 - 0.6$, respectively.

5.2   Results and Discussion

Table 1 summarizes the average center location error [6] results on ten sequences whose ground-truth data is available. For space limitations we show the comparisons with five methods only. Please check the YouTube channel http://www.youtube.com/ssptracker for further experimental results. The quality metric we used is the average center location error [6]. In most sequences, our method (SSP) most accurately tracked the target even with the presence of occlusions, pose variations, illumination changes and abrupt motions. In spite of the motion blur and heavy occlusions in the long Liquor sequence, our method achieved a significantly lower error than all other methods. Also, our error result for the Lemming sequence is very low although this sequence experiences large scale variations and motion blur. The Singer1 sequence contains large scale and illumination variations. Still, our tracker follows the singer accurately thanks to the robust adaptivity of our model. The Tiger1 and Tiger2 sequences exhibit fast motion, heavy occlusion and drastic appearance changes. Despite all of these challenges, our tracker robustly tracks the tiger faces in both sequences. Numerical error results in Table 1 support this conclusion. The Faceocc1, Faceocc2 and Woman sequences all suffer from severe occlusion and heavy appearance changes. However, because of the spatial information encoded into the proposed appearance model, our tracker managed to keep track of the respective objects and achieve the lowest errors on these three sequences. Figure 2 compares the performance of our algorithm with other algorithms on a few selected frames. As we can see from the examples, our tracker recovers from severe occlusions and appearance changes while most of the other trackers fail. For example, in the Board sequence, our tracker detects the moving circuit accurately while other trackers drift away. Similarly, for the Box sequence, our tracker closely matches the PROST tracker in following the target.

Table 1. Quantitative evaluation of the SSP tracking algorithm. The numbers indicate the average center location errors (in pixels) of the tracking windows. The number of frames for each sequence is shown in the parenthesis next to the sequence name.

	SSP (Ours)	MIL [6]	SB[5]	SPT [12]	PROST[4]	FRAG [1]
Board (698)	**14.2**	51.2	-	-	39.0	90.1
Box (1161)	17.1	104.6	-	-	**12.1**	57.4
Lemming (1336)	9.4	14.9	-	**7.0**	25.4	82.8
Liquor (1741)	**5.3**	165.1	-	9.0	21.6	30.7
Tiger1 (354)	10.0	15.0	46.0	-	**7.0**	40.0
Tiger2 (360)	**14.0**	17.0	53.0	-	-	17.0
Sylvester (1344)	**7.0**	9.4	16.0	-	11.0	11.0
Faceocc1 (886)	6.9	18.4	7.0	-	7.0	**6.5**
Faceocc2 (812)	**13.1**	20.0	23.0	-	17.0	45.0
Woman (539)	**5.0**	120.0	-	9.0	-	112.0

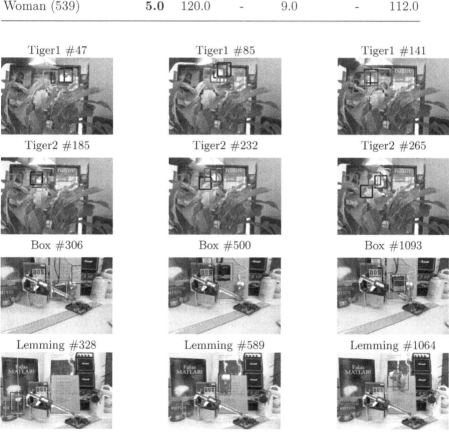

Fig. 2. Visual comparison of tracking results obtained using different algorithms. Tracking results by our method (SSP), MIL, PROST and FRAG are represented by red, blue, cyan and green rectangles, respectively.

6 Conclusions and Future Work

In this paper, we described a simple, reliable, and easy-to-update appearance model for non-articulated object tracking using structured superpixel (SSP). The SSP tracker successfully tracks targets undergoing severe shape, scale and pose variations. As well, the SSP tracker robustly handles occluded targets. Our tracker outperforms many state-of-the-art tracking algorithms on challenging sequences. For future work, we will investigate methods for automatic tuning of the structured superpixel model parameters.

References

1. Adam, A., Rivlin, E., Shimshoni, I.: Robust fragments-based tracking using the integral histogram. In: Proceedings of IEEE Conference on Computer Vision and Pattern Recognition, pp. 798–805 (2006)
2. Ross, D.A., Lim, J., Lin, R.S., Yang, M.H.: Incremental learning for robust visual tracking. International Journal of Computer Vision 77(1-3), 125–141 (2008)
3. Kwon, J., Lee, K.M.: Visual tracking decomposition. In: Proceedings of IEEE Conference on Computer Vision and Pattern Recognition, pp. 1269–1276 (2010)
4. Santner, J., Leistner, C., Saffari, A., Pock, T., Bischof, H.: Prost: Parallel robust online simple tracking. In: Proceedings of IEEE Conference on Computer Vision and Pattern Recognition, pp. 723–730 (2010)
5. Grabner, H., Leistner, C., Bischof, H.: Semi-supervised on-line boosting for robust tracking. In: Forsyth, D., Torr, P., Zisserman, A. (eds.) ECCV 2008, Part I. LNCS, vol. 5302, pp. 234–247. Springer, Heidelberg (2008)
6. Babenko, B., Yang, M.H., Belongie, S.: Robust object tracking with online multiple instance learning. IEEE Transactions on Pattern Analysis and Machine Intelligence 33(8), 1619–1632 (2011)
7. Mei, X., Ling, H.: Robust visual tracking using l1 minimization. In: Proceedings of the International Conference on Computer Vision, pp. 1436–1443 (2009)
8. Yang, M., Yuan, J., Wu, Y.: Spatial selection for attentional visual tracking. In: Proceedings of IEEE Conference on Computer Vision and Pattern Recognition, pp. 1–8 (2007)
9. Veksler, O., Boykov, Y., Mehrani, P.: Superpixels and supervoxels in an energy optimization framework. In: Daniilidis, K., Maragos, P., Paragios, N. (eds.) ECCV 2010, Part V. LNCS, vol. 6315, pp. 211–224. Springer, Heidelberg (2010)
10. Levinshtein, A., Stere, A., Kutulakos, K.N., Fleet, D.J., Dickinson, S.J., Siddiqi, K.: Turbopixels: Fast superpixels using geometric flows. IEEE Transactions on Pattern Analysis and Machine Intelligence 31(12), 2290–2297 (2009)
11. Moore, A.P., Prince, S.J.D., Warrell, J., Mohammed, U., Jones, G.: Superpixel lattices. In: Proceedings of IEEE Conference on Computer Vision and Pattern Recognition, pp. 1–8 (2008)
12. Wang, S., Lu, H., Yang, F., Yang, M.H.: Superpixel tracking. In: Proceedings of the International Conference on Computer Vision, pp. 1–8 (2011)
13. Swain, M.J., Ballard, D.H.: Color indexing. International Journal of Computer Vision 7, 11–32 (1991)
14. Grabner, H., Grabner, M., Bischof, H.: Real-time tracking via on-line boosting. In: Proceedings of the British Machine Vision Conference, pp. 47–56 (2006)
15. Saffari, A., Leistner, C., Santner, J., Godec, M., Bischof, H.: On-line random forests. In: IEEE International Conference on Computer Vision Workshops (ICCV Workshops), pp. 1393–1400 (2009)

Carried Object Detection and Tracking Using Geometric Shape Models and Spatio-temporal Consistency

Aryana Tavanai, Muralikrishna Sridhar, Feng Gu, Anthony G. Cohn,
and David C. Hogg

School of Computing, University of Leeds
Leeds, LS2 9JT, United Kingdom
{fy06at,scms,f.gu,a.g.cohn,d.c.hogg}@leeds.ac.uk*

Abstract. This paper proposes a novel approach that detects and tracks carried objects by modelling the person-carried object relationship that is characteristic of the *carry event*. In order to detect a generic class of carried objects, we propose the use of geometric shape models, instead of using pre-trained object class models or solely relying on protrusions. In order to track the carried objects, we propose a novel optimization procedure that combines spatio-temporal consistency characteristic of the carry event, with conventional properties such as appearance and motion smoothness respectively. The proposed approach substantially outperforms a state-of-the-art approach on two challenging datasets PETS2006 and MINDSEYE2012.

1 Introduction

Detection and tracking of carried objects is an important component of vision systems whether these are surveillance systems that aim to detect events such as leaving, picking up or handing over a luggage, or robots that learn to perform better in indoor environments by analysing events where humans manipulate carried objects. Despite significant progress in object detection and tracking, the task of detecting and tracking carried objects well enough to be able to use them for activity analysis is still a challenging problem. This task is elusive due to the wide range of objects that can be carried by a person and the different ways in which carried objects relate to the person(s) carrying it e.g. carrying, dropping, swinging, picking it up, occluding etc.

An early approach [2] demonstrated that pre-trained object-class models for specific types of objects may be useful in domains where the variety of carried objects is relatively small and is known in advance, the objects are of sufficient size and there is limited clutter in the background. To generalise to a more realistic setting, researchers have focused on *indirect* ways of characterising carried

---

* The financial support of the EU Framework 7 project Co-RACE (FP7-ICT- 287752), and the DARPA Mind's Eye program (project VIGIL, W911NF-10-C-0083) is gratefully acknowledged.

M. Chen, B. Leibe, and B. Neumann (Eds.): ICVS 2013, LNCS 7963, pp. 223–233, 2013.
© Springer-Verlag Berlin Heidelberg 2013

objects, which first aim to identify the person region and background and then attempt to explain the remaining regions in terms of carried objects. The first of these approaches looked for carried objects in protrusions which are regarded as the part of foreground that is different from the person region. This approach evolved starting from an early work - *Backpack* [6] - that proposed temporal templates as a way of characterising the person region. Subsequent researchers have extended this approach by introducing refinements - such as modelling variances from the temporal templates [1] and 3-D exemplar temporal templates corresponding to different viewpoints of a walking person together with spatial priors in a very recent work [4]. Other indirect approaches have built a pre-trained appearance model of *persons without carried objects* and they detect *person carrying objects* as anomalies [9].

We propose a novel approach for carried object detection and tracking with the following contributions. (1) we perform object detection by using geometric shape models to characterise carried objects. In this way, we avoid using specific pre-trained object class models as in [2]. (2) our approach integrates detection and tracking by incorporating normal motion properties that apply generically to most carried objects such as spatio-temporal smoothness that have been widely used in the tracking literature, but have not been exploited for the carried object task. (3), and most importantly, we propose a novel approach for carried object detection and tracking by characterising carried objects given that only the *carry* event occurs i.e. that these objects follow a person's trajectory with a temporally continuous and characteristically consistent spatial relationship with respect to the person. Accordingly, we introduce an optimisation strategy that starts with a small set of detections with possibly false positives and increasingly incorporates a learned person-object spatial relationship that characterises the carry event. This procedure starts building longer tracks that tend to approximate the true carried object trajectory, while also rejecting the false positives. The learned spatial relationship leads to significant improvement compared to using a static spatial prior [4]. §5 shows that the proposed approach significantly improves the performance over a state-of-the-art carried object detector [4] on the PETS2006 and MINDSEYE2012 (www.visint.org) datasets. Dataset and code can be found at: http://www.engineering.leeds.ac.uk/computing/research/vision/CODT.

2   Proposed Formulation

We consider a video $\mathcal{I}$ which is a time series of images $\{I^1, ..., I^t, ..., I^N\}$. For this video, we obtain a corresponding sequence of foreground regions $F = \{f^1, ..., f^t, ...f^N\}$ and a set of person tracks $P = \{p_1, ..., p_M\}$. Here a person track $p_i \in P$ is a time series of *segmented person regions* $\{..., p_i^t, ...\}$. In addition, we define $\mathcal{R}$ as a set of candidate object regions, from which a set $\mathcal{O}$ of all possible candidate object tracks may be sampled. We describe the procedure for obtaining the foreground, person tracks, object detections in §4.

In this work, we make the simplifying assumption that *carry* is the only event that governs the relationship between a person p_i and an associated set of carried object tracks $O \subseteq \mathcal{O}$ i.e. the carried objects are not picked up, dropped or given to another person. That is, if a carried object track $o_j \in O$ is associated with a person track p_i, then there exists a bijective relationship between the corresponding regions $o_j^t \in o_j$ and $p_i^t \in p_i$. We also assume that the carried object tracks are independent of each other.

Under these assumptions, our task is to find a set of carried object tracks O associated with each person track p_i. Accordingly, for each person track p_i we formulate our task as finding an optimal set of carried object tracks $\hat{O}$ that maximises the following objective.

$$\hat{O} = \arg\max_{O \subseteq \mathcal{O}} \prod_{o_j \in O} \mathcal{P}(o_j|\Theta_O)\mathcal{P}(o_j|p_i, F, \Theta_C)\mathcal{P}(o_j|\Theta_S) \tag{1}$$

In the above equation, the probability distribution $\mathcal{P}(o_j|\Theta_O)$ prefers tracks that consists of regions which correspond to certain geometric shapes, as detailed in §2.1. The probability distribution $\mathcal{P}(o_j|p_i, F, \Theta_C)$ models the person-object relationship that is characteristic of the carry event (§2.2). The probability distribution $\mathcal{P}(o_j|\Theta_S)$ parametrised by the smoothness model Θ_S in the above equation regards a track o_j being more likely, if the sequence of carried object regions constituting this track are smooth with respect to motion and appearance and if it has other desirable properties such as minimum overlap with other tracks, minimum gap and maximum possible length. These measures are computed similarly to [15].

2.1   Geometric Object Shape Models $\mathcal{P}(o_j|\Theta_O)$

We regard a candidate object track $o_j \in O$ as more likely to be a carried object if the shape of the region is likely to be any of the pre-defined generic geometric shapes. The distribution $\mathcal{P}(o_j|\Theta_O)$ in equation 1 measures this likelihood with respect to a set of geometric shape models Θ_O. Assuming independence between an object region o_j^t and the rest of the object regions in an object track o_j, we factorise the likelihood $\mathcal{P}(o_j|\Theta_O)$ as $\mathcal{P}(o_j|\Theta_O) = \prod_{o_j^t \in o_j} \mathcal{P}(o_j^t|\Theta_O)$. We marginalise across each of the object shape models $\theta \in \Theta_O$ and assume a uniform prior distribution $\mathcal{P}(\theta)$ across these models to obtain $\mathcal{P}(o_j^t|\Theta_O) = 1/|\Theta_O|\left(\sum_{\theta \in \Theta_O} \mathcal{P}(o_j^t|\theta)\right)$.

We consider a convex shape model with parameter $\theta_c \in \Theta_O$ and an elongated shape model with parameter $\theta_e \in \Theta_O$ since many carried objects have a shape that is approximately convex (e.g. briefcases, suitcases, petrol cans) or elongated (e.g. objects with an elongated part - shovels, guns, brooms). We evaluate the probabilities $\mathcal{P}(o_j^t|\theta_c)$ and $\mathcal{P}(o_j^t|\theta_e)$ for the convex and elongated model as an exponential distribution $1/z_0 \exp(\theta_c \mathcal{C}(E(o_j^t)))$ and $1/z_1 \exp(\theta_e \mathcal{E}(E(o_j^t)))$ over a convexity measure $\mathcal{C}(E(o_j^t))$ and a parallel measure $\mathcal{E}(E(o_j^t))$ respectively. Here, $E(o_j^t)$ refers to the set of edges that form the boundary of the object region o_j^t. In §4, we describe our novel level-wise mining approach for extracting the set $\mathcal{R}$ of candidate object regions, where each such region is formed by a set of edges. We compute the degree of convexity $\mathcal{C}(E(o_j^t))$ for a region o_j^t, using the method in [16]. In order to compute the degree of parallelism, $\mathcal{E}(E(o_j^t))$, we only consider those candidate sets of contour segments $E(o_j^t)$ which can be partitioned into two non-overlapping proximal groups of nearly co-linear contour segments, that are roughly parallel to each other. We combine a measure of co-linearity [13] within each group with the degree of parallelism across the two groups.

2.2 Person-Carried Object Relationship $\mathcal{P}(o_j | p_i, F, \Theta_C)$

We regard a candidate object track $o_j \in O$ as more likely to be a carried object associated with a person p_i if: (i) the track o_j follows p_i's trajectory with spatio-temporal consistency characterised by the *carry event*; (ii) the object regions $o_j^t \in o_j$ overlaps with protrusions corresponding to the person region $p_i^t \in p_i$. Both these person-carried-object relationships are modelled by the probability distribution $\mathcal{P}(o_j | p_i, F, \Theta_C)$ with carriedness parameter set Θ_C. Given model parameters θ_r for protrusions, θ_s for spatio-temporal consistency and the foreground regions F, we factorise this distribution whose two terms that capture person-object spatial relation and protrusions respectively, as explained below.

$$\mathcal{P}(o_j | p_i, F, \Theta_C) = \prod_{o_j^t \in o_j} \mathcal{P}(o_j^t | p_i^t, \theta_s) \mathcal{P}(o_j^t | p_i^t, f^t, \theta_r)$$

Person-Object Spatial Relation. A novel way of characterising carried objects given that only the *carry* event occurs is that they follow a person's trajectory with a temporally continuous and characteristically consistent spatial relationship with respect to the person. To quantify this, we propose a voting measure that counts the number of times the relative position of a pixel with respect to the centroid of a person's region falls within a detection.

Let $dx_{p_i^t}, dy_{p_i^t}$ be the offset of a pixel relative to the centroid $(x_{p_i^t}, y_{p_i^t})$ of the i'th person's bounding box p_i^t at time t i.e. $(x_{p_i^t} + dx_{p_i^t}, y_{p_i^t} + dy_{p_i^t})$ is the absolute position of the pixel relative to the image frame I^t. We define a function $\delta(dx_{p_i^t}, dy_{p_i^t}, o_j^t)$ as follows.

$$\delta(dx_{p_i^t}, dy_{p_i^t}, o_j^t, i) = \begin{cases} 1, & \text{if } (x_{p_i^t} + dx_{p_i^t}, y_{p_i^t} + dy_{p_i^t}) \in o_j^t \\ 0, & \text{if } (x_{p_i^t} + dx_{p_i^t}, y_{p_i^t} + dy_{p_i^t}) \notin o_j^t \end{cases}$$

Using the above definition we define the heatmap H of a relative offset $(dx_{p_i^t}, dy_{p_i^t})$ position as the following.

$$H(dx_{p_i^t}, dy_{p_i^t}) = \sum_{o_j \in O} \sum_{o_j^t \in o_j} \delta(x_{p_i^t} + dx_{p_i^t}, y_{p_i^t} + dy_{p_i^t}, o_j^t, i)$$

Given a set of tracks O associated with a person p_i, the intensity values in the heatmap measure the number of votes for each relative offset pixel $(dx_{p_i^t}, dy_{p_i^t})$ given by the tracks in O. Since we expect carried objects to have a consistent relative location with respect to the person and noise to be more randomly distributed, the heatmap captures the locations relative to the person where carried objects is most likely to exist. This is as a result of these locations receiving higher votes in the heatmap due to the repeated presence of potential carried objects even though they may be sparsely detected in the video.

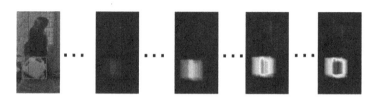

Fig. 1. An illustration of the learned spatial distribution of the object relative to the person approximates the true relative position in the leftmost figure

We regard a detection o_j^t as more likely to be a carried object if it covers pixels with high intensity values in the heatmap. We model the *relative positional probability* $\mathcal{P}(o_j^t|p_i^t, \theta_s)$ as follows.

$$\mathcal{P}(o_j^t|p_i^t, \theta_s) = \frac{1}{z_3} \exp\left(\theta_s \sum_{(x,y)\in o_j^t} H(x - x_{p_i^t}, y - y_{p_i^t})\right) \tag{2}$$

This distribution tends to get closer to the true distribution of the carried objects' relative location with respect to a person (Fig. 1) with the increasing number of true detections over the false detections, as further described in §3.

Protrusions. Areas corresponding to protrusions have been shown to be likely carried object regions with respect to the region of the person carrying it. For each person region p_i^t, we obtain a protrusion region α_i^t by subtracting the person region p_i^t from the foreground region f^t in frame I^t and considering only a subregion of α_i^t in the vicinity of the person (defined by the detected person bounding box). We regard a region o_j^t as more likely to be a carried object if it overlaps significantly with α_i^t. Accordingly we compute the degree of overlap $\mathcal{V}(\alpha_i^t, o_j^t) = (\alpha_i^t \cap o_j^t)/(\alpha_i^t \cup o_j^t)$ and then evaluate $\mathcal{P}(o_j^t|p_i^t, f^t, \theta_r)$ using an exponential model $1/z_2 \exp(\theta_r(\mathcal{V}(\alpha_i^t, o_j^t)))$.

3   Event Driven Optimisation

We now describe the main novelty of the paper which is an event driven optimisation. According to this scheme, the optimal solution of the objective function in equation 1 emerges as a result of iterations which involve cyclic interactions between the two components of the objective function. We define the first component, $\mathcal{P}(o_j|\Theta_O)\mathcal{P}(o_j|\Theta_S)$, as a product of the probability distributions corresponding to the detection strengths and spatio-temporal continuity respectively. The second novel component $\mathcal{P}(o_j|p_i, F, \Theta_C)$ is the relative positional probability distribution that models the person-object spatial relationship which is characteristic of the *carry event*.

We first describe the basic search procedure in the optimisation process before discussing the role of these two components. For each person track p_i, the optimisation involves starting with an initial set of tracklets O^0 and then applying a sequence of moves to iteratively obtain a sequence of hypothesised tracklets $(O^1, ..., O^k, ...)$. The objective function given in equation 1 is used at each step k

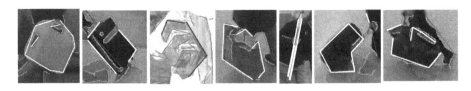

Fig. 2. Examples of using Geometric Shape Models for carried object detection. Green segments represent edges from the Canny edge detector and the solid convex/elongated objects mined in a level-wise fashion.

in the iteration to decided whether to accept the new hypothesis O^k or to persist the previous hypothesis O^{k-1}. We adopt two simple moves, (i) form larger tracklets from smaller ones by randomly choose a tracklet and then linking this tracklet to a neighbouring tracklet, which is chosen uniformly at random (u.a.r) from the set of neighbouring tracklets. (ii) split larger tracklets into smaller ones by choosing a tracklet u.a.r from the set of tracklets and then selecting a location along this chosen tracklet u.a.r and finally breaking it into two smaller tracklets at this location. After a relatively large number of iterations, we terminate the optimisation process and regard the final set of tracklets of length more than one as the optimal set of carried objects $\hat{\mathcal{O}}$. In the following we first introduce the basic tracking system to which we add the contribution of the heatmap and an attention-like mechanism leading to three variants of the optimisation process. We evaluate each of these variations in the experimental section.

Basic Tracking System (BTS). When this procedure is used *only* with the first component, it tends to result in carried object tracks that have higher detection probabilities $\mathcal{P}(o_j|\Theta_O)$ and are smooth with respect to the properties captured in $\mathcal{P}(o_j|\Theta_S)$. We call such a system as the basic tracking system, that we refer to in our experimental section.

Heatmap Driven System (HDS). The introduction of the 2nd component i.e. the relative positional probability distribution $\mathcal{P}(o_j|p_i, F, \Theta_C)$ tends to favour the formation of object tracks whose objects firstly overlap with protrusions, and secondly (more importantly) those tracks that overlap with the heatmap given in equation 2. That is these tracks tend to accumulate higher values of the positional probability distribution and therefore have the characteristics of a carried object, as described in §2.2.

Attention Driven System (ADS). To further capitalise on the potential of this relative positional probability distribution, we introduce an *attention-like mechanism* into the optimisation process, where we start by considering only those object detections that have high detection likelihoods and we call these initial tracklets of length one as initial seed tracklets. At each iteration, the link move forms larger seed tracklets by *focussing* on connecting *only* seed tracklets to other seed tracklets or non-seed detections (tracklet of length one). Similarly the split move operates only on the seed tracklets.

At each iteration, only the seed tracklets contribute to the computation of the heatmap. As the heatmap becomes more well defined with further iterations, some of those non-seed tracklets with higher positional probability distributions (although they may have relatively lower detection likelihoods) tend to be included as seed tracklets. These updated seed tracklets are used for applying moves in the next iteration. In this manner, an attention-like mechanism begins to evolve with a tendency to *select* object tracklets that correspond to the true carried objects, *against* other false positive candidate tracks. Due to the cyclic interactions between the two components of the objective function, the optimisation often starts with a sparse set of detections with possibly several false positives and starts building longer tracks that tend to approximate the true carried object trajectory, while rejecting the false positives.

4 Object Detection

We now describe the procedure for obtaining foreground, person regions and carried object detections (Fig. 2) respectively. We start by computing a sequence of foreground regions for a video using an off the shelf foreground extraction technique [11]. We then obtain person tracks by detecting a set of person regions in each frame and then we track all these detections using a dynamic programming based tracker [10]. The person regions in each frame are obtained in three steps. First we detect bounding boxes corresponding to the person detections obtained using a standard object detector with a trained person model [5]. Second, we obtain bounding boxes that are body part estimates inside each of the person bounding boxes using articulated pose estimation code [14]. Finally we take

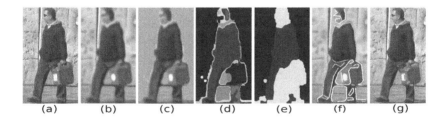

(a)   (b)   (c)   (d)   (e)   (f)   (g)

Fig. 3. The process of obtaining candidate carried object detection. (a) We first obtain the image corresponding to the person detection; (b) We then apply the method in [8] to enhance edges corresponding to natural boundaries; (c) We apply foreground extraction on b (background shown in green); (d) We apply colour based segmentation to c; (e) We identify the two largest segments (given in red) in d, which tend to correspond to regions on the person. The carried object is more likely to be present in the non-person regions (shown in green); (f) Using the regions identified in e, many of the line segments belonging to the person are removed (coloured with cyan); (g) The result of applying level-wise mining to the remaining edges (coloured yellow in f) to obtain candidate carried object regions (coloured in green), as an input to the event driven optimisation.

the union of the regions circumscribed by each part to be a segmentation of the person.

In order to find likely candidates for carried object detections, we first remove a majority of line-segments that form the boundaries of persons but not of the objects using a procedure illustrated in Fig. 3 (a-f). This approach drastically reduces the set of line segments enabling us to generate a smaller set of candidate object regions from the remaining set of line segments. We then search this set for candidate object detections o_j^t, where each detection is just a subset of line segments forming a fully or partially connected chain (Fig. 3.g), that are likely to belong to any of the geometric shapes under consideration. In order to search efficiently, we use a level-wise mining procedure, where two candidate $k - 1$ subsets are merged if they share $k - 2$ segments and accepted as a k candidate set o_j^t, if the likelihood score $\mathcal{P}(o_j^t|\theta)$ of o_j^t, with respect to a geometric shape model $\theta \in \Theta_O$ is above a minimum conservative threshold.

5   Experimental Setup

The experimentation consists of two aspects, first of which is a comparison between the proposed approach and the state-of-the-art protrusion based Damen and Hogg's carried object detector [4], henceforth DHD. Secondly, we would like to further explore the true potential of our approach, by alternating certain key components and identifying their effects in terms of detection performance. As a result, a benchmark dataset, namely the PETS2006 dataset is used for the first aspect of baseline comparison. On the other hand, a much more complex dataset, the MINDSEYE2012 dataset, is used in a set of more extensive experiments, which are aimed at the exploration of key components of the proposed approach. The corresponding evaluation is concentrated on the detection

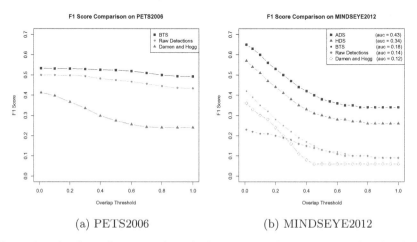

(a) PETS2006   (b) MINDSEYE2012

Fig. 4. Result plots of compared methods in terms of F1 scores as the threshold of overlap increases on both PETS2006 and MINDSEYE2012

performance of the compared approaches and thus it is done with respect to spatio-temporal localisation of each carried object per frame by computing the standard overlap ratio also used in [4], except that we also vary the overlap threshold and report results for each value.

Datasets. All seven videos of the third camera were chosen, due to its view angle, for PETS2006, similar to [4]. Overall 70 video clips were created by a third party from the MINDSEYE project year 2 dataset, with an average length of 200 frames. The complexity of this dataset results from variations in camera settings, environmental factors, e.g. changes in light conditions (e.g. brightness due to weather), moving trees and grasses in the background, as well as a greater variety of carried object types. The ground-plane homography estimation of PETS2006 was provided as part of the sample set, while that of MINDSEYE2012 is done for each camera setting. Human tracks of both datasets are generated through first applying basic background subtraction to obtain foreground segmentation and then using an off-the-shelf tracker [10].

Parameter Settings. In our experiments, we tune the parameter set Θ_O (corresponding to the geometric shape models), Θ_S (modelling smooth trajectories), and $\theta_r \in \Theta_C$ (concerning the overlap between the protrusion and the object mask respectively), on a separate subset of the Mindseye project. Values of these parameters are independent from any particular selection of subset, containing a reasonable number of videos. This is because general geometric properties Θ_O (e.g. convexity) are invariant across samples from any dataset. As focus of this work is to prove a concept, only the convex shape model is investigated. Similarly Θ_S are generic due to similar motion patterns in the datasets (e.g. people

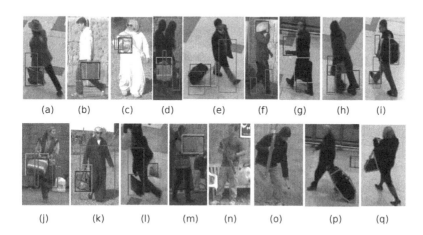

Fig. 5. Illustration of the successes and the failures of our approach and also a comparison with [4]. For images (a)-(m), boxes coloured in green correspond to ground truth, red to [4] and blue to those obtained using the proposed approach. Note that the ground truth is sometimes imperfect eg. (l). Images (n)-(q) illustrate the obtained contour of the detected object using the proposed method.

walking). Finally, for $\theta_r \in \Theta_C$, irrespective of the dataset and the perspective, it is reasonable to assume that the protrusion mask corresponds to a part or whole of the object. This is due to the assumption that the person and the carried object together constitute the foreground mask. In addition, we set the parameter $\theta_s \in \Theta_C$ equal to 1 over the length of the person track in consideration, acting as a normalisation factor. Default parameter settings of the detector [4] are used for both datasets, as it is often considered most suitable for general uses.

6   Results and Analysis

Results. Fig. 4a gives F1 curves for DHD, raw detections (RD) and the BTS, with Fig. 4b additionally showing HDS and ADS, with each being better than the previous. Even though BTS out-performs DHD on both datasets, ADS significantly outperforms DHD and all other variations of the system.

Qualitative Analysis. In this section we also present a qualitative analysis of the results on PETS2006 and MINDSEYE2012 by summarising successes and failure cases Fig 5. (a)-(f) illustrate how our approach is able to detect different types of objects such as boxes, bags, plastic bags and suitcases. This highlights the merits of performing generic object detection without specific object models. (g)-(i) show a few cases where our approach performs poorly, as the edges do not sufficiently demarcate the object from the person. The (c,d,n,o) images illustrate that our approach is also able to detect objects that are not protrusions. (a,b,c,f,j,k,l) highlight some typical cases where the protrusion based approach [4] fails whilst ours succeeds. (d) illustrates a situation when multiple persons are close by, or when the person's bounding box is displaced. (f) illustrates a case where the influence of a relatively strong prior on the position of the object in relation to the person can hinder the detection of an object (e.g. basket) above a person's head. (n,o,p,q) also illustrate that our approach can localise an object accurately with a contour around it.   .

7   Summary and Future Work

We have introduced a vision system that performs carried object detection and tracking. Our approach characterises carried objects in terms of generic shape properties such as convexity, whilst taking account of the fact that they are often, but not always, protrusions on a person silhouette, and exploiting the property that they have continuous and spatially consistent trajectories relative to the person carrying them. In addition, an iterative event driven optimisation process, which uses a heatmap and attention like mechanism, is introduced to obtain an optimal set of object detections. Experimental results show that our approach significantly outperforms a state-of-the-art technique [4], especially the ADS system where both a heatmap and attention-like mechanism are employed, on two challenging datasets. A future extension of this work would be to include other geometric shapes and events such as drop, pick-up, give etc.

References

1. Benabdelkader, C., Davis, L.S.: Detection of people carrying objects: A motion-based recognition approach. In: Proc. Intl Conf. Automatic Face and Gesture Recognition, pp. 378–384 (2002)
2. Branca, A., Leo, M., Attolico, G., Distante, A.: Detection of objects carried by people. In: Proc. Int. Conf. Image Processing, vol. 3, pp. 317–320 (2002)
3. Cutler, R., Davis, L.: Robust real-time periodic motion detection, analysis, and applications. PAMI 22(8) (2000)
4. Damen, D., Hogg, D.: Detecting carried objects from sequences of walking pedestrians. PAMI 34(6), 1056–1067 (2012)
5. Felzenszwalb, P.F., Girshick, R.B., McAllester, D.A., Ramanan, D.: Object detection with discriminatively trained part-based models. PAMI 32(9), 1627–1645 (2010)
6. Haritaoglu, I., Cutler, R., Harwood, D., Davis, L.S.: Backpack: Detection of people carrying objects using silhouettes. In: CVPR, vol. 1, pp. 102–107 (1999)
7. Harwood, D., Haritaoglu, I., Davis, L.S.: W4: Real-time surveillance of people and their activities. PAMI 22(8) (2000)
8. Kroon, D., Slump, C.H.: Coherence filtering to enhance the mandibular canal in cone-beam ct data. In: Proceedings of the 4th Annual Symposium of the IEEE-EMBS Benelux Chapter, pp. 41–44 (2009)
9. Nanda, H., Benabdelkedar, C., Davis, L.S.: Modelling pedestrian shapes for outlier detection: A neural net based approach. In: Proc. Intelligent Vehicles Symp., pp. 428–433 (2003)
10. Pirsiavash, H., Ramanan, D., Fowlkes, C.C.: Globally-optimal greedy algorithms for tracking a variable number of objects. In: CVPR, pp. 1201–1208 (2011)
11. Stauffer, C., Grimson, W.E.L.: Learning patterns of activity using real-time tracking. PAMI 22, 747–757 (2000)
12. Tao, D., Li, X., Maybank, S.J., Xindong, W.: Human carrying status in visual surveillance. In: CVPR (2006)
13. Tsuda, K., Minoh, M., Ikeda, K.: Extracting straight lines by sequential fuzzy clustering. Pattern Recognition Letters 17(6), 643–649 (1996)
14. Yang, Y., Ramanan, D.: Articulated pose estimation using flexible mixtures of parts. In: CVPR (2011)
15. Yu, Q., Medioni, G.: Multiple-target tracking by spatiotemporal monte carlo markov chain data association. PAMI 31 (2009)
16. Zunic, J., Rosin, P.L.: A convexity measurement for polygons. PAMI 26, 173–182 (2002)

Robust Multi-hypothesis 3D Object Pose Tracking

Georgios Chliveros[1], Maria Pateraki[1], and Panos Trahanias[1,2]

[1] Foundation for Research and Technology Hellas, Institute of Computer Science,
Heraklion, Crete, GR-70013
[2] Dept. of Computer Science, University of Crete, Heraklion, GR-71409

Abstract. This paper tackles the problem of 3D object pose tracking from monocular cameras. Data association is performed via a variant of the Iterative Closest Point algorithm, thus making it robust to noise and other artifacts. We re-initialise the hypothesis space based on the resulting re-projection error between hypothesised models and observed image objects. This is performed through a non-linear minimisation step after correspondences are found. The use of multi-hypotheses and correspondences refinement, lead to a robust framework. Experimental results with benchmark image sequences indicate the effectiveness of our framework.

Keywords: Robot Vision, Object Tracking, Relative Pose Estimation.

1 Introduction

Tracking of 3D objects from a monocular camera is important for numerous applications, including robotic control, grasping and manipulation. Several advances have been made but remains a difficult problem due to issues raised from both a theoretical and a practical perspective. Various approaches have been suggested (see survey in [1]), with most commonly employed being those of 'model-based' methods (see survey in [2]).

Early work by Harris [3] utilised a 3D CAD *model* which is projected onto the image frame and registered to the image extracted contour. A similar approach is employed in [4], where the model takes the form of a parametrised 3D object. Since these early works, great effort has been taken to improving upon the correspondence between the object's model and image contours. For example, Drummond and Cipolla [5] use binary space partition trees to determine the model contour (edge points) and subsequently perform a 1D search for corresponding points along the normal of the projected contour on the image. In [6], registration is based on the iterative closest point (ICP), but it considers the re-projection error as a non-linear minimization problem that is solved via the Levenberg–Marquardt (LM) algorithm. Non-linear error minimisation is also utilised in [4,7] but with a combined 1D point search.

Even though the aforementioned approaches do consider refinement of the estimated object pose, they do not consider it as a means to *re-initialisation*:

M. Chen, B. Leibe, and B. Neumann (Eds.): ICVS 2013, LNCS 7963, pp. 234–243, 2013.
© Springer-Verlag Berlin Heidelberg 2013

i.e. evaluating new model hypotheses. Inasmuch most tracking algorithms assume that a given 'start' or previous estimate of the object pose is sufficient for algorithm initialisation / re-initialisation. Alas, for erroneous pose initialisation values the tracker either does not converge to the true pose, or loses track of the object after some time in long image sequences.

To compensate for initialisation / re-initialisation issues, multiple pose hypotheses have been considered. An initialisation procedure is offered in [4], but it relies on motion segmentation, based on the displacement of extracted image features (contour / edges) between consecutive frames. Vacchetti *et al.* [8] employ a limited number of low level hypotheses and the tracking problem is solved via 'local' bundle adjustment. The incorporation of multi-hypotheses has recently been given particular attention when formulated within probabilistic frameworks (e.g. in [9,10]). In [11], a Sequential Monte Carlo (SMC) framework has been suggested, where a greater number of pose hypotheses (i.e. particles) is generated and maintained. Unfortunately the search space may be too large to converge at a good initialisation pose and within reasonable time limits. Re-initialisation is considered for establishing and generating a higher number of hypotheses (particles), when degenerate pose estimates occur based on the *effective particle size* defined in [12]. Unfortunately, SMC frameworks are computationally expensive. For example in [11], roughly a single pose estimate per second can be provided.

In this paper we propose the application of image extracted features (Section 2) in a multiple hypotheses 3D object tracking (MH3DOT) framework (Section 3) from known 3D models. However, for finding correspondences in dissimilar model and image point feature sets, we utilise the least median of squares error (Section 3.1). To compensate for re-initialisation issues we further perform a short term adjustment over given correspondence sets via non-linear minimisation (Section 3.2). We apply our MH3DOT method on benchmark sequences and illustrate that it is sufficiently robust for tracking over long time period and for a number of challenges in visual tracking systems (Section 4).

2   Extracted Image Features

To extract image features (contours and edges) we extend the 2D tracking approach of [13,14] to apply for multiple objects, according to which foreground coloured pixels are identified based on their colour and grouped together based on their colour histograms. Location and shape of each tracked colour pixels group is maintained by a set of pixel hypotheses which are initially sampled from the observed histograms and are propagated from frame t to $t+1$ according to linear object dynamics computed by a Kalman filter. The distribution of the propagated pixel hypotheses provides a representation for the uncertainty in both the 2D position and the shape of the tracked object. There are no explicit assumptions about the objects motion, shapes and dynamics.

Based on said templates and histograms a number of colour classes $c_i, i \in \mathbb{N}^*$ are formed. The posterior probability for each pixel $I_{n,m}$ with color c to belong to a color class c_i is computed according to Bayes rule $P(c_i|I_{n,m}) =$

Fig. 1. Extracted image features. From left to right: the original image; the result of thresholding operations; pixel probabilities after labelling; resulting point features, where the contour is shown in yellow and the internal edge is depicted in green.

$(P(c_i)/P(I_{n,m})) P(I_{n,m}|c_i)$, where $P(I_{n,m}) = \sum_j P(I_{n,m}|c_j)P(c_j)$. The prior probabilities of foreground pixels having $P(I_{n,m})$ specific colour c and $P(c_i)$ specific colour class, are computed via off-line training. $P(I_{n,m}|c_i)$ is the likelihood of colour c foreground regions for specific colour class.

The algorithm handles the issue of assigning a pixel in more than one color classes / objects, by assigning to the class with the highest probability. Using multi-level thresholding operations [15] and standard connected components labeling in the totality of the image [13], we acquire all regions that have high probability of belonging to the tracked object. A further query within contour's pixel regions reveals internal edges of the object (see example of Fig. 1).

3   Methodology for Tracking

In our methodology the model and image point features correspondences are found via a *'correspondence process'*. This is performed using an Iterative Closest Point variant, which makes for robustness to noise and other artifacts. Hypotheses are formed from rendered 3D models and are re-initialised by incorporating a non-linear minimisation step over a short term window. This is the 'interpretation process', which adjusts and bounds the pose error.

3.1   Correspondence Process

Given the (intrinsic) camera calibration matrix $\mathbf{K}$ and a projection matrix $\mathbf{P} = [\mathbf{R}|\mathbf{t}]$, then model 3D vectors $\mathbf{m}_i$ can be projected to the image plane; that is $\acute{\mathbf{m}}_i = \mathbf{KPm}_i$, where $\mathbf{m}_i$ are 3D points from model database and $\acute{\mathbf{m}}_i$ represents the 3D-to-2D projection model points. From the rendered model $\acute{\mathbf{m}}_i$, we subsequently extract the projected feature model points $\hat{\mathbf{m}}_i$. In the model feature extraction case, no multi-thresholding and labeling operations are performed, since the rendered down-projection is much simpler. The set of such points $\mathbb{M} = \{\hat{\mathbf{m}}_i\}_1^{n_m}$ is the employed model representation in our work. Observed image feature points are $\mathbb{P} = \{\hat{\mathbf{p}}_j\}_1^{n_p}$ are extracted using the procedure of Section 2.

Iterative Closest Point (ICP) algorithm and its variants have been extensively studied for matching. However, all points from $\mathbb{P}$, $\mathbb{M}$ (or subsets thereof) need be

Fig. 2. The TrICP correspondence process: the blue line defines the observed image feature points; the green line illustrates the down-projected model points; the red lines denote the trimmed least squares point correspondences

matched due to the iterative least mean squares error. Thus, in the presence of noise and artifacts (e.g. cluttered background) the matching process can rapidly deteriorate. For these reasons we employ ICP with a least median of squares error [16] with a 'trimming' operation. The Trimmed Least Squares ICP (TrICP) [17], allows for the two point sets to contain unequal number of points $(i \neq j)$. In our implementation, TrICP calculates the translation and rotation between the feature point sets by 'minimizing' the sum of the least median squared individual Mahalanobis distances [16], defined as

$$\mathbf{d}_{ij}^2 = (\hat{\mathbf{m}}_i - \hat{\mathbf{p}}_j)^{\mathrm{T}}(\mathbf{S}_{m_i} + \mathbf{S}_{p_j})^{-1}(\hat{\mathbf{m}}_i - \hat{\mathbf{p}}_j) \qquad (1)$$

where $\mathbf{S}_{m_i}$ is the covariance, thus the uncertainty, on the position of point feature $\hat{\mathbf{m}}_i$; and respectively for $\mathbf{S}_{p_j}$ of $\hat{\mathbf{p}}_j$.

To improve speed we first employ nearest neighbour search in $\mathbb{P}$, $\mathbb{M}$ using uniform grid structures[1]. The best possible alignment between data / model sets is found by 'sifting' through at most i nearest-neighbour combinations in an attempt to find a subset of size less than j, which yields the lowest sum of ordered $\mathbf{d}_{ij}^2$ values. When performing the least median search two thresholds are employed: (i) max distance to be used between valid point combinations, and (ii) max percentage of points allowed for the 'trimming' operation. An example of the correspondence loop can be found in Fig. 2, where the trimmed least squares point correspondences can also be seen.

Hypotheses initialisation: The starting point for finding correspondences is models generation from a parametrised pose estimate $\mathbf{s} = (t_x, t_y, t_z, \alpha_x, \alpha_y, \alpha_z)$ given at the previous frame instance, where t and α are the translation and rotation elements respectively. However, at the start of an image sequence this may not be the case (no prior pose is provided). Thus, we need to have in place an initialisation procedure, so that we generate a representative search space over rotations $(\alpha_x + \delta\alpha_x, \alpha_y + \delta\alpha_y, \alpha_z + \delta\alpha_z)$. The term $\delta\alpha$ can be assigned as dictated by a

---

[1] Other structures like 'range-trees' would cost with each query $\mathcal{O}(N \log N)$ as opposed to $\mathcal{O}(N)$ in the uniform case.

number of increment steps (N) over the full rotation range $(0, \pi)$ of the corresponding axis. However, this results in at least $3N(N^2 + 1)$ model hypotheses, which will require a great computational effort. In our implementation, rotations over the x, y axes, are constrained by the use of of monitoring the displacement of image extracted observed features, based on the assumption that for the first few frames, neighbouring moved image features represent projected features of the object we wish to initialise for our tracking process. It can be estimated that this constraint reduces the model hypothesis space to approximately N^2. The advantage of this procedure is that there will always exist a pose estimate, reflecting the system's 'best guess' of what the actual pose of the object is.

With respect to the covariance matrix $\mathbf{S}_{p_j}$, this is a 2×2 matrix with predetermined values modelling the observation noise on the camera frame, such that $0 < \sigma_x, \sigma_y < 0.2$; experimentally verified as an appropriate threshold. It should be evident that the higher the σ_x, σ_y values, the higher the uncertainty expected over the x and y axis respectively. The covariance matrix $\mathbf{S}_{m_i}$ is initialised as a unit matrix, and is subsequently updated within the interpretation process of Section 3.2.

3.2 Interpretation Process

The 're-initialisation' problem mentioned in Section 1, can be formulated as a minimisation problem either within small image frames sequence window (local) or a large window (global) bundle adjustment framework. Inspired by [4], we use an 'interpretation' loop because the correspondence sets' found in Section 3.1 process, need to be assessed for their 'validity' (i.e. reduce the number of outliers) as time passes over a sequence of neighbouring frames. Therefore the resulting set of model interpretations, are those that result in the smallest residuals between models and observed point features. Only those with the smallest residual are referenced as potential solutions and maintained over the next few frames. The aforementioned residuals are thus re-evaluated via non-linear minimisation of the re-projection error, between the model(s) and observed feature points. This is expressed as the sum of squares of a large number of nonlinear real-valued functions; i.e. a non-linear least squares problem. Thus, the objective function is formulated as:

$$\hat{\mathbf{s}}_t = \underset{\mathbf{s}}{\mathrm{argmin}} \sum_{i=1}^{n} ||\mathbf{p}_i - f(\mathbf{s}, \mathbf{m}_i)||^2 \qquad (2)$$

where $f(\cdot)$ is the function that projects the 3D model points to the image plane, according to $\mathbf{s}$.

Assuming an initial pose estimate $\hat{\mathbf{s}}$ equal to the current TrICP pose estimate, found during the correspondence process, the pose is updated iteratively according to $\hat{\mathbf{s}}_t = \hat{\mathbf{s}}_t + \Delta t$, where Δt is given by:

$$\Delta t = -(\mathbf{J}^\mathrm{T}\mathbf{J} + \mu\mathbf{I})^{-1}\mathbf{J}^\mathrm{T}\epsilon_t \qquad (3)$$

and $\mathbf{J}$ is the Jacobian resulting from $f(\cdot)$ computed at $\mathbf{s}_t$, and $\epsilon_t = |f(\hat{\mathbf{s}}_t) - f(\mathbf{s}_t)|$. The scalar μ, computed after every iteration, is a 'dumping term' and controls

Fig. 3. The interpretation process: an example of pose model best hypothesis after the LM optimisation step takes place

the behavior of a Levenberg-Marquardt (LM) algorithm. If the updated pose leads to a reduction in the error, the update is accepted and the process repeats with a decreased damping term μ. Otherwise, the damping term is increased, and the process iterates until a value of Δt that decreases the error is found.

An example output of this process can be seen in Fig. 3, 4. In Fig. 3 we illustrate a case where we selected the best hypothesis out of the initial N number of hypothesis generated. The realisation of these N number of hypotheses is illustrated in Fig. 4. At run-time execution we have set the generation of 35 hypotheses when the error is deemed to be large. In Frame 1300 the error was at 0.1689, i.e. greater than the preset value of 0.0025. Of the total number of formed hypotheses, and at Frame 1302 they are reduced to 6. In total, from Frame 1300 to Frame 1304, only three hypotheses survive (from a least squares fitting error of 0.1688 to 0.0022.

In this local framework, the normal equations have a sparse block structure. This is due to the fact that there is a lack of interaction among parameters for different (down-projected) 3D points and camera extracted feature points. This can be exploited to the overall algorithm computational benefit by avoiding storage and operation upon zero elements. Thus a sparse variant of the LM algorithm that takes advantage of the normal equations zeros pattern, greatly reduces the computational effort involved [18].

Hypotheses re-initialisation: Contour and edge points of an object may not provide enough information to uniquely identify the objects pose. This would become more prominent when occluded areas of the object and natural obstructions as well as the object coming in and out of the field of view of the camera.

To remedy for the aforementioned, if in the TrICP correspondence loop the best pose estimate has a large error attached to it, then an LM interpretation process is initiated. For a large LM error a greater number of rendered model hypotheses are generated. Hypotheses are generated by rotating the object model with respect to a previous frame's pose estimate. The number of frames is dictated by the number of frames LM is allowed to operate upon.

Each of these model hypotheses is assigned a value of the goodness-of-fit with respect to the current image frame. The values are updated from frame to frame based on the minimization of the objective function. Hence, multiple hypotheses are generated only when the error returned by the minimization algorithm exceeds a threshold. The covariance matrix calculated in the LM minimisation step, is assigned for $\mathbf{S}_{m_i}$ in the correspondence process'.

Frame	No. Hyps	Input	Generated Hyps

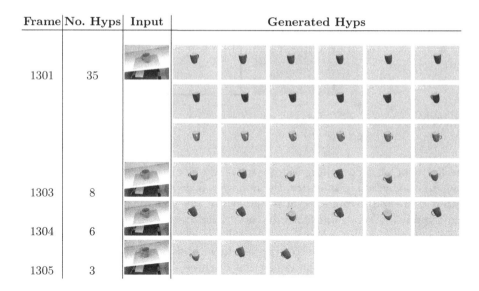

Fig. 4. An initialisation / re-initialisation case with hypotheses maintenance: a large re-projection error initiates a threshold number of hypothesis. For illustration purposes only few of the true number of generated hypotheses is reported.

Particle filters perform re-initialisation using Doucet's *effective particle size* N_{eff} [12]. In [11], and to avoid getting trapped in local minima, an additional rule is considered whereas if $N_{\text{eff}} < N_{\text{threshold}}$ then a set max number of pose hypotheses are generated. In our methodology a max number of model hypotheses is generated only when $\epsilon_t < \epsilon_{\text{threshold}}$, i.e. the error returned by the minimization algorithm exceeds a given threshold, or when a max number of LM iterations has been reached. We derive our '*efficient number of hypotheses*' N_{hyp} using Chebyshev's inequality for n independent random variables. It follows that, for some mean value $\mu = \max(\mu_i)$ and variance $\sigma = \max(\sigma_i)$ over the observations made for the set of image frames and for pose vector values $\mathbf{s} = \{S_i\}$, the probability within an expected sensitivity k is:

$$P\left\{\left|\sum_{i=1}^{n}(S_i/n) - \mu \geq k\right|\right\} \leq \sigma/nk^2 \tag{4}$$

For example, if $\sigma = 1$ and we wish to be 95% confident that our estimations are within $k = \epsilon_t = 0.5$ units at some model hypotheses of pose $\mathbf{s}$ then $\sigma/nk^2 = 1/0.25n = 4/n$ and our $N_{\text{hyp}} = 4/0.05 = 80$, where the estimate n is assumed to be *sufficient*. An example of re-initialisation ($N_{\text{hyp}} = 35$) is provided in Fig. 4.

4   Results

In order to evaluate our approach we have used the BoBoT[2] benchmark on tracking sequences which include partial ground truth data. For evaluation over

---
[2] http://www.iai.uni-bonn.de/~kleind/tracking/, /~martin/tracking.html

Table 1. Average total error in full image sequence taken per frame in image sequence. The total translational error is in mm and rotation in degrees. Reported time is in msec.

Sequence	Challenges	Methodology	Time	Total error					
				X	Y	Z	Roll	Pitch	Yaw
Panda toy	illumination, clutter	BLORT	84	3.8	6.6	3.3	2.1	3.2	1.3
		LM-ICP	31	20.2	32.0	11.7	2.7	6.3	4.7
		ViSP	40	12.7	21.1	13.4	7.5	4.4	3.4
		MH3DOT	132	3.9	5.5	3.1	2.2	2.1	1.9
Coffee box	viewpoint, scale	BLORT	147	1.2	2.3	1.8	3.0	4.2	1.7
		LM-ICP	54	11.3	7.6	4.4	4.1	11.0	6.8
		ViSP	62	6.2	4.7	2.1	3.1	5.1	4.9
		MH3DOT	195	1.4	2.5	1.9	3.2	4.1	1.5
Mug/Cup	viewpoint, clutter	BLORT	150	2.2	1.7	2.9	13.1	11.7	3.5
		LM-ICP	85	13.1	12.5	12.9	6.8	9.6	8.2
		ViSP	98	7.0	5.1	8.6	6.6	23.1	11.0
		MH3DOT	224	1.3	1.9	2.3	2.8	5.6	2.3

model based with no hypotheses generation and maintenance we applied the ViSP[3] software toolbox and a variant of LM-ICP. To evaluate performance of our MH3DOT and other multiple pose hypotheses methods, we have applied the BLORT[4] software toolbox, which implements a particle filter. The results are summarised in Table 1. It should be noted that both ViSP and BLORT use hardware acceleration. Our implementation does not currently support hardware acceleration. Optimisations are performed in the sense of custom matrix and array operations, based on uBLAS and Lapack libraries. For completeness we also report the computational time required by each method. We note that our method is close to BLORT in terms of computational performance and certainly applicable for on-line applications. A quantitative analysis on the sequences used alongside the aforementioned software solutions, is presented in Table 1.

For our experimental test, we set $n = 100$ for both BLORT (max particles number) and MH3DOT (effective number of hypotheses). In the case of LM-ICP and ViSP, the methods do not employ multiple hypotheses ($n = 1$). It should be noted from the error results of Table 1, that BLORT reports less errors in the 'coffee box' complex background sequence, whilst it shows large errors in the 'mug' simpler background sequence. In contrast, our hybrid method performs consistently in both image sequences. BLORT error results are slightly better than our MH3DOT method in the X and Z translation. However, BLORT severely suffers from increased errors in angular rotations. Furthermore, the pose results of ViSP, and to some extent BLORT, indicate increased error in rotation, which under certain conditions, is not desirable for robot vision applications. We postulate that the superiority of our MH3DOT method may be due to the fact that use of an interpretation process (Section 3.2), constrains this type of pose errors. That is, do not propagate into inferences for subsequent frames.

---

[3] http://www.irisa.fr/lagadic/visp/visp.html
[4] http://users.acin.tuwien.ac.at/mzillich/?site=4

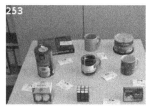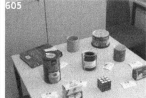

Fig. 5. Snapshot images with super imposed pose results from BoBoT's 'cup' image sequence: MH3DOT tracker versus BLORT. The green line is the object pose from MH3DOT and the yellow line corresponds to BLORT.

An example from the 'mug' sequence (three frames), with tracking superimposed, is provided in Fig. 5. From the sequences tested we can conclude that methods with multi-hypothesis generation and maintenance (MH3DOT green line in Fig. 5) track with good accuracy the target objects. We also observed that for the used case Particle filter tracker (BLORT yellow line in Fig. 5) at some point in time they converge to an erroneous result.

As evidenced in Fig. 5, by frame 869 BLORT pose estimation deteriorates, whilst MH3DOT remains consistent. Thus, the target object will no longer be tracked after some time has elapsed within the image sequences. This becomes even worse for single hypothesis implementations. In said cases, tracking fails to recover the target, and the object remains as 'lost' without successful recovery until the end of the sequence. This explains (in-part) the increased errors reported in Table 1. This is not the case with our MH3DOT approach and thus the reported error is smaller.

5   Conclusions

This paper presents a model based approach to tracking the pose of an object in 3D based on 2D derived contours and edges, using a monocular camera. To enhance the performance of our method under occlusions and other artifacts, we have established a generation of multiple hypothesis, in the form of rendered objects. For this purpose, we have formulated an efficient number of hypotheses criterion within our framework's implementation. Experimental results have demonstrated that our method achieves good pose tracking resolution at a relatively fast frame rate. The results have indicated that our tracking method exhibits better performance over the tested methods with reported parameters.

Further research is required to establish potential cases under which the method may not work robustly. However, in the current challenges posed by the image sequences used, the algorithm has shown to operate robustly even under situations where environmental (e.g. lighting, clutter) and motion conditions (e.g. motion, scale changes) are realistic. Finally, the criterion for efficient number of hypotheses will constitute a topic for further study.

Acknowledgments. This work was partially supported by the European Commission under contract numbers FP7-248258 (First-MM project) and FP7-270435 (JAMES project).

References

1. Yilmaz, A., Javed, O., Shah, M.: Object tracking: A survey. ACM Computing Surveys 38(4), 1–46 (2006)
2. Lepetit, V., Fua, P.: Monocular model-based 3D tracking of rigid objects: a survey. In: Foundations and Trends in Computer Graphics and Vision (2005)
3. Harris, C., Stennet, C.: RAPiD – A video-rate object tracker. In: British Machine Vision Conference, pp. 73–77 (1990)
4. Koller, D., Daniilidis, K., Nagel, H.: Model-based object tracking in monocular image sequences of road traffic scenes. International Journal of Computer Vision 10, 257–281 (1993)
5. Drummond, T., Cipolla, R.: Real-time visual tracking of complex structures. IEEE Transactions on Pattern Analysis and Machine Intelligence 24, 932–946 (2002)
6. Fitzgibbon, A.: Robust registration of 2D and 3D point sets. Image and Vision Computing 21(13), 1145–1153 (2003)
7. Paragios, N., Deriche, R.: Geodesic active contours and level sets for the detection and tracking of moving objects. IEEE Transactions on Pattern Analysis and Machine Intelligence 22(3), 266–280 (2000)
8. Vacchetti, L., Lepetit, V., Fua, P.: Stable real-time 3D tracking using online and offline information. IEEE Transactions on Pattern Analysis and Machine Intelligence 26, 1385–1391 (2004)
9. Azad, P., Münch, D., Asfour, T., Dillmann, R.: 6-DoF model-based tracking of arbitrarily shaped 3D objects. In: IEEE Int. Conf. on Robotics and Automation (2011)
10. Puppili, M., Calway, A.: Real time camera tracking using known 3D models and a particle filter. In: IEEE Int. Conf. on Pattern Recognition (2006)
11. Choi, C., Christensen, H.I.: Robust 3D visual tracking using particle filtering on the special Euclidean group: A combined approach of keypoint and edge features. The International Journal of Robotics Research 31(4), 498–519 (2012)
12. Doucet, A., Godsill, S., Andrieu, C.: On Sequential Monte Carlo sampling methods for Bayesian filtering. Statistics and Computing 10(3), 197–208 (2000)
13. Argyros, A.A., Lourakis, M.I.A.: Real-time tracking of multiple skin-colored objects with a possibly moving camera. In: Pajdla, T., Matas, J. (eds.) ECCV 2004. LNCS, vol. 3023, pp. 368–379. Springer, Heidelberg (2004)
14. Baltzakis, H., Argyros, A.A.: Propagation of pixel hypotheses for multiple objects tracking. In: Bebis, G., et al. (eds.) ISVC 2009, Part II. LNCS, vol. 5876, pp. 140–149. Springer, Heidelberg (2009)
15. Liao, P.S., Chen, T.S., Chung, P.C.: A fast algorithm for multi-level thresholding. Journal of Information Science and Engineering 17, 713–727 (2001)
16. Rousseeuw, P.J.: Least median of squares regression. Journal of the American Statistical Association 79(388), 871–880 (1984)
17. Chetverikov, D., Stepanov, D., Krsek, P.: Robust Euclidean alignment of 3D point sets: the trimmed iterative closest point algorithm. Image and Vision Computing 23, 299–309 (2005)
18. Lourakis, M.I.A.: Sparse non-linear least squares optimization for geometric vision. In: Daniilidis, K., Maragos, P., Paragios, N. (eds.) ECCV 2010, Part II. LNCS, vol. 6312, pp. 43–56. Springer, Heidelberg (2010)

Automatic Parameter Adaptation for Multi-object Tracking

Duc Phu Chau, Monique Thonnat, and François Brémond

STARS team, INRIA Sophia Antipolis, France
{Duc-Phu.Chau,Monique.Thonnat,Francois.Bremond}@inria.fr
http://team.inria.fr/stars

Abstract. Object tracking quality usually depends on video context (e.g. object occlusion level, object density). In order to decrease this dependency, this paper presents a learning approach to adapt the tracker parameters to the context variations. In an offline phase, satisfactory tracking parameters are learned for video context clusters. In the online control phase, once a context change is detected, the tracking parameters are tuned using the learned values. The experimental results show that the proposed approach outperforms the recent trackers in state of the art. This paper brings two contributions: (1) a classification method of video sequences to learn offline tracking parameters, (2) a new method to tune online tracking parameters using tracking context.

Keywords: Object tracking, parameter adaptation, machine learning, controller.

1 Introduction

Many approaches have been proposed to track mobile objects in a scene. However the quality of tracking algorithms always depends on scene properties such as: mobile object density, contrast intensity, scene depth and object size. The selection of a tracking algorithm for an unknown scene becomes a hard task. Even when the tracker has already been determined, it is difficult to tune online its parameters to get the best performance.

Some approaches have been proposed to address these issues. The authors in [1] propose an online learning scheme based on Adaboost to compute a discriminative appearance model for each mobile object. However the online Adaboost process is time consuming. In [2], the authors present an online learning approach to adapt the object descriptors to the current background. However, the training phase requires the user interaction. This increases significantly the processing time and is not practical for the real time applications.

Some approaches integrate different trackers and then select the convenient tracker depending on video content [3][4]. These approaches run the tracking algorithms in parallel. At each frame, the best tracker is selected to compute the object trajectories. These two approaches require the execution of different trackers in parallel which is expensive in terms of processing time. In [5], the

M. Chen, B. Leibe, and B. Neumann (Eds.): ICVS 2013, LNCS 7963, pp. 244–253, 2013.
© Springer-Verlag Berlin Heidelberg 2013

authors propose a tracking algorithm whose parameters can be learned offline for each tracking context. However the authors suppose that the context within a video sequence is fixed over time. Moreover, the tracking context is manually selected.

These studies have obtained relevant results but show strong limitations. To solve these problems, we propose in this paper a new method to tune online the parameters of tracking algorithms using an offline learning process. In the online phase, the parameter tuning relies entirely on the learned database, this helps to avoid slowing down the processing time of the tracking task. The variation of context over time during the online phase is also addressed in this paper.

This paper is organized as follows. Section 2 and 3 present in detail the proposed approach. Section 4 shows the results of the experimentation and validation. A conclusion as well as future work are given in the last section.

2   Offline Learning

The objective of the learning phase is to create a database which supports the control process of a tracking algorithm. This database contains satisfactory parameter values of the controlled tracking algorithm for various scene conditions. This phase takes as input training videos, annotated objects, annotated trajectories, a tracking algorithm including its control parameters. The term "control parameters" refers to parameters which are considered in the control process (i.e. to look for satisfactory values in the learning phase and to be tuned in the online phase). At the end of the learning phase, a learned database is created. A learning session can process many video sequences. Figure 1 presents the proposed scheme for building the learned database.

The notion of "context" (or "tracking context") in this work represents elements in the videos which influence the tracking quality. More precisely, a context of a video sequence is defined as a set of six features: density of mobile objects, their occlusion level, their contrast with regard to the surrounding background, their contrast variance, their 2D area and their 2D area variance. For each training video, we extract these contextual features from annotated objects and then

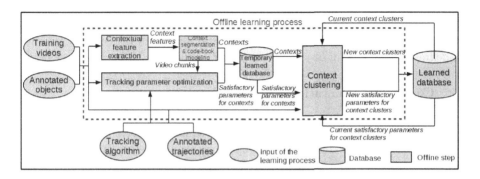

Fig. 1. The offline learning scheme

use them to segment the training video in a set of consecutive chunks. Each video chunk has a stable context. The context of a video chunk is represented by a set of six code-books (corresponding to six features). An optimization process is performed to determine satisfactory tracking parameter values for the video chunks. These parameter values and the set of code-books are inserted into a temporary learned database. After processing all training videos, we cluster these contexts and then compute satisfactory tracking parameter values for context clusters.

In the following, we describe the four steps of the offline learning process: (1) contextual feature extraction, (2) context segmentation and code-book modeling, (3) tracking parameter optimization and (4) context clustering.

2.1 Contextual Feature Extraction

For each training video, the context feature values are computed for every frame.

1. Density of Mobile Objects: A high density of objects may lead to a decrease of object detection and tracking performance. The density of mobile objects at t is defined by the sum of all object areas over the 2D camera view.

2. Occlusion Level of Mobile Objects: An occlusion occurrence makes the object appearance partially or completely invisible. The occlusion level of mobile objects at instant t is defined as the ratio between the 2D overlap area of objects and the object 2D areas.

3. Contrast of Mobile Objects: The contrast of an object is defined as the color intensity difference between this object and its surrounding background. An object with low contrast decreases the discrimination of the appearance between different objects. The contrast of mobile objects at instant t is defined as the mean value of the contrasts of objects at instant t.

4. Contrast Variance of Mobile Objects: When different object contrast levels exist in the scene, a mean value cannot represent correctly the contrast of all objects in the scene. Therefore we define the variance of object contrasts at instant t as their standard deviation value.

5. 2D Area of Mobile Objects: 2D area of an object is defined as the number of pixels within its 2D bounding box. Therefore, this feature characterizes the reliability of the object appearance for the tracking process. The 2D area feature value at t is defined as the mean value of the 2D areas of mobile objects at instant t.

6. 2D Area Variance of Mobile Objects: Similar to the contrast feature, we define the variance of object 2D areas at t as their standard deviation value.

2.2 Context Segmentation and Code-book Modeling

The contextual variation of a video sequence influences significantly the tracking quality. Therefore it is not optimal to keep the same parameter values for a long video. In order to solve this issue, we propose an algorithm to segment a training video in consecutive chunks, each chunk is defined as having a stable context (i.e. the values of a same context feature in each chunk are close to each other). This algorithm is described as follows.

First, the training video is segmented in parts of l frames. Second, the contextual feature values of the first part is represented by a context code-book model. From the second video part, we compute the distance between the context of the current part and the context code-book model of the previous part. If their distance is lower than a threshold Th_1 (e.g. 0.5), the context code-book model is updated with the current video part. Otherwise, a new context code-book model is created to represent the context of the current video part. At the end of the context segmentation algorithm, the training video is divided into a set of chunks (of different temporal lengths) corresponding to the obtained context code-book models. The following sections present how to represent a video context with a code-book model; and how to compute the distance between a context code-book model and a context.

1. Code-book Modeling: During the tracking process, low frequent contextual feature values play an important role for tuning tracking parameters. For example, when mobile object density is high in few frames, the tracking quality can decrease significantly. Therefore, we decide to use a code-book model [6] to represent the values of contextual features because this model can estimate complex and low-frequency distributions. In our approach, each contextual feature is represented by a code-book, called **feature code-book**, denoted cb^k, $k = 1..6$. So a video context is represented by a set of six feature code-books, called **context code-book model**, denoted CB, $CB = \{cb^k, k = 1..6\}$. A feature code-book is composed of a set of code-words describing the values of this feature. The number of code-words depends on the diversity of feature values.

Code-word definition: A code-word represents the values and their frequencies of a contextual feature. A code-word i of code-book k ($k = 1..6$), denoted cw_i^k, is defined as follows:

$$cw_i^k = \{\overline{\mu_i^k}, \ m_i^k, \ M_i^k, \ f_i^k\} \tag{1}$$

where $\overline{\mu_i^k}$ is the mean of the feature values belonging to this code-word; m_i^k and M_i^k are the minimal and maximal feature values belonging to this word; f_i^k is the number of frames when the feature values belong to this word. For each frame t, the code-book $cb^k(k = 1..6)$ is updated with the value of context feature k computed at t.

2. Context Distance: Table 1 presents the algorithm to compute the distance between a context c and a context code-book model $CB = \{cb^k, k = 1..6\}$. The function $distance(\mu_t^k, \ cw_i^k)$ is defined as a ratio between μ_t^k and $\overline{\mu_i^k}$. This distance is normalized in the interval $[0, 1]$.

2.3   Tracking Parameter Optimization

The objective of the tracking parameter optimization task is to find the values of the control parameters which ensure the tracking quality higher a given threshold

Table 1. Algorithm for computing the distance between a context code-book CB and a video context c

```
function contextDistance(c, CB, l)
Input: context code-book model CB, context c, l (number of frames of context c)
Output: context distance between code-book model CB and context c

countTotal = 0;
For each code-book cb^k in CB (k = 1..6)
    count = 0;
    For each value μ_t^k of context c at time t
        For each codeword cw_i^k in code-book cb^k
            if (distance(μ_t^k, cw_i^k) < ε) { count++; break; }
    if (count / l < 0.5) return 1;
    countTotal + = count;
return ( 1 − countTotal/(l * 6) )
```

for each video chunk. These parameters are called "satisfactory parameters". This task takes as input annotated objects, annotated trajectories, a tracking algorithm, a video chunk and control parameters for the considered tracker. The annotated objects are used as object detection results. Depending on the search space size and the nature of the control parameters, we can select suitable optimization algorithm (e.g. enumerative search, genetic algorithm).

2.4 Context Clustering

The context clustering step is done at the end of each learning session when the temporary learned database contains the processing results of all training videos. In some cases, two similar contexts can have different satisfactory parameter values because optimization algorithm only finds local optimal solutions. A context clustering is thus necessary to group similar contexts and to compute satisfactory parameter values for the context clusters.

In this work, we decide to use the Quality Threshold Clustering algorithm for this step because this algorithm does not require the number of clusters as input. Once contexts are clustered, all the code-words of these contexts become the code-words of the created cluster. The tracking parameters for a cluster is defined as a combination of tracking parameters belonging to clustered contexts.

3   Online Parameter Adaptation

In this section, we describe the proposed controller which aims at tuning online the tracking parameter values for obtaining satisfactory tracking performance. The online parameter adaptation phase takes as input the video stream, the list of detected objects at every frame, the learned database and gives as output the satisfactory tracking parameter values for every new context detected in the video stream (see figure 2). In the following sections, we describe the two main steps of this phase: the context detection and parameter tuning steps.

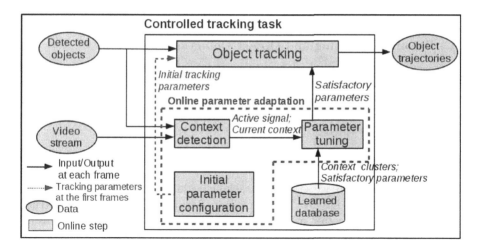

Fig. 2. The online parameter adaptation scheme

3.1 Context Detection

This step takes as input for every frame, the list of the current detected objects and the image. For each video chunk of l frames, we compute the values of the contextual features. A contextual change is detected when the context of the current video chunk does not belong to the context cluster (clusters are learned in the offline phase) of the previous video chunk. In order to ensure the coherence between the learning phase and the testing phase, we use the same distance defined in the learning phase (section 2.2) to perform this classification. If this distance is lower than threshold Th_1, this context is considered as belonging to the context cluster. Otherwise, the "Parameter tuning" task is activated.

3.2 Parameter Tuning

The parameter tuning task takes as input an active signal and the current context from the "context detection" task, and gives as output satisfactory tracking parameter values. When this process receives an activate signal, it looks for the cluster in the learned database to which the current context belongs. Let $\mathfrak{D}$ represent the learned database, a context c of a video chunk of l frames belongs to a cluster C_i if both conditions are satisfied:

$$contextDistance(c,\ C_i,\ l)\ <\ Th_1 \tag{2}$$

$$\forall C_j\ \in\ \mathfrak{D}, j \neq i:\ contextDistance(c, C_i, l) \leq contextDistance(c, C_j, l) \tag{3}$$

where Th_1 is defined in section 2.2. The function $contextDistance(c,\ C_i,\ l)$ is defined in table 1. If such a context cluster C_i is found, the satisfactory tracking parameters associated with C_i are considered as good enough for parameterizing the tracking of the current video chunk. Otherwise, the tracking algorithm parameters do not change, the current video chunk is marked to be learned offline later.

4   Experimental Results

4.1   Parameter Setting and Object Detection Algorithm

The proposed control method has two predefined parameters. The distance threshold Th_1 to decide whether two contexts are close enough (sections 2.2 and 3.2) is set to 0.5. The minimum number of frames l of a context segment (sections 2.2 and 3.1) is set to 50 frames. A HOG-based algorithm [7] is used for detecting people in videos.

4.2   Tracking Evaluation Metrics

In this experimentation, we select the tracking evaluation metrics used in several publications [1][9][10]. Let GT be the number of trajectories in the ground-truth of the test video. The first metric MT computes the number of trajectories successfully tracked for more than 80% divided by GT. The second metric PT computes the number of trajectories that are tracked between 20% and 80% divided by GT. The last metric ML is the percentage of the left trajectories.

4.3   Controlled Tracker

In this paper, we select an object appearance-based tracker [5] to test the proposed approach. This tracker takes as input a video stream and a list of objects detected in a predefined temporal window. The object trajectory computation is based on a weighted combination of five object descriptor similarities: 2D area, 2D shape ratio, RGB color histogram, color covariance and dominant color. For this tracker, the five object descriptor weights w_k ($k = 1..5$) are selected for testing the proposed control method. These parameters depend on the tracking context and have a significant effect on the tracking quality.

4.4   Training Phase

In the training phase, we use 15 video sequences belonging to different contexts (i.e. different levels of density and occlusion of mobile objects as well as of their contrast with regard to the surrounding background, their contrast variance, their 2D area and their 2D area variance). These videos belong to four public datasets (ETISEO, Caviar, Gerhome and PETS) and to the two European projects (Caretaker and Vanaheim). They are recorded in various places: shopping center, buildings, home, subway stations and outdoor.

Each training video is segmented automatically in a set of context segments. In the tracking parameter optimization process, we use an Adaboost algorithm to learn the object descriptor weights for each context segment because each object descriptor similarity can be considered as a weak classifier for linking two objects detected within a temporal window. The Adaboost algorithm has a lower complexity than the other heuristic optimization algorithms (e.g. genetic algorithm, particle swam optimization). Also, this algorithm avoids converging to the local optimal solutions. After segmenting the 15 training videos, we obtain 72 contexts. By applying the clustering process, 29 context clusters are created.

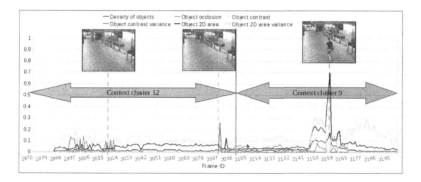

Fig. 3. Variations of the contextual feature values and of the detected contexts in the subway sequence from frame 2950 to frame 3350

4.5   Testing Phase

All the following test videos do not belong to the set of the 15 training videos.

1. Caretaker video
The first tested video sequence belongs to the Caretaker project[1] whose video camera is installed in a subway station. The length of this sequence is 1 hour 42 minutes. It contains 178 mobile objects. The graph in figure 3 presents the variation of contextual feature values and of the detected contexts in the test sequence from frame 2950 to frame 3200. The values of object 2D areas are normalized for displaying. From frame 2950 to 3100, the area and area variance values of objects are very small most of the time (see the brown and light blue curves). The context of this video chunk belongs to cluster 12. In this cluster, the color histogram is selected as the most important object descriptor for tracking mobile objects ($w_3 = 0.86$). This parameter tuning result is reasonable because compared to the other considered object descriptors, the color histogram descriptor is quite reliable for discriminating and tracking objects of low resolution (i.e. low 2D area). From frame 3101 to 3200, a larger object appears, the context belongs to cluster 9. For this context cluster, the dominant color descriptor weight is the most important ($w_5 = 0.52$). In this case, the object appearance is well visible. The dominant color descriptor is then reliable for tracking object.

The proposed controller helps to increase the *MT* value from 61.24% to 71.32%, and to decrease the value of *ML* from 24.72% to 20.40%.

2. Caviar Dataset
The Caviar videos are recorded in a shopping center corridor. They have 26 sequences in which 6 sequences belong to our training video set. The other 20 sequences including 143 mobile objects are used for testing. Figure 4 shows the correct tracking results of four persons while occlusions happen. Table 2 presents the tracking results of the proposed approach and of some recent trackers from

---

[1] http://cordis.europa.eu/ist/kct/caretaker_synopsis.htm

Fig. 4. Tracking results of four persons in the sequence ShopAssistant2cor (Caviar dataset) are correct, even when occlusions happen

the state of the art. The proposed controller increases significantly the performance of the tracker [5]. The MT value increases 78.3% to 85.5% and the ML value decreases 5.7% to 5.3%. We obtain the best MT value compared to state of the art trackers.

3. PETS 2009 Video

In this test, we use the CLEAR metrics presented in [8] to compare with other tracking algorithms. The first metric MOTA computes Multiple Object Tracking Accuracy. The second metric MOTP computes Multiple Object Tracking Precision. The higher these metrics, the better the tracking quality is. We select the sequence S2_L1, camera view 1, time 12.34 for testing because this sequence is experimented in several state of the art trackers. This sequence has 794 frames, contains 21 mobile objects and several occlusion cases. With the proposed controller, the tracking result increases significantly. Table 3 presents the metric results of the proposed approach and of different trackers from the state of the art. The metric $\overline{M}$ represents the average value of MOTA and MOTP. With the proposed approach, we obtain the best values in all the three metrics.

Table 2. Tracking results for the Caviar dataset. The proposed controller improves significantly the tracking performance. The best values are printed in **bold**.

Approaches	MT (%)	PT (%)	ML (%)
Xing et al.[9]	84.3	12.1	3.6
Li et al.[10]	84.6	14.0	1.4
Kuo et al.[1]	84.6	14.7	**0.7**
Appearance Tracker [5] without the proposed controller	78.3	16.0	5.7
Appearance Tracker [5] with the proposed controller	**85.5**	9.2	5.3

Table 3. Tracking results for the PETS sequence S2.L1, camera view 1, time 12.34. The best values are printed in **bold**.

Approaches	MOTA	MOTP	$\overline{M}$
Berclaz et al. [11]	0.80	0.58	0.69
Shitrit et al. [12]	0.81	0.58	0.70
Henriques et al. [13]	0.85	0.69	0.77
Appearance Tracker [5] without the proposed controller	0.62	0.63	0.63
Appearance Tracker [5] with the proposed controller	**0.87**	**0.72**	**0.80**

5   Conclusion and Future Work

In this paper, we have presented a new control approach for tuning online the tracker parameters. The proposed offline learning phase helps to decrease effectively the computational cost of the online control phase. The experiments show a significant improvement of the tracking performances while using the proposed controller. Although we test with an appearance-based tracker, other tracker categories can still be controlled by adapting the context definition to the principle of these trackers. In future work, we will extend the context notion which should be independent from the object detection quality.

Acknowledgments. This work is supported by The PACA region, The General Council of Alpes Maritimes province, France as well as The Vanaheim, Panorama and Support projects.

References

1. Kuo, C.H., Huang, C., Nevatia, R.: Multi-target tracking by online learned discriminative appearance models. In: CVPR (2010)
2. Borji, A., Frintrop, S., Sihite, D.N., Itti, L.: Adaptive Object Tracking by Learning Background Context. In: CVPR (2012)
3. Santner, J., Leistner, C., Saffari, A., Pock, T., Bischof, H.: PROST: Parallel Robust Online Simple Tracking. In: CVPR (2010)
4. Yoon, J.H., Kim, D.Y., Yoon, K.-J.: Visual Tracking via Adaptive Tracker Selection with Multiple Features. In: Fitzgibbon, A., Lazebnik, S., Perona, P., Sato, Y., Schmid, C. (eds.) ECCV 2012, Part IV. LNCS, vol. 7575, pp. 28–41. Springer, Heidelberg (2012)
5. Chau, D.P., Bremond, F., Thonnat, M.: A multi-feature tracking algorithm enabling adaptation to context variations. In: ICDP (2011)
6. Kim, K., Chalidabhongse, T.H., Harwood, D., Davis, L.: Background modeling and subtraction by codebook construction. In: ICIP (2004)
7. Corvee, E., Bremond, F.: Body parts detection for people tracking using trees of Histogram of Oriented Gradient descriptors. In: AVSS (2010)
8. Bernardin, K., Stiefelhagen, R.: Evaluating Multiple Object Tracking Performance: The CLEAR MOTMetrics. EURASIP J. on Img. and Video Processing (2008)
9. Xing, J., Ai, H., Lao, S.: Multi-object tracking through occlusions by local tracklets filtering and global tracklets association with detection responses. In: CVPR (2009)
10. Li, Y., Huang, C., Nevatia, R.: Learning to Associate: HybridBoosted Multi-Target Tracker for Crowded Scene. In: CVPR (2009)
11. Berclaz, J., Fleuret, F., Turetken, E., Fua, P.: Multiple object tracking using k-shortest paths optimization. TPAMI 33, 1806–1819 (2011)
12. Shitrit, J., Berclaz, J., Fleuret, F., Fua, P.: Tracking multiple people under global appearance constraints. In: ICCV (2011)
13. Henriques, J.F., Caseiro, R., Batista, J.: Globally optimal solution to multi-object tracking with merged measurements. In: ICCV (2011)

Probabilistic Cue Integration for Real-Time Object Pose Tracking*

Johann Prankl, Thomas Mörwald, Michael Zillich, and Markus Vincze

Automation and Control Institute
Vienna University of Technology, Austria
{prankl,moerwald,zillich,vincze}@acin.tuwien.ac.at

Abstract. Robust real time object pose tracking is an essential component for robotic applications as well as for the growing field of augmented reality. Currently available systems are typically either optimized for textured objects or for uniformly colored objects. The proposed approach combines complementary interest points in a common tracking framework which allows to handle a broad variety of objects regardless of their appearance and shape. A thorough evaluation of state of the art interest points shows that a multi scale FAST detector in combination with our own image descriptor outperforms all other combinations. Additionally, we show that a combination of complementary features improves the tracking performance slightly further.

1 Introduction

Vision systems for detection and tracking of objects are dominated by approaches based on interest points and local descriptors. While successful for textured objects the performance decreases if objects are uniformly colored. In industrial applications the variety of objects is limited and the environment can be adapted, but home and service robotic scenarios require systems which are able to handle different kinds of objects and a cluttered environment in a common framework. This can be achieved by designing a framework with multiple components, each optimized for the detection of one object category. In contrast, we propose a single detection and tracking approach which is able to handle a broad variety of objects by integrating complementary features. We evaluate state of the art interest point detectors and descriptors and develop a strategy to combine different feature types by learning a probabilistic reliability model. Note that in the remaining text we use the term interest point to indicate a salient image point plus the descriptor computed from the surrounding patch.

Starting with the *scale invariant feature transform (SIFT)* developed by Lowe [1] numerous successful interest point types have been proposed. A comparison of affine region detectors and descriptors can be found in [2] and [3].

---

* The work described in this article has been funded by the European project under the contract no. 600623, as well as by the Austrian Science Fund under the grant agreements I 513-N23 and TRP 139-N23 and the Austrian Research Promotion Agency under the grant agreement 836490.

M. Chen, B. Leibe, and B. Neumann (Eds.): ICVS 2013, LNCS 7963, pp. 254–263, 2013.
© Springer-Verlag Berlin Heidelberg 2013

Most of them are optimized for object recognition and are able to handle a limited number of objects with a fair amount of texture. More recently, interest points which are faster to compute and thus are more appropriate for object tracking have been proposed (FAST [4], MSER [5], SURF [6], ORB [7]. We focus on these interest point types and compare them to our own SIFT-like descriptor which we simply call *image gradient histogram descriptor (ImGD)*.

Our work is placed in the context of robotics applications where an accurate object pose is necessary for path planning or visual servoing. Hence, we evaluate the interest points within a complete tracking system. The tracker uses a monocular image sequence to compute the object pose and it is based on an iterative particle filter framework similar to the approach proposed by Mörwald [8]. In contrast to Mörwald who renders complete textures of 3D models into the image in order to compute particle quality, our object model consists of a sparse set of interest points of possibly different types and their 3D location on the object surface. A problem when trying to integrate interest points of different types is how to compare their matching quality. Therefore, we propose to learn a probabilistic confidence measure for each interest point detector/descriptor pair using Bayes theorem, which is used during tracking to compare and rank matched point pairs.

In this paper we propose a probabilistic framework for tracking objects by combining complementary interest point types. Concretely, our contributions are:

- A probabilistic tracking approach using Bayes theorem to combine complementary interest points.
- A framework for learning and evaluation of the probabilistic model.
- An evaluation of state of the art interest points including Harris [9] FAST [4], MSER [5], SIFT [1], SURF [6] and our own ImGD.

The paper proceeds with a discussion of the related work in Section 2. After that, the method, including learning of the probabilistic model and object tracking is described in Section 3. Then the interest point detectors and descriptors are reviewed in Section 4 which are evaluated in Section 5.

2   Related Work

State of the art interest points are reviewed in Sec. 4. In what follows we summarize related work for object pose tracking.

Robustness has always been a concern for visual tracking [10–12]. Especially the introduction of particle filtering to visual tracking [13] boosted robustness [14–16], aided by the increased use of GPU-optimised algorithms [17, 18]. Also the combination of complementary cues proved to boost robustness and broaden the range of objects that could be handled. [19] extended earlier work on tracking based on planar patches to take into account contour information, but remain limited to planar objects. [20] extended their earlier feature-point based 3D tracker with the ability to integrate edge information, handling the problem of ambiguities resulting from spurious background edges.[21] start with a 3D wire-frame model based tracker and augment this with point features (small image patches around Harris corners [9]) collected online from front-facing surfaces and fuse measurements using an Iterated Extended Kalman Filter (IEKF). [22] combine edges and texture (again image patches around Harris corners) in a single non-linear minimization scheme, which they apply to 2D tracking (homography estimation) of planar objects delineated by straight edges or NURBS, as well as full 3D tracking of objects such as boxes and balls. [23] combine depth data, appearance features, silhouettes and even tactile data within an Unscented Kalman Filter (UKF) and achieve high robustness tracking an articulated robotic manipulator and complexly shaped work piece.

In our work we are interested not in a particular choice of feature combination, but in the methodology to evaluate and combine different features. This is then applied to full 3D tracking of arbitrarily shaped 3D objects.

3   Method

Algorithms for object pose estimation need three or more corresponding 2D/3D point pairs [24]. To tolerate inaccurate and false correspondences these methods are typically embedded in a robust estimation schemes (e.g. RANSAC). In order to ensure convergence a set of "good" point correspondences with a high probability of being correct is necessary. In case of using a single feature type this is often implemented by comparing interest point descriptors and applying a threshold. If different types are combined a solution would be to provide individual thresholds for each descriptor. Instead of using *heuristic* thresholds, we propose to learn a mapping of descriptor distances to a probabilistic confidence measure using Bayes theorem. In detail, given an object model consisting of interest points, their 3D location on the object surface and interest points detected in a query image, the goal is to compare model descriptors with descriptors of query points and compute the probability of being a correct match. *Good* matches are then used to estimate the 3D location of the object with respect to the camera.

3.1   Training of the Probabilistic Model

Object models are reconstructed by collecting a sequence of RGB-D images and using a standard RGB-D SLAM approach [25, 26] to compute the camera pose.[1] For training of the probabilistic model we need positive training examples, i.e., correct matches (tp) and negative examples (tn). Positive and negative examples are directly acquired from the image sequence used for reconstruction. In each frame interest points are detected and reprojected to the object surface. Then neighboring reprojected points from all frames are clustered and marked as positive training example if the size of the corresponding image patches for descriptor

---

[1] There is no restriction to RGB-D images. The reconstruction pipeline could easily be substituted by a SfM approach using a monocular image sequence.

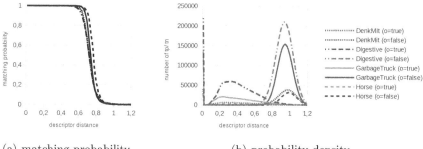

(a) matching probability   (b) probability density

Fig. 1. Example of a learned matching probability (multi scale FAST detector and ImGD)

calculation is similar. Patch similarity is given if the difference of the semi-axes of circumscribed ellipses is smaller than a threshold t_e and if the orientation is similar ($\Delta\theta_{i,j} < t_\theta$). Negative training examples are sampled from matches of one descriptor of a cluster and a randomly selected interest point outside of the cluster or of an interest point detected in a dedicated "false positive" image set.

With $d = ||D(i) - D(j)||_2$ being the descriptor distance of matched interest point pairs $m(i,j)$ the training set is used to compute the prior probability $p(m = true)$ of correct matches, the prior probability $p(d)$ of the occurrence of each distance d in the training set and the conditional probability $p(d|m = true)$ of a descriptor distance d being a correct match ($m = true$). During tracking the posterior probability $p(m = true|d)$ of being a correct match can then be computed using Bayes rule:

$$p(m = true|d) = \frac{p(d|m = true)p(m = true)}{p(d)}. \tag{1}$$

Probability density functions are approximated with histograms of the descriptor distances. In our implementation we pre-compute the posterior probabilities and use a lookup table during tracking, resulting in probabilities as shown in Fig. 1.

3.2 Object Tracking

Our tracking framework is based on a Sequential Importance Resampling (SIR) particle filter proposed by Doucet et al. [27] and adapted by Mörwald et al. [8] for tracking the 3D pose of objects. In contrast to Mörwald, who renders textured 3D models to the image and counts consistent edgels in order to evaluate the pose hypotheses of particles we project the 3D location of matched interest points to the image and use the distance of these point pairs to compute a confidence value.

In detail, first complementary interest points are detected in a query image (e.g. SURF and FAST+ImGD) and matched to descriptors stored in the object database. For each match we use the descriptors D and the pre-calculated lookup table presented in Section 3.1 to derive the posterior probability $p(m = true|d)$.

Matches of different interest point types are then combined and sorted in decreasing $p(m = true|d)$ and the best N matches are passed on to the pose tracking system. Pose tracking is the problem of finding the transformations T_t of an object with respect to a camera given a sequence of images (observations). This results in an estimation of 6 parameters for each observed image. For sampling pose hypotheses directly in a 6 DOF space an untractable number of trials would be necessary. Hence, we bootstrap our system with pose hypotheses computed with the three point pose (P3P) algorithm [24] and a robust RANSAC scheme.

The quality measure

$$c(T) = \sum_{i=1}^{N} \max(0, t_{inl} - ||\mathbf{p}_{im,i} - C\,T\,\mathbf{p}_{model,i}||_2^2) \qquad (2)$$

for P3P-RANSAC and for particles, is computed from the best N interest point matches. Where t_{inl} stands for an inlier threshold, $\mathbf{p}_{im,i}$ is a matched query point, $\mathbf{p}_{model,i}$ is the corresponding 3D model point in homogeneous coordinates and C is the intrinsic camera matrix. In comparison to the tracking framework proposed in [8] which needs a separate recognizer to reinitialize, our framework continuously adds poses from the P3P-RANSAC algorithm and thus automatically reinitializes if the object is lost.

4   Interest Point Detectors and Descriptors

In the following paragraphs we review the interest point detectors and descriptors evaluated with our system. For all detectors and descriptors we use implementations available in OpenCV[2], except SIFT, where we use the implementation of Wu[3], and MSER and ImGD where we use our own implementations.

4.1   Interest Point Detectors

SIFT detector (DoG) is proposed by Lowe [1]. The idea is to approximate the Laplacian of Gaussian with the difference of adjacent Gaussian images which is faster to compute. Additionally Lowe eliminates minima and maxima detected at edges and computes the dominant image gradient orientation. Hence, SIFT detects blob-like structures and it is scale and rotation invariant.

SURF detector (Hes) is developed by Bay et al. [6]. They propose to use an Hessian matrix approximation. The implementation is based on integral images which reduces the computation time drastically. SURF also detects blob-like structures and it is scale and rotation invariant.

Maximally Stable Extremal Regions (MSER), developed by Matas et al. [5] is an affinely-invariant region detector. It detects the extremal property of

---

[2] http://www.opencv.org
[3] http://cs.unc.edu/~ccwu/siftgpu/

| (a) Digestive | (b) DenkMit | (c) GarbageTruck | (d) Horse |

Fig. 2. Example images of our evaluation sequences including the ground truth coordinate system (yellow) detected with the ARToolKit [29] and the tracking coordinate system (red-green-blue)

the intensity function of regions by increasing/decreasing a brightness threshold and reporting stable parts of the image.

Harris detector is the classical corner detector developed by Harris et al. [9]. To achieve rotation invariance we compute the dominant gradient orientation.

Features from Accelerated Segment Test (FAST), proposed by Rosten et al. [4] is a heuristic for feature detection which uses machine learning to classify corner candidates by considering a circle of 16 pixels around a point. We use an implementation proposed in [7] where FAST corners are detected in an image pyramid to cover the scale space and the intensity centroid is used to detect the dominant orientation.

4.2   Interest Point Descriptors

SIFT descriptor, proposed by Lowe [1] describes a patch with histograms of gradient orientations sampled from 4×4 subregions. Each orientation sample is weighted with its magnitude and a Gaussian weight.

SURF descriptor, developed by Bay et al. [6] uses the first order Haar wavelet responses in x and y direction, exploiting integral images for speed, to describe the patch around interest points.

Image Gradient Descriptor (ImGD), our own descriptor is similar to the original SIFT descriptor proposed by Lowe. We use the same grid layout to compute 4×4 orientation histograms. To speed up computation we skip the interpolation used to distribute the value of each gradient sample into adjacent histogram bins. Instead, we compute an element wise square root of the L1 normalized descriptor proposed by Arandjelović et al. [28]. This transformation is equivalent to using the Hellinger kernel for comparing descriptors instead of the Euclidean distance.

5   Evaluation

To evaluate the interest points we propose two methods. First the *meaningfulness* of the descriptor is compared by computing the probability density function and the corresponding matching probability $p(m = true|d)$. Then we evaluate different interest points and combinations of them with our complete tracking system. In all experiments the Euclidean distance is used to compare descriptors.

5.1 Comparison of Interest Point Detectors and Descriptors

For learning the probabilistic model in order to evaluate the meaningfulness of descriptors we use the reconstruction and training pipeline described in Section 3.1. We select four objects ranging from highly textured surfaces with a simple repetitive shape 2(a) to a single colored surface with a more complex shape 2(d). For each object we used about 800 RGBD-frames, compute the camera poses and reconstruct the upper hemisphere of the objects. The interest points detected in each frame and reprojected to the object surface are used to generate true and false training examples. Depending on the interest point type and the object surface this results in up to $500k$ positive and $1.5M$ negative examples.

In general, it can be seen in Figs. 1 and 3, that different interest point detectors result in different matching probabilities even if the same descriptors are used. In every case ImGD leads to a better separation of true and false matches, i.e., a steeper slope of the posterior matching probability, no matter which interest point detector is used. It can also be seen, that the density functions have a similar behavior for each object which results in almost identical posterior curves. Hence, in the following tracking evaluation we use the posterior curve for *Garbage Truck* which is approximately the mean in every case.

5.2 Evaluation of the Object Pose Tracking System

For evaluation of tracking we place each object on a ground truth pattern and capture a trajectory covering different orientations and scales (see Fig. 2). Each sequence is annotated with the ARToolKit [29] by detecting the camera pose of about 600 frames per object. Then different interest point detectors, descriptors and combinations of them are used to track the object pose. To compare the results we compute the precision

$$p_{pr} = \frac{n_{tp}}{n_{tp} + n_{fp}}, \tag{3}$$

where n_{tp} is the number of true object detections and respectively n_{fp} is the number of false detected objects. To decide which object pose is correct and which is

Table 1. Tracking evaluation using different detector and descriptor combinations

detector / descriptor	precision	x [mm]	y [mm]	z [mm]	time [ms]
Harris/ImGD	0.59	4.6	5.6	18.9	83
MSER/ImGD	0.38	3.2	4.0	10.4	106
MultiFAST/ImGD	0.98	2.1	2.2	13.8	62
SIFT/SIFT	0.89	2.2	3.2	12.6	163
SURF/SURF	0.47	3.1	5.6	19.2	100
SURF/ImGD	0.81	3.3	3.8	14.4	77
Harris/ImGD + MSER/ImGD	0.60	3.9	7.5	18.5	172
Harris/ImGD + SURF/SURF	0.62	4.7	6.7	17.3	159
Harris/ImGD + SURF/ImGD	0.82	3.2	4.0	15.1	130
MultiFAST/ImGD + MSER/ImGD	0.98	2.0	2.2	13.4	149
MultiFAST/ImGD + SURF/SURF	0.98	2.2	2.3	13.4	134
MultiFAST/ImGD + SURF/ImGD	0.98	2.0	2.1	12.2	108

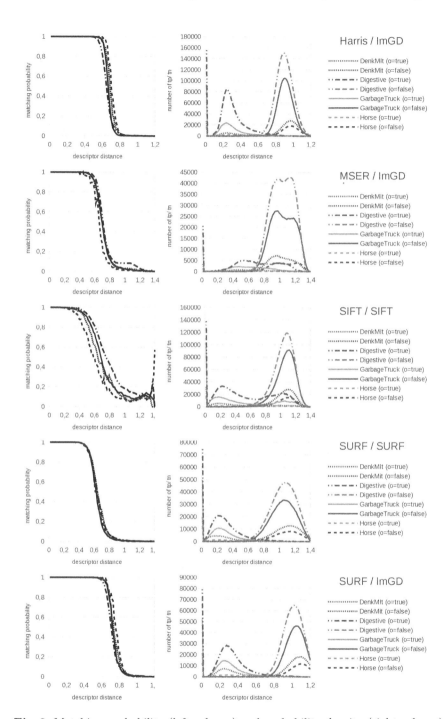

Fig. 3. Matching probability (left column) and probability density (right column) for different detector/descriptor combinations

false we compare the tracked pose with the pose computed with the ARToolKit and use an inlier threshold $t_{detection} = 40mm$ which is about half of the object size. In addition to the precision we record the pose accuracy in x, y and z direction (camera coordinate system) and the overall computation time per frame.

Results are shown in Table 1. It can be seen, that the MultiFAST detector in combination with our ImGD achieves the highest precision as well as the highest frame rat (for the Horse up to 20fps). An interesting insight is, that SIFT has almost the worst matching probability curve (see Fig. 3) but it achieves the second best tracking result. As proposed by Lowe [1], this motivates using the second nearest neighbor ratio to prune weak matches instead of using a fixed threshold. The results in Table 1 also indicate, that the performance can (slightly) be increased if different interest point types are combined. No improvement has been achieved for combinations with *MultiFAST/ImGD* where the precision is already at a very high level when using it alone.

6 Conclusion

We presented a system for real time object pose tracking. By learning probabilistic confidence measures for interest points the proposed system is able to integrate complementary features in a common tracking framework. This allows to handle a broad variety of objects regardless of their appearance and shape. We evaluate state of the art interest points and compare them to our own image gradient histogram descriptor (ImGD). Results show that a multi scale FAST detector in combination with our ImGD outperforms all other detector/descriptor combinations, which could be only slightly improved by combining it with another feature type. Future work will explore the possibly more pronounced improvements using more complementary feature types beyond the point-like features above (e.g. object contours), in handling even broader object classes such as partly transparent or shiny objects.

References

1. Lowe, D.G.: Distinctive image features from scale-invariant keypoints. IJCV 60(2), 91–110 (2004)
2. Comparison of Affine-Invariant Local Detectors and Descriptors. In: European Signal Processing Conference (2004)
3. Mikolajczyk, K., Tuytelaars, T., Schmid, C., Zisserman, A., Matas, J., Schaffalitzky, F., Kadir, T., Van Gool, L.: A comparison of affine region detectors. IJCV 65(1), 43–72 (2005)
4. Rosten, E., Porter, R., Drummond, T.: Faster and better: A machine learning approach to corner detection. PAMI 32, 105–119 (2010)
5. Matas, J., Chum, O., Urban, M., Pajdla, T.: Robust wide-baseline stereo from maximally stable extremal regions. Image and Vision Computing 22(10), 761–767 (2004)
6. Bay, H., Ess, A., Tuytelaars, T., Van Gool, L.: Speeded-up robust features (surf). CVIU 110(3), 346–359 (2008)
7. Rublee, E., Rabaud, V., Konolige, K., Bradski, G.: Orb: An efficient alternative to sift or surf. In: ICCV, pp. 2564–2571 (2011)

8. Mörwald, T., Zillich, M., Prankl, J., Vincze, M.: Self-monitoring to improve robustness of 3D object tracking for robotics. In: IEEE International Conference on Robotics and Biomimetics (ROBIO), pp. 2830–2837 (2011)
9. Harris, C., Stephens, M.: A combined corner and edge detector. In: Proc. of Fourth Alvey Vision Conference, pp. 147–151 (1988)
10. Drummond, T., Cipolla, R.: Real-Time Visual Tracking of Complex Structures. PAMI 24(7), 932–946 (2002)
11. Comport, A.I., Kragic, D., Marchand, E., Chaumette, F.: Robust Real-Time Visual Tracking: Comparison, Theoretical Analysis and Performance Evaluation. In: ICRA (2005)
12. Babenko, B., Yang, M.H.: Robust Object Tracking with Online Multiple Instance Learning. PAMI 33(8), 1619–1632 (2011)
13. Isard, M., Blake, A.: Condensation - conditional density propagation for visual tracking. IJCV 29(1), 5–28 (1998)
14. Klein, G., Murray, D.: Full-3D Edge Tacking with a Particle Filter. In: BMVC, vol. 3, pp. 1119–1128 (2006)
15. Cai, Y., de Freitas, N., Little, J.J.: Robust Visual Tracking for Multiple Targets. In: Leonardis, A., Bischof, H., Pinz, A. (eds.) ECCV 2006. LNCS, vol. 3954, pp. 107–118. Springer, Heidelberg (2006)
16. Choi, C., Christensen, H.I.: 3D textureless object detection and tracking: An edge-based approach. In: IROS, pp. 3877–3884 (2012)
17. Chestnutt, J., Kagami, S., Nishiwaki, K., Kuffner, J., Kanade, T.: GPU-Accelerated Real-Time 3D Tracking for Humanoid Locomotion. In: IROS (2007)
18. Sánchez, J.R., Álvarez, H., Borro, D.: Towards Real Time 3D Tracking and Reconstruction on a GPU using Monte Carlo Simulations. In: ISMAR, pp. 185–192 (2010)
19. Masson, L., Jurie, F., Dhome, M.: Contour/texture approach for visual tracking. In: Bigun, J., Gustavsson, T. (eds.) SCIA 2003. LNCS, vol. 2749, pp. 661–668. Springer, Heidelberg (2003)
20. Vacchetti, L., Lepetit, V., Fua, P.: Combining Edge and Texture Information for Real-Time Accurate 3D Camera Tracking. In: ISMAR (2004)
21. Kyrki, V., Kragic, D.: Integration of model-based and model-free cues for visual object tracking in 3D. In: ICRA, pp. 1566–1572 (2005)
22. Pressigout, M., Marchand, E.: Real-time Hybrid Tracking using Edge and Texture Information. IJRR 26(7), 689–713
23. Hebert, P., Hudson, N., Ma, J., Howard, T., Fuchs, T., Bajracharya, M., Burdick, J.: Combined shape, appearance and silhouette for simultaneous manipulator and object tracking. In: ICRA, pp. 2405–2412 (2012)
24. Haralick, R., Joo, H., Lee, C., Zhuang, X., Vaidya, V., Kim, M.: Pose estimation from corresponding point data. IEEE Transactions on Systems, Man and Cybernetics 19(6), 1426–1446 (1989)
25. Zillich, M., Prankl, J., Mörwald, T., Vincze, M.: Knowing your limits - self-evaluation and prediction in object recognition. In: IROS, pp. 813–820 (2011)
26. Engelhard, N., Endres, F., Hess, J., Sturm, J., Burgard, W.: Real-time 3d visual slam with a hand-held camera. In: Proc. of the RGB-D Workshop on 3D Perception in Robotics at the European Robotics Forum, Vasteras, Sweden (2011)
27. Doucet, A., de Freitas, N., Gordon, N.: Sequential Monte Carlo Methods in Practice. Statistics for Engineering and Information Science Series. Springer (2001)
28. Arandjelović, R., Zisserman, A.: Three things everyone should know to improve object retrieval. In: CVPR (2012)
29. Kato, H., Billinghurst, M.: Marker tracking and hmd calibration for a video-based augmented reality conferencing system. In: IEEE/ACM International Workshop on Augmented Reality (IWAR), pp. 85–94

Depth Estimation during Fixational Head Movements in a Humanoid Robot

Marco Antonelli[1], Angel P. del Pobil[1,*], and Michele Rucci[2]

[1] Robotic Intelligence Lab, Universitat Jaume I
12070 Castellón, Spain
{antonell,pobil}@uji.es
[2] Department of Psychology and Graduate Program in Neuroscience
Boston University, Boston, MA 02215, USA
mrucci@bu.edu

Abstract. Under natural viewing conditions, humans are not aware of continually performing small head and eye movements in the periods in between voluntary relocations of gaze. It has been recently shown that these fixational head movements provide useful depth information in the form of parallax. Here, we replicate this coordinated head and eye movements in a humanoid robot and describe a method for extracting the resulting depth information. Proprioceptive signals are interpreted by means of a kinematic model of the robot to compute the velocity of the camera. The resulting signal is then optimally integrated with the optic flow to estimate depth in the scene. We present the results of simulations which validate the proposed approach.

1 Introduction

Accurate 3D judgments are critical in many computer vision tasks, from visuomotor control of robots to object recognition. Unfortunately, extraction of depth and distance is a complex operation, as this information is lost when the three-dimensional world is projected onto the two dimensional surface of a camera sensor during the process of image acquisition. To circumvent this problem, many techniques have been proposed, but no optimal solution exists, as each method presents both pros and cons. For example, stereopsis—arguably the most common 3D approach in computer vision [2,7]—requires solving a correspondence problem: the determination of the positions of identical features in the images acquired from cameras at different locations. Decades of research have shown that this is an extremely challenging operation.

A popular 3D approach in computer vision as in biology is depth (or structure) from motion [10], the use of depth/distance information that emerges in a moving agent. The underlying principle is similar to that of stereopsis, but,

* This work was supported in part by Ministerio de Ciencia y Innovación (FPI grant BES-2009-027151, DPI2011-27846), by Generalitat Valenciana (PROMETEO/2009/052) and by Fundació Caixa-Castello-Bancaixa (P1-1B2011-54).

M. Chen, B. Leibe, and B. Neumann (Eds.): ICVS 2013, LNCS 7963, pp. 264–273, 2013.
© Springer-Verlag Berlin Heidelberg 2013

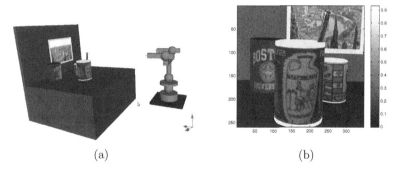

(a)   (b)

Fig. 1. Simulated environment. (a) An anthropomorphic head/eye system observes a scene composed by three objects at different distances. (b) The scene as viewed by the robot's camera.

in this case, separate views of the scene are obtained from the same camera at different instants in time, rather than from multiple cameras as in stereo-vision. In this case, the underlying cue to extract is no longer disparity, but motion parallax [12], and if the inter-frame movement of the camera is sufficiently small, the correspondence problem becomes an estimation of the optic flow in the temporal sequence [4]. The use of this cue has the advantages of (a) enabling 3D vision with a single camera; (b) eliminating the need for precise alignment of multiple cameras and complex calibration procedures; and (c) building upon an extensive literature on optic flow computation, which can be directly applied to the estimation of motion parallax.

Research on depth from motion or visual SLAM (simultaneous localization and mapping) has historically focused almost exclusively on relatively large movements of the agent [13,1,5,11]. However, in humans, useful motion parallax also emerges during much smaller movements, such as the minute involuntary head and body movements that humans continually perform during fixation [3]. These small relocations are particularly interesting, as they yield relatively small changes in the images, which greatly facilitate the reliable estimation of motion parallax. Furthermore, this approach opens the possibility for actively closing the sensory-motor control loop to optimize the extraction of 3D information. That is, if the establishment of 3D representations does not occur instantaneously, but is progressively refined based on the integration of new information acquired over the period of fixation, it becomes possible to control the agent on the basis of the available knowledge.

Previous studies have shown that small movements similar to those performed by humans, including small isolated camera rotations [14] and coordinated head/camera rotations [9], provide useful 3D information also in robotic systems. In these previous studies, the authors extracted distance information by means of triangulation, using an approach similar to stereopsis on two images acquired at successive times during fixation. Here, we present a full model for the extraction of the motion parallax that emerges during active fixation in a humanoid robot that replicates the coordinated head/eye movements normally performed by humans. Unlike the previous studies, this model optimally integrates motor/position information with optic flow to continually extract depth from the inflowing temporal sequences of images acquired during fixation and progressively refine 3D representations.

The reminder of the paper is organized as follows. Section 2 describes the optic flow generated by fixational head/eye movements. Section 3 describes the motion of the system. Section 4 summarizes the proposed approach. Finally, in section 5 we report results obtained with simulations of our humanoid robot.

2   Motion Equations

This section reviews the equations of the optic flow induced by the camera motion. Let consider an ideal point light source placed at the position $P = [X, Y, Z]^T$, where coordinates are given in a frame of reference centered on the camera's nodal point and oriented in such a way that the z-axis coincides on the optic axis. Modeling the camera as a pinhole system with focal length f, the point P is projected on the sensor surface at the coordinate $p = [x, y]^T$, as provided by equation (1).

$$\begin{bmatrix} x \\ y \end{bmatrix} = \frac{f}{Z} \cdot \begin{bmatrix} X \\ Y \end{bmatrix} \tag{1}$$

During active fixation, compensatory movements of the cameras and neck result in translational and angular velocities of the nodal point, that we denote with $v = [v_x, v_y, v_z]^T$ and $\omega = [\omega_x, \omega_y, \omega_z]^T$, respectively. This movement causes an apparent motion of the observed scene on the camera's sensor, so that, the point P is seen as moving with velocity $\dot{P} = -v - \omega \times P$. Taking the temporal derivatives of equation (1) and by writing the components of the apparent motion in terms of the instantaneous velocity of the camera, we obtain the classical equation of the optic flow [8], which is reported in equation (2).

$$\begin{bmatrix} \dot{x} \\ \dot{y} \end{bmatrix} = \begin{bmatrix} \frac{x \cdot y}{f} & -\frac{x^2 + f^2}{f} & y \\ \frac{y^2 + f^2}{f} & -\frac{x \cdot y}{f} & -x \end{bmatrix} \cdot \begin{bmatrix} \omega_x \\ \omega_y \\ \omega_z \end{bmatrix} + \frac{1}{Z} \cdot \begin{bmatrix} f & 0 & x \\ 0 & f & y \end{bmatrix} \cdot \begin{bmatrix} v_x \\ v_y \\ v_z \end{bmatrix} = \begin{bmatrix} r_x \\ r_y \end{bmatrix} + \frac{1}{Z} \cdot \begin{bmatrix} t_x \\ t_y \end{bmatrix} \tag{2}$$

Each component of the optic flow $(\dot{x}, \dot{y})$ is divided into two elements, r and t, which depend on the angular and translational velocities of the camera, respectively. It is important to remark that equation (2) is only valid for sufficiently small velocities and under the assumption that no motion occurs in the scene.

3   Coordinated Head/Eye Fixation

This section describes the robot's motor behavior. The robot replicates the strategy by which humans and primates maintain fixation under normal viewing condition. Neck rotation causes motion parallax. Since the centers of rotation of these motors do not lie on the nodal point of the camera, any movements resulting from these motors would generate both rotational and translational

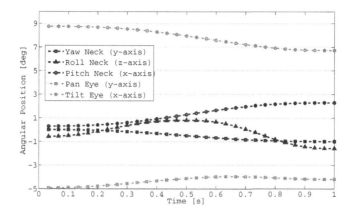

Fig. 2. Angular position of the neck motors (yaw, pitch, roll) and of the left eye motors (pan, tilt) during fixational head movements

velocities. Translational velocities cause motion on the image that depends on the distance of the various objects. Thus, we can use the optic flow in the images acquired from the camera to estimate distance directly from equation (2).

Since the measurement process is affected by noise and the magnitude of the signals is small, reliable depth estimation can be achieved by keeping the scene in the field of view and integrating depth cues over time. The scene is maintained in the visual field by means of visually-guided eye movements: the eyes rotate in the opposite direction with respect to the neck to compensate the shift of the gaze.

These compensating movements ensure that the instantaneous velocity of the camera is small, so that, equation (2) keeps its validity. Moreover, the viewed scene change slightly, thus the computational cost required to compute the optic flow decreases.

Figure 1(a) shows a simulation of our humanoid robot. Four simulated objects (three mugs and a postcard) are placed at a different distance. The scene, as viewed by the robot, is shown in Fig. 1(b).

Figure 2 shows an example of fixational eye movements. The yaw, roll and pitch angles of the head move following a minimum jerk trajectory, while the pan and tilt of the left camera counteract the head motion to maintain fixation on the mug (i.e. keep the mug at the center of the acquired image).

4   Model

The proposed model is summarized in Fig. 3. At each time step, we obtain the head/eye position from proprioceptive cues and the viewed scene from the camera. Proprioceptive cues are used by the kinematic model of the robot to provide the motion of the camera. In parallel, the system extracts a dense optic flow from the sequence of images. The iconic filter integrates the camera velocity

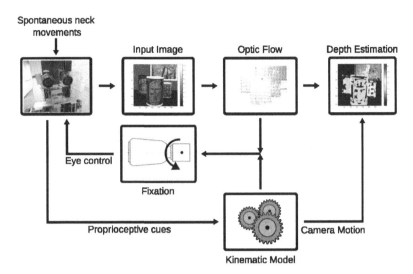

Fig. 3. System architecture. Images are acquired during coordinated head/eye fixation in which the cameras compensate for small random movements of the neck. The optic flow estimated by the images and the camera motion, as estimated by means of proprioceptive signals, are integrated to extract distance information from the scene.

with the optic flow in order to estimate distance at each point in the scene (see section 4.3). The fixation is maintained by a controller that combines both feed-forward (kinematic model) and feed-back (optic flow) contributions.

4.1   Camera Motion

The motion of the camera is provided by proprioceptive cues by using the kinematics model of the robot. Under the assumption of small movements, the camera velocity can be extracted directly from the homogeneous matrix M_{t-1}^t, which describes the displacement of the camera with respect to its previous position. This matrix is a function of the angular positions of the neck and the eye motors and can be approximated as described by equation (3).

$$M_{t-1}^t = \begin{bmatrix} 1 & -\omega_z & \omega_y & v_x \\ \omega_z & 1 & -\omega_x & v_y \\ -\omega_y & \omega_x & 1 & v_z \\ 0 & 0 & 0 & 1 \end{bmatrix} \tag{3}$$

Figure 4 shows the translational and the angular velocities of the nodal point obtained by the Fixational head movements showed in figure 2.

4.2   Optic Flow

Head fixational movements create an apparent motion of the viewed scene. We extracted the optic flow from two subsequent images using the probabilist version of the Lucas-Kanade algorithm proposed by Simoncelli et al.[15].

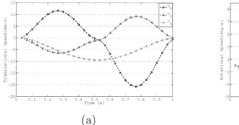
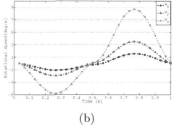

(a)   (b)

Fig. 4. (a)Translational (v) and (b) angular (ω) velocities of the nodal point as estimated from proprioceptive signals

The algorithm is based on the assumption that the brightness of the image
($\mathbf{I}$) is constant over time: $\mathbf{I}(x, y, t) = const$. This assumption implies that the
first order derivative is zero:

$$\mathbf{I}_x(x, y, t) \cdot \dot{x} + \mathbf{I}_y(x, y, t) \cdot \dot{y} + \mathbf{I}_t(x, y, t) = 0 \tag{4}$$

where $\mathbf{I}_x$ and $\mathbf{I}_y$ are the spatial derivatives of the image, $\mathbf{I}_t$ the temporal derivative and $\dot{x}$, $\dot{y}$ the horizontal and vertical components of the optic flow. Eq. (4)
provides one constraint for two unknowns, so that, it allows us to compute only
the normal component of the optic flow (*aperture problem*). For each pixel, the
aperture problem is solved by using the Lucas-Kanade algorithm which assumes
the optic flow is constant inside a neighborhood. In this way we set multiple
constraints and we find the two unknowns using the least squares method.

The probabilistic version of the algorithm introduces a prior information about
the optic flow, and *measurement* and *model* noises. Simoncelli et al.[15] modeled
the prior information as a zero mean Gaussian distribution. Conversely, we considered the optic flow as a stochastic constant process. On the other hand, white
Gaussian noise (η_t) affects the temporal derivative of the image (*measurement
noise*), while the spatial derivatives are assumed to be noise free in order to
keep the whole noise Gaussian[15]. The assumption that the velocity is constant
inside a patch is usually not verified so that Gaussian noise ($\eta_{\dot{x}}, \eta_{\dot{y}}$) is added to
the optic flow. Equation (4) becomes:

$$\mathbf{I}_x \cdot (\dot{x} + \eta_{\dot{x}}) + \mathbf{I}_y \cdot (\dot{y} + \eta_{\dot{y}}) + \mathbf{I}_t + \eta_t = \mathbf{I}_x \cdot \dot{x} + \mathbf{I}_y \cdot \dot{y} + \mathbf{I}_t + \eta_m = 0 \tag{5}$$

Using this model we can estimate the optic flow using a Kalman filter. The
system of equations that describes the state-transition is:

$$\begin{bmatrix} \dot{x}(t+1) \\ \dot{y}(t+1) \end{bmatrix} = \begin{bmatrix} 1 & 0 \\ 0 & 1 \end{bmatrix} \cdot \begin{bmatrix} \dot{x}(t) \\ \dot{y}(t) \end{bmatrix} + \begin{bmatrix} \xi_{\dot{x}}(t) \\ \xi_{\dot{y}}(t) \end{bmatrix} \tag{6}$$

where $\xi_{\dot{x}}(t)$ and $\xi_{\dot{y}}(t)$ represent the error that we introduce by assuming the
optic flow as constant in time.

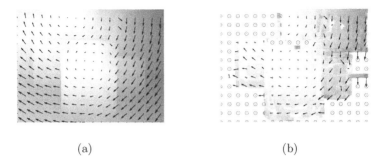

(a)   (b)

Fig. 5. (a) Ideal optic flow. (b) Optic flow estimated by means of Eq.6 and 7. Circles represent one standard deviation.

The system of equations that describes the measurement process is:

$$\begin{bmatrix} \mathbf{I}_{t1}(t) \\ \mathbf{I}_{t2}t) \\ \dots \\ \mathbf{I}_{tn}(t) \end{bmatrix} = \begin{bmatrix} \mathbf{I}_{x1}(t) \ \mathbf{I}_{y1}(t) \\ \mathbf{I}_{x2}(t) \ \mathbf{I}_{y2}(t) \\ \dots \\ \mathbf{I}_{xn}(t) \ \mathbf{I}_{yn}(t) \end{bmatrix} \cdot \begin{bmatrix} \dot{x}(t) \\ \dot{y}(t) \end{bmatrix} + \begin{bmatrix} \eta_{m1}(t) \\ \eta_{m2}(t) \\ \dots \\ \eta_{mn}(t) \end{bmatrix} \quad (7)$$

where the subscripts $1, 2, \dots, n$ denote the pixels inside the neighborhood.

Figure 5 compares the theoretical optic flow (Fig. 5(a)) and the estimated one (Fig. 5(b)). Different colors represent different orientations while the intensity is proportional to the magnitude of the optic flow. The circumferences in figure 5(b) represent the standard deviation of the optic flow. We can observer small radii in high textured regions and big radii in homogeneous regions. Moreover, the standard deviation assumes an elliptic shape in correspondence of the edges.

4.3   Iconic Depth Map

The optic flow and the instantaneous velocity of the camera are used by an iconic Kalman-filter to estimate the inverse of depth, also called disparity (d). Disparity is employed instead of the depth to work with a linear system [10]. Thanks to the small amplitude of the head movements, changes of the distance are negligible with respect to the distance of the objects. Also, the fixation movements keep the visual features practically in the same visual position, so that each pixel-centered filter observes features that are almost at the same depth. Indeed, in the acquired sequence of images the optic flow is always smaller than 2 pixels. For this reason we consider the disparity of the scene as constant in time (see equation 8). The small error due to this assumption is modeled by Gaussian noise η_d.

$$d(t+1) = d(t) + \eta_d(t) \quad (8)$$

The measurement of the disparity is time-variant and depends on the angular and translational velocities of the camera:

$$\begin{bmatrix} \dot{x}(t) \\ \dot{y}(t) \end{bmatrix} = \begin{bmatrix} t_x(t) \\ t_y(t) \end{bmatrix} \cdot d(t) + \begin{bmatrix} r_x(t) \\ r_y(t) \end{bmatrix} + \begin{bmatrix} R(t) \end{bmatrix} \quad (9)$$

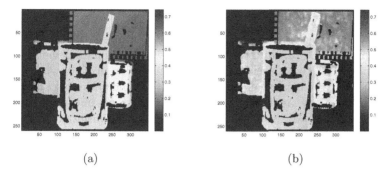

(a)   (b)

Fig. 6. Resulting map of distance in the scene. The ideal map (a) is compared to the map obtained from Eq. 8 and 9 (b). Distance estimation is possible only within textured regions.

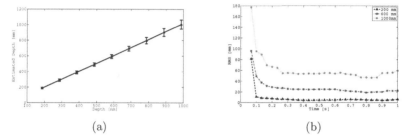

(a)   (b)

Fig. 7. Accuracy of the method. (a) Estimation of a single object (a cup) placed in front of the left camera at a variable distance in the range 0.2-1 m. The robot's neck moved as shown in Fig. 2 while the camera compensated to maintain fixation on the object. Data points represent means ± std. (b) Dynamics of error variance with targets at three different distances.

The covariance matrix of the error R is the covariance matrix provided by the computation of the optic flow described in the previous section.

Figure 6 shows the true depth of the scene (Fig. 6(a)) and the depth computed by the proposed algorithm (Fig. 6(b)). The depth is shown only where the result of the algorithm is reliable, that is, in the textured regions.

5 Experiments and Results

The simulation was performed using OpenRave [6] and we implemented the code in MATLAB. We simulated a robotic head (Fig. 1(a)) that moved with 7 degrees of freedom (d.o.f.s), three in the neck (yaw, roll and pitch) and two in each eye (pan and tilt). We simulated a vision system that acquires images at 30 frame/s from a high-resolution (1392×1040 pixels) monochrome camera. The pixel size of the camera was set almost as small as the cones in the retina ($4.65\mu m$). The focal length was set to $15mm$ and we did not take into account lens distortion.

During the experiments, the images acquired from the simulated environment were resized to 348×260 pixels to reduce computational time. For each pixel the optic flow was measured into a neighborhood of 7×7 pixels. The state transition error is represented by a white Gaussian noise with a standard deviation ($\xi_{\dot{x}}$ and $\xi_{\dot{y}}$) of 0.5 pixels. On the other hand, the standard deviation of the white Gaussian noises that affect the measurements, that is $\eta_{\dot{x}} = \eta_{\dot{y}}$ and η_t, were set to 0.002 and 0.1 pixels respectively. At the first frame the optic flow was initialized to zero and with a big standard deviation (10 pixels). A similar initialization was used also for the depth estimator, so that at the beginning we treated the whole scene as background (zero disparity). The algorithm was tested by executing fixational head movements described in section 3. While the neck moved following the trajectory shown in Fig. 2, the eye moved to keep the fixation.

Figures 5 and 6, described in the previous sections, provide a qualitative demonstration of the functioning of the algorithm. However, in figure 6(b) we can note that the error of the estimation grows with the depth of the object. In this section we provide some quantitatively results obtained in simulation. The experimental setup was composed of only a mug which was placed at variable distance within a range of a meter. For each scene we executed the fixational behavior described above.

Figure 7(a) shows the estimated depth (mean and standard deviation) for the mug placed at nine different distances. As expected, the error increases with the depth and, at a distance of 1 m, the standard deviation of the measure is approximately 100mm (10%). The proposed system improves the performance of previous work, in which the error at the same distance was around 150 mm [14,9]. Moreover, our algorithm works with smaller interframe displacements and with 4 times smaller images. Figure 7(b) shows how the estimation error evolves with the time. The plot is shown for the object placed at three different distances (0.2 m, 0.6 m and 1 m). The result shows that the convergence time increases with the depth of the object. However, in the worst case (1 m), it converges in less than ten frames, that is, 0.3 s with a frame rate of 30 fps.

6   Conclusions

We have presented a novel framework that combines visual, motor, and proprioceptive signals to extract distance/depth information in a humanoid robot. The robot replicates the coordinated head and eye movements that human normally perform while maintaining fixation. Because of these movements, depth information emerges in the form of parallax. A probabilistic filter in our model extracts the optic flow from the sequence of the incoming images and combines it with proprioceptive cues to extract 3D information. Results obtained by means of simulations have shown that the methods is efficient and robust. This method can be used alone or combined with other cues, such as stereopsis, to obtain more reliable 3D vision systems.

References

1. Aloimonos, Y., Duric, Z.: Estimating the heading direction using normal flow. International Journal of Computer Vision 13(1), 33–56 (1994)
2. Ayache, N.: Artificial vision for mobile robots - stereo vision and multisensory perception. MIT Press (1991)
3. Aytekin, M., Rucci, M.: Motion parallax from microscopic head movements during visual fixation. Vision Research (August 2012)
4. Barron, J.L., Fleet, D.J., Beauchemin, S.S.: Performance of optical flow techniques. International Journal of Computer Vision 12(1), 43–77 (1994)
5. Davison, A.J., Reid, I.D., Molton, N.D., Stasse, O.: Monoslam: Real-time single camera slam. IEEE Transactions on Pattern Analysis and Machine Intelligence 29(6), 1052–1067 (2007)
6. Diankov, R., Kuffner, J.: Openrave: A planning architecture for autonomous robotics. Robotics Institute, Pittsburgh, PA, Tech. Rep. CMU-RI-TR-08-34 (2008)
7. Faugeras, O.D., Luong, Q.T., Papadopoulo, T.: The geometry of multiple images - the laws that govern the formation of multiple images of a scene and some of their applications. MIT Press (2001)
8. Higgins, L.H.C., Prazdny, K.: The Interpretation of a Moving Retinal Image. Proceedings of the Royal Society of London. Series B, Biological Sciences (1934-1990) 208(1173), 385–397 (1980)
9. Kuang, X., Gibson, M., Shi, B.E., Rucci, M.: Active vision during coordinated head/eye movements in a humanoid robot. IEEE Transactions on Robotics PP(99), 1–8 (2012)
10. Matthies, L., Kanade, T., Szeliski, R.: Kalman filter-based algorithms for estimating depth from image sequences. International Journal of Computer Vision 3(3), 209–238 (1989)
11. Ramachandran, M., Veeraraghavan, A., Chellappa, R.: A fast bilinear structure from motion algorithm using a video sequence and inertial sensors. IEEE Trans. Pattern Anal. Mach. Intell. 33(1), 186–193 (2011)
12. Rogers, B., Graham, M.: Motion parallax as an independent cue for depth perception. Perception 8(2), 125–134 (1979)
13. Sandini, G., Tistarelli, M.: Active tracking strategy for monocular depth inference over multiple frames. IEEE Transactions on Pattern Analysis and Machine Intelligence 12(1), 13–27 (1990), doi:10.1109/34.41380
14. Santini, F., Rucci, M.: Active estimation of distance in a robotic system that replicates human eye movement. Robotics and Autonomous Systems 55(2), 107–121 (2007)
15. Simoncelli, E., Adelson, E., Heeger, D.: Probability distributions of optical flow. In: Proceedings of the IEEE Computer Society Conference on Computer Vision and Pattern Recognition, CVPR 1991, pp. 310–315. IEEE (1991)

LaserGun: A Tool for Hybrid 3D Reconstruction

Marco Fanfani and Carlo Colombo

Computational Vision Group
Dip. di Ingegneria dell'Informazione
Universitá di Firenze
Via S. Marta 3, 50139 Firenze, Italy
{marco.fanfani,carlo.colombo}@unifi.it
http://cvg.dsi.unifi.it/

Abstract. We present a tool for the acquisition of 3D textured models of objects of desktop size using an hybrid computer vision framework. This framework combines active laser-based triangulation with passive motion estimation. The 3D models are obtained by motion-based alignment (with respect to a fixed world frame) of imaged laser profiles backprojected onto time-varying camera frames. Two distinct techniques for estimating camera displacements are described and evaluated. The first is based on a Simultaneous Localization and Mapping (SLAM) approach, while the second exploits a planar pattern in the scene and recovers motion by homography decomposition. Results obtained with a custom laser-camera stereo setup — implemented with off-the-shelf hardware — show that a trade-off exists between the greater operational flexibility of SLAM and the higher model accuracy of the homography-based approach.

Keywords: 3D Reconstruction, Active Triangulation, Motion Estimation, SLAM.

1 Introduction

Visual reconstruction of 3D object shape is typically accomplished through either active or passive methods.

Active methods rely on the observation of a light pattern while it interacts with the scanned object [1,2]. Accurate models are obtained also for textureless objects, working in structured conditions with sophisticated hardware and relatively simple algorithms. In [3], the authors use a pattern with several light stripes arranged in a regular way; object shape is obtained through the so called *active triangulation* approach of single image points. In [4,5] two 3D reconstruction approaches based on active triangulation of a hand-held laser device are described. The former uses a laser blade and requires a background with known geometry to simultaneously estimate the laser plane equation and reconstruct small-size objects. The latter — used also to reconstruct room-size environments — uses an ad-hoc pointer array device and requires an initial calibration step.

M. Chen, B. Leibe, and B. Neumann (Eds.): ICVS 2013, LNCS 7963, pp. 274–283, 2013.
© Springer-Verlag Berlin Heidelberg 2013

A different approach, called *active rectification* and based on image warping transformations of entire laser profiles, is described in [6].

Passive methods use only unstructured illumination, and focus instead on low cost hardware and sophisticated software, by which a reasonable accuracy and a high flexibility can be obtained. Typical passive approaches encompass multi-view reconstruction from either image collections [7,8] or image sequences [9], real time stereo [10] and shape from shading [11].

In [12], an active/passive method is presented where cast shadows produced with a wand are used instead of projected light. Another hybrid approach extending standard shape from shading is photometric stereo [13], where a collection of photos of the object is taken from a single viewpoint by varying the light source.

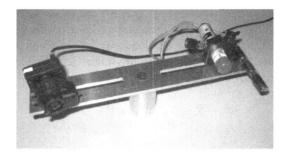

Fig. 1. The camera-laser group for free-hand 3D acquisition

In this paper, a hybrid solution to the 3D reconstruction problem is proposed, where classical active triangulation based on a single laser stripe is combined with a passive technique for motion estimation. System operation is performed with the device shown in Fig. 1, composed of a laser illuminator and an off-the-shelf camera kept in a fixed relative position. The device is moved manually in front of the object to reconstruct. As with the other hybrid active/passive approaches mentioned above, ours combines good accuracy and flexibility of use. Note that, unlike other hand-held acquisition systems, both the camera and the laser are moved during the scanning. Motion estimation is carried out with two different approaches. The first one is based on Simultaneous Localization and Mapping (SLAM). The second one relies on tracking of a checkerboard pattern in the scene and planar homography decomposition.

In the next Section, a general description of the approach is given. Then Sect. 3 and 4 discuss respectively the SLAM and the homography-based motion estimation approaches. In Sect. 5, a comparison between the motion estimation strategies is addressed, and experimental results are given. Finally, conclusions and directions for future work are discussed in Sect. 6.

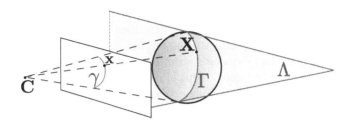

Fig. 2. An example of the device layout while scanning an object. C is the camera center, Λ the laser plane, Γ the 3D laser trace and γ the 2D laser image.

2   The Approach

Figure 2 shows the basic projection geometry of laser profile Γ onto the image. At any time t, each point $\mathbf{x}$ of the imaged laser profile γ can be backprojected onto the laser plane Λ, thus obtaining its pre-image $\mathbf{X} \in \Gamma$. The backprojection equation can be expressed as

$$ {}^{c}\tilde{\mathbf{X}} = \frac{d_\Lambda}{\mathbf{n}_\Lambda^\top \mathsf{K}^{-1}\mathbf{x}} \mathsf{K}^{-1}\mathbf{x} \ , \tag{1}$$

where $\mathbf{n}_\Lambda^\top {}^{c}\tilde{\mathbf{X}} - d_\Lambda = 0$ is the laser plane equation in inhomogeneous camera-centered coordinates, $\mathbf{x}$ is a homogeneous 3-vector, and K is the camera calibration matrix.

In our approach, object reconstruction is achieved by collating all laser profiles into a single 3D model. This is done by expressing all the backprojected laser profiles in a unique, world-centered reference frame, as

$$ {}^{w}\tilde{\mathbf{X}} = \mathsf{R}_t^\top \left[{}^{c}\tilde{\mathbf{X}} - \mathbf{t}_t \right] \ , \tag{2}$$

where $\{\mathsf{R}_t, \mathbf{t}_t\}$ is the roto-traslation of the camera w.r.t. the world reference frame at time t.

Note that the backprojection map of Eq. (1) does not change with time, since the camera and the laser are in a fixed relative position. Conversely, the camera-world coordinate transformation of Eq. (2) is time-dependent, and must be re-estimated for collating each new laser profile. The approach can be decomposed into four main phases as follows.

1. *System Calibration.* This phase is aimed at estimating the matrix K and the laser plane parameters to be used in Eq. (1) for the purpose of model building. In this phase, a planar checkerboard pattern is moved by hand in front of the camera-laser system, which is kept in a fixed position. Camera calibration is carried out with the method presented in [14]. For the purpose of laser calibration, a reference frame is attached to the planar calibration pattern, referred to as π, with the normal of the plane coincident with the Z axis, so that the plane equation is simply ${}^{\pi}Z = 0$. For each frame, the

roto-translation $\{Q, b\}$ such that $^{\pi}\tilde{X} = Q^{\top}[^{c}\tilde{X} - b]$ can be easily obtained as a sub-product of camera calibration [14]. The time-varying pattern plane parameters (n_{π}, d_{π}) can be then computed as

$$n_{\pi} = q_3 \qquad d_{\pi} = q_3^{\top} b \ , \tag{3}$$

where q_3 is the third column of Q. Once the pattern plane parameters are computed for all the calibration frames, the set of back-projected laser points $\{^{c}\tilde{X}_i \in \Lambda \cap \pi\}_{i=1}^{N}$ can be computed using Eq. (1) with (n_{π}, d_{π}) in the place of $(n_{\Lambda}, d_{\Lambda})$. Since the set contains (thanks to the different planar pattern orientations) at least three non-aligned points, the laser plane parameters are estimated by solving an over-constrained linear system.

2. *Laser Extraction* During the reconstruction process the laser profile is automatically extracted from each image. Given the acquisition video we start by tracking the scanned object using an implementation of the Adaptive Mean Shift [15] in the HSV color space, so to isolate a region of interest (ROI) in each video frame. Then the laser search is performed in a color subspace that depends on the real laser color. For example, using a red laser profiler, only the red channel of the image is used during the extraction. The resulting image is converted into gray levels and the highest intensity pixels are chosen as laser point candidates. Then the gray image is convolved with a Sobel filter to enhance the laser stripe edges. Starting from the candidate pixels, we search the left and right edges of the laser on the filtered image and only those points surrounded by both edges are kept. Finally a Center of Mass algorithm [16] is used to achieve subpixel accuracy.

3. *Model Building.* In this phase the 3D laser profiles are obtained using Eq. (1). Then, the roto-traslation $\{R_t, t_t\}$ between the world and camera frames is needed to collate each single 3D profile in an unique reference frame, using Eq. (2). To estimate the camera-laser group movements, two strategies have been implemented and tested. In the first case (see Sect. 3) SLAM algorithm is used to recover the roto-traslation at any time. Alternatively, a homography-based motion estimation algorithm, based on the tracking of a planar pattern, is used in the second case (see Sect. 4).

4. *Texture Acquisition* To augment the raw 3D shape model, the texture of the object is recovered by simply projecting each 3D point back onto the image plane, and then sampling color at the nearest pixel.

3   SLAM Motion Estimation

SLAM algorithms [17,18] are mainly used to estimate the camera position in an unknown environment. Building an incremental 3D representation of the scene (referred to as map), these algorithms are capable to estimate the camera roto-traslation exploiting the known 2D-3D correspondences between the images and the world. In this work a keyframe-based iterative approach, similar to an incremental structure and motion algorithm, was used. Fig. 3 shows its main steps.

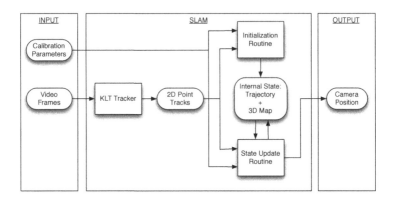

Fig. 3. A block representation of the implemented SLAM algorithm

Between each subsequent video frame a set of 2D matches is obtained, using an implementation of the KLT tracker [19,20] and, by linking subsequent matches, the system is able to group the movements of each 2D point in *tracks* — e.g., if A matches with B and B matches with C, than {A,B,C} defines a track for a single point movements.

Given the calibration matrix K, to estimate the first two camera positions and to obtain an initial map representation an *initialization routine* is needed. To achieve this, the world reference frame is attached to the first camera position and a second frame, with sufficient baseline, is manually chosen. After robustly estimating the essential matrix E from 2D correspondences and decomposing it in $\{R_1, t_1\}$ [21], the first two camera matrices are given as $P_0 = K[I \mid 0]$ and $P_1 = K[R_1 \mid t_1]$. Note that to correctly initialize the real scene scale factor and set the magnitude of t_1, a metric reference (here a checkerboard pattern) has to be visible in the first frames of the sequence. The 3D map is computed by triangulation, storing in a look-up table the correspondence between a 2D track and a 3D point. Finally a bundle adjustment [22] optimization is performed. In this way the system internal state, defined as the camera trajectory and the 3D map, is initialized.

As time progresses, the internal state grows through a *state update routine*. By exploiting the 2D-3D correspondences — easily computed using the updated 2D tracks and the look-up table defined above — the camera matrix at time t is obtained with a robust implementation of a pose estimation algorithm.

To increase the map and to minimize the estimation global error, at specific times a frame is chosen as new keyframe. In this case, in addition to the camera matrix estimation, a new triangulation step is performed, so as to add new 3D points in the map. All the parameters (the keyframe's camera matrices and the map) are then further optimized with a new bundle adjustment iteration.

4   Homography-Based Motion Estimation

In this case, while the camera-laser device is moved to scan the object, a planar pattern has to be kept still and in view of the camera. This allow us to estimate, as time goes by, the homography H_π between the (moving) image plane and the (fixed) pattern, and eventually compute the roto-traslation $\{R_t, t_t\}$ used in Eq. (2) for collating profiles. This is done as follows. The homography has the form

$$H_\pi = \mu K \begin{bmatrix} r_1 & r_2 & t_t \end{bmatrix} , \tag{4}$$

where $R_t = [r_1 \ r_2 \ r_3]$ and μ is an unknown scale factor. Defined $H_\pi = [h_1 \ h_2 \ h_3]$, it holds $r_i = \frac{1}{\mu} K^{-1} h_i$ for $i = 1, 2$ and $t_t = \frac{1}{\mu} K^{-1} h_3$. Now, for the orthonormality of R_t, the scale factor and the last column of the rotation matrix can be respectively computed as $\mu = \| K^{-1} h_1 \|$ and $r_3 = r_1 \times r_2$.

5   Results

A comparison of the results obtained with the two motion estimation solutions is given hereafter. Operationally speaking, SLAM is preferable, as it guarantees a higher flexibility in terms of objects size and choice of viewpoint. In fact the homography-based solution is more constrained in this sense since users must take care that the checkerboard patter always remain in view during the acquisition. However, as evident from the qualitative result of Fig. 4, homography-based approach outperforms SLAM for what concerns 3D model accuracy. Indeed, as it's possible to see in Fig. 5, the SLAM and the homography-based computed trajectories show an increasing divergence. Motion estimates are initially very similar but then SLAM performance gradually degrades. The main reason of this behavior is to be found in the scale factor drift that generally affects single camera structure and motion algorithms.

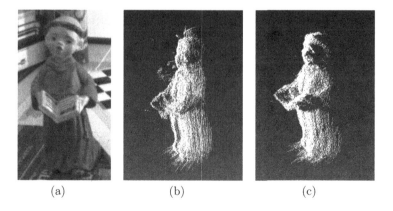

(a)   (b)   (c)

Fig. 4. An example of reconstruction obtained with the SLAM (Fig. 4(b)) and the Homography-based (Fig. 4(c)) solutions

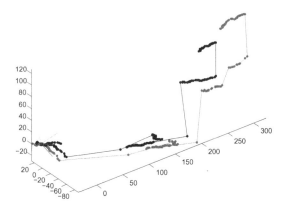

Fig. 5. Results of camera trajectory estimation for the reconstruction of Fig. 4. In red the trajectory computed with the SLAM algorithm. In black the homography-based estimated trajectory. As we can see, while the estimation goes on, the differences between the two trajectories increase. Note that the points on the trajectories are the camera center positions. Instead the straight lines where no points are drawn represent sub-sequences where no laser stripe was found over the scanned object and so no motion estimation was carried out.

More reconstruction tests were carried out with the homography-based approach. Figure 6 shows the results of the 3D reconstruction algorithm for other two different objects. To evaluate the accuracy of the reconstructions, we compared the 3D models with several measurements manually done on the real objects with an high precision caliber. Table 1 reports on the measurements and errors for the *Book* object of Fig. 6(a). Table 2 summarizes the accuracy result in terms of average and maximum error. The results are good and comparable to other approaches requiring either more constrained acquisition scenarios or more sophisticated hardware. On the other hand, a closer inspection to Fig. 6 reveals that the acquired 3D models present some gaps, that are mainly due to the fact that manual operation does not guarantee that all surface points are illuminated at least once by the laser stripe.

Table 1. Measurements (cm) of the *Book* model

Dim.	Real	Model	Error
Height	22.50	22.13	0.37
Width	14,80	14,71	0.09
Length	2.08	2.38	0.30

Table 2. Average and max errors (cm) for the *Book* and *Horse* models

Model	Avg. Error	Max Error
Book	0.25	0.37
Horse	0.23	0.4

(a) Example 1: Book

(b) Example 2: Horse

Fig. 6. Reconstruction examples: in the first column the photos, in the second the 3D models

6   Conclusions and Future Work

In this work we described a tool based on an active/passive framework for reconstruction of realistic 3D models of limited size objects, and we compared two motion estimation solutions. System operation includes a simultaneous camera and laser calibration phase, followed by backprojection and collation of all imaged laser profiles. As shown in Sect. 5, the implemented (mono) SLAM solution, which has been found to be perfectly adequate for augmented reality applications (see Fig. 7 and its description), appears to be less accurate than the homography-based approach for 3D reconstruction applications. On the other hand, the homography-based approach is less flexible than SLAM, but nevertheless allows us to obtain good quality models using a very simple procedure and an inexpensive hardware. The software is currently implemented as a prototype with partial manual operation — as for example the checkerboard detection step.

Future work will address code optimization — including the removal of all manual operations — and the development of suitable point cloud densification strategies aimed at filling the model gaps. In addition a new device with a stereo pair and a laser emitter is currently under study. Using a stereo approach for SLAM is likely to lead to a more robust motion estimation, avoiding any

Fig. 7. An augmented reality (AR) application using our SLAM algorithm. The virtual wire-frame cube undergoes the correct perspective deformations and remains stable upon the desk. Although the algorithm is the same used for 3D reconstruction, here the perceived quality of motion estimation is higher. In fact, differently from Fig. 4(b), the inaccuracies in camera motion estimates do not appear as flaws. This shows that 3D reconstruction requires a higher estimation accuracy than AR to achieve a similar perceptual quality.

scale factor uncertainty, and yield an even more efficient an flexible tool for 3D structure recovery.

Acknowledgements. This work has been carried out during the THESAURUS project, founded by Regione Toscana (Italy) in the framework of the "FAS" program 2007-2013 under Deliberation CIPE (Italian government) 166/2007.

References

1. Chen, F., Brown, G.M., Song, M.: Overview of Three-Dimensional Shape Measurement using Optical Methods. Optical Engineering 39, 10–22 (2000)
2. Bernardini, F., Rushmeier, H.E.: The 3D Model Acquisition Pipeline. Computer Graphics Forum 21, 149–172 (2002)
3. Rocchini, C., Cignoni, P., Montani, C., Scopigno, R.: A low cost 3D scanner based on structured light. Computer Graphics Forum 20, 299–308 (2001)
4. Winkelbach, S., Molkenstruck, S., Wahl, F.M.: Low-cost laser range scanner and fast surface registration approach. In: Franke, K., Müller, K.-R., Nickolay, B., Schäfer, R. (eds.) DAGM 2006. LNCS, vol. 4174, pp. 718–728. Springer, Heidelberg (2006)

5. Habbecke, M., Kobbelt, L.: Laser brush: a flexible device for 3D reconstruction of indoor scenes. In: Proceedings of the 2008 ACM Symposium on Solid and Physical Modeling, pp. 231–239. ACM, New York (2008)
6. Colombo, C., Comanducci, D., Del Bimbo, A.: Shape reconstruction and texture sampling by active rectification and virtual view synthesis. Computer Vision and Image Understanding 115, 161–176 (2011)
7. Agarwal, S., Snavely, N., Simon, I., Seitz, S.M., Szeliski, R.: Building Rome in a Day. In: Proceedings of the International Conference on Computer Vision, ICCV 2009, Kyoto, Japan (2009)
8. Farenzena, A.M., Fusiello, A., Gherardi, R.: Structure-and-Motion Pipeline on a Hierarchical Cluster Tree. In: Proceedings of the IEEE International Workshop on 3-D Digital Imaging and Modeling, Kyoto, Japan (2009)
9. Vogiatzis, G., Hernàndez, C.: Video-based, real-time multi view stereo. Image and Vision Computing (2011)
10. Wang, L., Liao, M., Gong, M., Yang, R., Nistèr, D.: High-quality real-time stereo using adaptive cost aggregation and dynamic programming. In: 3rd Int. Symposium on 3D Data Processing, Visualization and Transmission (3DPVT), pp. 798–805. Springer (2006)
11. Zhang, R., Tsai, P.S., Cryer, J.E., Shah, M.: Shape from shading: A survey. IEEE Transactions on Pattern Analysis and Machine Intelligence 21(8), 690–706 (1999)
12. Bouguet, J.Y., Perona, P.: 3D Photography Using Shadows in Dual-Space Geometry. International Journal of Computer Vision (IJCV) 35, 129–149 (1999)
13. Hernàndez, C., Vogiatzis, G., Cipolla, R.: Multi-view Photometric Stereo. IEEE Transactions on Pattern Analysis and Machine Intelligence 30 (2008)
14. Zhang, Z.: A flexible new technique for camera calibration. IEEE Transactions on Pattern Analysis and Machine Intelligence 22, 1330–1334 (2000)
15. Bradski, G.R.: Computer Vision Face Tracking for Use in a Perceptual User Interface. Intel Technology Journal (1998)
16. Fisher, R.B., Naidu, D.K.: A Comparison of Algorithms for Subpixel Peak Detection. In: Image Technology, Advances in Image Processing, Multimedia and Machine Vision, pp. 385–404. Springer (1996)
17. Klein, G., Murray, D.: Parallel tracking and mapping for small AR workspaces. In: Proc. Sixth IEEE and ACM International Symposium on Mixed and Augmented Reality (ISMAR 2007), Nara, Japan (November 2007)
18. Mei, C., Sibley, G., Cummins, M., Newman, P., Reid, I.: RSLAM: A system for large-scale mapping in constant-time using stereo. International Journal of Computer Vision, 1–17 (2010); Special issue of BMVC
19. Shi, J., Tomasi, C.: Good features to track. Technical report, Ithaca, NY, USA (1993)
20. Bouguet, J.Y.: Pyramidal implementation of the Lucas-Kanade feature tracker description of the algorithm (2000)
21. Hartley, R.I., Zisserman, A.: Multiple View Geometry in Computer Vision, 2nd edn. Cambridge University Press (2004) ISBN: 0521540518
22. Lourakis, M.I.A., Argyros, A.A.: SBA: a software package for generic sparse bundle adjustment. ACM Transactions on Mathematical Software, 1–30 (2009)

Accurate Dense Stereo Matching of Slanted Surfaces Using 2D Integral Images

Gwnag Yul Song[1], Seong Ik Cho[2], Dong Yong Kwak[2], and Joon Woong Lee[1,*]

[1] Dept. of Industrial Engineering, College of Engineering, Chonnam National University 300, Yongbong-dong Buk-gu, Gwangju, Korea
skyclass@nate.com, joonlee@chonnam.ac.kr
[2] Electronics and Telecommunications Research Institute, 218 Gajeong-ro, Yuseong-gu, Daejeon, 305-700, Korea
{chosi,dykwak}@etri.re.kr

Abstract. This paper presents an advanced algorithm providing accurate stereo correspondences of two frames through concise disparity gradient estimation at the per-pixel level and 2D integral images. The key contributions of this novel algorithm are twofold: First, combining an upright cross-based support region with disparity gradient estimation realizes the implicit construction of a 3D support region for each anchor pixel. This approach yields the disparity accuracy for slanted surfaces as well as fronto-parallel surfaces. Second, the 2D integral image technique leads to a speedup of matching cost aggregation in the implicit 3D support regions. The experimental results show that the proposed algorithm can successfully convey the correspondences of actual sequence of outdoor stereo images and Middlebury stereo images with high accuracy in near real time.

Keywords: stereo matching, disparity gradient, integral image, cross-based support region.

1 Introduction

Stereo matching has been extensively studied as an important computer vision topic, which involves finding correspondences between two images. The stereo correspondences can be applied to various fields, such as a 3D reconstruction. We are specifically interested in using this approach to determining a drivable-region for unmanned vehicles. The most important component of this task is to obtain accurate disparities corresponding to the road surface and obstacles.

Stereo matching methods are broadly divided into local and global methods [1]. Most local algorithms commonly compute pixel-based matching cost over all pixels and all disparities and form a disparity space image $C(x,y,d)$ – namely a cost volume(CV), in which (x, y) represents a pixel position and d means a disparity. The costs are then aggregated over a support region. A support region can be either

---

* Corresponding author.

M. Chen, B. Leibe, and B. Neumann (Eds.): ICVS 2013, LNCS 7963, pp. 284–293, 2013.
© Springer-Verlag Berlin Heidelberg 2013

two-dimensional at a fixed disparity, or three-dimensional in CV [1]. Yoon et al. [2] assigned a support weight to the pixel in a fixed 2D support window based on color similarity and geometric proximity. Zhang et al. [3] and Mei et al. [4] proposed a shape adaptive local support region construction. After the region construction, they aggregate costs within the 2D constant disparity planes using an orthogonal integral image technique under the assumption that the pixels in a local region of similar colors or intensities have the same disparity. This assumption does not favor slanted surfaces, such as road surfaces in outdoor road traffic images, but rather fronto-parallel surfaces.

In the methods developed by Klaus et al. [5] and Yang et al. [6], the image is first segmented into homogeneously-colored regions, and a 3D region is constructed based on disparity plane fitting. Zhang et al. [7] introduced a per-pixel non-fronto-parallel disparity plane model and performed adaptive-weight cost aggregation in CV along slanted planes. Their approaches provide acceptable correspondences for slanted surfaces, but take a long time. For these reasons, we develop a new stereo correspondence solution capable of realizing near real time processing that can provide good correspondences for slanted surfaces as well as fronto-parallel surfaces. The structure of our method is shown in Fig. 1, which includes the following key techniques:

- Several well-known algorithms, such as AD-Census to construct the initial CV, scanline optimization (SO) to alleviate the noise effect in the initial matching costs, and upright cross-based region construction [4], are employed. After SO, we estimate the initial disparities and then remove outliers in the disparities by the left-right consistency check proposed by Mühlmann et al. [8].
- For all pixels in an image, a 3D support region is implicitly constructed by estimating disparity gradients along an upright cross. The estimation is performed using linear regression [9] because the regression can be implemented in high speed. But the method is in general sensitive to noise, so a refinement process based on a voting paradigm is incorporated to enhance the estimation.
- The cost aggregation over an implicit 3D support region is performed. However, this process is very time-consuming. Thus, this problem is solved by using a novel 2D integral image technique proposed in this paper.

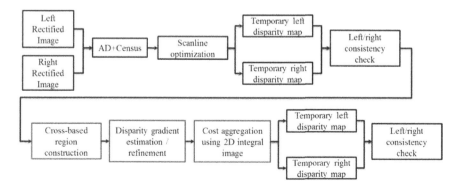

Fig. 1. Structure of the proposed algorithm

2   Cross-Based Support Region Construction

The region construction uses a smoothness constraint that neighboring pixels with a similar color should have similar disparities. For further details with respect to the construction, refer to Mei et al. [4]. The region is constructed with two stages. First, an upright cross of a pixel $\mathbf{p}=(x,y)$ in a color image I is formed by using the following conditions. The conditions can be explained with the formation of the left arm by finding an end pixel $\mathbf{p}_1$.

1. $D_c(\mathbf{p}_1,\mathbf{p}) < \tau_1$ and $D_c(\mathbf{p}_1,\mathbf{p}_1+(1,0)) < \tau_1$
2. $D_s(\mathbf{p}_1,\mathbf{p}) < L_1$
3. $D_c(\mathbf{p}_1,\mathbf{p}) < \tau_2$, if $L_2 < D_s(\mathbf{p}_1,\mathbf{p}) < L_1$

where $D_c(\mathbf{p}_1,\mathbf{p})$ is the color difference between $\mathbf{p}_1$ and $\mathbf{p}$, and τ_1 and $\tau_2(\tau_1 > \tau_2)$ are preset threshold values. $D_s(\mathbf{p}_1,\mathbf{p})$ is the spatial distance between $\mathbf{p}_1$ and $\mathbf{p}$, and L_1 and $L_2(L_1 > L_2)$ are preset lengths measured in pixels. Both differences are defined by following equations (1) and (2), respectively.

$$D_c(\mathbf{p}_1,\mathbf{p}) = \max_{i=R,G,B} |I_i(\mathbf{p}_1) - I_i(\mathbf{p})| \tag{1}$$

$$D_s(\mathbf{p}_1,\mathbf{p}) = |\mathbf{p}_1 - \mathbf{p}| \tag{2}$$

The right, up and bottom arms of $\mathbf{p}$ are built in a similar way. Fig. 2 shows an example of an upright cross depicted by a shaded region, in which $\mathbf{p}_t$, $\mathbf{p}_b$, $\mathbf{p}_l$ and $\mathbf{p}_r$ represent end points of the top, bottom, left and right arms, respectively. For every pixel in I, a vertical arm { $\mathbf{p}_t$ and $\mathbf{p}_b$ } and a horizontal arm { $\mathbf{p}_l$ and $\mathbf{p}_r$ } are constructed. Second, the support region of $\mathbf{p}$ is formed by merging the horizontal arms of all pixels lying on $\mathbf{p}$'s vertical arm. In Fig. 2, the red line represents the support region.

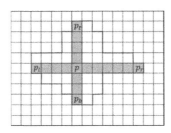

Fig. 2. An example of a cross-based support region

3   Disparity Gradient Estimation

3.1   Disparity Gradient

The disparity gradient is composed of partial derivatives, $\partial d/\partial x$ and $\partial d/\partial y$ in CV, $C(x,y,d)$. This gradient is used when costs are aggregated in CV. For the estimation of disparity gradient, we use linear regression [9], which provides the slope of a line, because even if the regression is affected by noises it is possible to reduce the processing time. In addition, to use this estimated gradient to aggregate costs we assume that a curved surface like a road surface can be depicted by plane patches. The gradient components along the x-axis and y-axis are calculated as follows:

$$g_x = \frac{\partial d}{\partial x} = \frac{n\sum_{i\in[\mathbf{p}_l,\mathbf{p}_r]}x_i d_i - \sum_{i\in[\mathbf{p}_l,\mathbf{p}_r]}x_i \sum_{i\in[\mathbf{p}_l,\mathbf{p}_r]}d_i}{n\sum_{i\in[\mathbf{p}_l,\mathbf{p}_r]}x_i^2 - (\sum_{i\in[\mathbf{p}_l,\mathbf{p}_r]}x_i)^2}$$

$$g_y = \frac{\partial d}{\partial y} = \frac{n\sum_{i\in[\mathbf{p}_t,\mathbf{p}_b]}y_i d_i - \sum_{i\in[\mathbf{p}_t,\mathbf{p}_b]}y_i \sum_{i\in[\mathbf{p}_t,\mathbf{p}_b]}d_i}{n\sum_{i\in[\mathbf{p}_t,\mathbf{p}_b]}y_i^2 - (\sum_{i\in[\mathbf{p}_t,\mathbf{p}_b]}y_i)^2}$$

(3)

where $\mathbf{p}_l$ and $\mathbf{p}_r$ represent end pixels of pixel $\mathbf{p}$'s horizontal arm, and $\mathbf{p}_t$ and $\mathbf{p}_b$ represent end pixels of pixel $\mathbf{p}$'s vertical arm. In this calculation we only use the pixels that pass the left-right consistent check. In calculating the terms $\sum x_i$, $\sum y_i$, $\sum d_i$, $\sum x_i d_i$, $\sum y_i d_i$, $\sum x_i^2$, $\sum y_i^2$, we employ the orthogonal integral image technique [3] to save computation time. This is one of the reasons why we use linear regression to estimate the disparity gradient.

3.2   Disparity Gradient Refinement

Since the gradient from Eq. (3) can be affected by noises, it is necessary to enhance the accuracy of the disparity gradient. This refinement is carried out by introducing a voting paradigm. The process consists of successive passes of two steps applied to both of g_x and g_y. We explain the process with g_x.

In step 1, a voting is performed along the vertical arm $[\mathbf{p}_t,\mathbf{p}_b]$ of a pixel $\mathbf{p}$'s upright cross skeleton. For this voting, we subdivide the gradient range $[1,-1]$ into twenty one cells of equal distance. If the gradient value exceeds this range, we regard it as an outlier and it is excluded from voting. At each vote for a cell, the gradient value g_x is accumulated and the number of pixels is counted. After voting is completed, g_x of the pixel $\mathbf{p}$ is replaced by the arithmetic mean of the accumulated value in a cell of the maximum vote. After step 1 is applied to all pixels over an image, then step 2 is applied to the resulting data from step 1.

In step 2, the same process described in step 1 is applied to all pixels over an image except the voting direction is changed from the vertical arm to the horizontal one $[\mathbf{p}_l,\mathbf{p}_r]$ in order to enhance the smoothness effect over $\mathbf{p}$'s support region. We perform these two steps twice in order to obtain a precise g_x. For updating g_y, the same process as g_x is applied except the voting direction is changed.

4   2D integral Image Technique for Cost Aggregation

4.1   2D Integral Image Technique

As proposed by Zhang et al. [3], the cross-based cost aggregation is fulfilled using a two-step process as shown in Fig. 3(b) and (c). This approach assumes all surfaces in the scene are fronto-parallel and aggregates matching costs within the same disparity planes in CV using an orthogonal integral image (OII) technique as shown in Fig. 4 to accelerate the processing speed.

However, the surfaces are generally slanted and accordingly an implicit 3D support region is required. For the slanted surfaces, the original OII technique is not appropriate, because it is one-dimensional. Therefore, instead of the 1D OII, we propose an advanced integral image technique. This new method is called the two-dimensional orthogonal integral image (TDOII) technique, which is shown in Fig. 5.

As shown in Fig. 5, the steps to build the TDOII, (a), (b) and (c) correspond to the steps used to build OII, (a), (b) and (c) in Fig. 4, respectively. The advantage of the proposed technique is that it can integrate costs on different disparity planes in CV. Therefore, we can aggregate matching costs in implicit 3D support regions. The technique is composed of two steps.

The first step involves accumulating the matching costs along the disparity gradient (g_x, g_y), which corresponds to Fig. 5(a) and (b). Basically, the accumulation continues moving forward. However, the accumulation direction is not constant but changing. Therefore, it is necessary to specify for which cell in CV the accumulation is intended. For this specification, a map is newly designed. We call it a jumping map (J-map). The value in the J-map specifies the change in the accumulation direction.

The second step is a subtraction step that is used to obtain an aggregated value within a range as shown in Fig. 5(c). When this step is started, it is also necessary to search for the cells corresponding to the both ends of the range quickly. For this quick search, we design a map called an integral jumping map (IJ-map). The IJ-map is created by accumulating values in the J-map.

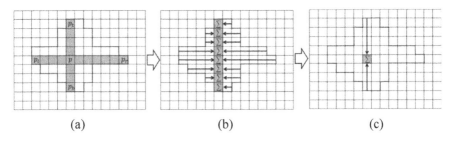

| (a) | (b) | (c) |

Fig. 3. Cross-based cost aggregation

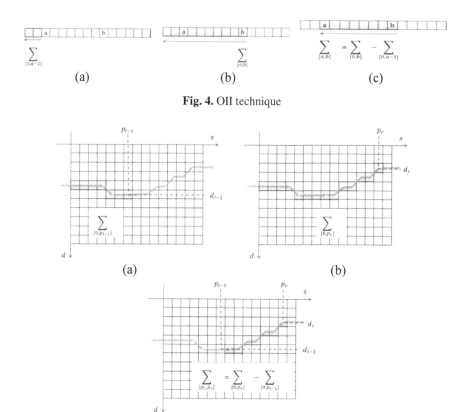

Fig. 4. OII technique

Fig. 5. TDOII technique

4.2   Jumping Map

The value in a J-map will determine whether or not the accumulation direction coincides with the previous direction. The size of the map is same as the size of an image. There are two J-maps, j_x and j_y – maps for the x-axis and y-axis, respectively. Here, we develop a map building algorithm by considering the case of j_x. j_y is also built using a similar approach except the gradient component is switched from g_x to g_y. Fig. 6 shows a part of j_x and its role.

$j_x(\mathbf{p})$ of a pixel $\mathbf{p}$ is constructed by taking the difference in the cumulative sum of g_x between two consecutive pixels as follows:

$$j_x(\mathbf{p}) = \begin{cases} round(t_x(\mathbf{p})) - round(t_x(\mathbf{p} - (1,0))), & \text{if } D_c(\mathbf{p}, \mathbf{p} - (1,0)) < \tau_1 \\ 0 & \text{otherwise} \end{cases} \tag{4}$$

where *round*($\cdot$) returns the nearest integer of a real number, $t_x(\mathbf{p})$ is the cumulative sum of g_x, and D_c is the color difference defined in Eq. (1). $t_x(\mathbf{p})$ is built depending on D_c as follows:

$$t_x(\mathbf{p}) = \begin{cases} t_x(\mathbf{p}-(1,0)) + g_x(\mathbf{p}), \text{if } D_c(\mathbf{p},\mathbf{p}-(1,0)) < \tau_1 \\ g_x(\mathbf{p}) \qquad\qquad\qquad \text{otherwise} \end{cases} \tag{5}$$

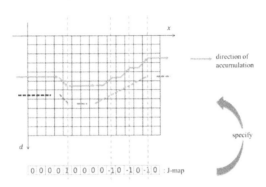

direction of accumulation

specify

0 0 0 0 1 0 0 0 -1 0 -1 0 1 0 : J-map

Fig. 6. A part of j_x and its role

The value 0 in $j_x(\mathbf{p})$ means that the accumulation direction is not changed, whereas the other value, for example 1, means that the coordinate of the d-axis is incremented by 1 as shown in Fig. 6. The accumulated sum of matching costs in CV is obtained using the J-map as follows:

$$C_s(\mathbf{p},d) = C_s(\mathbf{p}-(1,0),d-j_x(\mathbf{p})) + C_I(\mathbf{p},d) \tag{6}$$

where $C_I(\mathbf{p},d)$ is the initial matching cost obtained from AD-Census [4].

4.3   Integral Jumping Map

As mentioned in section 4.1, after accumulation over all pixels in an image the subtraction process starts. This process requires the positions $(\mathbf{p},d)$ of cells along the accumulation path. For this purpose, we design two IJ-maps, J_x and J_y for the x-axis and y-axis, respectively. Here we introduce an IJ-map building with J_x as follows:

$$J_x(\mathbf{p}) = \sum_{\mathbf{i}=[\mathbf{p}_0,\mathbf{p}]} j_x(\mathbf{i}) \tag{7}$$

where $\mathbf{p}_0 = (0,y)$. J_y is built by using a similar approach as J_x. The aggregated sum between $[\mathbf{p}_l,\mathbf{p}_r]$ is obtained by

$$C_a(\mathbf{p},d_p) = \frac{C_s(\mathbf{p}_r,d_r) - C_s(\mathbf{p}_{l-1},d_{l-1})}{|\mathbf{p}_r - \mathbf{p}_{l-1}|} \tag{8}$$

where $\mathbf{p}_{l-1} = \mathbf{p}_l - (1,0)$ is the previous pixel of $\mathbf{p}_l$, d_{l-1} and d_r are coordinates of the d-axis of $\mathbf{p}_{l-1}$ and $\mathbf{p}_r$, respectively. These coordinates are obtained by using J_x as follows: $d_r = d_p + J_x(\mathbf{p}) - J_x(\mathbf{p}_r)$ and $d_{l-1} = d_p + J_x(\mathbf{p}) - J_x(\mathbf{p}_{l-1})$.

Fig. 7 shows an example of how to use the IJ-map in exploring cell positions to aggregate matching costs. After the horizontal cost aggregation is completed for all pixels in an image, the vertical cost aggregation starts. In the vertical cost aggregation, j_y and J_y are used. In addition, instead of $C_l(\mathbf{p},d)$ in Eq. (6), the resulting data $C_a(\mathbf{p},d_p)$ from the horizontal cost aggregation is used. The remaining procedures are very similar to the horizontal cost aggregation. A combination of the horizontal cost aggregation and the vertical cost aggregation yields one cycle of cost aggregation.

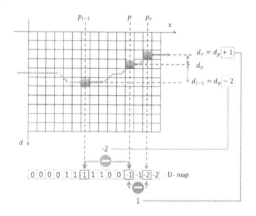

Fig. 7. An exploration of cell coordinates using an IJ-map

5   Experimental Results

The proposed algorithm was evaluated using indoor images as well as outdoor images. The test platform was a PC with a Core i7-3770 3.40GHz CPU and NVIDIA GeForce GTX 680 graphics card. The threshold values used in the equations are given in Table 1.

Table 1. Threshold values

L_1	L_2	τ_1	τ_2
34	17	20	6

The cost aggregation runs two cycles to obtain stable cost values. For cost aggregation, we followed the strategy proposed by Mei et al. [4]. For the first cycle, we first aggregated horizontally and then vertically. For the second cycle, we switched the order of the aggregation directions.

Fig. 8. Experimental results

Experimental results are shown in Fig. 8, where the first image was from Middlebury site, and the last two images were actual outdoor road traffic images. The leftmost column represents the left image of a pair of stereo images, the center column represents the disparity map obtained by applying the method proposed by Mei et al. [4] and the rightmost column represents the disparity map obtained by applying the proposed algorithm. The algorithm developed by Mei et al. was good for fronto-parallel surfaces as shown in the first image and the rectangle region indicated by the dash lines in the second image. However, their algorithm did not work well for the slanted surfaces as shown in the rectangles indicated by solid lines in the last two images. In contrast, our algorithm worked well regardless of the surface structures.

The processing time of our algorithm was 0.09 sec as shown in Table 2. The outdoor images used in the experiment were 320×240 pixels and the maximum disparity was 50.

Table 2. Processing time

	Disparity gradient estimation	Cost aggregation
Time(sec)	0.007	0.07

6   Conclusion

This paper presents an advanced local stereo matching algorithm. The proposed algorithm can be classified into per-pixel non-fronto-parallel disparity modeling. We showed that the algorithm can be processed in a near real-time. The key attributes of this algorithm were disparity gradient estimation using linear regression, disparity gradient refinement using a voting paradigm and cost aggregation using TDOII technique. The TDOII technique was developed by newly designing the J-map and IJ-map. Even if the support region for cost aggregation was three-dimensional, the proposed method can be used to build a disparity map within a practical amount of time.

Acknowledgement. This work was supported by MKE/ISTK (Mega Convergence Core Technology Development) and Basic Science Research Program through the National Research Foundation of Korea funded by the Ministry of Education, Science and Technology (grant number: 2011-0012323).

References

1. Scharstein, D., Szeliski, R.: A taxonomy and evaluation of dense two-frame stereo correspondence algorithms. Int. J. Computer Vision 47(1), 7–42 (2002)
2. Yoon, K.J., Kweon, S.: Adaptive support-weight approach for correspondence search. IEEE Trans. Pattern Anal. Mach. Intell. 28(4), 650–656 (2006)
3. Zhang, K., Lu, J., Lafruit, G.: Cross-based local stereomatching using orthogonal integral images. IEEE TCSVT 19(7), 1073–1079 (2009)
4. Mei, X., Sun, X., Zhou, M., Jiao, S., Wang, H.: On building an accurate stereo matching system on graphics hardware. In: ICCV Workshops, pp. 467–474 (2011)
5. Klaus, A., Sormann, M., Karner, K.: Segment-Based Stereo Matching Using Belief Propagation and a Self-Adapting Dissimilarity Measure. In: 18th International Pattern Recognition (ICPR), pp. 15–18 (2006)
6. Yang, Q., Wang, L., Yang, R., Stewenius, H., Nister, D.: Stereo matching with color-weighted correlation, hierarchical belief propagation and occlusion handling. In: CVPR (2006)
7. Zhang, Y., Gong, M., Yang, Y.: Local stereo matching with 3D adaptive cost aggregation for slanted surface modeling and sub-pixel accuracy. In: 19th International Conference on Pattern Recognition (ICPR), pp. 1–4 (2008)
8. Mühlmann, K., Maier, D., Hesser, J., Männer, R.: Calculating Dense Disparity Maps from Color Stereo Images, an Efficient Implementation. International Journal of Computer Vision 47, 79–88 (2002)
9. Chapra, S.C., Canale, R.P.: Numerical methods for engineers, 4th edn., pp. 440–445. McGraw-Hill (2002) ISBN 0-07-112180-3

Integrating Multiple Viewpoints for Articulated Scene Model Aquisition

Leon Ziegler[1], Agnes Swadzba[1], and Sven Wachsmuth[1,2]

[1] Applied Informatics, Faculty of Technology, Bielefeld University
[2] Central Lab Facilities, CITEC
Universitätstraße 25, 33615 Bielefeld, Germany
{lziegler,aswadzba,swachsmu}@TechFak.Uni-Bielefeld.DE

Abstract. In this paper we present a method to generate an *Articulated Scene Model* for a system's current view, which allows to integrate multiple egocentric models previously gathered from different viewpoints. The approach is designed to build up separate representations for the static, movable and dynamic parts of an observed scene. In order to make already gathered information available for subsequent viewpoints of the same location, a merging algorithm is needed that considers view-dependent aspects like occlusion and limitations of the view frustum. We show in our experiments that the proposed algorithm correctly merges multiple scene models and can be applied profitably in an integrated vision system for detecting movable objects on a mobile robot.

1 Introduction

For the encoding of spatial information in human memory it has been shown that both egocentric and allocentric representations play an important role [6]. Allocentric representations relate objects to visual landmarks. Being the cognitive basis of human navigation [2], robotics has focused on using global coordinate systems for representing space for navigation. Egocentric representations have a special role in self-motion [5]. Wang and Simons [16] show that visual tasks are significantly impaired, if self-motion is disturbed, e.g. by causing visual change through moving a human subject in a wheelchair. They suggest that "the representation [. . .] of viewpoint changes is not environment-centered. The representation must be viewer-centered and the difference between observer and display movements results from a difference in the nature of the transformation." In robotics, the role of egocentric representations of spatial information acquired through locomotion has been underestimated so far. In our paper, we systematically deal with this aspect and present a method to generate a scene model of a system's current view incorporating past egocentric views by utilizing self-motion. Thereby, we exclusively rely on egocentric representations for perception tasks, while allocentric representations are used for navigation purposes and localization.

A mobile robot can benefit from this approach in several ways. Imagine a robot detecting movable objects and agents by observing changes in the scene

M. Chen, B. Leibe, and B. Neumann (Eds.): ICVS 2013, LNCS 7963, pp. 294–303, 2013.
© Springer-Verlag Berlin Heidelberg 2013

from a first egocentric viewpoint. After moving to a subsequent location the robot is able to infer a new egocentric representation of the same scene including information of the movable parts of the scene previously observed. We do this by computing an accumulative background model incorporating previous views.

As a basis for the presented approach we use the *Articulated Scene Model* (ASM) introduced by Swadzba *et al.* [14]. This model enables an artificial system to categorizes the current vista space into three different layers: The static background layer which contains those structures of the scene that ultimately limit the view as static scene parts (e.g. walls, tables); second, the movable objects layer which contains those structures of the scene that may be moved, i.e. have a background farther perceived after moving (e.g. chairs, doors, small items); and third, the dynamic objects layer which contains the acting, continiously moving agents like humans or robots.

After discussing related work (Sec. 2), we describe the original *Articulated Scene Model* algorithm (Sec. 3) and then explain our new merging algorithm in detail (Sec. 4) proving its applicability in Sec. 5.

2   Related Work

Much work has been done in segmenting objects from a scene in order to facilitate a tracking or classification task. Many of those applications expect a detailed model (e.g. CAD) of the object to be segmented. Algorithms pursuing this approach make use of decomposition [4] of the scene or rely on local hierarchical features combined with a matching algorithm [12]. However, there was also research done on segmenting structures with more instance independent, but category specific properties [13]. However, our approach targets a bottom-up segmentation of the scene, rather than a semantic interpretation of the objects.

Campbell *et al.* [3] suggest a model-free approach for segmenting and 3D model creation through observation of multiple frames. In contrast to our approach which employs passive observation, the object is expected to stand still and the camera is actively moved around the object.

Traditional background subtraction algorithms apply the assumption that the static background does not change over time to identify moving objects by detecting changes in the scene. E.g. Sheikh *et al.* [10] describe a sophisticated background subtraction algorithm that can be applied on freely moving systems like robots, which analyses trajectories of salient features over time. However, these approaches only detect moving objects, whereas for many scenarios movable objects as described by Sanders *et al.* [9] are of greater interest.

In robotics most of the previous work make use of allocentric representations for meaningful instances in the robot's environment. There are several semantic map approaches like Nuechter *et al.* [7]. They build up a complete 3D representation of the whole environment and use it for navigation and detection of objects alike. An allocentric semantic map representation for navigation and attention, also containing global object locations which were locally detected, is presented in [17]. Vasudevan *et al.* [15] describe a hierarchical solution containing a allocentric topological representation of places combined with local probabilistic object graphs.

3   The Articulated Scene Model

This section describes the underlying principles that form a basis for the work presented in this paper. The *Articulated Scene Model* approach introduced by Swadzba *et al.* [14] aims to segregate the three previously described semantic scene parts in one single view. It is motivated by the definition of *motion* and *change* proposed by Rensink [8]. Concretely, we focus on detection of completed changes which involves a comparison of currently visible structures with a representation in memory. Hence, our approach detects articulated parts and adapts the static background model of the scene simultaneously. The detection of dynamic object parts (like moving humans) is modeled in a separate layer and requires a tracking mechanism. For the implementation in the presented system, the body tracking algorithms in the NiTE Middleware[1] in combination with the OpenNI SDK[2] was used.

Algorithm 1. Background adaptation and detecting movable/dynamic objects

---

Require: $F_t = \{\boldsymbol{f}_t^i\}$ (current frame)
Require: $D_t \subset F_t$ (current dynamic clusters)
Require: $S_{t-1} = \{\boldsymbol{s}_{t-1}^i\}$ (current background model)

1: $F_t' \leftarrow F_t \setminus D_t$
2: **for** $i = 1$ to n **do**
3:      **if** $|\boldsymbol{s}_{t-1}^i - \boldsymbol{f}_t'^i| < \theta_d^i$ **then**
4:          $\boldsymbol{s}_t^i \leftarrow \boldsymbol{s}_{t-1}^i + \frac{1}{w^i}(\boldsymbol{f}_t'^i - \boldsymbol{s}_{t-1}^i)$
5:          $w^i \leftarrow w^i + 1$
6:      **else**
7:          **if** $|\boldsymbol{f}_t'^i| > |\boldsymbol{s}_{t-1}^i|$ **then**
8:              $\boldsymbol{s}_t^i \leftarrow \boldsymbol{f}_t'^i$
9:              $w^i \leftarrow 1$
10:         **else**
11:             $\boldsymbol{s}_t^i \leftarrow \boldsymbol{s}_{t-1}^i$
12:             $O_t \leftarrow O_t \cup \boldsymbol{f}_t'^i$
13:         **end if**
14:     **end if**
15: **end for**
16: **return** $S_t = \{\boldsymbol{s}_t^i\}$ (new background)
17: **return** O_t (movable objects)

The algorithm introduced by Swadzba *et al.* [14] (see Algorithm 1) works on depth images and assumes that the view direction remains still while the processing of the model is active. At each time step t the algorithm is presented the depth image of the current frame $F_t = \{\boldsymbol{f}_t^i\}_{i=1...n}$ and the current dynamic regions $D_t \subset F_t$ provided by the tracking module. In the default version of the

---

[1] http://www.openni.org/files/nite/, accessed 2013-02-19.
[2] http://www.openni.org/openni-sdk/, accessed 2013-02-19.

algorithm the dynamic regions are excluded from the current frame. Now the algorithm compares the input frame F_t with the currently known static background $S_{t-1} = \{s^i_{t-1}\}_{i=1...n}$. For each pixel f^i_t a decision is made whether it supports the background model S_{t-1}, defines a new background observation, or represents an articulated part O_t of the scene. These decisions incorporate an adaptive noise model which defines the noise level θ^i_d for a pixel linearly to its depth value. Additionally, for every pixel a weight value w^i is saved which represents the reliability of the background model. If the distance of the observed depth f^i_t to the corresponding background depth s^i_{t-1} is smaller than θ^i_d then it is accumulated to an updated static background point s^i_t with improved reliability (line 4). Otherwise, if the input is farther than the known background, the background point is reset to the new measurement (line 8). If the input is nearer, it is assumed to be part of a foreground object (line 11).

In contrast to the original implementation, in our case the static scene model is not directly fed back into the tracking system, because the tracking implementation works on the raw depth data. However, a slight alteration of the algorithm allows a more accurate combination of both detection mechanisms. Instead of subtracting the dynamic parts from the input, it may also be subtracted from the detected articulated parts O_t, which gives the new movable objects model $O'_t \leftarrow O_t \setminus D_t$ and the new dynamic objects model $D'_t \leftarrow O_t \cap D_t$. This altered algorithm confides more strongly in the movable object detection. Only articulated parts of the scene can be dynamic objects.

4   Integration of Multiple Viewpoints

In order to utilize previously gathered information on a mobile robot, the system must be able to integrate multiple scene models from different viewpoints. Beuter et al. [1] suggest to use the ICP method to accurately reconstruct the current view from the previous model. However, they assume a subsequent combination of scene models and only small changes in the camera position. This is problematic when the robot travels greater distances. Also this prevents the system to consider knowledge from older scene models.

But most importantly, the background model can not be transformed and used as it is from a different viewpoint, because at the new location different environmental structures may provide the actual static background (see Fig. 1). For example, if the current view contains background structures that were not visible from the previous location, but do now occlude the previously assumed background, the naive method would mark these structures as articulated. On the other hand, the new view may contain objects, that would have been foreground in the previous location because the background was known. At the current location the object has different background structures, which previously may not have been visible. So the naive method would mark this object as background although all necessary information is available to label it correctly.

In the following we will present a method to reliably fuse multiple scene models from different locations into a new model representing the current view.

The method only transfers previously generated background models to the new scene, because articulated parts can be calculated if the background is known. Because of the movable or even dynamic nature of the remaining parts it is likely that their location changed since the last observation. Further, it is possible for smaller objects that the previously discovered front of the object is not fully visible anymore and therefore occluded by the object's back, which would result in an inaccurate model. The distinction between movable and dynamic parts of the scene must therefore be done after merging the background models using the methods explained in Sec. 3.

When initializing a scene model at a new location, all previously generated static background models S_u^j (or a reasonable subset) are transformed into the current position of the camera. The transformation is calculated from the memorized self-motion from the models' positions to the current one provided by a navigation component. It is then applied to the point cloud representation of the background model. Because of the possible inaccuracy of the position estimate for the current or previous locations, the resulting point clouds are aligned to the current view using the ICP method. Afterwards they are again rasterized as a depth image. Thereby the smallest distance is chosen if two or more points fall in the same cell. For fusing the models with the current frame we developed a new merging algorithm which is similar to the basic articulated scene model algorithm, but utilizes the spatial relations of the merged models.

The merging algorithm (see Algorithm 2) subsequently merges the transformed static background models S_u^j into the new accumulated background model S_v which initially contains the currently perceived depth camera frame F_t.

Algorithm 2. Merging multiple scene models from different viewpoints

---

Require: $F_t = \{f_t^i\}$ (current frame)
Require: $S_u^j = \{s_u^{j,i}\}$ (transformed background models)
Require: $S_v = \{s_v^i\}$ (accumulated background model)
Require: $O_t = \varnothing$ (current movable clusters)
 1:   $S_v \leftarrow F_t$
 2:   **for** $j = 1$ to m; $i = 1$ to n **do**
 3:      **if** $|s_u^{j,i} - s_v^i| < \theta_d^i$ **then**
 4:         $s_v^i \leftarrow s_u^{j,i} + \frac{1}{w}(s_v^i - s_u^{j,i})$
 5:      **else**
 6:         **if** $|s_u^{j,i}| > |s_v^i|$ **and** all premises apply for s_v^i **then**
 7:            $o_t^i \leftarrow s_v^i$
 8:            $s_v^i \leftarrow s_u^{j,i}$
 9:         **else if** $s_u^{j,i}$ is unknown **and** all premises apply for s_v^i **then**
10:            $o_t^i \leftarrow s_v^i$
11:            $s_v^i \leftarrow$ projection of s_v^i onto rear view frustum of S_u^j
12:         **end if**
13:      **end if**
14: **end for**
15: **return** $S_v = \{s_v^i\}$ (accumulated background)
16: **return** O_t (movable objects)

For each pixel the same tests as for the basic ASM algorithm are performed. If the incoming transformed pixel s_u^i is in range of the current accumulated background value s_v^i the model is updated with increased reliability (line 4).

If the transformed measurement is nearer than s_v^i it is ignored, because it is already known that the static background is behind this pixel. If it is farther than the currently believed background or unknown, a refinement of the accumulated model may be necessary (line 6-11). As described before, a few special cases must be ruled out in order to ensure a correct model. If the transformed pixel does not meet the corresponding premises, it is ignored. The premises are:

Field of View. The corresponding 3D point of the pixel s_v^i representing the accumulated background must have been in the field of view at the time when the incoming model S_u^j was generated. Otherwise it is not safe to assume that the object was moved. It may just not have been visible.

Occlusion. The currently assumed background point s_v^i must not have been occluded by any other point for the location of the camera of the incoming model S_u^j. Otherwise the object may again have been invisible because it was hidden.

Neighborhood. The candidate point s_v^i of the accumulated model must not have neighboring points in the incoming transformed model S_u^j. Because of the transformation of the scene models it is possible that small holes or inaccurate borders of the objects appear when re-rasterizing the image. In order to not propagate these errors into the accumulated model, the neighborhood in the transformed model must be checked.

If the premises apply for s_v^i, it is marked as movable (lines 7, 10) and the accumulated background model is either set to $s_u^{j,i}$ (line 8) or – if it is unknown – the model is set to the rear projection of s_v^i on the view frustum of the camera corresponding to S_u^j (line 11).

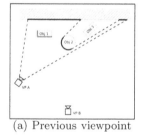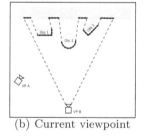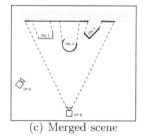

(a) Previous viewpoint   (b) Current viewpoint   (c) Merged scene

Fig. 1. Scene from different viewpoints. In *viewpoint A* the static background (solid black) is known for *object 1*, so it is marked as movable (sold gray) (1(a)). In *viewpoint B* everything is assumed to be background (dashed black) before the merging algorithm is applied (1(b)). After merging (1(c)) *object 1* can be marked as movable, because the transformed model provides the required background data. However, although the background is known for *object 2* it can not be marked as movable, because the previous front is known to be static and the back is ignored because it does not fulfill the occlusion premise. *Object 3* is assumed to be background as well because of the premises.

Figuratively speaking, the algorithm refines the currently perceived static background using evidences from other viewpoints and thereby fills areas that

Table 1. Quantitative results: recall values for the movable pixels. The columns distinguish the viewpoint (VP) on the respective scene. In scene 3 from VP 2 the moved object was completely occluded, so no pixels could be measured.

(a) ASM from one viewpoint

	VP 1	VP 2	VP 3	VP 4	VP 5
Scene 1	0.840	0.955	0.736	0.725	0.771
Scene 2	0.870	0.947	0.876	0.852	0.867
Scene 3	0.044	—	0.531	0.465	0.618
Scene 4	0.938	0.956	0.769	0.889	0.773
Scene 5	0.976	0.934	0.914	0.874	0.883

(b) Accumulated ASM

	VP 1	VP 2	VP 3	VP 4	VP 5
Scene 1	0.838	0.707	0.820	0.880	0.915
Scene 2	0.908	0.895	0.900	0.922	0.968
Scene 3	0.858	0.957	0.775	0.415	0.826
Scene 4	0.875	0.946	0.827	0.943	0.908
Scene 5	0.905	0.955	0.950	0.939	0.967

were not yet measured, e.g. because of shadows or reflecting surfaces. From the knowledge of the static parts of the scene at different times in the past, the algorithm can implicitly detect if an object was manipulated. Certain parts of the current scene will be marked as articulated if one of the merged models provides evidence that the corresponding object was not present at the time the model was built up or it was already known to be movable. The premises prevent that an object is falsely marked as movable because it was simply not visible from older views, but appeared in a subsequent view. So this algorithm allows the system to gain a much more informative articulated scene model without observing any change in the scene from the current viewpoint.

5   Evaluation

To evaluate our approach, we conducted two experiments. For a quantitative analysis of the performance, we presented the system several scenes (Fig. 2). We created an *Articulated Scene Model* A_0 of the presented scene using the basic ASM algorithm. While generating the model one object from the scene was moved. We rotated the camera around the center of the scene in order to generate five different test viewpoints V_i with an angular distance of $45°$. For each viewpoint we applied our merging algorithm to merge the original scene model A_0 into the new view to gain an accumulated test model T_i. For a second test set we generated an accumulated scene model A_1 from two different viewpoints (with two moved objects) in order to merge it with each of the views from the test viewpoints.

For measuring the performance we analyzed the movable objects layer of the test models T_i. As a quantitative measure we chose the number of pixels representing the believed movable objects. For comparison we generated a ground truth by labeling the depth image of the same frame by hand. We analyzed the recall of those values. The precision was not incorporated on the pixel level, because the high number of noise pixels at structure borders does not allow a reasonable analysis.

The results show that the system successfully finds the movable objects. Overall the system marked an amount of 0.807 of the hand labeled pixel correctly

Fig. 2. Examples from the quantitative evaluation results. First row: The different test setups used (White arrows: Background model was recorded, Black arrows: Test viewpoints). Second row: Results from one exemplary viewpoint for each setup (detected movable pixels are white).

(standard deviation: 0.181). It is not surprising that not all pixels were found because the adaptive noise model of the ASM algorithm (Sec. 3) induces that pixels close to the static background are ignored. Further, the tolerance of the occlusion and neighborhood tests (Sec. 4) causes pixels close to other objects or their shadows to being ignored. Not surprisingly the amount of correctly marked pixels for the tests with the accumulated ASM (0.854) is significantly higher than for the tests with the simple ASM from only a single viewpoint (0.759). This becomes particularly clear in *scene 3* (Table 1). Here the moved object is partly occluded by another object (Fig. 2). In the case of the simple ASM only a small amount of the object's pixels is found in viewpoint 2, whereas in the case of the accumulated ASM – which incorporates information from a viewpoint where the object was not hidden – nearly the complete object is detected.

In addition we tested how many moved objects can be found by the system. The analysis for objects is done by the system through counting the connected movable pixels in one region and applying a threshold. In the previously described scenario the system found an amount of 0.969 of all moved objects (recall) with a precision of 0.873. The false positives can be explained through suboptimal alignment when applying the ICP method which causes false foreground regions. The false negatives occure when objects are occuded.

For a qualitative analysis we implemented the extended *Articulated Scene Model* into our mobile service robot BIRON [11]. The robot was confronted with the following scenario. A Human guides the robot through an apartment and interacts with the environment. The robot has to build up a scene model while observing these actions. Through analysis of the changes in the scene, the robot has to detect whether objects were removed or added to the scene. A very simple reasoning mechanism tries to infer which object was moved from where to where. In a second phase, the robot is asked to bring the moved objects back to their original location. Now the robot has to approach the locations where objects where placed and detect the movable object by utilizing the previously accumulated scene model. The actual grasping and transport of the object to its previous location is omitted in this evaluation. For navigation and reasonable positioning

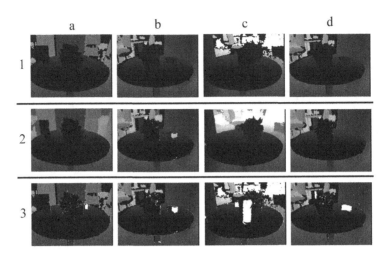

Fig. 3. Subsequent results from scene 3 (see Fig. 2). Row 1: Raw depth image; Row 2: merged background model; Row 3: detected movable pixels (white); (a) center viewpoint, one moved object (b) diagonal right viewpoint, only half of the object is detected (c) far left viewpoint, both objects were moved (d) diagonal right viewpoint, visible parts of both objects are detected with accumulated model.

– while observing the human as well as approaching the moved objects – the system uses the allocentric representation of the environment described in Ziegler *et al.* [17] and the associated methods. The detection of removed and added objects is realized by applying the resulting ASM at one location to keyframes at the beginning (F_0) and at the end of the observation (F_1).

The task was performed four times with three objects being relocated in each run. In total the robot successfully inferred the correct origin and target locations from 13 of 15 objects. In all of the 13 cases it correctly approached the target locations and was able to extract movable objects.

6   Conclusion

We presented a novel algorithm for integrating egocentric scene models from different viewpoints into one coherent accumulated model for the current viewpoint. The important aspect is that the integration is based on some basic fusion rules in the egocentric reference system of the current view point and self-motion information. We were able to show that the algorithm generates correct results and we proved the applicability of the approach for real world scenarios on a mobile robot. Scenarios like the presented one encourage the need for transforming previously gathered knowledge to new viewpoints.

The presented approach allows an accurate spatio-temporal analysis of movements in the robot's field of view. The back propagation of a current model into models from previous viewpoints promises a powerful mechanism for longterm observation tasks.

Acknowledgements. This work was funded by the German Research Foundation (DFG) within the Collaborative Research Center 673 "Alignment in Communication".

References

1. Beuter, N., Swadzba, A., Kummert, F., Wachsmuth, S.: Using articulated scene models for dynamic 3d scene analysis in vista spaces. 3D Research 1 (September 2010)
2. Burgess, N., Spiers, H.J., Paleologou, E.: Orientational manoeuvres in the dark: dissociating allocentric and egocentric influences on spatial memory. Cognition 94, 149–166 (2004)
3. Campbell, N.D.F., Vogiatzis, G., Hernández, C., Cipolla, R.: Automatic 3d object segmentation in multiple views using volumetric graph-cuts. Image Vision Comput. 28(1), 14–25 (2010)
4. Gelfand, N., Guibas, L.J.: Shape segmentation using local slippage analysis. In: Proceedings of the 2004 Eurographics/ACM SIGGRAPH Symposium on Geometry Processing, SGP 2004, pp. 214–223. ACM, New York (2004)
5. Hartley, T., Trinkler, I., Burgess, N.: Geometric determinants of human spatial memory. Cognition 94, 39–75 (2004)
6. Mou, W., McNamara, T.P., Rump, B., Xiao, C.: Roles of Egocentric and Allocentric Spatial Representations in Locomotion and Reorientation. Journal of Experimental Psychology: Learning, Memory, and Cognition 32(6), 1274–1290 (2006)
7. Nüchter, A., Hertzberg, J.: Towards semantic maps for mobile robots 56, 915–926 (2008)
8. Rensink, R.A.: Change Detection. Annual Review of Psychology 53, 245–277 (2002)
9. Sanders, B., Nelson, R., Sukthankar, R.: A theory of the quasi-static world. In: Proceedings of the 16th Int. Conf. on Pattern Recognition, vol. 3, pp. 1–6 (2002)
10. Sheikh, Y., Javed, O., Kanade, T.: Background subtraction for freely moving cameras. In: 2009 IEEE 12th Int. Conf. on Computer Vision, September 29-October 2, pp. 1219–1225 (2009)
11. Siepmann, F., Ziegler, L., Kortkamp, M., Wachsmuth, S.: Deploying a modeling framework for reusable robot behavior to enable informed strategies for domestic service robots. Robotics and Autonomous Systems (2012)
12. Steder, B., Grisetti, G., Van Loock, M., Burgard, W.: Robust on-line model-based object detection from range images. In: IEEE/RSJ Int. Conf. on Intelligent Robots and Systems, IROS 2009, pp. 4739–4744 (October 2009)
13. Sturm, J., Konolige, K., Stachniss, C., Burgard, W.: Vision-based detection for learning articulation models of cabinet doors and drawers in household environments. In: 2010 IEEE Int. Conf. on Robotics and Automation (ICRA), pp. 362–368 (May 2010)
14. Swadzba, A., Beuter, N., Wachsmuth, S., Kummert, F.: Dynamic 3d scene analysis for acquiring articulated scene models. In: IEEE Int. Conf. on Robotics and Automation. IEEE, Anchorage (2010)
15. Vasudevan, S., Gächter, S., Nguyen, V., Siegwart, R.: Cognitive maps for mobile robots – an object based approach 55, 359–371 (2007)
16. Wang, R.F., Simons, D.J.: Active and passive scene recognition across views. Cognition 70, 191–210 (1999)
17. Ziegler, L., Siepmann, F., Kortkamp, M., Wachsmuth, S.: Towards an informed search behavior for domestic robots. In: SIMPAR 2010 Workshop on Domestic Service Robots in the Real World (2010)

Explicit Context-Aware Kernel Map Learning
for Image Annotation

Hichem Sahbi

CNRS - TELECOM ParisTech
`hichem.sahbi@telecom-paristech.fr`

Abstract. In kernel methods, such as support vector machines, many existing kernels consider similarity between data by taking into account only their content and without context. In this paper, we propose an alternative that upgrades and further enhances usual kernels by making them context-aware. The proposed method is based on the optimization of an objective function mixing content, regularization and also context. We will show that the underlying kernel solution converges to a positive semi-definite similarity, which can also be expressed as a dot product involving "explicit" kernel maps. When combining these context-aware kernels with support vector machines, performances substantially improve for the challenging task of image annotation.

Keywords: Context-Aware Kernels, Explicit Kernel Maps, SVMs.

1 Introduction

Image annotation is a major challenge in computer vision, which consists in assigning a list of keywords to a given image [14,20,6]. These keywords may either correspond to physical entities (pedestrians, cars, etc.) or to high level concepts resulting from the interaction of many entities into scenes (races, fights, etc.). In both cases, image annotation is challenging due to the perplexity when assigning keywords to images especially when the number of possible keywords is taken from a large vocabulary and when analyzing highly semantic contents.

Existing annotation methods usually model image observations using low level features (color, texture, shape, etc.), and then assign keywords to these observations using a variety of machine learning and inference techniques such as latent Dirichlet allocation [2], hidden Markov models [14], probabilistic latent semantic analysis [17] and support vector machines (SVMs) [7]. These learning machines are used to model correspondences between keywords and low level features and make it possible to assign keywords to new images. Among learning techniques those based on kernel methods, mainly SVMs, are particularly successful [1] but their success remains highly dependent on the choice of kernels. The latter, defined as symmetric and positive semi-definite functions [23], should reserve large values to very similar contents and vice-versa.

---

[1] See for instance the periodic and the challenging ImageCLEF benchmark [20].

M. Chen, B. Leibe, and B. Neumann (Eds.): ICVS 2013, LNCS 7963, pp. 304–313, 2013.
© Springer-Verlag Berlin Heidelberg 2013

Considering a collection of images, each one seen as a constellation of primitives (eg. interest points) [8]. Two families of kernels were introduced, in the literature, in order to handle these types of data; *holistic* and *alignment-based* kernels. Holistic kernels first map constellations of primitives to feature vectors, by estimating their first or high order statistics or by aggregating them [13,18]. Then, similarity is defined as any decreasing function of a distance between these feature vectors, via usual kernels (such as gaussian or histogram intersection). Note that the resulting kernels are positive semi-definite per construction. In the second family of kernels, methods proceed differently [1,9,5,16,27] and consider similarity proportional to the quality of aligning primitives. In contrast to the first family, the positive definiteness of this second family of kernels is not straightforward and not always guaranteed. Notice also that holistic kernels are naturally more flexible and invariant to geometric transformations, but alignment-based kernels are more discriminating; it is clear that kernels that gather the advantages of the two aforementioned families of kernels are preferred.

We are interested, in this work, in the integration of context in kernels in order to further enhance their discrimination power while keeping their flexibility to handle constellations of primitives, their invariance to geometric transformations and also their efficiency. Context is important and has, indeed, played an important role in leveraging the performances of many computer vision tasks, and mainly those based on Markov models (see for instance [11,25,12,22,19]), but the novel part of this work aims to integrate context, in kernel design useful for classification and annotation, and plug these kernels in support vector machines in order to take benefit from their well established generalization power [26]. Again, given a collection of images, each one described as a constellation of interest points, the proposed method is based on the optimization of an objective function mixing a fidelity term, a context criterion and a regularization term. The fidelity term, takes into account the visual content of interest points in order to measure the quality of their alignments, so high quality alignments encourage high kernel values. The context criterion, considers the global scene structure and allows us to further enhance the relevance of our designed kernel, by restoring the similarity *iff* pairs of aligned interest points are *also* surrounded by good quality alignments that should also share the same context (see § 2.1). The regularization term controls the smoothness of the learned kernel and makes it possible to obtain a closed form solution.

Note that this work is built upon [24] but includes many differences (see § 2):
- A simplification of the learning model; which now includes an *unconstrained* objective function, easier-to-solve. Furthermore, the number of parameters of our model reduces now to one, and corresponds to the weight of context.
- A new study of the theoretical properties of our solution; mainly (i) the introduction of a loose upper-bound, about the weight of context, that guarantees convergence of the learned kernel to a fixed-point and (ii) the study of the positive definiteness which shows that the obtained kernel solution can be written as a dot product, involving "explicit" kernel maps. Indeed, in spite of the non-linearity of our kernel, its map is explicit, so one may use extremely fast SVM

solvers in order to handle large scale datasets[2] and without the overhead of pre-computing gram matrices and solving quadratic programming (QP) problems.

2   Explicit Context-Aware Kernel Map Learning

Let $\{\mathcal{I}_p\}_p$ be a collection of images and let $\mathcal{S}_p = \{\mathbf{x}_1^p, \ldots, \mathbf{x}_n^p\}$ be the list of interest points of an image $\mathcal{I}_p$ (the value of n may vary with the image $\mathcal{I}_p$). The set $\mathcal{X}$ of all possible interest points is the union over all possible images of $\{\mathcal{I}_p\}$: $\mathcal{X} = \cup_p \mathcal{S}_p$. Consider $\mathcal{S}_p, \mathcal{S}_q \subseteq \mathcal{X}$ as two finite subsets of $\mathcal{X}$, the convolution kernel $\mathcal{K}$, between $\mathcal{S}_p = \{\mathbf{x}_i^p\}_{i=1}^n$ and $\mathcal{S}_q = \{\mathbf{x}_j^q\}_{j=1}^{n'}$, is defined as $\mathcal{K}(\mathcal{S}_p, \mathcal{S}_q) = \sum_{i,j} \kappa\left(\mathbf{x}_i^p, \mathbf{x}_j^q\right)$, here κ may be any symmetric and continuous function on $\mathcal{X} \times \mathcal{X}$, so $\mathcal{K}$ will also be continuous and symmetric, and if κ is positive semi-definite (p.s.d) then $\mathcal{K}$ will also be p.s.d [10]. Since $\mathcal{K}$ is defined as the sum of all the pairwise similarities between all the possible sample pairs taken from $\mathcal{S}_p \times \mathcal{S}_q$, its evaluation does not require any (hard) alignment between these pairs. Nevertheless, the value of $\kappa\left(\mathbf{x}_i^p, \mathbf{x}_j^q\right)$ should ideally be high only if $\mathbf{x}_i^p$ actually matches $\mathbf{x}_j^q$, so κ needs to be appropriately designed while being p.s.d.

Formally, an interest point $\mathbf{x}$ is defined as $\mathbf{x} = (\psi_g(\mathbf{x}), \psi_o(\mathbf{x}), \psi_s(\mathbf{x}), \psi_f(\mathbf{x}), \omega(\mathbf{x}))$ where the symbol $\psi_g(\mathbf{x}) \in \mathbb{R}^2$ stands for the 2D coordinates of $\mathbf{x}$ while the orientation and scale of $\mathbf{x}$ (respectively denoted $\psi_o(\mathbf{x}) \in [-\pi, +\pi]$ and $\psi_s(\mathbf{x}) \in]0, \max]$) are provided by the SIFT gradient and scale respectively. We have an extra information about the visual content or features of $\mathbf{x}$ (denoted $\psi_f(\mathbf{x}) \in \mathbb{R}^s$); in our case, these visual features result from the concatenation of (i) 128 SIFT coefficients; [15], (ii) 3-channel color histograms, of 20 dimensions each and (iii) shape context dartboard [3] of 8 bands and 8 sectors; both (ii) and (iii) are computed locally, in a disk centered at $\mathbf{x}$ with a radius proportional to $\psi_s(\mathbf{x})$. We also use $\omega(\mathbf{x})$ to denote the image from which the interest point comes from, so that two interest points with the same location, feature, scale and orientation are considered different when they are not in the same image (since we want to take into account the context of the interest point in the image it belongs to). Introduce the context of $\mathbf{x}$, $\mathcal{N}^{\theta,\rho}(\mathbf{x}) = \{\mathbf{x}' : \omega(\mathbf{x}') = \omega(\mathbf{x}), \mathbf{x}' \neq \mathbf{x} \text{ s.t. (1) holds}\}$,

$$\|\psi_g(\mathbf{x}) - \psi_g(\mathbf{x}')\|_2 \in \left[\frac{\rho - 1}{N_r} \epsilon_p, \frac{\rho}{N_r} \epsilon_p\right], \text{angle}\left(\psi_o(\mathbf{x}), \psi_g(\mathbf{x}') - \psi_g(\mathbf{x})\right) \in \left[\frac{\theta - 1}{N_a}\pi, \frac{\theta}{N_a}\pi\right].$$
$$(1)$$

Here ϵ_p is the radius of a neighborhood disk surrounding $\mathbf{x}$ and $\theta = 1, \ldots, N_a$, $\rho = 1, \ldots, N_r$ correspond to indices of different parts of that disk. In practice, N_a and N_r correspond to 8 sectors and 8 bands. In the remainder of this paper, $\mathcal{N}^{\theta,\rho}(\mathbf{x})$ will simply be denoted as $\mathcal{N}^c(\mathbf{x})$, with $c = (\theta - 1)N_r + \rho$.

2.1   The Method

We can view a kernel κ on $\mathcal{X}$ as a matrix $\mathbf{K}$ in which the "$(\mathbf{x}, \mathbf{x}')$−element" is the similarity between $\mathbf{x}$ and $\mathbf{x}'$: $\mathbf{K}_{\mathbf{x},\mathbf{x}'} = k(\mathbf{x}, \mathbf{x}')$. Let $\mathbf{P}_c$ be the intrinsic adjacency

---

[2] Such as stochastic gradient descent [4]. When the kernel map is explicit, the complexity of this method is linear in the size of the training data instead of quadratic.

matrix defined as $\mathbf{P}_{c,\mathbf{x},\mathbf{x}'} = g_c(\mathbf{x}, \mathbf{x}')$, where g is a decreasing function of any (pseudo) distance involving $(\mathbf{x}, \mathbf{x}')$, not necessarily symmetric. In practice, we consider $g_c(\mathbf{x}, \mathbf{x}') = \dfrac{1}{m}\mathbb{1}_{\{\mathbf{x}' \in \mathcal{N}^c(\mathbf{x})\}}$, with $m = |\mathcal{X}|$. Let $\mathbf{S}$ be a matrix with $\mathbf{S}_{\mathbf{x},\mathbf{x}'} = \langle \psi_f(\mathbf{x}), \psi_f(\mathbf{x}') \rangle$. We propose to use the kernel on $\mathcal{X}$ defined by solving

$$\min_{\mathbf{K}} tr(-\mathbf{K}\mathbf{S}')) \; - \alpha \sum_c tr(\mathbf{K}\mathbf{P}_c\mathbf{K}'\mathbf{P}'_c) + \frac{\beta}{2}\|\mathbf{K}\|_2^2, \tag{2}$$

with $\alpha, \beta \geq 0$, $'$, tr denote matrix transpose and trace operator respectively. The first term, in the above optimization problem, measures the quality of matching two features $\psi_f(\mathbf{x})$, $\psi_f(\mathbf{x}')$ (this is considered as the inner product, $\langle \psi_f(\mathbf{x}), \psi_f(\mathbf{x}') \rangle$, between the visual features of $\mathbf{x}$ and $\mathbf{x}'$). A small value of this inner product should result into a small value of $\kappa(\mathbf{x}, \mathbf{x}')$ and vice-versa. The second term is a neighborhood (or context) criterion which considers that a high value of $\kappa(\mathbf{x}, \mathbf{x}')$ should imply high kernel values in the neighborhoods $\mathcal{N}^c(\mathbf{x})$ and $\mathcal{N}^c(\mathbf{x}')$. This criterion also makes it possible to consider the spatial configuration of the neighborhood of each interest point in the matching process. The third term is a regularization criterion that controls the smoothness of the learned kernel and also helps getting a closed form kernel solution.

Proposition 1. *Let $\gamma = \alpha/\beta$ and $\|.\|_1$ denote the entrywise L_1-norm. Provided that the following inequality holds,*

$$\gamma < \Big\| \sum_{\mathcal{L}} \mathbf{P}_c \, \mathbb{1}_{mm} \, \mathbf{P}'_c \Big\|_1^{-1} \tag{3}$$

the optimization problem (2) admits a unique solution $\tilde{\mathbf{K}}$ as the limit of

$$\mathbf{K}^{(t+1)} = \psi(\mathbf{K}^{(t)}), \tag{4}$$

here $\psi : \mathbb{R}^{m \times m} \to \mathbb{R}^{m \times m}$ is defined as $\psi(\mathbf{K}) = \mathbf{S} + \gamma \sum_c \mathbf{P}_c \mathbf{K} \mathbf{P}'_c$, and $\mathbb{1}_{mm}$ is a $m \times m$ square matrix of ones. Furthermore, the kernels $\mathbf{K}^{(t)}$ in (4) satisfy the convergence property: $\|\mathbf{K}^{(t)} - \tilde{\mathbf{K}}\|_1 \leq L^t \|\mathbf{K}^{(0)} - \tilde{\mathbf{K}}\|_1$, with $L = \gamma \| \sum_c \mathbf{P}_c \, \mathbb{1}_{mm} \, \mathbf{P}'_c \|_1$ and $\mathbf{K}^{(0)} = \mathbf{S}$.

Proof. See appendix.

Now, we will show how explicit kernel maps can be obtained from this solution.

2.2   Explicit p.s.d Kernels

Definition 1. *Let κ be symmetric and continuous similarity function. κ is referred to as explicit p.s.d kernel if κ is p.s.d (i.e. $\exists \phi : \forall \mathbf{x}, \mathbf{x}' \in \mathcal{X}, \kappa(\mathbf{x}, \mathbf{x}') = \langle \phi(\mathbf{x}), \phi(\mathbf{x}') \rangle$) and its mapping ϕ is explicit and finite dimensional.*

Example. following the above definition, the polynomial kernel defined, between $\mathbf{x}_a = (a_1 \; a_2)^t$, $\mathbf{x}_b = (b_1 \; b_2)^t$, as $\kappa(\mathbf{x}_a, \mathbf{x}_b) = \langle \mathbf{x}_a, \mathbf{x}_b \rangle^2$, is explicit p.s.d since $\langle \mathbf{x}_a, \mathbf{x}_b \rangle^2 = \langle \phi(\mathbf{x}_a), \phi(\mathbf{x}_b) \rangle$, with $\phi(\mathbf{x}_a) = (a_1^2 \; \sqrt{2}a_1a_2 \; a_2^2)^t$ and $\phi(\mathbf{x}_b) = (b_1^2 \; \sqrt{2}b_1b_2 \; b_2^2)^t$, while the gaussian kernel $\kappa(\mathbf{x}_a, \mathbf{x}_b) = \exp(-\frac{1}{\sigma}\|\mathbf{x}_a - \mathbf{x}_b\|_2^2)$ is p.s.d but not explicit p.s.d as its mapping is infinite dimensional.

Proposition 2. *The similarity functions* $\mathbf{K}_{\mathbf{x},\mathbf{x}'}^{(t+1)}$, $(t = 0, 1, \dots)$ *defined, in proposition (1), as* $\mathbf{K}_{\mathbf{x},\mathbf{x}'}^{(t+1)} = \left(\mathbf{S} + \gamma \sum_c \mathbf{P}_c \, \mathbf{K}^{(t)} \, \mathbf{P}'_c\right)_{\mathbf{x},\mathbf{x}'}$ *are explicit p.s.d kernels.*

Proof. See appendix.

Algorithm (1) shows the iterative process of kernel map learning. According to this algorithm and the previous proposition, it is clear that the mapping $\mathbf{\Phi}^{(t+1)}$ is not equal to $\mathbf{\Phi}^{(t)}$ since the dimensionality of the map increases w.r.t. t. However, the convergence of the inner product $\mathbf{\Phi}'^{(t+1)}\mathbf{\Phi}^{(t+1)}$ to a fixed point is guaranteed when (3) is satisfied, i.e., the gram matrices of the designed kernel maps are convergent.

Resulting from the definition of the adjacency matrices $\{\mathbf{P}_c\}$, in (2.1), it is easy to see that the latter are block diagonal so learning kernel maps could be achieved image per image with obviously the same number of iterations, i.e., the evaluation of kernel maps of a given image is independent from others and hence not transductive; and this makes it incremental. Now, considering $\tilde{\mathbf{K}}$ as the limit of $\psi(\mathbf{K})$, the new form of the convolution kernel $\mathcal{K}$ between two sets of interest points $\mathcal{S}_p$, $\mathcal{S}_q$ can be rewritten $\mathcal{K}(\mathcal{S}_p, \mathcal{S}_q) = \sum_{(\mathbf{x},\mathbf{x}') \in \mathcal{S}_p \times \mathcal{S}_q} \langle \tilde{\mathbf{\Phi}}_\mathbf{x}, \tilde{\mathbf{\Phi}}_{\mathbf{x}'} \rangle$, again $\tilde{\mathbf{\Phi}}$ is the learned kernel map obtained after convergence of algorithm (1) and the subscript in $\tilde{\mathbf{\Phi}}_\mathbf{x}$ denotes the restriction of this map to an interest point $\mathbf{x}$. It is easy to see that $\mathcal{K}$ is an explicit p.s.d kernel as it can be rewritten as a dot product involving finite dimensional and explicit maps, i.e., $\mathcal{K}(\mathcal{S}_p, \mathcal{S}_q) = \langle \phi_\mathcal{K}(\mathcal{S}_p), \phi_\mathcal{K}(\mathcal{S}_q) \rangle$, with $\phi_\mathcal{K}(\mathcal{S}_p) = \sum_{\mathbf{x} \in \mathcal{S}_p} \tilde{\mathbf{\Phi}}_\mathbf{x}$, which clearly shows that each constellation of interest points $\mathcal{S}_p$ can be indexed simply with the explicit kernel map $\phi_\mathcal{K}(\mathcal{S}_p)$.

Algorithm 1. Recursive kernel map learning

Input: The union of all interest points $\{\mathbf{x}_i\}$ in $\mathcal{X}$.
Output: Learned kernel maps $\tilde{\mathbf{\Phi}}$.

Set $t = 0$, γ using condition (3) and set the adjacency matrices $\{\mathbf{P}_c\}$ and $\mathbf{\Phi}^{(0)}$ with $\mathbf{\Phi}_{\mathbf{x}_i}^{(0)} = \psi_f(\mathbf{x}_i)$

repeat

$$\mathbf{\Phi}^{(t+1)} \longleftarrow \left(\mathbf{\Phi}'^{(0)} \quad \gamma^{\frac{1}{2}} \, \mathbf{P}_1 \mathbf{\Phi}'^{(t)} \quad \dots \quad \gamma^{\frac{1}{2}} \mathbf{P}_{N_r N_a} \mathbf{\Phi}'^{(t)} \right)',$$

Set $t \leftarrow t + 1$

until $\left\| \mathbf{\Phi}'^{(t+1)} \mathbf{\Phi}^{(t+1)} - \mathbf{\Phi}'^{(t)} \mathbf{\Phi}^{(t)} \right\|_1 \rightsquigarrow 0$ *or* $t > T_{max}$;

Set $\tilde{\mathbf{\Phi}} \leftarrow \mathbf{\Phi}^{(t)}$

---

3   Experiments

We plugged the learned kernel $\mathcal{K}$ into SVMs in order to evaluate its performance. The targeted task is image annotation; given a picture of a database, the goal is to predict which concepts (classes) are present into that picture. For this purpose, we trained "one-versus-all" SVM classifiers for each concept; we use three random folds (75% of a database) for SVM training and the remaining

Fig. 1. Sample of images from Swedish leaf (left) and ImageCLEF (right) databases

fold for testing. We repeat this training process through different folds, for each concept, and we take the average equal error rates (EERs) of the underlying SVM classifiers. This makes classification results less sensitive to sampling.

We run these experiments on different databases ranging from simple ones such as the Olivetti face database to relatively more challenging ones such as the Swedish and the extremely challenging ImageCLEF Photo Annotation database (see Fig. 1). The latter contains $18,000$ pictures split into 93 categories; a subset of $8,000$ images was used for training and testing as ground truth was publicly available for this subset only. The Swedish database contains 15 leaf species, each one represented by 75 examples, resulting into $1,125$ images while the Olivetti set is a well known face database of 40 persons each one contains 10 instances. For each image in these databases, we run the SIFT detector [15] in order to extract a constellation of interest points, and each one is described with the visual features discussed in Section (2).

Our goal is to show the improvement brought when using the learned kernel maps $\{\mathbf{\Phi}^{(t)}\}_{t\in\mathbb{N}^+}$, so we tested them against context-free kernel maps (i.e., $\mathbf{\Phi}^{(t)}$, $t = 0$). For that purpose, we trained the "one-versus-all" SVM classifiers for each class in Olivetti, Swedish and ImageCLEF sets using the convolution kernel $\mathcal{K}(\mathcal{S}_p, \mathcal{S}_q) = \left\langle \sum_{\mathbf{x}\in\mathcal{S}_p} \mathbf{\Phi}_{\mathbf{x}}^{(t)}, \sum_{\mathbf{x}'\in\mathcal{S}_q} \mathbf{\Phi}_{\mathbf{x}'}^{(t)} \right\rangle$. The influence (and the performance) of the context term in $\mathbf{\Phi}^{(t)}$ (and hence $\mathbf{K}^{(t)}$) increases as γ increases (see example in Fig. 2), nevertheless and as shown earlier, the convergence of $\mathbf{K}^{(t)}$ to a fixed point is guaranteed only if Eq. (3) is satisfied. Intuitively, the parameter γ should then be relatively high while also satisfying condition (3). Larger values of γ (in practice $\gamma > 1$), do not always guarantee convergence of the learned kernels and the classification performances may not converge to the best ones.

Table. (1) shows EERs of different baseline kernel maps and their upgraded context-aware versions. These baselines include: Linear: $\mathbf{K}_{\mathbf{x},\mathbf{x}'}^{(0)} = \langle \psi_f(\mathbf{x}), \psi_f(\mathbf{x}') \rangle$, Polynomial: $\langle \psi_f(\mathbf{x}), \psi_f(\mathbf{x}') \rangle^2$, RBF: $\exp\left(-\|\psi_f(\mathbf{x}) - \psi_f(\mathbf{x}')\|_2^2/0.1\right)$, Triangular: $-\|\psi_f(\mathbf{x}) - \psi_f(\mathbf{x}')\|_2$, Histogram intersection: $\sum_i \min(\psi_f(\mathbf{x})_i, \psi_f(\mathbf{x}')_i)$ and Chi-square: $1 - \frac{1}{2}\sum_i \frac{(\psi_f(\mathbf{x})_i - \psi_f(\mathbf{x}')_i)^2}{(\psi_f(\mathbf{x})_i + \psi_f(\mathbf{x}')_i)}$. Each initialization $\mathbf{K}_{\mathbf{x},\mathbf{x}'}^{(0)}$ should be expressed as an explicit dot product $\langle \mathbf{\Phi}_{\mathbf{x}}^{(0)}, \mathbf{\Phi}_{\mathbf{x}'}^{(0)} \rangle$. As this explicit kernel map is not available for the above kernels (excepting the linear), we apply kernel principal component analysis (KPCA) in order to decompose the matrix $\mathbf{K}^{(0)}$ into $\mathbf{\Phi}'^{(0)}\mathbf{\Phi}^{(0)}$ and hence

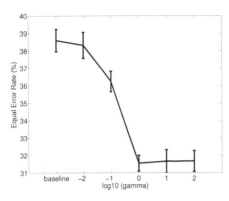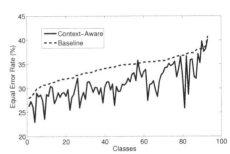

Fig. 2. The left-hand side figure shows the evolution of the overall (average) EER + standard deviation, of our context-aware kernel (with $N_a = N_r = 8$ and $t = 3$), w.r.t γ; these EERs are obtained on the ImageCLEF set. The right-hand side figure, shows this EER class-by-class (when $\gamma = 1$) and a comparison against the underlying baseline kernel (i.e., $t = 0$); for ease of visualization we sort classes according to their difficulty (i.e., increasing error rates when using the baseline kernel). It is clear that our context-aware kernel (with $\gamma = 1$) decreases the EERs for almost all the classes.

approach these maps, i.e., each $\mathbf{x}$ is mapped to a finite dimensional vector $\mathbf{\Phi}_{\mathbf{x}}^{(0)}$ using the principal axes of KPCA[3].

According to Table (1) and Fig. (2), results obtained on different databases, clearly and consistently illustrate the out-performance of the learned context-aware kernel maps with respect to context-free ones for almost all the cases, with only few iterations ($t = 3$ in practice).

Table 1. This table shows EERs (in %) and standard deviations, of image annotation using SVMs, for different baseline kernels (denoted CF) and the underlying context-aware versions (denoted CD). In all these experiments, $N_a = N_r = 8$, the number of iterations = 3 and $\gamma = 1$.

Kernels	Lin (CF)	Lin (CD)	Poly (CF)	Poly (CD)	RBF (CF)	RBF (CD)
Olivetti	1.50 ± 0.31	$\mathbf{0.28 \pm 0.21}$	1.44 ± 0.30	$\mathbf{0.26 \pm 0.17}$	1.36 ± 0.34	$\mathbf{0.66 \pm 0.30}$
Swedish	2.58 ± 0.90	$\mathbf{0.12 \pm 0.11}$	2.47 ± 0.97	$\mathbf{0.08 \pm 0.01}$	2.44 ± 0.85	$\mathbf{2.32 \pm 0.94}$

Kernels	Tri (CF)	Tri (CD)	χ^2 (CF)	χ^2 (CD)	HI (CF)	HI (CD)
Olivetti	1.00 ± 0.26	$\mathbf{0.30 \pm 0.20}$	1.50 ± 0.27	$\mathbf{0.28 \pm 0.19}$	0.90 ± 0.26	$\mathbf{0.28 \pm 0.18}$
Swedish	1.42 ± 0.72	$\mathbf{0.14 \pm 0.13}$	2.72 ± 0.91	$\mathbf{0.12 \pm 0.12}$	1.54 ± 0.77	$\mathbf{0.10 \pm 0.01}$

4   Discussion

Similarity Diffusion. Our kernel is able to recursively diffuse the similarity from/to larger and more influencing contexts (i.e., two primitives are considered

---

[3] Note that KPCA approximation is exact when principal axes are learned using the whole set $\mathcal{X}$ [21] but computation is expensive, so we learn the principal axes on a small subset of $\mathcal{X}$.

similar if their neighbors, with close spatial configurations, are similar and if the neighbors of their neighbors are similar too, etc.) so resulting into a recursive definition and propagation/diffusion of similarity through the spatial structure of primitives (interest points in particular). Therefore, our context-aware kernel exploits pairwise (local) as well as higher order interactions (resulting from recursion). Our comparison in Table (1) corroborates this statement as the learned context-aware kernel maps show consistent gain compared to baseline kernel maps built upon shape context, SIFT and color histograms.

Invariance. It is easy to see that the adjacency matrices $\{\mathbf{P}_c\}$ are translation and rotation invariant and can also be made scale invariant when ϵ_p (see Eq. 1) is proportional to $\psi_s(\mathcal{S}_p)$. It follows that the context term of our kernel is invariant to 2D similarity transformations. Notice, also, that $\mathbf{S}$ in $\mathbf{K}^{(t)}$ involves similarity invariant (or at least tolerant) visual features $\psi_f(.)$ (including 128 SIFT features, color and shape context, see § 2), so both the kernels $\mathbf{K}^{(t)}$ and their explicit maps $\mathbf{\Phi}^{(t)}$ are similarity invariant.

Computational Complexity. let's consider a collection of N images including n interest points each. Assuming $\mathbf{\Phi}^{(t-1)}$, $\mathbf{K}^{(t-1)}$ known at iteration $t-1$, the worst complexity of evaluating the kernel map $\mathbf{\Phi}^{(t)}$ is $O(n^2 N)$ and the complexity of the underlying SVM training using stochastic gradient descent is $O(N)$. This complexity reaches $O(n^4 N^2)$ if one considers instead the evaluation of the gram matrix $\mathbf{K}^{(t)}$. As for testing, the complexity of evaluating the kernel map for a test image is $O(n^2)$ while the complexity of extending the gram matrix with that test image is $O(n^4 N)$. Therefore, it becomes clear that the proposed kernel map evaluation method is at least an order of magnitude faster (than gram matrix based evaluation) both for training and testing.

If the adjacency matrices $\{\mathbf{P}_c\}$ are sparse, the method becomes even faster and its complexity reduces to $O(nM\ N)$, here $M = \max_{\mathbf{x} \in \mathcal{X}} |\mathcal{N}^c(\mathbf{x})| \ll n$. In practice, it takes less than 20 mins (on a standard 2Ghz PC) in order to evaluate the kernel maps and train the SVMs on the $N = 8{,}000$ pictures of ImageCLEF, instead of 5 hours when evaluating gram matrices before SVM learning.

5   Conclusion and Take-Home Message

We introduced in this paper a kernel map learning procedure that takes into account the context. The purpose of this contribution is not to design another kernel; the main take home message is how to *upgrade* usual and widely used kernels, with context, in order to enhance their performances when used in SVM classification.

The proposed kernel design method shows a substantial gain compared to usual kernels for the challenging task of image classification. The method is also generic and could easily be extended to classification tasks in other neighboring fields and applications.

Acknowledgments. This work was supported in part by a grant from the Research Agency ANR (Agence Nationale de la Recherche) under the MLVIS project and a grant from DIGITEO under the RELIR project.

Appendix

Proof (of Proposition 1). Following (2), let us consider the function defined on the set of matrices in $\mathbb{R}^{m \times m}$

$$E : \mathbf{K} \mapsto -tr(\mathbf{KS'}) \; - \alpha \sum_c tr(\mathbf{KP}_c \mathbf{K'P'}_c) + \tfrac{\beta}{2} \|\mathbf{K}\|_2^2 \tag{5}$$

The necessary condition of the fixed-point relation in (4) results from $\partial E / \partial \mathbf{K} = 0$ (details about derivative are omitted in this proof). We will now prove that the function ψ is L-Lipschitzian, with $L = \gamma \| \sum_c \mathbf{P}_c \, \mathbf{1}_{mm} \, \mathbf{P}'_c \|_1$.
Given two matrices $\mathbf{K}^{(1)}$, $\mathbf{K}^{(2)}$, we have

$$
\begin{aligned}
\left\| \mathbf{K}^{(2)} - \mathbf{K}^{(1)} \right\|_1 &= \sum_{\mathbf{x},\mathbf{x'}} \left| \mathbf{K}^{(2)}_{\mathbf{x},\mathbf{x'}} - \mathbf{K}^{(1)}_{\mathbf{x},\mathbf{x'}} \right| \\
&= \gamma \sum_{\mathbf{x},\mathbf{x'}} \left| \sum_{u,u',c} \mathbf{P}_{c,\mathbf{x},u} \, \mathbf{P}_{c,\mathbf{x'},u'} \, (\mathbf{K}^{(1)}_{u,u'} - \mathbf{K}^{(0)}_{u,u'}) \right| \\
&= \gamma \sum_{\mathbf{x},\mathbf{x'}} \left| \sum_{u,u'} (\mathbf{K}^{(1)}_{u,u'} - \mathbf{K}^{(0)}_{u,u'}) \sum_c \mathbf{P}_{c,\mathbf{x},u} \, \mathbf{P}_{c,\mathbf{x'},u'} \right| \\
&\leq \gamma \sum_{\mathbf{x},\mathbf{x'}} \sum_{u,u'} \left| \mathbf{K}^{(1)}_{u,u'} - \mathbf{K}^{(0)}_{u,u'} \right| \left| \sum_c \mathbf{P}_{c,\mathbf{x},u} \, \mathbf{P}_{c,\mathbf{x'},u'} \right| \\
&\leq \gamma \sum_{u,u'} \left| \mathbf{K}^{(1)}_{u,u'} - \mathbf{K}^{(0)}_{u,u'} \right| \times \sum_{\mathbf{x},\mathbf{x'}} \sum_{u,u',c} \left| \mathbf{P}_{c,\mathbf{x},u} \, \mathbf{P}_{c,\mathbf{x'},u'} \right| \\
&\qquad (\text{as } \sum_i |a_i|.|b_i| \leq \sum_{i,j} |a_i|.|b_j|, \; \forall \, \{a_i\}, \{b_j\} \subset \mathbb{R}) \\
&= L \left\| \mathbf{K}^{(1)} - \mathbf{K}^{(0)} \right\|_1
\end{aligned}
$$

with $L = \gamma \| \sum_c \mathbf{P}_c \, \mathbf{1}_{mm} \, \mathbf{P}'_c \|_1$ $\square$

Proof (of Proposition 2). We proceed by induction; $\mathbf{K}^{(0)}_{\mathbf{x},\mathbf{x'}} = \langle \psi_f(\mathbf{x}), \psi_f(\mathbf{x'}) \rangle$ is explicit p.s.d as it is per definition p.s.d and the mapping $\psi_f(.)$ is known and finite dimensional. Assuming $\mathbf{K}^{(t)}_{\mathbf{x},\mathbf{x'}}$ explicit p.s.d, we obtain

$$
\begin{aligned}
\mathbf{K}^{(t+1)}_{\mathbf{x},\mathbf{x'}} &= \left(\mathbf{\Phi}'^{(0)} \mathbf{\Phi}^{(0)} + \gamma \sum_c \mathbf{P}_c \mathbf{K}^{(t)} \mathbf{P}'_c \right)_{\mathbf{x},\mathbf{x'}} = \left(\mathbf{\Phi}'^{(0)} \mathbf{\Phi}^{(0)} + \gamma \sum_c \mathbf{P}_c \mathbf{\Phi}'^{(t)} \mathbf{\Phi}^{(t)} \mathbf{P}'_c \right)_{\mathbf{x},\mathbf{x'}} \\
&= \left(\mathbf{\Phi}'^{(t+1)} \mathbf{\Phi}^{(t+1)} \right)_{\mathbf{x},\mathbf{x'}}
\end{aligned}
\tag{6}
$$

$$\text{where} \quad \mathbf{\Phi}^{(t+1)} = \left(\mathbf{\Phi}'^{(0)} \quad \gamma^{\frac{1}{2}} \, \mathbf{P}_1 \mathbf{\Phi}'^{(t)} \quad \dots \quad \gamma^{\frac{1}{2}} \mathbf{P}_{N_r N_a} \mathbf{\Phi}'^{(t)} \right)', \tag{7}$$

so $\mathbf{K}^{(t+1)}_{\mathbf{x},\mathbf{x'}}$ is also symmetric, continuous and p.s.d. Since $\mathbf{\Phi}^{(t)}$ is finite dimensional, $\mathbf{\Phi}^{(t+1)}$ defined in (7) is also finite dimensional so $\mathbf{K}^{(t+1)}_{\mathbf{x},\mathbf{x'}}$ is explicit p.s.d $\square$

References

1. Bahlmann, C., Haasdonk, B., Burkhardt, H.: On-line handwriting recognition with support vector machines, a kernel approach. In: IWFHR, pp. 49–54 (2002)
2. Barnard, K., Duygululu, P., Forsyth, D., Blei, D., Jordan, M.: Matching words and pictures. The Journal of Machine Learning Research (2003)

3. Belongie, S., Malik, J., Puzicha, J.: Shape context: A new descriptor for shape matching and object recognition. In: NIPS (2000)
4. Bottou, L.: Large scale machine learning with stochastic gradient descent. In: Proc. of the 19th Int Conference on Computational Statistics, pp. 177–187 (2010)
5. Boughorbel, S., Tarel, J., Boujemaa, N.: The intermediate matching kernel for image local features. In: IEEE International J. Conference on Neural Networks (2005)
6. Carneiro, G., Vasconcelos, N.: Formulating semantic image annotation as a supervised learning problem. In: Proc. of CVPR (2005)
7. Gao, Y., Fan, J., Xue, X., Jain, R.: Automatic image annotation by incorporating feature hierarchy and boosting to scale up svm classifiers. ACM Multimedia (2006)
8. Gartner, T.: A survey of kernels for structured data. Multi Relational Data Mining 5(1), 49–58 (2003)
9. Grauman, K., Darrell, T.: The pyramid match kernel: Efficient learning with sets of features. Journal of Machine Learning Research (JMLR) 8, 725–760 (2007)
10. Haussler, D.: Convolution kernels on discrete structures. Technical Report UCSC-CRL-99-10, U. of California in Santa Cruz, CS Department (July 1999)
11. He, X., Zimel, R., Carreira, M.: Multiscale conditional random fields for image labeling. In: CVPR (2004)
12. Jaakkola, T., Diekhans, M., Haussler, D.: Using the Fisher kernel method to detect remote protein homologies. In: ISMB, pp. 149–158 (1999)
13. Kondor, R., Jebara, T.: A kernel between sets of vectors. In: Proccedings of the 20th International Conference on Machine Learning (2003)
14. Li, J., Wang, J.Z.: Automatic linguistic indexing of pictures by a statistical modeling approach. IEEE Trans. on PAMI 25(9), 1075–1088 (2003)
15. Lowe, D.: Distinctive image features from scale-invariant keypoints. International Journal of Computer Vision 60(2), 91–110 (2004)
16. Lyu, S.: Mercer kernels for object recognition with local features. In: The Proceedings of the IEEE Computer Vision and Pattern Recognition (2005)
17. Monay, F., GaticaPerez, D.: Plsa-based image autoannotation: Constraining the latent space. In: Proc. of ACM International Conference on Multimedia (2004)
18. Moreno, P., Ho, P., Vasconcelos, N.: A kullback-leibler divergence based kernel for svm classification in multimedia applications. In: NIPS (2003)
19. Moser, G., Serpico, B.: Combining support vector machines and markov random fields in an integrated framework for contextual image classification. TGRS (2012)
20. Nowak, S., Huiskes, M.: New strategies for image annotation: Overview of the photo annotation task at imageCLEF 2010. In: Working Notes of CLEF 2010 (2010)
21. Scholkopf, B., Smola, A., Muller, K.-R.: Nonlinear component analysis as a kernel eigenvalue problem. Neural Computation 10, 1299–1319 (1998)
22. Semenovich, D., Sowmya, A.: Geometry aware local kernels for object recognition. In: Kimmel, R., Klette, R., Sugimoto, A. (eds.) ACCV 2010, Part I. LNCS, vol. 6492, pp. 490–503. Springer, Heidelberg (2011)
23. Shawe-Taylor, J., Cristianini, N.: Support vector machines and other kernel-based learning methods. Cambridge University Press (2000)
24. Sahbi, H., Audibert, J.-Y., Keriven, R.: Context-Dependent Kernels for Object Classification. IEEE Trans. on PAMI 33(4) (April 2011)
25. Singhal, A., Jiebo, L., Weiyu, Z.: Probabilistic spatial context models for scene content understanding. In: CVPR (2003)
26. Vapnik, V.-N.: Statistical learning theory. A Wiley-Interscience Publication (1998)
27. Wallraven, C., Caputo, B., Graf, A.: Recognition with local features: the kernel recipe. In: ICCV, pp. 257–264 (2003)

Integrating Cue Descriptors in Bubble Space for Place Recognition

Özgür Erkent and Işıl Bozma

Intelligent Systems Lab,
Electrical and Electronics Engineering, Boğaziçi University, Turkey

Abstract. This paper presents a new approach to the integration of different sensory cues in bubble space for place recognition. In bubble space, bubble surfaces enable the representation of all features in a manner that is implicitly dependent on robot pose while preserving their local S^2-geometry. In the proposed approach, for each place, distinct groups of bubble surfaces conduce different cue descriptors which are then combined together. Unlike most previous work, merging cues of different nature is very simple regardless of the number of observations associated with each cue. Comparative experiments on a benchmark dataset indicate that while learning times are decreased considerably, recognition rates are comparable to state-of-the art approaches in place recognition.

1 Introduction

Sensory knowledge is essential in place representation and recognition. Within each scene, information is delivered in many different forms including various visual filter responses, color and possibly range data. Each sensory cue conveys a separate aspect of the scene which may be either redundant or complementary in nature. However, with its individual limits on accuracy and availability, it will rarely suffice alone. This problem is alleviated via the integration of information provided by different cues [1,2]. Previous work has shown this to be the case for place recognition as well where more cues are shown lead to improved recognition performance [3,4]. Our focus is on another aspect of the problem in place recognition - namely the effect of particular form of cue representation and the associated reasoning.

1.1 Related Literature

The vision science community has studied the problem of cue integration extensively. Experimental findings suggest a mixture of cue selection and statistical integration depending on viewing conditions or context [5,6]. Within robot vision community, there is a variety of approaches to cue integration depending on the assumptions regarding the sources of uncertainty in sensory signals as well as the overall task [2]. The simplest approach is based on building a new representation that combines different cues in a single feature vector and using

M. Chen, B. Leibe, and B. Neumann (Eds.): ICVS 2013, LNCS 7963, pp. 314–323, 2013.
© Springer-Verlag Berlin Heidelberg 2013

a standard pattern recognition approach [7,8,9]. Even if these approaches may lead to good performances for specific tasks, they have two shortcomings [10]. First, as the number of cues increases, so does the dimension of the feature vector which implies longer learning and recognition times and greater memory requirements [11]. Second, if new cues become available, the whole learning procedure needs to be repeated.

Alternatively, a variety of cue integration schemes have been developed. Here, the incoming sensory data is organized as a group of cue vectors of smaller dimensions rather than a single feature vector of much bigger dimension. Voting based approaches [12] are easy to implement, however as information provided by a minority of cues are completely ignored, they may lead to poor performance in cases when this information is vital. Minimum-variance unbiased estimators are simple linear integrators where cues - weighted based on their reliability - are summed [2]. Such an approach is taken in accumulation approach where cue integration for object recognition is based on weighting and summing margins of each cue as obtained from the associated pre-learned support vector machines (SVM) [4,10]. This framework is extended to a probabilistic Bayesian reasoning where each cue is represented by a posterior probability distribution [2,13]. Bayesian schemes, while providing for more accurate cue integration, are associated with high computational complexity which can be problematic in real-time applications [14]. In all these methods, additional processing needs to be employed if the number of observations associated with each cue changes in time.

1.2   General Approach

In this paper, we present cue integration in bubble space for place recognition [9]. In bubble space, bubble surfaces and descriptors enable both local and holistic representation of places. In the proposed approach, for each place, distinct groups of bubble surfaces conduce different cue vectors - which are referred to as cue descriptors. Similar to bubble descriptors, each cue descriptor can accommodate any number of observations - hence its dimension is independent of the number of observations. Thus, as the number of observation changes, no relearning is required. Furthermore, no extra processing is required for finding correspondences among observations taken at different times. Thus, it is very simple to construct the cue descriptors. This is because each cue is represented by an associated subset of bubble surfaces where the relative S^2 geometries of the individual cue observations are preserved. Thus, different observations or sensory modalities can be added without requiring special processing for data adaptation. Cue descriptors are combined together based on a weighted cumulation scheme using pre-learned SVMs similar to [4,10]. As expected, introducing new cues improves recognition performance. We further show that place learning times are shortened considerably. The outline of the paper is as follows: First, we give a short overview of bubble space for completeness in Section 2. We then explain cue decomposition, learning and recognition in Section 3. Experimental results on a commonly used dataset with comparison to other methods are discussed in Section 4. The paper concludes with a brief summary.

2   Bubble Space - Surfaces and Descriptors

In this Section, we shortly review bubble space for completeness. The interested reader is referred to [9] for details. Consider a robot positioned at location $c \in R^2$ with a heading $\alpha \in S^1$. Its base is defined as $x = [c, \alpha]^T$ and the base space is defined to be the set of all possible viewpoints $\mathcal{X} = R^2 \times S^1$. Let the robot camera state space (pan and tilt movements) be denoted by $\mathcal{F} \subset S^2$. The bubble space $\mathcal{B} = \mathcal{X} \times \mathcal{F}$ is an abstract representation of the robot's base along with its viewing directions. Each point $b \in \mathcal{B}$ is defined as $b = [x\ f]^T$ where $x \in \mathcal{X}$ and $f \in \mathcal{F}$. The robot's base point is given by $\pi : \mathcal{B} \to \mathcal{X}$ - defined as the projection of b onto $\mathcal{X}$ as $\pi(b) = x$. The section is a continuous map $h : \mathcal{X} \to \mathcal{B}$ such that $\forall x \in \mathcal{X}, \pi(h(x)) = x$. The image of a section h – namely $Im(h(x))$ – is the set of viewing directions from a given base position x.

Assume that at time t, the robot is at base $x \in \mathcal{X}$. For each viewing direction $f \in \mathcal{F}$, it applies a set of sensory filters $\mathcal{V}$ with $|\mathcal{V}| = N_v$. The choice of $\mathcal{V}$ will vary depending on the task at hand. Let $q(b,t) = [q_1(b,t), \ldots, q_{N_v}(b,t)]^T$ denote the observation vector that consists of all individual responses. Now, for each filter $i \in \mathcal{V}$, visualize the robot to be surrounded by an hypothetical spherical surface that is deformed at each f by an amount that is dependent on the filter response in that direction. This surface is referred to as bubble surface $B_i(x,t)$. As the robot's camera moves through a sequence of N_s viewing directions $\{f^0, \ldots, f^{N_s}\}$ over time, this in turn generates a sequence of visual observations which are then encoded by a bubble surface $B_i(x,t)$ after being deformed exactly at N_s points. From place representation perspective, it is an egocentric representation of its surroundings based on its associated visual feature. As this is done for each visual feature $i \in \mathcal{V}$, a set of N_v bubble surfaces $B_i(x,t)$ is generated.

Mathematically, each bubble surface is a deformed sphere embedded in R^3 with an intrinsic parametrization:

$$B_i(x,t) = \left\{ \begin{bmatrix} f \\ \rho_i(b,t) \end{bmatrix} \mid \forall f \in \mathcal{F} \text{ and } b = [x\ f]^T \right\} \tag{1}$$

where $\rho_i : \mathcal{B} \times R^{\geq 0} \to R^{\geq 0}$ is a Riemannian metric that encodes the response to the ith visual feature. Each bubble surface can be explicitly represented by the double Fourier series as:

$$\rho_i(b,t) = \sum_{m=0}^{H_1} \sum_{n=0}^{H_2} \lambda_{mn} z_{xi,mn}^T(t) e_{mn}(f)$$

While bubble surface coefficients are not rotationally invariant with respect to changes in robot's heading, a series of rotational invariants can be defined as [9]:

$$I_{i,mn}(x,t) = z_{xi,mn}^T(t) z_{xi,mn}(t)$$

Each set of bubble surfaces $\{B_i(x,t) \mid i \in \mathcal{V}\}$ is associated with a bubble descriptor $I(x,t) \in R^{N_I}$ where $N_I = N_v(H_1 + 1)(H_2 + 1)$ as:

$$I(x,t) = [I_{1,00}(x,t), \ldots, I_{N_v,H_1 H_2}(x,t)]^T$$

Please note that we will omit the second argument and use $I(x)$ for notational simplicity. In each place $p \in \mathcal{P}$, for each base point $x_j(p)$, $j = 1, \ldots, M_p$, the robot generates a bubble descriptor $I(x_j(p))$. Hence, each place is associated with a set $\mathcal{I}_p$ of bubble descriptors:

$$\mathcal{I}_p = \{I(x_j(p)) \mid j = 1, \ldots, M_p\}$$

A bubble descriptor is a single feature vector of fixed dimension that embeds data from different sensors or sensor modalities. It can accommodate any number of observations from each cue since each new observation simply means an added deformation on the bubble surface. In recognition, a bubble descriptor is constructed and compared with previously learned vectors as shown in Fig. 1(left). However, if new features are introduced into the system or some features are removed, its dimension needs to be adjusted accordingly.

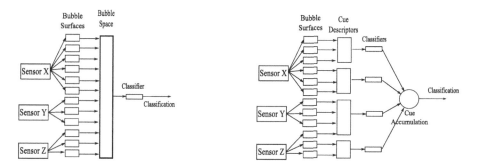

Fig. 1. Recognition in bubble space. Left: Bubble descriptor representation; Right: Multiple cue descriptors.

3   Integrating Cue Descriptors

Each set of bubble surfaces is a collection of representations that encode different sensory features of the respective scene. In this perspective, each bubble descriptor $I(x_j(p))$ is really an aggregation of N_v different components - again each component corresponding to one different sensory feature as:

$$I(x_j(p)) = \sum_{l=1}^{N_v} e_l \otimes I_l(x_j(p))$$

where the vectors e_k are the unit vectors in $\mathbb{R}^{N_v}$. and $\otimes$ is the Kronecker product [15]. The vectors $I_l(x_j(p)) \in \mathbb{R}^{(H_1+1)(H_2+1)}$ are subvectors in $I(x_j(p))$ that embed invariants associated with one particular sensory feature l as:

$$I_l(x_j(p)) = [I_{l,00} \ldots I_{l,H_1 H_2}]^T$$

If the sensory features can be categorized into $N_c << N_v$ groups, then accordingly the bubble surfaces can be decomposed into N_c subsets where each subset consists of bubble surfaces whose features are related. Each subset of bubble surfaces can be viewed as corresponding to one different cue. Let $\{\mathcal{V}_c\}_{k=1}^{N_c}$ be a partition of N_v features into N_c groups where $\forall j, k = 1, \ldots, N_c; k \neq j, \mathcal{V}_c \cap \mathcal{V}_j = \emptyset$ and $\cup_{c=1}^{N_c} \mathcal{V}_c = \mathcal{V}$. Assume that each cell in this partition is defined as cue features $\mathcal{V}_c = \{\mathcal{V}_1c, \ldots, \mathcal{V}_{N_k}c\}$ where the cardinality of each group is $\|\mathcal{V}_c\| = N_k$ and $\mathcal{V}_k c$ is the sensory feature element of the cue feature. The corresponding cue descriptor $\bar{I}_c \in R^{N_k(H_1+1)(H_2+1)}$ is defined as:

$$\bar{I}_c = \begin{bmatrix} I_{k1}^T, \ldots, I_{kN_c}^T \end{bmatrix}^T$$

where I_{kc} corresponds to the bubble descriptor of the sensory feature $\mathcal{V}_k c$. For each place p and for each cue k, the associated cue set is simply obtained as:

$$\mathcal{C}_{pc} = \left\{ \bar{I}_c(x_j(p)) \mid j = 1, \ldots, M_p \right\}$$

With cue formulation, as shown in Fig.1(right), instead of a single vector (bubble descriptor) with a very large dimension, a set of N_c cue vectors (cue descriptors) with much smaller dimensions are generated. The strength of integration in bubble space is that correspondences among different cues are easily established regardless of the number of observations or the inherent nature of the associated cue. This is because all the sensory responses and their relative S^2-geometry are encoded by the bubble surfaces which - in turn - are encoded as cue descriptors in a compact and rotationally invariant manner. Hence different sensors or sensing modalities can easily be merged together.

3.1   Cue Learning

In learning mode, at each place p, for each base point x_j, the robot generates a set of cues $\bar{I}_c(x_j(p))$ with $c = 1, \ldots, N_c$. Once it visits all N_p places, using the complete set of labeled cues as training data, the following is done:

- For each place and for each cue $c = 1, \ldots, N_c$,
- Each set $\mathcal{C}_{pc}$ is divided into two groups as learning $\mathcal{C}_{pc}^+$ and test groups $\mathcal{C}_{pc}^-$.
- For the samples in the learning group $\mathcal{C}_{pc}^+$, a one-against-all SVM classifier is constructed via computing the parameters w, d of a separating hyperplane $w^T \bar{I}_c(x_j(p)) + d = 0$.

3.2   Individual Cues

In recognition mode, when the robot enters into a place p, as it starts looking around, it constructs all the different cues $\bar{I}_c'$, $c = 1, \ldots, N_c$. It then uses the SVM model constructed during learning. The decision value $c_{pc}(\bar{I}_c')$ is computed using the learned one-against-all (*oaa*) SVM classifier model as:

$$c_{pc}(\bar{I}_c') = \sum_{\bar{I}_c(x_j(p)) \in \mathcal{C}_{pc}^+} \zeta_i y(\bar{I}_c(x_j(p))) K(\bar{I}_c', \bar{I}_c(x_j(p))) + d$$

The value $y(\bar{I}_c(x_j(p))) \in \{-1,1\}$ specifies whether a cue descriptor belongs to the place p or not in a one-against-all comparison model. The parameters ζ_i are obtained via solving dual Lagrangian form of the aforementioned optimal hyperplane problem.

3.3 Recognition with Cues

The integration of different functions is done via an objective function that encodes all the different cues together. We choose a linear function for simplicity. Recognition is based on finding the place with maximum value as:

$$p^* \in \arg\max_{p \in \mathcal{P}} \sum_{c=1}^{N_c} r_c^{u_c} c_{pc}(\bar{I}_c')$$

where r_c, $c = 1, \ldots, N_c$ are cue weights obtained using the training data and u_c is the associated power factor that is preselected.

3.4 Cue Weights

Cue weights r_c are defined based on the recognition rates of individual cue sets $\mathcal{C}_{pc}^-$. The SVM model for each cue c is input all the samples in $\mathcal{C}_{pc}^-$, $p = 1, \ldots, N_p$ and is made to classify with respect to one of the N_p places. Let $\mathcal{C}_{pc}^{-+} \subseteq \mathcal{C}_{pc}^-$ be set of correctly recognized cue samples. Then, the associated cue weight is computed as:

$$r_c = \frac{1}{N_p} \sum_{p=1}^{N_p} \frac{|\mathcal{C}_{pc}^{-+}|}{|\mathcal{C}_{pc}^-|}$$

The cue weight serves as a measure of the reliability of the associated cue in the corresponding learning set.

4 Experiments

This Section presents experimental results to evaluate the proposed cue integration approach. The experiments are similar to those that were done in recent, related work [16,17,9]. The bubble surface deformation parameters are $\rho_{min} = 0.5$, $\rho_{max} = 1.5$ and $\rho_0 = 1$ respectively with $\epsilon = 2°$. It stops this process after it has gotten sensory observations from $N_s = 40$ different viewing directions. These viewing directions are determined automatically via looking around in a free viewing mode as described in detail in [18]. The robot learns a place by using half of the learning samples for constructing an SVM model of the environment. The SVM parameters are obtained via libSVM library [19] by using RBF (radial basis functions) Kernel. It then uses the other half of the learning samples to obtain the recognition rate weight r_k for a specific cue set k. In recognition, a sample image from the test data is given. All the processing is done on a processor with an Intel Xeon W3250 @2.67 GHz, 6 GB RAM.

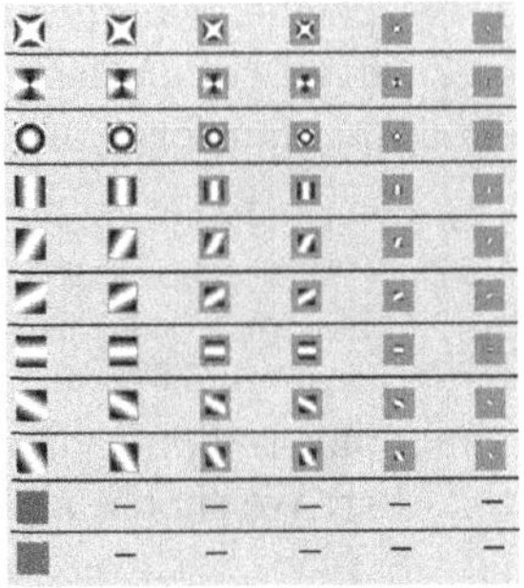

Fig. 2. Cues that are used in the experiments. The cue sets are separated by solid lines. Each cue consists of 6 different filter response type. The remaining two cues at the bottom are a and b color channels of CIELAB color space.

4.1 Visual Data Only

In the first set of experiments, the robot has only vision data from two different laboratories of the COLD dataset [20]. Both laboratories have five different places: printer area (PA), corridor (CR), two-person office (2PO1), washroom (TL) and stairs area (ST). A robot equipped with an omnidirectional camera travels a standard route that passes through each of these places and acquires images from $150 < M_p < 350$ base points at each place. This is repeated three times under three different illumination conditions (cloudy, sunny and night). Hence, there are 9 sets of data. For learning, we use one set associated with one particular illumination condition. The remaining two sets acquired under the same illumination condition are considered to be "similar" test conditions while the image sets acquired under other illumination conditions are considered to be "different" test conditions. Thus, the test data differs either in run or illumination or any combination of. The robot applies $N_v = 56$ visual filters at each viewing direction – including Cartesian and non-Cartesian filters and two color channels of CIELAB color space as shown in Fig. 2. Simultaneously, the corresponding bubble descriptors are constructed with $H_1 = H_2 = 6$ number of harmonics, however only the first 40 rotational invariants are used since the remaining are observed to be nondiscriminating. Hence, each bubble descriptor is of dimension $56 \times 40 = 2240$. For cue integration approach, the visual filters are categorized into $N_j = 11$ cues as shown in Fig.2 where the dimension of the first nine cue descriptors is 240 while the two color cues are of dimension 40. The weights r_c are computed for each learning set separately with power factor $u_c = 10$. The contribution of each cue in recognition has a different weight according to the illumination condition of training.

We conduct a comparative study similar to [17] including three other representations - bubble space (BuS) [21], extended-HCT (e-HCT) [17] and CPAM [22] that have been shown to have better performance in comparison to SURF [23] used together with HIST [24] or classic BoW [25] [17]. Recognition rates

Table 1. Recognition rates

Learn & Test Conditions	Freiburg				Ljubljana			
	Cue-BuS	BuS	e-HCT	CPAM	Cue-BuS	BuS	e-HCT	CPAM
Similar	82.6	85.5	85.6	86.2	82.5	86.0	87.3	93.6
Different	65.7	72.3	62.9	53.2	71.0	71.4	71.8	76.1

are based on the average of performance under the three illumination conditions. The results are as shown in Table 1. With similar testing conditions, it is observed that recognition rates with cue-BuS representation are only slightly lower as compared to other three approaches. We attribute this to the fact that as cue descriptors are of much smaller dimensions, the discrimination capability of the simple linear integrator in cue-BuS integration scheme will be lower in cases where the linear separation of the feature space is not possible. In case of different testing conditions, the performance degrades to some extent for all the approaches. This is in agreement with similar results obtained in previous work on cue integration [4] – where a different dataset is used. Again, the performance of cue-Bus is slightly lower than that of the BuS approach. We attribute this again to lower discrimination capability of the simple linear integrator.

4.2 Adding 2D Laser Cue

In the second set of experiments, we introduce a new cue - laser data to our already existing set of eleven cues that were learned previously. Hence, the augmented cue set contains twelve cues. As only two-dimensional laser data is available with the COLD dataset, the bubble surface is constructed only with deformation along its equator. The associated cue descriptor is of dimension 40. We compare performance with regular BuS approach where the bubble descriptor dimension increases from 2240 to 2280. In the case of cue descriptors, simply a new cue with dimension 40 is added. First, as discussed previously, more cues improve recognition performance [3,4]. We expect this to be the case here as well. This is indeed the case as shown in Table.3. Interestingly, the effect of the newly added cue is much greater in the cue-BuS approach on recognition rates as the performance of cue-BuS method increases from 65 % to 73 % in different illumination conditions while that of BuS approach goes up from roughly 72% to 73%. Thus, it is observed that adding new cues to a larger feature vector has a smaller effect on its discriminative power as compared to the smaller cue descriptors - possibly due to reaching the upper bound in the recognition performance with the available data.

What is really interesting is the effect of this approach on learning time. As expected, the retraining time for cue-BuS is much lower as compared to BuS approach. When the new sensory data is included in the system, the new cue-Bus approach becomes superior as the average re-learning time (which includes the SVM modeling time and modifying the parameters r_k.) is about 4 times faster – which is a significant improvement.

Table 2. Recognition rates for Freiburg Lab with added 2D laser cue

	Freiburg	
Learn & Test Conditions	BuS	Cue-BuS
Similar	87.6	85.6
Different	73.1	75.2

Table 3. Re-Learning with 2D Laser

	BuS	Cue-BuS
Avg. Modeling Time (sec)	23.4	0.6
Avg Re-Learning Time (sec)	30.6	7.8

5   Conclusion

This paper has presented the integration of different sensory cues in bubble space for place recognition. In bubble space, bubble surfaces enable representation of all features in a manner that is implicitly dependent on robot pose while preserving their local S^2-geometry. In the proposed approach, taking advantage of this representation, distinct groups of bubble surfaces conduce different cue descriptors for each place which are then combined together. Unlike most previous work, merging cues - even of different nature - is very simple regardless of the number of observations associated with each cue. As expected, introducing new cues improves recognition performance. We also show a new sensor modality such as laser range data can easily be added in this framework without any relearning or special processing of the sensory data - thus shortening the relearning times significantly.

Acknowledgments. This work has been supported in part by TUBITAK Project 111E285.

References

1. Clark, J.J., Yuille, A.L.: Data Fusion for Sensory Information Processing Systems. Kluwer Academic Publishers (1990)
2. Landy, M.S., Banks, M.S., Knill, D.C.: Ideal-Observer Models of Cue Integration. In: Trommershauser, J., Kording, K., Landy, M.S. (eds.) Sensory Cue Integration, pp. 5–29. Oxford University Press (2011)
3. Pronobis, A., Caputo, B.: Confidence-based cue integration for visual place recognition. In: IEEE/RSJ Int. Conf. on Intelligent Robots and Systems, pp. 2394–2401 (2007)
4. Pronobis, A., Martinez Mozos, O., Caputo, B., Jensfelt, P.: Multi-modal Semantic Place Classification. The Int. J. of Robotics Research 29(2-3), 298–320 (2010)

5. Bulthoff, H., Yuille, A.: Bayesian models for seeing shapes and depth. Comments on Theoretical Biology 4(2), 283–313 (1991)
6. Trommershauser, J., Kording, K., Landy, M.: Sensory Cue Integration. Oxford University Press (2011)
7. Leibe, B., Schiele, B.: Analyzing appearance and contour based methods for object categorization. In: IEEE Conference on Computer Vision and Pattern Recognition, vol. 2, pp. II-409–415 (2003)
8. Rottmann, A., Mozos, O.M., Stachniss, C., Burgard, W.: Semantic place classification of indoor environments with mobile robots using boosting. In: National Conference on Artificial Intelligence, pp. 1306–1311 (2005)
9. Erkent, O., Bozma, I.: Place representation in topological maps based on bubble space. In: IEEE Int. Conf. on Robotics and Automation, pp. 3497–3502 (2012)
10. Nilsback, M.E., Caputo, B.: Cue integration through discriminative accumulation. In: IEEE Conf. on Computer Vision and Pattern Recognition, vol. 2, pp. 578–585 (2004)
11. Joachims, T., Yu, C.N.J.: Sparse kernel SVMs via cutting-plane training. Machine Learning 76(2-3), 179–193 (2009)
12. Brautigam, C.G.: A Model-Free Voting Approach to Cue Integration. PhD thesis, Kungl Tekniska Hogskolan (1998)
13. DeCarlo, D.: Towards real-time cue integration by using partial results. In: Heyden, A., Sparr, G., Nielsen, M., Johansen, P. (eds.) ECCV 2002, Part IV. LNCS, vol. 2353, pp. 327–342. Springer, Heidelberg (2002)
14. Alpert, S., Galun, M., Brandt, A., Basri, R.: Image Segmentation by Probabilistic Bottom-Up Aggregation and Cue Integration. IEEE Trans. on Pattern Analysis and Machine Intel. 34(2), 315–327 (2012)
15. Horn, R.A., Johnson, C.R.: Topics in Matrix Analysis, vol. 2. Camb. Univ. Press, England (1991)
16. Ullah, M.M., Pronobis, A., Caputo, B., Luo, J., Jensfelt, R., Christensen, H.I.: Towards robust place recognition for robot localization. In: IEEE Int. Conf. on Robot. and Aut., pp. 530–537 (2008)
17. Wang, M.L., Lin, H.Y.: An extended-HCT semantic description for visual place recognition. The Int. J. of Robotics Research 30(11), 1403–1420 (2011)
18. Erkent, O., Bozma, H.I.: Artificial potential functions based camera movements and visual behaviors in attentive robots. Autonomous Robots 32, 15–35 (2012)
19. Chang, C.C., Lin, C.J.: {LIBSVM}: A library for support vector machines. ACM Transactions on Intelligent Systems and Technology 2(3), 1–27 (2011)
20. Pronobis, A., Caputo, B.: Cold: Cosy localization database. The Int. J. of Robotics Research 28(5), 588–594 (2009)
21. Erkent, O., Bozma, H.I.: Bubble space and place representation in topological maps. The Int. J. of Robotics Research (to appear, 2013)
22. Qiu, G.: Indexing chromatic and achromatic patterns for content-based colour image retrieval. Pattern Recognition 35(8), 1675–1686 (2002)
23. Bay, H., Tuytelaars, T., Van Gool, L.: SURF: Speeded up robust features. In: Leonardis, A., Bischof, H., Pinz, A. (eds.) ECCV 2006, Part I. LNCS, vol. 3951, pp. 404–417. Springer, Heidelberg (2006)
24. Ulrich, I., Nourbakhsh, I.: Appearance-based place recognition for topological localization. In: IEEE Int. Conf. on Robot., vol. 2, pp. 1023–1029 (2000)
25. Nowak, E., Jurie, F., Triggs, B.: Sampling Strategies for Bag-of-Features Image Classification. In: Leonardis, A., Bischof, H., Pinz, A. (eds.) ECCV 2006. LNCS, vol. 3954, pp. 490–503. Springer, Heidelberg (2006)

A Hierarchical Scheme of Multiple Feature Fusion for High-Resolution Satellite Scene Categorization

Wen Shao[1], Wen Yang[1,2], Gui-Song Xia[2], and Gang Liu[1]

[1] School of Electronic Information, Wuhan University, Wuhan, 430072, China
[2] Key State Laboratory LIESMARS, Wuhan University, Wuhan, 430079, China
{shaowen1989,yangwen94111,gsxia.lhi,liugang.spl}@gmail.com

Abstract. Scene categorization in high-resolution satellite images has attracted much attention in recent years. However, high intra-class variations, illuminations and occlusions make the task very challenging. In this paper, we propose a classification model based on a hierarchical fusion of multiple features. Highlights of our work are threefold: (1) we use four discriminative image features; (2) we employ support vector machine with histogram intersection kernel (HIK-SVM) and L1-regularization logistic regression classifier (L1R-LRC) in different classification stages, respectively. The soft probabilities of different features obtained by the HIK-SVM are discriminatively fused and fed into the L1R-LRC to obtain the final results; (3) we conduct an extensive evaluation of different configurations, including different feature fusion schemes and different kernel functions. Experimental analysis show that our method leads to state-of-the-art classification performance on the satellite scenes.

Keywords: Scene Categorization, Hierarchical Fusion, Histogram Intersection Kernel, Logistic Regression.

1 Introduction

Scene categorization is a challenging problem in remote sensing image interpretation. It is difficult due to the high intra-class variability and low inter-class disparity in remote-sensing images. Other factors, such as changes of viewpoint, illuminations and shadows, partial occlusions, background clutter and multiple instances, further complicate these problems. Simultaneously, with the substantial increase of the resolution of images, details of the targets become more clear, and a multitude of cues also become more distinctive, such as structure, shape, texture and color. Thus, it is essential to design highly discriminative image features and to reasonably combine them based on different aspects. In the past few years, tremendous efforts have been made to develop advanced image features and classification techniques for boosting the classification accuracy[1,2].

Designing comprehensive and complementary image features is one of recent trends in image classification domain. Unlike the case of low-resolution satellite images, where texture and intensity cues have been proved to be effective and

M. Chen, B. Leibe, and B. Neumann (Eds.): ICVS 2013, LNCS 7963, pp. 324–333, 2013.
© Springer-Verlag Berlin Heidelberg 2013

efficient enough for recognition [3], structure, shape and color information also play important roles in analyzing high-resolution satellite images. For example, Xia *et al.* [4] have confirmed the applicability of their shape-based image indexing scheme to satellite scene categorization, named tree of shapes.

Another trend is how to properly combine different features. Many approaches have been reported in the literature. A prominent kernel level fusion instance is the Multiple Kernel Learning (MKL). MKL linearly combines similarity functions between images, which yields good results on the application of object classification. However, although the MKL solution is sparse for every class separately, it is not sparse jointly in the multi-class setup. Based on the observation that higher computation efficiency and classification accuracy can be achieved by simple feature combination strategies than that by MKL, Gehler and Nowozin [5] concluded that the performance of MKL has been overestimated in the past. Recently, a frequently used approach is score level fusion, where scores from different feature channels are combined. Sheng *et al.* [6] designed a high-resolution satellite scene classification using a sparse coding based multiple feature fusion, simplified as SCMF. SCMF set the final fused result as the concatenation of the probabilities obtained by the individual feature channel, the approach turned out to work surprisingly well with the linear SVM classifier, while dramatically reducing the computational complexity. Furthermore, many breakthroughs have been made by discriminative feature fusion. Fernando *et al.* [7] presented a new logistic regression-based fusion method, called LRFF. LRFF first created a visual dictionary for each feature, and then used a Logistic Regression (LR) method to deduce the most class-specific discriminative visual words from the multiple dictionaries, finally applied the LR outputs to design an efficient marginalized kernel for the purpose of learning a new SVM classifier. Experimental results have demonstrated the effectiveness of their approach.

Inspired by the above two trends, this paper describes a robust two-level classification model by discriminatively fusing multiple features. The remainder of this paper is organized as follows. First, multiple feature extraction procedure is presented in Section 2. Then, Section 3 gives a detailed description of our hierarchical feature fusion method. Further, Section 4 shows the experimental results and performance evaluation. Finally, Section 5 ends up with conclusions and future work.

2   The Hierarchical Categorization Framework

In this section, we build a hierarchical categorization framework by discriminatively fusing multiple features, shown in Figure 1. Observe that our method is also flexible to other features and classifiers.

2.1   Multi-feature Extraction

Since a high-resolution satellite image usually consists of several kinds of information cues, capturing these cues is very helpful in recognizing and distinguishing categories. Thus, we exploit four channels of features to characterize the images. For structural cues, we extract SIFT gradient orientation histograms within the support region and quantize local feature descriptors using a bag of features (BoF) model [8]. For shape cues, we incorporate color information into the shape-based invariant image indexing framework of Xia *et al.* [4], and the resulting output is the concatenation of R, G and B three channeled edge information, termed tree of colored shapes (tree of c-shapes). For textural cues, a supervised three-layered model is adopted, and the discriminative CLBP feature (disCLBP) [9] is obtained by concatenating pattern occurrence histograms of sign and magnitude operators. For color cues, we use the simple yet effective bag-of-colors [10] signature as an additional global color descriptor, which brings in the idea of a Lab-color-palette.

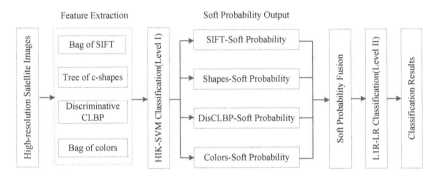

Fig. 1. The two-level categorization framework

2.2   Level-I Classification by HIK-SVM

Support vector machine (SVM) with histogram intersection kernel (HIK-SVM) [11] remains an extremely popular choice for histogram feature classification. Moreover, the HIK SVM is able to provide probabilistic output for the test image. After feature extraction, we therefore serve HIK-SVM as the base classifier for Level-I classification.

Let $\mathbf{x}_I^k$ and $\mathbf{x}_J^k$ denote the kth ($k = 1, 2, 3, 4$) feature vector extracted in image I and J, respectively. The similarity between $\mathbf{x}_I^k$ and $\mathbf{x}_J^k$ can be defined by the histogram intersection kernel K_{int} as

$$K_{int}(\mathbf{x}_I^k, \mathbf{x}_J^k) = \sum_{i=1}^{M} \min\{\mathbf{x}_I^k(i), \mathbf{x}_J^k(i)\} \tag{1}$$

where M is the dimension of the feature vectors. The histogram intersection can be used as a similarity measure for histogram-based representations of images. Integrating histogram intersection kernel into a SVM framework, a classification can be obtained by:

$$h(\mathbf{x}^k) = \sum_{l=1}^{m} \alpha_l^k y_l K(\mathbf{x}^k, \mathbf{x}_l^k) + b^k \tag{2}$$

where $K(\mathbf{x}^k, \mathbf{x}_l^k)$ represents the value of a kernel function for the lth training image $\mathbf{x}_l^k$ and the test image $\mathbf{x}^k$, α_l^k and y_l are weight and class label c $(c = 1, 2, ..., C)$ of $\mathbf{x}_l^k$, and b^k is the learned threshold.

Multi-class categorization is implemented using a set of binary classifiers and taking the majority vote. In terms of four feature channels of the image, we obtain four kinds of soft posteriori probabilities $\mathbf{P}_1, \mathbf{P}_2, \mathbf{P}_3, \mathbf{P}_4 \in \mathbb{R}^C$ in parallel using HIK-SVM, their lengths are equivalent to the number of categories C within a dataset.

2.3   Level-II Classification by L1R-LR and Other Kernel Classifiers

Several data fusion methods have been reported in the literature [5]. In what follows, four representative fusion strategies are employed to combine the intermediate soft probabilities,

$$\mathbf{Y}_1 = \max\left(\mathbf{P}_1, \mathbf{P}_2, \mathbf{P}_3, \mathbf{P}_4\right) \in \mathbb{R}^C \tag{3}$$

$$\mathbf{Y}_2 = \mathrm{sum}\left(\mathbf{P}_1, \mathbf{P}_2, \mathbf{P}_3, \mathbf{P}_4\right) \in \mathbb{R}^C \tag{4}$$

$$\mathbf{Y}_3 = \mathrm{cat}\left(\mathbf{P}_1, \mathbf{P}_2, \mathbf{P}_3, \mathbf{P}_4\right) \in \mathbb{R}^{4C} \tag{5}$$

$$\mathbf{Y}_4 = \mathrm{multiply}\left(\mathbf{P}_1, \mathbf{P}_2, \mathbf{P}_3, \mathbf{P}_4\right) \in \mathbb{R}^C \tag{6}$$

In order to keep the consistency of data, most of the multi-stage classification tasks use the same classifier in each stage [6]. However, different classifiers may be more capable of helping each other by focusing on different aspects of the data, and not making the same mistakes. Here, we use an L1-regularization logistic regression (L1R-LR) model [7] to train the Level-II classifier, by taking $\mathbf{Y}_t$ $(t = 1, 2, 3, 4)$ as the input feature vectors.

Suppose an image I can be described as a normalized feature vector $\mathbf{x}$, multivariate logistic regression models the probability that the image label y belongs to class c as follows:

$$P\left(y = c \mid \mathbf{x}; \mathbf{b}, \mathbf{W}\right) = \frac{\exp\left(\mathbf{b}_c + \mathbf{w}_c^T \mathbf{x}\right)}{N} \tag{7}$$

where $\mathbf{b}$ is a class-bias vector, $\mathbf{W}$ is a weight vector-matrix with columns $\mathbf{w}_n$, and $N = N\left(\mathbf{x}; \mathbf{b}, \mathbf{W}\right) = \sum_c \exp(\mathbf{b}_c + \mathbf{w}_c^T \mathbf{x})$ is a probability normalization term. L1-regularized logistic regression-based training [12] actually solves following unconstrained optimization problem,

$$\arg\min \sum_c \| \mathbf{w}_c \|_1 - A \sum_i \log\left(\frac{\exp(\mathbf{b}_{c_i} + \mathbf{w}_{c_i}^T \mathbf{x}_i)}{N_i}\right) \tag{8}$$

where $\| \cdot \|_1$ denotes the L1-regularization, A is a regularization parameter and i runs over the training samples with features $\mathbf{x}_i$, labels c_i, and normalizations N_i.

Unlike the L2-regularization that only restricts large values, the L1-regularization term penalizes all factors equally, which can create sparse answers.

For comparisons, we further consider other kernel functions, such as HIK, RBF kernel, χ^2 kernel, and especially logistic regression marginalized kernel (LRMK) [7], which is a new marginalized kernel designed by making use of the output weight and condition probability of logistic regression model. More details are discussed in the subsequent experiments.

3   Experimental Evaluation and Analysis

In the experiments, we report the experimental results on two datasets: a 19-class satellite scene[1], and a 21-class land-use dataset[2].

3.1   19-Class Satellite Scene

Data Description. Our first dataset is composed of 19 classes of scenes, including airport, beach, bridge, commercial area, desert, farmland, football field, forest, industrial area, meadow, mountain, park, parking, pond, port, railway station, residential area, river and viaduct. Each class has 50 images, with the size of 600×600 pixels. To make the results as robust and quantitative as possible, we randomly divided the dataset into five equal sets, three of which were chosen for training and the remainder for test the same as [6]. The classification accuracy is the mean and standard deviation over five evaluations.

Implementation Details and Results. To obtain the optimal parameter configuration, SIFT descriptors from 16×16 pixel patches were densely extracted from each image on a grid with a spacing of 8 pixels. During BoF processing, a visual dictionary with a size of 1024 was used. In addition, codebook sizes of 1400 and 512 were set separately for the tree of c-shapes and bag-of-colors methods to achieve satisfactory classification accuracies. Since different training sets produced different global dominant pattern sets, the dimension of disCLBP feature over five runs were unfixed (4135, 3955, 4144, 4173, 4243) but converged to a constant 4000. Table 1 gives the dimensions and classification rates of four features independently using HIK-SVM. We can find that bag of SIFT accounts for the largest importance and bag of colors the lowest on the 19-class satellite scene. An empirical combination of feature concatenation was also realized to classification, the accuracy increases at the expense of the reduced computational speed due to the high-dimensional vector.

In order to further improve the performance, four data fusion strategies were proposed to combine the intermediate results from four feature channels, five kernels were also considered to perform classification tasks. Table 2 shows the classification rates of different fusion methods using different kernels. Experimental results show

---

[1] http://dsp.whu.edu.cn/cn/staff/yw/HRSscene.html
[2] http://vision.ucmerced.edu/datasets

that all kernels under maximum, sum and concatenation fusion can dramatically improve the classification accuracy as opposed to the above single feature channels and simple feature concatenation, and their performances almost keep pace with each other. However, L1R-LRC shows a significant advantage over other kernels under multiplication fusion and explicitly performs the best in all experiments. The superiority can be attributed to at least two reasons. On the one hand, the four features we chose are relatively independent, which exactly meets the requirement of multiplication fusion. On the other hand, the choice of L1R-LRC is important since L1-regularization provides for robustness in the case that no categories matching all feature attributes of the image. Furthermore, multiplying probabilities from all feature channels would tend to favor the category where all features are somewhat likely, but none is particularly low.

Table 1. Performance comparison with different features using HIK-SVM on 19-class

Feature	Dimension	Accuracy (%)
Bag of SIFT	1024	**85.52 ± 1.23**
Tree of c-shapes	1400	80.42 ± 1.80
DisCLBP	~ 4000	80.42 ± 1.37
Bag of colors	512	70.63 ± 1.44
concatenation	~ 6936	90.79 ± 0.65

Table 2. Performance comparison of different fusions using different kernels on 19-class

Fusion method	Maximum	Sum	Concatenation	Multiplication
L1R-LR Accuracy (%)	90.11 ± 1.05	93.21 ± 1.02	92.37 ± 0.51	**94.53 ± 1.01**
LRMK Accuracy (%)	90.16 ± 0.76	93.23 ± 0.74	92.68 ± 1.08	53.46 ± 0.68
HIK Accuracy (%)	90.21 ± 1.02	93.26 ± 1.06	93.16 ± 0.97	58.74 ± 0.53
RBF Accuracy (%)	**90.21 ± 0.63**	93.42 ± 0.43	**93.26 ± 0.82**	50.36 ± 0.75
χ^2 Accuracy (%)	89.82 ± 0.33	**93.59 ± 0.96**	93.15 ± 0.70	60.18 ± 0.59

Table 3. Classification results using L1R-LRC under multiplication fusion with two features

Two features	Accuracy (%)
Bag of SIFT, Tree of c-shapes	89.05 ± 0.97
Bag of SIFT, DisCLBP	90.16 ± 0.71
Bag of SIFT, Bag of colors	**90.37 ± 0.72**
Tree of c-shapes, DisCLBP	87.89 ± 0.78
Tree of c-shapes, Bag of colors	88.58 ± 0.35
DisCLBP, Bag of colors	88.46 ± 0.46

Table 4. Classification results using L1R-LRC under multiplication fusion with three features

Three features	Accuracy (%)
Bag of SIFT, Tree of c-shapes, DisCLBP	91.89 ± 0.51
Bag of SIFT, Tree of c-shapes, Bag of colors	**93.84 ± 0.47**
Bag of SIFT, DisCLBP ,Bag of colors	93.79 ± 0.60
Tree of c-shapes, DisCLBP, Bag of colors	92.68 ± 0.79

Meanwhile, we have redone the two-level classification experiments using L1R-LRC under multiplication fusion with two and three features, and the corresponding classification results are shown in Table 3 and Table 4. It is clear that the overall performance with two features is worse than three features, and the performance with three features is inferior to four features. The results show the benefits and complementarities of the four features we chose.

For comparison, we also give results for two competitive methods in Table 5. In the "sparse coding-based multiple feature combination (SCMF)" method [6], *SIFT, CH, LTP-HF* were processed with the same dictionary size 512. In the "logistic regression-based feature fusion (LRFF)" method [7], the descriptors *SIFT+Hue+CN+Opp.SIFT* were with sizes of 1024+300+300+2000. The comparative results demonstrate the effectiveness of our hierarchical multiple feature fusion method.

Table 5. Performance comparison with state-of -the-art methods on 19-class

Method	SCMF	LRFF	Ours
Accuracy (%)	92.75 ± 0.64	91.26 ± 0.47	**94.53 ± 1.01**

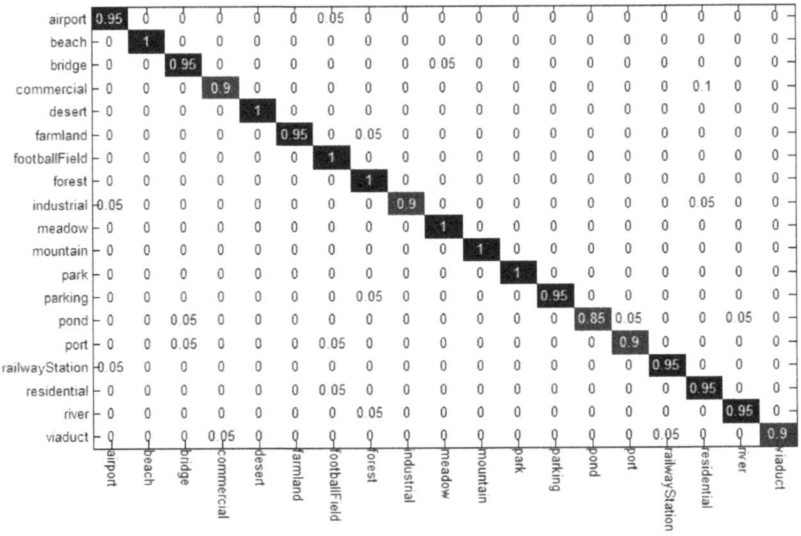

	airport	beach	bridge	commercial	desert	farmland	footballField	forest	industrial	meadow	mountain	park	parking	pond	port	railwayStation	residential	river	viaduct
airport	0.95	0	0	0	0	0	0.05	0	0	0	0	0	0	0	0	0	0	0	0
beach	0	1	0	0	0	0	0	0	0	0	0	0	0	0	0	0	0	0	0
bridge	0	0	0.95	0	0	0	0	0	0	0.05	0	0	0	0	0	0	0	0	0
commercial	0	0	0	0.9	0	0	0	0	0	0	0	0	0	0	0	0	0.1	0	0
desert	0	0	0	0	1	0	0	0	0	0	0	0	0	0	0	0	0	0	0
farmland	0	0	0	0	0	0.95	0	0.05	0	0	0	0	0	0	0	0	0	0	0
footballField	0	0	0	0	0	0	1	0	0	0	0	0	0	0	0	0	0	0	0
forest	0	0	0	0	0	0	0	1	0	0	0	0	0	0	0	0	0	0	0
industrial	0.05	0	0	0	0	0	0	0	0.9	0	0	0	0	0	0	0	0.05	0	0
meadow	0	0	0	0	0	0	0	0	0	1	0	0	0	0	0	0	0	0	0
mountain	0	0	0	0	0	0	0	0	0	0	1	0	0	0	0	0	0	0	0
park	0	0	0	0	0	0	0	0	0	0	0	1	0	0	0	0	0	0	0
parking	0	0	0	0	0	0	0	0.05	0	0	0	0	0.95	0	0	0	0	0	0
pond	0	0	0.05	0	0	0	0	0	0	0	0	0	0	0.85	0.05	0	0	0.05	0
port	0	0	0.05	0	0	0	0.05	0	0	0	0	0	0	0	0.9	0	0	0	0
railwayStation	0.05	0	0	0	0	0	0	0	0	0	0	0	0	0	0	0.95	0	0	0
residential	0	0	0	0	0	0	0.05	0	0	0	0	0	0	0	0	0	0.95	0	0
river	0	0	0	0	0	0	0	0.05	0	0	0	0	0	0	0	0	0	0.95	0
viaduct	0	0	0	0.05	0	0	0	0	0	0	0	0	0	0	0	0.05	0	0	0.9

Fig. 2. Confusion matrix of the 19-class satellite scene using our classification method

In particular, using L1R-LRC under multiplication fusion, our method can even achieve a overwhelming accuracy of 95.26%, which exceeds the highest accuracy 93.62% previously obtained in [6]. An overview of the best performance from one run of our approach for all 19 categories is given by the confusion matrix presented in Figure 2. Performance is measured as the average classification accuracy per class. Totally 7 classes of satellite scenes achieve 100% classification accuracy using our fusion method. The visually complex classes appear to be the main source of confusion. Especially some scenes that should belong to commercial area are misclassified into residential area, perhaps because commercial area images often contain patterns such as dense houses, horizontal and vertical lines which are also characteristics of residential area images. In addition, it is not surprising that pond areas filled with waters are easily classified into ports and rivers.

3.2   21-Class Land-Use Dataset

Data Description. To provide more comprehensive analysis, the 21-class land-use dataset was additionally introduced, and it has been quantitatively evaluated in the literature [8]. The dataset consists of 21 classes of images which was manually extracted from aerial orthoimagery with a pixel resolution of one foot, including agricultural, airplane, baseball diamond, beach, buildings, chaparral, dense residential, forest, freeway, golf course, harbor, intersection, medium density residential, mobile home park, overpass, parking lot, river, runway, sparse residential, storage tanks, and tennis courts. Each class separately contains 100 images with 256×256 pixels. To make a quantitative comparison with representative methods [6,7], we chose 80 samples of each class for training and 20 for test. This setup was selected based on the comparative evaluation of [8], which just applied one feature and the best classification accuracy was only 76.81%. At the same time, the experiments were also repeated over five runs.

Implementation Details and Results. Similar to the case of 19-class satellite scene, the parameter configuration was also selected by a linear search process. Table 6 shows the performance comparison with different type of features indendently using HIK-SVM across all 21 classes of land-use scene. We can observe that all features work very well. Thus, there is a need to reasonably combine these four features to further improve the classification performance, certainly feature concatenation is a general alternative. As expected, using soft probabilities from four feature channels together, our proposed data fusion strategies drastically improve the performance, which is in consistence with the results of the 19-class satellite scene. Under maximum, sum and concatenation, the performance of L1R-LRC is almost on a par with other kernels, while far more surpasses others under multiplication fusion. From Table 7 we can draw up a same conclusion that our level-II implementation with L1R-LRC under multiplication fusion satisfies the optimal configuration.

In addition, we also compared our approach with SCMF (*SIFT+CH+LTP-HF* with sizes of 512+512+512) [6] and LRFF (*SIFT+Hue+CN+Opp.SIFT* with sizes of 512+300+300+1000) [7] on the 21-class dataset. Table 8 shows the overall results of these representative methods.

Table 6. Performance comparison with different features using HIK-SVM on 21-class

Feature	Dimension	Accuracy (%)
Bag of SIFT	512	83.33 ± 1.64
Tree of c-shapes	1400	**83.52 ± 0.94**
DisCLBP	~ 2000	82.52 ± 1.75
Bag of colors	512	83.46 ± 1.57
concatenation	~ 4424	89.48 ± 0.81

Table 7. Performance comparison of different fusions using different kernels on 21-class

Fusion method	Maximum	Sum	Concatenation	Multiplication
L1R-LR Accuracy (%)	89.43 ± 0.98	91.38 ± 0.69	91.19 ± 1.24	**92.38 ± 0.62**
LRMK Accuracy (%)	**89.68 ± 1.09**	91.48 ± 0.56	91.14 ± 0.86	73.33 ± 0.84
HIK Accuracy (%)	89.57 ± 0.83	**91.62 ± 0.83**	91.57 ± 1.06	77.14 ± 0.58
RBF Accuracy (%)	89.57 ± 0.83	91.52 ± 1.03	91.52 ± 0.61	71.67 ± 0.31
χ^2 Accuracy (%)	88.86 ± 0.37	91.33 ± 0.52	**91.57 ± 0.30**	80.81 ± 0.56

Table 8. Performance comparison with state-of -the-art methods on 21-class

Method	SCMF	LRFF	Ours
Accuracy (%)	91.03 ± 0.48	90.76 ± 0.59	**92.38 ± 0.62**

Compared to the results reported in the literature [6,7], our proposed method is capable of gaining the best performance of 92.62%. To get a convincing completion, confusion matrice from one run of our method demonstrating the highest classification rate on the 21-class dataset is shown in Figure 3. On the whole, 9 land-use classes are absolutely recognized by our proposed method. Of course, there are also a few explainable confusions between some classes. It is obvious that there exists certain resemblance in the structure and texture between baseball diamond and storage tanks, and many buildings are just next to the airport. In particular, the most difficult categories are dense residential and medium density residential. This can be explained by the fact that both categories share similar image components such as trees, buildings and roads. These are partial factors for misclassifications.

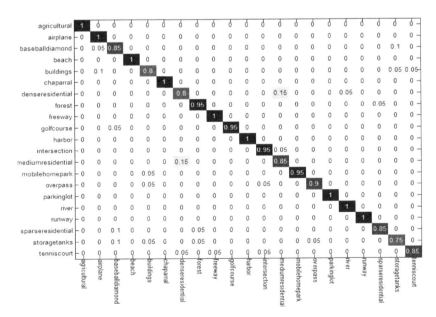

Fig. 3. Confusion matrix of the 21-class land-use dataset using our classification method

4   Conclusions and Future Work

This paper has presented a hierarchical multiple feature fusion approach for high-resolution satellite scene categorization. More specifically, we made three main contributions. First, we selectively extracted four complementary image descriptors. Further, we used HIK-SVM and L1R-LRC in different classification stages. Above all, the posteriori information we applied in Level-II classification was the product of four probabilities from Level-I outputs. Based on the presented experimental results and analysis, we can conclude that the proposed two-level classification model can yield state-of-the-art results. Furthermore, our classification model is also flexible to other extensions, such as new features, classifiers, and fusion methods. In future work, we will also extend our work to large-scale satellite scene categorization.

Acknowledgments. The research was supported in part by the Chinese National Natural Sciences Foundation grants (NSFC) 61271401 and China Postdoctoral Science Foundation (CPSF) 20110491187.

References

1. Dai, D.-X., Yang, W.: Satellite Image Classification via Two-layer Sparse Coding with Biased Image. IEEE Geoscience and Remote Sensing Letters 8, 173–176 (2011)
2. Amarsaikhan, D., Douglas, T.: Data Fusion and Multisource Image Classification. International Journal of Remote Sensing 25, 3529–3539 (2004)
3. Li, C.-S., Castelli, V.: Deriving Texture Feature Set for Content-Based Retrieval of Satellite Image Database. In: Proceedings of International Conference on Image Processing, vol. 1, pp. 576–579 (1997)
4. Xia, G.-S., Yang, W., Delon, J., Gousseau, Y., Sun, H., Maitre, H.: Structural High-resolution Satellite Image Indexing. In: Proceedings of ISPRS, pp. 298–303 (2010)
5. Gehler, P., Nowozin, S.: On Feature Combination Methods for Multiclass Object Classification. In: IEEE International Conference on Computer Vision, pp. 221–228 (2009)
6. Sheng, G.-F., Yang, W., Xu, T., Sun, H.: High-resolution Satellite Scene Classification Using Sparse Coding Based Multiple Features Combination. International Journal of Remote Sensing 33, 2395–2412 (2012)
7. Fernando, B., Fromont, E., Muselet, D., Sebban, M.: Discriminative Feature Fusion for Image Classification. In: IEEE International Conference on Computer Vision and Pattern Recognition (CVPR 2012) (2012)
8. Yang, Y., Newsam, S.: Bag-of-visual-words and Spatial Extensions for Land-use Classification. In: ACM SIGSPATIAL GIS, California, America (2010)
9. Guo, Y.-M., Zhao, G.-Y., Pietikäinen, M.: Discriminative Features for Texture Description. Pattern Recognition 45(10), 3834–3843 (2012)
10. Wengert, C., Douze, M., Jégou, H.: Bag-of-colors for Improved Image Search. In: Association for Computing Machinery, Multimedia (2011)
11. Maji, S., Berg, A.C., Malik, J.: Classification Using Intersection Kernel Support Vector Machines is Efficient. In: Proceedings of IEEE Computer Society Conference on Computer Vision and Pattern Recognition (2008)
12. Lee, S.I., Lee, H., Abbeel, P., Andrew, Y.N.: Efficient L1 Regularized Logistic Regression. In: Proceedings of the Twenty-First National Conference on Artificial Intelligence (AAAI 2006), Boston, MA, USA (2006)

A Validation Benchmark for Assessment of Medial Surface Quality for Medical Applications

Agnés Borràs, Debora Gil, Sergio Vera, and Miguel Angel González

Computer Vision Center, Comp. Science Dep. UAB, Spain
Alma I.T. Systems, Barcelona, Spain
{agnesba,debora}@cvc.uab.es,
{sergio.vera,miguel.gonzalez}@alma3d.com

Abstract. Confident use of medial surfaces in medical decision support systems requires evaluating their quality for detecting pathological deformations and describing anatomical volumes. Validation in the medical imaging field is a challenging task mainly due to the difficulties for getting consensual ground truth. In this paper we propose a validation benchmark for assessing medial surfaces in the context of medical applications. Our benchmark includes a home-made database of synthetic medial surfaces and volumes and specific scores for evaluating surface accuracy, its stability against volume deformations and its capabilities for accurate reconstruction of anatomical volumes.

Keywords: Medial Surfaces, Shape Representation, Medical Applications, Performance Evaluation.

1 Introduction

Medial manifolds (skeletons in 1D, medial surfaces in 2D) are powerful descriptors of shapes that have been used in many computer vision areas such as object recognition, computer graphics, animation or shape modelling [23,10,2]. Their associated medial representation [1] defines a coordinate system for volumetric shapes that allows easy localization of internal points from the volume boundary surface. Given the usefulness of such a coordinate system, in recent years several medial representations have been adapted to medical imaging tasks:

- *Localization of injured tissue.* The radial coordinate of medial representations allows parameterizing [7,16] the (possibly diseased) parenchyma of organs, as well as their internal vascular system, powerful sources of information in organ functionality, analysis and diagnosis
- *Segmentation of medical images.* Techniques such as M-Reps [4] and CM-Reps [25] have shown the potential to describe complex shapes in a versatile manner. Using information of a medial surface for medical imaging segmentation has proven to improve segmentation results [12,19]. It follows that deformable medial modelling has been used in a variety of medical imaging analysis applications, including computational neuroanatomy [27,17], 3D cardiac modelling [18] or cancer treatment planning [15,3].

M. Chen, B. Leibe, and B. Neumann (Eds.): ICVS 2013, LNCS 7963, pp. 334–343, 2013.
© Springer-Verlag Berlin Heidelberg 2013

- *Anatomy Modelling.* In shape analysis, medial representations can model not only the shape but also the interior variations [26]. Medial manifolds of organs have proved robust and accurate to study group differences in internal structures of the brain [17,16]. They also provide more intuitive and easily interpretable representations of complex organs [24] and their relative positions [11].

In order to be suitable for the above listed tasks, anatomical medial manifolds should satisfy some requirements. First, they should be simple enough to allow an easy generation of the radial coordinate, as well as, provide a good representation of organs positions and shapes. A main requirement for a confident representation of shapes valid for clinical applications is that medial manifolds present branches that correspond to changes in object boundary convexity [5]. In this manner, they could be useful for detecting pathological components [22]. Finally, medial surfaces should reach a compromise between simplicity and a satisfactory reconstruction of the whole volume. In particular, they should ensure that finest details on the organ boundary are preserved in order to allow early identification of pathological deformations.

Although there are plenty of approaches addressing computation of medial surfaces, existing methods often generate useless spikes or loose connectivity at main branches. A main concern is that validation of accuracy of medial surfaces for medical applications lacks of a solid benchmark. Validation in the medical imaging field is a delicate issue due to the difficulties for generating ground truth data and quantitative scores valid for reliable application to clinical practice.

We propose a benchmark for evaluating medial surface quality in the context of medical applications. The benchmark is divided in three tests. The first test evaluates the quality of the medial surface generated, the second one checks medial branch stability for detection of volume deformations and the third one explores the capabilities of the generated surfaces to recover the original volume and describing anatomical structures. We have applied our benchmark to two representative algorithms for medial surface computation in order to illustrate its performance.

2   Validation Benchmark

In order to address the representation of organs for medical use, medial representations should achieve a good reconstruction of the full anatomy and guarantee that the boundaries of the organ are reached from the medial surface. Given that small differences in algorithm criteria can generate different surfaces, we are interested in evaluating the quality of the generated manifold as a tool to recover the original shape. In this context, a validation benchmark should cover three topics:

1. **Medial Surface Accuracy.** Representations of the original anatomical geometry are accurate as far as the extracted medial manifold satisfies three main properties [13]: 1) preservation of the topology of the original object

(homotopy); 2) one-pixel thin structures (thinness); 3) structures equidistant to object boundaries (medialness). A first test should evaluate to what extent medial surfaces satisfy these 3 quality requirements.

2. **Medial Surface Stability.** A main requirement for a confident representation of shapes valid for clinical applications is the stability of medial manifolds under perturbations of the object boundary [14]. In order to fully describe anatomical shapes, medial manifolds should present branches that correspond to changes in object boundary convexity [5]. A second test should evaluate the stability of the medial surface branches for known volumes undergoing a controlled deformation.

3. **Medial Surface Reconstruction Power.** For a confident application in medical applications, medial representation have to achieve a good reconstruction of the full anatomy and guarantee that the boundaries of the organ are reached from the medial surface [22]. Therefore, a third test should assess the capabilities of the generated surfaces to recover the original volume and describing anatomical structures.

In order to illustrate our validation benchmark, we have applied it to two representative methods of current approaches to medial surface computation. The ridge based method (labelled $GSM2$) described in [21] and the morphological thinning approach (labelled $Th26P$) described in [13].

2.1 Medial Surface Accuracy

Surface quality tests start from known medial surfaces, that will be considered as ground truth. From these surfaces, volumetric objects can be generated by placing spheres of different radii at each point of the surface. The newly created object is the input to medial surface algorithms, which output is compared to the surfaces used to generate synthetic volumes.

The test set of synthetic volumes / surfaces aims to cover different key aspects of medial surface generation (see first row in Fig.1). The first batch of surfaces (labelled 'Simple') includes objects generated with a single medial surface. A second batch of surfaces is generated using two intersecting medial surfaces (labelled 'Multiple'), while a last batch of objects (labelled 'Homotopy') covers shapes with different number of holes. We have used a 3D modelling software called 3D Studio Max to produce the ground truth medial sufaces containig several deformations and holes. Surfaces are exported to voxel format in Matlab where the volumes are computed.

The volumetric object obtained from a surface can be generated either using spheres of uniform radii (identified as 'UnifDist') or spheres of varying radii (identified as 'VarDist'). Volumes are constructed by assigning a radial coordinate to each medial point. In the case of UnifDist, all medial points have the same radial value, while for VarDist they are assigned a value in the range $[r_1, r_2]$ using a polynomial. The values of the radial coordinate must be in a range ensuring that volumes will not present self intersections. Therefore, the maximum range and procedure this radius is assigned depends on the medial topology:

- *Simple.* In this case, there are no restrictions on the radial range.
- *Multiple.* For branching medial surfaces, especial care must be taken at surface self-intersecting points. At these locations, radii have to be below the maximum value that ensures the medial representation defines a local coordinate change [8]. This maximum value depends on the principal curvatures of the intersecting surfaces [8] and it is computed for each surface. Let X be the medial surface, Z denote the self-intersection points and $d(Z)$ the distance map to Z. The radial coordinate is assigned as follows:

$$R(X) = min(R(X), max(r_Z, d(Z)))$$

for $R(X)$ the value of the polynomial function and r_Z the maximum value allowed at self-intersections. In this manner, we obtain a smooth distribution of the radii ensuring volume integrity.

- *Homotopy.* In order to be consistent with the third main property of medial surfaces [13], volumes must preserve all holes of medial surfaces. In order to do so, the maximum radius r_2 is set to be under the minimum of all surface holes radii. In the case that the medial surface contains multiple branches, r_2 is also set to be under the radius of the self-intersection points r_Z.

Our database, which is publicly available [6], has a total number of 120 samples, distributed in 6 families (20 samples each) covering the 3 medial topologies and the 2 volume distance types. Figure 1 shows an example of the synthetic volumes in the first row (labelled GT). Columns exemplify the different families of volumes generated: one (Simple in 1st and 2nd columns) and two (Multiple in 3rd and 4th columns) foil surfaces, as well as, surfaces with holes (Homotopy in 5th and 6th columns). For each kind of topology we show a volume generated with constant (1st, 3rd and 5th columns) and variable distance (2nd, 4th and last columns). We show medial surfaces in solid meshes and the synthetic volume in semi-transparent color.

The quality of medial surfaces has been assessed by comparing them to ground truth surfaces in terms of surface distance [9]. The distance of a voxel y to a surface X is given by: $d_X(y) = min_{x \in X} \|y - x\|$, for $\| \cdot \|$ the Euclidean norm. If we denote by X the reference surface and Y the computed one, the scores considered are:

1. *Standard Surface Distances*:

$$AD = \frac{1}{\#Y} \sum_{y \in Y} d_X(y) \qquad MD = \max_{y \in Y}(d_X(y))$$

for $\#$ the number of elements of a set.

2. *Symmetric Surface Distances*:

$$ASD = \frac{1}{\#X + \#Y} \left(\sum_{x \in X} d_Y(x) + \sum_{y \in Y} d_X(y) \right)$$

	Simple		Multiple		Homotopy	
	UnifDist	VarDist	UnifDist	VarDist	UnifDist	VarDist
GT	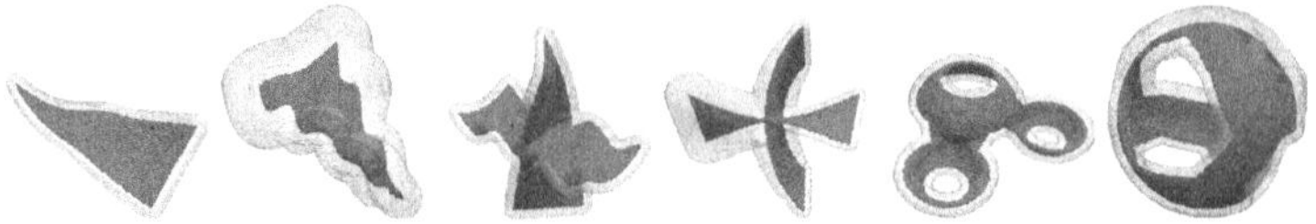					
Th26P	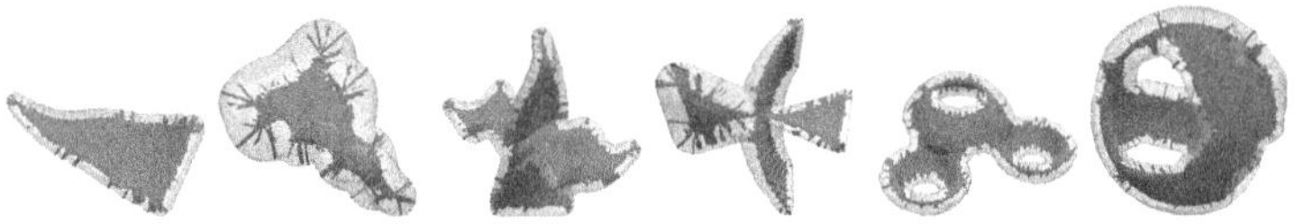					
AD, MD	0.6, 5.5	3.3, 16.2	0.7, 5.6	1.4, 10.7	0.6, 5.5	1.3, 12.1
ASD, MSD	0.5, 5.5	1.9, 16.1	0.5, 5.6	1.1, 11.1	0.4, 5.7	0.8, 11.0
GSM2	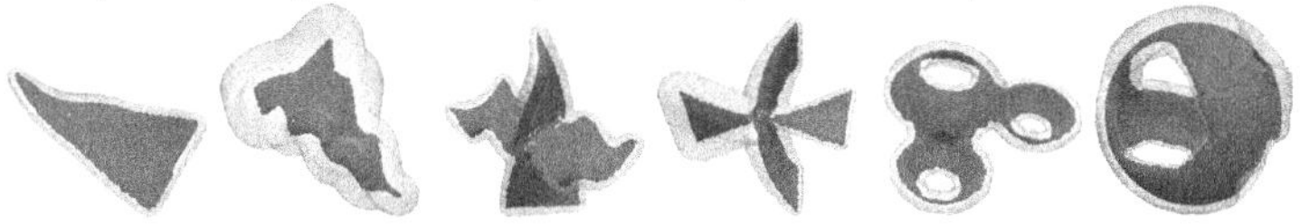					
AD, MD	0.3, 3.0	0.3, 4.6	0.4, 3.6	0.4, 4.8	0.4, 3.4	0.3, 3.7
ASD, MSD	0.3, 3.1	0.3, 4.1	0.4, 4.1	0.4, 4.8	0.3, 3.4	0.3, 3.7

Fig. 1. Representative examples of the data base medial surfaces and the medial accuracy validation

$$MSD = \max \left(\max_{x \in X}(d_Y(x)), \max_{y \in Y}(d_X(y)) \right)$$

All distance scores are in the range $[0, \inf)$, being 0 the best matching.

Standard distances measure deviation from medialness, while differences between standard and symmetric distances indicate the presence of homotopy artifacts and presence of unnecessary medial segments. Figure 1 shows an example of the computed medial surfaces using $GSM2$ and $Th26P$, as well as, their quality scores for the shown surfaces. The visual quality of the morphological $Th26P$ is worse by the presence of multiple spikes. We note that extra spikes in surfaces are detected by higher distance scores.

2.2   Medial Surface Stability

Stability of medial surfaces is checked by assessing that their branches correspond to changes in object boundary convexity for known volumes undergoing a controlled deformation. The volumes generated for assessment of medial surface accuracy have been deformed in order to generate branches at specific sites. These sites are points selected among a triangular mesh of the volume boundary. For each point, we displace its position, $\overrightarrow{P}$, a given distance, δ_P, along the boundary normal direction at the point, $\overrightarrow{N}_P$:

$$\overrightarrow{P} \rightarrow \overrightarrow{P} + \delta_P \overrightarrow{N}_P$$

Fig. 2. Generation of volume spikes from original ground truth volumes

for $\delta_P \in [0, D_{max}]$. It should be clear that volume spikes should generate a medial branch if their height is large enough to introduce a significant change in volume boundary curvature. Therefore, normal distances are gradually increased from 0 to a maximum distance D_{max} in order to check the critical deformation that generates a new branch. Given that for $\delta_P = 0$, we have the original volumes, the connected components of the difference between volumes for $\delta_P = 0$ and $\delta_P > 0$ is the collection of volume spikes, namely $\mathcal{VS} = \{VS_i\}_{i=1}^{N_{VS}}$ generated by the deformation process. Figure 2 shows an example of the volume deformation process. The left mesh shows an original ground truth volume which has been deformed to the mesh shown in the middle. The most-right image shows the deformed volume with its spikes in green and the volume for $\delta_P = 0$ in red.

Medial surfaces for $\delta_P = 0$ give the baseline accuracy by comparison to the database ground truth surfaces [20]. For $\delta_P > 0$, computed medial surfaces should generate new branches for each volume spike if the deformation size δ_P is large enough to introduce a significant change in volume curvature. Branches not arising from volumetric spikes changing boundary convexity profile are useless and should as least as possible.

The quality of medial branching arising from volumetric spikes has been assessed in terms of spike detection and its accurate localization. Branches arising from the volume deformation are given by the connected components of the difference between medial surfaces for $\delta_P = 0$ and $\delta_P > 0$. We will note them by $\{B_j\}_{j=1}^{N_B}$. Spike detection rate has been measured in terms of medial branch false and true positives A branch is considered a true positive if it intersects any of the volume spikes VS_i. In order to measure the impact of false branches arising during volume deformation (i.e. detection instability), we have also considered the percentage of area that false positives represent over all medial branches:

1. *Detection Rates*:

$$TB = \frac{\#\{VS_i \text{ s. t. } \exists B_j, \, B_j \bigcap VS_i \neq \emptyset\}}{N_{VS}}$$

2. *Detection Instability*:

$$DIA = 100 \frac{\sum_{B_j \bigcap VS_i = \emptyset} \|B_j\|}{\sum_{j=1}^{N_B} \|B_j\|}$$

for $\| \cdot \|$ denoting the area of a surface.

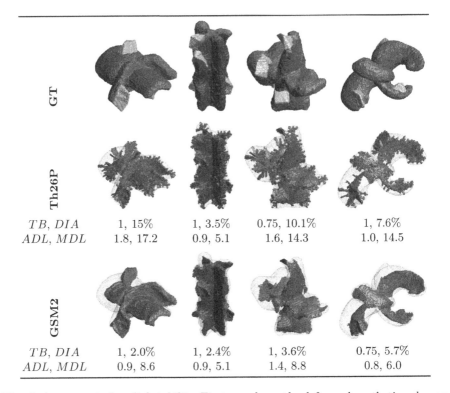

TB, DIA	1, 15%	1, 3.5%	0.75, 10.1%	1, 7.6%
ADL, MDL	1.8, 17.2	0.9, 5.1	1.6, 14.3	1.0, 14.5
TB, DIA	1, 2.0%	1, 2.4%	1, 3.6%	0.75, 5.7%
ADL, MDL	0.9, 8.6	0.9, 5.1	1.4, 8.8	0.8, 6.0

Fig. 3. Assessment of medial stability. First row shows the deformed synthetic volumes, 2nd and 3rd computed medial surfaces and stability scores.

TB is the range $[0,1]$, with best performance achieved for $TB = 1$ and DIA is in the range $[0,100]$ with best value for 0%.

We define spike localization in terms of the distance to the volume spikes, namely d_{VS}, and the ground truth medial surfaces, namely d_X. For each point in computed medial surfaces $y \in Y$, we have that the minimum between $d_X(y)$ and $d_{VS}(y)$ reflects a compromise between medial branches size and its proximity to a volume spike. Let $DL(y) := min(d_X(y), d_{VS}(y))$ denote such minimum. Then, our localization scores are given by the average and maximum values of DL over the computed surface:

1. *Spike Localization*:

$$ADL = \frac{1}{\#Y} \sum_{y \in Y} DL(y) \quad MDL = \max_{y \in Y} DL(y)$$

Spikes are best localized when ADL and MDL take value 0.

Figure 3 illustrates assessment of medial branch stability for $GSM2$ and $Th26P$. The detection rate TB drops as a main volume spike is lost as it clearly illustrates the last surface computed using $GSM2$. Meanwhile, DIA scores perfectly agree with the visual quality of surfaces and increase in the presence of

Th26P extra spikes. Finally, distance scores also detect extra structures not associated to a volume spike.

2.3   Reconstruction Power for Clinical Applications

In medical imaging applications the aim is to generate the simplest medial surface that allows recovering the original volume without losing significant voxels. Volumes recovered from surfaces generated with the different methods are compared with ground truth volumes. Volumes are reconstructed by computing the medial representation [1] with radius given by the values of the distance map on the computed medial surfaces.

Let A, B be, respectively, the original and reconstructed volumes and ∂A, ∂B, their boundary surface. Completeness of reconstructed volumes is assessed using the following volumetric and distance measures:

1. *Volume Overlap Error:*

$$VOE(A, B) = 100 \times \left(1 - 2\frac{\|A \cap B\|}{\|A\| + \|B\|}\right)$$

2. *Maximum Volume Boundary Difference:*

$$MVD = \max\left(\max_{x \in \delta A}(d_{\delta B}(x)),\ \max_{y \in \delta B}(d_{\delta A}(y))\right)$$

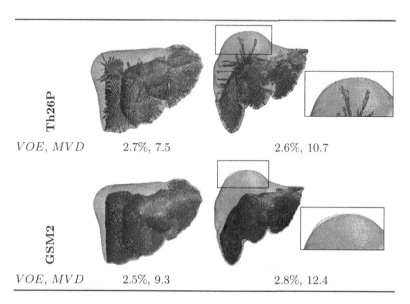

Th26P		
VOE, MVD	2.7%, 7.5	2.6%, 10.7
GSM2		
VOE, MVD	2.5%, 9.3	2.8%, 12.4

Fig. 4. Reconstruction Power for Clinical Applications

The minimum error in the reconstruction is observed when VOE and MVD are 0, where $VOE \in [0, 100]$ and $MVD \in [0, \inf)$. We would like to note that reconstruction scores do not require a ground truth for medial surfaces, only volumes. Therefore they can be computed over any database.

Figure 4 illustrates assessment of reconstruction power for clinical applications. In order to provide a real scenario for the reconstruction tests we have used livers from the SLIVER07 challenge [9] as a source of anatomical volumes. Volumes reconstructed using the computed medial surfaces (colored in red) are shown in transparent blue over true anatomical volumes shown in transparent gray. Difference between reconstructions and original volumes is better appreciated in the right image close-ups of the liver lobe. Gross differences between volumes are detected by VOE and, in spite of the right liver lobe, none of the cases seem to be significantly better. In medical applications, restoring local deformations can be important for early diagnosis. In this context, the surface distance score MVD is suitable for detection of local differences.

3   Conclusions

We have presented a complete benchmark for evaluating medial surface generation in the context of shape description. Our benchmark includes a battery of synthetic medial surfaces and volumes that cover different medial topologies and volume deformations. We have also defined several scores for measuring 3 different quality aspects: accuracy, stability and reconstruction power. Our benchmark has been applied to 2 representative methods for medial computation. Results show that the proposed scores and methodologies agree with the visual quality of surfaces and, thus, they are valid for quantitative systematic evaluation.

Acknowledgments. Work supported by Spanish projects TIN2009-13618, TIN2012-33116, the Catalan project 2009-TEM-00007 and **HEAR-EU**.

References

1. Blum, H.: A transformation for extracting descriptors of shape. MIT Press (1967)
2. Chang, M., Leymarie, F., Kimia, B.: 3d shape registration using regularized medial scaffolds. In: Proc. 3DPVT, pp. 987–994 (2004)
3. Crouch, J.R., Pizer, S.M., Chaney, E.L., Hu, Y.-C., Mageras, G.S., Zaider, M.: Automated Finite-Element analysis for deformable registration of prostate images. IEEE Transactions on Medical Imaging 26(10), 1379–1390 (2007)
4. Fletcher, P.T., Lu, C., et al.: Principal Geodesic Analysis for the study of nonlinear statistics of shape. IEEE Trans. Med. Imag. 23(8), 995–1005 (2004)
5. Giblin, P.J., Kimia, B.B., Pollitt, A.J.: Transitions of the 3d medial axis under a one-parameter family of deformations. PAMI 31(5), 900–918 (2009)
6. Gil, D., Borràs, A.: Medial surfaces database, http://iam.cvc.uab.es/downloads/medial-surfaces-database (accessed: April 25, 2013)
7. Gil, D., Garcia-Barnes, J., Hernandez, A.A.: Manifold parametrization of the left ventricle for a statistical modelling of its complete anatomy. In: SPIE 2001. LNCS, pp. 304–314 (2010)

8. Gray, A.: Tubes. Birkhäuser (2004)
9. Heimann, T., van Ginneken, B., Styner, M.A., Arzhaeva, Y., Aurich, V.: Comparison and evaluation of methods for liver segmentation from CT datasets. IEEE Trans. Med. Imag. 28(8), 1251–1265 (2009)
10. Keim, D., Panse, C., North, S.C.: Medial-axis-based cartograms. IEEE Comput. Graph. Appl. 25, 60–68 (2005)
11. Liu, X., Linguraru, M.G., Yao, J., Summers, R.M.: Organ pose distribution model and an MAP framework for automated abdominal multi-organ localization. In: Liao, H., "Eddie" Edwards, P.J., Pan, X., Fan, Y., Yang, G.-Z. (eds.) MIAR 2010. LNCS, vol. 6326, pp. 393–402. Springer, Heidelberg (2010)
12. Pizer, S.M., Fletcher, P.T., et al.: A method and software for segmentation of anatomic object ensembles by deformable M-Reps. Medical Physics 32(5), 1335–1345 (2005)
13. Pudney, C.: Distance-ordered homotopic thinning: A skeletonization algorithm for 3D digital images. Comp. Vis. Imag. Underst. 72(2), 404–413 (1998)
14. Siddiqi, K., Zhang, J., Macrini, D., et al.: Retrieving articulated 3-d models using medial surfaces. Mach. Vis. Appl. 19(4), 261–275 (2008)
15. Stough, J.V., Broadhurst, R.E., Pizer, S.M., Chaney, E.L.: Regional appearance in deformable model segmentation. In: Karssemeijer, N., Lelieveldt, B. (eds.) IPMI 2007. LNCS, vol. 4584, pp. 532–543. Springer, Heidelberg (2007)
16. Styner, M., Gerig, G., Lieberman, J., Jones, D., Weinberger, D.: Statistical shape analysis of neuroanatomical structures based on medial models. Med. Im. Ana. 7(3), 207–220 (2003)
17. Styner, M., Lieberman, J.A., Pantazis, D., Gerig, G.: Boundary and medial shape analysis of the hippocampus in schizophrenia. Medical Image Analysis 8(3), 197–203 (2004)
18. Sun, H., Avants, B.B., Frangi, A.F., Sukno, F., Gee, J.C., Yushkevich, P.A.: Cardiac medial modeling and time-course heart wall thickness analysis. In: Metaxas, D., Axel, L., Fichtinger, G., Székely, G. (eds.) MICCAI 2008, Part II. LNCS, vol. 5242, pp. 766–773. Springer, Heidelberg (2008)
19. Sun, H., Frangi, A.F., Wang, H., Sukno, F.M., Tobon-Gomez, C., Yushkevich, P.A.: Automatic cardiac mri segmentation using a biventricular deformable medial model. In: Jiang, T., Navab, N., Pluim, J.P.W., Viergever, M.A. (eds.) MICCAI 2010, Part I. LNCS, vol. 6361, pp. 468–475. Springer, Heidelberg (2010)
20. Vera, S., Gil, D., Borras, A., George Linguraru, M., Gonzalez, M.A.: Geometric steerable medial maps. Machine Vision Applications (in press)
21. Vera, S., Gil, D., Borràs, A., Sánchez, X., Pérez, F., Linguraru, M.G., González Ballester, M.A.: Computation and evaluation of medial surfaces for shape representation of abdominal organs. In: Yoshida, H., Sakas, G., Linguraru, M.G. (eds.) Abdominal Imaging. LNCS, vol. 7029, pp. 223–230. Springer, Heidelberg (2012)
22. Vera, S., Gonzalez, M.A., Gil, D.: A medial map capturing the essential geometry of organs. In: Proceedings of ISBI. IEEE (2012)
23. Wade, L., Parent, R.E.: Automated generation of control skeletons for use in animation. The Visual Computer 18, 97–110 (2002)
24. Yao, J., Summers, R.M.: Statistical location model for abdominal organ localization. In: Yang, G.-Z., Hawkes, D., Rueckert, D., Noble, A., Taylor, C. (eds.) MICCAI 2009, Part II. LNCS, vol. 5762, pp. 9–17. Springer, Heidelberg (2009)
25. Yushkevich, P.A.: Continuous medial representation of brain structures using the biharmonic PDE. NeuroImage 45(1), 99–110 (2009)
26. Yushkevich, P.A., Zhang, H., Gee, J.C.: Continuous medial representation for anatomical structures. IEEE Trans. Medical Imaging 25(12), 1547–1564 (2006)
27. Yushkevich, P.A., Zhang, H., Simon, T.J., Gee, J.C.: Structure-specific statistical mapping of white matter tracts. NeuroImage 41(2), 448–461 (2008)

When Is a Confidence Measure Good Enough?

Patricia Márquez-Valle[1], Debora Gil[1], Aura Hernàndez-Sabaté[1],
and Daniel Kondermann[2]

[1] Computer Vision Center, Universitat Autònoma de Barcelona
{pmarquez,debora,aura}@cvc.uab.cat
[2] Heidelberg Collaboratory for Image Processing at the IWR, University of Heidelberg
daniel.kondermann@iwr.uni-heidelberg.de

Abstract. Confidence estimation has recently become a hot topic in image processing and computer vision. Yet, several definitions exist of the term "confidence" which are sometimes used interchangeably. This is a position paper, in which we aim to give an overview on existing definitions, thereby clarifying the meaning of the used terms to facilitate further research in this field. Based on these clarifications, we develop a theory to compare confidence measures with respect to their quality.

Keywords: Optical flow, confidence measure, performance evaluation.

1 Introduction

The aim of confidence estimation in image processing can be intuitively described: Given the input as well as the output of a given algorithm (*e.g.* an image pair and a flow field), how can we evaluate the "amount of uncertainty" of the result at each pixel location? Knowing how much we can trust these results is crucial for all applications with legal obligations and possibly lethal consequences in domains such as driver assistance and medical imaging systems.

In this paper, we focus on confidence measures in dense correspondence problems such as optical flow, image registration and stereo depth estimation. Without loss of generality, we will focus on optical flow algorithms. In optical flow, the accuracy is commonly computed by the end-point error [1]. If we could estimate the accuracy of the result at each pixel, we could use this information by either improving the model or by removing all results above a given error threshold.

Yet, in general, given a model together with the input as well as output data, it is impossible to estimate the accuracy. To illustrate this case, consider the example of a white image pair (*i.e.* all pixels have equal intensity). Given that the pairing of such two images could be achieved by any flow field, the output of any optical flow method will only depend on the prior knowledge added to the model, L^2-regularization for instance. But not being able to estimate the accuracy, does not mean that we cannot find out anything about the error in the flow field. By analyzing the input data along with the model we can try to estimate the *upper bound* of the error at each pixel location. This information will not help to improve the flow field, but it reveals the *risk* of assuming that the outcome is actually correct in such location.

M. Chen, B. Leibe, and B. Neumann (Eds.): ICVS 2013, LNCS 7963, pp. 344–353, 2013.
© Springer-Verlag Berlin Heidelberg 2013

This paper contributes to analysis of confidence measures in three aspects. First, we clarify the definitions of the terms accuracy, confidence and error prediction; second, we group existing confidence measures using these terms and third, we propose an approach to assess how good a confidence measure is with respect to its capabilities for error bounding. Our explanations will be accompanied by various examples showing the usefulness of our approach. Please note that actual comparisons between existing confidence measures is beyond the scope of this paper.

1.1 Related Work

In their seminal work on optical flow evaluation, Barron et al. [2] emphasized the importance of confidence measures to examine optical flow methods and also carried out a first comparison. A few years later, Bainbridge-Smith and Lane [3] compared seven different confidence measures for two image sequences. These results have been first steps towards a comparison of confidence measures within a single framework. The importance of such a framework and a general roadmap for the evaluation of optical flow was recently discussed by an international group of researchers in [4]. In this section, we exemplarily review the literature explicitly dealing with confidence measures of several types.

Early papers were mainly based on local image properties. Chronologically, [5] only evaluate flow where the determinant of the local Hessian (i.e. the product of the eigenvectors of the second image derivatives) of the image is non-zero. In contrast to analyzing the eigenvalues of the image itself, [6] analyzes the eigenvalues of the energy distribution resulting from block-matching. This idea was later picked up and relabeled as surface measure in [7]. Similar methods can be found throughout local optical flow literature. All these measures either use the energy or the image curvature as indicators for confidence. In [8] the authors aim for a statistical analysis of the resulting flow vectors. For each pixel, they compute a two-dimensional distribution of flow vectors conditioned on the local image gradient. As the authors choose this condition to be a Gaussian based on the local image structure, this method basically is an anisotropic version of Lucas and Kanade [9] defined in a probabilistic framework. Therefore, as in [5] the inherent confidence measure is also based on local image curvature.

An early general attempt to define a type of confidence measures for global flow computation methods has been made by Bruhn et al. [10]. The authors argue that for global approaches one should always use the inverse of the energy at every pixel as a confidence measure, since it shows exactly how well the flow vectors fit the model. They compare their method to using the image gradient magnitude as confidence measure and validate the quality of the results based on sparsification curves. To create such curve, the flow field is systematically sparsified by a fixed percentage of flow vectors which are sorted according to their confidence. For each such threshold, the remaining average angular error is plotted.

Furthermore, the authors state in [10] that any other confidence measure with better performance should be integrated into the flow computation method. They conclude that for these reasons the inverse of the energy is the only real confidence measure for global optical flow methods. Hence, the authors understand the term confidence to be synonymous to error prediction. As discussed in Section 2, this holds true in the special case when not only the upper bound of the flow error can be evaluated but also a lower bound. Yet, in general, confidence estimation can only estimate upper error bounds. As a consequence, they can not be inserted into the model since a low confidence does not necessarily imply an erroneous flow vector. Besides, as explained in [11], sparsification plots are not suitable for evaluating the quality of a confidence measure. The main problem is that the removal of pixels ordered by confidence not necessarily removes pixels with high errors. This results in possibly unfair comparisons between measures.

More recently, a confidence measure has been defined based on the statistics of empirically measured distributions of flow fields [12]. They are independent of the particular model used for flow estimation and require a database of motion patterns which is representative for the application at hand. The flow field is sparsified by the continuous p-values computed from the mahalanobis distances on the previously computed principal components. The bootstrap method proposed in [13] computes the variability of the computed flow with respect to a perturbation of the variational model, by excluding randomly selected pixels in the data term. Pixels with high variability are associated to model inconsistencies and, thus, discarded. Finally, in [14], the authors train a random forest to classify errors in the flow field which are larger than a given threshold. The features used in their approach are based on a combination of all confidence measures described above, including the image data on several scales as well as the output of the algorithm itself. Sparsification is based on the continuous output of the random forests.

2   Accuracy, Confidence and Prediction

2.1   Sources of Inaccuracies

Confidence measures aim at measuring the uncertainty of flow fields at each image pixel from the input data along with the model output. Inaccuracies in the output of optical flow algorithms follow from three main reasons: Model Assumptions, Multiple Global Minima and Numerical Stability of Local Minima.

Model Assumptions. The goal of optical flow approaches is to find the vector that best matches two consecutive frames in a sequence. Given that motion vectors are at least 2D, there is not enough information in the image data alone for producing a unique solution. Consequently, optical flow algorithms need to assume some conditions on the output vector in order to compute it. Intuitively, these conditions favor a particular kind of vector field satisfying some theoretical requirements (the model assumptions) for being the final solutions to the problem. Model assumptions on optical flow can be of either analytical or probabilistic type. In the first case, the flow vector must satisfy some degree of regularity. This is usually enforced by adding the norm of the flow in some Sobolev space (usually L^2 or L^1) to a variational formulation of the optical flow problem [15]. In the second case, the flow vector should follow a given probabilistic distribution or be generated by a finite number of basic functions [15]. In any case, the restriction of possible vectors given by model assumptions might not be right for all image patches and flows. This implies that even if we have a unique stable solution, the final output might not resemble the true motion at all (see fig. 1 (a)).

Multiple Global Minima. Optical flow computation follows from the minimization of an energy functional including a data term and model assumptions. Unless simplified models are used (such as classic Horn and Schunck [16]), this functional will not be, in general, convex. Lack of convexity introduces multiple local minima that hinder the performance of gradient descent approaches based on Euler-Lagrange equations. On one hand, varying initial conditions might lead to different solutions. On the other hand, the iterative solution might get trapped in a saddle point not reaching a minimum of the energy. Multiple minima follow from non-convexity of the energy functional that is minimizing. Although theoretically convexity can be analyzed by means of the second derivative of the variational [15], in practice it is difficult to have a friendly analytical expression and some sort of heuristics should be used. Besides, a main concern is that, even if we are able to find all possible local minima, there might not be any objective criterion to decide which is the optimal solution. This uncertainty is illustrated in the plot representing an energy function shown in figure 1(b). The energy has three local minima (depicted by dots) that have equal energy and, thus, are also global.

Numerical Stability of Local Minima. The minimum of the energy modeling optical flow requires a numeric scheme in almost all cases. In this setting, it is important ensuring that any variability in the input data will not introduce a large deviation in the solution (see bottom sketches in fig.1(c)). In mathematical numerical analysis this is called error propagation or numerical stability [17]. The main concern of numerical stability is to bound errors of the output data (ε_{out}) in terms of the error of the input data (ε_{in}) by means of a constant K such that $\|\varepsilon_{out}\| < \text{K} \cdot \|\varepsilon_{in}\|$ for $\|\cdot\|$ a given norm of the space the data belongs to, usually $\mathbb{R}^n$. The constant K is an intrinsic property of the algorithm and it is computed using the energy derivatives [17]. In the special case of local minima, error propagation is directly related to the flatness of the energy around each local solution. Intuitively, if the energy local profile at a minimum is flat, the number of points locally having a low energy value increases. Thus, the position of the local minimum is less accurate. On the contrary, its location accuracy increases as the profile becomes more acute. In other words, flat profiles magnify differences in initial inputs more than acute ones (see fig. 1(c)).

2.2   Confidence Measures and Error Prediction

Confidence measures can be formulated from either an analytic or a probabilistic point of view. Analytic approaches either use the energy [10,6] or the image structure (gradient magnitude [2], structure tensor [18]) as indicators of confidence. Energy-based approaches are linked to the capability of finding the energy minima and, thus, energy convexity. Whereas structure-based approaches are related to numerical stability and model assumptions. Probabilistic approaches define confidence in terms of probabilistic distributions of either flow fields itself [12] or its variability with respect perturbations in the model [13]. Probabilistic approaches are more flexible and not necessarily linked to any source of error. Furthermore, they can even be used to get a confidence fusing all previous measures [14] and, thus, relate to all three error sources. Table 1 categorizes existing confidence measures according to their formulation and source of error they mainly focus on.

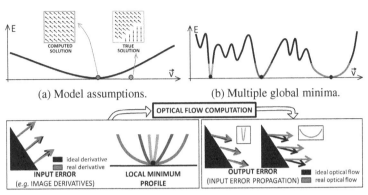

(a) Model assumptions.   (b) Multiple global minima.

(c) Numerical stability of local minima.

Fig. 1. Three main sources of error in optical flow algorithms: model assumptions (a), multiple global minima (b) and numerical stability of local minima, (c)

Table 1. Categorization of Confidence Measures according to Error Types

			Model Assumptions	Multiple Minima	Numerical Stability
Measure Formulation	Analytic	gradient-based [2]	✓	✗	✓
		image local structure [18]	✓	✗	✓
		energy-based [10]	✗	✓	✗
	Probabilistic	bootstrap [13]	✓	✗	✓
		p-val [12]	✗	✗	✗
		random forest [14]	✓	✓	✓

In an ideal case, we would expect the values of a confidence measure to be correlated to the flow endpoint error. In this case, the relation between measure and error could be estimated by means of non-linear regression. The confidence values would provide an estimation of the flow error and they could be further used for predicting it in sequences without ground truth. Unfortunately, this is not possible in the general case, given that errors either follow a random distribution or can not be estimated (as the white sequence example illustrates). A more realistic approach is to define quantities that estimate an upper bound for the flow error. This is consistent with the bounds on error propagation defined in the context of numerical stability. In order that a measure is useful for bounding errors, the plot between the measure and endpoint errors should show a monotonic tendency.

The plots in figure 2 illustrate the difference between the concepts of error prediction and error bounding. For both plots, the confidence measure (cm) is plotted in the x-axis and its corresponding End-point Error (EE) [1] in the y-axis. In the first case, shown in fig. 2 (a), there is a clear functional correlation between cm and EE. The scatter along the curve determines the quality (confidence interval around the value EE_0) of the error prediction given by the measure values. In the second case, fig. 2 (b), we do not have a

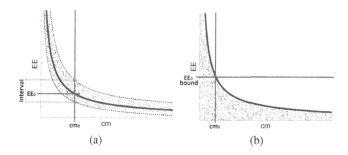

Fig. 2. Difference between Error Prediction, (a) and Error bounding, (b)

functional dependency but a sparse plot following a decreasing pattern. It follows that a given value of cm is able to provide, at most, an upper bound of the error values. In particular, we have that low values for the confidence do not necessarily imply a large error. That is, errors can take any possible value.

3   The Confidence of the Confidence

Once we have a confidence measure we still need a way to evaluate it. As discussed in the previous section, a confidence measure can, at most, provide a bound on the flow error. Therefore, we should be confident on cm in the measure it is good for bounding error. At a first intuitively approach, we would like the lowest possible error bound for all pixels.

In an ideal world, cm should give an upper bound for EE everywhere. That is, $\forall cm_0$, EE values should be bounded for all cm values above cm_0, so that the following probability is zero:

$$\forall cm_0, \exists EE_0 \text{ s.t. } P(cm > cm_0, EE > EE_0) = 0 \tag{1}$$

In practice, there is a percentage of points with an error that can not be bounded by the measure:

$$\exists cm_0 \text{ s.t. } \forall EE_0, P(cm > cm_0, EE > EE_0) = \alpha > 0 \tag{2}$$

We define the risk of a confidence measure as the percentage of points, α, which bound can not be determined by cm values. It should be clear that the lower the risk, the higher the power for bound prediction of cm.

The scatter plot in fig. 3(a) showing cm versus EE illustrates the concept of risk. The vertical line represents the threshold for cm at the value cm_0 and the horizontal lines several bounds on EE_0 having different risks ($risk_1 > risk_2 > risk_3$). For each EE_0 its risk is given by the percentage of points on the upper right square defined by the two lines. Given that EE_0 can take any possible value and this holds for all $cm > cm_0$, it is clear that cm can not provide a bound on the error everywhere. This is not the case for the scatters shown in fig. 3(b), where, for each cm value, equation (1) holds.

Not all $cm - EE$ scatters having the same risk have equal properties for error bound prediction. Also, for a given risk, there are several curves that could be fitted to the data

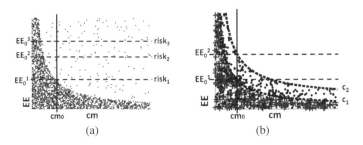

Fig. 3. Concepts involved in the quality of a confidence measure: risk in error bound prediction, (a), and optimal error bound for a given risk, (b)

for error bound setting, since the only requirement for error bounding is that curves should be monotonically decreasing. Figure 3 (b) shows two scatter plots (one in blue crosses and the other one in black dots) achieving risk zero for their envelope curves plot in dashed lines and labeled c_1 for the cross scatter and c_2 for the dot one. Yet, having both a zero risk, c_1 is better than c_2 because for any cm_0 value we have $EE_0^1 < EE_0^2$. On the other hand, note that c_1 is also a valid curve for error bounding for the second scatter plot. It provides a better error bound than c_2, but it increases the risk. This is because the curve c_1 does not enclose all points belonging to the second scatter. Those points above c_1 represent the risk.

Under the considerations above, a confidence of the confidence measure should quantify, for each risk, how good for error bounding the measure is. That is, for a given risk, each cm value should provide the lowest possible bound EE_0. We observe that the best scatter in terms of error bounding is the one having a maximum decay or, in other words, the one having a minimal area of points without risk. Given a decreasing curve fitted to the scatter, this area corresponds to the Area Under the Curve (AUC) while the risk is given by the percentage of points above the fitted curve. The trade off between the risk and EE_0 for all decreasing curves fitting the scatter data measures how good for error bounding our confidence measure is. Meanwhile, the optimal fitting curve should reach the best compromise (prone to vary across applications) between risk and AUC.

The plot showing AUC versus risk, for curves of increasing risk is our confidence of the confidence measure and we will name it RAUC. By the previous considerations, it should be clear that the steeper the RAUC is, the better the confidence measure is. The curve of minimum risk is given by the envelope to the scatter plot. It represents the worst EE_0. The convex curve enclosing the maximum number of pixels gives the lower bound for EE_0. Its risk is a measure of the maximum risk for the best EE_0 bound. The intermediate curves are computed iteratively removing a percentage of these points.

Figure 4 shows the RAUC (first on the left) and scatter plots (second to fourth) for three representative examples of a confidence measure: an ideal case ($C1$, second), expected case ($C2$, third) and worst case ($C3$, fourth). Some representative decreasing curves fitted for a given risk are also shown on each scatter. For the ideal case (C_1), the envelope of the scatter (the curve of risk 0) is the first convex curve enclosing all the points (that one with the best EE_0). It is ideal because it is able to produce a convex curve achieving zero risk. Consequently, its RAUC first point starts with the lowest

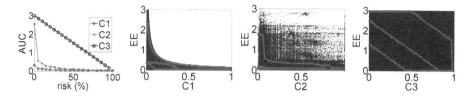

Fig. 4. Synthetic example. From left to right: the RAUC for the three different cases, ideal case ($C1$), expected case ($C2$) and worst case ($C3$).

value, and its profile is flat. The middle scatter (C_2) achieves the first convex curve at a moderate risk, which is parsed by the fitted curves. Its RAUC is worse than the case before and has positive area, so that there are still points under the curve. Finally, the right scatter (C_3) is the worse possible case, because EE is random for all cm values and thus, cm is unable to bound the error. In this case, assuming more risk, does not imply lower values for EE. Consequently, the RAUC has a linear decreasing pattern. Any confidence measure should have a RAUC under this line.

3.1 Benchmark Examples

In order to show the main concepts developed in this section, we show some examples over benchmark sequences selected from two different databases: Middelbury [1] and Sintel [19]. Optical flow was computed using the local-global approach with warping implemented by [20]. Concerning confidence measures, we chose two representative examples of each formulation category. The structured based measure defined in [11] and the energy based [10] for analytic formulations and p-val [12] and bootstrap [13] for probabilistic approaches. They are denoted as C_k, C_e, C_s and C_b respectively. We also plot C_u as a uniform confidence measure (as seen in fig.4), that is, the worst case.

For each sequence, we show the $cm - EE$ scatter plot with some of the fitted confidence curves in red and the RAUC plot for all confidence measures, as well as, the baseline worst performance C_u. Figure 5 shows results for the Middlebury sequences hydrangea and grove3 and for the Sintel sequences cave2 and sleeping1. In general, C_s scatters resemble a uniform distribution as the synthetic one shown in fig.4. This is reflected by the RAUC curves which are among the worse for all cases and are, indeed, the worst ones for sleeping1, grove3 and hydrangea. Concerning the remaining $cm's$, they show a monotonic decreasing tendency which risk and bounding capabilities vary across sequences. There is not a clear best performer for all cases due to the fact that, as discussed in Sec.2, each measure focus on a different source of error.

4 Conclusions

Confidence estimation is of prime importance for decision support systems and quite a lot of research has been recently done. Yet, there is little consensus about the meaning of some usual terms and the best way to assess the quality of a confidence measure. In this paper, we have introduced a setting for categorizing confidence measures in terms of accuracy and capabilities for error bound prediction. We have also developed a validation

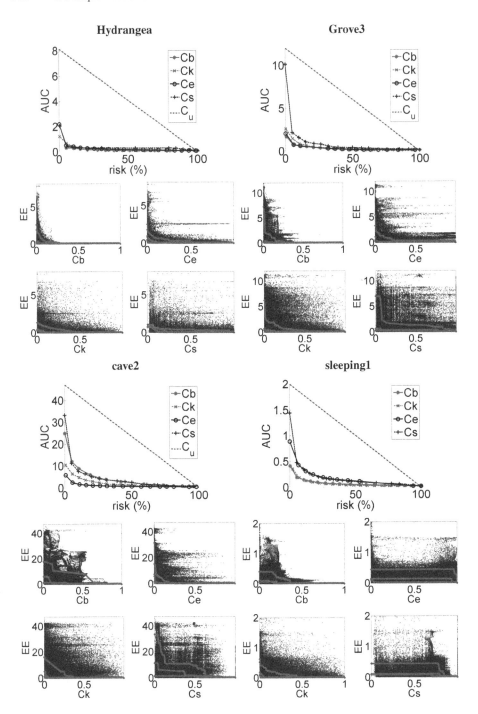

Fig. 5. RAUC and $cm\text{-}EE$ scatter plots for Middlebury sequences Hydrangea and Grove3 and Sintel sequences cave2 and sleeping1

framework for assessing their quality. Being far from presenting a deep comparison between existing confidence measures, our examples clearly support the arguments about error sources given in this position paper. Our examples, also illustrate the usefulness of the concepts and tools introduced for facilitating research in confidence measure definition and evaluation of the best optical flow model. This encourages further research in comparison of confidence measure performance using a complete set of benchmark sequences for different applications.

Acknowledgements. Work supported by the Spanish projects TIN2009-13618, TIN2012-33116 and TRA2011-29454-C03-01 and first author by FPI-MICINN BES-2010-031102 program.

References

1. Baker, S., Scharstein, D., Lewis, J.P., et al.: A database and evaluation methodology for optical flow. IJCV 92(1), 1–31 (2011)
2. Barron, J.L., Fleet, D.J., Beauchemin, S.: Performance of optical flow techniques. IJCV 12(1), 43–77 (1994)
3. Bainbridge-Smith, R.G., Lane, A.: Measuring confidence in optical flow estimation. IET Electronics Letters 32(10), 882–884 (1996)
4. Kondermann, D., et al.: On performance analysis of optical flow algorithms. In: Dellaert, F., Frahm, J.-M., Pollefeys, M., Leal-Taixé, L., Rosenhahn, B. (eds.) Real-World Scene Analysis 2011. LNCS, vol. 7474, pp. 329–355. Springer, Heidelberg (2012)
5. Uras, S., Girosi, F., Verri, A., Torre, V.: A computational approach to motion perception. Biol. Cybern. 60, 79–97 (1988)
6. Singh, A.: An estimation-theoretic framework for image-flow computation. In: ICCV, pp. 168–177 (1990)
7. Kondermann, C., Kondermann, D., Garbe, C.S.: Postprocessing of optical flows via surface measures and motion inpainting. In: Rigoll, G. (ed.) DAGM 2008. LNCS, vol. 5096, pp. 355–364. Springer, Heidelberg (2008)
8. Simoncelli, E., Adelson, E., Heeger, D.: Probability distributions of optical flow. In: CVPR, pp. 310–315 (1991)
9. Lucas, B., Kanade, T.: An iterative image registration technique with an application to stereo vision. In: DARPA Image Understanding Workshop, pp. 121–130 (1981)
10. Bruhn, A., Weickert, J.: A confidence measure for variational optic flow methods. In: GPID, pp. 283–298 (2006)
11. Márquez-Valle, P., Gil, D., Hernández-Sabaté, A.: A complete confidence framework for optical flow. In: ECCV Workshops, pp. 124–133 (2012)
12. Kondermann, C., Mester, R., Garbe, C.S.: A statistical confidence measure for optical flows. In: Forsyth, D., Torr, P., Zisserman, A. (eds.) ECCV 2008, Part III. LNCS, vol. 5304, pp. 290–301. Springer, Heidelberg (2008)
13. Kybic, J., Nieuwenhuis, C.: Bootstrap optical flow confidence and uncertainty measure. In: CVIU, pp. 1449–1462 (2011)
14. Mac Aodha, O., Humayun, A., Pollefeys, M., Brostow, G.J.: Learning a confidence measure for optical flow. IEEE PAMI (2012)
15. Evans, L.C.: Partial Differential Equations. American Mathematical Society (1998)
16. Horn, B., Schunck, B.: Determining optical flow. AI 17, 185–203 (1981)
17. Burden, R., Douglas Faires, J.: Numerical Analysis. Thompson (2005)
18. Shi, J., Tomasi, C.: Good features to track. In: CVPR, pp. 593–600 (1994)
19. Butler, D.J., Wulff, J., Stanley, G.B., Black, M.J.: A naturalistic open source movie for optical flow evaluation. In: Fitzgibbon, A., Lazebnik, S., Perona, P., Sato, Y., Schmid, C. (eds.) ECCV 2012, Part VI. LNCS, vol. 7577, pp. 611–625. Springer, Heidelberg (2012)
20. Liu, C.: Beyond pixels: exploring new representations and applications for motion analysis. Ph.D. thesis (2009)

Parallel Deep Learning with Suggestive Activation for Object Category Recognition

Karthik Mahesh Varadarajan and Markus Vincze

{kv,mv}@acin.tuwien.ac.at

Abstract. The performance of visual perception algorithms for object category detection has largely been restricted by the lack of generalizability and scalability of state-of-art hand-crafted feature detectors and descriptors across instances of objects with different shapes, textures etc. The recently introduced deep learning algorithms have attempted at overcoming this limitation through automatic learning of feature kernels. Nevertheless, conventional deep learning architectures are uni-modal, essentially feedforward testing pipelines working on image space with little regard for context and semantics. In this paper, we address this issue by presenting a new framework for object categorization based on Deep Learning, called Parallel Deep Learning with Suggestive Activation (PDLSA) that imbibes several brain operating principles drawn from neuroscience and psychophysical studies. In particular, we focus on Suggestive Activation – a schema which enables feedback loops in the recognition process that use information obtained from partial detection results to generate hypotheses based on long-term memory (or knowledge base) to search in the image space for features corresponding to these hypotheses thereby enabling activation of the response corresponding to the correct object category through multimodal integration. Results presented against a traditional SIFT based category classifier on the University of Washington benchmark RGB-D dataset demonstrates the validity of the approach.

1 Introduction

Recognition of object categories has been traditionally regarded as a major challenge in the field of computer vision. While early approaches to solving the problem focused on building global shape descriptors (such as shape primitives) to characterize the classes, modern approaches since 2000 have largely focused on local feature based schemes with additional steps such as clustering, pose estimation and geometric validation to obtain better consensus. Primary among these methods include SIFT [1], G-RIF [2], SURF [3], GLOH [4] and MSER [5]. Nevertheless, these approaches, while being quite successful in performing instance recognition of target objects, fail to generalize across object categories due to the inability to capture object constancy features. In order to alleviate this concern, approaches such as Bag of Visual Words [6] that collate local feature descriptors across large representative databases have been developed. Nevertheless, such hand-crafted local feature descriptors provide poor performance with the state-of-art algorithms showing a mean average precision of 40-60% in the best case [7].

M. Chen, B. Leibe, and B. Neumann (Eds.): ICVS 2013, LNCS 7963, pp. 354–363, 2013.
© Springer-Verlag Berlin Heidelberg 2013

An alternative to using such engineered local feature descriptors is to build a system that learns the kernel functions that generate these feature descriptors. The recently introduced family of Deep Learning (DL) algorithms [8] achieves this by defining a multi-layered architecture which automatically learns the feature kernels or bases defining the structure underlying the data.

These algorithms thus provide for better characterization of the data and the level of sparsity of the representation, enabling efficient sparse coding, thereby mimicking processes in the brain for object representation [9, 10, 11]. Since the learning units in deep learning are organized hierarchically in multiple levels, they also result in efficient non-linear encoding of the data. Furthermore, the intermediate representations in a deep learning typically characterize properties of the training images that are transferable across multiple categories or tasks. Hence, they are very useful from the standpoint of Multi-Task Learning (MTL) [12] and help provide for better regularization with respect to noise in comparison with other regularizers [8].

2   Deep Learning Networks and Deficiencies

DL algorithms represent the current direction of research in building cognitive models of human visual perception and object recognition. However, there are a number of Brain Operating Principles (BOPs) that DL systems do not account for. Firstly, DL systems solely use local feature descriptors while global descriptions (such as geons) are also known to be used in the human visual system [13]. Secondly, all DL systems are inherently serial (though providing for parallel evaluation of feature kernels at each level or layer), while parallel computing is a well known BOP [14]. Thirdly, DL systems are essentially uni-modal while the processing underlying visual perception is known to encompass integration of multi-modal and multi-sensory stimuli. Fourthly, the recognition phase in DL systems is composed traditionally of feedforward circuits with no loops. However, on the other hand, the human perception system uses both feedforward and feedback loops to improve the quality of the results of the perception process through nested iteration [14]. Fifthly, most DL based recognition systems try to detect objects from its intrinsic properties without regard for the semantic context in which the object is placed. On the other hand, it has been proven through psychophysical tests [15], that object context and semantics play a crucial role in recognizing as well as improving the confidence of recognition of objects. Besides these cognitive deficiencies, there are several other problems with DL systems from the standpoint of implementation. For example, deciding the number of levels in a DL system and efficient training of multi-level DL systems remain only partially solved.

3   Proposed System - Parallel Deep Learning with Suggestive Activation

In order to alleviate these concerns as well as to build an object categorization system that closely mimics the functioning of the brain, we present an alternate framework –

Parallel Deep Learning with Suggestive Activation (PDLSA). The PDLSA imbibes several brain operating principles, thereby providing for a better cognitive model for object recognition as opposed to traditional DL systems. The primary characteristics of PDLSA are described below.

1. **Hierarchical Network:** Similar to DL systems, PDLSA is organized as a hierarchical graphical network drawing parallels with columnar architecture in the brain. However, the PDLSA is a heterogeneous network with multiple hand-coded parallel levels (each parallel level corresponding to a unimodal feature type) and with automatically learnt serial levels (by deep learning).

2. **Global Affordance Features:** PDLSA is based on global features that encompass shape, color, local texture and semantic contexts. Specifically, affordance features [16], that generalize over the wide variety of abstract and metric shape and local feature definitions, based on reasoning about the underlying functionality of the feature, leading to object constancy and categorization are used. These provide convenient cognitive schemas for recognition of object categories based on the functional properties of the object. Such a functional approach to categorization is cognitively grounded based on Gibson's theory of affordances [17] and functional form fits as well as the Common Coding Theory [18]. The Common Coding Theory postulates that the brain circuits used for perception as well as motor actuation are shared and coding process is also common. Thus affordances (as functions actuated by the motor processes) are intrinsically tied with visual perception. This is also evidenced in the case of Mirror neurons and Anti-mirror neurons that link real or imagined endo- and exo- functional actuation with perception [19].

3. **Parallel Affordance Feature Detection:** The affordance features are primarily categorized into two – (a) Structural features and (b) Material features [20, 21], along with Affordance Semantics [22] that describes the positional relationships between entities exhibiting the affordance features. While structural features are recognized using shape information (2D/3D shapes), material features are recognized using color and texture information (Gabor, DCT). Each of these individual features form a modality corresponding to a parallel level. Each of the parallel detection units operate asynchronously – hence based on the computational complexity of the process, some units will complete earlier than the others. Furthermore, such a multi-feature integration approach helps handle a wide variety of environmental conditions during perception. For example, recognition of an object in the dark for the case of the human visual system is largely based on luminosity differences along the contour, rather than color or local feature information. Thus, PDLSA is robust to ore environmental variations than DL systems.

4. **Knowledge base for Recognition:** Unlike DL systems, PDLSA uses long-term memory based on the k-TR theory of visual perception [20]. Long-term knowledge about objects and object categories is organized in the form of a knowledge base using affordance or functional features of the objects. In the PDLSA architecture, we use the AfNet affordance knowledge base [23] that describes objects in terms of parts and part relationships, with each part offering function(s) or affordance

feature(s). Hence unlike traditional DL, PDLSA uses multi-modal features as well as knowledge bases for recognition.

5. **Suggestive Activation:** Unlike DL, PDLSA uses feedforward as well as feedback systems. As noted earlier, some parallel asynchronous units can finish their computation faster than the others. The units which complete computation faster can help prune/prioritize the processing of other units. This pruning or prioritization works in consonance with the knowledge base. If for example, some units of the material affordance detection (say, detection of wood like material) completes earlier, it can be used with information from the knowledge base to select possible candidate objects that might be made of wood and prune or prioritize the structural processing algorithms to look for structural features that are typical of objects made of that specific material (in this case, rectangular – such as desks, windows, doors etc.). Furthermore, once a single part of the object is identified in the course of parallel execution and matches in the knowledge base are obtained, PDLSA goes back to the image domain to search for other parts of the object corresponding to the candidate match. This is termed as Suggestive Activation and helps greatly to identify objects in the case of clutter and poor segmentation. For example if the cylindrical part of a cup is identified, PDLSA through Suggestive Activation can go back and look for a possible handle(s) through generation of candidate 2D/3D corners, surface patches and contour structures and find a match for these in the image, thereby enabling identification of the handle even if a very small portion of it is visible and cannot be modeled as a part in the course of the feedforward operation. Thus, unlike the DL system, Suggestive Activation through feedforward and feedback loops entertains the possibility of better recognition.

6. **Semantic Grounding:** Unlike the DL system, PDLSA uses Affordance Semantics. These semantics are of three types [22], namely – a) Localizer affordances b) Affordance Duals c) Affordance Co-occurrences. For example, there is a high incidence of a pen and book occurring together – since they provide complementary affordances, essentially the affordance duals of engrav-ability and display-ability. Similarly, other semantics can also be identified from the scene of interest. By using these semantics, it is possible to improve the confidence of the recognition or bias the category labels towards those expected from the affordance relationships. For example, if the noise in the perception system results in ambiguity between the classes pen and spoon for a candidate object, the occurrence of a book or a plate nearby can be used to bias the detected result class towards the one supported by the affordance relationship.

4 Implementation Details

Traditional deep learning approaches use multi-layer frameworks such as Deep Belief Networks (DBN), Stacked Denoising Auto-Encoders (SdA), Convolution Neural Networks (CNN), Convolution Auto-Encoders (CAE) or combinations of the above [8]. The state-of-art implementations of Deep Learning approaches use convolution layers trained using greedy layer-wise unsupervised learning (DBN) based on Restricted Boltzmann Machine (RBM) that uses output of lower layers to train higher ones, sandwiched between layers of Maxpooling (non-linear down-sampling) with the option of supervised task based fine-tuning of hidden layers typically using gradient descent along with a classifier such as logistic regression. Additional pure classification layers may also be added in order to improve the classification accuracy. Shift and rotation invariance may also be introduced by creating local regional processing units in the computation. These Deep Learning modules operate on the raw image pixel domain to yield the required recognition processing. In essence, these DL algorithms can be defined as using short-term memory of auto-encoded features.

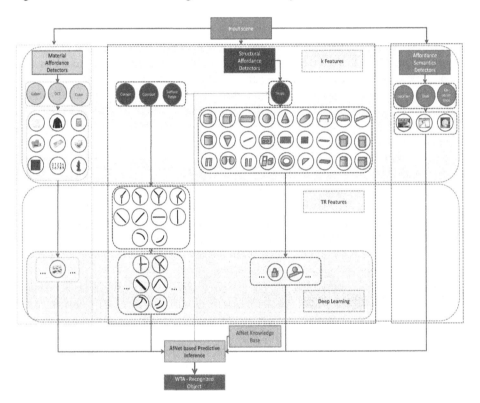

Fig. 1. PDLSA architecture

In contrast, the PDLSA being based on the k-TR theory uses both short-term of auto-encoded (TR features) as well as long-term memory of hand-crafted affordance features (k features). These k features, being the primary recognition mechanism form the first layer of the recognition process. Deep Learning for TR detection in PDLSA is incorporated in two stages. Firstly, it is incorporated in the feedforward stage (marked by red arrows) in the definition of complex feature schema (analogous to complex cells or geon assemblies). Thus Deep Learning in this stream is carried out on k feature labels that are converted to indices in order to generate vectorized inputs for the neural network. Secondly, DL is also used in the feedback stage (marked by green arrows - the Suggestive Activation stage). Here, DL is carried out not on the original image pixels but on synthetic image pixels produced from k feature labels yielding contours, edges, junctions, corners, patches, textures, color configurations.

As noted earlier, the various k feature detectors operate in a parallel asynchronous mode. Hence, some modules (such as the material affordance detectors) complete earlier than the others. In the testing phase, detection of some k features triggers the AfNet based inference schema leading to Suggestive Activation. The Suggestive Activation primes the processing of other k feature detectors (that are still running) towards predicted object characteristics (in terms of material and structural affordances for current and other possible parts). Suggestive Activation also selects deep learning neurons that have previously been trained for simulated image pixel structures (composed of corners, contours etc.) corresponding to the object structures predicted by the AfNet inference module. This suggestive activation also draws parallels to the operation of Spiking Neural Networks (SNN), wherein neurons are not activated at every neuronal cycle but only when the membrane potential exceeds a certain threshold. The final categorization is obtained by applying a Winner-Take-All (WTA) model to the various hypotheses suggested by the AfNet inference module and the results of both the feedforward and the feedback pathways.

4.1   Implementation of k Feature Detectors

Detection of affordance or 'k' features is a well-studied topic [16]. Traditionally, material affordance features are detected using color and texture information (DCT/ Gabor). For example, while colors such as red, gray, white, black, gold etc. trigger certain material affordance mechanisms, textures such as that of wood trigger other mechanisms. Structural affordance features (as shown in the flowchart) are largely detected by using Superquadric fitting of segmented 2.5D point cloud data and geometric primitive analysis. For a full list of affordance features used here, please refer to [23]. For mechanisms used in the detection of affordance features please refer to [21].

4.2   Implementation of TR Feature Detectors

As described earlier, suggestive activation changes flow of the algorithmic pipeline in traditional DL systems by introducing feedback loops from the visual reasoning space to the perception space. This reactivation of specific perception modules is based on possible candidate suggestions for the type of object from AfNet.

As described earlier, while k features are essentially affordance features, TR features are obtained through deep learning – these include 2D/3D contours, corners and complex pixel configurations learnt by higher levels of the deep learning network. In order to achieve deep learning, we employ a Deep Belief Network (DBN). In the case of the feed-forward stream, the DBN learns higher-order relationships between the affordance features (that are converted to vectors by indexing) in an unsupervised fashion by training on AfNet definitions. Each layer of the DBN is trained greedily using an RBM. The output of each layer is used as input for the next subsequent layer. Thus the DBN learns successively complex definitions of affordance feature combinations that occur in the AfNet database. The DBNs thus effectively model the joint distribution between the observed vector i and N hidden layers h_k as

$$P(i, h_1, h_2, \ldots, h_N) = (\prod_{k=0}^{N-2} P(h_k|h_{k+1}))\, P(h_{N-1}, h_N)$$

Where $i = h_0$ and the first term in the product indicate conditional distributions for the visible units with respect to the hidden units and the second term indicates the distribution of the visible-hidden top-level.

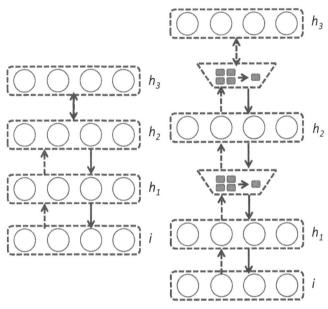

Fig. 2. DBN for Feedforward and Feedback pathways. i is the input layer, hk are the hidden layers and the trapezoids describe MaxPooling

On the other hand, the feedback stream of PDLSA employs Deep Learning using an alternate mechanism. While the construction of the DL network is almost identical to the previous case with the DBN forming the core of the network, the learning is carried out on image pixels that are obtained from synthesized views of predicted part shapes. In other words, based on the partially or wholly identified parts (using the affordance detectors), other parts of the object can be hypothesized using AfNet. For example, if the cylindrical portion of a cup is identified, the handle (in the case of a mug) or the lid (in the case of a canister) are examples of candidate parts. Based on the configuration of these parts as defined by AfNet, synthetic geometries can be generated for each of these objects. By choosing an arbitrary viewpoint for the synthesized geometry, the DBN can be made to learn features such as corners, junctions, contours, surface patches and shapes which can then be used to detect such structures in the input image. Using such an approach enables the recognition of occluded parts as well objects in the case of heavy clutter. Figure 2 shows the basic structure of the DBN used in the training process. In order to make the problem more tractable, the hidden layers are interspersed by MaxPooling layers that resample or reduce the resolution of the data.

5   Evaluation and Results

In order to test performance of the proposed generic category recognizer, tests were carried out on the University of Washington RGB-D Dataset. The performance of the

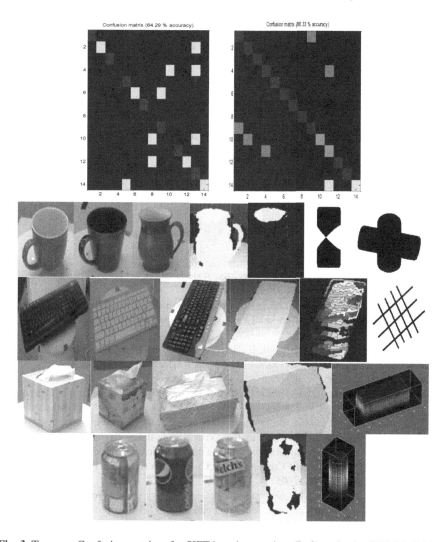

Fig. 3. Top row: Confusion matrices for SIFT based recognizer (Left) and using PDLSA (Right). Subsequent rows: In each of the example rows, the first two im-ages indicate cases where recognition was successful using SIFT owing to similari-ty to the training set. The third image shows an instance where SIFT fails, but PDLSA uses affordance features – concavity (for the cup), textures (keyboard) (with detection shown in the fifth image) and simulates artificial image descriptors (shown in sixth) for deep learning. Similarly, detection of affordance features in the form of cubo-id and cylinder leads to enhanced recognition in the case of the Kleenex box and the Soda can (example rows three and four). This process results in a recognition rate of 88% as opposed to 64% with SIFT in this case of similar category different shape test bed.

PDLSA recognizer was compared with that of a SIFT based categorization system based on VLFeat. The SIFT categorizer uses PHOW features (dense SIFT), spatial histograms of visual words for feature representation and Pegasos Chi^2 SVM for classification (based on kd-trees and homogeneous kernel maps). The performance of the two systems were evaluated on 14 categories of objects with 20 resampled training images. The results from the SIFT system are shown in Fig 3 along with results using PDLSA. The use of multi-modal features and suggestive activation enables the higher recognition rate in PDLSA (88.33%) as opposed to PHOW-SVM (64.29%).

6   Conclusion

In this paper we have presented a novel brain inspired cognitive framework for object category recognition using deep learning algorithms. The framework imbibes a number of brain operating principles and demonstrates a better prospect towards generalizability and scalability as opposed to traditional local feature based category recognition approaches.

References

1. Lowe, D.G.: Distinctive image features from scale-invariant keypoints. International Journal of Computer Vision 60(2), 91–110 (2004)
2. Kim, S., Yoon, K.-J., Kweon, I.S.: Object recognition using a generalized robust invariant feature and Gestalt's law of proximity and similarity. Pattern Recognition 41(2), 726–741 (2008)
3. Bay, H., Tuytelaars, T., Van Gool, L.: SURF: Speeded up robust features. In: Leonardis, A., Bischof, H., Pinz, A. (eds.) ECCV 2006, Part I. LNCS, vol. 3951, pp. 404–417. Springer, Heidelberg (2006)
4. Mikolajczyk, K., Schmid, C.: Scale & affine invariant interest point detectors. International Journal of Computer Vision 60(1), 63–86 (2004)
5. Forssen, P.-E., Lowe, D.G.: Shape descriptors for maximally stable extremal regions. In: IEEE 11th International Conference on Computer Vision, ICCV 2007. IEEE (2007)
6. Fei-Fei, L., Perona, P.: A bayesian hierarchical model for learning natural scene categories. In: IEEE Computer Society Conference on Computer Vision and Pattern Recognition, CVPR 2005, vol. 2. IEEE (2005)
7. Jarrett, K., et al.: What is the best multi-stage architecture for object recognition? In: 2009 IEEE 12th International Conference on Computer Vision. IEEE (2009)
8. Bengio, Y.: Learning deep architectures for AI. Foundations and Trends in Machine Learning 2(1), 1–127 (2009)
9. Cover, T.M., Thomas, J.A.: Elements of information theory. Wiley-Interscience (2006)
10. Field, D.J.: Relations between the statistics of natural images and the response properties of cortical cells. J. Opt. Soc. Am. A 4(12), 2379–2394 (1987)
11. Field, D.J.: What is the goal of sensory coding? Neural Computation 6(4) (1994)
12. Caruana, R.: Multitask learning. Machine Learning 28(1), 41–75 (1997)
13. Biederman, I.: Recognition-by-components: a theory of human image understanding. Psychological Review 94(2), 115 (1987)
14. Arbib, M.A. (ed.): The handbook of brain theory and neural networks. MIT Press

15. Rogers, T., et al.: Object recognition under semantic impairment: The effects of conceptual regularities on perceptual decisions. Language and Cognitive Processes 18(5-6), 625–662 (2003)
16. Varadarajan, K.M., Vincze, M.: AfNet: The affordance network. In: Lee, K.M., Matsushita, Y., Rehg, J.M., Hu, Z. (eds.) ACCV 2012, Part I. LNCS, vol. 7724, pp. 512–523. Springer, Heidelberg (2013)
17. Gibson, J.J.: The concept of affordances. Perceiving, Acting, and Knowing, 67–82 (1977)
18. Prinz, W.: Modes of linkage between perception and action. Cognition and motor processes, pp. 185–193. Springer, Heidelberg (1984)
19. Kohler, E., et al.: Hearing sounds, understanding actions: action representation in mirror neurons. Science 297(5582), 846–848 (2002)
20. Varadarajan, K.M.: k-TR: Karmic Tabula Rasa – A Theory of Visual Perception. In: Conference of the International Society of Psychophysics - ISP (2011)
21. Varadarajan, K.M., Vincze, M.: Knowledge representation and inference for grasp affordances. In: Crowley, J.L., Draper, B.A., Thonnat, M. (eds.) ICVS 2011. LNCS, vol. 6962, pp. 173–182. Springer, Heidelberg (2011)
22. Varadarajan, K.M., Vincze, M.: AfRob: The affordance network ontology for robots. In: 2012 IEEE/RSJ International Conference on Intelligent Robots and Systems (IROS). IEEE (2012)
23. AfNet: The Affordance Network (2013), http://www.theaffordances.net

Author Index

Antonelli, Marco   264
Arens, Michael   1
Argyros, Antonis   143

Bakshi, Ainesh   173
Benedek, Csaba   21
Boben, Marko   93
Borràs, Agnés   334
Bozma, Işıl   314
Brémond, François   244

Cai, Hongping   103
Čehovin, Luka   93
Chau, Duc Phu   244
Chen, Weixia   163
Chetverikov, Dmitry   21
Chliveros, Georgios   234
Cho, Seong Ik   284
Cohn, Anthony G.   223
Colombo, Carlo   52, 274
Comanducci, Dario   52
Conradt, Jörg   133

Dellaert, Frank   183
del Pobil, Angel P.   264
Donath, Axel   193
Douvantzis, Petros   143
du Buf, J.M.H.   113

Erkent, Özgür   314

Fanfani, Marco   274
Farrajota, Miguel   113
Fath, Thilo   42
Fritz, Gerald   62
Fuchs, Stefan   31

Gao, Chunming   163
Gavrila, Dariu M.   203
Gil, Debora   334, 344
Goel, Kratarth   173
González, Miguel Angel   334
Grosselfinger, Ann-Kristin   1
Gu, Feng   223

Haas, Harald   42
Hellwich, Olaf   31
Hernández-Sabaté, Aura   344
Ho, Jeffrey   213
Hoffmann, Raoul   133
Hofmann, Albert   62
Hogg, David C.   223
Horváth, Csaba   21
Hübner, Wolfgang   1

Jankó, Zsolt   21

Kapur, Salil   173
Kiss, Andras   11
Kondermann, Daniel   193, 344
Kristan, Matej   93
Kulkarni, Ninad   173
Kwak, Dong Yong   284
Kyriazis, Nikolaos   143

Lee, Joon Woong   284
Lei, Yuan   163
Leonardis, Aleš   93
Li, Songnan   153
Liem, Martijn C.   203
Liu, Gang   324
Lobato, David   113
Lodron, Gerald   62
Lourakis, Manolis   83

Márquez-Valle, Patricia   344
Martins, Jaime   113
Matas, Jiří   103
Mayer, Heinz   62
Molnár, Dömötör   21
Mörwald, Thomas   254
Münch, David   1

Nagy, Zoltan   11
Nejhum, Shahed   213
Nemeth, Mate   11
Ngan, King Ngi   153

Oikonomidis, Iason   143

Paletta, Lucas   62
Pan, Huawei   163
Pateraki, Maria   234
Prankl, Johann   254

Richtsfeld, Andreas   73
Roberts, Richard   183
Rodrigues, J.M.F.   113
Rucci, Michele   264
Rushdi, Muhammad   213

Sahbi, Hichem   304
Saleiro, Mário   113
Sant, Rohit   173
Santner, Katrin   62
Savchenko, Andrey V.   123
Schubert, Falk   42
Shao, Wen   324
Sheng, Lu   153
Song, Gwnag Yul   284
Sridhar, Muralikrishna   223
Srinivasan, Natesh   183
Suppa, Michael   31
Swadzba, Agnes   294
Szirányi, Tamás   21

Tabernik, Domen   93
Tavanai, Aryana   223
Terzić, Kasim   113
Thallinger, Georg   62
Thonnat, Monique   244
Trahanias, Panos   234

Vanek, Balint   11
Varadarajan, Karthik Mahesh   354
Vera, Sergio   334
Vincze, Markus   73, 254, 354

Wachsmuth, Sven   294
Weikersdorfer, David   133
Werner, Tomáš   103

Xia, Gui-Song   324

Yang, Wen   324

Zabulis, Xenophon   83
Zarandy, Akos   11
Ziegler, Leon   294
Zillich, Michael   73, 254
Zsedrovits, Tamas   11